Athletic Director's DESK REFERENCE

SECOND EDITION

DONNA A. LOPIANO, PhD
Sports Management Resources

CONNEE ZOTOS, PhD
Sports Management Resources

Human Kinetics

Library of Congress Cataloging-in-Publication Data

Names: Lopiano, Donna A., author. | Zotos, Connee, author.
Title: Athletic director's desk reference / Donna A. Lopiano, PhD, Connee Zotos, PhD.
Description: Second edition. | Champaign, IL : Human Kinetics, [2023] | Includes bibliographical references and index.
Identifiers: LCCN 2021020574 (print) | LCCN 2021020575 (ebook) | ISBN 9781718208490 (paperback) | ISBN 9781718208506 (epub) | ISBN 9781718208513 (pdf)
Subjects: LCSH: Athletic directors--Handbooks, manuals, etc. | Sports administration--Handbooks, manuals, etc.
Classification: LCC GV713 .L66 2023 (print) | LCC GV713 (ebook) | DDC 796.069--dc23
LC record available at https://lccn.loc.gov/2021020574
LC ebook record available at https://lccn.loc.gov/2021020575

ISBN: 978-1-7182-0849-0 (print)

The online learning content that accompanies this product is delivered on HK*Propel*, HKPropel.HumanKinetics.com. You agree that you will not use HK*Propel* if you do not accept the site's Privacy Policy and Terms and Conditions, which detail approved uses of the online content.

The web addresses cited in this text were current as of July 2021, unless otherwise noted.

Acquisitions Editor: Andrew L. Tyler; **Developmental Editor:** Melissa J. Zavala; **Permissions Manager:** Dalene Reeder; **Graphic Designer:** Joe Buck; **Cover Designer:** Thom Whitaker; **Art Director:** Keri Evans; **Cover Design Specialist:** Susan Rothermel Allen; **Photographs (interior):** © Human Kinetics, unless otherwise noted; **Photo Production Manager:** Jason Allen; **Senior Art Manager:** Kelly Hendren; **Illustrations:** © Human Kinetics, unless otherwise noted; **Production:** Westchester Publishing Services; **Printer:** Sheridan Books

Printed in the United States of America

10 9 8 7 6 5 4 3 2 1

The paper in this book is certified under a sustainable forestry program.

Human Kinetics
1607 N. Market Street
Champaign, IL 61820
USA

United States and International
Website: **US.HumanKinetics.com**
Email: info@hkusa.com
Phone: 1-800-747-4457

Canada
Website: **Canada.HumanKinetics.com**
Email: info@hkcanada.com

E8408

Tell us what you think!
Human Kinetics would love to hear what we can do to improve the customer experience. Use this QR code to take our brief survey.

Contents

An extended table of contents can be found on page iv.

Preface xv
Acknowledgments xvii

CHAPTER 1 Developing Leadership Style and Philosophy 1
CHAPTER 2 Governance of the Athletic Program 59
CHAPTER 3 Vision, Mission, and Goals 87
CHAPTER 4 Operational Structure of the Athletic Program 113
CHAPTER 5 Office Operations, Finance, and Budgeting 153
CHAPTER 6 Managing a Staff to Accomplish Program Goals 181
CHAPTER 7 Ethics, Rules Compliance, and Professional Conduct .. 235
CHAPTER 8 Student-Athlete Support Programs 247
CHAPTER 9 Sports Medicine and Athletic Training Programs 269
CHAPTER 10 Diversity, Inclusion, and Nondiscrimination 281
CHAPTER 11 Team Administration 311
CHAPTER 12 Event Management and Scheduling 335
CHAPTER 13 Revenue Acquisition and Fund-Raising 351
CHAPTER 14 Communications, Media Relations, and Promotions .. 405
CHAPTER 15 Facilities and Operations 421

Index 453
About the Authors 462

Extended Table of Contents

Preface xv

Acknowledgments xvii

Chapter 1 Developing Leadership Style and Philosophy 1

In the book	Online in HK*Propel*
Characteristics and Skills of the Athletic Director	
1.1 **Management Tip**–Required Skills of an Athletic Director	
1.2 **Management Tip**–Personal Attributes of Leaders	
	1.3 **Educational Resource**–All Employees Should Aspire to Be Leaders
	1.4 **Educational Resource**–Personal Leadership Self-Evaluation
1.5 **Management Tip**–Critical Thinking and Decision Making	
1.6 **Planning Tool**–Basic Qualifications of the Athletic Director	
1.7 **Planning Tool**–Ongoing Training Needs of the Athletic Director	
	1.8 **Educational Resource**–Monitoring Legal Decisions and Understanding Legal Concepts
1.9 **Management Tip**–Decision Making and Employee Relationships	
1.10 **Management Tip**–Political Acumen: A Skill Necessity	
1.11 **Management Tip**–Wise Use of Power	
Philosophy, Values, and Operating Principles	
1.12 **Planning Tool**–Program and Operating Values and Principles	
	1.13 **Policy**–Program Operating Philosophy and Principles
1.14 **Management Tip**–Developing a Culture of Shared Learning	
1.15 **Planning Tool**–Communicating Performance Expectations	
	1.16 **Educational Resource**–Completed Staff Work: Performance Expectations of All Employees
1.17 **Management Tip**–Role and Function of Sport in Education	
1.18 **Planning Tool**–Management Training of Employees	
1.19 **Management Tip**–Keys to Managing Change	
1.20 **Management Tip**–Preventing Resistance to Change	
Relationship Building	
1.21 **Management Tip**–It's All About Relationship Building	
	1.22 **Policy**–Relationship-Building Responsibilities of All Employees
	1.23 **Evaluation Instrument**–Employee Relationship-Building Scorecard and Development Plan
	1.24 **Educational Resource**–10 Commandments for Management Success
Problem Solving	
1.25 **Management Tip**–Politically Effective Problem-Solving Strategies	
1.26 **Management Tip**–Confronting Title IX Challenges	
1.27 **Management Tip**–Asking Permission to Recruit a Coach at Another Institution	
1.28 **Management Tip**–Firing a Coach	
1.29 **Management Tip**–Leading an Environmentally Responsible Organization	
Bibliography	
1.B **Bibliography**–Developing Leadership Style and Philosophy	

Chapter 2 Governance of the Athletic Program 59

In the book	Online in HK*Propel*
Accountability to Institutional Stakeholders	
2.1 **Management Tip**–Never Go It Alone! Navigating Layers of Governance	
2.2 **Planning Tool**–Accreditation and Certification	
2.3 **Management Tip**–Reliance on Professional Legal Advice	
2.4 **Management Tip**–Athletic Director Responsibilities Related to Rules Compliance	
	2.5 **Policy**–Institutional Governance and Rules Compliance
2.6 **Management Tip**–Chain of Command	
Governance and Advisory Mechanisms	
2.7 **Planning Tool**–Composition and Function of the Athletic Advisory Council	
	2.8 **Policy**–Athletic Advisory Council
2.9 **Planning Tool**–Involvement of Student-Athletes in Athletic Governance	
	2.10 **Policy**–Student-Athletes' Advisory Council
2.11 **Planning Tool**–Alumni and Fan Involvement in Athletic Affairs	
	2.12 **Policy**–Athletic Development Advisory Council
	2.13 **Policy**–Athletic Hall of Fame Committee
2.14 **Planning Tool**–Sport Performance Advisory Group	
2.15 **Planning Tool**–Policy Manuals and Operations Handbooks	
	2.16 **Form**–Athletic Department Policy Manual: Sample Table of Contents
	2.17 **Form**–Athletic Department Operations Handbook: Sample Table of Contents
Bibliography	
2.B **Bibliography**–Governance of the Athletic Program	

Chapter 3 Vision, Mission, and Goals 87

In the book	Online in HK*Propel*
3.1 **Management Tip**–Articulating a Philosophy of Educational Sport	
3.2 **Planning Tool**–Creating Powerful Vision and Mission Statements	
3.3 **Management Tip**–Developing a One-Page Strategic Plan	
3.4 **Planning Tool**–Developing Strategies, KPIs, and Action Plans	
3.5 **Planning Tool**–Strategies, KPIs, and Action Plans for Sport Teams	
3.6 **Planning Tool**–Strategies, KPIs, and Action Plans for Fund-Raising	
3.7 **Planning Tool**–Five-Year KPI Targets for Academic Excellence Goal	
3.8 **Planning Tool**–Installing a Mechanism to Review the Strategic Plan	
Bibliography	
3.B **Bibliography**–Vision, Mission, and Goals	

Chapter 4 Operational Structure of the Athletic Program 113

In the book	Online in HK*Propel*
4.1 **Planning Tool**–Articulating the Presence of a Tiered Funding Model	
4.2 **Management Tip**–Communicating the Benefits of a Tiered Program	
4.3 **Management Tip**–Confronting the Challenges of a Tiered Program	
4.4 **Planning Tool**–A Complete Guide to Creating a Tiered Program	
	4.5 **Policy**–Adding New Sports or Eliminating Existing Sports
4.6 **Management Tip**–Due Diligence When Adding New Sports	
4.7 **Management Tip**–Adding Esports to the Athletic Program: Is It the Right Fit?	
Bibliography	
4.B **Bibliography**–Operational Structure of the Athletic Program	

Chapter 5 Office Operations, Finance, and Budgeting 153

In the book	Online in HK*Propel*
Staff Preparation	
5.1 **Management Tip**–Orientation on Office Operations for New Employees	
	5.2 **Form**–Checklist of Office Operations for New Employees
	5.3 **Educational Resource**–Acronyms That All Staff Members Should Know
	5.4 **Educational Resource**–Professional Communication Guidelines
	5.5 **Educational Resource**–Instructions on Preparing a Position Playbook
Office Operations	
	5.6 **Policy**–Buildings and Grounds
	5.7 **Policy**–Staff Meetings
	5.8 **Policy**–Mail, E-Mail, and Social Media Communications
	5.9 **Policy**–Computer and Software Use
	5.10 **Policy**–Appearance Code
Contracts and Insurance	
5.11 **Management Tip**–Production and Approval of Legal Agreements	
	5.12 **Policy**–Contracts and Signature Authority to Expend Funds
	5.13 **Form**–Contract-Processing Checklist
	5.14 **Form**–Cover Memo: Request for Approval of Contract
5.15 **Management Tip**–Insurance Issues Confronting Athletic Directors	
Financial Affairs	
	5.16 **Policy**–Financial Policies
	5.17 **Policy**–Staff Travel
	5.18 **Form**–Staff Travel Reimbursement Request
	5.19 **Form**–Advance Travel Authorization
	5.20 **Form**–Request for Payroll Payment
	5.21 **Form**–Staff Nontravel Expense Reimbursement Request
	5.22 **Form**–Request for Payment to Vendor
	5.23 **Form**–Report of Credit Card Use
	5.24 **Risk Assessment**–Checklist: Finance, Insurance, and Contracts
Budgeting	
5.25 **Planning Tool**–Basic Characteristics of the Well-Conceived Budget	
5.26 **Planning Tool**–Why Multiple Budget Managers Should Be Appointed	
5.27 **Planning Tool**–Implementing the Budget Preparation Process	
	5.28 **Policy**–Policies Regarding the Development, Approval, and Control of the Annual Budget
	5.29 **Form**–Project Budget Form
5.30 **Planning Tool**–How to Cut a Budget	
Bibliography	
5.B **Bibliography**–Office Operations, Finance, and Budgeting	

Chapter 6 Managing a Staff to Accomplish Program Goals 181

In the book	Online in HK*Propel*
Organizational Structure	
6.1 **Management Tip**–Creating a Culture of Excellence	
6.2 **Planning Tool**–Organizational Chart and Supervisor Responsibilities	
Supervisor Responsibilities	
6.3 **Management Tip**–Critical Management Behaviors for Supervisors	
Hiring Process	
6.4 **Planning Tool**–Assembling a Talented Workforce	
	6.5 **Policy**–Procedures Governing the Hiring of Employees
	6.6 **Form**–Letter Acknowledging Receipt of Application
	6.7 **Form**–Candidate Evaluation Form
	6.8 **Form**–Summary of Candidates' Evaluations

In the book	Online in HK*Propel*
Staff Evaluation	
6.9 **Planning Tool**–Program and Employee Evaluation and Corrective Action Techniques	
	6.10 **Policy**–Evaluation, Corrective Action, and Termination
	6.11 **Evaluation Instrument**–Annual Athletic Program Achievement Report
	6.12 **Evaluation Instrument**–Current Year and Five-Year Sport Achievement Report
	6.13 **Evaluation Instrument**–Current Year and Five-Year Development Program Report
	6.14 **Evaluation Instrument**–Annual Performance Review
	6.15 **Evaluation Instrument**–Annual Coach and Team Practice Assessment
	6.16 **Evaluation Instrument**–Evaluation of the Coach by the Student-Athlete
	6.17 **Evaluation Instrument**–Peer Assessment
	6.18 **Evaluation Instrument**–Evaluation of the Athletic Director by Senior Staff
	6.19 **Evaluation Instrument**–Staff Evaluation of the Athletic Director
	6.20 **Evaluation Instrument**–Evaluation of Supervisor
	6.21 **Form**–Performance Improvement Plan
Employment Administration	
6.22 **Management Tip**–General Personnel Policies	
	6.23 **Risk Assessment**–Checklist: Employment
	6.24 **Policy**–Conflict Resolution
	6.25 **Form**–Corrective Action Record
	6.26 **Policy**–Outside Employment and Compensation of Personnel
	6.27 **Form**–Request for Approval of Outside Employment
	6.28 **Form**–Acknowledgment of Outside Compensation Rules
	6.29 **Form**–Letter: Coach Participation in Camps or Clinics
	6.30 **Policy**–Time Reports, Overtime, and Outside Work
	6.31 **Policy**–Work-Study, Volunteers, and Other Part-Time Personnel
6.32 **Planning Tool**–Designing Compensation, Benefits, and Employment Agreements	
	6.33 **Policy**–Compensation, Benefits, and Employment Agreements
	6.34 **Form**–Employee at Will Appointment Letter
	6.35 **Form**–Multiyear Employment Agreement
	6.36 **Form**–Term Sheet Preceding Official Employment Agreement
6.37 **Management Tip**–Donor Car Programs	
	6.38 **Policy**–Donor Car Program
	6.39 **Form**–Request for Approval of Donor Car Assignment
	6.40 **Form**–Employee Acceptance of Responsibilities for a Donor Car
	6.41 **Form**–Monthly Report of Donor Car Use
Job Descriptions	
	6.42-6.85 **Forms**–Sample job descriptions for 44 positions typically found in a Division I athletic department
Bibliography	
6.B **Bibliography**–Managing a Staff to Accomplish Program Goals	

Chapter 7 Ethics, Rules Compliance, and Professional Conduct 235

In the book	Online in HK*Propel*
7.1 **Management Tip**–Setting Standards of Ethical Conduct	
	7.2 **Policy**–Ethical and Professional Conduct of Athletic Department Employees
	7.3 **Policy**–Standards of Professional Coaching Conduct
	7.4 **Form**–Coaches Code of Conduct Agreement
	7.5 **Policy**–Compliance With Athletic Governance Rules
	7.6 **Policy**–Gambling Prohibition
	7.7 **Policy**–Rules Compliance for Student-Athletes

In the book	Online in HK*Propel*
	7.8 **Educational Resource**–Rules Advisory for Alumni, Donors, Friends, and Fans
7.9 **Planning Tool**–Compliance With Governance Association Rules	
	7.10 **Policy**–Academic Eligibility of Student-Athletes
	7.11 **Policy**–Eligibility Lists and Participation Reports
	7.12 **Policy**–Ethical Recruiting
	7.13 **Policy**–Report of Participation in Athletic-Related Activities
	7.14 **Form**–Verification of Academic Eligibility Report
	7.15 **Form**–Degree-Countable Coursework to Be Certified by Dean
	7.16 **Educational Resource**–Instructions for Hosting Visiting Prospects
	7.17 **Form**–Official Visit: Prospect and Host Agreement
	7.18 **Form**–Weekly Report of Athletic-Related Activities
	7.19 **Form**–Amateurism Questionnaire
	7.20 **Policy**–Athletic Scholarship Awards
	7.21 **Form**–Athletic Scholarship Agreement
	7.22 **Form**–Recruiting Log
Bibliography	
7.B **Bibliography**–Ethics, Rules Compliance, and Professional Conduct	

Chapter 8 Student-Athlete Support Programs 247

In the book	Online in HK*Propel*
Academic Support Programs	
8.1 **Planning Tool**–Best Practices in the Development of Academic Support Programs	
	8.2 **Policy**–Academic Performance of Student-Athletes
	8.3 **Policy**–Tutoring Services
	8.4 **Form**–Request for Student-Athlete Academic Progress Report
	8.5 **Form**–Student-Athlete Academic Contract
	8.6 **Form**–Tutor Application Form
	8.7 **Form**–Tutor Employment Agreement
	8.8 **Form**–Payment and Verification of Tutoring Session
8.9 **Management Tip**–Assisting Academically At-Risk Student-Athletes	
	8.10 **Policy**–Study Hall and Computer Lab Rules
	8.11 **Policy**–Oversight of Student-Athlete Academic Performance
Student-Life Programs	
8.12 **Planning Tool**–Design of Model Student-Life Program	
	8.13 **Educational Resource**–Guidelines for Student-Athlete Peer Mentors
	8.14 **Policy**–Student-Life Program
	8.15 **Policy**–Student-Athlete Exit Interviews
	8.16 **Evaluation Instrument**–Student-Athlete Exit Survey
8.17 **Planning Tool**–Student-Athlete Community Service and Fund-Raising Issues	
	8.18 **Policy**–Participation in Events Sponsored by Outside Organizations
	8.19 **Form**–Response to Requests for Participation in Outside Events
	8.20 **Form**–Request for Coach or Student-Athlete Participation in Outside Event
8.21 **Management Tip**–Addressing Student-Athlete Mental Health Issues: Prevention, Access to Services, and Treatment	
Bibliography	
8.B **Bibliography**–Student-Athlete Support Programs	

Chapter 9 Sports Medicine and Athletic Training Programs. 269

In the book	Online in HK*Propel*
Program and Facility Operations	
	9.1 **Policy**–Sports Medicine and Athletic Training Program and Authority
	9.2 **Policy**–Athletic Training Room Operations

In the book	Online in HK*Propel*
Preparticipation Requirements	
	9.3 **Policy**—Medical Screening, Records, and Emergencies
	9.4 **Evaluation Instrument**—Student-Athlete and Family Medical History
	9.5 **Policy**—Student-Athlete Insurance Coverage and Treatment of Athletic Injuries
	9.6 **Form**—Insurance Authorization, Medical and Health Treatment, Informed Consent, and Release of Liability
	9.7 **Form**—Proof of Insurance
	9.8 **Form**—Preparticipation Physician's Examination and Participation Clearance
Injury Documentation	
	9.9 **Form**—Emergency Case Report
	9.10 **Form**—Nonemergency Injury Report and Treatment Record
	9.11 **Form**—Medical Referral Form
	9.12 **Form**—Medical and Participation Status Report to Coach
Drug-Testing Program	
	9.13 **Policy**—Drug Education, Testing, and Rehabilitation Program
	9.14 **Form**—Informed Consent for Institutional Drug Testing
	9.15 **Form**—Request for Documentation of Prescribed Medications
	9.16 **Risk Assessment**—Checklist: Drug Testing and Education
Critical Sports Medicine Issues	
	9.17 **Policy**—Distribution of Drugs, Supplements, and Other Ingestible Substances
	9.18 **Policy**—Treatment of Pregnant or Parenting Student-Athletes
	9.19 **Policy**—Treatment of Eating Disorders
	9.20 **Evaluation Instrument**—Screening Tool for Eating Disorders
	9.21 **Form**—Eating Disorder Contract 1
	9.22 **Form**—Eating Disorder Contract 2
	9.23 **Policy**—Blood-Borne Pathogens and Infectious Diseases
	9.24 **Policy**—Dehydration and Heat- and Cold-Related Illnesses
	9.25 **Risk Assessment**—Checklist: Sports Medicine and Athletic Training
9.26 **Planning Tool**—Concussion: Protecting Student-Athletes and the Institution	
	9.27 **Policy**—Concussion
Bibliography	
9.B **Bibliography**—Sports Medicine and Athletic Training Programs	

Chapter 10 Diversity, Inclusion, and Nondiscrimination 281

In the book	Online in HK*Propel*
10.1 **Planning Tool**—Elements of a Model Diversity and Inclusion Program	
	10.2 **Evaluation Instrument**—Diversity Evaluation Based on Key Performance Indicators
10.3 **Planning Tool**—Strategic Planning for Diversity: Goals and Objectives	
	10.4 **Policy**—Diversity, Inclusion, and Nondiscrimination
10.5 **Planning Tool**—Aggressive Marketplace Search and Recruiting Practices	
10.6 **Planning Tool**—Staff and Student-Athlete Diversity Education	
10.7 **Management Tip**—Retention Strategies and Inclusion Issues	
10.8 **Management Tip**—Role of the Athletic Policy Board in Advancing Diversity	
10.9 **Planning Tool**—Staff Incentives to Advance Diversity Objectives	
10.10 **Management Tip**—Issues Related to Individuals With Disabilities	
	10.11 **Evaluation Instrument**—Title IX Compliance (Gender Equity): Includes a Title IX Assessment Workbook with 27 Excel spreadsheets for data collection and analysis
10.12 **Management Tip**—Sexual Abuse and Harassment	
	10.13 **Policy**—Inclusivity and Nondiscrimination for LGBTQ Individuals
Bibliography	
10.B **Bibliography**—Diversity, Inclusion, and Nondiscrimination	

Chapter 11 Team Administration 311

In the book	Online in HK*Propel*
Roster Management	
11.1 **Management Tip**–Athletic Director's Role in Team Roster Decisions	
	11.2 **Policy**–Roster Management and Tryouts
11.3 **Management Tip**–Proper and Improper Use of Roster Management	
Athlete Selection, Participation, and Preparation	
	11.4 **Form**–Clearance to Participate in Tryouts
	11.5 **Policy**–Clearance for Athletic Participation
	11.6 **Form**–Student-Athlete Participation Agreement
	11.7 **Form**–Limited Privacy Waiver (FERPA and HIPAA Release)
	11.8 **Form**–Unsupervised Preseason Conditioning Agreement
	11.9 **Policy**–Athlete Preparation: Conditioning and Practice Sessions
	11.10 **Form**–Preseason Conditioning Program Communication
	11.11 **Risk Assessment**–Checklist: Athlete Preparation and Participation
Coach and Student-Athlete Conduct	
11.12 **Management Tip**–Managing the Coach–Athlete Relationship	
	11.13 **Risk Assessment**–Checklist: Student-Athlete Discipline and Behavior
11.14 **Planning Tool**–Handling a Complaint Related to Coach Behavior	
11.15 **Planning Tool**–Student-Athlete Handbook, Team Rules, and Athlete Rights	
	11.16 **Policy**–Team Rules and Disciplinary Procedures
	11.17 **Policy**–Alcohol, Tobacco, and Drug Use
	11.18 **Policy**–Hazing, Sexual Harassment, and Other Intimidation Tactics
11.19 **Management Tip**–Consider Retaining a Substance Abuse Counselor	

In the book	Online in HK*Propel*
Equipment and Uniforms	
11.20 **Management Tip**–Uniforms and Equipment: Model Practices and Risk Mitigation	
	11.21 **Policy**–Equipment Selection, Purchase, Maintenance, Issuance, and Safety
	11.22 **Form**–Equipment Inventory and Replacement Schedule
	11.23 **Form**–Equipment Inspection, Repair, and Maintenance Record
	11.24 **Policy**–Uniform Selection, Purchasing, and Issuance
	11.25 **Form**–Student-Athlete Equipment and Uniform Checkout and Return Record
	11.26 **Risk Assessment**–Checklist: Athletic Equipment and Apparel
Travel	
	11.27 **Policy**–Team Travel
	11.28 **Policy**–Ground Transportation
	11.29 **Policy**–Air Transportation
	11.30 **Form**–Travel Arrangements Request Form
	11.31 **Form**–Hotel Confirmation Request and Rooming List
	11.32 **Form**–Team Travel Itinerary
	11.33 **Form**–Approval of Student-Athlete Not Traveling With Team
	11.34 **Policy**–Band and Cheerleader Travel
	11.35 **Risk Assessment**–Checklist: Team Travel
Awards	
	11.36 **Policy**–Annual Participation Awards
	11.37 **Policy**–Special Awards
	11.38 **Policy**–Conference Championship Awards
	11.39 **Policy**–National Championship Awards
	11.40 **Policy**–Annual Awards Banquet
Bibliography	
11.B **Bibliography**–Team Administration	

Chapter 12 Event Management and Scheduling.......................335

In the book	Online in HK*Propel*
Scheduling of Practices and Contests	
	12.1 **Policy**–Facility Scheduling for Athletic Activities
	12.2 **Form**–Facilities Request
	12.3 **Policy**–Competition Schedules
	12.4 **Policy**–Contest Contracts
	12.5 **Form**–Contest Agreement
	12.6 **Form**–Request for Schedule Change
	12.7 **Policy**–Offering and Accepting Guarantees
Event Operations	
	12.8 **Policy**–Hiring, Assignment, and Evaluation of Sports Officials
	12.9 **Form**–Official's Payment Voucher
	12.10 **Form**–Evaluation of Contest Officials
	12.11 **Policy**–Arrangements for Visiting Teams
	12.12 **Policy**–Tickets
	12.13 **Policy**–Cash-Handling Procedures at Events and Summer Camps
	12.14 **Form**–Cash Box Request and Reconciliation
12.15 **Management Tip**–Alternatives to Concessions Outsourcing	
	12.16 **Policy**–Bidding to Host Special and Championship Events
	12.17 **Policy**–Support of Print and Electronic Media
	12.18 **Policy**–Signage, Distribution of Commercial Products, and Promotional Activities
12.19 **Planning Tool**–Factors Dictating Preevent Risk Assessment	
	12.20 **Policy**–Event Accessibility and Safety
	12.21 **Policy**–Security Management
12.22 **Management Tip**–Effective Crowd Control	
	12.23 **Policy**–Crowd Control
	12.24 **Form**–Security Incident Report
	12.25 **Form**–Letter to Spectators Removed for Misconduct
	12.26 **Risk Assessment**–Checklist: Event Management
12.27 **Management Tip**–Fan Engagement and Broadband Capability	

In the book	Online in HK*Propel*
Camps and Clinics	
12.28 **Planning Tool**–Management of Camps and Clinics	
	12.29 **Policy**–Camps and Clinics
	12.30 **Form**–Camp or Clinic Participant Acknowledgments, Authorizations, and Releases
	12.31 **Form**–Camp or Clinic Participant Proof of Insurance
	12.32 **Form**–Medical Information and Physician Clearance for Camp or Clinic Participation
	12.33 **Form**–Parent Acknowledgment of Drop-Off and Pick-Up Policies
	12.34 **Form**–Parent Acknowledgment of Participant Behavior Expectations
	12.35 **Policy**–Residence Hall Policies for Overnight Camps
	12.36 **Policy**–Protocol for Missing Child During a Camp or Clinic
	12.37 **Form**–Camp or Clinic Staff Acknowledgment of Policy Review
	12.38 **Form**–Responsibility for Participant Safety
	12.39 **Risk Assessment**–Checklist: Camps and Clinics
Bibliography	
12.B **Bibliography**–Event Management and Scheduling	

Chapter 13 Revenue Acquisition and Fund-Raising 351

In the book	Online in HK*Propel*
Overview of General Considerations	
13.1 **Planning Tool**–Elements of a Model Revenue Acquisition and Fund-Raising Program	
13.2 **Planning Tool**–Critical Staffing, Technology, and Integration Issues	
13.3 **Planning Tool**–Relationship Building by Coaches and Staff	
13.4 **Planning Tool**–Fund-Raising Events That Make Sense	
	13.5 **Form**–Approval for Team Fund-Raising Activity

In the book	Online in HKPropel
Annual Giving and Major Giving	
13.6 **Planning Tool**–Annual Giving Programs and Booster Clubs	
	13.7 **Policy**–Governance of External Booster Clubs
13.8 **Planning Tool**–Major Donor and Endowed Gift Programs	
	13.9 **Policy**–Permanently Restricted Endowments
	13.10 **Form**–Establishment of an Endowment
Fund-Raising Campaigns	
13.11 **Planning Tool**–Building Construction and Other Major Fund-Raising Campaigns	
	13.12 **Educational Resource**–Campaign Leadership Committee Guidelines
Corporate-Giving and Sponsorship Programs	
13.13 **Planning Tool**–Sponsorship and Corporate-Giving Programs	
	13.14 **Policy**–Corporate Sponsorships
	13.15 **Form**–Corporate Sponsorship Proposal
	13.16 **Educational Resource**–Guidelines for Soliciting Corporate Sponsors
Athletic Event Income	
13.17 **Planning Tool**–Maximizing Event Income: Ticketing, Concessions, Parking, and Guarantees	
13.18 **Planning Tool**–Seating Priority Points Systems	
Multimedia Rights and Advertising Income	
13.19 **Planning Tool**–Selling Event and Multimedia Rights	
	13.20 **Form**–Request for Proposal: Athletic Event and Multimedia Rights
13.21 **Planning Tool**–Assessment of Radio, Television, and Internet Streaming Production Capability	
Other Sources of Revenue	
13.22 **Planning Tool**–Launching a New Sport as a Revenue Producer	
13.23 **Planning Tool**–Licensed Merchandise	
13.24 **Management Tip**–Student Fees and Pay to Play	
	13.25 **Policy**–Pay-to-Play Program
13.26 **Planning Tool**–Tuition Waivers, Facility Rentals, Land Leases, Vending Machines, and Other Income Sources	
13.27 **Planning Tool**–More Than Summer Camps for Children	
Bibliography	
13.B **Bibliography**–Revenue Acquisition and Fund-Raising	

Chapter 14 Communications, Media Relations, and Promotions 405

In the book	Online in HKPropel
Positioning the Brand	
14.1 **Planning Tool**–Getting the Message Out Versus Selling	
14.2 **Planning Tool**–Branding: Why Expert Help Is Necessary	
14.3 **Management Tip**–Establishing Guidelines for Social Media	
	14.4 **Educational Resource**–Wise Use of Social Media
Media Relations	
14.5 **Planning Tool**–Media Relations, Promotions, and Public Relations	
	14.6 **Policy**–Media Relations
	14.7 **Policy**–Media Responsibilities of Coaches
	14.8 **Form**–Media Relations: Student-Athlete Information
	14.9 **Form**–Media Relations: Coach Information
	14.10 **Form**–Request for Media Credentials
	14.11 **Policy**–Crisis Communications
Publications	
14.12 **Planning Tool**–Checklist: Basic Communications Vehicles	
	14.13 **Policy**–Athletic Department Publications
	14.14 **Policy**–Copyright Releases
	14.15 **Form**–Student-Athlete Communications Copyright Release
	14.16 **Form**–Employee Communications Copyright Release
	14.17 **Form**–Visiting Student-Athlete and Staff Copyright Release

In the book	Online in HKPropel
	14.18 **Form–**Publications Production Action Plan
	14.19 **Policy–**Website Publishing
	14.20 **Policy–**Photography Services

Bibliography

In the book	Online in HKPropel
14.B **Bibliography–**Communications, Media Relations, and Promotions	

Chapter 15 Facilities and Operations 421

Building or Significantly Renovating a Sport Facility

In the book	Online in HKPropel
15.1 **Planning Tool–**First Step: Facility Planning Committee	
15.2 **Planning Tool–**Justification for a New Building or Renovation Project	
15.3 **Planning Tool–**Site Selection for a New Facility	
15.4 **Planning Tool–**Feasibility Study Part I: Facility Cost	
15.5 **Planning Tool–**Feasibility Study Part II: Facility Financing	
15.6 **Planning Tool–**Feasibility Study Part III: Fiscal Sustainability	
15.7 **Planning Tool–**Outsourcing Facility Construction and Operations	
15.8 **Planning Tool–**Virtual Walk-Through: Functionality, Efficiency, and Safety	

Facility Operations

In the book	Online in HKPropel
15.9 **Planning Tool–**Adequate Supervision of Sport Facilities	
	15.10 **Policy–**Supervision of Sport Facilities
	15.11 **Form–**Facility Emergency Action Plan
15.12 **Planning Tool–**Facility Operating and Deferred Capital Budgets	
	15.13 **Form–**Basketball Gymnasium Maintenance, Inspection, Repair, and Replacement Schedule
	15.14 **Form–**Basketball Gymnasium Rotation Budget
15.15 **Planning Tool–**Mitigation of Risk Through Proper Facility Management	
	15.16 **Policy–**Facility Inspection and Maintenance
	15.17 **Form–**General Release, Waiver, and Consent
	15.18 **Form–**General Incident or Injury Report
	15.19 **Risk Assessment–**Checklist: Ball Fields Inspection
	15.20 **Risk Assessment–**Checklist: Facility Safety and Supervision
15.21 **Planning Tool–**Considerations in Scheduling a Multiuse Facility	

Facility Rentals

In the book	Online in HKPropel
	15.22 **Policy–**Use of Sport Facilities by Community Groups
	15.23 **Form–**Application for Use of Facilities
	15.24 **Form–**Notification of Decision for Facility Use Application
	15.25 **Form–**Facility Use Agreement
	15.26 **Policy–**Volunteer Groups and Concessions at Home Athletic Events
	15.27 **Form–**Volunteer Consent and Release From Liability
	15.28 **Form–**Charitable Organization Application for Concessions Booth
	15.29 **Risk Assessment–**Checklist: Facility Use by Third Parties

Bibliography

In the book	Online in HKPropel
15.B **Bibliography–**Facilities and Operations	

Index 453

About the Authors 462

Preface

Over the past five decades, we have been coaches, athletic directors in all three NCAA membership divisions, and leaders of nonprofit organizations. This collection of materials is the resource we wish had been available at the beginning of our administrative careers rather than a reference that we later developed showing how we corrected every mistake we made during those careers. Through decades of interactions with colleagues, it is clear that we have learned more from our on-the-job experience than we did from formal education. Our books and classes never completely connected the dots between theory and practice, and rarely did they cover the most difficult challenges we had to handle. Thus, this collection is intended to be the most comprehensive practical resource on the market, a desk reference that every high school and college athletic director consults to find help with almost every typically encountered situation, and one that provides information that can be used immediately in a format that fulfills the policy and system needs of the athletic manager.

This compilation is not a traditional textbook that is intended to be read from cover to cover. Rather, it is a comprehensive resource that includes management tips, planning tools, educational resources, policies, forms, evaluation instruments, and risk assessments that can be used as a desk reference as topics become important to the athletic manager. Seven types of documents are included, the definitions of which are as follows:

- Management tip—Factual background information, insights, problem-solving strategies, and suggestions for the athletic director. Management tips can be found in the book.
- Planning tool—Steps to take or factors that should be considered in the development of strategic plans, action plans, professional development plans, and governance systems. Planning tools can be found in the book.
- Educational resource—Informational handouts that can be used to educate staff members, campus constituents, volunteers, or student-athletes. Educational resources can be found in the online web resource.
- Policy—Sample policies and procedures that should be adopted by an athletic department after customization and review by appropriate expert institutional or school district officials. These can be found in the online web resource.
- Form—Sample forms, letters, or job descriptions. These can be found in the online web resource.
- Evaluation instrument—Administrative tools that help the athletic director, a supervisor, or an employee assess job performance and evaluate program content. These can be found in the online web resource.
- Risk assessment—Checklists that help the athletic director, a supervisor, or an employee identify risks and prevent litigation. These can be found in the online web resource.

Together, the book and web resource focus on the practical application of educational and management theory by athletic directors, senior managers, and head coaches—the issues that they will confront and the practices that dictate a sound course of action. This desk reference is really a collection of three things: (1) information that every athletic manager needs to know; (2) a description of how the athletic department should operate on a daily basis; and (3) a collection of policies, procedures, and other systems that, if followed, should prevent the occurrence of many problems.

Although a resource-rich program at an NCAA Division I FBS institution differs considerably from a limited-resource program that might be found at a rural high school, the management principles are the same. What differs are (1) the number of people who must be managed, (2) whether the institution can afford staff members with specialty skills and high levels of expertise, and (3) the sheer complexity of a more intense political and media climate. With money comes a heightened risk for corruption and even greater concern for ethics policies and continuing education that may protect the integrity of the institution and the athletic program. Thus, although we tried to write to the complexity of a large collegiate athletic program, the material is generally applicable to the smallest high school athletic program, and athletic directors at smaller schools can focus on the policies, instruments, and forms most applicable to them.

The online resource available in HK*Propel* contains downloadable documents that are easily customized by the user. The differences in institutional policies and philosophies or in state laws are so vast that it is impossible to say that any policy, procedure, or program contained herein is perfectly usable as presented. Additionally, reference to specific NCAA rules, other governing body rules, or legal documents that regularly change should be checked for accuracy. Some documents should be reviewed by institutional legal counsel or institutional experts in human resources, medical services, campus security, risk management, or other areas, depending on the nature of the topic being addressed and the type of institution promulgating the policy. What these materials represent are model programs and policies developed by experienced managers. We hope that most of these documents can be used immediately after simple modifications, which will save the athletic director from investing significant time and the necessary attention to detail required to produce effective policies and procedures.

Like all policies and procedures, they are written from the ethical and philosophical perspective of the authors. This perspective may differ from that of other athletic directors. For instance, we believe that student-athlete academic support programs should not be overseen by the athletic department because of an inherent conflict of interest. Also, we have strong beliefs about the responsibilities of all staff members in the area of relationships with student-athletes or others over whom they have supervisory responsibility. We believe that the heart of professional satisfaction lies in a commitment to excellence in both the athletic director's work performance and that of the staff members supervised. We believe that another key ingredient in the career success of managers is that they conduct themselves in an exemplary professional manner and always stand up for what they believe is the right and fair thing to do.

At the beginning of our management careers, we were young, inexperienced, and naive athletic directors. We thought that how we operated was what all athletic directors were supposed to do and that everyone did it that way. As we got older, we came to understand that many administrators were more concerned about retaining power, having people comply with their wishes, and not confronting what was wrong with the system. They avoided change and embraced the status quo. We realized that taking the easy road often meant taking the wrong road, that being a leader involved trying to determine what was right and fair, and that embracing change was a perpetual way of leading. We also learned that change wasn't always about correcting a wrong; it was about simply finding a more efficient way to do something. The administrator who is committed to learning and changing because of what he or she learns is committed to managing an environment of change.

After the completion of successful administrative careers, each of us was delighted to learn that we carried identical life mantras for which we credited our parents:

"Work hard, give unselfishly to others, and always do good. If you do these things, good things will always happen to you."

"The joy of work is rarely a result of personal success but more often revealed through team accomplishments and enduring relationships with others."

Acknowledgments

A comprehensive compilation of policies, forms, evaluation tools, and practical management advice required the input and feedback of many professionals. We are deeply indebted to and would like to thank the following people for their invaluable expert assistance in the development of these resources.

We give significant credit to our former employees, to every colleague we've ever worked with or consulted with, and to our mentors. All of these policies, programs, and systems were created with the input of many others; it was truly a team effort. Because these programs and policies affected many others, they needed the review of higher administration, other experts on campus and off, and other athletic department staff members whose experience provided different insights and knowledge. We are particularly grateful for the contributions of all the staff members of the Department of Intercollegiate Athletics for Women at the University of Texas at Austin who, during the period from 1975 through 1992 in particular, helped create many model documents, programs, and systems that were used as the basis of materials developed for this collection. We especially want to thank these colleagues:

- Dr. Randa Ryan, former senior associate athletic director for student services, who was instrumental in the development of materials related to student support programs
- Dr. Sheila Rice, former assistant director for academic affairs, for her contributions to policy development in the area of academic affairs
- Lynn Wheeler, former associate athletic director for events and operations, for her contributions in the area of event management
- Jody Conradt, now special assistant to the athletic director and former athletic director and head women's basketball coach, for her expertise in numerous team administration and management areas
- Becky Bludau Marshall, former head athletic trainer, for her advice and contributions in this area
- Tina Bonci, MS, ATC, LAT, former associate athletic director for sports medicine and athletic training, now deceased, for her forward thinking and incredible work in documenting the operation of athletic training and sports medicine programs

At Drew University, the following people were instrumental in developing and reviewing educational resources, personnel evaluation systems, facility and event policies, and business processes:

- Vincent Masco, former associate director of athletics and former head baseball coach
- Christa Racine, now director of athletics and head soccer coach
- Tom Leanos, former director of facilities and head lacrosse coach
- Rosemari Renahan, former business manager and assistant to the director of athletics

Special thanks are also extended to the following people who made significant contributions of content to this book:

- Dr. Bob Frederick, former University of Kansas teacher, coach, and athletic director, now deceased, who contributed to the development of materials related to event management, facility maintenance and safety, team travel, insurance and supervision, emergency medical protocols, and other policies developed for the University of Kansas program of intercollegiate athletics
- Dr. Christine H.B. Grant, former director of women's athletics at the University of Iowa, for her contributions related to drug testing and alcohol policies and procedures, hiring and evaluation of employees, diversity, event management, eligibility, gender equity, and other policies developed for the University of Iowa Intercollegiate Athletics Policy Manual
- Dr. Lauren Costello, MD, former team physician at Princeton University and former assistant professor at the University of Medicine and Dentistry of New Jersey, for

her contributions related to eating disorders, blood-borne pathogens, and infectious diseases

- Zachary Lewis, former New York University graduate research assistant in the Preston Robert Tisch Center for Hospitality, Tourism and Sports Management, who worked diligently to collect best practice documents from countless high school, college, and university athletic departments

We would also like to thank Chris Voelz, former director of women's athletics at the University of Minnesota, and Francine Nocella, former athletic director of Wantagh Public Schools, Wantagh, New York, who were instrumental in the conceptual organization of this book. We also appreciate the contributions of Tuti B. Scott, president of Imagine Philanthropy, for her forward-thinking approach to fund-raising and relationship building and her contributions to the revenue section of this desk reference.

Good policy is never developed in a vacuum. Good policy is the result of dedicated and passionate staff members who care about their profession, the student-athletes they serve, and the stakeholders who support educational sport programs. We owe them our thanks and appreciation for work well done.

CHAPTER

1

Developing Leadership Style and Philosophy

Every athletic director must have a firm grounding in the role and function of educational sport based on a clear moral compass, a respectful leadership style, and enunciated values that all employees are expected to honor. Above all other factors, these management characteristics and beliefs will dictate organizational culture, generate passion for achieving mission, and result in the highest levels of operational integrity and performance. By adding critical-thinking skills and political acumen to the process used to approach every challenge, the manager will prevent crises, help employees adapt quickly to change, and lead deftly during times of calm as well as unexpected events. The documents in this chapter, in both the book and the HK*Propel*, are intended to help athletic directors define and improve these leadership and communications skills toward the end of building trusting and productive relationships with all staff members and stakeholders.

TYPES OF DOCUMENTS

Management tip—Factual background information, insights, problem-solving strategies, and suggestions for the athletic director

Planning tool—Steps to take or factors that should be considered in the development of strategic plans, action plans, professional development plans, or governance systems

Educational resource—Handouts that can be used to educate staff members, campus constituents, volunteers, or student-athletes

Policy—Sample policies and procedures that should be adopted by an athletic department after customization and review by appropriate expert institutional or school district officials

Form—Sample forms, letters, or job descriptions

Evaluation instrument—Administrative tools that help the athletic director, a supervisor, or an employee assess job performance and evaluate program content

Risk assessment—Checklists that help the athletic director, a supervisor, or an employee identify risks and prevent litigation

1.1 MANAGEMENT TIP

Required Skills of an Athletic Director

The athletic director is the head coach of a team, a master teacher, and a leader who has the ability to organize and inspire a group of people to achieve common goals. The athletic department team will vary with regard to numbers of employees, size of budget, and age of student-athletes (middle school, high school, and college programs). The goals of the team will vary according to the competitive level of the program and its related definition of success. But every effective athletic director is a highly organized person who has a great deal of responsibility and is committed to pulling the best out of his or her players and pursuing the highest level of excellence in the specified philosophical context of the program.

The success of the athletic director lies in five dimensions:

1. Making informed, ethical, and fair decisions
2. Hiring and retaining competent, passionate, and committed employees
3. Fulfilling the educational, resource, and inspirational needs of employees and student-athletes
4. By example and action, inspiring excellence in the performance of employee and student-athlete duties and responsibilities
5. Creating policies and procedures that enable employees to work efficiently and effectively in mitigating the occurrence or repetition of problems

Success in all these dimensions, the difference between being good and being great, depends on specific skills, all of which can be learned:

- **Leadership**—Exhibiting decision-making behavior, a manner of communicating instructions, and intrapersonal behavior that produce respect, trust, and an enjoyable working environment that inspires employees and student-athletes to want to demonstrate excellence and meet the expectations of the leader
- **Values and principles**—Setting ethical standards and requiring ways of working together that engender feelings of pride, dignity, and honor in what all employees do and how they are expected to work together
- **Knowledge**—Demonstrating a mastery of the subject matter of educational sport and administration coupled with critical-thinking skills that produces wise decisions and solutions to problems
- **Management philosophy**—Clearly communicating beliefs about how people are expected to work together to produce a desired outcome that creates an efficient and productive team of workers
- **Political acumen**—Demonstrating wise strategic and diplomatic skill in influencing the decisions of others so that the organization can acquire the resources necessary to support its work
- **Change management**—Embracing the importance and inevitability of change and guiding employees and stakeholders through the change process
- **Commitment to learning**—Creating an athletic department culture of shared learning that affirms the value of each employee's knowledge and contributions to the success of the team

1.2 MANAGEMENT TIP

Personal Attributes of Leaders

Leadership is a composite of commendable personal attributes and ways of acting that causes employees and student-athletes to believe in the leader's judgment and direction and want to execute or fulfill the leader's assignments and expectations. Attributes refer to a person's manner of acting as contrasted with decision making or other skills. Is there such a thing as a person being a natural leader, like a natural athlete or a gifted artist or musician whose talent appears to come easily? To an extent, the answer is yes. Leadership qualities come more easily to some than others, but all of the following personal attributes of a good leader can be developed by intent.

Patient and understanding communicator—Able to explain tasks clearly and inspire others of varying capacities, educational backgrounds, and philosophical perspectives.

Confidence—Poised, clear thinker under pressure and demonstrates conviction in the course being set and decisiveness, characteristics that earn the respect and loyalty of others.

Fairness—Treats people fairly and makes decisions consistent with clearly expressed standards of right and wrong. When handling disputes, the leader's resolution engenders a feeling of justice, equal treatment, and evenhandedness. The leader's decisions are sought by others because they generate a feeling of dependability, reliability, and stability.

Generosity—A giver rather than taker; a giver of time, knowledge, and support.

Honesty—Truthful and openly self-critical with regard to acknowledgment of own errors.

Humility—Modest about his or her abilities.

Mastery—Decision making and performance demonstrate high personal commitment to acquisition of fact-based information, new knowledge, skill mastery, and thoughtful action. A leader is a role model whom others would like to emulate.

Passion—Performs work and approaches every task with passion and enthusiasm.

Optimism—Believes that everyone has something important to contribute to the success of the organization and creates an environment that is positive, hopeful, and buoyant, a place of working, playing, and human interaction that employees and student-athletes enjoy and value.

Respectful—Always respectful of others.

Selflessness—Puts the needs, interests, and wishes of others before his or her self-interest. When the leader asks someone to do something, the person knows that what is being asked is for the larger good or the good of another or the organization.

Trustworthiness—Team members confide in, rely on, and follow advice and instruction of the leader because they trust and have faith that he or she is acting in their best interest and will not reveal confidential information.

Model behavior—"Do as I say and as I do." The leader models all behaviors that employees are expected to emulate and that the organization wants student-athletes, fans, donors, and alumni to see and respect.

Not surprisingly, research demonstrates that people with these characteristics are successful leaders. For example, McCall and Lombardo (1983) found that the successful leaders they studied had the following key traits: (1) emotional stability (calm, composed, predictable), (2) acknowledged own errors, (3) breadth of knowledge, and (4) excellent communications and interpersonal skills.

Collins (2001) identified level 5 executive leadership as a combination of humility, strong confidence, and mastery. Bass (1999) and others pointed to the ability to inspire as key to transformational leadership. Lewin et al. (1939) found that democratic or participatory leadership was more effective than autocratic or diffused leadership but was dependent on the subject matter requiring decision making. Hersey, Blanchard, and Johnson (2007), proponents of situational leadership, noted that every situation is different and that each situation calls upon different traits and skills on the part of a manager, including the skill to adapt to the personality and motivation of employees involved. Tannenbaum and Schmitt (1958) suggested that good leadership depends on accurate identification and management of leader, employee, and situational forces. Stogdill (1974) identified 13 traits and 9 skills of successful leaders, all among those already mentioned.

The athletic director should go beyond working to develop his or her own leadership competencies and think about ways to encourage all employees to become leaders. Sharing thoughts on leadership and encouraging all employees to aspire to becoming leaders may be as simple as distributing a memo on the topic. Educational Resources 1.3 and 1.4 are examples of such communications.

Of course, the most effective way to develop employee leadership is to give employees the authority and responsibility to practice being leaders. The leader should continually challenge others to be accountable for performing important functions and tasks.

1.3 **Educational Resource**—All Employees Should Aspire to Be Leaders

A sample memo from the athletic director to all employees that describes positive traits of employees and managers and defines competencies that differentiate leaders.

1.4 **Educational Resource**—Personal Leadership Self-Evaluation

A sample memo from the athletic director to all managers and supervisors that cautions employees about abuses of power and encourages them to complete a self-evaluation that emphasizes important leadership behaviors.

Available in HK*Propel*.

1.5 MANAGEMENT TIP

Critical Thinking and Decision Making

Even when the athletic director is well educated in a particular subject area, wise decision making or effective problem solving isn't guaranteed. What a person knows and how he or she applies that knowledge are very different circumstances. The application of knowledge to decision making and problem solving requires critical-thinking skills. Critical thinking is a persistent effort to process information rationally while simultaneously being aware of the often-competing forces of (1) the rights and needs of others, (2) the fiduciary duty to the educational institution as employer, and (3) the decision maker's inclination to act with self-interest or unintentional prejudice. Critical thinking requires a disciplined approach to decision making. Checking your gut feeling is fine, but making a decision based only on such intuition is never good enough.

The more complex or important the issue is, the more important it is to take the time necessary to complete the critical-thinking process. Too often managers wrongly believe that a quick answer is a measure of intelligence or analytical acumen. The critical-thinking process (Foundation for Critical Thinking, 2007) has the following characteristics:

- Formulate clear questions and problems about the issue
- Seek to recognize and acknowledge bias, prejudice, or other indicators of lack of open-minded consideration; understand who benefits and who is disadvantaged by the decision
- Gather and evaluate relevant information about the issue
- Test possible conclusions and solutions against applicable criteria or standards, choosing the best option
- Review the implications and practical consequences of conclusions and solutions with others from diverse perspectives and be willing to refine thinking and options accordingly

Especially with regard to this last point, before discussing conclusions and solutions with others, the athletic director must be sure that he or she has completed this process. Only then will the athletic director be able to respond to questioning by a superior. Completing the critical-thinking and decision-making process requires the athletic manager to follow all of the following specific steps (Facione, 2006):

- **Analysis**—Looking at an issue in detail, separating the whole into its component parts
- **Evaluation**—Judging the value or importance of an issue
- **Inference**—Drawing a conclusion through reasoning from the consideration of evidence
- **Explanation**—Ascribing significance to an issue or its related parts
- **Interpretation**—Giving reasons for the existence or origin of the issue
- **Self-regulation**—Reexamining or reconsidering a position in light of new information or after determining bias and then considering new conclusions

Critical thinking is essential when addressing complex problems, establishing new policies, taking positions on important issues, and dealing with situations that affect the well-being of student-athletes, employees, or others. A commitment to critical thinking in such situations means patience, doing your homework, and being confident and secure enough to ask others to critique your conclusions. Most of all, critical thinking is committing to a thorough thought process commensurate with the importance of the decision to be made.

This commitment is similar to that of a great pitcher who, before throwing any pitch, has studied the hitter, determined the batter's strengths and weaknesses, prioritized the best pitches to be thrown given the count or game situation, and is continuously self-evaluating both the quality of his or her pitches and the choice of pitches when the at-bat and game are over. A talented pitcher can pitch a good game without doing any of this homework or preparation, but the difference between good and great is consistently working at being fully prepared and having a strong work ethic in that preparation. Anyone can make a decision, fewer can consistently make good decisions, and fewer still can make good decisions in crisis environments. Like any skill, critical thinking requires practice and commitment.

1.6 PLANNING TOOL

Basic Qualifications of the Athletic Director

Athletic Department as a Professional Bureaucracy Substructure

The athletic department resides within what is most often an already predetermined professional bureaucracy, an organization primarily consisting of educators whose occupations require extensive specialized training, skill, and competence in an academic area and whose status causes the public to give them a high degree of control over their own work. The larger educational institution is run by professional educators who are secondarily trained in the administration of such institutions.

Educational institutions are structured as classic bureaucracies in which a clear hierarchy of educator decision makers controls the work of specialized departments. Departments consist of highly trained teachers who provide primary educational services to student consumers, talented researchers who are expected to advance the state of their fields of study, and specialized personnel who provide the support services that enable teachers and researchers to spend the majority of their time on their work assignments. Educational institutions also have nonacademic departments with managers trained in specific institutional support skills like human resources, campus security, and buildings and grounds. As with most bureaucracies, numerous standardized operating policies are in place, including job categories and titles, policies related to salaries and benefits, basic information technology systems, and so on. The athletic director must adhere to these policies but has considerable flexibility in determining the design of internal athletic department operations.

An athletic director operating within this professional bureaucracy is often expected to have management training specific to educational administration, not just sport management. At the middle or high school level, an administrative certificate indicative of such training may be a required or preferred job qualification. At the college level, a master's or doctoral degree or coursework in educational administration may be required. Although many educational institutions have hired athletic directors without such qualifications, the complexities of athletics and education and today's litigious society argue for strong training in education administration and sport management.

Sport Management Training The breadth and complexity of high school and college athletic programs justifies requiring comprehensive undergraduate and graduate preparation for athletic administrators. The following subject areas constitute the prerequisite knowledge base for athletic directors:

- Philosophy of educational sport, ethics, and professional conduct
- Theories of leadership
- Administrative theory and structure
- Change management
- Athletic program models
- Athletic governance organizations
- Athletic finance
- Critical thinking
- Legal issues in sport and physical activity environments
- Athletic event management
- Strategic planning and program evaluation
- Sport pedagogy and evaluation of coaches
- Personnel management and evaluation
- Design and management of support programs for student-athletes
- Management of facilities, equipment, and supplies
- Fund-raising and revenue development
- Communications, marketing, and promotion

- Information management and technology in athletics
- Sociology of sport and critical issues

Degree, Certification, and Continuing Education Credentials Whether a prospective employee has to demonstrate experience, degree certification, or training in athletic management as prerequisites for being hired as an athletic director is unilaterally determined by the hiring agency—the respective school district, college, or university. Requirements range from the minimal, such as previous management experience in any field and no formal coursework, certification, or degree requirements (or such requirements listed as preferred rather than required qualifications) to higher standards such as athletic administration certification or a master's or other advanced degree in athletic or sport management. Surprisingly, as with the absence of certification or degree requirements for coaches, high professional management training standards for athletic directors are the exception rather than the rule. School district and college leaders seem reluctant to surrender any flexibility in hiring the person they want as an athletic director. A highly revered former coach, a former chief executive officer with no nonprofit or education experience, or a proven athletic director who lacks credentials are options that they want to keep open.

The absence of high standards in the marketplace, however, does not mean that aspiring athletic directors should minimally prepare. The better an applicant's experience, academic preparation, and certification credentials are, the more likely it is that the applicant will be carefully considered. Prospective athletic directors can obtain knowledge or experience credentials acceptable to employers in numerous ways.

Institutions of higher education are accredited by respected expert agencies through a peer review process that assesses conformance with a predetermined set of standards related to the award of undergraduate or graduate degrees. Similarly, specialized degree or certificate programs may be accredited as proofs of training in specialized subject areas. For instance, from the early 1990s through 2009, the North American Society for Sport Management (NASSM) and the National Association for Sport and Physical Education (NASPE) jointly sponsored a Sport Management Program Review Council (SMPRC) that certified sport management preparation programs at the university level (NASSM, 2007). That system has evolved into a peer review accreditation program established in 2009 and governed by the Commission on Sport Management Accreditation (COSMA). The NASSM maintains a list of all bachelor's, master's, and doctoral sport management degree programs in the world (NASSM, 2020).

Professional organizations such as coaches associations or athletic administrators associations also establish certification programs or training programs in their respective fields. For instance, the National Interscholastic Athletic Administrators Association (NIAAA) sponsors a four-level certification program: registered athletic administrator (RAA), registered middle school athletic administrator (RMSAA), certified athletic administrator (CAA), and certified master athletic administrator (CMAA) (NIAAA, 2020). College courses required by the program are offered by accredited universities. An undergraduate degree, experience as an athletic administrator, and completion of an examination administered by NIAAA are required for CAA and CMAA certification. The Women Leaders in College Sports (WLCS) offers a three-level executive training program: the Institute for Administrative Advancement, the Leadership Enhancement Institute, and the Executive Institute (WLCS, 2021).

Is certification required in addition to completion of a degree program, as with the certification or licensing of teachers? Again, the answer depends on the hiring agency and sometimes the degree program. For instance, many teacher education institutions specialize in offering both the pedagogy training and subject matter required for teacher certification or licensure as part of the undergraduate degree or a five-year program. Similarly, an undergraduate or graduate degree in sport management may fulfill all the experience and subject matter requirements of a certification program. The certifying agency may accept proof of such extensive preparation in lieu of a certification examination. Some certification programs count years of experience as an athletic director in lieu of some requirements.

Although administrative certificate programs have been long required in K–12 public education, athletic administration certification programs for K–12 are comparatively new and still don't exist at the college level. The need for these certification programs for athletic management is the result of an increasingly litigious environment and the visibility of athletic programs. Lawsuits and embarrassing media coverage are catalysts for professions to create more stringent training programs. Heightened standards of credentialing are one way that superintendents of schools or college presidents seek to protect their institutions from financial losses or a damaged reputation.

A number of online education programs offer certificates of completion to those who pass sport management courses, and some offer degree programs in athletic administration. Some of these online programs are accredited in the same way as institutions that require classroom attendance. Prospective students should be clear about the differences between certification as part of a higher education degree program accredited though a peer review process according to established standards in contrast to certification that simply indicates the completion of a course or program that may not be offered according to such standards.

Another important category of knowledge acquisition is continuing education programming. Many school districts require teachers, coaches, and administrators to demonstrate continuing education in their respective fields through the completion of educational programs each year. Such continuing education may consist of formal coursework offered by an institution of higher education or verification of attendance at workshops or conferences that have been approved for acceptable continuing education credits.

1.7 PLANNING TOOL

Ongoing Training Needs of the Athletic Director

Although every athletic director requires basic training in all areas of sport and education management, the unique nature of athletic programs requires that the sport manager stay up to date on developments in those critical program areas, which carry the highest reputation and legal liability risk for the educational institution. In addition, the lack of stable funding for athletic programs places a premium on fund-raising and revenue production. These constantly changing areas of knowledge require a strong commitment to continuing education. For instance, three decades ago

- concussions and decisions about returning to play following such injuries were not identified as critical health issues,
- revenue production through seat licenses and point systems for seating priorities were almost nonexistent,
- court cases and government agencies did not provide adequate guidance regarding legal liability related to sexual harassment,
- background checks for students and athletes as they relate to campus safety were not even discussed,
- conducting athletic programs in the midst of a pandemic was not contemplated,
- embarrassing student-athlete behavior on the Internet and use of social media was almost nonexistent, and
- fear of terrorism as it relates to security at major events did not exist.

Risk Management

Extensive participation in off-campus athletic events creates the need for the highest standards of supervision of student-athletes and sound policy related to the travel of athletic teams. The physical nature of athletics and the risk of injury inherent in such activity requires

- high standards of facility construction and maintenance;
- provision of protective sports equipment and adequate instruction on its use;
- well-maintained sports implements;
- strict policies for preparticipation and postinjury health assessment; and
- physician oversight of athletic employees who provide athletic training, weight training, and other injury prevention, treatment, and physical development support for student-athletes.

The effect of performance-enhancing drugs on the efficacy of the competition and the health of student-athletes may require drug testing, an intrusion into student-athlete privacy that requires an extremely high standard of care in process and procedure. The athletic department is frequently responsible for overseeing the construction, maintenance, and operation of physical activity facilities in which spectator events are conducted, creating another element of safety and liability consideration. Even suspending an athlete for violation of team rules or declaring a student-athlete ineligible for academic or other reasons are situations that have generated lawsuits on the part of parents concerned about the loss of collegiate athletic scholarships or professional sport opportunities. Numerous laws prohibiting discrimination based on sex, race, ethnicity, disability, age, and other characteristics affect hiring processes and program decisions related to distribution of resources and provision of athletic opportunities. All these areas are fraught with liability concerns. Thus, every athletic director needs a strong and continuing grounding in sport law. Likewise, senior managers in charge of various program areas and head coaches need to have relevant knowledge of sport law with regard to practice and competition facilities, team rules, and relationships with student-athletes.

First, people in these positions must be careful observers at all times, looking at everything from the perspective of anticipating what can go wrong. Second, structured risk assessments should be regularly scheduled. Risk assessment checklists should be distributed to senior staff members in charge of various program areas and facilities. The athletic director should request a comprehensive review of designated risk elements, a written report on deficiencies, and recommendations for steps required to correct those deficiencies. The following risk assessment and cautionary legal documents are available in this book, and asterisked documents are downloadable instruments that can be found in HK*Propel*:

- *1.8 Educational Resource—Monitoring Legal Decisions and Understanding Legal Concepts
- 2.3 Management Tip—Reliance on Professional Legal Advice
- 5.11 Management Tip—Production and Approval of Legal Agreements
- *5.24 Risk Assessment—Checklist: Finance, Insurance, and Contracts
- *6.23 Risk Assessment—Checklist: Employment
- *9.16 Risk Assessment—Checklist: Drug Testing and Education
- *9.25 Risk Assessment—Checklist: Sports Medicine and Athletic Training
- 10.10 Management Tip—Issues Related to Individuals With Disabilities
- *10.11 Evaluation Instrument—Monitoring Title IX Compliance (Gender Equity)
- 10.12 Management Tip—Sexual Abuse and Harassment
- *11.13 Risk Assessment—Checklist: Student-Athlete Discipline and Behavior
- *11.26 Risk Assessment—Checklist: Athletic Equipment and Apparel
- *11.35 Risk Assessment—Checklist: Team Travel
- 12.19 Planning Tool—Factors Dictating Pre-event Risk Assessment
- *12.26 Risk Assessment—Checklist: Event Management
- *12.38 Risk Assessment—Checklist: Camps and Clinics
- *15.19 Risk Assessment—Checklist: Ball Fields Inspection
- *15.20 Risk Assessment—Checklist: Facility Safety and Supervision
- *15.29 Risk Assessment—Checklist: Facility Use by Third Parties

Third, although athletic directors don't have to be and seldom are attorneys by training, as high-level managers they must understand basic legal concepts and legal obligations, and must develop policies, procedures, and training programs that reduce or eliminate the risk of litigation. If the athletic director is not a formally trained sport manager, at the very least he or she should take a course in sport law. After taking such a course, the athletic director as well as senior staff members must make a commitment to ongoing education in risk management. All athletic conferences have two or three athletic directors meetings each year. The athletic director should speak to the conference commissioner to ask that the organization's legal counsel conduct a legal update on an annual basis. In larger athletic departments, the athletic director may wish to appoint the compliance director or business manager to attend appropriate conferences; be responsible for ongoing communication with the institution's legal counsel, risk manager, or compliance director; or track recent legal developments through review of sport law newsletters. This person should report on such developments at regular staff meetings.

All senior staff members should share risk management responsibilities. The athletic director should advance this concept by sharing legal and risk management resources and requiring senior staff to subscribe to online sport business and sport litigation newsletters. Educational Resource 1.8 can be customized and distributed to senior staff for this purpose.

Media Attention and Public Pressure

No educational program receives more media attention than athletics. The sports section usually makes up 25 percent of a daily newspaper

1.8 Educational Resource—Monitoring Legal Decisions and Understanding Legal Concepts

A sample memo from the athletic director to senior staff members that (1) details specific and continuing risk management monitoring and sport law education responsibilities, (2) provides a glossary of legal terms and concepts, and (3) recommends online sport business and sport litigation e-newsletters.

Available in HK*Propel*.

and a significant part of radio and television news. Local print and electronic media cover local school and college sport on a daily basis. As a result, at many schools and colleges, the quality of the athletic program may be closely tied to the public's perception of the quality of the educational institution's brand. Likewise, in many small communities, the quality of the athletic program may be closely tied to the brand identity of the community itself. The existence of such brand identity relationships may put inordinate pressure on the athletic department to have successful athletic programs in those sports most covered by the media. Athletes, coaches, and administrators need to know how to speak to and serve the media. Athletic department employees need to know how to protect the privacy of athletes. Controlling public expectations by educating them about the differences between professional or commercial sport and educational sport is essential and requires the athletic director to have considerable communications skill and knowledge and a solid background in branding.

Revenue Production

Professional sport is a for-profit business in which profits (excess revenues over expenses) go to the owners of the business or shareholders. Educational sport is a not-for-profit business. Excess revenues over expenses belong to the school or college as a whole (not individual departments) and are reinvested in educational programs based on where the principal or president determines they are needed most. To make matters more complex, because of the ambiguous position of sport within the educational curriculum, many states prohibit the use of state education funds for the support of athletic programs, fearing abuse of tax dollars and that the popularity of sport might result in substantial use of state funds and insufficient funds for higher priority academic programs.

Because athletics is not funded like regular academic subjects, the principal of the school or president of the college most often chooses to allow the athletic department to keep all or part of the excess revenues it produces to offset some of the cost of the athletic program. In most educational institutions, these revenues are not substantial, but they may be large enough to support the operating costs of one or more sports. At institutions where revenues are substantial, considerable pressure may exist to maximize those revenues to perpetuate and support a large and successful athletic program.

Unlike most academic departments, the athletic department has athletic events, a product attractive to the public, for which the public will pay admission. The athletic program may be so popular that the public consents to contributing annually to its support as members of booster clubs or alumni groups. Therefore, unlike academic departments, the athletic department may be expected to produce revenues for its own support. In many instances, athletic program growth or even meeting normal cost-of-living and overhead increases requires considerable revenue development effort on the part of athletic personnel. Thus, the athletic director must be well trained in all aspects of revenue development: marketing, promotions, fund-raising, sale of licensed products, operation of concessions, acquisition of television and radio advertising and rights fees, and so forth. Athletic directors with such training and a track record of success are in high demand.

Managing educational sport as both a service and product industry is a significant challenge. Sport participation is a tool used to educate student-athletes, and coaches provide instructional services to student-athlete consumers. The athletic department also produces athletic events that may be offered for sale to spectators, students, and the public. In addition, the athletic department may have the right to use the school logo on T-shirts and other products and operate licensing or merchandising programs for the sale of such products. Thus, training in athletic event management, product sales management, and financial management is required, more so than in almost any other academic area.

Ethical Conduct of Educational Sport

A sound philosophy of educational sport is essential to achieving the right balance between achieving student-athlete development goals and taking advantage of commercial and other revenue development opportunities. As athletic program revenues and rewards to coaches responsible for such revenues increase, so does dependence on the acquisition and eligibility of top athletes and temptations to use inappropriate means to maintain and increase those revenues and human assets. Winning championships or important contests and basking in the glow of public and media admiration are powerful forces that can easily cloud good judgment. Inappropriate sexual relationships between coaches and athletes and issues of sexual harassment and abuse are garnering elevated media attention. Therefore, continuing to stay informed on sport governing body rules, campus oversight of rules compliance, and issues related to the ethical conduct of educational sport is mandatory for athletic administrators.

Athletic Event Management

The educational nature of the athletic event also affects the nature of the contract between the spectator and the athletic department. Athletic events can be likened to classroom tests in which students demonstrate what they have learned. The personal performance and improvement of each player is the test that is most important, rather than the outcome of the game or the number of tickets sold to spectators who are interested in watching students being tested. Spectators have no right to interfere with this learning environment and the teacher–student relationship. Their presence is a privilege, and their ticket purchase affords them no rights. Accustomed to the loose nature of commercial sport spectator environments or the lack of rules in the open amateur sport environment, school sport and youth sport must devote time and expertise to training spectators on appropriate and positive behavior at sport contests. Crowd control, sportsmanship education, and event security represent essential areas of knowledge for the athletic director.

1.9 MANAGEMENT TIP

Decision Making and Employee Relationships

Many theories describing how organizations should be structured and should function have been implemented. The athletic director needs to find an organizational structure and decision-making philosophy or develop his or her own composite that fits with his or her leadership style, values, and beliefs—one that he or she believes is the best and can sell to employees as the best. It has been said about great coaches that their philosophies of the game can be vastly different as long as (1) their system works, (2) they unequivocally believe that their system is the best system, and (3) they can convince others to believe the same. For example, a basketball coach may believe in a system that relies on a single basic offense and perfecting all options off that offense. Another coach may believe in multiple offenses—a different offense to use against each defense encountered. Both coaches can be successful. Success depends on how well they explain and teach their system and motivate their players to achieve excellence. The same is true of the athletic director—the head coach of a larger and more complex team.

Manager's Decision-Making Philosophy

Will group decision making occur depending on the subject or project? Is the decision-making system transparent? Are employees kept informed? Can decisions be appealed? Is employee input required before decisions are made? Many of these answers are based on knowledge of how people within organizations work, how employee behavior affects other employees, and how employees contribute to the effectiveness of organizational output. Athletic directors often come from the coaching ranks or have had coaching or playing experience. They understand the importance of developing teams. The choice of an operating system will be rooted in the manager's philosophy of how people best work together as a team to achieve excellence. Reviewing the research and literature on this topic will help the athletic director develop a philosophy about how to run his or her department.

Unique Needs of Service Organizations

Most of the early management theorists, because they were coping with the demands of the new industrial age of the late 1800s and early 1900s, were concerned about the efficient mass production of material products. Managers were perceived to be the educated class that established training programs and systems of production that resulted in directions that could be followed by workers, the uneducated class. Workers were not respected for their own insights, judgment, and experience. Today, especially in developed countries, service industries like education have required a careful rethinking and modification of industrial management theory. Rather than designing an administrative system for workers who will exercise little individual initiative or decision making, service organizations highly value and encourage independent assessment and thinking of employees who must respond to the needs of an incredibly diverse pool of consumers seeking to use their product. In addition, as industrial products become more complex (from computers to iPads), servicing the consumer after product purchase has increased the importance of workers skilled in developing strong and lasting relationships with those they serve. Developing those skills and applying them with efficiency, getting the best and most work done with the lowest expenditure of energy and resources, is a timeless management challenge.

In service industries like education, everyone, even those supporting the direct service providers (teachers and coaches), must be responsible for fulfilling the needs of consumers (students) and those who financially support the nonprofit service industry (donors, elected public officials).

Think about a major donor to the athletic program who, on a visit to campus, encounters a field maintenance worker caring for the field on which he or she used to play.

- When asked about the composition of the artificial turf, how will that worker respond?
- Will that employee be a part of the athletic department team that is committed to relationship building with alumni, parents, fans, faculty, and students?
- Has that employee been trained in effective consumer interaction? Who is responsible for that training?
- Will that donor leave the conversation thinking about the importance of an investment in artificial turf?
- Has that employee been inspired by the athletic director to believe that he or she is a critical component in the success of the athletic department's development program?
- Is it the athletic director or the employee's supervisor who is responsible for communicating to that employee his or her responsibility to develop positive personal relationships with everyone they meet?

Importance of Management Theory

The answers to these questions are what management theory is all about. And the manager needs to be able to answer many more questions through an expressed system of how the organization will work. Should employees refuse requests from those who are not their supervisors? How does the athletic director want those outside the athletic department to think about how the department does business? How does the operating system of the organization make a positive first impression?

For instance, an autocratic athletic director who believes that his or her word is God's word and that either people do a task the way the manager wants it done or they can "hit the highway" will likely design an internal athletic department operating system with a sacrosanct structure or chain of command that will not permit the athletic director's decisions to be questioned. Tasks within the organization will be explicitly defined. Employees will be valued if they follow orders, complete their assigned tasks efficiently, and never question the system or the decision. The function of supervisors, with the approval of the athletic director, is to break down the job to be done into easily definable smaller tasks, define what task each employee is expected to complete, and specify how the job is to be performed. Such an administrative system would be a fair description of scientific management as described by one of the first management theorists, Frederick Taylor (Taylor, 1911). Many head coaches run their sport teams according to this management theory. They believe that to score the greatest number of points in a specified time, they should have strict control over as many variables as possible to maximize their control over the outcome of the game. Although this system may be effective in many cases and result in consistency of performance, it may not be as effective if

- opponents don't act as the coach has predicted,
- a key player gets injured and is replaced by someone less competent and predictable to teammates,
- one or more players don't accomplish their assigned tasks, or
- an opportunity appears during a game that can be exploited by a creative but not commonly allowed response by someone who can think on his or her own.

In many respects, the administrative system chosen by a coach to direct the performance of players within the time-limited, rigidly prescribed game is different from the systems that are most effective in the governance and complex daily processes that occur in a large athletic organization. A well-run organization can be highly organized and have clarity of duties and responsibilities without controlling employees so rigidly that the organization cannot benefit from their initiative, thinking, and experience.

Balancing Employee Trust, Creativity, and Efficiency

Commonly credited with defining the pros and cons of bureaucracies, Max Weber cautioned that although bureaucracies are required to achieve efficiencies in production by replacing emotion and tradition with rational rules, the flaw of this structure lay in its excesses such as not allowing exceptions for unusual individual cases and not realizing the positive benefits of teamwork across department units (Mommsen, 1989). Elton Mayo's research, the Hawthorne Studies, clearly demonstrated that the more management trusts employees, allows for their participation in decision making, encourages group and team approaches to accomplishing tasks, and creates an open and information-sharing environment, the more productive the employees are (Accel Team Development, 2003). Douglas McGregor popularized Mayo's human relations approach with his X and Y theory, suggesting that theory X, a manager's view of the limited motivation and inferior ability of employees, was flawed. He emphasized in theory Y that employees could be creative and self-directed, and would enjoy work if they and their work were respected and if they were committed to the goals of the organization (McGregor, 2006).

As the study of organizations and the way in which people best work together became more complex and sophisticated, the variables that managers needed to heed became both greater in number and even more apparent. Examples of this complexity include

- the influence of technology on work and efficiency,
- increased specialization of workers,
- concepts of organic rather than mechanistic systems,
- interaction between people and technology,
- predictability and lack thereof of decision making,
- workers' reactions to change and the pace of change, and
- competing interests and ethics.

Old thinking was not discarded as much as it was revised to adjust to these new or newly recognized variables. More study and deeper analyses created new ways of organizing or communicating with people or suggested policies that more effectively accommodated new challenges. This growth in the sophistication of administrative theory could be likened to adding more flexible branches and leaves to the more rigid hierarchal and pyramidal main decision-making trunk of a tree.

Athletic Manager's Challenge

In other words, if the manager can create the right environment and hire competent employees who work well with others and are passionate about what they do, the organization will flourish as an operating system. Unfortunately, creating the right environment isn't as simple as it sounds. Managers must be adept in applying organizational and human relations theory in varying situations with different types of employees engaged in different types of work. Just as the great coach has probably read every book on Xs and Os in his or her sport, the great manager should be committed to lifelong education, to reading about new research and ideas that may be applicable to the athletic environment. Numerous excellent and comprehensive online resources are available. A good place to start is on two free online sites:

American Management Association Online Library

Wide variety of quick-read tips and resources:

www.amanet.org/individualsolutions/parameters-solution1.aspx?SelectedSolutionType=Articles+%26+White+Papers

Free Management Library

650 topics, 5,000 links, easily the most comprehensive site:

http://managementhelp.org

Unique Athletic Environment and Avoiding Conflict of Interest

Besides keeping abreast of the general literature on administrative theory, the athletic manager must also understand how athletic programs differ from other service industries and nonprofit organizations. Unique forces at play in athletics may require departures from or adjustments to commonly accepted theory and practice. For instance, in general, administrative subunits (e.g., athletic training services, academic support services) that exist to support primary program units (teams) that deliver direct service to consumers (student-athletes) are usually subservient to those primary units. At times, however, public pressure to win and the monetary or power rewards of winning may create a significant temptation for coaches to break recruiting rules, play athletes who are injured or not completely rehabilitated, allow improper types of academic assistance to keep athletes academically eligible, or engage in similar practices that constitute wrongdoing. How does the athletic director design an administrative system that trusts coaches as professionals but also contains built-in mechanisms that can prevent dysfunctional practices?

Whenever a potential conflict of interest is present, a departure from traditional line authority to create a rational check and balance system that protects student-athletes and the organization from wrongdoing is necessary. For example, the manager would structure the administration of a student-athlete health support program to include a medical doctor working with a certified athletic trainer as the head decision makers on releasing an injured athlete to return to competition, never involving the coach in such decisions. Another example would be the athletic director or senior athletic department manager responsible for academic affairs who supervises the hiring and assignment of tutors and the provision of academic support services, rather than a coach. Such systems that recognize the potential for impropriety and prevent the reality or perception of its occurrence are also used when handling cash, a commonly recognized temptation. These check and balance systems and the unique forces affecting athletics must always be considered.

1.10 MANAGEMENT TIP

Political Acumen: A Skill Necessity

Although relationship building is a basic skill required of all employees, the athletic director and senior staff members need to be adept at sophisticated forms of influencing others, especially understanding the nature of and mastering the art of politics. The athletic director needs to mentor all employees on acquiring this knowledge and developing the skills necessary to operate successfully in complex external environments.

A good working definition of politics is "the ability to influence another person's thinking or actions." The athletic director must be a master of politics, able to persuade others to support the resource requirements and other needs of the athletic department. Developing political acumen should start with a self-assessment. Ann Richards, a now-deceased former governor of Texas, once said, "You can say anything to anyone as long as you dress like a lady and smile." This statement was not sexist. It was her way of saying that dressing professionally and having a positive and smiling demeanor influences someone's first impression of a person, before verbal interaction even occurs. Even after meeting someone and beginning the verbal interaction process, the effective influencer remains calm, smiling, and positive, even when imparting negative information. This commitment to a positive and professional style of dealing with others on the part of everyone in the organization is important. The athletic director is expected to be a role model in this regard, especially in a crisis where all eyes are looking for guidance and leadership from the head administrator.

The athletic director should have a policy that is explicitly communicated to every employee: "The only person in the athletic department who is permitted to make an enemy or engage in conflict is the athletic director." In effect, what this policy says is that nothing is more important than the reputation of the organization and that no employee has the right to risk that reputation.

Influencing others to respect the athletic department and provide it with what it needs requires the athletic director and other employees to master the following influencer skills:

1. **Do your homework.** Knowledge of situational needs and the way in which those needs will be communicated, the rationale behind policies or procedures offered for adoption, or the facts of situations to be resolved requires mastery of the knowledge surrounding the subject area in question. Before meeting and interacting with others, do everything you can to know more than who you are conferring with regarding the issue to be discussed.
2. **Demonstrate respect for those you are trying to influence.** Respect is demonstrated by (*a*) tone of voice, (*b*) professional greeting and thanks upon departure, (*c*) asking for the opinion or advice of another, (*d*) listening to the opinion or advice of another, and (*e*) accepting or rejecting recommendations based on good and unbiased reasoning. Respect is also demonstrated by always thanking people for their time as a first order of business, thanking them again for sharing their time and knowledge as closure to any meeting, and thanking them more formally, in writing by electronic or snail mail, the day following the meeting.
3. **Create a win–win.** Be able to explain why the person you are dealing with, the larger institution or community, or the business of the person you are speaking with will benefit from the action you are proposing. In designing what is commonly referred to as a win–win situation, the good influencer always thinks about the needs of others and how those needs intersect with the influencer's proposed action.
4. **Align with the larger institutional mission.** Show how the proposed action is consistent

with and advances the mission of the educational institution.

The athletic director should consider placement of the topic of political acumen on the agenda of a senior staff or all-employee staff meeting at which those expectations are explicitly discussed. Good politics should never be left to chance.

1.11 MANAGEMENT TIP

Wise Use of Power

Every manager tends to think about how the status of his or her position will affect how others respond to requests. A manager may even consider how much additional pressure can be created by using the influence of powerful people he or she knows. Good managers also understand that the use of power can be a double-edged sword. Each of the various types of power has upsides and downsides. Thus, the athletic director needs to understand the three traditional sources of power: (1) the power of position or internal sanction, (2) the power of external sanction, and (3) the power of knowledge.

Power of Position

The power of position is the title and status of the athletic director. The title itself signifies the athletic director's decision-making authority within the organizational hierarchy, a measure of the degree of control that the athletic director has over athletic department employees. This title and status gives the athletic director the power to sanction (to impose a penalty or to reward) athletic department employees based on the responsiveness of the employee to the athletic director's requests, such as by determining a person's evaluation, salary, hiring, termination, or recommendation for advancement. Internally, the athletic director seldom has to threaten the use of his or her power to sanction because employees commonly understand this power and act accordingly. But this power to have a negative effect on an employee's career, salary, or advancement should not be taken lightly. Such actions must be governed by stated policies and procedures and fairly exercised. Managers who commonly threaten sanction outside such processes are perceived to be insecure and unfair. The status of the athletic director title may or may not have any influence on others within the institution outside the athletic department. But if the athletic program is considered an important institutional asset, this power may be considerable. For instance, athletics may receive priority over all other programs with regard to facility requests.

Power of External Sanction

The power of external sanction occurs when a person who is not in a formal organizational hierarchy has power over those within that system. For example, a donor who just gave $50 million to the institution persuades the president of the institution that the losing football coach should be fired, and the president tells the athletic director to do so. Or the winning football coach, who has not been given the power within the institution's hierarchy to control the decisions of the admissions office, threatens to leave the institution unless a top recruit receives an admissions exception. Or the athletic director, who doesn't control parking permits on campus, gets the best assigned parking space and a permit to park anywhere on campus because he or she makes sure that the person in charge of this area gets good football tickets.

When an athletic director uses connections to ignite the power of external sanction, such control is an abuse of power even if the power is used to make something good happen. Athletic directors commonly have the opportunity to use this influence. Major donors may simply ask, "Can I help you with something?" or they might say, "Let me know if you need help getting approval for the renovation of a new locker room. I'd be happy to make my donation to the microbiology building contingent on a new facility for Coach Smith."

Use of this power of external sanction can be a double-edged sword. In the previous example, if the locker room renovation proposal is rejected, the donor may become angry because his or her help was not sought. If the donor intercedes with the threat of withdrawal of the microbiology building donation if the locker room isn't renovated, the college president may become angry with the athletic director and possibly express this anger when the time comes to consider next year's athletic budget or another athletic department request. Even someone as seemingly powerless as a student and his or her parents may be able to intercede in the internal workings of a department through the power of external sanction. What would the athletic director do if a parent threatens to go to the press or file a lawsuit because of the transgressions of a coach? These external forces are challenges that must be addressed by the athletic director and require a focus on right and wrong. Think of bypassing the decision-making hierarchy of an organization as a decision to cheat. The hierarchy was established to permit the development of a stable management system and the achievement of the goals of the larger educational structure. Inappropriately pursuing an athletic department priority is a threat to the integrity of the system.

One last thought about using the power of others is that longevity in a position is power. The longer that a manager stays with an organization, the more relationships he or she develops. Inevitably, some of these relationships will be with influential people who want to help. Thus, longevity does translate to increased influence. Quality of managerial performance also affects that manager's ability to garner the support of those outside the institutional hierarchy. Never underestimate the value of many people thinking well of the leader of the athletic program. Think of longevity as a synonym for reputation. Developing a reputation takes time. Reputation is a function of performance over time and the opinion of others about that performance.

Power of Knowledge

The power of knowledge comes into play when the athletic director gets the decision, action, or resource sought because of the persuasiveness of the facts and reasons marshaled in support of the request. The skill of assembling and communicating this knowledge is the primary method by which the athletic director exercises power outside the athletic department. This process is critical to the success of the department. If higher salaries for coaches are desired, compelling factual and statistical arguments must be made in support of such a proposal. What are coaches earning at institutions with which the institution traditionally compares itself (i.e., other schools in the conference, other schools who have achieved the level of athletic excellence to which the school aspires)? How will the school benefit if the salaries necessary to attract better quality coaches are provided? Do legal considerations support arguments for salary increases, such as laws requiring nondiscrimination on the basis of sex? Does the marketplace require a higher salary to attract an employee who is key to the success of a program? The athletic director should have a reputation for doing his or her homework, preparing logical and factually compelling written requests or reports, communicating this information in a persuasive way, and always being the most knowledgeable person concerning the issue being addressed.

Wise Use of Power

The wise manager seeks to use the power of knowledge first, coupled with relationship-building skills, to acquire the decisions and resources needed. The use of the power of position or the power of external sanction should be secondary choices given the fact that they pose other risks.

1.12 PLANNING TOOL

Program and Operating Values and Principles

Every organization reflects the values and principles of its leader. A value is a belief about what is important with regard to individual conduct or an expectation that managers and employees must hold in common, the absence of which may result in sanction. Operating principles are guidelines for everyday action and decision making that are consistent with stated values but more explicit about how the leader wants people to conduct the business of the organization.

Values and operating principles are primary expectations that must be communicated explicitly and frequently to employees, student-athletes, donors, parents, and fans. They should be expressed in print as official athletic department policy, as well as by spoken word. Policy 1.13 is an example of how to express the operating philosophy and principles of a program.

> **1.13 Policy**—Program Operating Philosophy and Principles
>
> A sample policy defining the core values and principles that govern the operation of the athletic program.
>
> Available in HK*Propel*.

These concepts represent the core substance of the athletic director's leadership and are the tenets to be used for everyday decision making as well as the behaviors that employees and student-athletes are expected to demonstrate when they relate to each other and the external public.

Think of what a working environment would feel like if every employee and student-athlete heard expressions of higher-order values like "fairness," "honesty," and "trust" repeated every day. Think of how employees and student-athletes would feel about an organization dedicated every day to green environmental values and actions. The athletic director's most important leadership responsibility is making those values and principles explicit and repeating them as often as possible so that they become internalized:

- Write them down as organizational policy.
- Distribute them at the staff meeting at the beginning of each year.
- Distribute them at a meeting of all student-athletes at the beginning of each year.
- Put them on a central place on the athletic department's website.
- Print them in event programs and department newsletters.
- Express them in public address announcements at events (i.e., requests for respectful conduct).
- Require that the statement of values and appropriate operating principles be a part of the team rules of every sport team.
- At every staff meeting, select one value or operating principle for comment or discussion.
- Be sure that the values are reflected in the department's annual employee evaluation instrument.
- Incorporate them as locker room or office signage.
- Use moving value words or statements as screen savers on all department computers.
- Once a week, send a text message to all students and employees that includes a quote expressing a program value or principle.

In short, these words and statements should be mantras, repeated frequently orally and in print by the athletic director, coaches, and managers. Such repetition is required to facilitate internalization and adoption. The goal should be that all student-athletes and employees in the organization will feel proud and comfortable voicing these rules of conduct and will do so as explanations for their everyday decisions and actions.

1.14 MANAGEMENT TIP

Developing a Culture of Shared Learning

Achieving athletic department goals is a team sport. The manager cannot do it alone, even if he or she is a superstar. The more good players who are on staff and the more those players share information with each other, the greater the chances are of program success. Therefore, the athletic director must be committed to creating a culture in which everyone is committed to making everyone else better—a culture of shared learning.

Learning From Others

Like a head coach, an athletic director must be a master teacher. The athletic director's team is just larger, consisting of players of all ages and skill levels, and the range of subject matter is much broader than just one sport. Being a good teacher first requires a commitment to learning, not only through formal and continuing education but also through watching people and identifying programs to emulate. The latter requires getting out into the world and putting oneself in a position to learn from the best. Before the athletic director takes the gift of knowledge from others, he or she should be willing to give time and effort in return.

The workload and time required to run an athletic department would be reasonable excuses for any athletic director to stay close to home and become isolated. But the leader of the athletic program simply cannot let this happen. Study of the careers of top athletic directors shows that they said yes when asked to chair or serve on committees, run for elected office, give speeches to local groups, or become involved in conference and athletic association committees in highly visible ways. Giving of self professionally is a commitment that results in accruing benefits. Being involved in national professional associations for athletic directors or managers, volunteering to serve on committees of athletic governance and professional organizations, and being a member of the local Rotary Club are just a few ways to observe and learn from other leaders of sport and nonsport organizations and, in turn, share knowledge to help others. Likewise, every employee should be encouraged to participate in professional organizations and attend professional conferences.

One of the challenges for the athletic director is accessing colleagues at the same level of responsibility who can help with advice. Every athletic director should have at least three or four other athletic directors as colleagues and mentors whom they can call upon.

Doing as the Ultimate Test of Learning

The application of knowledge and theory and verifying that it works is what a manager does every day. Developing a strategic plan, creating measurable objectives, designing action plans to accomplish those objectives, and evaluating how well those action plans worked are the guts of doing. Having everyone in the organization participating in all these tasks is a teaching necessity. People learn best by doing. And doing must be a process that includes commitment to a plan, execution of the plan, evaluation, adjustment, and finally renewed and informed additional effort. And then the cycle repeats itself.

Commitment to Teaching

Sharing everything learned is an obligation of the athletic director and should be a mantra for every employee in the organization. The athletic department policy manual and office policies and procedures handbook are formal teaching mechanisms. Alternatively, sharing knowledge might be as simple as having conversations with other athletic directors and offering suggestions for solving a particular problem with senior staff members during a staff meeting. Maybe it's a weekly employee electronic newsletter that shares tips from all employees. Sharing knowledge could become a specific agenda item at every department or senior staff meeting. Consider establishing a professional development policy that institutionalizes the principle of sharing such as requiring any employee who attends a professional development activity, as a condition of athletic department funding, to provide a written summary of what was learned or to conduct a learning seminar upon his or her return. Consider requiring senior managers, as a community service obligation, to share their management knowledge with local nonprofit organizations. The athletic director who takes the time to focus on developing a culture of shared learning and the responsibility of all employees to share what they know affirms the value of each employee's knowledge.

1.15 PLANNING TOOL

Communicating Performance Expectations

The athletic department organizational structure depicts the decision-making hierarchy and is a skeletal structure that gives an organization its basic strength and predictability. The department's organizational chart provides employees and consumers with basic information on the design of an organization with regard to who is in charge of each area or program and responsible for dealing with the program or service that they need. This skeletal structure also clearly delineates decision-making responsibility. But management is more than the skeletal structure of an organization. Although the skeleton is important, the quality of the musculature, its operating system, determines what that skeleton can accomplish. The operating system consists of all mechanisms used to communicate performance expectations to employees.

In the athletic department, the athletic director has both the freedom and the responsibility to determine the organization's operating system. Think of this operating system as the offensive and defensive philosophy of the team—how the athletic director wants the team to operate and how team members are trained to play at the top of their game. All these performance expectations—the operating system—are formally communicated using four primary mechanisms: (1) policies; (2) position descriptions; (3) performance tools such as strategic plans, measurable objectives, action plans, and evaluation tools; and (4) educational materials. All these mechanisms must be in place.

Policies

A policy is a written statement or procedure that defines a specific course of action determined by the athletic director with regard to how employees are to handle a service or issue. Policies frequently are created after something has gone wrong and the manager wants to make sure that it doesn't happen again. It has been said that an organization's policy manual is a compilation of solutions to all the mistakes that were ever made in that organization. Policies not only prevent repetition of errors but also set performance standards in that they describe how the athletic director expects employees to act, both generally and in response to specific circumstances. This book is a compilation of policies dealing with all aspects of managing an athletic program. Think of policies as basic governing laws or guidelines that set performance standards and expectations for all employees.

Position Descriptions

Position descriptions communicate the functions of employees, the education and competencies they are expected to bring to their jobs, to whom they report, and the responsibilities for which they will be held accountable. Whereas policies communicate how the team is expected to function, a position description communicates the duties and scope of responsibility of the individual employee.

Performance Tools

Performance tools consist of strategic plans, measurable objectives, action plans, and evaluation tools, all of which are interrelated and work in synchrony. The athletic department strategic plan is a document that defines what the program wants to accomplish in a time-delimited period, usually three to five years. Measurable objectives are that part of the strategic plan and describe desired athletic program achievements in measurable terms. Action plans are those things that each employee or unit is expected to do to produce the measurable objective. Evaluation instruments include all forms of evaluation used to demonstrate achievement of objectives and the effectiveness of employees, including annual performance evaluations. All these instruments communicate performance expectations.

Educational Materials

Policies, job descriptions, and performance tools communicate expectations to employees and are quasi dictatorial in nature. Educational materials and efforts are investments in the professional growth of employees that will enable them to be better able to fulfill these expectations. Often, athletic managers think that educational investments in their employees involve formal education through conferences, workshops, courses, in-service training programs with guest speakers, and so on. Employee education, however, need not be expensive or formal. For instance, at the core of any high-performance organization is the individual accountability of each employee to produce his or her best effort or work product. The athletic director should consider producing clear instructions that define acceptable and unacceptable work product—a concrete and practical guide for individual performance expectations. See Educational Resource 1.16 for such a suggested employee handout.

1.16 Educational Resource—
Completed Staff Work: Performance Expectations of All Employees

A sample handout designed to be distributed by the athletic director to all employees that details employee performance expectations when a supervisor assigns a project.

Available in HK*Propel*.

Regularly disseminating similar performance improvement advice, assigning mentors to younger employees, and taking the time in staff meetings to include agenda items that focus on improving employee performance are all effective ways to enhance employee performance.

1.17 MANAGEMENT TIP

Role and Function of Sport in Education

In its most pure educational form, sport can be treated as a performing art, like dance, drama, or music. Sport contains subject matter (physical skills and strategic game theory) that must be mastered in a learning laboratory (the game or competition) where those skills can be demonstrated or tested as part of a broader study of kinesiology (the study of human movement). It could be argued that varsity sport is part of a comprehensive physical education curriculum, serving the function of honors courses for the exceptionally gifted athlete. Unfortunately, few educational institutions offer sport as such an educational construct.

At the scholastic level, physical education may be a required or elective curricular or cocurricular course. Few credit hours are awarded for its completion. Practice for varsity sports, cheerleading, band, and drill team may be accepted in lieu of formal physical education classes. At the college level, physical education or kinesiology departments typically do not have jurisdiction over varsity sport, which is most often operated as an extracurricular activity. Physical education majors, however, may be granted credit for participation.

Because of such ambiguity with regard to curricular subject designation, although the larger educational institution consists of professional teachers, trained and certified to teach in the specific subject delivered to student-consumers, in many athletic departments, coaches and assistant coaches are often not certified teachers of sport (trained physical educators or certified coaches). In many cases, a winning record, successful assistant coach apprenticeships under a head coach, or previous coaching experience suffices in lieu of a teaching credential. At the middle or high school level, some minimal requirements for head coaches often exist, such as proof of completion of a first-aid course, full-time employment by the school district (not necessarily as a teacher), or maybe the completion of an online basic coaching course. At the college level, few qualifications other than previous experience as a coach are required.

Thus, to the extent that it is possible, an effort by the athletic director to express the role and function of sport in education will be appreciated by higher administration. Similarly, efforts to hire coaches and other staff who are certified educators and have the same credentials as the faculty or have coaching licenses issued by national sport governing associations will contribute to increased respect for the athletic program and serve to reduce the ambiguity between sport and education programs. In light of this discussion, the athletic director should hold the highest educational credential possible.

Efforts to establish certification requirements for coaches have had limited success primarily because school districts have a high demand for coaches and assistant coaches and a relatively small applicant pool. Many administrators therefore believe that they will be unable to fill those positions if certification is required because it will reduce the pool of qualified candidates. Accentuating the problem is the fact that many trained physical educators do not wish to coach in addition to fulfilling full-time teaching loads because of the tremendous number of hours required for after-school practice, competition, and travel. This absence of certified coaches and the existence of a large number of part-time coaches place an unusual burden on the athletic director, who is held responsible for the safety of students in the hazardous environment of high-level sport participation. Given such circumstances, a high level of supervision, evaluation, and in-service training is essential rather than suggested. This reality also argues for managers who have been coaches or physical educators, well versed in pedagogy and the evaluation of teachers.

This ambiguous nature of varsity sport as it relates to other subjects in the academic curriculum, coupled with the fact that athletic staff members are located in facilities separate from academic facilities, creates an isolation dilemma. When coaches and athletic administrators are not faculty members, are perceived to be educationally less qualified, and physically do not work side by side or interact with faculty, the athletic department is less likely to be as fully valued as academic departments are. The athletic director who understands this circumstance can counter this perception by (1) effectively communicating the educational benefits of sport for student participants to the faculty through an annual report to the faculty, (2) requiring that coaches possess the same educational credentials as faculty, (3) communicating graduation rates and overall grade point averages of student-athletes to demonstrate respect for and commitment to the institution's primary mission, (4) insisting that the treatment of student-athletes be identical to the treatment of other students, and (5) being active on institutional committees. Failure to attend to the need to integrate athletics in the larger institutional mission can generate significant problems ranging from placing athletics in lower funding priorities to fueling negative coach and athlete stereotypes. Thus, the athletic director must embrace the responsibility to communicate frequently and effectively to nonathletic institutional constituents.

1.18 PLANNING TOOL

Management Training of Employees

Educational institutions (secondary and higher education) are professional bureaucracies. Managers are educators first, recognized for their professional credentials and expertise in the general subject of education or a specialized academic discipline. These professional educators are so well respected and highly trained that they are also entrusted with the administration of the business of the school or college in addition to what happens in the classroom. But school principals or presidents of educational institutions will likely be required to undergo additional training as managers and demonstrate their competency as administrators before they are hired.

The larger the institution is and the higher the position is in the professional bureaucracy, the more likely it is that professional management training and experience will be required. The lower the position is in the bureaucracy, especially among middle managers in academic or athletic departments, the less likely it is that those professionals will have had formal training in managerial and supervisory skills or that it will be required. For instance, in college academic departments, department chairs may be elected by the faculty without having to attain any administrative credentials. At a small high school, the football coach may also be the athletic director, and no administrative credentials would be required to be an athletic director. Therefore, two of the challenges of every athletic director are to (1) avoid the mistake of assuming that employees have had management training or that administrative experience equals management training, and (2) recognize the need to require or provide leadership and management training for employees.

Professional development of managers needs to be a regularly addressed priority. One of the easiest mechanisms to reach this goal is to install a professional development evaluation section as part of the annual performance evaluation of each employee. Section IV of Evaluation Instrument 6.14 demonstrates how this might be done.

> **6.14 Evaluation Instrument**—Annual Performance Review
>
> This sample annual performance evaluation is designed to be used for all employees and is fully aligned with each employee's job description and the department's strategic plan. The instrument covers (*a*) assigned measurable objectives, (*b*) performance of primary job responsibilities, (*c*) general performance qualities, (*d*) professional growth and development plans, and (*e*) succession planning.
>
> Available in HK*Propel*.

Requiring a conversation about succession planning (see section VI of that instrument) performs a similar function in that it should identify current staff members with management potential who should be supported with regard to further professional development. These conversations force supervisors to focus on the professional development of individual employees at least once a year.

Other more general professional development efforts should include (1) requiring those who attend professional conferences to share conference notes with other staff upon returning, (2) funding professional development experiences for promising staff members, (3) distributing educational resources on management skills, (4) identifying department or external mentors to help managerial prospects advance, (5) giving challenging assignments to prospective managers so that they have to work for an experienced supervisor, and (6) nominating young managers to serve on campus and conference committees or to chair department committees.

1.19 MANAGEMENT TIP

Keys to Managing Change

Inevitability of Change—Key to Organization Resiliency

From the cellular level of all plants and animals to the human organism as a whole to the organization as a collection of individuals, how each of these entities responds and adapts to the pressure of external stimuli determines its strength and resilience. Failure to respond and adapt to these changes leads to stagnation, brittleness, and eventually death. The growth of knowledge is exponential. Governance association rules change every year. New institutional policies are promulgated regularly. The nature of every new class of students and generation of employees reflects significant differences in views toward the importance of everything from material wealth to personal fulfillment. Budgetary resources fluctuate from year to year. As the organization's leader, the athletic director is responsible for ensuring that the organization and employees in the organization positively respond and adapt to these changes. Thus, accepting the importance and inevitability of change, understanding the stages of change, and developing the skills required to guide employees and stakeholders through the change process are essential competencies of the athletic director.

Responses to Change

Key to influencing others to be successful in the constantly changing environment of an athletic department requires understanding and respect for the mechanisms of change. What the athletic director is really trying to do when he or she seeks to manage the change process is to ask others to think in a certain way or act differently based on newly identified circumstances or information. An athletic director will have to deal with the challenge of persuading others to accept the change—not only all employees but also possibly parents, student-athletes, and donors. Think of what will go through the hearts and minds of athletic program stakeholders who are asked to accept and support a new coach after the termination of a much respected but not sufficiently successful predecessor.

In general, the athletic director needs to grasp two important facts: (1) People accept change at different rates because change is a process, and (2) several predictable stages of and responses to change need to be anticipated and handled. With regard to the latter, the athletic director needs a simple paradigm about the stages of change to anchor his or her analysis and decision making:

- Stage 1 involves a negative emotional reaction to change.
- Stage 2 usually is characterized by behavioral resistance to change.
- Stage 3 includes acceptance and adjustment.

In stage 1, people who are asked to change initially encounter emotions ranging from loss, fear, confusion, and anxiety to anger and resentment. These emotions vary according to the experience and personality of the individual and her or his level of confidence and security. The second stage usually includes some form of resistance, which can range from skepticism to passive and overt forms of undermining behaviors such as retribution against those who benefit from the change or efforts to sabotage change implementation systems. In stage 3, acceptance and changed behavior begins, and positive anticipation and excitement develops about doing something in a different way.

Helping Employees Navigate Change

Therefore, the primary focus of the manager is to get as many people as possible, especially those employees or donors most respected and emulated by others, through the first two stages of change with minimal angst and into the acceptance and celebration stages as quickly as possible. Helping employees cope with stage

1 emotional reaction or resistance to change should involve three basic concepts: (1) having face-to-face individual meetings to discuss concerns, (2) making sure to allow time between the announcement of change and the implementation of change to allow for employee processing, and (3) installing an anonymous feedback mechanism that encourages employees fearful of expressing concerns to do so. The athletic director should schedule one-on-one meetings with key senior staff members and supervisors, and senior staff members should do the same in their units. A powerful tactic is for a manager to ask an employee to help other employees adjust to the change and to invite that employee to discuss any concerns about adaptation whenever he or she observes an issue. All-staff and subunit staff meetings should be scheduled and devoted to this single agenda item. Change should never be announced by e-mail or the dissemination of written policies or directives. Allowing employees to express concerns and suggest adjustment solutions in response to anonymous online surveys is an effective strategy if managers sense fear or reticence of employees to share their feelings or concerns. The manager should recognize that time is required for these meetings and employee interactions, so a coping and discussion period should precede the implementation of change. Management needs to be transparent about concerns, share such concerns with all employees, and indicate how it intends to respond to the concerns. This practice serves the function of communicating to employees that management values and is responsive to employee opinions and advice. Communication of employee-identified problems and solutions also promotes a culture of teamwork—we are in this together and will be successful in adapting to this change.

Navigating stage 2 is somewhat more challenging because the manager is often confronting verbal or behavioral expressions of resistance. The first step is making sure that senior managers are not part of this problem. Senior staff must be required to accept their responsibility to manage change in a positive way. The athletic director may have to make clear that resistance will not be tolerated. Senior management must be the solution, not the problem. Retribution should not be tolerated (employees engaging in verbal comments or behaviors disrespectful to employees who might benefit from the change or supervisors responsible for implementing the change). A culture of respect and beneficence (do no harm; do good) must be maintained. Performance resistance should be approached as if it were any performance concern—a one-on-one meeting to discuss the performance deficiency and management expectations, with no written corrective action or penalty, but escalating corrective action up to and including termination if the performance deficiency continues. Key to any corrective action is confronting the issue as soon as it occurs and not stockpiling behaviors to be confronted only during scheduled annual performance reviews. Another key is to keep employees informed of the positive effect or reaction to the change. Was money or time saved? Did positive response occur from student-athletes, donors, spectators, or other consumers? Did revenue increase, or did complaints decrease?

In short, the athletic director must use knowledge (education) and direct face-to-face communication to provide reasons for the need to change, confront concerns about and negative reactions to change, and convey the positive effects of change implementation to help employees adjust to a new way of acting. If necessary, the athletic director may be required to exercise the power of position (potential sanction or reward) to indicate and reinforce new desired behaviors. Many times, navigating and leading the change process is incredibly complex, requiring keen insight and moral strength to get others to adopt a position that is right but unpopular at the moment. Managing change is difficult and time consuming. Doing the homework, understanding the issues, and being prepared to support taking the morally right course of action, even though it may not be a popular position, is essential. In the long run, even when positions are diametrically opposed, the right position always wins out over the most popular decision.

Key Considerations in the Face of Resistance

Even when the manager is absolutely right, she or he may be unsuccessful in accomplishing needed changes, like gaining approval for a budget request or a getting a principal or vice president to approve a new policy or procedure. Even within the athletic department, the manager may be unsuccessful in getting genuine support for what needs to be done. At some point in your career as an athletic director, you may need to challenge the system or the boss and know that in undertaking this effort, the result might be losing the argument, the esteem in which you are held, or maybe even your job. In these cases, it might be helpful to ask the following questions:

- If I don't insist on this change, am I breaking the letter or spirit of the law, an institutional policy, or an athletic association governance rule?
- Can I find someone with more power who might be willing to carry the ball on this issue—a major donor, a respected alumnus, a member of the media, a tenured faculty member?
- Do I have to take a major action immediately? Significant change often results from making steady progress toward a goal that requires persistence over time. In such cases, longevity in your position is important, especially if you outlast those who are barriers to successful action. Is there a way to keep advocating for change while maintaining your position and credibility and making steady progress toward the objective by taking smaller steps?
- Do I have enough allies to achieve change? The bigger the change is, the more important it may be to spend time getting powerful people on your side and not trying to do it alone.
- Will this change result in creating a significant enemy? Always think twice before you burn a bridge; the creek has a tendency to rise whenever you do. Doing the right thing is always a priority, but how you do it is also important. "Are you making the fewest enemies possible in pursuing this course of action?" may be the right question.
- If you move forward and face unfair termination, have you kept good written records to support your case? Is the issue important enough to risk your job? At times, the issue may be that important. Note that robust whistleblower laws may protect you. If the stakes are this high, seek legal counsel before you make your move.
- Is the larger institution or your boss ready for the idea that you want to bring to fruition? Can it wait? Every manager should have a file folder labeled "Ideas Whose Time Has Not Yet Come." You can always pull out the great idea when the time is right.

Like administrative theory in general, change theory and resistance to change have received much attention. Almost every theory contains nuggets of knowledge that are useful in the administrator's efforts to lead change. Therefore, managers need to make a personal commitment to continuing education in this subject through reading and attendance at conferences. Understanding and managing change is an important responsibility of every manager.

1.20 MANAGEMENT TIP

Preventing Resistance to Change

A new or significant revision to the athletic department strategic plan presents a useful case study of how a leader should think through what obstacles might be encountered in getting staff members to embrace different and probably higher performance standards. Typically, such change requires significant revision in the way tasks were previously done. Consider the following situation:

- The new athletic director has a vision and strategic plan to advance the athletic program to higher levels of achievement.
- Higher administration officials, including the president of the institution, who hired the athletic director to institute such changes, have bought into the vision and pledged their support.
- Several key senior athletic department staff members have made it clear that they are philosophically opposed to increasing the program emphasis on winning, especially the plan to make a number of head coach changes to increase the energy and intensity of the program.
- The new athletic director wants to do everything that he or she can to prevent senior staff members or others from undermining the strategic plan.

How should he or she proceed?

Step 1: Proving the Vision Is Achievable

The athletic director must be committed to using fact-based data to show that his or her vision is achievable. Behind closed doors with his or her most trusted group of advisors and executives, the senior staff, the strategic plan must be developed and all concerns must be answered. Thus, the strategic planning process with the senior staff is the most critical step in selling the new athletic director's vision. The athletic director must directly oversee the production of data required to support the need for change and the strategic plan that would implement his or her vision. The need for change is the outcome of three processes: (1) a formal SWOT (strength, weaknesses, opportunities, and threats) analysis, (2) assembling baseline data that establish where the department stands (salary, budget, facilities, and other important variables) compared with like institutions that are operating at the success level desired, and (3) higher administration designation of comparable institutions and the measure of athletic and academic success desired. Never underestimate the importance of ensuring that the president, school principal, or superintendent specifies the level of success that he or she wants the athletic program to achieve. Such success will always depend on the resources that the institutional CEO is willing to provide. Specific goals and measurable objectives (see chapter 3 for goal formulation) must be established by this group, including a timetable and projected costs.

During this process, the athletic director must persuade the senior staff naysayers to put all their doubts on the table so that they can be addressed before the plan is presented for the review and critique of any other group. This test of leadership must be passed. If intransigent individuals and their fears are identified during this process, the leader must then meet with each person, one on one, to figure out how to win him or her over to the vision and gain commitment to supporting the plan. Although obtaining support from everyone may not be possible, the majority of the department's senior staff leadership must be convinced of the desirability and achievability of the plan.

Step 2: Selling the Plan to All Staff

After the senior staff produces the strategic plan (taking care to include all supporting data), it is presented to the full athletic department professional staff (coaches, middle managers, and professional staff). Again, all questions and concerns must be answered. This group will be responsible for executing the plan.

Step 3: Selling the Plan to Key Stakeholders

Next, the athletic policy board (which should include student-athlete representatives) and a strategic planning committee made up of alumni and donors should receive, review, and critique the document recommended by senior staff. Before these meetings, key members of these groups should be targeted for individual meetings in which the athletic director presents a personal preview of the plan and asks for their support in getting their respective groups to support the new vision. These groups will likely debate and tweak the plan, but if the senior staff has done what it was supposed to do, changes at this stage will be minimal. The greater the number of stakeholders involved in developing and supporting the plan, the greater the likelihood of successful implementation.

Step 4: Selling the Plan to Other Stakeholders

Presentations should be made by the athletic director to additional groups of stakeholders, such as the student-athlete advisory committee, the faculty senate, the alumni association executive committee, and the association of former student-athletes. At the high school level, these groups might be the parent–teacher association, the school board, and the senior staff of the superintendent of the school district. In these presentations, groups are not asked for advice. Rather, they are told who was responsible for developing the plan, that alumni and students are members of the athletic policy board, and that a select alumni and donor committee was also involved in developing the plan. Comments should not be refused, but neither should the impression be given that these groups can change the plan.

Step 5: Implementation Meetings With Senior Staff

After the plan is adopted, the athletic director must pay attention to the needs of supervisors who will be overseeing the change process. In one-on-one conversations, as well as in weekly senior staff meetings, the athletic director should ask supervisors to identify details of implementation that most concern them. In areas like fundraising, staff may have to be trained. Problems usually occur after plans are adopted because the details of implementation were not anticipated or the effect was not felt until implementation. Thus, this step is important.

Step 6: Everyone Must Be on Board

If senior staff naysayers will not fully support the team effort, the athletic director may have to deliver an employment ultimatum. The athletic staff is just like a sport team. After the offensive and defensive systems are established, all players must give their best effort toward executing the game plan or risk sitting on the bench or even being removed from the team to make room for a contributing player.

The primary point of this case study is to demonstrate that a good leader never assumes that plans will be implemented just because the athletic director or the president of the institution gives such orders. Staff commitment to the best executional effort is a function of staff involvement in plan development, staff belief in the feasibility of execution based on hard data rather than wishing it so, and anticipation of the challenges that must be overcome to succeed. The athletic director must orchestrate all of this and be the consummate coach who is able to convince every player on the team that greatness is within reach.

1.21 MANAGEMENT TIP

It's All About Relationship Building

The athletic department does not exist in a vacuum. On a daily basis, the athletic director and most of the department's employees interact with numerous people who work for the educational institution at large or members of the public such as vendors, parents, ticket buyers, sports officials, and the media. In fact, the athletic program probably has more contacts with people outside the institution than any other department does. The success of such external interaction will determine whether the athletic department gets the resources that it needs to be successful. For instance, a typical day for a college program might look like this:

- The athletic director has a full schedule of meetings:

  9:00 a.m. Meeting with the director of recreation and intramurals and the chairperson of the physical education department to discuss policies governing the scheduling of physical activity facilities

  11:00 a.m. Meeting with the local Coca-Cola distributor to ask for $10,000 to be the title sponsor of the department's annual basketball invitational tournament

  12:30 p.m. Lunch with a major donor to discuss the need for an ice hockey facility and to ask the donor to lead and assemble a capital campaign committee for that purpose

  2:30 p.m. Meeting with the athletic department academic advisor and the vice president for student affairs and her staff to review the new admissions standards and procedures for early determination of the status of athletes being recruited

  4:00 p.m. Meeting with the head baseball coach, a student-athlete, and his parents to discuss the recent dismissal of the student-athlete from the baseball team

- The assistant athletic director in charge of event management meets the head of buildings and grounds for the university to discuss the problem with drainage at the lower soccer field.
- The head athletic trainer meets with a salesperson who represents the major training-room supplies vendor to discuss the specifications and price for a bulk purchase of tape and other supplies and to ask whether he will buy a foursome in the department's annual benefit golf tournament this spring.
- The sports information director and head volleyball coach are at a local radio station to participate in a morning-drive-time talk show to promote the upcoming conference championships being hosted by the athletic department.

The situation is typically no different for the high school athletic director:

- The athletic director has a full schedule of meetings:

  8:00 a.m. Meeting with the director of custodial services to discuss maintenance of the basketball court and dead spots on the floor under the west basket

  9:00 p.m. Meeting with the assistant principal to discuss an incident in which a group of football players harassed girls exiting the cafeteria after lunch

  11:00 a.m. Authorized by central administration as meeting school district protocol, meeting with the local Coca-Cola distributor to ask for $5,000 for a Coca-Cola advertisement to be placed on the scoreboards of the softball field, baseball field, and football and soccer field

  12:15 p.m. Meeting with the assistant principal, chief of school security, the director of city emergency medical services, the cheerleader advisor, an assistant football coach, and the person in charge of scheduling game officials to discuss crowd control at the big game Friday night with an archrival high school

1:30 p.m. Meeting with the principal to discuss the need for new dugouts and the addition of bleachers for spectators on the softball field to comply with a federal gender equity mandate

6:00 p.m. Meeting with the head soccer coach, a student-athlete, and her parents to discuss the recent dismissal of the student-athlete from the soccer team

- The head athletic trainer meets with a salesperson who is the major training-room supply vendor to discuss the specifications and price for a bulk purchase of tape and other supplies and to ask whether she will buy a foursome in the department's annual benefit golf tournament this spring.
- The head basketball coach is at a local radio station to participate in a morning-drive-time talk show to promote the start of the upcoming season.

Successful communication focused on building good relationships with numerous external entities is a responsibility of all employees and should be considered a responsibility at the heart of accomplishing the business of the athletic department. These meetings and relationships may yield everything from goodwill and increased ticket sales to approval of a new facility and better media coverage. Influencing people to think well of the department and to provide it with increased resources are keys to success. In particular, the athletic director must be an exceptional relationship builder and purposely educate all employees to interact effectively with a variety of constituencies so that the athletic department can get the resources it needs.

The athletic director can use several tools to advance the importance of relationship building as an employee responsibility. Consider establishment of a department policy related to relationship-building responsibilities such as Policy 1.22, which also serves as an educational tool. By making these performance expectations policies instead of delivering this information as an educational resource, the athletic director effectively elevates the importance of and employee accountability for demonstrating such behavior.

Educational tools should be used to reinforce policy obligations. Evaluation Instrument 1.23 enables employees to self-assess their relationship-building skills and identify areas that need improvement. Consider distributing this to employees in preparation for their annual performance evaluation meeting and a discussion of professional development goals. The instrument should be used by the employee for self-reflection and should not be turned in to the supervisor. Another educational tool that could be used to reinforce relationship-building policy can be found in Educational Resource 1.24.

1.22 **Policy**—Relationship-Building Responsibilities of All Employees

A sample policy that communicates model relationship-building practices while establishing such behaviors as expectations of all employees.

1.23 **Evaluation Instrument**—Employee Relationship-Building Scorecard and Development Plan

A sample self-evaluation tool that enables employees to assess their relationship-building skills and develop a plan for improvement.

1.24 **Educational Resource**—10 Commandments for Management Success

A handout that can be given to employees who demonstrate interest in becoming managers, or have the skills to be managers, to encourage wise political and relationship behavior.

Available in HK*Propel*.

1.25 MANAGEMENT TIP

Politically Effective Problem-Solving Strategies

Athletic directors usually discover the need to think about details after they make a mistake that could have been avoided. Just the opposite should occur. Attention to detail related to political, personality, and problem-specific issues, even when confronting the most basic problems, is a characteristic of a successful manager and respected leader. Also, speaking about attention to detail and understanding what that really means in the context of a daily athletic problem are two different things. The purpose of this tip is to illustrate that difference—to present what on its face is a simple typical athletic issue and to illustrate how an athletic director has to think through all the political, personality, and problem-specific issues.

Consider this scenario: The soccer field has a significant drainage problem. The athletic director goes to the head of buildings and grounds, a manager known to be difficult to work with and typically described as a bear, to ask for his or her assistance in solving the problem. The athletic director should have done the necessary homework before the meeting, thought through how to create a calm and positive communication environment, and anticipated what to do if the head of buildings and grounds does not respond positively. The athletic director might have developed the following plan:

- Thank the person for his or her time.
- Express how much you would appreciate his or her help and advice in solving an athletic facility problem.
- Provide a detailed description of the problem that includes a discussion of the following:
  - How much rain produces the problem
  - How much of the playing field is affected
  - How many practices or competitions had to be canceled because of the problem
  - How moving teams to other areas affects other programs (e.g., intramurals canceled because athletic practice takes priority)
  - The cost of such canceled programs such as paying cancellation fees to officials, renting of water vacuums to alleviate the condition, re-sodding costs, and the cost of rescheduling such as rental fees for indoor or outdoor space
  - How the condition affects the safety of coaches and students
- Detail what actions you have taken to date to address the problem.
- Express that you understand how tight the facilities budget must be but that you are worried about the safety issues of trying to play on wet facilities and the unacceptable cost of injured athletes or litigation.
- Ask whether there is any way that you can help get the resources necessary to resolve the issue.
- Listen.
- Agree on the next step, including whom you might meet with next to try to get the problem addressed if the person says that nothing can be done to alleviate the problem.
- Thank the person again for his or her time.
- Ask the person to let you know whether you can ever do anything to help him or her.

If the person responds positively with a plan to address the problem, follow up with a thank-you note expressing your appreciation for what was specifically promised and asking him or her to call you if you can provide further assistance. Create a memorandum for your files that reiterates the preceding as a record of the meeting.

If the person says that he or she can do nothing to solve the problem, follow up the meeting with a formal written communication to him or her that reiterates the preceding, thanks the person for recommending that you schedule a meeting with the superior who was suggested, and concludes with a thank-you for his or her time and assistance, even if the meeting was not cordial or the person was not helpful. You would use this document to start the meeting with the person's supervisor.

If the person you met with is so obstinate that you can't get him or her to recommend a next step, state that you hope that he or she will not object if you go to your boss (who you hope is not his or her boss) to ask for advice in handling the matter. Never say anything in a threatening tone. Always ask (rather than tell) the person whether they would object to your consulting with someone who is more powerful than either of you.

1.26 MANAGEMENT TIP

Confronting Title IX Challenges

When the athletic regulations implementing Title IX of the Education Amendments of 1972 (the federal law prohibiting sex discrimination in educational programs receiving federal funds) were adopted in 1975, athletic directors were asked to embrace gender equity and lead this major civil rights change within their athletic departments. Few administrators were able to rise to the challenge. Most athletic programs are still not in full compliance with this legal mandate. The Title IX athletic challenge is a perfect example of the complexity of change that athletic directors are asked to handle. This challenge will not go away, and the risk of litigation to institutions not in compliance is real. Athletic directors need to master this issue.

Few would dispute the fact that before the passage of Title IX, athletic programs served only male athletes and hired only male employees, with the exception of secretarial personnel. Thus, many athletic department cultures were both macho and sexist. Staff members and supporters believed that sport was a male domain and that women could never be and did not aspire to be superior athletes and competitors. Lacking role models and never having had the opportunity to develop their talents, female athletes had little sense of their potential. Think of the magnitude of change that had to occur for equal opportunity to be realized:

- A huge redistribution of resources to create equal treatment and opportunity for female student-athletes
- Sharing employment opportunities with women
- Removing sexual harassment (also prohibited by Title IX) as an acceptable expression and behavior within athletic department culture
- Convincing donors who wanted their resources to support only men's sports to support women's sports as well
- Convincing coaches of men's teams that their support for doing the right thing was essential

As soon as the mandate for equal opportunity for women in educational sport became known, most athletic department employees started thinking that effecting change would be a zero-sum game. In other words, if women gained opportunity and resources, men would lose opportunity and resources. This assumption has made embracing the right thing difficult. Has it been a zero-sum game? No, few things are in the arena of social change. When you give rights to a previously disadvantaged group and bring that group into an economic system as productive contributors, they expand the economic pie.

Between 1972 and 2019, high school girls' sport participation grew by 1,057 percent (NFHS, 2019). Over 3.4 million girls were participating in high school sport in 2018–19, up from 300,000 in 1972–73, which represented an increase from 1 in 27 high school girls participating in varsity sport to 1 in 2.5 (NFHS, 2019). NCAA college women's sport participation grew during this same period by 632 percent, with 221,052 women participating (NCAA, 2020). By 2017–18 NCAA college women were receiving \$1.57 billion in college athletic scholarships (EADA, 2020), up from \$100,000 in 1972 (NCAA, 2012). Yet, although the Title IX athletic regulations have been in force since 1975, female athletes are still not receiving equal treatment or participation opportunities:

- In 2017–18, the female participation gap (the difference between the participation opportunities females actually received and what they are entitled to receive under prong 1 of Title IX) at the high school level was 971,000; at the college level it was 140,000. Although girls comprise 49 percent of the high school population, they receive only 43 percent of all high school athletic opportunities. At the college level, women comprise

54 percent of the full-time undergraduate student body but receive only 46 percent of athletic opportunities at NCAA institutions.

- Female college athletes received $241 million less in athletic scholarships than their male counterparts in 2017–18 (EADA, 2019).
- Recruiting spending for women's teams was $124 million less than it was for men's teams at the college level, a 237 percent difference (EADA, 2019).

During this period, contrary to media reports, sport opportunities for males were not losing as a result of gains for women. In fact, opportunities for males grew during this period. Look at the high school data in figure 1.26.1—girls still haven't caught up!

The situation is identical at the college level. Contrary to some media reports, male athletes have not lost opportunities as a result of Title IX. See figure 1.26.2.

From 2004–05 to 2018–19, NCAA member institutions added more new sport participation opportunities for male athletes than they did for females (61,353 for men and 54,314 for women) (NCAA, 2020, *2018–2019 Sports Sponsorship and Participation Rates Report*). Thus, the male–female participation gap is increasing rather than decreasing.

The media occasionally report the elimination of a men's college team. Such events usually occur among the richest Division I institutions, which are choosing to drop male sport participation opportunities to put more resources into men's football and basketball. Institutions regularly add and drop sports from their athletic program menus. A look at net adds and drops is illuminating. From 1988–89 to 2017–18, NCAA Division I schools suffered a net loss of 329 men's teams whereas Divisions II (+595) and III (+859) enjoyed net gains (NCAA, 2019, *2017–2018 Sports Sponsorship and Participation Rates Report*). In a study of both NCAA and NAIA schools from 1981–82 to 1998–99, the net outcome of added and discontinued teams was +36 for men. Similarly, a federal government report found that Division II and III schools were more likely to add teams and less likely to drop teams compared with Division I schools (United States Government General Accounting Office, 2001).

The previously cited facts support the following conclusions: (1) women continue to

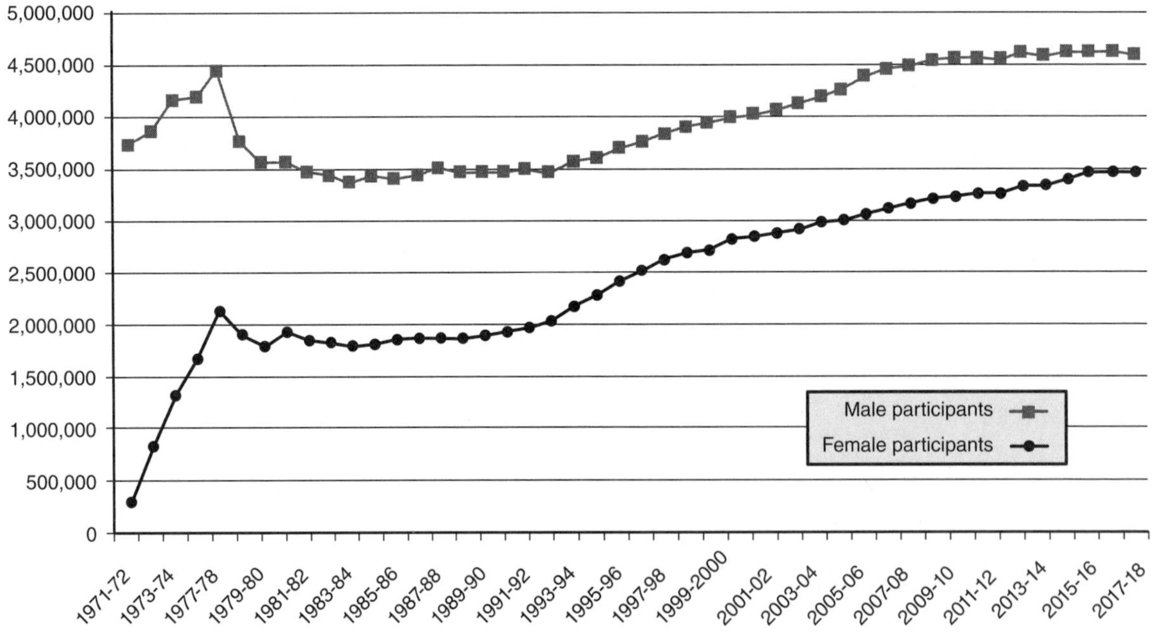

Figure 1.26.1 High school athletic participation, 1971–72 to 2018–19. Note that no data were reported for 1972–73, 1973–74, or 1974–75.

Data from National Federation of State High School Associations (2020).

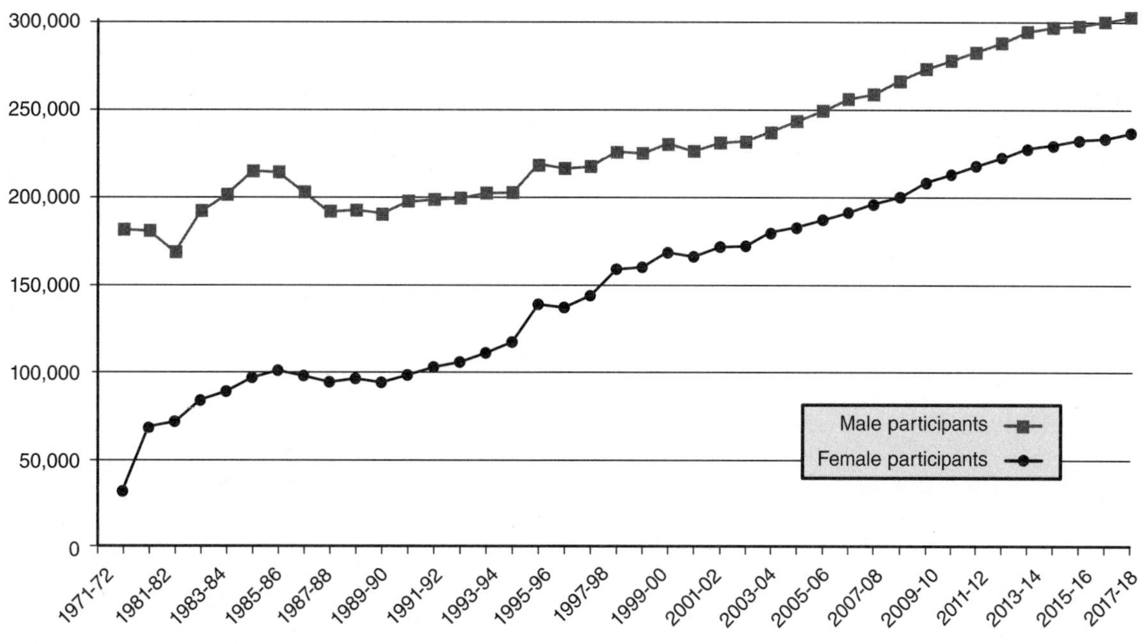

Figure 1.26.2 College (NCAA) athletic participation, 1971–72 to 2018–19.

Data from National Collegiate Athletic Association (2019).

be significantly underrepresented among high school and college athletes, (2) the gap between men's and women's sport participation and support is not closing, and (3) research shows that if men's sports teams are being discontinued, it's not because of Title IX and the growth of women's sports (which has stalled) but because the wealthiest athletic programs in NCAA Division I are dropping these nonrevenue men's sport programs and shifting these monies to compete in the football and men's basketball arms race. They are not dropping women's sports teams because they are more likely to face a lawsuit alleging Title IX noncompliance.

Gender equity change is occurring, but why is it occurring so slowly, and why is it still a major challenge for athletic directors? A number of reasons are contributing to this resistance to change:

1. Challenging economic times and the insatiable arms race in popular men's sports, at both the high school and college level, have intensified the competition for resources needed to achieve gender equity. Rather than keeping men's sport participation and budgets constant or reducing expenditures on men's sports while women's sports catch up, men's sports, or at least the priority men's sports, continue to grow as a percentage of operating expenditures (NCAA, 2012, *2004–2010 NCAA Gender Equity Report*). Thus, the continued growth of women's sports is stalled because of lack of resources needed for expansion or equal treatment. Gender equity is simply not a priority for athletic directors.
2. Historically, women's sports were housed within women's physical education departments, separate from men's physical education and men's athletics. When Title IX was adopted, the control of women's sports moved under the previously all-male athletic department and athletic directors who were primarily male. Because of this separation of women's sport from women's physical education, women's sports lost the protection of tenured and powerful female faculty members while at the same time being placed within the male sport culture that could not be characterized as welcoming.
3. Women's sports were underdeveloped spectator products that were not valued. Little effort was expended to develop either

women's sports or men's minor sports into revenue-producing programs because most attention was directed to mining successful men's football and basketball programs.

4. Faced with fears of litigation or having to share resources, many male athletic directors hired and promoted weak female administrators who were afraid to bring up Title IX concerns and questions. Thus, consistent internal pressure to achieve gender equity was absent.
5. Male athletic directors, who still hold over 80 percent of all top administrative positions in athletic departments, controlled hiring. Although 90 percent of all coaches and administrators in women's sports were female before Title IX, male athletic directors began hiring males with whom they had greater connections and comfort levels to work in women's sports. As a result, in 2019 women held 25 percent of the head coaching jobs in NCAA men's and women's college sport—41 percent of the head coach positions in women's sports and only 6 percent of the head coach positions in men's sports (NCAA Demographics Database, 2020).
6. Subtle employment discrimination is also at play. Athletic directors are more likely to make "paper hires" (select coaches from among a formal paper applicant pool) for coaches of women's teams, whereas they are more likely to go aggressively into the marketplace to identify and pay what it takes to attract the best coach for men's teams, ignoring the paper hire process.
7. Double standards and outright discrimination continue to exist; athletic directors privately express concerns about pregnancy limiting a female coach's longevity, homophobia, and fear of strong, outspoken women who might raise Title IX issues and initiate litigation. If women are hired, many times they receive less encouragement and support within a predominantly male system, creating retention problems.

Although these factors explain resistance to change, another host of factors has been at play to support change:

1. Eighty-two percent of voters support Title IX, including support from those of all political parties and among voters with and without children (Mellman Group, 2007). The American public believes that sport participation is as important for our daughters as it is for our sons. The media were responsible for this public education, having to provide both sides of the argument. Women's Sports Foundation research and numerous other research studies pointed to physical activity as a fundamental solution to many of the health and societal problems faced by girls today (Sabo et al., 2004).
2. Dad led support for Title IX, filing lawsuits if he had to, because for the first time he was able to share something important in his life with his daughter. Dad took her out into the backyard and taught her to play, and he was the biggest champion for her continued opportunities.
3. Mom, who never had the chance to play, didn't know the importance of sport participation when Title IX was adopted. Now, the first generation of Title IX babies, girls who had the chance to play, are coaching their daughters and are fully committed to supporting Title IX for their daughters.
4. The older male athletic directors who grew up in a culture that did not respect the athletic abilities of females and resisted change are finally retiring. In their place are the first generation of men and women who grew up playing with each other and respecting each other's athletic skills.
5. Even among the old-timers, donors who were initially against Title IX, fearing that it would detract from football or other men's sports, have had their minds changed by the first generation of granddaughters who won over their grandparents with their love of the game.
6. When lawsuits have been filed, plaintiffs are batting close to 1.000. Schools fighting Title IX stand to lose large sums to their lawyers and to pay for the legal representation of the plaintiffs (required if the plaintiff wins).

As can be seen in this Title IX perspective, the athletic director is confronted with myriad factors as he or she attempts to manage the change required to eliminate sex discrimination—a decades-old change process that is not going to disappear. Most of the solutions that should be considered involve controlling costs to permit the redistribution of resources to achieve gender equity while maintaining existing men's sports programs at a competitive level. So, what strategies and perspectives can enable this and future generations of athletic directors to achieve gender equity and maximize the success of men's sports? The following suggestions are worthy of consideration:

1. At the institutional level, invest in major donor fund-raising and revenue production in all sports. Having a diversified revenue strategy protects against down years in one or two sports, as does a sophisticated donor development strategy across all sports.
2. At the institutional level, make sure that a gender equity plan in writing has been approved by higher administration. Even if the institution is not in compliance with Title IX, it will be in a better position to come into compliance in response to a Title IX complaint or lawsuit. Not knowing the gender equity status of the athletic program and not advising higher administration of this issue places the athletic director in a position of being blamed.
3. At the institutional level, if financial resources are tight, create a tiered athletic program that complies with Title IX. Ensure that an equal proportion of male and female athletes are in each tier, which differs based on level of scholarship, staffing, and operating budget support. See Management Tips 4.2 and 4.3 for an explanation of tiering and Planning Tool 4.4 for a comprehensive how-to guide.
4. At the institutional level, if the institution has to make financial reductions to achieve gender equity, eliminating a team should be the last choice. Significant downsides in alumni fund-raising and public relations result from such actions. Moving a team to a lower funding tier is a more responsible choice. Consider the following order of budget cuts:
    a. Cut indirect student services (communications, advertising, and so on)
    b. Reduce salary expenditures (eliminate lowest priority positions, move some full-time positions to part-time, and so on)
    c. Reduce scholarships (i.e., reduce scholarship allocations for low-priority sports)
    d. Make across-the-board percentage budget cuts to ensure that the higher budgeted sports contribute a reasonable share
    e. Limit out-of-country and out-of-state travel for as many sports as possible or eliminate airline travel
    f. Institute maximum limits to numbers of players and personnel traveling to away events
    g. Institute a moratorium on construction of new facilities
    h. Move to a conference that better restricts spending for all member institutions
    i. Move to a lower competitive division
5. At the conference level, consider the following actions:
    a. Adopt strict limits on travel squads for all member institutions
    b. Split conference competition geographically and play off to reduce travel expenses
    c. Institute maximum roster limit legislation in all sports
    d. Institute limits lower than NCAA levels on number of assistant coaches
    e. Significantly reduce maximum football rosters
    f. Establish maximum competition schedules lower than NCAA levels (or state levels for high schools)
    g. Reduce scholarship maximums in all sports while factoring in gender equity concerns
    h. Legislate caps on recruiting budgets by sport

i. Prohibit film staffing other than production of running-time game film and reinstitute the trading of film
j. Prohibit resort or out-of-state meetings and noninstitutional entertainment and return savings to schools
k. Prohibit training tables and athletics-only facilities
l. Add the same women's sport at the same time as all conference institutions

6. Work to reduce the cost of men's football and basketball and the pressures of the arms race. This concern is primarily a Division I and II college issue, but it is also present among larger high school sport programs. These cost reductions cannot occur unilaterally without damaging the competitiveness of the program that initiates such action. Thus, this action should occur through state legislation at the high school level (high schools do not have a national governance system) and at the national governance level for colleges. Even conference-level legislation can be effective when the athletic director realizes that as long as the conference has an automatic championship berth, teams can be successful in often unpredictable national championship competitions. Reducing exorbitant expenses will enable gender equity and prevent further cutting of men's sports programs. Other national-level legislation that should be supported include the following:
   a. Institute maximum roster limits in all sports
   b. Limit the numbers of coaches
   c. Institute significant cutbacks in maximum football rosters
   d. Reduce scholarships and go to equivalencies in all sports
   e. Prohibit all training tables
   f. Prohibit athletics-only facilities
   g. Prohibit coach contract provisions that require sport operating, recruiting, or new facility expenditures
   h. Aggressively pursue an NCAA antitrust exemption that would permit control of exorbitant coaches' salaries

The point is clear: Managing gender equity change is difficult and time consuming. Doing the necessary homework, understanding the issues, having a clear plan of strategies that can be applied, and being prepared to support doing the right thing, even though it may not be a popular position, is essential. In the long run, when positions are diametrically opposed, the right position always wins out over the popular decision.

1.27 MANAGEMENT TIP

Asking Permission to Recruit a Coach at Another Institution

This management tip presents a typical athletic issue and illustrates how important it is for an athletic director to think through and question commonly accepted assumptions. In the athletic culture, the athletic director will often encounter unwritten rules of etiquette such as "Before contacting a coach at another institution, the athletic director wishing to make such a contact should seek permission from that institution's athletic director." Although this courtesy seems reasonable, a careful examination of the issue reveals otherwise. First, most coach employment agreements in high schools and colleges are employee-at-will agreements in which either party can exit at any time. Some coaches, however, especially those in the NCAA's Division I football and basketball programs and in some high-powered high school football and basketball programs, have multiyear contracts. In this case the athletic director does have an obligation not to interfere with a contract already in place between two parties if it is known that such a contract exists. Technically, such a situation is referred to as tortious interference (Chelladurai & Madella, 2017; Sharp, Moorman, & Claussen, 2007; Spengler, Anderson, Connaughton, & Baker, 2009; Wong, 2010). Proving a claim of tortious interference requires proof not only that a binding contract existed but also that (1) the third party knew of its existence and intended to interfere with the contract, (2) damages were suffered, and (3) the interference caused the damages. A defense against tortious interference in some states may be the existence of a fair competition doctrine in which the new employer need only prove its purpose in advancing competition against the old employer and demonstrate that it did not use wrongful means. Yet the disadvantages of this practice of etiquette should be considered, especially when legal considerations can be accommodated. We argue that the practice of asking permission of another athletic director to recruit one of his or her staff members contributes to an unhealthy hiring environment. Consider the following points:

1. **How does the institution know whether an employment agreement exists?** Except at the Division I major-sport level (football, basketball, and maybe one or two other sports), a multiyear contract may not exist. Before recruiting a coach or considering a coach for the finalist applicant pool, a required question to that coach should be whether he or she has other than an at-will current employment contract. If the answer is yes, the institution should ask the employee whether he or she has permission from the current institution to speak to another prospective employer. If the employee says that he or she will seek that permission only if he or she is definitely offered the position, the prospective employee can go ahead with the interview process as long as the actual offer of position is contingent on the current employer's approval. The new employer needs to be careful not to advise other finalist candidates that they were not selected in the case that the current institution and employee cannot come to terms or the new employer does not wish to buy out the contract.
2. **What will happen if the athletic director says no?** As a practical matter, the athletic director seeking to hire the employee may have no obligation to honor this response in the case of an employee with an at-will employment agreement. If the employee has a multiyear contract, the employee must deal with this obligation while the new employer waits for resolution before making an offer. Although the employee may eventually ask the new employer to buy out the remainder of his or her contract, that issue is separate and must be handled entirely by the employee, who knows the

terms of his or her agreement, and only if an actual employment offer is forthcoming.

3. **Someone will be the bad guy.** Even if permission is given by the current employer, the requesting athletic director may be perceived as a raider. The institution performing the courtesy is the bad guy if the current employer denies permission and the athletic director goes forward anyway.
4. **The hiring athletic director has to rush a decision.** Making a real (assuming no one has contacted the prospective coach) permission phone call increases the pressure to conclude the hiring process. The coach being sought can pressure the hiring athletic director to move faster than might be desirable, pleading pressure from his institution, alumni, and players and wanting to be fair to recruits. Before the athletic director formally offers the position, the current employer may up the ante for the coach being sought by changing the salary and other considerations. If the contact becomes public knowledge, pressure increases from all stakeholders at the new institution who may second-guess the athletic director regarding the quality of a prospective hire.
5. **Increased possibility of abuse.** The practice of asking another athletic director to call an applicant's current athletic director can be too easily abused by coaches who will use interest expressed by another institution to gain additional salary, years on contract, or other benefits from their current employee. This situation may occur with no certain offer of alternative employment ever being made and maybe not even a desire of the coach to move elsewhere.
6. **Increasing the likelihood that everyone will know.** In this age of social networking and incredibly fast communication, the chance of such a conversation leaking to all stakeholders is high. When stakeholder pressure starts building, the hiring athletic director's job as well as that of the current employer just gets more difficult.
7. **Multiple media downsides.** Especially in the case of high-profile coach searches, all or some of the following can occur if the contact leaks or the media is searching the marketplace for proof of such contact:
   a. At the institution currently employing the coach, the athletic director has three options if contacted by the media and asked if permission to leave was sought by the current coach or another institution: (1) admit to a true answer, opening the door to media investigation and conjecture by media, the institution, and alumni; (2) be dishonest by saying no, risking an allegation of dishonesty if the truth comes out after further investigation or following a hire; or (3) be neutral by saying, "By policy, the athletic department doesn't discuss personnel matters with the media," risking ignition of further media investigation or conjecture anyway. The pressure surrounding keeping or letting the coach go immediately ratchets up at the coach's current institution.
   b. At the institution making the ask for permission to speak with the coach employed by another institution, revealing one of the candidates being considered for the position may negatively influence the consideration of the job by other viable candidates. As soon as information about the candidate pool gets into the coach community, whatever the sport, it travels like wildfire.
   c. Parents and student-athletes at both institutions may be motivated to offer their opinions about the prospective coach.
8. **Institutional and alumni downsides.** The prospective coach's loyalty to his or her current employer is immediately questioned. Or, alumni may be ignited to put unreasonable pressure on the athletic director to keep the coach, even if the athletic director may not want to retain that coach.
9. **Use of search firms antiquates the practice.** When search firms are used, prospects are contacted without knowledge of the hiring athletic director. Asking permission after a coach reaches the finalist prospect list of the search firm means that the conversation with

the coach has already taken place before the employer is asked for permission, rendering the ask meaningless because making the list means that the coach wants to be considered. Why, then, should an athletic director risk a no-permission response from the institution?

10. **The prospective coach may not want the hiring athletic director to contact his or her employer.** In numerous instances the coach wants to be considered an applicant only under the condition of confidentiality or only if he or she is offered the position. The coach does not want to risk letting the current employer know that he or she is actively in the marketplace; the coach does not want his or her loyalty or commitment questioned if he or she is not offered the job. Thus, if the athletic director does make the ask, the risk of losing the applicant is real.

Following the practice of asking forgiveness rather than permission appears to be a much more sensible approach. After the job has been accepted by the coach in the case of an at-will employee or just before the offer is made in the case of an employee with a multiyear contract at another institution, a call from the hiring athletic director to the employer athletic director honestly explaining why the asking-for-permission call wasn't made—because of downsides for both parties—is likely to be a much healthier conversation.

These considerations argue against automatically honoring this unwritten rule of asking permission before approaching a coach employed by another institution. The practice does not appear to be used anywhere else in the education, nonprofit organization, or corporate marketplace, and the downsides suggest cautious consideration before doing so.

1.28 MANAGEMENT TIP

Firing a Coach

Most managers agree that one of the most difficult tasks they face is firing an employee. When that employee is a coach, especially a popular coach or one who is highly visible in the community, the process is even more stressful. Yet few textbooks help the athletic director deal with this common challenge. The problem to be solved is how to terminate a popular coach while handling all of the stakeholders interested or upset about this personnel decision. Although chapter 6 deals with personnel and building a staff, the following discussion approaches this issue from a leadership and complex problem-solving perspective.

Consultation With Human Resources

As soon as nonrenewal or termination of employment is being considered by any supervisor, coach, or any staff member, the institutional or school district human resources office should be contacted for advice. Having a written record of evaluations, corrective action, or other evidence supporting the decision is critical if a lawsuit eventually ensues. The earlier the athletic director is reminded of these responsibilities, the more likely it is that the employee's personnel file will fully support the termination or nonrenewal decision.

Consultation With Legal Counsel

In any termination decision for cause (such as violation of NCAA or high school association rules, commission of a felony, or refusal to follow instructions of a supervisor), if a multiyear employment agreement exists, or the termination is either for cause or not (dissatisfaction with performance of a team) of a high-profile coach, even if he or she is an at-will employee, the human resources office will most likely recommend that legal counsel become an additional advisor.

Consultation With Higher Administration

Any individual's employment might be terminated for many reasons, and whenever this happens, both the athletic director and the employee face challenging emotional stress. But the decision to fire a coach is even more difficult because of the number of stakeholders directly and indirectly affected—from the coach's current student-athletes, their parents, and the assistant coaching staff and their families to athletes being recruited, their families, former student-athletes, alumni, and fans. The stakeholders increase in number and importance for a high-profile athletic program, which may be just as true for a small, tight-knit community with regard to its high school program as it is for a nationally recognized university. At some institutions, major donors, powerful business people, members of the institution's governing board or school board, and state legislators or city council members may try to get involved. Thus, consultation with higher administration is essential. The athletic director must remember that the president or principal is ultimately responsible for the conduct of the athletic program and the institution. Any contact with elected officials, influential alumni, important members of the business community, or major donors should be made by the president or principal or superintendent of schools, or such contact agreed upon through a conversation with the athletic director. At the college level, when consulting with higher administration, the athletic director and the athletic department faculty representative should be operating as a team.

When the Termination Should Occur

Although most personnel actions take place at the end of an academic year, decisions on termination of coaches at the college level usually occur at the end of a season to try to recoup some portion of the recruiting period. In some cases, coaches are fired midseason. If a midseason termination does occur, every effort must be made to make sure that the transition staff (current assistant coaches) are prepared and supported through this period. Even if the coach is terminated at the end of the sport season, plans must be put in place to deal with the period until the new coach is in place and through the orientation and introduction of the new coach to key stakeholders. As the athletic director thinks through this process, a first priority must be personally communicating with and meeting the needs of student-athletes, who are the least prepared to deal with a significant life change.

Dealing With Media Pressures Before the Announcement of a Decision

Often, especially in high-profile programs, the media may sense that the coach is in trouble and pressure the athletic director for his or her thoughts on retaining the coach. The best response is to refer to athletic department policy on employee evaluation: "We annually evaluate the performance of all our coaches. This evaluation does not happen until the end of the season. Any decision on employee retention will not be made until that time."

Thoughts on Reasons for Termination

Termination for cause is an easier decision in many ways than firing a coach for other reasons because the decision is clear. The coach has crossed a well-defined line—he or she has broken rules, committed a felony, violated a contract, or committed some other such action. Termination for other reasons such as lack of control of player behavior; poor graduation rates or substandard academic performance of players; lack of competitive success; or poor effort, performance, or attitude on the part of players is a more difficult decision because this lack of essential coaching skills is realized gradually over time. Usually no clear line has been crossed or no specific thing has happened. Most likely, the athletic director has made a number of efforts to inform the coach of these deficiencies, the coach has probably been given time to remedy the issues, and clear communication may have been made that failure to show improvement would result in termination of employment. But these situations are often less clear with regard to determining that the coach cannot make the necessary changes. For instance, improvement may occur, but it is insufficient or uneven. Or, a revered and well-liked coach who was initially successful shows deteriorating performance as the nature of student-athletes changes, recruiting becomes more competitive, or his or her coaching skills are not continually updated. Ultimately, the athletic director is the one who understands the deficiencies and is the closest observer of daily performance and relationships with players and staff. The decision rests with the athletic director.

Even if internal or external stakeholders ratchet up the pressure, the proverbial buck stops on the athletic director's desk. The athletic director must be comfortable with his or her assessment, which really comes down to the student-athlete experience not being what it should be and lack of confidence that the coach has the ability to remedy the situation over the near term. Notice this focus on the student-athlete experience. Even the most successful coach, as measured by wins and losses or conference and national championships won, cannot be salvaged if student-athlete health and well-being is sacrificed in the process.

What happens if the athletic director is told to fire the coach? If the athletic director agrees with the action, the decision becomes his or hers. If the athletic director disagrees, only two choices remain: (1) refuse to terminate the employee and offer his or her resignation or (2) agree to do the termination or an alternative to a termination as described later. In the case of the latter, the termination must become the athletic director's decision. Blame cannot be placed elsewhere, publicly or privately.

Alternatives to Termination

Especially in the case of long-time coaches who have earned the respect of generations of student-athletes, faculty, and alumni but have lost their effectiveness on the playing fields or in the recruiting wars, consideration should be given to moving that coach to another position in the department, the university, or the school system. Could the relationships developed over decades serve the athletic department well in the athletic or institutional development office at the college level? Is a place available in the physical education department where years of coaching experience can be used to train future coaches? Is early retirement an option? Is resignation a possibility, and if so, can this decision by the coach be enhanced by the offer of an attractive severance package? Sometimes the athletic director has the luxury of negotiating a departure at a specified time. The athletic director may inform the coach that employment will be terminated at the end of the next season, giving the coach time to seek another job and having the option of tendering a resignation instead of being fired. In certain situations, all these possibilities should be explored with the intent of producing a win–win as opposed to facing the challenge of a termination of employment.

Laying Out the Termination Sequence

But let's assume that the situation is such that the coach is unwilling to resign and is going to be fired or the coach is going to resign under the threat of termination. The athletic director should be aware that after the departure decision is communicated to the coach, chances are that the decision will quickly leak to assistant coaches, student-athletes, the media, and others. Thus, to control the accuracy of communication, a plan must be developed to have the following actions happen sequentially, one immediately after the other, and some actions possibly occurring simultaneously:

1. Inform the head coach.
2. Meet with the assistant coaches.
3. Meet with the student-athletes.
4. The president places personal phone calls to the chair of the board of trustees (or the superintendent calls the school board) and selected other influential stakeholders.
5. Conduct press conference or inform the press.
6. Inform other stakeholders (athletic department staff, institution administrative officers, faculty, other donors, parents of current student-athletes, former student-athletes of the coach).
7. At the college level, communicate with student-athletes who are being recruited.

The athletic director must do all items except item 4; the president or principal or superintendent should communicate with the trustees, elected officials, administrative officers, faculty, and top donors by personal phone calls or messages. At the college level, the vice president for development can help with other major donors. Communications with the parents of student-athletes and former student-athletes can be by e-mail followed by formal letter. In this day of instant communication, snail mail is a formality and e-mail is the optimum choice.

Executing the Termination Plan

Following are some thoughts about executing the termination plan. The athletic director, higher administration, the vice president for development (at the college level), and the head of athletic and institutional or school district communications should meet to develop the exact timeline; determine who will attend each session; and approve formal press releases, e-mail communications, the formal statements to be made at the press conference, and so on. This planning process is much like managing a football or basketball game; a timeline should be produced that specifies when everything is supposed to happen.

Step 1: Communicating the Termination Decision to the Head Coach Coach termination meetings are of two types: one in which the purpose of the meeting is a done deal in that when the meeting ends, the coach's employment will be terminated by the institution, and the other in which the coach has accepted the alternative of resignation, retirement, or acceptance of an alternative noncoaching position. In both, the decision is final with regard to termination of the coaching position. In the case of the latter, the termination meeting may focus on the athletic department, institution, and coach statements regarding the departure and a review of the timetable for meetings with assistant coaches, the team, and the media. With regard to the former situation (termination is the only option), the athletic director needs to walk into this meeting with full confidence in the finality of his or her decision and be prepared to take full responsibility for it. At this point, laying blame on the president, alumni, or the board of trustees is unprofessional, even if there was pressure. If details to the severance are present, such as the institution's meeting contractual obligations to pay out the remainder of the contract, or being relieved of such obligations because of the reasons for termination, or offering a buyout or severance even though one is not required in order to avoid media debate, the athletic director must be prepared to deliver all these messages clearly, finalize the deal and any conditions, and have the result be closure.

Step 2: Communicating the Head Coach Termination to the Assistant Coaches

The next meeting for the athletic director is with the assistant coaches. The head coach should not be present. The athletic director should communicate (1) the reasons for his or her decision, being frank, (2) the commitment of the institution to fulfill the institution's employment commitment to the assistant coaches, (3) the desire of the athletic director to work closely with the assistant coaches in dealing with student-athlete issues and ensure a smooth transition to the new head coach, (4) whether assistant coaches will be considered for the head coach position if they wish to apply, (5) that the decision to renew the employment agreements of assistant coaches shall rest with the new head coach, and (6) that assistant coaches are immediately free to seek new employment and that if the athletic director can be of assistance with recommendations, he or she will provide such help. The athletic director should state that any assistant coach who thinks that he or she cannot operate in a positive and professional manner that is fully supportive of the institution's decision should consider resigning immediately, knowing that the institution will provide two weeks of severance pay (or none, or whatever the institution decides). The athletic director should also make clear that the institution is committed to hiring an outstanding replacement and that this is the message that all staff members should be delivering to student-athletes, who will be represented on the search committee.

The athletic director should also explain the sequence of meetings occurring after the assistant coaches' meeting—the meeting with athletes, press conference, and so forth. Consideration should be given to having the sports information director or school district communications officer present to distribute copies of the press release to the assistant coaches and discuss appropriate responses to media questions. Time should be allotted for questions. If an assistant coach has a multiyear employment agreement, which may be the case in a Division I college institution, the athletic director has to make additional decisions with regard to offering a buyout or other action, which should occur, of course, in a separate one-on-one meeting.

The assistant coaches should then be invited to the student-athletes' meeting, but it should be explained that the meeting is for the athletes and that assistant coaches should not be asking questions or raising issues. They should just be listening carefully so that they understand the athletes' concerns and can ensure that their subsequent conversations with student-athletes are in full alignment with the athletic director's position. Last but not least, at the college level, all the assistant coaches should meet with the athletic director or senior staff administrator overseeing their sport to determine the contents of e-mails or phone calls that are to be made to all recruiting prospects that evening.

Step 3: Meeting With Student-Athletes

The athletic director should meet with the entire team without the head coach (unless the head coach is resigning or moving to another noncoaching position), setting aside at least an hour for this meeting. The athletic director should communicate (1) the reasons for the termination decision and an assurance that a great deal of care and deliberation preceded the decision or, in the alternative, how much the institution appreciates the service of the resigning or reassigned head coach and with the head coach making an appropriate statement in this regard; (2) that the athletic director will work closely with the assistant coaches in dealing with student-athlete issues and ensuring a smooth transition to the new head coach; (3) that the team will be asked to select a representative to serve on the search committee to select a new head coach and that this person is responsible for communicating to the search committee those criteria or qualifications of candidates most important to student-athletes; (4) whether assistant coaches will be considered for the head coach position if they wish to apply, being frank that only applicants with at least X number of years' experience as a head coach will be considered if that is the case; and (5) that the decision to renew the employment agreements of assistant coaches shall rest with the new head coach.

The floor should then be open for questions. Again, the sports information director or district communications officer should be present and should distribute copies of the press release to the student-athletes, explaining that a press conference or meetings with the athletic director and the media will occur next. Recommendations should be made about responding to media questions, urging students to focus on the positives of their experience with the departing head coach and their appreciation for his or her commitment. A discussion should occur about the importance of not being drawn into making negative comments. If the student-athletes don't agree with the institution's decision, they should be assured that no one is stopping them from saying anything, but they should be urged to think about how they want to communicate whatever they think. Respectfully disagreeing with the institutional decision is one thing; responding emotionally or with anger is another, especially if the student-athlete is not knowledgeable of everything that went into the decision. Student-athletes should also be told that not speaking to the media is fine, if they are not comfortable doing so.

A question may be asked like, "What if we want our captain to respond for the entire team?" This approach should be acceptable and may be an excellent learning experience for all team members. At this point, the team should be allowed to meet for this purpose. The sports information director or district communications officer should offer to help student-athletes draft or issue a press release.

Step 4: Informing the Chair of the Board of Trustees and Selected Major Donors As the athletic director moves into the meeting with student-athletes, if the president determines that the board of trustees of the institution needs to be informed, or at the high school level, if the principal and superintendent agree that the school board members should be informed, these calls should be made by the president or principal or superintendent, respectively. The same approach should be used with the most influential donors and stakeholders. The athletic director should be involved in these decisions, and at the college level the vice president for development and the head of development for the athletic department should be part of these strategic conversations. Typically, there will be collaboration and agreement about which staff member will call these supporters and donors. All these decisions are made in the preliminary meeting with higher administration before the start of the termination sequence.

Step 5: Meeting With the Media For a high-profile college or high school program that attracts high media interest, conducting a press conference is the best way to prevent one media company from scooping another. For high schools or colleges with low media profiles, the sports information director may simply make phone calls and then e-mail press releases to local radio, television, and newspaper sports reporters. These contacts should occur immediately after the meetings with the coach, assistant coaches, and student-athletes are completed. The athletic director should be available for phone calls or one-on-one interviews with the media. If a press conference is conducted regarding coach termination, the terminated coach should not be present. The athletic director would read a prepared statement and then be open to questions. If the situation is a resignation, retirement, or reassignment, the athletic director would open with an announcement of the coach's departure, thank the coach for his or her service, and then have the coach make his or her own statement, which has been jointly developed in concert with the institution. The coach and the athletic director will have met with the sports information director and possibly the institutional or school district communications director to discuss responses to all possible questions that might be raised.

Step 6: Informing Other Stakeholders In any situation in which a head coach is terminated and a press release is issued to that effect, the athletic director should communicate this decision by e-mail to all athletic department coaches and staff members and issue a copy of the press release. This should be done immediately after the meetings with the coach, assistant coaches, and student-athletes of the affected team. If necessary, a larger institutional e-mail to faculty and staff should occur at this time. All institutions have electronic communication mechanisms to make announcements to all faculty and staff. Communication by e-mail, if possible, followed by snail mail may also need to be initiated to all donors to the sport program, parents of current student-athletes, and former student-athletes. Such decisions are made based on analysis of circumstances. These broad announcements should be made only in the case of high-profile decisions, not all coach personnel decisions. If the decision rises to this level of broad interest, the faculty and staff announcement should be a statement from the president, announcing the athletic director's decision and his or her support for it along with a copy of the press release. Communications to lower-level athletic donors, parents of current student-athletes, and former student-athletes should come from the athletic director.

Step 7: Communicating With Recruits at the College Level Immediately after the press conference, the athletic director and senior staff member overseeing the affected sport program should meet with the assistant coaches to determine the appropriate way to communicate with recruits—those who have already signed letters of intent and those who are still undecided. Rules regarding whether athletes are obligated to attend the institution should be reviewed. Formal communications should be drafted depending on recruiting status. Personal phone calls may precede e-mails and snail mail. Every effort must be made to encourage undecided recruits to wait until the new coach is appointed before they make their college decision.

Planning for a Positive Transition

Attention must be directed to ensuring that the student-athlete experience during the period following termination and before the arrival of the new coach on campus is as positive and organized as possible. The athletic director or senior staff administrator over the affected sport should have a planning meeting with assistant coaches to determine all the tasks that need to be accomplished and who is assigned responsibility for each duty. The need for additional team or personal meetings with student-athletes should be discussed. Athletic department senior student affairs and academic support staff members should be included in this meeting. After that plan has been determined, the senior staff member over the affected sport should have a weekly meeting with the assistant coaches to review the plan's progress, make necessary adjustments, or make decisions regarding new problems encountered.

Concluding Comment

The bottom line in any termination process is that the athletic director must think through all possible situations and know how to handle them. The termination announcement sequence is important, requiring both precise timing and planning. The difference between a successful and unsuccessful coaching transition often lies in this incredible attention to detail.

1.29 MANAGEMENT TIP

Leading an Environmentally Responsible Organization

Environmentally responsible, or sustainable, sport cannot be considered an option. It is an economic and ethical necessity. Unfortunately, athletic directors receive little or no training in this area and thus think themselves less capable of adopting a leadership role. Sport programs can have a significant impact on the environment:

- Sports fields and golf courses increase water consumption, pollute water and soil with pesticides and fertilizers, consume energy for field lighting, generate greenhouse gases through the operation of grounds maintenance equipment, increase soil erosion and compaction when accommodating large groups of spectators, and often are placed on fragile or scarce land types.
- Traveling teams create greenhouse gases when they use various forms of transportation.
- Indoor facilities use tremendous amounts of energy for heating, cooling, and lighting; ice rinks use ozone-depleting refrigerants; swimming pools use hazardous chemicals, huge amounts of water, and much energy to maintain water and deck temperatures.
- Major athletic events generate huge amounts of paper, plastic, and human waste and produce greenhouse gas emissions associated with travel to and traffic surrounding such events.

Seldom discussed is the impact of polluted or poor-quality air environments on the student-athletes forced to perform in them. Notable effects result from the emissions of plastic, petroleum, and cleaning products in training rooms, locker rooms, and indoor facilities in general and by poorly circulated indoor air and chlorine gas in the pool. Being environmentally responsible by addressing these pollutants clearly advances the health and well-being of student-athletes.

Most sustainable sport initiatives involve zero costs or minimal costs, and most of those that involve capital costs pay for themselves over the long term. No cost is involved in lowering or manually shutting off thermostats; turning off unnecessary lights; reducing water temperatures in showers, arenas, and other facilities; imposing fewer ice or water changes in rinks and pools; and removing lights from excessively lit areas. Similarly, many minimal-cost actions can be initiated. We simply cannot afford to continue to advance a disposable and wasteful sport culture.

That being said, the athletic department doesn't have the time or expertise to determine what needs to be done. Expert help from qualified professionals is needed to create a comprehensive action plan to serve as the sustainable sport blueprint. In short, specialized assistance must be requested from the school district or university because higher administration has ready access to city waste, energy, and water consultants. Most large institutions have already instituted cost-saving energy audits and other audits, but few have looked into the highly specialized and unique sport environment. Larger institutions may be willing to pay for retaining a specialized consultant to do an environmental audit of athletic operations and create sustainable sport recommendations. Thus, the athletic director's leadership comes into play in three places: (1) strongly insisting that the school district or university provide the resources necessary to get experts to define everything that could possibly be done by the athletic department to be environmentally responsible, (2) when those recommendations are received, determining how many of those actions can be reasonably afforded and implemented by who and by when, and (3) motivating employees to embrace the behavioral changes required to become a sustainable sport program. The first step is easy. Consider writing a formal request to the administration now!

DEVELOPING LEADERSHIP STYLE AND PHILOSOPHY

Accel Team Development. (2011). *Elton Mayo's Hawthorne experiments*. www.accel-team.com/motivation/hawthorne_03.html.

American Management Association. (2011). *Articles and white paper solutions*. www.amanet.org/individualsolutions/parameters-solution1.aspx?SelectedSolutionType=Articles+%26+White+Papers.

Bass, B.B. (1999). Two decades of research and development in transformational leadership. *European Journal of Work and Organizational Psychology, 8*(1).

Bridges, F.J., & Roquemore, L.L. (2004). *Management for athletics/sport administration: Theory and practice* (4th ed.). Decatur, GA: ESM Books.

Chelladurai, P., & Madella, A. (2017). *Human resource management in sport and recreation* (3rd ed.). Champaign, IL: Human Kinetics.

Chernushenko, D., van der Kamp, A., & Stubbs, D. (2001). *Sustainable sport management: Running an environmentally, socially, and economically responsible organization*. Nairobi, Kenya: United Nations Environment Programme.

Cheslock, J. (2007). *Who's playing college sports? Trends in participation*. East Meadow, NY: Women's Sports Foundation.

Collins, J. (2001). *Good to great: Why some companies make the leap and others don't*. New York: Harper Collins.

Commission on Sports Management Accreditation. (2020). *Sport management accreditation*. https://www.nassm.com/InfoAbout/NASSM/ProgramAccreditation.

Connolly, P.M. (2006). *Navigating the organizational lifecycle*. Washington, DC: Board Source.

Covey, S.R. (2004). *The 7 habits of highly effective people*. New York: Free Press.

Drucker, P. (2006). *Classic Drucker*. Boston: Harvard Business School.

Facione, P.A. (2011). Critical thinking: What it is and why it counts. *Insight Assessment*. www.insightassessment.com/pdf_files/what&why2006.pdf.

Faludi, S. (1991). *Backlash: The undeclared war against American women*. New York: Crown.

Faludi, S. (1999). *Stiffed: The betrayal of the American man*. New York: William Morrow.

Foundation for Critical Thinking. (2011). *Defining critical thinking*. www.criticalthinking.org/aboutCT/define_critical_thinking.cfm.

Free Management Library. (2011). *Historical theories of management*. www.managementhelp.org/mgmnt/cntmpory.htm.

Hersey, P., Blanchard, K.H., & Johnson, D.E. (2013). *Management of organizational behavior: Leading human resources* (10th ed.). Upper Saddle River, NJ: Pearson.

Hums, M.A., & MacLean, J.C. (2018). *Governance and policy in sport organizations* (4th ed.). New York: Routledge.

Jensen, C.R., & Overman, S.J. (2003). *Administration and management of physical education and athletic programs*. Prospect Heights, IL: Waveland Press.

Lewin, K., Lippitt, R. & White, R.K. (1939). Patterns of aggressive behavior in experimentally created social climates. *Journal of Social Psychology, 10*, 271–301.

Likert, R. (1967). *The human organization: Its management and value*. New York: McGraw-Hill.

McCall, M.W., Jr., & Lombardo, M.M. (1983). *Off the track: Why and how successful executives get derailed*. Greensboro, NC: Centre for Creative Leadership.

McGregor, D. (2006). *The human side of enterprise*. New York: McGraw-Hill.

Mellman Group. (2007, June 8). *Memorandum from the Mellman Group, Inc. on Title IX to the National Women's Law Center*, 1 (on file with the National Women's Law Center).

Messer, D. (2008). *Skills of good networking*. www.canadaone.com/ezine/expert/expert_qa.html?id=09Sep23_1.

Mommsen, W.K. (1989). *The political and social theory of Max Weber: Collected essays*. Chicago: University of Chicago Press.

National Association of Collegiate Directors of Athletics (NACDA). Membership information at http://nacda.com.

National Association for Sport and Physical Education (NASPE). Membership information at www.aahperd.org/NASPE.

National Collegiate Athletic Association (NCAA). (2012). *1981–82 to 2018–19 NCAA sports sponsorship and participation rates report*. www.ncaapublications.com/p-4293-2011-12-ncaa-sports-sponsorship-and-participation-rates-report.aspx.

National Collegiate Athletic Association (NCAA). (2012). *2004–2010 NCAA gender-equity report*. www.ncaapublications.com/productdownloads/GEQS10.pdf.

National Collegiate Athletic Association (NCAA). (2020). *Finances of Intercollegiate Athletics Database.* http://www.ncaa.org/about/resources/research/finances-intercollegiate-athletics-database.

National Collegiate Athletic Association (NCAA). (2020). *NCAA Demographics Database.* http://www.ncaa.org/about/resources/research/ncaa-demographics-database.

National Federation of State High School Associations (NFHS). (2021). *1971–72 to 2018–19 high school participation data.* www.nfhs.org/Participation/HistoricalSearch.aspx, www.nfhs.org/content.aspx?id=5752, and www.nfhs.org/content.aspx?id=7495.

National Interscholastic Athletic Administrators Association (NIAAA). (2021). *Certification program.* http://niaaa.org/Certification/certification.asp.

North American Society for Sports Management. (2011). *Academic programs.* www.nassm.org/Programs/AcademicPrograms.

Pederson, P. & Thibault, L. (Eds.) (2022). *Contemporary sport management* (7th ed.). Champaign, IL: Human Kinetics.

Pike Masteralexis, L., Barr, C.A., & Hums, M.A. (Eds.) (2014). *Principles and practice of sport management* (5th ed.). Sudbury, MA: Jones and Bartlett.

Robin, D. *Sailing the seven seas of collaborative business relationships.* www.abetterworkplace.com/038.html.

Sabo, D., Miller, K.E., Melnick, M.J. & Heywood, L. (2004). *Her life depends on it: Sport, physical activity, and the health and well-being of American girls.* East Meadow, NY: Women's Sports Foundation.

Sharp, L.A., Moorman, A.M., & Claussen, C.L. (2014). *Sport law: A managerial approach.* New York: Routledge.

Slack, T., & Parent, M.M. (2021). *Understanding sport organizations: Applications for sport managers* (3rd ed.). Champaign, IL: Human Kinetics.

Spengler, J.O., Anderson, P.M., Connaughton, D.P., & Baker, T.A., III. (2016). *Introduction to sports law* (2nd ed.). Champaign, IL: Human Kinetics.

Stogdill, R.M. (1974). *Handbook of leadership: A survey of the literature.* New York: Free Press.

Straker, D. Changing Minds.org. www.changingminds.org.

Tannenbaum, A.S., & Schmitt, W.H. (1958). How to choose a leadership pattern. *Harvard Business Review, 36,* 95–101.

Taylor, F.W. (1911). *The principles of scientific management.* New York: Harper Brothers.

United States Government General Accounting Office. (2001, March 8). *Intercollegiate athletics: Four-year colleges' experiences adding and discontinuing teams.* GAO report.

US colleges awarded over $4 billion in athletic scholarships during 2019–20. *ScholarshipStats.com.* 2020. https://scholarshipstats.com/average-per-athlete.

Women Leaders in College Sports (WLCS). (2021). *Coach and administrator training programs.* www.womensleadersincollegesports.org.

Wong, G.M. (2010). *Essentials of sports law* (4th ed.). Santa Barbara, CA: Praeger.

Yiamouyiannis, A., Lawrence, J.J., Hums, M.A., & Ridpath, R.D. (2010). Use of the responsible decision making model for athletics (RDMMA) to address conflicting priorities at NCAA Division I member institutions. *Sports Management Education Journal, 4*(1), 60–75.

CHAPTER

2

Governance of the Athletic Program

No cocurricular or extracurricular educational program matches the complexities of interscholastic and intercollegiate athletics from a risk management, accountability, and authorities perspective. Navigating multiple layers of internal and external governance while being responsive to enthusiastic fans and stakeholders and the needs of athletic staff members and program participants can be daunting. Key to mastery of this challenging environment is reliance on expert advice from others in specialized areas, an understanding of the chain of command, and the design of internal systems that provide clear operational guidance to employees and allow the expression of advice but not control from those without authority. The documents in this chapter, in both the book and HK*Propel*, define essential organizational structures and governing documents that provide a strong and stable skeleton for athletic program operations that will meet the tests of certification and accreditation agencies.

TYPES OF DOCUMENTS

Management tip—Factual background information, insights, problem-solving strategies, and suggestions for the athletic director

Planning tool—Steps to take or factors that should be considered in the development of strategic plans, action plans, professional development plans, or governance systems

Educational resource—Informational handouts that can be used to educate staff members, campus constituents, volunteers, or student-athletes

Policy—Sample policies and procedures that should be adopted by an athletic department after customization and review by appropriate expert institutional or school district officials

Form—Sample forms, letters, or job descriptions

Evaluation instrument—Administrative tools that help the athletic director, a supervisor, or an employee assess job performance and evaluate program content

Risk assessment—Checklists that help the athletic director, a supervisor, or an employee identify risks and prevent litigation

2.1 MANAGEMENT TIP

Never Go It Alone! Navigating Layers of Governance

Governance is the formal control of the operation of the athletic program through decision making according to specified authorities. The athletic director is only one decision maker in a chain of school district or institutional decision makers. Decisions by these institutional or school district authorities are affected by external governmental and nongovernmental decision makers such as lawmakers (local, state, and federal governments and their education agencies), accreditation agencies, and athletic program governance organizations (conference, state, and national). See figure 2.1.1.

Although the athletic director is expected to be the internal institutional expert on athletic program governance organization rules and, if applicable, athletic program certification conducted by those athletic governance associations, he or she is not expected to be an expert in local, state, and federal laws and policies or to be responsible for the institutional accreditation process. Key to successful athletic program governance is identifying a team of internal and external experts who are always accessible to the athletic director for help with athletic program governance issues. This arrangement is particularly important for high school or small-college athletic departments that have small athletic administrative staffs or none at all. If an associate athletic director for compliance or athletic eligibility officer is not on staff, a probably overextended athletic director must depend on others to help with compliance responsibilities. He or she can never go it alone. The stakes are too high to risk the reputation of the educational institution. Violation of athletic association rules, misbehavior of coaches or student-athletes, misuse of funds, a Title IX lawsuit, or other transgressions are readily chronicled by the media. Remember, sports and politics account for nearly half of all stories in newspapers (Farrell & Cupito, 2010).

Understanding the chain of command is also important politically. In numerous instances, donors, members of boards of trustees, school board members, and others try to exercise unofficial power to influence athletic program decisions. When people who are important to the institution ask the athletic director to take certain actions or make particular decisions, the athletic director must both inform and seek counsel of higher administrative officials in handling such situations. In addition, formally constructed and appointed advisory groups, such as faculty-dominated intercollegiate athletic committees, have no official authority in decision making but play critical political and integrity functions. Regular communication and consultation with such groups is important to the institution because these groups are often turned to for expressions of support for formal decision making.

Governance isn't just about rules compliance. Governance, or decision making, is about every operational decision, from budgeting to hiring a new employee. It is about fairness, about being consistent about the reasons for a decision from case to similar case. It is about being able to explain the reasons behind every decision so that people understand the reasoning process and being open to questions about decisions. It is about being willing to reconsider a decision whenever a mistake has been made or new information is brought forward.

Finally, all decision making involves consideration of both the letter and spirit or intent of rules, laws, and policies. Rules and laws simply cannot cover every situation. Thus, the athletic director will always have interpretive latitude. But the consequences of bad decisions

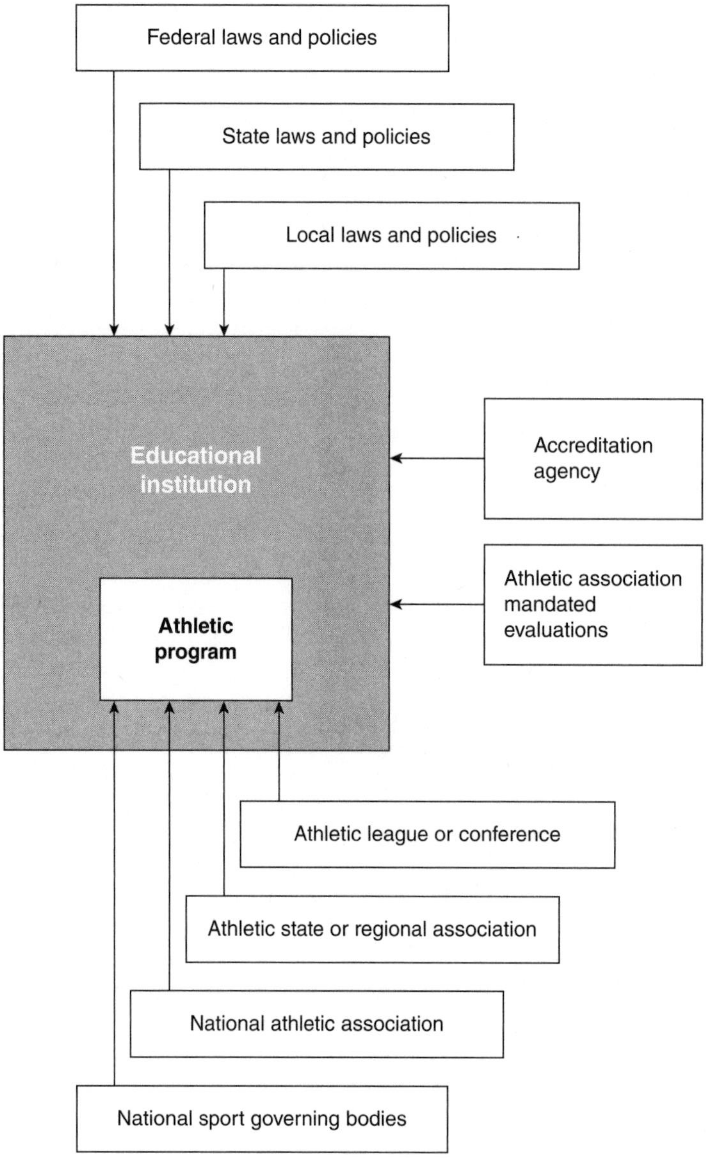

Figure 2.1.1 The formal governance environment of an athletic program.

in a sport-sensitive media environment are significant. Thus, the athletic director must hold himself or herself accountable to both the letter and spirit of rules, displaying a commitment to high ethical standards and embracing a duty of care for the student-athletes being served as well as the reputation of the institution and program.

Suggested Governance Team

Athletic program governance is too complex for the athletic director to handle alone. A team of advisors should be formally assembled by invitation of the athletic director to perform the following critical functions upon request:

- Principal or president—Considered by most athletic governance organizations to be ultimately responsible for the conduct of the athletic program. In some institutions the athletic director may have a direct reporting relationship to the president or principal.
- Direct-report vice president or assistant principal (immediate supervisor of athletic director)—Serves primarily as a political advisor; should be

informed of any concern or when the athletic director is directly contacted by a member of the board of trustees or school board, an elected official, or a major donor.

- Registrar—To produce or verify eligibility reports, must be fully educated in athletic association regulations.
- Human resources director—School district or university administrator, to help with all personnel issues, one of the most difficult areas for the athletic director.
- Director of admissions—For colleges and universities, makes decisions related to admission of all recruited student-athletes; must be fully educated in athletic association rules.
- Legal counsel—School district or university administrator, to help with all legal issues.
- Title IX compliance coordinator—School district or university staff member required by law to deal with Title IX and gender equity, pregnancy, and sexual harassment issues.
- Compliance director—For colleges and universities, an assigned athletic department staff member.
- Conference or league compliance officer.

This group of advisors doesn't meet or act by committee. These individuals are true advisors who will be contacted based on specific situations. They should be identified beforehand because the athletic director must make a concerted effort to educate each on athletic governance association rules and, in the case of eligibility, establish strict procedures and timetables for the production of required documents. A relationship should also be established with a member of the state (for high schools) or national (for colleges) athletic governance association rules staffs.

Keys to responsible governance are (1) educating internal decision makers who will be responsible for making sure that the athletic program conforms to legal and athletic governance association rules; (2) ensuring that eligibility, admissions, and other critical and ethical decisions related to student-athlete academic status are made independent of the athletic department and according to clearly documented procedures; (3) establishing clear written policies holding athletic personnel (staff and student-athletes) accountable for following governance rules; (4) being transparent by sharing all information with administrative superiors or those in the institution responsible for decision making or oversight; (5) self-reporting any discovered violations of rules and showing that systems have been established to prevent reoccurrence of violations; and (6) always asking expert advisors before taking action if any question arises regarding the application of rules to specific situations.

2.2 PLANNING TOOL

Accreditation and Certification

One of the key characteristics of a profession is self-policing and self-regulation through voluntary peer review. Regarding the profession of education, institutions of higher education are members of regional organizations that exist for the sole purpose of establishing standards of quality and conducting regular peer review accreditation of their members. The U.S. Department of Education requires accreditation in order to participate in federal student aid programs. For instance, the Commission on Colleges of the Southern Association of Colleges and Universities conducts accreditation of colleges and universities in an 11-state southern region from Virginia to Texas. The members of the association adopt accreditation standards, and each institution periodically undertakes an evaluation process in which the institution first conducts a self-evaluation that is then reviewed by noninstitutional peers. This institutional accreditation covers athletics. For example, two principles in the Commission on Colleges of the Southern Association of Colleges and Universities standards are directly on point: principle "1.1—The institution operates with integrity in all matters" and principle "5.2.b—The institution's chief executive officer has ultimate responsibility for, and exercises appropriate administrative and control over . . . (b) the institution's intercollegiate athletics program" (Commission on Colleges, 2017).

Schools and school districts have similar associations and processes except that schools must meet state standards for performance and there are no federal K–12 requirements (Oldham, 2017). Athletic directors must therefore familiarize themselves with the accreditation requirements for middle school and high school athletic programs in their respective states.

During the institutional accreditation self-evaluation, the athletic director will be asked to contribute data in support of the institution's contention that it meets the accreditation standard or may be asked to serve on a committee or subcommittee responsible for conducting the self-evaluation required under the accreditation process. Demonstrating control of athletics will require proof of oversight, documented policies and procedures to determine eligibility, demonstration of the absence of violations of athletic association rules, and so on. Throughout the process of assembling accreditation data, the athletic director will be assisted by the institution's self-evaluation committee and myriad school, district, or university administrators who are responsible for submitting the institution's report.

In addition to gaining institutional accreditation, athletic governance associations may require compliance reviews or athletic program self-assessments or offer institutional performance assessments. The NCAA's Division I certification program, established in 1993 as a rigorous peer review program analogous to regional accreditation programs but solely focused on athletic programs, was discarded in 2011 and replaced with an Institutional Performance Program (IPP). This certification program was transparent to all members of the institution's community as well as the general public while the IPP program is not. The NCAA's IPP program involves the collection of data from the athletic department on academics, inclusion, and fiscal management, which is then fed back to a limited number of institutional leaders together with comparable information on other institutions (NCAA D-I IPP Program, 2021). The certification standards, peer review, and campus-wide committee aspects of the certification program have been eliminated. A similar IPP program was established for Division II (NCAA D-II IPP Program, 2021). Division's III's IPP program includes only graduation rates, sports sponsorship, and demographic information as required elements (NCAA D-III IPP Program, 2021). Division III reporting of financial data is voluntary.

IPP data are not publicly transparent; obtaining such data requires a Freedom of Information Act (FOIA) request for public institutions and is not available for private institutions.

NCAA Division I athletic programs must also submit to external review of their rules compliance processes on a regular basis. These reviews are usually performed by third-party consultants or the institution's conference office compliance director. NCAA Division II and III members mandate completion of self-evaluation processes as a condition of membership, but such reviews are internal and not overseen or conducted by external peer review panels. Division II and III members must also conduct an athletic program self-study every five years. Similar self-studies are also required in all NCAA divisions for institutions seeking reclassification (change to another membership division or subdivision) (*NCAA Division II and III Manuals*, 2020 and *Division II and III Self-Study Guides*).

Whether an institution is required to engage in an accreditation process, compliance process review, or a self-evaluation, the purpose of such processes is to improve the quality of the institution's program and not to penalize institutions. Thus, when deficiencies are identified, institutions are put on probation or certification is withheld until the deficiencies are remedied. The general practice is that such remedies must be accomplished within established time limits. The institution may also be obliged to monitor or complete an established plan developed in conjunction with the accreditation process.

Key to successful completion of the accreditation or self-study review is advance preparation. The actual self-evaluation is usually an 18-month process. But an understanding of the accreditation or compliance standards, the data required to meet standards, and annual collection of such data should be an ongoing process rather than an activity done once in five years or once in a decade. Such preparation enables the athletic department to develop policies and procedures essential to demonstrating control of program areas and to establish refined systems to gather necessary data so that the self-evaluation process is relatively painless. Regular tracking of key performance indicators should be installed as standard operating procedures for the athletic department. Thus, the key preparation messages to the athletic director are (1) gain full understanding of the standards that must be met from the applicable accreditation agency or compliance publication, (2) review the most recent institutional self-evaluation conducted according to those standards to be sure that all identified deficiencies have been remedied, (3) ensure that ongoing athletic department data collection is aligned with self-evaluation requirements, and (4) keep up to date with national and state or conference regulations to determine necessary changes in requirements and obligations to collect additional data.

2.3 MANAGEMENT TIP

Reliance on Professional Legal Advice

An important governance responsibility is compliance with legal obligations. Local, state, and federal laws place myriad obligations on athletic decision makers in a variety of areas such as equal employment opportunity laws related to employment searches, local health regulations affecting athletic event food and beverage concessions, taxation on the sale of certain kinds of merchandise, and so on. Laws such as Title IX also affect the structure of the athletic program, requiring equal participation opportunities, scholarship support, and equal treatment of male and female athletes. Further, in this highly litigious society, the athletic director must be constantly vigilant about the management of risk, from promulgating policies related to the stoppage of play because of dangerous weather to routine inspection of facilities to ensure that they do not present a danger to participants or spectators. The nature of athletics involves risk of injury to participants. Accommodating the public at athletic events requires attention to security, crowd control, safe food concessions, and the possible need for emergency medical treatment in the case of accident, illness, or injury. The media's interest in athletics requires attentiveness to privacy issues. The value of a scholarship and the effect of ineligibility on the career of a prospective professional athlete requires due diligence with regard to student-athlete due process rights.

Throughout this resource, legal requirements, restrictions, or risks are identified for each program area and suggestions are offered about how to manage them. Risk Assessments are offered as web-based downloadable resources. Management Tips and Educational Resources that are risk management–related are designated throughout the book (see document listing in Planning Tool 1.7). But many laws vary by state, and it is neither possible nor desirable to rely on publications for legal advice. Thus, the athletic director must have easy access to school district or university legal counsel and must take advantage of this expert resource. Legal counsel should review all policies related to personnel management, student-athlete discipline, and risk management before they are adopted. Never take a sample athletic program policy model or a policy used by another institution and assume that it will pass legal muster in your state or even that it has ever been reviewed by legal counsel.

2.4 MANAGEMENT TIP

Athletic Director Responsibilities Related to Rules Compliance

The athletic director must be knowledgeable of the various athletic governance associations of which the institution is a member. Although the institution's association with recognized state or national associations or conferences and leagues that promulgate rules on the conduct of athletic programs contributes to the educational credibility of the program, the primary reason for such affiliations is access to regular season and postseason competition opportunities. The intra-institutional nature of varsity sport programs requires institutions that compete against each other to (1) commit to a fair and level playing field, (2) agree on playing by the same sport rules, (3) abide by academic eligibility rules for athletes, (4) use the same limits on the numbers of athletic scholarships that can be awarded, (5) enforce the prohibition and policing of the use of performance-enhancing substances, (6) abide by established limits on recruiting practices and expenditures, and (7) abide by the selection or qualification procedures for postseason competition. These regulations to ensure a level playing field are democratically decided by votes of member institutions in governance associations that exist for the purpose of imposing such controls and ensuring that members comply with them. These governance associations also enhance competitive opportunities by offering postseason championship play, and some, like the NCAA and many collegiate conferences, commercially exploit such championship properties and share the proceeds with members.

For high schools, the primary governance association affiliations are the state high school athletic federation and the institution's local league or conference. The state association is responsible for promulgating eligibility rules, establishing limits on playing and practice seasons and numbers of competitions, and conducting state championship play. The local league is responsible for determining the regular season schedule with other schools in the league and usually takes responsibility for assigning officials. Local leagues are geographically determined for public schools and are usually within reasonable geographic proximity for private schools. For colleges and universities, the primary governance association affiliations are (1) one of the national collegiate governance associations (i.e., National Collegiate Athletic Association [NCAA], National Association for Intercollegiate Athletics [NAIA], National Junior College Athletic Association [NJCAA], National Christian College Athletic Association [NCCAA], Association for Christian College Athletics [ACCA]), (2) their respective conferences, and (3) national sport governing bodies (e.g., USA Swimming, USA Rowing) if institutions want to participate in open national championships or invitational tournaments.

Conference membership for colleges and universities is determined by the institution. Institutions seek affiliation with a group of schools that are similar in size, location, academic orientation, and athletic program philosophy, including a common competitive division (Division I, II, or III). For those few but powerful NCAA athletic programs that generate substantial revenue through their football or basketball programs, conference affiliation may also be based on the potential for shared revenue through conference television packages. In the case of NAIA and smaller national associations, conference affiliations are more likely to be based on geographic proximity because of financial considerations. The institutional representative to these various organizations may be the athletic director or, at the college level, a faculty representative appointed by the president of the institution. Both are usually in attendance at all meetings of the collegiate organizations.

The athletic director has several responsibilities related to these affiliations:

- Understand the structure and function of each organization in order to offer and influence legislation
- Establish a close working relationship with the faculty voting representative of his or her institution to make sure that philosophies are aligned and information is shared to ensure adequate program oversight
- Understand the rules and regulations of each organization and make sure that all coaches, staff, and student-athletes are fully educated about and comply with all rules
- Install policies and procedures in the athletic department to ensure accurate production of all eligibility reports and monitoring of compliance with all recruiting and other rules

Educating coaches, staff, and student-athletes as well as providing them clear instructions regarding their obligation to report any inadvertent violation of the rules and to "ask before you do" are crucial responsibilities of the leader of the athletic department. These instructions begin with a clear and strong policy statement concerning responsibility to follow rules and accountability for violation of athletic governance association rules and regulations. Policy 2.5 is a sample of what should be contained in such a policy.

2.5 **Policy**—Institutional Governance and Rules Compliance

A sample policy that communicates staff, student-athlete, and other personnel accountabilities related to compliance with institutional, conference or league, and state or national athletic governance association rules and regulations.

Available in HK*Propel*.

2.6 MANAGEMENT TIP

Chain of Command

Board of Trustees or Board of Education

The placement of athletics in the institution's organizational structure is relatively consistent across various types of educational institutions, for both high school and college. See figure 2.6.1.

Few educational institutions operate as for-profits. Almost all educational institutions are not-for-profit organizations that have either elected or appointed boards of directors. Legally, these boards have fiduciary responsibility for the financial well-being and proper operation of the organization. In the case of a local public high school, the members of the board of education might be elected by all citizens as part of a general election ballot. In the case of a private high school or private college or university, the board of directors may be responsible for electing its own new members or renewing the terms of members by majority vote. At a public university, the members of the board may be appointed by the governor of the state. In turn, the board is responsible for appointing the leader of the educational institution. If that institution is a school district, the board hires the superintendent who in turn hires principals for each school in the district. If the school is a private school, the board hires the headmaster. In the case of colleges and universities, the board hires the president of the institution. In addition to hiring the administrative leader of the educational institution, the board is responsible for approving the annual budget and making all major governance decisions that affect the financial health of the organization. In turn, the administrative leader is responsible for appointing his or her staff and running the daily business of the institution.

Although members of the board may be interested in athletics or other educational programs, they should not be directly interacting with the program leaders in the educational institution. Thus, the president or principal of the institution should know whenever a trustee or director comes to campus and should be orchestrating such visits. If a trustee wants tickets to athletic events, that request should be fulfilled by the office of the president. The athletic director should not seek to establish independent relationships with members

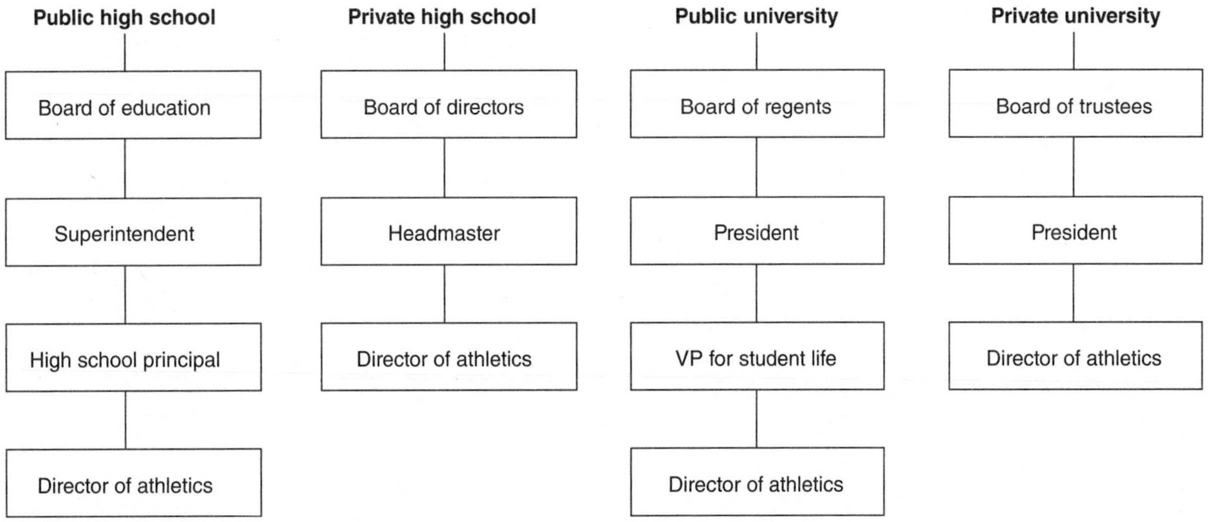

Figure 2.6.1 Location of athletics in the educational institution.

of the board and should never make requests directly to trustees.

Superintendents or Chancellors

Whenever multiple institutions are governed by a single board of directors, such as a school district with elementary, junior high, and high schools or a state university system made up of a number of colleges and universities, an administrative leader of all institutions may exist. In the case of a school district, this person is the superintendent of schools. In the case of a state university system, the position may be the chancellor, although in some university systems the head of the system is the president and the head of the institution is the chancellor. These individuals are usually responsible for hiring the head of each institution within the system at the high school level. At the college level, the board of trustees may have this role. As in the case of relationships with trustees or members of a board of directors, the athletic director should not deal directly with the superintendent or the chancellor. All requests for tickets or other athletic department services should come through the office of the principal or the office of the president of the institution. The chain of command must always be honored.

Presidents or Principals

The appointed leader of the educational institution determines whether the athletic director reports directly to him or her or through another senior but lower officer. Where the athletic program is a politically sensitive program of highest interest to trustees and alumni or at the high school or small-college level where there are few significant administrative layers, the athletic director may report directly to the president or principal. In high schools or at smaller institutions, the athletic director may also be in charge of physical education, intramurals, and recreational sport. At larger institutions, the athletic director may report to a vice president for student life or student affairs or a vice president for administration, an arrangement that is often a preferable reporting line. The simple fact is that neither presidents nor principals have the time to provide the adequate daily oversight required to support the athletic program. As much as an athletic director might say that he or she wants direct access to the president because of the political importance of the athletic program, access on a situational basis is different from having a regularized reporting relationship to a senior officer who is always available and is highly educated about the ongoing affairs of the athletic department. A president or principal should want an attentive daily overseer over any program that has high political risk. When the athletic director reports to a senior officer, he or she should always have the option to meet with the president on important matters and they should attend such meetings together.

Specialized Administrative Authorities

Athletic department decision making is also constrained by numerous departments that hold higher delegated authority for activities in specialized areas involving high risk for liability, significant financial implications, or highly specialized knowledge and responsibilities. These authorities either take decision making out of the hands of the athletic department (e.g., admissions, purchasing, maintenance, buildings and grounds, the registrar, campus police) or require collaboration (e.g., development office, human resources, campus parking, recreation [shared facilities]). Thus, the athletic director must ensure that all staff members understand those areas that require the athletic department to obtain external or joint approval and the processes that must be followed in this regard. These areas usually have well-documented policies and procedures because they serve all programs and departments in the institution.

In the case of these services, the athletic director must think about managing relationship-building activities because, inevitably, a time will come when special requests need to be made for policy exceptions or a faster process. The athletic director wants the athletic department to be highly thought of with regard to respecting service personnel and established policies and procedures and asking for special treatment only in the case of emergency or special situations. A specific person in the athletic department should be designated as the respective liaison and relationship builder with each of these institutional units. These liaisons should invite their assigned counterparts to athletic events, be encouraged to write formal thank-you notes for good service (always copied to the head of the department involved), and engage those contacts in informal activities such as lunch with the coach. The importance of these relationships should never be underestimated. We have seen an entire maintenance department armed with leaf blowers and squeegees drying off tennis courts to make sure that an important competition can be played and a director of admissions speeding up review of the admissions application of the coach's top volleyball recruit as a result of attending to relationship building. These exceptional things happen when people and processes that form the chain of command are respected and institutional service units are knowledgeable about and invested in the success of athletics.

2.7 PLANNING TOOL

Composition and Function of the Athletic Advisory Council

Clear Expression of Authority and Purpose

The governance chain of command flowing from the principal or president down through the athletic director may be influenced by required consultation with groups that serve important expert, political, fund-raising, or oversight functions. Such groups should always be advisory rather than designated as governance or decision-making structures so that no question arises about ultimate authority residing in the institution with expert professionals. These groups promote transparency; improve communications with various stakeholders; and employ volunteer talent, expertise, and influence in service of athletic program success.

Care must be taken to ensure that the appointment of members is intentional with regard to gender and racial balance and operation of these groups is not simply a token or perfunctory process. Those who serve on these groups must believe that their time and opinions are respected. That being said, care must be taken to provide documentation to members of these groups that clearly defines the purpose and function of the group and the commitment required of each member to execute responsibilities. Athletic programs should have at least three advisory groups regularly functioning: (1) a faculty-majority athletic council, (2) a student-athlete advisory council (see Planning Tool 2.9 and Policy 2.10), and (3) a development, fund-raising, or booster club committee (see Planning Tool 2.11 and Policy 2.12). Other groups may be established but only if the athletic department is of sufficient size to create meaningful involvement and regularized communication with the group.

Athletic Advisory Council

The following comments are thoughts on the ideal composition and function of the athletic policy council or board. Policy 2.8 is a sample policy that defines the composition and function of this group.

2.8 Policy—Athletic Advisory Council

A sample policy that defines the composition, duties, and operating rules of a collegiate or high school athletic council, advisory to the athletic director and higher administration.

Available in HK*Propel*.

Advisory Function An intercollegiate athletic council or interscholastic athletic council should be advisory to the athletic director, principal, or president depending on the political importance of the athletic program. At high schools and smaller collegiate institutions that have low-key athletic programs, advisory to the athletic director is sufficient. At larger collegiate institutions, advisory to the president may be advisable, and members may include one or more appointees by the board of trustees.

Composition The majority of members should be members of the faculty. The conference or national athletic governance association with which the institution is affiliated may dictate such majority-faculty composition. Ultimately, the purpose of the educational institution is to educate students, and traditionally the faculty is charged with guarding the academic integrity of the institution. A majority-faculty composition acknowledges this responsibility. This acknowledgment is especially important given that institutional reputation risk related to academic integrity is at an all-time high because of the following factors:

- In higher education, media coverage of graduation rates and academic progress rates, publicly reported because of NCAA rules and state open-records mandates, has become the rule rather than the exception.
- Academic progress rate failure poses the risk of loss of athletic scholarships as a penalty at NCAA Division I institutions, which have the most highly visible athletic programs.
- The stakes to win at Division I institutions show no signs of abating, putting more pressure on coaches in the recruiting and admissions process.
- The academic rigor at top institutions and the competition for the best students is escalating, putting more pressure on academically underqualified students in the classroom.
- Academic support programs controlled by the athletic department carry a perception of conflict of interest, and questions have increased about whether tutors rather than student-athletes are producing required academic work.
- Coaches and athletic department academic counselors have been criticized for pushing student-athletes to register in selected easy courses, less-demanding majors, or independent study courses with less-than-rigorous professors.
- Faculties, charged with preserving the academic reputation of the institution, have become vocal critics of academic support systems that are controlled by the athletic department or programs not subject to faculty oversight.
- The NCAA mandates provision of academic support programs for student-athletes in Division I, and such programs may come under regular rules compliance or self-study review.
- At the high school level, coaches and parents have been accused of having athletes repeat a grade so that they are more physically mature and capable of excelling in sport and more likely to get college scholarships.

Such factors mandate ethical oversight relationships with the faculty and their involvement on committees to ensure the academic integrity of the athletic program.

Although there is no one correct composition for the athletic council or committee that serves in an athletic program oversight and policy advisory role, the following are important considerations:

- **Objective view.** No voting member of the committee should be in the normal decision-making line of authority over athletics. The committee is charged with oversight and advisory responsibilities. A conflict of interest would be present if a member of the committee was directly associated with the athletic department or was an administrator to whom the athletic director reports. This point would not prevent the athletic director from serving as a member in an ex-officio, nonvoting capacity.
- **Majority faculty.** Athletic department conformance with higher education's core belief in faculty control of academic integrity is essential. The majority of voting members of the committee should be members of the faculty. The faculty senate (or teachers' groups at the high school level) should nominate a slate of a minimum size (e.g., three members for every open position), and the president or high school principal should select and appoint these members from the slate.
- **Faculty athletic representative (FAR).** The FAR is usually a presidential or principal appointee charged with representing the institution to league, conference, state, or national governance associations of which the institution is a member. The FAR is responsible not only for voting on behalf of the institution but also for performing the oversight function. The FAR should normally chair the athletic council as a voting member to lend continuity, knowledge, and stability to the leadership of the board.
- **Student-athletes.** At least two current or former (one male and one female) student-athlete representatives should serve on the committee as voting members to ensure that the "customer" voice is heard. If the committee member is a former athlete, the representative should not be currently employed by the

athletic department. If the committee members are current student-athletes, these representatives should be appointed by or be the officers of the student-athlete advisory committee (see Planning Tool 2.9 and Policy 2.10).

- **Nonathlete students.** If the athletic department budget is supported by mandatory or optional student fees, a representative of the general student body, appointed by the president of the student body, should be considered.
- **Alumni.** At least one alumnus should be a voting member to be sure that the views of this important stakeholder and donor group are considered. The alumni member should be appointed or nominated by the alumni association.
- **Regent, trustee, or board appointment.** If the athletic program is of significant interest to the board of education, board of regents, or trustees of the institution, having at least one but no more than two representatives or appointees to enhance communication and transparency is advisable for high-visibility athletic programs.
- **Athletic director.** No member of the athletic department should be a member of the committee except the athletic director, who should serve in an ex-officio, nonvoting capacity to ensure that the committee operates based on the best information possible.
- **Terms.** Committee members should have term limits to avoid the awkwardness and political liability of removing board members against their will, and within each type of representative (e.g., faculty, student-athletes, alumni) terms should be staggered so that all members of a group aren't leaving or starting service at the same time. Consider requiring that all student members be at least juniors in good academic standing.

Oversight Functions Many athletic councils are underutilized, and many are mistrusted; the former case is often related to the latter. In such cases, the athletic director may not feel confident that members, particularly the faculty, are committed to providing strong support for the athletic program. Our experience has been that the more significant the representation and responsibilities of the faculty are and the greater the transparency of athletic program data is, particularly academic data, the more invested the faculty is in helping high-risk student-athletes and supporting the athletic program.

Typically, the athletic council serves the following important advisory functions related to oversight of the athletic program:

- Review of new or revised policies and procedures
- Annual review of the academic performance of student-athletes
- Review and recommendations related to rules violations or ethical issues
- Review and recommendations related to institutional positions taken in support of or against legislation promulgated by athletic governance organizations of which the institution is a member
- Review of the athletic department budget and financial reports
- Review and recommendations related to the strategic plan of the athletic department
- Review and recommendations related to gender equity and racial and ethnic diversity of employees and student-athlete participants

The academic community perceives competition between support of the academic program and the athletic program. The academic community is also concerned about athletic program transgressions damaging the integrity of the institution. Thus, it is critical to have supportive and highly involved faculty allies who can assure their colleagues that the operation of the athletic program is student centered and meets high standards.

Standing Committees

Standing committees of the athletic council, appropriately composed based on the expertise of members, should be specified. Standing committees reflect the most important oversight functions and need for ongoing attention. At a minimum, the following standing committees should be established: (1) academic review, (2) ethics, and (3) gender equity and diversity.

Academic Review Committee The academic review committee should consist of faculty members only, acknowledging the priority academic purview of faculty in educational institutions. Athletic department conformance with the institution's core belief in faculty control of academic integrity is essential. The extent to which the athletic department acknowledges this trust in faculty control and judgment by including and being transparent with the faculty corresponds to the likelihood that coaches and athletic personnel will work with the faculty to maximize the success of student-athletes and that general faculty trust of athletics will develop. Chaired by the faculty athletic representative (who should also be a member of the faculty), this group should be charged with making annual reports to the overall university faculty governance structure on the academic progress and graduation achievement of all student-athletes and the progress of all specially admitted student-athletes (if such special admissions exist). The academic review committee should meet annually with each head coach to review the academic progress and achievements of their respective student-athletes. Members should be asked to review and make recommendations about whether scholarships or special admission offers should be extended to student-athletes with high-risk academic profiles. We believe that a conflict of interest exists if the coach or athletic staff member is making sole direct recommendations for special-admit exceptions. Whether such policy exists or not, we believe that it is important for the credibility of the athletic department to use a faculty committee to review and support such coach recommendations. The coach and the athletic senior staff member overseeing academic affairs should have a face-to-face formal meeting with the academic review committee to present the case for such exemptions. The head coach and athletic department academic support personnel should be directly responsive to faculty queries regarding the reasons why the athletic staff believes that the student-athlete will be successful. This answering to the faculty is the epitome of acceptance of responsibility and accountability for the academic and athletic success of student-athletes. The academic review committee should consider all this information and make recommendations to the office of admissions. Such faculty recommendations will be viewed more positively than coach or athletic department recommendations. Such faculty review committees commonly not only support the admission of at-risk recruits but also, because of their decision-making responsibility, become invested in developing an academic support program that proves themselves right. Often, they take a personal interest in the academic success of these students, mentoring them outside the athletic program and recruiting other faculty members to help.

Ethics Committee Another standing subcommittee of the athletic council should be the ethics committee. This committee should consist of representatives of all stakeholders, but the majority should be faculty members. The committee should be charged with reviewing reports of rules violations, evaluating athlete or staff conduct issues, and making recommendations on policy and disciplinary action. See Policy 2.5 for a sample policy that defines responsibilities related to compliance with national and conference rules and regulations. In that sample policy are policies and procedures related to ethics committee functions in the case of such violations.

Gender Equity and Diversity Committee
Another standing subcommittee of the athletic council should be the gender equity and diversity committee. This committee should consist of representatives of all stakeholders, but a majority of members should be from underrepresented gender, racial, and ethnic groups. The committee should be consulted regarding appointments to all committees, charged with reviewing annual gender equity and diversity reports including the composition of all committees and employee diversity, serving on search committees, making recommendations, and reviewing progress related to gender equity or diversity plans.

2.9 PLANNING TOOL

Involvement of Student-Athletes in Athletic Governance

Why Student-Athletes Should Be Involved in Governance

The athletic program exists for its educational influence on the growth and development of student-athletes. Yet, in many athletic programs, the pressure on coaches to win or, at the high school level, to demonstrate that their athletes receive college athletic scholarships, creates incentives for these goals to take precedence over the educator's duty-of-care responsibilities. Thus, the athletic director must keep in touch with student-athlete issues and challenges. A formally constructed and regularly meeting student-athlete advisory council should be the cornerstone of the athletic director's communication with student-athletes. Student-athlete participation should also extend to voting membership on the athletic advisory council (or similarly titled athletic policy board), which is directly responsible for recommending all athletic department policies to the president or principal. Student-athletes should also serve on standing and ad hoc committees devoted to student-athlete life and welfare, leadership development programming, media training, career mentoring, and community service programs. Student-athlete representation on these committees and councils ensures that opportunities are available for student-athletes to learn how to govern and exercise leadership skills. In addition, the presence of student-athletes allows members of oversight bodies involved in the governance of athletics to make reality checks on whether the needs of athletic department consumers are being met.

How Student-Athletes Should Be Involved

Whenever student-athletes are given the opportunity to serve on committees and councils with faculty, alumni, and trustee representatives, consideration should be given to helping them prepare for such service. The athletic director or an assigned senior staff member should meet with the students for an orientation session that covers everything that they need to know. Don't assume that student-athletes have had extensive committee experience. A good orientation may remove any initial fears about interacting with authority figures. Several topics should be considered for discussion at such orientation meetings:

- Expectation for dress and punctuality at meetings
- Review of the policy or governance document that describes the structure and function of the committee or council on which they will serve
- Review of a sample agenda and materials and the way in which a meeting is conducted
- Review of the minutes of a previous meeting of the council or committee
- Review of a list of committee or council members and an explanation of who they are and what initial forms of address should be used (Mr., Dr., and so on)
- Discussion of expectations regarding confidentiality of documents and privacy laws related to employee and student-athlete data that they may be asked to review
- Discussion of how they should communicate what they learn to student-athletes on their teams

Consideration should also be given to the experience and maturity of student-athletes who will be asked to serve. For policy committees that require high levels of sophistication, consider establishing minimum requirements such as junior class status, good academic standing, or previous experience as a member of the athletes' advisory council or in student government. Allow former student-athletes who may be completing a fifth year or be enrolled in graduate school to serve. Consider always having at least two students on committees that also include faculty, staff, alumni, or trustees so that they don't feel isolated or alone. Consider legislating multiple-year and staggered student-athlete terms of service so that an experienced student-athlete is always teaching a newly appointed student-athlete.

Last but not least, at the end of the year of any student-athlete's service on a committee or council, assign a staff member to do a one-on-one follow-up interview to assess the student's experience and whether he or she needs additional mentoring. Consider whether the committee or council on which the student-athlete is serving should have another nonathlete committee member assigned to be a mentor.

Policy 2.10 is a sample policy that defines the function and composition of a student-athletes' advisory council.

2.10 **Policy**—Student-Athletes' Advisory Council

A sample policy that defines the composition, duties, and operating rules of a collegiate or high school student-athletes council, advisory to the athletic director, and athletic advisory council.

Available in HK*Propel*.

2.11 PLANNING TOOL

Alumni and Fan Involvement in Athletic Affairs

Donor and fan support of the athletic programs can be a double-edged sword. All athletic programs invite and value those who purchase event tickets, make financial and gift-in-kind contributions, lend political support and connections to assist the institution in obtaining legislative support, and become business sponsors. But all athletic directors also fear the possibility that these same people may violate the rules of the sport governing organization by engaging in nonpermissible contacts with prospective student-athletes or their parents, providing prohibited benefits to prospective or current student-athletes, or interfering with internal operations and authority (e.g., exert pressure to hire or fire coaching staff, condition large contributions on access to coaches or administrators). Athletic directors and development officers also know that cultivating major gifts requires years of relationship building and controlled involvement with influential coaches and staff. Thus, careful thought should be given to structuring formal associations with the athletic department and communicating rules and regulations to alumni, fans, and donors, including former student-athletes.

Following are formally structured committees or programs that operate within most athletic programs that provide excellent opportunities for controlled outside supporter involvement:

- **Intercollegiate athletic council**—One or two voting positions for donors or alumni on this policy advisory council that advances recommendations to the president of the institution (see Management Tip 2.7 and Policy 2.8 for extended discussion and sample policy).
- **Alumni and donor advisory council**—All positions on a committee whose primary purpose is to raise funds and acquire additional resources for the athletic program (see Policy 2.12 for sample policy).
- **Hall of fame and awards committee**—Any number of ex-student-athlete positions on the nominating or selection committee for athletic department awards and recognition (see Policy 2.13 for sample policy).
- **Annual giving benefit program or booster club**—Based on total annual gifts to the athletic program, donors are given access to athletic event hospitality areas, special events (e.g., annual golf tournament, awards banquet), and formal programs conducted by coaches and administrators (e.g., pre- or postgame meetings with the coach or student-athletes, athletic administrator speakers, weekly meeting or annual lunch with the coach) (see Planning Tool 13.6 and Policy 13.7 for additional information regarding the structure and operation of annual giving benefit programs).

The following guidelines and recommendations should be considered when making decisions concerning the structure and operation of such groups and the relationship of coaches and administrators to high-wealth donors:

1. Key to successful fund-raising, individual or corporate, is relationship building and networking with key influencer individuals who are well connected and respected in the community. Structured athletic department programs, many held in conjunction with competitive events, should advance this purpose. These programs provide convenient evening and weekend meeting times and places and donor personal contact with inspirational athletic directors, coaches, and student-athletes critical to fund-raising success.
2. Most donors and supporters appreciate and respond to authentic recognition for their contributions or the opportunity to serve on important committees. Awards programs and committee service opportunities are important elements in donor cultivation.

3. The institution is responsible for the actions of its supporters with regard to violations of governing association rules. The athletic program must make every effort to use ticket buyer and donor communication vehicles to transmit critical information about rules compliance responsibilities. This transmission of information must be regularly replicated, at least on an annual basis, and should be constantly available online. See Educational Resource 7.8 in HK*Propel* for such a sample publication.
4. Control of the use of the educational institution's name, the promulgation of policy, the purpose and methodology for fund-raising in the name of the athletic department, and program decision making should reside in the internal authority structure of the educational institution. Involvement of outside alumni, fans, and supporters should always be advisory to official institution authorities.
5. If an athletic fund-raising group is incorporated independent of the educational institution, bylaws and operating procedures of the entity must include (*a*) formal institutional approval related to use of the institution's name, fund-raising purpose, and use of funds; (*b*) requirements for independent audits or other controls related to financial affairs; and (*c*) formal involvement or oversight by designated institution representatives (see Planning Tool 13.6 for extensive discussion on and the issue of control of booster clubs).
6. A formal advisory structure consisting of respected donor fund-raisers and key influencers should exist and should include formal ex-officio participation of athletic department development staff and the athletic director. This group should meet and be communicated with on a regular basis rather than convened only when the athletic department needs money or other resources. The group needs to feel that they are knowledgeable about the program and are asked for advice on a regular basis. They should understand their responsibility for introducing coaches and athletic development and senior administrative staff to individuals and groups that will expand the reach of the department and community knowledge of the athletic program. Policy 2.12 is a model policy that defines the function and composition of a development advisory council.
7. Athletic department staff should engage in organized relationship-building activities with members of advisory committees, booster clubs, or development committees so that each member feels a personal affinity and relationship with the athletic director and the head coaches. Ultimately, donors give to people they like, trust, and believe are doing a great job.
8. A consistent, highly organized annual effort should be made to keep in touch with every student-athlete who has ever been in the athletic program. Every student-athlete is the recipient of years of significant institutional financial investment and major education, growth, and development efforts. During their participation time, these student-athletes established close relationships to coaches and support staff. Twenty or 30 years following graduation, a significant number of those student-athletes may be in positions to make major contributions to the program as donors, prominent business connectors, politicians, professional athletes, or celebrities.
9. Every athletic program should have a hall of fame, hall of honor, or similar recognition program that serves to maintain relationships and communication with former student-athletes, coaches, and staff. On occasion, these programs should also be authorized to recognize major donors or other unique contributors to the athletic program. Consider structuring the hall of fame committee to include at least one representative from every graduating class and reflect broad sports representation. The athletic director should meet with this group at least once annually. Built into the recognition function of this committee should be an athletic department advisory role. Policy 2.13 is a sample policy that defines the function and composition of a hall of fame committee.

10. Remember the fund-raiser's mantra, "Ask for money and you will get advice; ask for advice and you will get money." Athletic department officials should always be asking supporters for advice and counsel, making clear that final decision-making authority resides in the institution.
11. Regular communication is at the heart of successful relationship building. Every coach should be annually required to send all the alumni in their sport a personal letter and competition schedule. The athletic director should also communicate with all ex-student-athlete alumni, season ticket holders, and donors at least once a year, presenting an annual report on the accomplishments of the program. And, of course, every communication should provide the opportunity for the person to make a donation to support those student-athletes following in his or her footsteps.
12. Wealthy individuals are often too busy to serve on committees or councils and may have a desire to participate in more private ways. Regular face-to-face meetings with and phone calls to high-wealth donors and donor prospects are critical strategies that must be executed. See chapter 13 for more information and policies specifically related to fund-raising and revenue production.

2.12 **Policy**—Athletic Development Advisory Council

A sample policy that defines the composition, duties, and operating rules of a collegiate or high school athletic development or fund-raising committee, advisory to the athletic director and higher administration.

2.13 **Policy**—Athletic Hall of Fame Committee

A sample policy that defines the composition, duties, and operating rules of a collegiate or high school hall of fame committee, responsible for advising the athletic director on award and recognition programs that keep alumni involved with the athletic program.

Available in HK*Propel*.

2.14 PLANNING TOOL

Sport Performance Advisory Group

In the late 1970s the University of Texas at Austin (UT Austin) Department of Intercollegiate Athletics for Women, led by staff members Tina Bonci (athletic training and sports medicine) and Randa Ryan (student development and nutrition), pioneered the establishment of a "performance team" advisory group of experts to assist staff working in the sports medicine and athletic training, sport nutrition, strength and conditioning, coaching, and student-athlete support areas. At the cutting edge of elite collegiate sport programs, UT Austin realized that expert knowledge outside the athletic staff should be used to

1. install a strong check-and-balance system or determine whether more advanced protocols are required to monitor the effect of intense training on the health and well-being of student-athletes;
2. design testing programs and review existing testing protocols to identify causative factors of injuries or illness and learn whether there are ways in which they could be prevented or risks reduced;
3. provide research knowledge that coaches might not receive because of the two- to three-year time lag between completion of research and journal publication;
4. help understand differences among individual athletes and the way in which those differences might affect choices in training regimens;
5. raise ethical questions or concerns related to training methodology;
6. answer important questions asked by coaches, doctors, trainers, and allied health service professionals who are operating world-class training environments; and
7. contribute expertise in areas such as athlete nutrition, disordered eating, the training of elite female athletes, and other issues in which the application of knowledge to elite athlete training was minimal or which required scrutiny.

There was also a realization that bringing together experts in various disciplines to focus on a question might provide new and innovative views, ideas, or insights related to the solution of problems. Indeed, the group was successful and in a number of cases was responsible for collaborating with academic researchers to initiate research or data collection to validate recommendations. Thus, athletic departments should consider creating similar "performance groups" of advisors to provide such assistance. Consideration should be given to identification of experts in the following areas: (1) orthopedics, (2) neurology and concussion, (3) nutrition, (4) strength and conditioning, (5) asthma, (6) blood chemistry, (7) eating disorders, (8) rehabilitation, (9) vision, (10) motor learning, (11) ear, nose, and throat, (12) chiropractic, (13) sport psychology, (14) learning disabilities, and (15) dentistry. The focus of such a group should always be to improve student-athlete performance while minimizing student-athlete risk for injury and enhancing student-athlete health. Such experts always have limited time to devote to such volunteer service, so it is important to determine who should be assembled based on the specific nature of every problem or question and to provide this ad hoc group with as much fact-based data and clearly communicated questions as possible.

On an ongoing basis, every member of the expert group should be asked to send any research or articles that he or she thinks coaches or athletic staff should be aware of to the performance group liaison for distribution. The composition of the group should be expansive (no limit on number) rather than restrictive, and consideration should be given to attracting a broad range of applied sport science experts. Coaches and others should not be allowed to call these people independently. Rather, communication should be funneled through a primary internal liaison. This policy ensures that questions placed before the group are well thought out and not asked multiple times and that responses are broadly disseminated.

The head of sports medicine should be in charge of convening and communicating with the group, but the problems brought before these volunteers should be discussed with many athletic staff members who should shape the questions asked and facts presented for consideration. The athletic director, team physician, head trainers, and directors of various student-support services should nominate prospective expert members and decide on membership.

Consideration should be given to defining performance group responsibilities as follows:

1. To review, revise, or establish protocols that contribute to prevention of athletic injury, reduction of injury risk, or reduction of health deficiencies induced by sport training regimens that may negatively affect the health or safety of student-athletes
2. To share research findings and other knowledge that might be used by athletic staff to improve the quality of training or care and performance of student-athletes
3. To recommend the initiation of research or collection of data related to questions regarding improving athletic performance, factors contributing to injury or health deficiencies, or the clarification of information needed to respond to questions raised regarding health or performance effects
4. To advise the athletic staff members regarding policies or procedures related to the administration of treatment protocols or testing or prevention programs
5. To review the effectiveness of department procedures or training programs as they relate to improving athletic performance or reducing the incidence of injury
6. To raise ethical, health, safety, and procedural questions related to the adoption of new practices
7. To respond to questions and answers raised by coaches, trainers, and other athletic professional staff related to the expertise of the performance group member

Many of the issues encountered in high-performance sport are well beyond the normal expertise of athletic directors and even athletic trainers and student development specialists. Yet these training and injury and treatment issues are at the heart of sport team performance and student-athlete welfare. Similarly, training and treatment decisions often migrate into the area of litigation risk. Organizing expert assistance to manage these risks is essential, especially in programs in which coaches are constantly pushing to try the next new thing that might give their student-athletes a competitive edge.

2.15 PLANNING TOOL

Policy Manuals and Operations Handbooks

Policies and Procedures Versus Administrative Operating Rules and Processes

A policy is a primary or decision-making rule or guideline, whereas a procedure is a description of how the policy is to be implemented or how work is to be performed. Policies and procedures manuals grow in size over time because policy making often occurs following an administrative mistake. Policies are created to prevent repetition of errors. Some policies and procedures are so important that they require the approval of and oversight by higher authorities. Other less important policies and procedures involve rules for the production of consistent, quality administrative or operational work. The former will require approval by a policy board (intercollegiate or interscholastic athletic council) and usually a senior institutional executive official (principal, president, or vice president). The latter only requires athletic director or senior staff approval. For definitional convenience, the sport manager may wish to refer to important decision-making guidelines as policies and procedures and production requirements as administrative rules and protocols. In both cases, these decision-making instructions and processes represent decision-making guidance concerning commonly encountered circumstances, ensure consistency of decisions, and reflect a mature, well-organized organization.

Policy Exceptions and Review

Seldom does a policy cover every decision-making circumstance. Thus, a mechanism should be in place for a policy exception for a reason directly connected to the purpose of the policy. Such policy exceptions should result in a review of the policy to be sure it is still accomplishing its purpose. Policies should never be so sacrosanct that they require the organization to act in a way that is antithetical to its mission and purposes. Also, every policy needs to be regularly reviewed with regard to functionality and the need for revisions.

Policy Manuals and Operations Handbooks

Some athletic departments have a single policy manual that contains both important policy guidance and rules about how to make a software purchasing decision. But larger athletic departments often find it more convenient to have both a policy manual and an operations handbook. The policy manual contents are approved by the appropriate higher institutional officials and are primarily used by professional staff. The policy manual also defines decision-making authority and responsibilities. Ultimately, the policy manual is a historical record of the exercise of governance. A policy manual is more substantive in content, analogous to a book of laws and regulations that are of such high importance that failure to follow such directions may result in disciplinary action. An operations handbook is used by all employees for consistency and guidance in performing daily clerical, administrative, and office operations work. It provides employees with general information about programs to ensure a common understanding and instructions about the mechanics of everyday work—how to operate, how to find, and how to get. The operations handbook also serves as a primary training tool for all employees, orienting them to the structure, work, and operation of the athletic program and instructing them how to execute commonly encountered tasks or whom to ask for information. The operations handbook may contain some content from the policy manual as a mechanism to orient all employees regarding important obligations or treatment like rules compliance and annual employee evaluations.

Sample Tables of Contents

This *Athletic Director's Desk Reference* and the accompanying HK*Propel* is a collection of policies, procedures, and administrative protocols that is intended to reflect best practices or common practices that should be customized to the needs of the program or institution and considered for adoption. Each of these policies has been placed in a chapter according to topic. The athletic director may find it helpful to view a complete sample table of contents for both a policy manual and an operations handbook to gain a better understanding of the breadth of knowledge and information that must be assembled to conduct an athletic program.

Form 2.16 is a sample table of contents for a mature, well-developed Division I college athletic department policy manual, and Form 2.17 is a sample table of contents for its companion athletic department office operations handbook.

Employee Accountability

Just because a policy manual or operations handbook exists doesn't mean that employees will learn or follow these policies and procedures. Three additional mechanisms are required to ensure that employees comply. First, every new employee should be required to complete an orientation checklist that verifies that all procedures have been clearly explained and that he or she has been taught how to operate various machines or use essential software (see Form 5.2 in HK*Propel* for an example).

Second, each employee should have a comprehensive job description that defines his or her responsibilities (see Forms 6.42 through 6.85). Last, the annual performance evaluation of each employee (see Evaluation Instrument 6.14) completes the governance loop. This annual assessment should include whether the employee follows department rules and procedures, fulfills his or her position requirements, and responsibly uses institutional resources.

Education Commitment

Compliance with rules established by conference and state or national athletic governance organizations as well as with institutional rules and regulations requires a commitment by the athletic department to distribute rules manuals, conduct ongoing education programs for employees about these obligations, and hold employees accountable for transgressions. From orientation of new staff members to rules education, the athletic director is responsible for making sure that education programs are conducted and for ensuring that strong policies related to attendance at these programs are in place.

2.16 Form—Athletic Department Policy Manual: Sample Table of Contents

Sample table of contents that covers all areas in which athletic department policies and procedures should be developed.

2.17 Form—Athletic Department Operations Handbook: Sample Table of Contents

Sample table of contents that covers all internal operation areas in which athletic department rules and processes should be defined and communicated to employees.

Available in HK*Propel*.

GOVERNANCE OF THE ATHLETIC PROGRAM

Association of Governing Boards of Colleges and Universities. (2018). *AGB Board of Directors' statement on governing board responsibilities for intercollegiate athletics*. https://agb.org/sites/default/files/u27335/2018_statement_intercollegiateathletics.pdf.

Commission on Colleges, Southern Association of Colleges and Schools. (2017). *The principles of accreditation: Foundations for quality enhancement*. https://sacscoc.org/app/uploads/2019/08/2018PrinciplesOfAcreditation.pdf.

Connolly, P.M. (2006). *Navigating the organizational lifecycle*. Washington, DC: Board Source.

Drew University. (2008). *Intercollegiate athletics policy manual*. Unpublished. Madison, NJ: Department of Intercollegiate Athletics.

Farrell, M., & Cupito, M.C. (2010). *Newspapers: A complete guide to the industry*. New York: Peter Long Publishing.

Gardner-Webb University. (2007). *2007–2008 athletics department policy manual*. Boiling Springs, NC. www.gwusports.com//pdf2/92284.pdf.

Hums, M.A., & MacLean, J.C. (2018). *Governance and policy in sport organizations* (4th ed.). Scottsdale, AZ: Holcomb Hathaway.

Jensen, C.R., & Overman, S.J. (2003). *Administration and management of physical education and athletic programs*. Prospect Heights, IL: Waveland Press.

Oldham, J. (2017). K–12 accreditation's next move. *Education Next*. https://www.educationnext.org/k-12-accreditations-next-move-storied-guarantee-looks-to-accountability-2-0.

National Collegiate Athletic Association. (2015–16). *Instructions for completing the division II institutional self-study guide (2015–16)*. https://www.ncaa.org/sites/default/files/d3-online-issg-instructions.pdf.

National Collegiate Athletic Association. (2018). *Instructions for completing the 2018 division III institutional self-study guide*. https://www.ncaa.org/sites/default/files/d3-online-issg-instructions.pdf.

National Collegiate Athletic Association. (2020). *2020–21 Division I, II and III manuals*. Indianapolis, IN: NCAA.

National Collegiate Athletic Association. (2020). *2020–21 NCAA guide for the college bound student-athlete*. http://fs.ncaa.org/Docs/eligibility_center/Student_Resources/CBSA.pdf.

National Collegiate Athletic Association. (2021). *Division I institutional performance program*. https://www.ncaa.org/governance/division-i-institutional-performance-program.

National Collegiate Athletic Association. (2021). *Division II institutional performance program*. https://www.ncaa.org/governance/ncaa-division-ii-institutional-performance-program-resources.

National Collegiate Athletic Association. (2021). *Division III institutional performance*. https://www.ncaa.org/about/division-iii-institutional-performance-program-ippprogram.

Pedersen, P.M. & Thibault, L. (Eds.). (2022). *Contemporary sport management*. (7th ed.). Champaign, IL: Human Kinetics.

Rutgers University Athletics. (2017). *Policy manual*. https://scarletknights.com/sports/2017/6/11/compliance.aspx.

University of North Carolina, Charlotte. (2010). *Policy statement on the governance and oversight of intercollegiate athletics*. http://legal.uncc.edu/sites/legal.uncc.edu/files/media/GovernanceOversightIntercollegiateAthletics.pdf.

University of Texas at Austin. (1992). *Intercollegiate athletics for women policy manual*. Unpublished. Austin, TX: Department of Women's Intercollegiate Athletics.

University of Texas at Austin. (2010). *Intercollegiate athletics policy manual*. Austin, TX. No longer available.

CHAPTER

3

Vision, Mission, and Goals

The importance of creating and communicating a clear mission statement, as well as crafting and implementing specific performance goals and objectives, cannot be overstated in the management of a complex athletic program. All strategic plans, daily operations, and staff behaviors should ultimately reflect the overarching values and goals of the department. The documents in this chapter guide the athletic director through a process of formulating the mission, goals, and objectives of the athletic program in a way that ties their achievement to specific strategic plans, action plans, and key performance indicators.

TYPES OF DOCUMENTS

Management tip—Factual background information, insights, problem-solving strategies, and suggestions for the athletic director

Planning tool—Steps to take or factors that should be considered in the development of strategic plans, action plans, professional development plans, or governance systems

Educational resource—Handouts that can be used to educate staff members, campus constituents, volunteers, or student-athletes

Policy—Sample policies and procedures that should be adopted by an athletic department after customization and review by appropriate expert institutional or school district officials

Form—Sample forms, letters, or job descriptions

Evaluation instrument—Administrative tools that help the athletic director, a supervisor, or an employee assess job performance and evaluate program content

Risk assessment—Checklists that help the athletic director, a supervisor, or an employee identify risks and prevent litigation

3.1 MANAGEMENT TIP

Articulating a Philosophy of Educational Sport

One of the most important responsibilities of a high school principal or university president is to define the institution's mission and to measure the effectiveness of each department in promoting and supporting that mission. Equally responsible are program managers, such as athletic directors, who are expected to help articulate this philosophy as it applies to athletics and who must create, monitor, and evaluate department mission, goals, and objectives to ensure that they serve as appropriate complements to the central mission of the institution. Through this process, a clear articulation of the athletic department's value added to the educational institution should evolve, which in turn serves as a rationale for program existence and continued program support.

Historical Area of Weakness

Unfortunately, athletic directors have often not been required to define the mission and goals of the department in a way that connects the dots—how athletics is an integral part of the institutional mission. When addressing this topic from a college perspective, Zotos and others (1995) contend,

> It has become increasingly obvious that, as program managers, athletics administrators have been held to different standards when compared to their peers. Athletics departments are notorious for being permitted to work in a vacuum. There has been little oversight by deans or vice-presidents and, at best, casual assessments of how program practices affect the university at large.

In essence, some athletic directors have been given the right to administer their programs as an auxiliary enterprise that is only loosely coupled with the academy. Although this feature sounds like a benefit of autonomy, the result may be a department that lacks a clear vision, which in turn makes it susceptible to constant scrutiny and criticism by faculty, alumni, athletes, parents, and the media.

Personal Philosophy of Educational Sport as a Critical Anchor

The athletic director must take the lead in expressing the athletic department position in the institution because he or she is the expert in educational sport. Although alumni and donors may focus on school spirit and college presidents or principals may see the most beneficial role of sport as marketing the educational institution, the primary justification for the presence of sport in the educational institution must be its contribution to the growth and education of a student—its curricular connection. What is sport, and how is it analogous to traditional subjects? Does it exist in a curricular form, or is it purely extracurricular? Although it can serve secondary functions, what is the principal justification of its existence in education? Like dance and drama, sport is a performing art. Performing arts may have a curricular existence that allows students to major or minor in those subjects, or they may exist as extracurricular activities, recognizing that students want the opportunity to develop skill and mastery in such human movement forms. Alternatively, sport and dance may also exist in a curriculum focused on the cross-disciplinary study of human movement in its various forms. In most high schools and colleges, educational sport most commonly exists as an extracurricular activity focused on the development of student-athlete excellence in goal-oriented motor skills (sport), through which the student explores his or her physical and emotional capacity under highly competitive circumstances.

This proactive articulation by the athletic director of the central reason justifying the inclusion of sport in an educational environment is critical because it places the focus of the program squarely on serving the student-athlete by advancing his or her growth and development.

The fact that the program is extracurricular also mandates that athletic program goals be subservient to the success of the student-athlete in achieving his or her curricular commitments. Graduation, grades, and academic progress in chosen curricular programs must take priority over student-athlete sport participation and sport program success. These anchor beliefs and tenets serve as the philosophical foundation used to create the athletic department mission, goals, and objectives, which will formalize how athletics fits into the educational enterprise, highlight the values that it brings to the participants and other constituents whom it serves, and detail both primary and secondary functions in the educational environment. Without a commitment to these beliefs and tenets, strategic planning, day-to-day operations, and decision making tend to be situational and subject to lack of clarity rather than being solidly grounded. The pressures of secondary purpose can easily move to the forefront.

Successful leaders create a sense of shared philosophy among the entire staff. Having a clear view of program purpose, passionately stated by the athletic director, goes a long way toward creating such a shared belief system. Creating a unified vision centered on putting the well-being of the student-athlete first establishes a higher-order common purpose that will have broad appeal and be more likely to create a department-wide ethos in which employees can take pride in an amalgam of objectives that include student-body spirit, recruitment, winning championships, and generating revenues.

We suggest that this clear statement of student-athlete growth and development through sport always be presented as the number one priority because leaders sometimes find it difficult to formulate their own philosophy, especially when more powerful people seem to embrace another priority. Bertrand Russell (1990), who wrote *The Problems of Philosophy*, suggests that many people make the mistake of relying on commonly accepted beliefs and do not understand that the responsibility of philosophy is to question given answers. The athletic director should feel comfortable questioning the common sets of propositions that are often used when defining the value of educational sport and embracing multiple purposes, but there should be no doubt about core beliefs and priorities.

Following are the most common propositions offered to justify the presence of athletics in educational institutions with related questions that can be used to measure one's own views about relative importance. A useful initial exercise is to think about these propositions from a purely philosophical perspective without being burdened with the reality of institutional history or financial capabilities. Those factors will be added later when the philosophical principles must be transferred into realistic statements of department mission, goals, and action plans.

Athletics Is a Natural Extension of the Educational Mission

Athletic directors and coaches often contend that teaching student-athletes a sport is no different from teaching in the classroom. Therefore, athletics is a natural extension of the curriculum. Faculty may resist this notion, contending that educating the mind is different, and more important, than educating the body. Is the faculty correct? How should athletic professionals respond to this contention? Is learning how to throw a ball, in and of itself, purely physical, or is it a physical and intellectual pursuit that requires an understanding of physics and biomechanics? Are coaches expected to incorporate all intellectual components in sport instruction such as nutrition, biomechanics, exercise science, sports psychology, and so on? Are coaches expected to be deliberate about teaching student-athletes more than the basic mechanical skills needed to perform in a game or match? If so, what are the essential parts of the general sport curriculum? Does every coach's job description contain the expectation to advance each student-athlete's level of knowledge with regard to sport nutrition, biomechanics, exercise science, and sport psychology as it relates to improvement of sport performance? Do coaches have the adequate preparation or time to address these educational objectives? If not, does the athletic department have access to resource people on or off campus who can collaborate with staff to accomplish these educational objectives?

Athletics Enhances the Overall Development of Student-Athletes Sport professionals have made lofty claims about how the sport experience can have a positive effect on the overall development of each student-athlete. Learning to compete in a high-stress environment, setting and reevaluating goals, appreciating the benefits and expectations of cooperative effort, and winning and losing gracefully are just a few of the lessons frequently cited that may have value to everyday life. Most athletic programs explicitly link life-enhancing lessons through the sport experience as a primary part of their mission statement. These objectives complement the goals of campus student-life programs and help justify the existence of the athletic program as an important and effective extracurricular student activity.

Does sport participation really build character and enhance development? Should it? Does it just happen naturally through teamwork and the self-discipline of participation, or does it need to be taught in a focused and intentional manner by coaches? If developmental elements need to be addressed specifically and intentionally, which ones are important and how are they going to be addressed? Has the desire to win at all costs overshadowed the importance of the developmental values? If so, is that just the reality of it or should it be changed?

Athletics Serves as a Campus Community Integrator General student body and alumni involvement in athletic programs can undoubtedly produce a powerful campus and community life experience. From pep rallies to student attendance at sport competitions, athletic programs may create a sense of pride in the community, an affiliation with the institution, and camaraderie among students and alumni. In addition, athletics may also demonstrate the power of diversity in race and ethnicity.

Athletes are often called on to play leadership roles in activities on campus that are not sponsored by the athletic department. Team representatives may be asked to help first-year students move into their residence halls during orientation week or to take the lead in a campus fund-raising project. Managers from other campus offices often call coaches and request that student-athletes participate in new or ongoing initiatives.

Is it important for the athletic department to maximize opportunities for student-athletes to be campus community integrators? If so, why? Are athletes expected to do too much outside of practice and competitions? Are athletes held to higher academic, behavioral, and leadership standards than other students on campus? Should they be?

Athletics Enhances Town and Gown Relationships Teams and individual athletes are frequently asked to perform community service projects. As community celebrities, student-athletes may be active in mentoring elementary or middle school students. They may make youth sport program appearances and act as ambassadors for the institution. In return, the institution and the athletic department can become a source of pride for the entire town, and athletic contests can serve as a place for social gatherings. Is it important for the athletic department to maximize opportunities to enhance town and gown relationships? If so, why? Does participating in town and gown activities produce any value for the student-athlete and staff? Are athletes expected to participate in too many town and gown activities?

Athletics Contributes to the Business Objectives of the Institution The business objectives of an athletic program as they relate to those of the institution vary according to the size of an institution, its competitive level, and the perception of the importance of athletic success to the image of the institution. Typically, business objectives include meeting tuition goals; creating local, state, or national exposure for the institution; raising revenues; and increasing alumni involvement. Athletics has the unique capability of developing an institutional affinity among non-alumni members of the community and local businesses who express their sports enthusiasm as ticket buyers, advertisers, and sponsors of the athletic program. These non-alumni relationships represent new development opportunities for the institution beyond direct athletic department support. Does the athletic department recognize this possibility and actively work with non-athletic campus units to use athletic events to cultivate these prospective non-alumni assets for greater involvement with the institution?

Meeting Tuition Goals

Attracting students to preparatory schools or universities may be one of the most important and fundamental tasks of faculty and staff. The financial health of some institutions relies on meeting or exceeding the number of tuition-paying students necessary to fill each class. But the game involves more than numbers. Recruiting students who have a reasonable chance of success is just as important. If students are successful, retention can be positively affected and those yearly tuition dollars will not be lost through large numbers of students failing academically or transferring to other institutions. Athletic department personnel are expected to be active participants in the recruiting and retention process.

What is the appropriate role of the athletic department in the recruitment and retention of students? Should the athletic department have increased pressure to recruit a certain number of students per year? Should the department have a responsibility to monitor academics and post higher retention rates than departments that recruit nonathletes? Should winning on the athletic field be a more important measure of success than athlete retention? What is the appropriate relationship between the admissions department and the athletic department?

Local, State, Regional, and National Exposure

Every educational institution strives to be recognized as excellent in a variety of ways. Some pursue top overall rankings among peer institutions, whereas others may want to achieve recognition as the best in a specific discipline or rely on a few select departments to bring increased recognition to the institution. Many institutions see great benefits in sponsoring an athletic program or specific teams that are nationally prominent and win conference, state, regional, or national championships. As a business objective, the rationale is that the exposure of athletic success will lead to an enhanced image of institutional excellence, which in turn can lead to more selective admissions, increased alumni support, significantly more revenue generation, and a host of other benefits. Despite the fact that research does not necessarily support these contentions, university presidents still believe that a strong correlation exists. The 2010 Knight Commission study addressed this issue head-on by reporting,

> Although a number of presidents are aware of scholarly research questioning the relationship between big-time athletics and nonathletic benefits, personal experience plays a much more powerful role in defining presidents' attitude toward athletics than do the results of these studies. (p. 41)

Many athletic directors agree with the presidents' opinion that athletic success pays huge dividends to the university. Joan Cronan, the director of women's athletics at the University of Tennessee, sees a strong connection between the school's perennially powerful women's basketball team and university image. She refers to athletics as the front porch of an institution, stating that the excellence displayed by a nationally prominent team may be the first impression that people have of the institution at large (Cronan, 2009).

How should institutions take advantage of this perceived relationship between athletics and institutional excellence? What is the appropriate role of the athletic department in enhancing local, state, regional, or national exposure of the institution? In doing so, must compromises be made to enhance the chances of winning (e.g., increase slots in admission for those with special talent, provide more privileges to athletes, overlook negative athlete behavior)? To what extent will those compromises be made, and will they differ from team to team? Should select teams be better funded to improve the chance of winning, which will likely require reducing the financial support of other teams that may not have the fan appeal necessary to bring recognition to the institution even if they win championships?

Revenue Generation

Some institutions impose an expectation that the athletic department or specific teams will be self-sufficient or raise a significant portion of its annual operating budget. The reality is that few athletic programs come close to being self-sufficient. The NCAA publishes annual reports on the revenues and expenses of intercollegiate athletics among its 1,100 members (Archives of NCAA Revenue & Expense Reports, 1981–2019). In 2019 only 25 NCAA Division I member institutions reported revenues in excess of expenses on an operating expense basis (excluding debt service and capital construction). Thus 98 percent of all NCAA athletic programs operate on a deficit basis, requiring subsidization from institutional general funds or mandatory student athletic fees. What responsibility should the athletic department have to raise money for the institution or the athletic operating budget? Should athletes be expected to take part in fund-raising activities, and if so, to what extent? Should a pay-to-play component be in place by which athletes personally bear some of the cost? How are the relationships structured between the athletic department and corporate partners, booster clubs, licensing partners, and media? What role should other campus offices, such as development and public relations, play in these negotiations?

Increasing Alumni Involvement

The numerous studies relating athletic success with alumni giving have yielded mixed results. In the most recent comprehensive review of the literature on athletic success and its relationship to the quantity and quality of admission applications and alumni giving, Baumer & Zimbalist (2019) conclude that some support exists for the contention that "robust" athletic success can lead to increased admissions applications, whereas poor athletic performance can lead to declines in applications; there is "weak, if any" support for a relationship between sport success and quality of students; and there is a positive correlation between sport success and giving to athletics but not in giving to academics. But there is little doubt that at many institutions, athletic contests bring alumni to campus and can be a source of alumni pride. Homecoming activities center on major athletic rivalries and create a festive atmosphere with bands, cheerleaders, and parades. Development officers use athletic contests to cultivate and entertain current and prospective donors. Academic departments schedule alumni advisory council meetings on days of athletic contests to enhance the experience of returning to campus. At some large universities, seat locations at athletic contests are tied to alumni giving levels.

What role should the athletic department play in increasing alumni involvement? What is the appropriate relationship between the athletic department and the development office? What expectations should be placed on athletes regarding alumni interactions? Should the athletic department provide perquisites like game tickets, luxury boxes, access to golf facilities, and the like to important alumni who have no association with athletics?

Answering these questions, as well as others that arise from this exercise, will not only help determine the department's philosophy of educational sport but also identify areas of inconsistent or incompatible ideas that may cause problems in the future. Only when the basic beliefs or tenets are clearly established is it possible to formalize a coherent vision, mission, and set of goals for an athletic program.

3.2 PLANNING TOOL

Creating Powerful Vision and Mission Statements

One of the most difficult and time-consuming tasks of any leader is to capture the philosophical beliefs and values of the organization and transform those complex concepts into clear and powerful vision and mission statements. The importance of committing the time and energy needed to do so cannot be overestimated. Well-crafted philosophical statements essentially serve as the inspirational guiding principles for all the work that follows. Goals, objectives, strategic plans, action plans, and marketing the program to the public and the faculty will depend on and be aligned with these powerful descriptors.

Economou (2009) suggests five foundational elements for any organization (p. 15):

- **Purpose:** Why does the organization exist? What is its purpose in context to its marketplace?
- **Mission:** At the highest level, what does the organization plan to do to fulfill its potential and purpose?
- **Vision:** In which direction is the organization headed? Is this direction clearly articulated? Is this vision realistic?
- **Values:** What are four or five basic qualities that define the organization as a business and sport entity? Can every stakeholder recite each of them on command? Are these values communicated consistently to the organization's customers?
- **Value proposition/brand positioning:** What is the organization's promise to itself and its customers? Is this promise believable? Does this promise differentiate the brand from its competition?

Although Economou's model evolves from a commercial business perspective, each of these elements is important for an educational sport organization. These foundational pillars clearly define both the core and value-added program components discussed in 3.1, as well as create an internal focus and accountability that defines how the organization is going to fulfill its purpose in a realistic and believable way.

Economou also contends that solid foundational statements educate stakeholders about the way in which the organization describes itself and that these stakeholders will frequently refer to the organization using these memorable statements. This level of collective understanding and buy-in not only promotes organizational values but also creates and supports the organization's culture. Essentially, the athletic department's commitment to these foundational elements should make stakeholders so excited and inspired by the values of the organization that they incorporate these words into the way that they speak about the organization and, in turn, behave in ways that are consistent with organizational values. These actions become a clear testament to the effectiveness of the vision and mission statements.

The athletic director should approach the development of these statements with careful consideration. To assist the athletic director in this important exercise, we propose alternatives that should be considered. The final product depends on the nature of the institution and its athletic program in the view of the athletic director.

PURPOSE

Craft one statement that explains the specific purpose of the athletic program. Samples are provided.

Our athletic program exists . . .

- to provide student-athletes with an extracurricular experience that allows them to acquire the highest levels of skill and mastery in selected highly competitive sports.
- to support an athletic program ranked among the nation's top 10 with regard to total program success that provides student-athletes

with an unparalleled opportunity to explore their sport potential while completing an academic degree at a nationally top-10-ranked academic institution.

- to provide all students with a varsity or subvarsity athletic experience that permits them to experience an advanced level of fitness, teamwork, and the pursuit of excellence toward a common goal in a highly competitive environment.
- to provide an extracurricular competitive sport program that focuses on the development of skill mastery and the advancement of student-athlete knowledge with regard to sport nutrition, biomechanics, exercise science, and sport psychology as it relates to improvement of sport performance.
- to provide an extracurricular competitive sport experience in which the student explores his or her physical and emotional capacity to achieve excellence in a highly competitive environment.
- to provide a focal point for the experience of the general student body and alumni community that advances the spirit and success of the institution while providing student-athletes with an exceptional varsity sport experience.

MISSION

Craft one concise and inspirational statement that expresses how the organization will accomplish its purpose.

The mission of our athletic program is . . .

- to enhance the spirit, mind, and body of our students and contribute to the success of the institution through a nationally recognized and respected athletic program.
- to have academically successful student-athletes who also achieve a top-10 national ranking in every sport.
- to provide a rewarding, highly competitive varsity athletic experience for talented students whose aspirations to excel in sport are equal to their goals in the classroom.
- to provide an opportunity for athletically talented students to enhance their sport skills in an athletic program that aspires to finish consistently among the top three in the conference in every sport while providing experiences on the playing fields that are fully integrated with rewarding educational experiences.
- to provide student-athletes with exceptional instruction and competitive experiences, inspiration to excel in the classroom, and training in the development of leadership skills through participation in varsity sport.
- to provide a personalized learning environment with equitable participation opportunities for student-athletes to develop their sport skills, work ethic, leadership potential, and, win or lose, to demonstrate sportsmanship and poise under competitive pressure.

VISION

Choose or craft several statements that express a future vision of program outcomes—the ultimate result of program success, the desired effect of the program.

Our vision is a future in which . . .

- each student, upon leaving our institution, would say yes if asked whether he or she would want to repeat his or her experiences as a student-athlete.
- every student-athlete leaves our institution with the intellectual, human relationship, and personal leadership skills to meet life's challenges and pursue his or her dreams.
- all our faculty, staff, students, and alumni express pride in the honesty, integrity, and quality of the athletic program.
- all former student-athletes urge their children and those of their friends and colleagues to attend our institution.
- all former student-athletes remain connected to our institution, contribute to the athletic program, and participate in other areas of university development.

VALUES

Choose or craft several statements that express the values that guide the operation of the program and would make an alumnus and parent proud of the athletic program.

We are committed to the importance of . . .

- all club, intramural, recreational, and varsity sport and physical activity participants at all skill levels because sport and fitness play an important role in achieving a healthy lifestyle.
- diversity by including people of every age, color, gender, national origin, physical disability, race, religion, and sexual orientation.
- efficiency by carefully using the resources available to us.
- honesty by following the letter and spirit of all athletic governance association rules.
- integrity by always acting in the best interest of our student-athletes and our institution.
- support from our parents, alumni, and volunteers.
- faculty and staff knowledge, guidance, and encouragement of our student-athletes.
- the dedication of our coaches, student-athletes, and athletic department staff.
- respect for all officials, opponents, and fans.

BRAND POSITION

Compose a short but powerful expression of the unique position that the athletic department wishes to occupy—a succinct and impactful phrase that generates an emotional image of how the program wants to be thought of.

We are . . .

- champions—in the classroom and on the field.
- winners with integrity, respected by all.
- nationally ranked, nationally recognized, educationally sound.
- proud, hardworking, aspiring to greatness.
- serious about winning, graduation, and exemplary conduct on and off the field.
- proud of our tradition of winning and always giving 100 percent effort in everything we do.

Each of these statements should appear on the athletic department website and in all promotional materials. They should be repeated whenever possible as mantras that express purpose and commitment. These foundational statements create a strong framework upon which the athletic director will build strategies, measurable objectives, and action plans.

3.3 MANAGEMENT TIP

Developing a One-Page Strategic Plan

Goals and objectives are discussed in the literature in a variety of ways and are often used interchangeably. Chappelet and Bayle (2005) suggest that objectives can be used to reflect the mission statement in a more detailed way and should be statements of what the organization "wants to achieve (or can) in practical but not too detailed terms" (p. 10). What an organization wants to achieve must also be based on the reality of what is possible. Although mission statements often have idealistic underpinnings because they express the program philosophy, goals and objectives should ultimately generate operational strategies or action plans that can be measured. Therefore, they must be realistic and begin to reflect the structure and capability of the department based on institutional philosophy, funding capacity, and other relevant factors that are necessary to support goal attainment. To be truly effective, objectives should be "SMART . . . significant, measurable, action oriented and accepted, realistic, time related" (Chappelet & Bayle, 2005, p. 13).

For instance, a mission statement might be "to provide rewarding, highly competitive varsity and junior varsity sport experiences for students committed to academic success and community service" for a typical high school program, demonstrating the philosophical belief that sport participation must be integrated with academic objectives and higher-order values such as community service. For a highly visible Division I athletic program that is expected to contribute to institutional fund-raising and recruiting nonathlete students, a mission statement might be "to enhance the spirit, mind, and body of university student-athletes and contribute to the success of the university through athletics."

After the mission statement is established, the athletic director should then establish general goal statements covering six basic areas: athletic excellence, academic achievement, personal development, contributions to the university or high school community, acquisition of resources, and management excellence. Under each goal, more specific measurable objectives should be delineated. These goals and objectives should reflect realistic expectations of program performance. This expression of mission, goals, and objectives becomes the executive summary of the athletic department's strategic plan. See figures 3.3.1 and 3.3.2 for examples of how such goals and objectives might be stated.

The athletic director should be able to produce a one-page executive summary of the strategic plan. The department's purpose, vision, values, and brand position should be on one side and its mission, goals, and objectives on the other. This summary can be given to a supervisor, the principal or president of the institution, a parent, a donor, a faculty member, a student-athlete, and other important stakeholders, and it should affect how they feel and think about the athletic program. Would they think that the athletic department is well led? Would they think that the athletic program has purpose and direction? Would they be proud to be associated with this program? For examples of one-page strategic plans, see figure 3.3.1 for a highly competitive Division I collegiate athletic program and figure 3.3.2 for a high school athletic program. These can be an important and effective educational communication to staff, coaches, student-athletes, and others in the institution.

Review and Revision

Note that no strategic plan should be set in concrete. Plans should be reviewed annually and even changed midstream if circumstances change or unforeseen events occur. If a contractor is building a house according to a blueprint and finds an error in the blueprint during the process of construction, would he or she correct the blueprint or build the error into the house? We live in a world of uncertainty in which making accurate short-term predictions is difficult and making accurate predictions over long periods is almost impossible. Too often, this uncertainty translates into reluctance to develop mission, goals, and strategies. Managers may believe that because so many environmental factors affect athletic departments, it is easier to let mission and goals evolve from what the organization currently is rather than what they want it to be. We contend that proactive management is much better than reactive management. When the athletic director dictates where he or she wants the program to go and how, employees' confidence and comfort levels increase because they know what is expected of them. Confidence increases as clarity of purpose and action increase. In high-performing organizations, the goals and objectives of the team are clear and everyone is pulling in the same direction. Failing to state a clear direction demonstrates lack of good management practice and leadership.

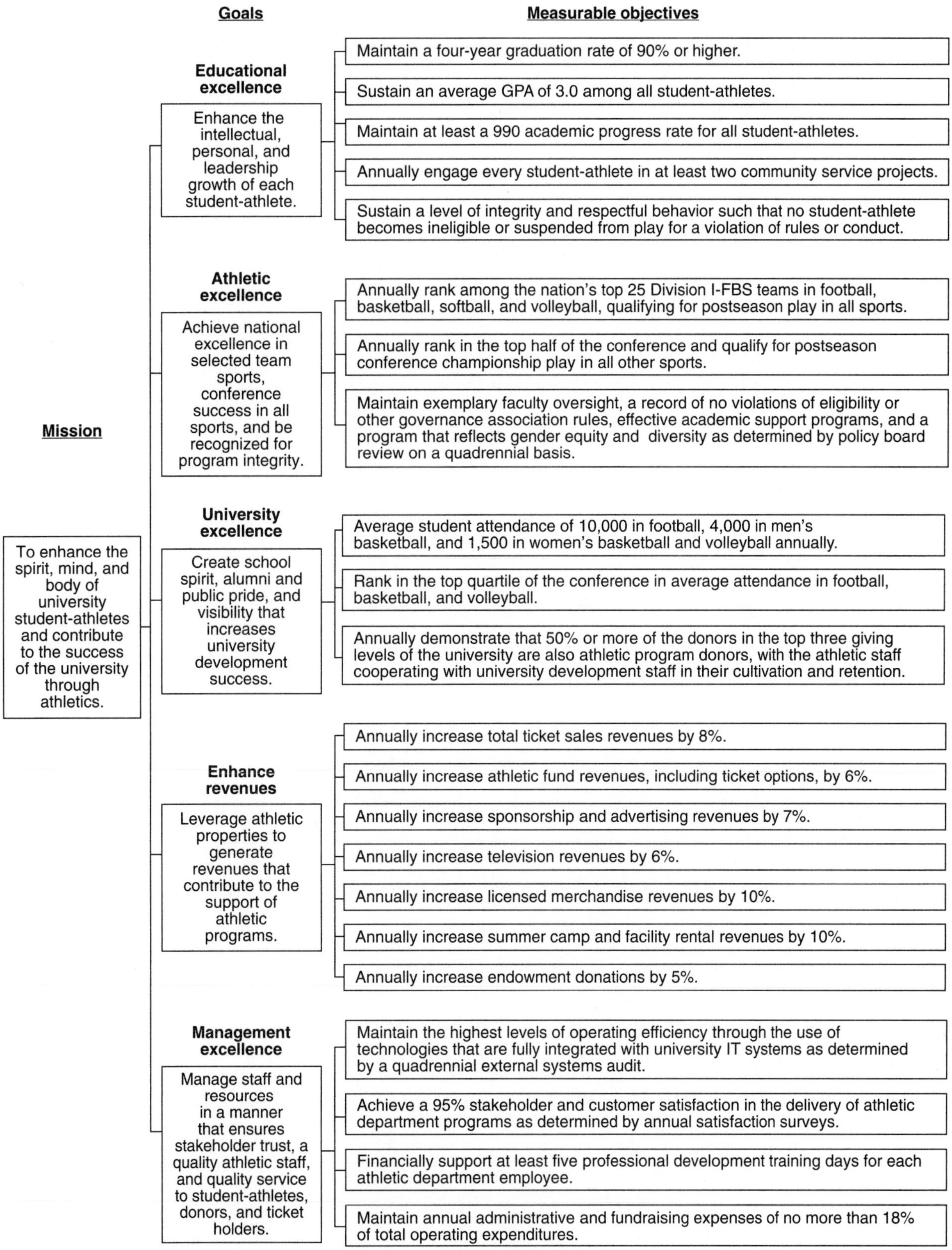

Goals
Measurable objectives
Mission
To enhance the spirit, mind, and body of university student-athletes and contribute to the success of the university through athletics.
Educational excellence
Enhance the intellectual, personal, and leadership growth of each student-athlete.
Maintain a four-year graduation rate of 90% or higher.
Sustain an average GPA of 3.0 among all student-athletes.
Maintain at least a 990 academic progress rate for all student-athletes.
Annually engage every student-athlete in at least two community service projects.
Sustain a level of integrity and respectful behavior such that no student-athlete becomes ineligible or suspended from play for a violation of rules or conduct.
Athletic excellence
Achieve national excellence in selected team sports, conference success in all sports, and be recognized for program integrity.
Annually rank among the nation's top 25 Division I-FBS teams in football, basketball, softball, and volleyball, qualifying for postseason play in all sports.
Annually rank in the top half of the conference and qualify for postseason conference championship play in all other sports.
Maintain exemplary faculty oversight, a record of no violations of eligibility or other governance association rules, effective academic support programs, and a program that reflects gender equity and diversity as determined by policy board review on a quadrennial basis.
University excellence
Create school spirit, alumni and public pride, and visibility that increases university development success.
Average student attendance of 10,000 in football, 4,000 in men's basketball, and 1,500 in women's basketball and volleyball annually.
Rank in the top quartile of the conference in average attendance in football, basketball, and volleyball.
Annually demonstrate that 50% or more of the donors in the top three giving levels of the university are also athletic program donors, with the athletic staff cooperating with university development staff in their cultivation and retention.
Enhance revenues
Leverage athletic properties to generate revenues that contribute to the support of athletic programs.
Annually increase total ticket sales revenues by 8%.
Annually increase athletic fund revenues, including ticket options, by 6%.
Annually increase sponsorship and advertising revenues by 7%.
Annually increase television revenues by 6%.
Annually increase licensed merchandise revenues by 10%.
Annually increase summer camp and facility rental revenues by 10%.
Annually increase endowment donations by 5%.
Management excellence
Manage staff and resources in a manner that ensures stakeholder trust, a quality athletic staff, and quality service to student-athletes, donors, and ticket holders.
Maintain the highest levels of operating efficiency through the use of technologies that are fully integrated with university IT systems as determined by a quadrennial external systems audit.
Achieve a 95% stakeholder and customer satisfaction in the delivery of athletic department programs as determined by annual satisfaction surveys.
Financially support at least five professional development training days for each athletic department employee.
Maintain annual administrative and fundraising expenses of no more than 18% of total operating expenditures.

Figure 3.3.1 Sample one-page Division I athletic program strategic plan.

From D. Lopiano and C. Zotos, *Athletic Director's Desk Reference*, 2nd ed. (Champaign, IL: Human Kinetics, 2023).

Mission

To provide rewarding, highly competitive varsity and junior varsity sport experiences for students committed to academic success and community service.

Goals	Measurable objectives
Educational excellence Enhance the intellectual, personal, and leadership growth of each student-athlete.	Maintain a graduation rate of 95% or higher. Sustain an average GPA of 3.0 among all student-athletes. Have 80% of all graduating student-athletes be accepted for college admission. Annually engage every student-athlete in at least two community service projects. Sustain a level of integrity and respectful behavior such that no student-athlete becomes ineligible or suspended from play for a violation of rules or conduct.
Athletic excellence Achieve conference success in all varsity and junior varsity sports and be recognized for program quality and integrity.	Annually rank among the top three and qualify for postseason conference play in all varsity sports. Annually rank in the top half of the conference in all junior varsity sports. Annually rank #1 or #2 in the conference sportsmanship rankings with no athlete or coach removed from the playing field for misconduct. Have 25% of graduating seniors receive athletic scholarship offers from colleges or universities.
School spirit Create school spirit and alumni and public pride in the athletic program.	Average 50% of all students attending home football games and average attendance of 1,000 at men's and women's basketball games. Rank in the top quartile of the conference in average attendance in football, basketball, and volleyball. Through an annual survey of the public, demonstrate that 75% of respondents approve or greatly approve of the success and integrity of the high school athletic program.
Acquire resources Leverage athletic properties to generate resources that contribute to the support of athletic programs.	Annually increase total ticket sales revenues by 3%. Annually increase booster club donations by 5%. Annually increase sponsorship and advertising revenues by 3%. Annually increase gift-in-kind donations from local businesses by 5%. Annually increase licensed merchandise revenues by 3%. Annually increase summer camp and facility rental revenues by 5%. Increase annual golf tournament profits by 5%.
Management excellence Manage staff and resources in a manner that ensures stakeholder trust, a quality athletic staff, and quality service to student-athletes, donors, and ticket holders.	Maintain the highest levels of financial prudence and operating efficiency through consistent use of bidding and purchasing procedures. Through an annual audit of athletic department and booster club finances, find no discrepancies or financial improprieties. Financially support at least two professional development training days for each athletic department employee. Principal or athletic director receives no parent, fan, donor, or student-athlete complaints about athletic operations.

Figure 3.3.2 Sample one-page high school athletic program strategic plan.

From D. Lopiano and C. Zotos, *Athletic Director's Desk Reference*, 2nd ed. (Champaign, IL: Human Kinetics, 2023).

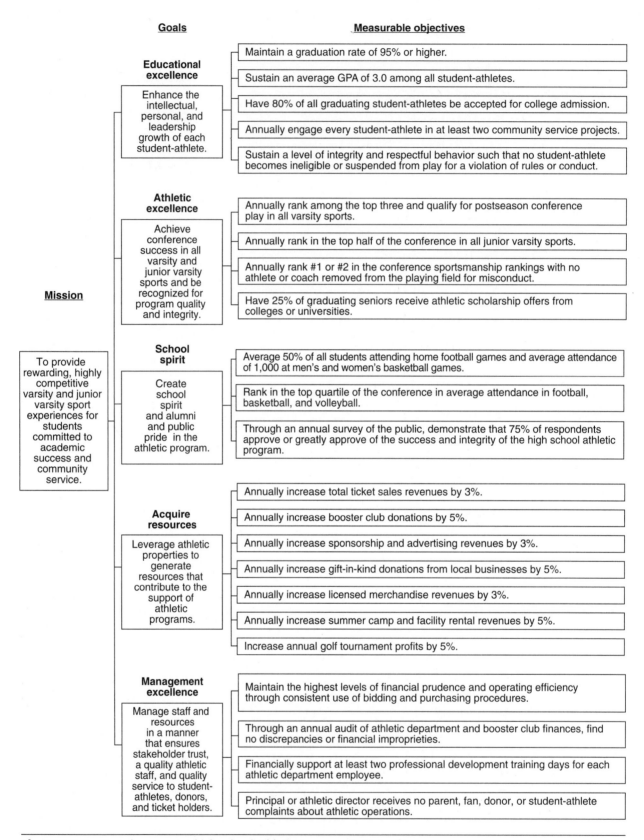

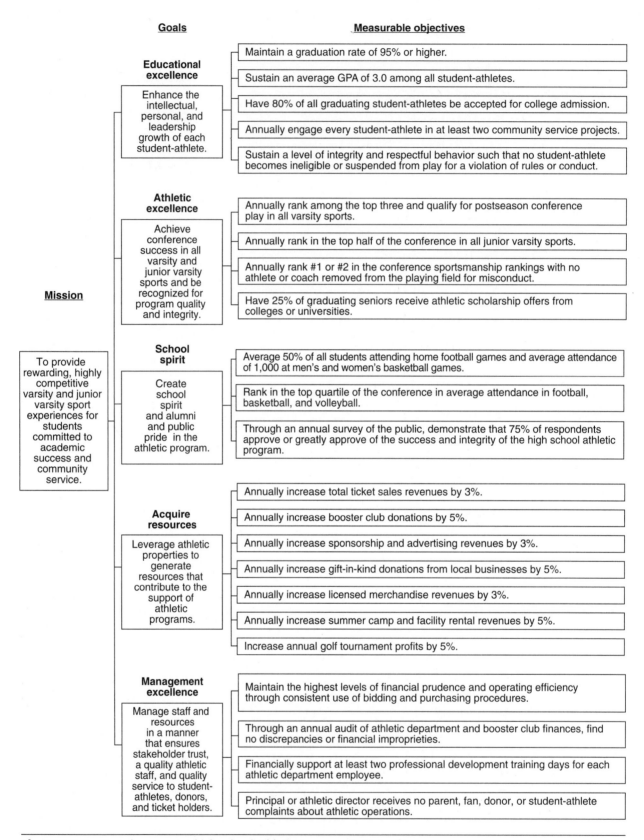

3.4 PLANNING TOOL

Developing Strategies, KPIs, and Action Plans

Many organizations fail to take the next and most important step in strategic planning—defining exactly how they are going to accomplish their goals and objectives. For each measurable objective, one or more overarching general strategies should be developed. For each measurable objective, one or more key performance indicators (KPIs) should also be specified. KPIs inform staff of what data are to be collected to assess progress toward the objective and determine whether the objective has been achieved. Then, aligned with the identified strategies, action plans follow. One person is designated as responsible for executing each action plan by a specified deadline. Each action plan must have a direct relationship to production of the desired result.

The athletic director's experience and understanding of sport business comes into play here. What makes for a winning sports program? Money? Coaches? Recruiting success? What are the critical pieces that result in goal attainment? The athletic director must analyze each measurable objective contained in the strategic plan as illustrated in figures 3.3.1 and 3.3.2 and answer the question, "What do we have to do to achieve this result?" Later in this chapter, Planning Tool 3.5 is an example of this process for team performance objectives. It illustrates the strategies, key performance indicators, and action plans that represent the guidance of the athletic director about those actions that would likely result in a highly successful Division I program in four selected sports. Planning Tool 3.5 deals with only one objective among the three related to achieving athletic program excellence as illustrated in figure 3.3.1.

This critical planning process requires the athletic director to focus on identifying specific actions that might result in a high-performing sport program. This level of in-depth analysis is essential. What are the overarching strategies or guiding rules that provide insights into the causative factors of excellence? How important is the head coach, and how do you define the quality of coach to be hired? What key performance indicators will the athletic director constantly examine to make sure that the program is on track? What action plans executed by the coach and others would be most likely to produce the desired results? This construction—strategies, KPIs, action plans—should be followed for each objective in the strategic plan illustrated in figures 3.3.1 and 3.3.2. The difference between being good and being great as an administrator is the manager's ability to think strategically and identify what makes a great sport program happen. He or she must pinpoint the specific activities by every person that can contribute to that outcome. Holding the head coach responsible and hoping that he or she can figure this out is not enough. The athletic director should collaborate with the head coach to review each of these action items, and both should agree that these and maybe others will make a positive contribution to overall success. By putting multiple action plans in play, the athletic director and head coach are also avoiding putting all of their eggs into one basket. If recruiting is substandard in one year, executing all other aspects of the plan may compensate.

If the athletic department's strategic plan encompasses 23 objectives (as illustrated in figure 3.3.2), the athletic director must go through this process of developing action plans 23 times. This attention to detail, the nuts and bolts of excellence, is the difference between being good and being great. Again, the athletic director should not do this alone. Each objective should be approached using the best thinking and deliberation of the coaches and senior managers who will be expected to achieve the objective. Planning Tool 3.6 is another example of strategy and action plan development for a single fundraising objective.

This level of planning takes time, but it is the most important and primary responsibility of the athletic director. This is what leadership is all about. The athletic director must insist that every sport, support program, and administrative unit has written action plans directly tied to the measurable objectives in the strategic plan, and, at the end of the year, each employee should be evaluated on whether he or she has executed the action plans assigned to him or her. This full and detailed alignment is missing in most athletic departments. Sometimes this level of planning and detail doesn't happen because the athletic director doesn't know how to do it. More often, the athletic director is too busy to do more than keep up with daily problem solving and operational responsibilities. But the bottom line is that if this level of planning and leadership championed by the athletic director doesn't occur, then success will not happen unless it is accidental (great team chemistry) or because of the efforts of one or more outstanding sport coaches or brilliant staff members who simply get the job done through their individual commitment to organizing their program areas and efforts. It is unrealistic for any athletic director to expect that he or she has hired such skilled and experienced professionals for every program area that program goals can be accomplished without action plans. Thus, the strategy–KPI–action plan blueprint for each strategic plan objective is an essential insurance policy that maximizes the possibility of success rather than leaves it to chance.

Long-Range Plans

Although a one-page strategic plan summary provides obvious communications advantages and a good snapshot of goals and objectives, KPIs and action plans for each objective are essential annual planning requirements. The strategic plan must also be presented as a planned-growth document that shows how much progress is expected each year toward reaching performance objectives. Thus, the athletic director should also create a three- to five-year measuring stick to ensure that efforts are on track and that reasonable success is being demonstrated annually and over the long term. Planning Tool 3.7 is an example of a format that can be used to accomplish this requirement.

3.5 PLANNING TOOL

Strategies, KPIs, and Action Plans for Sport Teams

Use the following template as a model to produce a strategy, key performance indicators, and an action plan for each measurable objective applicable to each sport program in the athletic department strategic plan. Through this process the athletic director can ensure that a measurable objective is achieved by a certain date because staff members are held accountable for performing specific tasks directly related to the objective to be achieved (see table 3.5.1).

Goal:	Achieve national excellence in selected team sports, have conference success in all sports, and be recognized for program integrity.
Objective 1:	**Annually rank among the nation's top 25 Division I-FBS teams in football, basketball (men and women), and women's volleyball, qualifying for postseason play in all sports.**
Strategies:	—Hire or retain coaches with demonstrated success at this level
	—Schedule as many nonconference games as possible versus top 25 opponents
	—Ensure that staffing and budgets for these programs are comparable with other top 25 programs
	—Hire top recruiting coordinators for each program
	—Assign specific strength and conditioning coaches to each program
KPIs:	—End-of-season national ranking or national championship finish in the top 25
	—Finish first or second in conference championship
	—Win–loss record of .750 or better

Table 3.5.1 Sample Strategy for Achieving Objective of Top 25 Ranking

Action plans	Accountable	Deadline
Complete football coach search, hire candidate with top 20 credentials	Athletic director	March 1
Issue nonrenewal notice to head men's basketball coach and begin search for replacement	Athletic director	April 1
Get athletic policy board and president approval for contract extension and salary increase for women's basketball and volleyball coaches in recognition of top 10 national finishes	Athletic director	April 15
Complete schedule showing 75 percent of nonconference opponents in top 25	Head football, basketball, and volleyball coaches	June 1
Complete survey of top 25 football, basketball, and volleyball programs showing operating budgets, staff, and staff salaries	Associate athletic director	Jan. 15
Establish next year's budgets for football, basketball, and volleyball in top quartile of top 25 programs	Athletic director	April 1
Produce next year's recruiting prospect list for football, basketball, and volleyball showing national ranking of each prospect and status regarding serious consideration of XU	Recruiting coordinator	Feb. 1
Produce report on strength and fitness levels of all current players with next year's goals and spring and summer individualized training programs	Strength and conditioning coach for football, basketball, and volleyball	April 1
Meet with each head coach to review status of program in all 10 strategic areas including review of performance evaluations of all assistant coaches	Football, basketball, and volleyball head coaches with athletic director	May 1
Meet with each head coach and associate director of student affairs to review academic performance and eligibility status of current athletes	Football, basketball, and volleyball head coaches with athletic director	May 1

3.6 PLANNING TOOL

Strategies, KPIs, and Action Plans for Fund-Raising

Use the following template as a model to produce a strategy, key performance indicators, and an action plan for each measurable objective for the fund-raising program in the athletic department strategic plan. With this method the athletic director can ensure that a measurable objective is accomplished by a certain date because specific staff members are held accountable for performing specific tasks that relate directly to the objective to be achieved (see table 3.6.1).

Goal: Leverage athletic properties to generate revenues that contribute to the support of athletic programs.

Objective 1: Increase athletic fund (annual giving) revenues by 10 percent.

Strategies:

—Invest in development capacity by hiring and retaining sufficient development staff to cultivate and solicit qualified major donor prospects

—Maximize relationship-building activities and prospective major donor contacts by the athletic director, coaches, and student-athletes

—Initiate a priority-seating program to incentivize and reward those who give most

—Centralize, consolidate, and relocate fund-raising leader, fund-raising staff, and ticketing staff to maximize information and relationship synergies

—Relieve athletic director from daily operational responsibilities to enable greater donor cultivation and solicitation activities

—Enhance benefits for donors who give $500 or more annually as incentives to increase annual giving

KPIs:

—By month and year to date overall:

- Total number of donors
- Total dollars from all donors
- Average donation, all donations
- Percentage increase over previous year

—By month and year to date by donor category (less than $100; $101–$250; $251–$500; $501–$1,000; $1,001–$2,500; $2,501–$5,000; over $5,000)

- Total number of donors
- Total dollars from all donors
- Average donation, all donations
- Percentage increase over previous year

—Total number of major donor prospects being cultivated

- Number of face-to-face visits to date by staff member, weekly average
- Number of personal phone calls by staff member, daily average
- Number of donor prospects entertained as guest coaches, at athletic events, or at other arranged activities; weekly average

- Average number of major donors and donor prospects assigned per staff member
- New prospect lists obtained (number of lists and total number of prospects)

Table 3.6.1 Sample Strategy for Achieving Objective of Increasing Revenues by 10 Percent

Action plans	Accountable	Dead-line
Move university development staff and ticket office staff into athletic fund-raising staff area	Assistant athletic director of operations	Aug. 20
Appoint Sue Smith associate athletic director for external relations and move ticket office from associate athletic director for business affairs to associate athletic director for external relations	Athletic director	July 15
Hire two additional fund-raisers to bring major donor cultivation ratio down from 1:250 to 1:125	Sue Smith	Sept. 1
Complete priority-seating program research and get president's approval for next year implementation	Jack Jones	Oct. 1
Develop detailed plan for meetings and communications with all stakeholders regarding new priority-seating program to take place during the current year	Sue Smith	Nov. 1
Review and revise athletic fund benefit chart to add additional benefits at higher levels and move three-star members to new game-day entertainment area	Pete Smith	May 1
Schedule athletic director and selected head coach speaking engagements at 15 alumni, social, or business group meetings and obtain mailing lists for each	Mary Steed	Oct. 1
Send out current unresearched prospect list for wealth overlay prospect screening and assign top prospects to fund-raising staff	Sue Smith	Nov. 1
Execute quarterly mass mailings to new prospect lists Sept. through Nov. about becoming members of athletic fund	Joe Black	Feb.–April
Assign each head coach 10 alumni or donor prospects to invite as guest coaches for team at away events and conduct training session about communication and activities	Sue Smith	Sept. 1
Develop and implement athletic director face-to-face meeting plan for the year to be executed by athletic director administrative secretary for top 25 donors and top 50 prospects and schedule three thank-you calls per day to donors or prospects	Sue Smith	Sept. 1
Confirm 15 alumni- or friend-hosted house parties to introduce friends to athletic program; provide execution support	Mary Steed	Oct. 15
Audit and add new parents and friends to team lists	Head coaches	Oct. 1
Finalize invitations for guest coaches for all home events for all fall sports	Fred and each head coach	Aug. 30
Finalize invitations for guest coaches for all home events for all winter sports	Fred and each head coach	Nov. 1
Finalize invitations for guest coaches for all home events for all spring sports	Fred and each head coach	Jan. 15

3.7 PLANNING TOOL

Five-Year KPI Targets for Academic Excellence Goal

Use the following template as a model to produce a long-range planning tool that enables tracking of key performance indicators (KPI) and the setting of targets over a five-year period. This management chart can also be used to demonstrate trends and achievements for such reports as the required NCAA Division I certification self-evaluation or other certification and evaluation processes.

Table 3.7.1 2021–2028 Strategic Plan: Five-Year KPI Targets for Academic Excellence

Goal 1 Targets: Academic Excellence, Enhance the Intellectual, Moral, and Leadership Growth of Each Student-Athlete

			TARGETS (REPLACE TARGET WITH ACTUAL FOR COMPLETED YEARS)							
	Measurable objectives	**Critical indicator**	**2021–22**	**2022–23**	**2023–24**	**2024–25**	**2025–26**	**2026–27**	**2027–28**	**Data collector**
Objective 1.1	Maintain a four-year average graduation rate of 90% or higher	Graduation rate	90%	90%	90%	90%	90%	90%	90%	Mary
Objective 1.2	Maintain at least a 985 academic progress rate for all student-athletes	Overall APR	985	985	985	985	985	985	985	Mary
Objective 1.3	Sustain an average GPA of 3.0 among all student-athletes	Overall GPA	3.0	3.0	3.0	3.0	3.0	3.0	3.0	Mary
Objective 1.4	Sustain a level of integrity and respectful behavior for the rules of society, the game, officials, and opponents such that no student-athlete becomes ineligible or is suspended from play for a violation of NCAA, game, or university rules or local, state, or federal laws	Number of NCAA or conference rules violations	0	0	0	0	0	0	0	Joe
		Number of game suspensions or ejections	0	0	0	0	0	0	0	Joe
		Number of athletes suspended or dismissed by university rules	0	0	0	0	0	0	0	Joe
		Number of athletes declared ineligible (behavioral)	0	0	0	0	0	0	0	Joe
Objective 1.5	Provide at least one international sport experience before graduation that enhances the student-athlete's appreciation and understanding of people from other nations and cultures	Percentage of current senior student-athletes with one or more international experiences	100%	100%	100%	100%	100%	100%	100%	Peter
Objective 1.6	Recruit varsity teams that set an example for the university in celebrating racial and ethnic diversity, increasing student-athlete diversity (35.5%) to 2% higher than university goals by 2028	Percentage of student-athletes of color or ethnicity	33.5%	35.5%	37.5%	39.5%	41.5%	43.5%	45.5%	Sherri

From D. Lopiano and C. Zotos, *Athletic Director's Desk Reference*, 2nd ed. (Champaign, IL: Human Kinetics, 2023).

3.8 PLANNING TOOL

Installing a Mechanism to Review the Strategic Plan

The larger an athletic department grows, the more specialized and isolated sport and support programs become. The more developed and organized the program is, the greater the focus is on individual responsibility for the achievement of objectives and key performance indicators. Thus, staff and even the athletic director may lose sight of the big picture and the interdependence of all the moving parts. Given this propensity toward lack of integration and considering the need to review the strategic plan each year to see whether the organization is meeting its goals, consider having a strategic-planning meeting in each sport at the end of each academic year.

The athletic director or senior staff member assigned to supervise the sport would be responsible for calling and conducting the meeting. Schedule the meeting for at least three to four hours. The focus of the meeting would be "How are we doing, and what can we do to be better?" A representative from each service area serving the sport program (athletic training, communications, strength and conditioning, marketing and fund-raising, academic support, student life, business office, event management) would be required to attend with all the coaches in that sport.

The format of the meeting would be for each service area representative to review a one-page summary that he or she brings to the meeting (enough copies for all attendees) covering the following topics: (1) the aspect that the person most appreciated in working with that sport program, (2) factual data demonstrating performance this year based on strategic plan KPIs for his or her respective program area, (3) a current SWOT (strengths, weaknesses, opportunities, threats) for his or her respective program area, and (4) recommendations for changes in his or her program area that would enhance sport program performance. With regard to recommendations, any budgetary cost associated with the recommendation should be noted.

The head coach should be the first to present and should review team performance, coaching performance, and recruiting—not any service area. Each presentation should be restricted to five minutes. Questions should be entertained immediately following each presentation, but no discussion should occur. The one-page summary should be distributed before each person begins his or her presentation so that all present can use the information to take notes. After all representatives have presented, the senior staff chair asks the group to review the recommendations for each area and asks whether any additional recommendations to enhance that program offering should be considered. This discussion is conducted one area at a time. Following the discussion of recommendations for each area, the group shall determine, by consensus, which recommendations should and could be implemented in the next academic year. The last item on the agenda of the meeting is whether there are any recommendations to revise the department's one-page strategic plan.

The athletic director or senior staff member chairing the meeting must remember to open the meeting by stating the rules of the meeting, as described earlier, and to emphasize (1) the five-minute presentation limit, (2) the importance of not taking criticism or additional recommendations for improvement of the service area or sport program in a personal manner, and (3) using a constructive tone of voice. The chair must keep the tenor of the meeting positive. At the end of the meeting, the chair should explain that all recommendations will be taken to the senior staff meeting for action, particularly those that have budgetary implications, and that the decisions will be reported back to everyone.

This type of meeting is an excellent planning session that should underpin action plans for the following academic year. More important, the coaching staff and all service areas will see the role played by and review the performance of all program areas critical to the success of the sport program. The senior staff member is responsible for bringing all recommendations made by the group to the senior staff group for action, which should consist of a one-day retreat scheduled at the end of the academic year. The senior staff group should first review all end-of-year reports on strategic plan critical indicators (KPIs), discuss recommendations in light of their alignment with the strategic plan as well as budgetary implications, and make decisions on each recommendation. These decisions might be to reject the recommendation, reconsider the recommendation next year, approve the recommendation, or approve with revisions. If any revision needs to be made to the department's strategic plan, it should be made at this meeting and as a predicate to the request for senior staff to prepare action plans for the following academic year. All actions should be reported back to all staff in writing or at the next all-staff meeting.

BIBLIOGRAPHY

VISION, MISSION, AND GOALS

Allison, M., & Kaye, J. (2005). *Strategic planning for nonprofit organizations: A practical guide and workbook.* Hoboken, NJ: Wiley.

Baumer, B., & Zimbalist, A. (2019, April). The impact of college athletic success on donations and applicant quality. *International Journal of Financial Studies, 7*(2), 1–23.

Chappelet, J.L., & Bayle, E. (2005). *Strategic and performance management of Olympic sport organizations.* Champaign, IL: Human Kinetics.

Clotfelter, Charles T. (2011). *Big-time sports in American universities.* Cambridge, United Kingdom: Cambridge University Press.

Covell, D., & Barr, C.A. (2010). *Managing intercollegiate athletics.* Scottsdale, AZ: Holcomb Hathaway.

Cronan, J. (2009, December 9). Athletics director's panel on financing intercollegiate athletics. IMG Intercollegiate Athletics Forum. New York.

Duderstadt, J. (2003). *Intercollegiate athletics and the American university: A university president's perspective.* Ann Arbor: University of Michigan Press.

Economou, G. (2009, February 23). Dynamic organizations build effectiveness from the inside out. *Street & Smith's Sports Business Journal.* https://www.sportsbusinessjournal.com/Journal/Issues/2009/02/23/From-The-Field-Of/Dynamic-Organizations-Build-Effectiveness-From-The-Inside-Out.aspx?hl=Dynamic+organizations+build+effectiveness+from+the+inside+out&sc=0.

Hums, M.A., & MacLean, J.C. (2018). *Governance and policy in sport organizations* (4th ed.). Scottsdale, AZ: Holcomb Hathaway.

Knight Commission on Intercollegiate Athletics. (2001). *A call to action: Reconnecting college sports and higher education.* www.knightcommission.org/images/pdfs/2001_knight_report.pdf.

Knight Commission on Intercollegiate Athletics. (2010). *Restoring the balance: Dollars, values, and the future of college sports.* www.knightcommission.org/images/restoringbalance/KCIA_Report_F.pdf.

Lopiano, D.A., & Zotos, C. (2021). *Restructuring a college athletic program to protect Olympic sports during financial uncertainty.* Champaign, IL: Human Kinetics. https://us.humankinetics.com/products/restructuring-a-college-athletic-program-to-protect-olympic-sports-during-financial-uncertainty-pdf.

Louisiana State University. (2019). *A strategic plan for LSU athletics.* https://issuu.com/lsuathletics/docs/13lsustrategicplan.

Martinez, J.M., Stinson, J.L., Kang, M., & Jubenville, C.B. (2010, March). Intercollegiate athletics and institutional fundraising: A meta-analysis. *Sports Marketing Quarterly.*

National Collegiate Athletic Association. (1981–2019). *Archives of NCAA revenues and expense reports by division.* https://www.ncaa.org/about/resources/research/archives-ncaa-revenues-and-expenses-reports-division.

National Collegiate Athletic Association. (2018). *Instructions for completing the 2018 division III institutional self-study guide.* https://www.ncaa.org/sites/default/files/d3-online-issg-instructions.pdf.

National Collegiate Athletic Association. (2015–16). *Instructions for completing the division II institutional self-study guide (2015–16).* https://www.ncaa.org/sites/default/files/d3-online-issg-instructions.pdf.

Pederson, P.M., & Thibault, L. (2022). *Contemporary sport management* (7th ed.). Champaign, IL: Human Kinetics.

Russell, B. (1990). *The problems of philosophy.* Indianapolis, IN: Hackett.

Shulman, J.L., & Bowen, W.G. (2001). *The game of life: College sports and educational values.* Princeton, NJ: Princeton University Press.

Slack, T., & Parent, M. (2021). *Understanding sport organizations: Applications for sport managers* (3rd ed.). Champaign, IL: Human Kinetics.

Spitzer, D.R. (2007). *Transforming performance measurement: Rethinking the way we measure and drive success.* New York: American Management Association.

Thelin, J. (1994). *Games colleges play: Scandal and reform in intercollegiate athletics.* Baltimore: Johns Hopkins University Press.

Villanova University. *Athletics department mission statement.* http://villanova.cstv.com/school-bio/mission-statement.html.

Yow, D. et al. (2000). *Strategic planning for collegiate athletics.* Binghamton, NY: Haworth Press.

Zimbalist, A. (1999). *Unpaid professionals: Commercialism and conflict in big-time college sports.* Princeton, NJ: Princeton University Press.

Zotos, C. et al. (1995). *Creating gender neutral coaches' employment and compensation systems: A resource manual.* East Meadow, NY: Women's Sports Foundation.

CHAPTER

4

Operational Structure of the Athletic Program

Few high schools or universities can financially afford to administer an athletic program in which all teams enjoy equal benefits related to credentials of coaches, travel, facilities, equipment, uniforms, and the like. The reality is that most schools will administer a major–minor sports model or a multitiered funding model. The documents in this chapter, in both the book and HK*Propel*, help the athletic director analyze and evaluate the current funding model, identify associated benefits and challenges, and create policies that formalize the funding model while ensuring compliance with gender equity laws.

TYPES OF DOCUMENTS

Management tip—Factual background information, insights, problem-solving strategies, and suggestions for the athletic director

Planning tool—Steps to take or factors that should be considered in the development of strategic plans, action plans, professional development plans, or governance systems

Educational resource—Handouts that can be used to educate staff members, campus constituents, volunteers, or student-athletes

Policy—Sample policies and procedures that should be adopted by an athletic department after customization and review by appropriate expert institutional or school district officials

Form—Sample forms, letters, or job descriptions

Evaluation instrument—Administrative tools that help the athletic director, a supervisor, or an employee assess job performance and evaluate program content

Risk assessment—Checklists that help the athletic director, a supervisor, or an employee identify risks and prevent litigation

4.1 PLANNING TOOL

Articulating the Presence of a Tiered Funding Model

Most athletic directors would like to say, "We treat all of our teams and student-athletes equally." Yet few athletic programs do. A clear distinction must be made between goals and objectives related to the growth and development of each student-athlete and those related to the development of each sport. In the case of the former, all growth and development objectives for student-athletes should be (1) equally applied to all sports, (2) clearly articulated and monitored, and (3) uncompromised by sport program revenue, media interest, or other objectives. These growth and development objectives for student-athletes should be clearly stated as the highest athletic program priorities. Consideration should be given to the following points:

- Meeting the highest standards of ethical and respectful conduct
- Maximization of academic achievement, which results in graduation with a meaningful baccalaureate degree that resulted from maintenance of good academic standing, consistent and normal progress toward meeting degree requirements, and the demonstration of academic commitment through class attendance and completion of course and other academic obligations
- Participation in community service
- Demonstrating growth and improvement in sport skills and strategies
- Acquisition of leadership skills
- Exemplary conduct as a public figure, school representative, and role model including the development of public speaking and media interview skills, and demonstration of skilled social interaction with children, alumni, spectators, and other members of the public

Why Team Objectives May Vary

Beyond common growth and development objectives for student-athletes, financial factors, long-standing tradition, success rates, and other considerations may result in some sport programs having different objectives than others. A simple example of this differentiation may be a school with a long-established tradition of excellence in one sport like ice hockey, which is the product of its location near the Canadian border in a region where youth ice hockey is immensely popular and superior ice hockey facilities are easily accessible. At that same institution, baseball and softball are not as popular. The combination of no indoor practice facilities and the cold climate always results in shortened competition schedules and an inability to recruit top players. Even at public high schools where recruiting is absent, factors such as access to facilities, community sport popularity, and local youth sport emphasis affect the school's feeder system and help determine which sports are going to be privileged in funding and other means of support. The long-time presence of an exceptional and venerable coach is another factor that may result in different treatment of the sport program.

It is important to recognize and communicate to parents and others who argue that all athletic programs should be equally supported that differences in program support and priorities are common in all educational institutions. Math and science may have more teachers or faculty and depth in course offerings because of state educational requirements, or a university may decide to have a nationally ranked economics or marine biology program. Foreign languages and psychology or history may not have the same financial support. No matter what the reason for program differentiation with regard to athletic program emphasis and financial support, acknowledgment of these differences should be transparent. Athletic program administrators must determine which business or success expectations apply to each sport and express why such differentiation makes sense. Also critical is the need to be sure that differences in team treatment are applied proportionally to each gender so that sex discrimination in violation of Title IX does not occur.

Differences in financial support may affect expectations of success or involvement in activities outside athletics. For instance, student-athletes in a high-profile sport that strengthens alumni involvement and provides national exposure for the university may not be asked to perform local community service projects but instead may be asked to participate in university alumni activities. The team that has a part-time coach and no fan base may not be required to fund-raise. Most universities and even many high school programs, by accident or by design, have created tiered athletic programs; they have multiple levels of financial support and various limitations that place teams at different levels, resulting in different treatment. Unfortunately, at most institutions, athletic program tiers, or differences in treatment, are neither acknowledged nor clearly defined. This absence of clarity creates challenges in articulating program objectives, creating policy, exercising fiscal controls, and providing a gender-equitable athletic program. The bottom line is that athletic departments are complex organizations in which objectives can vary from team to team. Trying to prioritize a single set of objectives for the unit as a whole may be an exercise in futility. When the athletic director does create such differentiation, it must be fully analyzed, gender neutral, and explainable to all stakeholders.

Need for Assessment and Formalization of Operational Structure

Every institution needs to formalize the structure and function of its athletic program by conducting a self-study that will aid administrators in prioritizing athletic department objectives, setting realistic program expectations, and evaluating team-by-team funding patterns. Such an assessment will also provide a clear picture of how well the athletic program is complying with gender equity requirements.

Administrators must also realize that there is no perfect model that should be emulated. Each institution has to create a unique model that is consistent with institutional and athletic department philosophy, is fiscally responsible, and is compliant with state and federal legal obligations. Though time consuming, a systematic analysis, evaluation, or revision of the current athletic department structure offers great benefits. Ultimately, the model that evolves serves as the foundation for day-to-day operations and effective strategic planning. In addition, the model serves five other primary purposes, as described in the following sections.

Planned Growth as an Economic Necessity Over the past 30 years, high school and university athletic programs have grown dramatically because of increased interest in emerging sports such as soccer and lacrosse, as well as the effect of gender equity laws. According to a report by the National Coalition for Women and Girls in Education (2017), in 1972, 29,977 female athletes and 170,384 male athletes participated in intercollegiate athletics (p. 3). By 2019 those figures had risen to 218,657 women and 280,560 men at NCAA member institutions (NCAA, 2020). The sheer volume of more athletes and more sports has created the need to have a plan in place that addresses program goals, gender equity objectives, and funding levels on a sport-by-sport basis. Such a plan is particularly important during times of economic recession. Also, if male–female athletic participation is not proportional to the male–female ratio of the undergraduate student population, prongs 2 and 3 of Title IX will require mechanisms that demonstrate regular assessment of interest in new sports and a policy mechanism for adding new sports. Policy 4.5 addresses adding or cutting teams from the athletic program.

4.5 Policy—Adding New Sports or Eliminating Existing Sports

Sample policy that establishes protocols and standards to follow when adding new sports or removing existing sports from the athletic program.

Available in HK*Propel*.

Communicating the Private School or University's Athletic Commitment to Prospective Athletes Prospective student-athletes require accurate information during the decision-making process involved in school selection. They and their parents have become sophisticated consumers of the sport product. They want every advantage possible and expect that coaches and athletic administrators will clearly present the benefits and limitations of participating in sport at their institution. Primarily, they are interested in the credentials and accessibility of the coach, the expectations for success of the program, the quality of the facilities, and the provision of athletic scholarships and support services. The recruiting process has become a negotiation similar to any other sales encounter. Coaches and athletic administrators must know their product and sell it on its own merits.

Communicating the Private School or University's Athletic Commitment to Prospective Coaches Communicating the advantages and limitations of specific sport programs in the employment recruiting process is also essential. One of the advantages of a clear statement of differences in sport program goals and objectives is to control a coach's expectations of financial support and program emphasis. Providing an unrealistic or unclear picture of program support to prospective coaches is unfair. They must know what will be expected of them and what types of resources will or will not be available to meet those expectations.

Accountability to Faculty and Other Constituents Being accountable to a variety of constituents creates another reason to have a clearly defined athletic program model. Faculty need to understand the diverse roles that the athletic department plays on campus, as well as the value of its existence. They must also know that a carefully crafted plan is in place for the attainment of program objectives and that oversight is sufficient to control the potential dysfunctions of the largest, most powerful student activity on campus. Students, parents, alumni, and booster groups are other constituents who need to understand how and why the athletic program functions the way that it does. For stakeholders who question the value of high school or collegiate athletics, a defined athletic program model justifies the department's existence and explains expenditures that may come at the cost of providing other student activities. For those groups who highly support athletic programs, the model sends a clear message of how important the program is to institutional life, sets limits on their involvement in athletic program decision making, and provides a clear rationale for the necessity of their financial support.

Responding to Aggressive Media Helping the media understand why an athletic program conducts business the way that it does is another reason for athletic departments to have a clear, identifiable structure. The media's interest in sport has evolved far beyond contest reporting. They have become much more active as watchdogs for the rights of student-athletes, sportsmanship, and commercialism. Educational administrators must be able to articulate the objectives of the program, define and justify differences in treatment from sport to sport, and provide rationale for how the structure relates to the central mission of the institution.

4.2 MANAGEMENT TIP

Communicating the Benefits of a Tiered Program

Historically, athletic administrators and coaches have been reluctant to admit that tiered models (treating some sports differently from others) exist in high schools and universities. Sometimes, athletic administrators and coaches will claim that their reluctance stems from a concern that athletes who participate on teams in lower tiers will feel undervalued. Less often, they will admit that they can't explain why the tiered model exists. In most cases, athletic directors and coaches have inherited a model that simply evolved over time. Treatment of teams may have become differentiated without a plan or with little evaluation. Even with the addition of women's sport teams and the implications of gender equity, few institutions considered the necessity of factoring gender equity into their placement of teams in various tiers. Many benefits result from formalizing and openly articulating the existence of a tiered sports program including (1) the accommodation of a variety of educational and business objectives, (2) fairness to student-athletes, (3) the promotion of effective and efficient management strategies, (4) compliance with legal standards, and (5) the ability to maintain or increase participation opportunities for student-athletes.

Accommodating a Variety of Educational and Business Objectives

The mission of an athletic department may be unique to each institution and will often encompass multiple objectives. For example, an institution may want to create national recognition through the success of the athletic department. Not every sport at that institution has to be exceptional to create that exposure. Therefore, administrators may select some male and female sports, categorize them in tier I, and provide a level of financial support in a way that brings about a successful, nationally recognized program. That same institution may want a group of tier II sports that help increase enrollment at the institution and provide a base of support for community service projects.

Fairness to Student-Athletes

Fairness to student-athlete consumers is another benefit associated with creating and openly articulating a clear, definable athletic program model. Student-athletes should know exactly what kind of program they will be participating in including the level of competition, the expectations of performance, and available benefits. Coaches and athletic administrators have demonstrated a reluctance to articulate the presence of a tiered funding model. They argue that student-athletes participating on teams in lower tiers will feel unappreciated because they do not receive benefits afforded other student-athletes. Student-athletes, however, know when they are being treated differently; what is important is to be able to explain why. Only then will it be clear that logical reasons led to such decisions, rather than arbitrary favoritism.

Promotion of Effective and Efficient Management Strategies

A tiered athletic program promotes efficient and effective management strategies. Tiers not only define institutional funding and treatment distinctions but also limit what coaches can do on their own. When supervisors allow coaches to administer their own program unilaterally with little regard for the department at large, the result is a fuzzy understanding of organizational mission and a variety of practices based on the diverse personalities and desires of staff rather than educationally sound objectives based on carefully considered priorities. A well-defined tier structure increases institutional control and creates consistent work standards and expectations.

Compliance With Legal Standards

Lack of a clearly defined athletic program model could make an institution more vulnerable to legal challenges. Continually espousing that all athletes and programs are treated equally and have unlimited potential for success, when practices indicate otherwise, increases an institution's risk related to accusations of sex discrimination under Title IX, Title VII, and the Equal Pay Act. In addition, some athletes are filing lawsuits that claim unrealistic or unfulfilled promises made by the coach or the institution, alleging an effect on potential opportunities and earnings in professional sport.

Maintaining or Increasing Participation Opportunities

One of the most compelling advantages of administering a tiered athletic program is the ability to maintain or increase participation opportunities for student-athletes. With the growth of participation in sport by women, the excessive spending on the high-profile sports of football and men's and women's basketball, and the escalating costs of officials' fees and athletic equipment at rates higher than inflation, athletic department resources have been stretched. Rather than eliminate a sport during difficult economic times, the sport can be dropped to a lower funding tier. Thus, a tiered athletic program allows a variety of funding levels that preserves opportunities. Varying perquisites, such as the provision of practice gear or year-round access to locker rooms, can be provided on a tier-by-tier basis. In addition, teams that receive higher levels of support could be expected to raise money. A multitude of options created by a tiered funding approach can help offset the high costs of running an athletic program without compromising opportunities to participate.

4.3 MANAGEMENT TIP

Confronting the Challenges of a Tiered Program

A number of challenges are inherent in adopting a tiered athletic program model: (1) creation of a class system, (2) difficulty in defining the true varsity experience, (3) finding a conference with homogenous competitive aspirations, and (4) denying top-tier designation when teams succeed.

Creation of a Class System

A tiered model in athletics does create an economic class system. The athletes in the top-tier sports are often treated like royalty. They receive many perquisites, practice and play in state-of-the-art facilities, and have access to outstanding coaches who can dramatically affect team and individual success. Simultaneously, athletes in lower-tier sports may be driving to contests in vans, have part-time coaches, and wear older uniforms. These class systems often create dissonance among student-athletes, coaches, and athletic administrators, which is one of the primary reasons why athletic administrators have failed to formalize the existence of the tiers. But the reality is that student-athletes and coaches have always known which teams were considered flagship programs that have privileges and perquisites and which teams were funded at moderate or base levels. A more sensible approach is to educate the athletes about why these tiers exist rather than pretend that they don't.

Defining the True Varsity Experience

The presence of a tiered model raises concerns about the quality of the student-athlete experience for members of teams that are placed in the lowest tiers. Administrators and coaches have to wrestle with the issue of defining the difference between a club sport and a varsity sport experience. When does a varsity sport really become a club sport that relies more on student or volunteer coaches, student fees, fund-raising, and out-of-pocket spending by participants? What minimum amount of funding or support should a high school or university give a team so that student-athletes have a true varsity experience? The line is not always clear. Many institutions struggle to preserve participation opportunities without totally compromising the quality of the experience.

Finding the Right Conference Affiliation

For universities and some private high schools, a dilemma of administering a multitiered model is finding the right competitive fit for all sport programs with regard to conference affiliation. Conferences provide a route to championship competition, guarantees of games, and a sense of identity. An institution may have one or two flagship sports that would be best served by playing in a highly competitive conference. But if the other schools in the conference support all their teams at either a tier I level or tier I and tier II levels, the institution that has four funding tiers may find that its lower-tier sports have no chance of success. Because each institution creates a unique athletic model, finding a set of institutions to compete against in all sports is difficult. If some teams are being continually embarrassed, the administration faces pressure to compress the tiers by providing better funding or it risks igniting the question of quality versus participation opportunities.

Denying Top-Tier Designation to Successful Teams

When a lower-tier sport team exceeds the performance expectations of one or more sport teams located in higher tiers, the system feels immediate pressure to elevate the team's status or defend not doing so. In such situations, the administration must reflect on the variety of reasons why sports were placed in different tiers. Winning cannot be the only criterion for tier placement. The other reasons for such placement must be resurrected to remind advocates of the overachieving sport that other considerations are involved in tier assignments. Frequently, lower-tier placement is simply a matter of economic limitations.

4.4 PLANNING TOOL

A Complete Guide to Creating a Tiered Program

This planning tool presents the issues that an athletic director needs to consider when creating a tiered athletic program. Seven topics guide the discussion:

Section 1: Determining Sport Program Differences
Section 2: Defining the Current Athletic Program Model
Section 3: Identifying Factors That Influence Preferential Treatment
Section 4: Evaluating the Current Athletic Program Model
Section 5: Gender Equitable Participation Opportunities in a Tiered Model
Section 6: Gender Neutral Policies and Practices by Tier
Section 7: Accommodating Differences in Each Tier

Section 1: Determining Sport Program Differences

The institution can develop tiers in two ways: (1) by starting from scratch with a theoretical model or (2) by examining current sport program differences and developing tiers that most closely approximate these differences. The advantages of the latter are that such an analysis (1) reveals the historical forces that created such differentiation, (2) provides important preliminary information about the selection of sports to be placed in the tiers eventually created, and (3) reveals differences in the current treatment of existing sport programs that would be helpful in defining tiers. Because tiers must meet Title IX gender equity requirements, we recommend examining current sport program differences through a legal requirements filter. Under the athletic regulations of Title IX of the Education Amendments Act of 1972, 13 elements are required for gender equity (*Achieving Gender Equity*, p. II-1):

1. Accommodation of interests and abilities
2. Athletic financial assistance
3. Coaching
4. Recruitment of student-athletes
5. Practice and competitive facilities
6. Equipment and supplies
7. Scheduling of games and practice times
8. Travel and daily allowance
9. Access to tutoring and academic support services
10. Housing and dining facilities and services
11. Medical and training facilities and services
12. Publicity
13. Support services

Element 1: Accommodation of Interests and Abilities Element 1 as it relates to participation opportunities and sports offered should be determined only after the athletic program tiers are established. This element is fully addressed in section 5 later in this Planning Tool. For the other 12 elements, the current practices in each sport should be examined and defined. The following sets of questions can be used to identify current practices.

Element 2: Athletic Financial Assistance
Answer the following questions for each sport in the program:

1. Are there limits on the total number of full scholarships permitted?
2. Are there limits on the number of in-state or out-of-state scholarships permitted?
3. With regard to partial scholarships, is there a minimum or maximum number of recipients permitted?
4. With regard to partial scholarships, is there a minimum scholarship amount for individual student-athletes?

5. Are there limits on the total amount of money awarded?
6. Are there limits on the use of scholarship money (need based, merit based, tuition only, and so on)?

Element 3: Coaching Answer the following questions for each sport in the program:

1. Is the head coach full time or part time?
2. What is the number of full-time assistant coaches?
3. What is the number of part-time assistant coaches?
4. Is a student-to-coach ratio used to determine the size of the coaching staff? What is it?
5. What is the number of volunteer coaches?
6. Is there a limit on numbers of volunteer or assistant coaches permitted?
7. Are minimum credentials required for head, assistant, or volunteer coaches (degrees, certifications, experience, and so on)?
8. What are the hiring practices for head coaches (national search, search committee required, athletic director appointment with no oversight, and so on)?
9. Which of the following job responsibilities are applicable to the head coaches?
   a. Recruiting student-athletes
   b. Fund-raising
   c. Limited-season or year-round team training (designate one or the other)
   d. Public speaking
   e. Academic advising
   f. Monitoring academic progress
   g. Managing the budget
   h. Purchasing uniforms and equipment
   i. Maintaining facilities and equipment
   j. Publicity and promotions
   k. Scheduling athletic contests
   l. Scheduling officials
   m. Teaching courses or job responsibilities other than those related to athletic coaching (describe)
   n. Other
10. Define the following expectations applicable to the head coach:
    a. Specific minimum win–loss record or other measures of team success (conference championship, national rankings, athlete awards such as All-American or all-conference, coach awards such as coach of the year, and so on)
    b. Specific number of recruited athletes
    c. Academic quality of recruited athletes
    d. Athletic quality of recruited athletes
    e. Academic success of student-athletes (retention, graduation rates, and so on)
    f. Behavior of student-athletes
    g. Minimum fund-raising yield
    h. Attendance minimums at home contests
    i. Season-ticket sales
    j. Public relations
    k. Community service
    l. Other
11. Describe the compensation and benefits packages for head and assistant coaches:
    a. Predetermined salary ranges
    b. Standard university benefits
    c. Special benefits (car, country club benefits, and so on)
    d. Additional compensation bonuses, merit increases, annuities, shoe contracts, and so on)
    e. Single- versus multiple-year employment agreements

Element 4: Recruitment of Student-Athletes Answer the following questions for each sport in the program:

1. Is there a quota system or other requirement regarding minimum number of matriculated athletes that must be recruited each year?
2. Are there geographical limitations to recruiting?
3. What is the recruiting budget?
4. Are there limitations on recruiting practices (off-campus visits, telephone, use of Federal Express, paid campus visits, and so on)?

Element 5: Practice and Competitive Facilities Answer the following questions for each sport in the program:

1. Rank the quality of the team's practice facilities: excellent, good, average, below average, poor.
2. Rank the quality of the team's competition facilities: excellent, good, average, below average, poor.
3. Is practice facility access unlimited or restricted? What are the restrictions (off campus, time, cost, and so on)?
4. Is competition facility access unlimited or restricted? What are the restrictions (off campus, time, cost, and so on)?
5. Rank the quality of the team's locker room: excellent, good, average, below average, poor.
6. Is access to the locker room unlimited or restricted? What are the restrictions?
7. Who maintains the facilities?
8. Rank the quality of facility maintenance: excellent, good, average, below average, poor.

Element 6: Equipment and Supplies Answer the following questions for each sport in the program:

1. Rank the adequacy of the team's equipment and supply budget: excellent, good, average, below average, poor.
2. How often can uniforms be replaced?
3. Rank the quality of uniforms: excellent, good, average, below average, poor.
4. How often is equipment replaced?
5. Are there limitations on the type of apparel or equipment that is issued to the team (athletic shoes, sport implements, outerwear, and so on)?
6. Rank the adequacy of equipment maintenance: excellent, good, average, below average, poor.

Element 7: Scheduling of Games and Practice Times Answer the following questions for each sport in the program:

1. Is the team permitted to play the maximum number of allowable contests specified by governing-body rules? If not, what percentage is permitted?
2. Is the scheduling of contests limited by location or other factors? What are the limitations?
3. Is the team limited in scheduling contests or practices in the nontraditional season?
4. Are there limitations on practice time (hours, prime time, and so on)? What are they?
5. Are there limitations on contest time (times of day, times of week, and so on)? What are they?
6. Is the team provided with ample practice opportunities in preseason? Describe if inadequate.
7. Is practice or competition limited during times when school is not in session (winter break, spring break, and so on)? If so, describe.
8. Are opportunities to compete in postseason competitions limited in any way? How?

Element 8: Travel and Daily Allowances Answer the following questions for each sport in the program:

1. Are there restrictions on the mode of transportation to contests? What are they?
2. Are there restrictions on overnight stays? What are they?
3. Are there restrictions on numbers of athletes in rooms for overnight stays? What are they?
4. Is there a limit on the quality of lodging based on cost per night for the team? What are the limitations?
5. Are there limitations on the time of arrival and length of stay for competitive events (permissible departure times, staying at site)? What are they?
6. What is the per diem allowance or limits on expenditures per meal?

Element 9: Access to Tutoring and Academic Support Services Answer the following questions for each sport in the program:

1. Are tutoring services provided to the team? If so, are there limitations to this service (time of day, numbers of hours, and so on)?

2. What other academic services are provided to student-athletes?
3. Are tutoring services charged to the operating budget or paid for by the athlete or other sources? What sources?
4. What is the quality of the tutors (other students, trained professionals, volunteer or paid, and so on)?
5. Is there a specific area designated for the team to access tutoring, study hall, or computer labs?
6. Are there limitations on the number of tutors available to the team?

Element 10: Housing and Dining Facilities and Services Answer the following questions for each sport in the program:

1. Are athletes provided with housing arrangements different from those of the general student body? Describe any special benefits or arrangements.
2. If different from the general student body, rate the quality of housing facilities: excellent, good, average, below average, poor.
3. Are athletes provided with dining arrangements different from the general student body? If so, describe any special arrangements.
4. If different from the general student body, rate the quality of the dining arrangements: excellent, good, average, below average, poor.
5. Are pregame meals provided before home contests? If so, are there any restrictions on this benefit?
6. Are housing and meals available during times when the institution is not in session? If so, describe any limitations.

Element 11: Medical and Training Facilities and Services Answer the following questions for each sport in the program:

1. Rate the quality of weight-training and conditioning facilities: excellent, good, average, below average, poor.
2. Are there limitations on access to weight-training and conditioning facilities (location, hours, and so on)? If so, what are they?
3. Rate the quality of strength and conditioning coaches assigned to the team (students, trained professionals, and so on): excellent, good, average, below average, poor.
4. Rate the quality of medical and training facilities: excellent, good, average, below average, poor.
5. Are there limitations on access to the training room (location, hours, and so on)? If so, what are they?
6. Describe and rate the quality of the trainers assigned to the team (students, trained professionals, and so on): excellent, good, average, below average, poor.
7. Do trainers attend all practices and home contests?
8. Do trainers travel to all away contests?
9. Does the team have access to a team doctor?
10. Is the team doctor on site for home and away contests?
11. Are athletes provided annual preseason physicals paid for by the athletic department or university?
12. Are athletes covered by full medical insurance? Describe any limitations.

Element 12: Publicity Answer the following questions for each sport in the program:

1. Rate the availability of sports information promotional services compared with other teams: excellent, good, average, below average, poor.
2. What sports information services are provided?
    a. Media guide
    b. Score reports to media
    c. Press releases
    d. Recruiting brochure
    e. Schedule poster
    f. Scheduling media interviews
    g. Arrangement of radio coverage and frequency of radio coverage
    h. Arrangement of television coverage and frequency of television coverage
    i. Promotion of All-American candidates

j. Travels with team to away contests
k. Present at home games
l. Maintains statistics
m. Other (describe)

3. Rate the quantity and quality of publicity compared with other teams: excellent, good, average, below average, poor.

Element 13: Support Services Answer the following questions for each sport in the program:

1. What clerical and secretarial support is provided? Describe the number and type of personnel and time assigned.
2. What administrative support and services are provided through the athletic department?
   a. Recruiting coordinator
   b. Laundry services
   c. Equipment manager
   d. Facilities director
   e. Business manager (invoicing, purchasing, and so on)
   f. Fund-raising coordinator
   g. Ticket office
   h. Event manager
   i. Counseling and student-life support
   j. Travel coordinator
   k. Other (describe)

Section 2: Defining the Current Athletic Program Model

The next step is to define the athletic program's current de facto tier system. Each element should be examined to identify how many different practices exist. This task can be done by listing the practices in hierarchical order from best supported to least supported. Indicating which teams benefit from each practice would also be helpful. See, for example, table 4.4.1.

As this exercise is completed for each element, a pattern of tiers will emerge. For some criteria one or two differences of treatment may occur among all sports, whereas for other criteria seven or eight differences may be apparent and little homogeneity may be seen in the treatment

Table 4.4.1 Defining the Athletic Program de Facto Tier System
Example for Element 6, Equipment and Supplies

CRITERIA: UNIFORM REPLACEMENT	
Scheduled replacement	**Sport**
Replacement annually	M basketball, W basketball, football
Replacement on a two-year rotation	M soccer, W soccer, baseball
Replacement on a three-year rotation	Softball, M lacrosse, W lacrosse
Fill-in replacement only as needed	M tennis, W tennis, M cross country, W cross country, M swimming, W swimming
CRITERIA: UNIFORM QUALITY	
Quality level	**Sport**
Excellent quality—custom	M basketball, W basketball, football
Above average quality—noncustom	Baseball
Average quality—custom	M soccer, W soccer
Average quality—noncustom	M lacrosse, W lacrosse, W swimming
Low quality—noncustom	M tennis, W tennis, M cross country, W cross country

of individual sports. The administrator must determine which criteria and what levels of difference in treatment are significant enough to define tiers. Careful attention should be paid to the elements that appear to have the greatest effect on team and individual athlete success and the quality of the athletic experience. These elements include (1) access to and quality of coaching, (2) support of the recruiting process, (3) availability of scholarship dollars, and (4) the quality of and access to practice and competitive facilities. The criteria in these elements should be evaluated first in any tier system. Table 4.4.2 is an example of how tiers may start to emerge based on these four elements.

After the number of tiers is established for the top four elements, the administration must decide how the other criteria will be accommodated. If a three-tier model seems to be the best choice, the decision may be made to compress practices in other criteria to create a good fit. For example, if four different practices currently govern uniform replacement, as indicated in table 4.4.1, the administration could decide to drop the two-year rotation and use a three-tier model consisting of an annual replacement cycle, a three-year rotation cycle, and fill-in replacements. There may be good reasons not to compress or expand practices to fit perfectly into the model. For example, because of wear and tear from sliding, the baseball and softball teams may have to stay on a two-year uniform rotation.

Each set of practices has to be evaluated to determine what would make the most sense. While going through this process, it is helpful to include all the Title IX elements that apply to the program in the model. This approach will help create practices in each tier that consider gender equity. See table 4.4.3 for an example of a four-tier athletic program that incorporates 11 elements of Title IX.

Section 3: Identifying Factors That Influence Preferential Treatment

After the tiered model has taken shape, administrators should examine the historical factors that influenced why some sports have received preferential treatment and others have not. Was emphasis on certain sports a result of a documented plan, or did it just happen? Most administrators will find that no plan was used. More often, the tiered athletic program model came about through a series of reactions to various pressures. A historical analysis will probably show that many factors drove the funding of selected teams upward and created a de facto tiered system. Following is a discussion of factors that have typically affected athletic department structure.

Competitive Success A history of competitive success is one of the primary reasons for a

Table 4.4.2 Sample of a Three-Tier Athletic Program Based on Four Elements

Element	Tier I	Tier II	Tier III
Scholarships	• Maximum allowable • No restriction on in state vs. out of state	• 50 percent of maximum • One-third out-of-state maximum	• None permitted
Coaching	• Full-time head coach • Full-time assistant coaches, maximum number allowable	• Full-time head coach • One assistant coach (part-time)	• Part-time head coach • No assistants
Recruiting	• National scope • 100 percent of team recruited	• Regional scope • 75 percent recruited	• Regional scope • 25 percent recruited
Facilities	• State of the art • Exclusive access	• Top three in conference • Priority access	• Adequate • In-season priority

Table 4.4.3 Sample of a Four-Tier Athletic Program

Title IX elements	Tier I policies	Tier II policies	Tier III policies	Tier IV policies
Scholarships	• Maximum • No geographical limits	• Up to 75 percent of maximum • 50 percent in state	• Up to 25 percent of maximum • All in state	• No scholarships
Access to coaching	• Head coach: national search, 12 months • Assistants 10:1, 12 months • Maximum graduate assistants • Volunteers 25:1	• Head coach: regional search, 10 months • 1 full-time assistant • Graduate assistants 15:1 • 1 volunteer	• Head coach: local search, 10 months • Assistants 15:1, part time only • 1 volunteer	• Head coach: part time • Assistants 15:1 • 1 volunteer
Recruiting	• National and international • 100 percent of roster • Paid visits	• National • 80 percent of roster minimum • 50 percent paid visits	• Regional • Paid visits on case by case	• Mail and phone • No paid visits
Practice and contest facilities	• State of the art • Exclusive use	• Above average • Year-round priority use	• Adequate • In-season priority use	• Adequate • In-season priority use
Equipment and supplies	• Fully funded • Yearly apparel replacement	• Fully funded • 2-year apparel replacement	• Athletes buy implements and shoes • 3-year apparel replacement	• Athletes buy implements and shoes • 4-year apparel replacement
Practice and contest scheduling	• Full schedule, national • Full nontraditional season • Championship funding	• Full schedule, national • Full nontraditional season • Championship funding	• Full schedule, regional • Limited nontraditional season • Championship funding	• Full schedule, regional • Limited nontraditional season • Championship funding
Travel and daily allowances	• Fly over 250 miles (400 km) • Bus less than 250 miles • Full per diem	• Fly over 400 miles (650 km) • Bus less than 400 miles • 80 percent per diem	• Bus over 150 miles (250 km) • Vans less than 150 miles • 80 percent per diem	• Vans only • 80 percent per diem
Tutors and academic support services	• Full access to athlete study hall facility and staff	• Full access to athlete study hall facility and staff	• Access to study hall facility and staff case by case	• Access to study hall facility and staff case by case
Housing and dining facilities	• Athlete dorms • Training table	• Same as other undergrads	• Same as other undergrads	• Same as other undergrads
Medical and training facilities	• Exclusive access to weight room and strength coaches • Practice and game medical staff	• Priority use of university weight room • Practice and game medical staff	• Priority use of university weight room • Practice and game student trainers	• Priority use of university weight room • Practice and game student trainers
Publicity	• Media guides • Full SID coverage • TV and radio	• Media guides • Full SID coverage	• Media guides • Student SID services	• Media guides

team to have moved into the top tier. Over a number of years, a team can develop a fan base of students, parents, boosters, community members, and alumni and become a source of pride for the institution. When that occurs, the expectation is that the administration will continue to support that team at almost any cost to preserve competitive excellence. Unfortunately, consistent, long-term success has not always been a prerequisite. One or two winning seasons can cause a sense of euphoria among constituents. The result is increased pressure on the institution to devote more resources to that team.

Leadership Influence A long-term analysis of the high school or university administration's support of athletics and the specific sport interests of principals, presidents, school boards, or trustees usually provides insight into why specific teams are more highly funded than others. A new administrator may arrive on campus and almost immediately reallocate resources to a program that he or she thinks will bring pride and notoriety to the institution. The same practices hold true for athletic directors. Many athletic directors have coached a specific sport for several years before going into administration and may be inclined to support that sport wherever they work.

Ability of a Coach The extraordinary ability and commitment of an individual coach who has put considerable time, energy, and effort into promoting his or her sport may be another reason why a particular team has risen to the top of the tiered structure. Some coaches are exceptional motivators who have the kind of charisma and energy that creates a sense of campus and community excitement. Athletes, parents, boosters, and alumni of the sport become devoted advocates for the growth and development of the team and its performance. The slightest amount of competitive success makes this group hungrier for additional resources. Their enthusiasm can spill over into the administration or put pressure on the administration and be a catalyst for increased funding to the program. Additional funds may come in small increments along with slight increases in expectations of success. Before anyone realizes it, the program is being funded at the tier I level, and the expectation to continue that amount of support exists.

Keeping Up With the Joneses How a high school and university's competitors are funding their athletic programs could have an effect on the tier structure. If institutional administrators think that successfully competing in athletics with a set of peer schools is important, decisions that they make about which sports to support at a higher level may be in direct response to what those schools are doing. This practice is prevalent among many institutions that are competitive in Division I football and basketball. Cedric Dempsey, former president of the NCAA, called it the "ever-growing arms race," which is still a topic of discussion today and the focus of the 2009 Knight Commission study of Division I college athletics. Dempsey purported that administrative decisions at Division I are often based on a spend-to-win mentality and have less to do with what is best for student-athletes (quoted in Brown, 2000, p. 14). We contend that, over the years, this mentality has trickled down to many college and high school programs and continues to do so.

Attracting Students Another reason why some private high schools and universities may have promoted one sport over another is to appeal to a specific type of student. If the institution is expensive, coaches may need to attract a high percentage of students who have the ability to pay. Certain sports like golf and equestrian are extremely costly to the participant. A high percentage of student-athletes who participate in these sports tend to come from higher socioeconomic backgrounds. By providing excellent competitive opportunities in those sports, the institution may fulfill one of its business objectives of attracting more full-paying students.

Facilities The quality of an institution's athletic facilities may be another factor that contributes to the creation of tiers. For example, if an institution has a rowing team but the river that they practice and compete on is 35 minutes from campus, the team may not have been able to create the kind of campus and alumni support needed to provide the rationale for increased funding. Conversely, if the river is at the base of the campus and is a focal point of the city, the rowing program may have evolved as a premier sport for the university and the local community.

Many other reasons may account for why certain sports have risen or fallen in the tiered athletic program structure at each university. Understanding those reasons is essential before administrators can evaluate whether the model is still a good fit with the current university mission and the goals and objectives of the athletic department.

Section 4: Evaluating the Current Athletic Program Model

The next step is to assess whether the current tiered model is compatible with the mission, goals, and objectives that have already been identified. In essence, the following questions must be answered:

1. How well does the current athletic program model reflect and accomplish the current educational and business objectives?
2. Are the objectives clearly delineated and prioritized for each tier? Are there defensible rationales for the differences in tier objectives and team expectations?
3. Have the objectives been clearly communicated to all constituents (student-athletes, coaches, faculty, alumni, the media, and so on)?
4. Are operational strategies in place to support attainment of stated objectives?

While wrestling with these questions and matching objectives to tiers, the administration may find that the existing model does not adequately support the desired program goals. At that point, the focus of analysis should switch to how the current model could be restructured to accommodate goal attainment. This process, in and of itself, is a time-consuming exercise that would need input from a multitude of sources. Determining what the ramifications would be if significant changes to the athletic program are needed can be a daunting task. The process would be relatively easy if all decisions led to providing additional resources for specific sports and not placing new limitations on any team. Of course, this circumstance assumes that the administration has sound justification for increased funding to athletics that would gain the support of the student body, school board, trustees, faculty, and alumni.

The harder choices occur when the decision is to pare down spending and create additional tiers, widen the funding gap between tiers, or drop sports. One of the mistakes often made during the decision-making process is that administrators do not include the concerns of constituents who will be most affected by the change. A prudent strategy is to give coaches, current athletes, their parents, school boards, trustees, and alumni the opportunity to have input before final decisions are made.

As is frequently reported in the media, schools announce plans to cut programs, elevate programs to a higher competitive division, move into new conferences, or realign tiers to create levels of treatment matching new aspirations. Oftentimes, institutions must change some of their initial decisions after trustees, athletes, or alumni create an unpredicted amount of dissension. For instance, a prominent Division I state university announces aspirations to build a nationally competitive football program and drops five sports to shift financial resources to football to enable that to occur. It is difficult to anticipate the effort that will be needed to mend the relationships that may have been compromised during the announced or actual change.

Dropping sports is one of the hardest decisions that administrators can make. In many cases, adjusting tiers by lowering benefits that are provided in the bottom tier and placing sports slated to be dropped there is a better alternative. Administrators should examine the existing tiers and decide which variables cost the most. Adjustment of those variables may allow expenses to be reduced and participation opportunities to be preserved. For instance, table 4.4.3 is an example of a four-tier athletic program. Tier II or III could be eliminated and more sports could be placed in the bottom tier. Or, tiers II and III could be eliminated and a new tier that has lower limits than tier II but slightly higher limits than tier III could be created in their place.

Section 5: Gender Equitable Participation Opportunities in a Tiered Model

After the athletic staff has created the tiers based on current program practices, an evaluation of which teams occupy each tier is essential. This exercise is significant in measuring whether the athletic program is providing participation opportunities in a gender-equitable way under Title IX. Title IX, a federal law that was passed in 1972, states, "No person in the United States shall, on the basis of sex, be excluded from participation in, be denied the benefits of, or be subjected to discrimination under any educational program or activity receiving Federal financial assistance" (20 U.S.C. §1681 et seq. ["Title IX"]).

In section 1, 12 of the 13 elements that must be assessed to measure compliance with Title IX were used to identify current practices that could aid in the delineation of funding tiers. This section will focus on the first variable, Element 1: Participation Opportunities, and the distribution of teams among tiers.

In athletics, compliance with the "accommodation of interest and abilities" or "participation opportunities" standard under Title IX can be achieved in three ways, often referred to as the three-prong test: proportionality, accommodation of interest and ability, and demonstrating a history of expansion of teams for the underrepresented sex. Following is an explanation of the three prongs. Each explanation assumes that women are the underrepresented sex.

The Proportionality Standard (Prong 1)

The test of proportionality, commonly referred to as the prong 1 option of the Title IX participation standard, is the easiest way to measure equitable participation opportunities. If the percentage of male athletes and female athletes is the same as the percentage of male students and female students on campus, an athletic program has met the proportionality standard of Title IX. For universities, only full-time undergraduates would be counted to determine population size. Table 4.4.4 is an example of a three-tier model that places teams in tiers along with the corresponding roster size. If the composition of students on campus is 50 percent male and 50 percent female, the participation opportunities depicted in table 4.4.4 demonstrate Title IX compliance based on the proportionality test. If the population is 56 percent female and 44 percent male, however, the proportionality standard has not been met. If meeting the proportionality test is the goal of this institution and the male athlete population of 207 participants is to be preserved, 56 more participation opportunities for female athletes would need to be provided.

Besides providing more opportunities, the administration should be cognizant of adding teams to the appropriate tier. In table 4.4.4,

Table 4.4.4 Placement of Teams in a Three-Tier Athletic Program to Meet the Proportionality Standard at a 50 Percent Male, 50 Percent Female Institution (Student Population = 50 Percent Male and 50 Percent Female)

Tier I	Tier II	Tier III
M football (85)	M soccer (24)	M tennis (12)
M basketball (15)	W soccer (24)	W tennis (12)
W basketball (15)	M swimming (20)	M track (22)
W lacrosse (27)	W swimming (20)	W track (22)
W crew (32)	M fencing (15)	M volleyball (14)
W field hockey (26)	W volleyball (15)	W squash (14)
Total: 100 males, 100 females	Total: 59 males, 59 females	Total: 48 males, 48 females
TOTAL ATHLETE POPULATION = 207 MALES (50 PERCENT) AND 207 FEMALES (50 PERCENT)		

approximately 48 percent of all male and female athletes participate on tier I teams, 29 percent participate on tier II teams, and 23 percent participate on tier III teams. Assuming that the administration would elect to leave male teams in the tiers they currently occupy, those same percentages would have to be maintained as female teams were added.

Table 4.4.5 demonstrates how teams could be added to ensure that an athletic program could still meet the proportionality standard if the student population is 56 percent female and 44 percent male. Maintaining equal percentages in each tier is representative of equal treatment.

Note that Title IX law does not mandate that the same male and female teams be placed in the same tiers. In other words, an institution could offer men's basketball and women's volleyball in tier I while placing women's basketball in tier II or III. Similarly, as demonstrated in table 4.4.4, women's volleyball occupies tier II and men's volleyball occupies tier III.

A dilemma that has plagued high school and university administrators is determining how close to the actual proportionality measure an institution has to be to attain compliance. The findings of court cases have resulted in mixed messages. Each regional court's application of the law to the specific circumstances of each institution causes this variation. The size of the athletic program alone could result in different findings. But that does not mean that there is or should be a wide range of variance in the proportionality measure. According to the Office of Civil Rights 1996 Clarification,

> participation is considered substantially proportionate to enrollment when the number of opportunities that would be required to achieve substantial proportionality is not sufficient to sustain a viable team, i.e., a team for which there is a sufficient number of interested and able students and enough available competition to sustain an intercollegiate team. (para. 17)

For example, if an athletic program has 400 total athletes and the overall student population is 52 percent female and 48 percent male, under the proportionality standard the athletic population should include 208 female athletes (52 percent) and 192 male athletes (48 percent). If this athletic program has 200 female athletes

Table 4.4.5 Placement of Teams in a Three-Tier Athletic Program to Meet the Proportionality Standard at a 44 Percent Male, 56 Percent Female Institution (Student Population = 44 Percent Male, 56 Percent Female)

Tier I	Tier II	Tier III
M football (85)	M soccer (24)	M tennis (12)
M basketball (15)	W soccer (24)	W tennis (12)
W basketball (15)	M swimming (20)	M track (22)
W lacrosse (27)	W swimming (20)	W track (22)
W crew (32)	M fencing (15)	M volleyball (14)
W field hockey (26)	W fencing (16)	W squash (14)
W softball (25)	W volleyball (15)	W cross country (12)
Tier total: 100 males, 125 females	Tier total: 59 males, 75 females	Tier total: 48 males, 60 females
Percentage of gender: 48 percent male, 48 percent female	Percentage of gender: 29 percent male, 29 percent female	Percentage of gender: 23 percent male, 23 percent female
TOTAL ATHLETE POPULATION = 207 MALES (44 PERCENT) AND 263 FEMALES (56 PERCENT)		

and 200 male athletes (a 50–50 split), it would need 15 additional participation opportunities for females to reach actual proportionality. At that point, the institution would have to determine whether a viable team could be established with 15 participation opportunities.

Roster management is one strategy that some institutions use to reach actual proportionality. This practice allows female teams to carry a few more players on their rosters compared with male teams or limits roster sizes for male teams. In the previous example, if this institution had 10 female teams, it could meet the proportionality standard by adding 1 or 2 players to the rosters of the female teams that are already offered to reach the target of 15 additional players. Care must be taken, however, to ensure that the women's team roster sizes are reasonable expectations that do not result in discriminatory treatment of women. Later in the book, Management Tip 11.3 addresses proper and improper use of roster management.

A History of Continued Expansion (Prong 2) A second way for an institution to comply with participation opportunities under Title IX law is to show a history and continuing practice of expansion for the underrepresented gender. This method is commonly referred to as the prong 2 option of the Title IX participation standard. To use this prong, the institution must show (1) that no decline has occurred in participation of the underrepresented sex since Title IX went into effect (1975) (other than normal fluctuations resulting from larger or smaller graduating or recruiting classes) and (2) that expansion has been occurring every two or three years over this period to reflect continuing practice. Using this means of compliance can be somewhat problematic because a time may come when expansion is complete. At that point an institution must meet either the proportionality standard or the accommodation of interest and ability standard. Continued expansion is more realistically used as a means to reach prong 1 or prong 3. Therefore, while expanding the athletic program for the underrepresented sex, institutional administrators need to know whether meeting the proportionality measure or the interest and ability measure is the ultimate goal.

While adding teams, an institution has to be mindful of where teams need to be placed in its tiered model. Because both accommodation of interest and proportionality are based on percentages of athletes in each tier, an analysis of which tier needs additional participation opportunities is essential before sports are added. In other words, all new female teams cannot be added at the tier III level if the percentages of opportunities for females in tiers I and II are not representative of equity under the applicable prong.

A review of court cases indicates that institutions have been found to be in compliance with the participation standards of Title IX using any one of the three prongs. A misperception in the athletic community is that the proportionality standard is really the only true measure that the Office of Civil Rights uses to evaluate cases. Although the proportionality test is the easiest way to assess compliance, it is not the only measure. Many institutions found in compliance with the participation opportunities standards of Title IX did so under the accommodation of interest and ability or the history of expansion standards. However, it is important to note that assessing interest is a rigorous process explained in section 6 in this chapter. Additionally, if an institution has ever dropped a women's sport it cannot use prong 2 or prong 3. Similarly, if an institution has not expanded opportunities for women in any three-year period, it cannot use prong 2 as justification for compliance.

Full Accommodation of Interest and Ability (Prong 3) The third way to comply with Title IX is more complex. In essence, this standard requires that the institution demonstrate that the athletic program has fully met the interest and ability of the underrepresented sex. This method is commonly referred to as the prong 3 option of the Title IX participation standard. In other words, if an athletic program has a higher percentage of male athletes than male students, the administrators must prove that the institution is offering all the sports to females in which they have interest and ability. This condition can be assessed through a variety of means. In the case of universities or private schools that recruit student-athletes, the assessment must include evaluating the interest and ability of females who are prospective student-athletes as well as current students.

The rationale for measuring the interest of females who are prospective student-athletes is clear. If an institution does not offer a sport, athletes who are interested in that sport may not elect to attend that institution and, in essence, will self-select themselves out of the pool. Therefore, limiting the scope of interest to current female students attending the institution is not a true measure of what the interest would be if the sport were offered.

Evaluating prospective student-athlete interest and ability can be a relatively easy process. One of the easiest and more comprehensive ways is to assess which high school sports for girls are offered in the areas from which the institution recruits students. For example, if an institution's student population is heavily recruited from the Northeast, high interest and ability in the sport of girls' field hockey likely exists. That circumstance may not hold true if most of an institution's students came from public schools in the Southwest where field hockey is almost nonexistent in public schools. If the institution recruits its students from all over the country, a good way to identify new sports might be to evaluate NCAA championship sports or conference championship sports not already offered by the institution.

As an additional means of measuring interest and ability of prospective female athletes, some institutions include questions on the standard admissions inquiry card that ask what sports the prospective student would like to participate in if he or she matriculates. Universities would be prudent to ask what level of experience and success the applicant has in the sport.

Institutions can measure interest and ability of females who are already part of the student body in several ways. One way is to investigate whether there has been a history of females requesting the addition of sports not already offered. A second way is to assess participation rates and ability levels of participants in female club sports. The third and more comprehensive way is to conduct a campuswide survey that measures interest as well as previous experience and levels of success in each sport.

Universities must make every effort to evaluate the athletic ability of females who indicate an interest in a sport. According to the National Federation of State High School Associations, 3,402,733 girls participated in high school sports in 2018–19. In the same year, 218,657 women participated in intercollegiate sports at NCAA member institutions (NCAA). Therefore, it is safe to assume that the majority of athletes at four-year colleges are more often recruited from the top 7 percent of the high school talent pool. Title IX does not mandate that an institution offer sports in which interest is high but ability is not up to the expectation of that particular athletic program. For example, if the results of a campuswide survey indicate that 40 women would be interested in an intercollegiate lacrosse team but none has played past the eighth grade, the ability level may not be high enough to create the need to institute a lacrosse team. This measure is less important when assessing prospective athletes because most coaches conduct targeted recruiting and pursue only student-athletes who have the ability to play at the collegiate level. But if a coach and the university are limited to recruiting prospective students in a small geographic area and the high school talent pool in that sport is not large enough to play at the competitive level articulated by the institution, the measure of ability for prospective student-athletes may apply.

Another caveat is relevant to the accommodation of interest standard. An institution is not expected to add a new sport for the underrepresented gender if no competition in that sport is available in the region where the institution normally competes. For example, if through the investigative process an institution learns that there is considerable interest and ability in the sport of fencing, that institution would not be required to add fencing if there are not enough fencing teams to compete against in their region. If an institution sends its teams nationwide to compete, however, this condition would not apply.

After an institution has undergone the process of measuring interest and ability and has met the goal of meeting participation opportunities through accommodation of interest and ability, the placement of teams in tiers still needs to be considered. Table 4.4.6 is an example of how teams with their corresponding roster sizes could be placed in a three-tier model under a program that has met prong 2 or prong 3.

Table 4.4.6 Placement of Teams in a Three-Tier Athletic Program to Meet the Requirements of Prong 2 or Prong 3 (Athlete Population = 207 Males and 187 Females)

Tier I	Tier II	Tier III
M football (85)	M soccer (24)	M tennis (11)
M basketball (15)	W soccer (24)	W tennis (11)
W basketball (15)	M swimming (20)	M track (22)
W lacrosse (27)	W fencing (16)	W track (22)
W softball (22)	M fencing (15)	M volleyball (15)
W field hockey (26)	W volleyball (14)	W squash (10)
Tier total: 100 males, 90 females	Tier total: 59 males, 54 females	Tier total: 48 males, 43 females
Percentage of gender: 48 percent male, 48 percent female	Percentage of gender: 29 percent male, 29 percent female	Percentage of gender: 23 percent male, 23 percent female

Table 4.4.6 shows that an institution has 207 male athletes and 187 female athletes. To comply with Title IX under the accommodation of interest test, although there is no requirement related to the proportion of male and female students in the general student population, each tier must have the same percentage of athletes as the overall population for male and female athletes to ensure equality of treatment and benefits. As shown, tier I sports for males include 48 percent of the overall male athlete population. Similarly, tier I sports for females must include 48 percent of the female athlete population. As demonstrated, this calculation applies to population percentages of male and female athletes in tiers II and III as well.

Section 6: Gender Neutral Policies and Practices by Tier

At this point in the process, the basic model, including how many tiers are in place and how teams occupy the tiers, should be completed. Going forward, a multitude of other policy decisions must be made that will help delineate any difference in philosophical principles and practical procedures that exist between the tiers. The types of decisions that must be addressed are separated into the following categories and continue to reflect a process that promotes gender equity.

Distributing Scholarship Dollars Simply stated, allotment of athletic scholarships is a dollar-for-dollar requirement under Title IX law (Bonnette, 2000, p. 1). This measure is attached to the percentages of males and females in the athlete population. Assuming that an institution is in compliance with participation standards under the proportionality test or the accommodation of interest and ability test described earlier, the allotment of scholarship dollars is a simple calculation. First, percentages of males and females must be calculated using an unduplicated count. Multisport athletes can be counted only once. For example, and assuming that there are no multisport athletes, if an institution is in compliance with the proportionality standard and their athlete population mirrors the full-time undergraduate population of 52 percent women and 48 percent men, 52 percent of the scholarship money would go to women and 48 percent to men. Similarly, if an institution is in compliance with the participation standard under the accommodation of interest measure and its athlete population is 53 percent men and 47 percent women, men would receive 53 percent of the scholarship dollars and women would receive 47 percent.

The analysis of scholarship allotments is a bit trickier if an institution is in the process of adding teams. Planning for scholarship allotments while adding teams reinforces the point made earlier requiring that an administrator know whether the ultimate goal for participation is to reach the proportionality standard or the interest and ability standard. For example, an institution has determined that it is adding women's teams to meet the accommodation of interest and ability standard, which would be met when the athlete population becomes 53 percent men and 47 percent women. If women were already receiving 47 percent of the scholarship dollars despite being only 40 percent of the population, then no new scholarship money would be provided for new women's teams. Conversely, if the current female athlete population is 40 percent of the overall athlete population and females are receiving only 32 percent of the scholarship money, the institution is already out of compliance with Title IX and should be adding scholarship money to the current population as well as more scholarship funding when new women's teams are added to reach the needed allotment of 47 percent of the scholarship money going to female athletes.

Under Title IX, allotment of scholarship money is calculated programwide. In other words, in a tiered model keeping scholarship dollar percentages equal between men and women within the same tier is not required. In fact, a review of the limitations that the National Collegiate Athletic Association (NCAA, 2020) places on the maximum number of scholarships allowable in each sport could make an institution's ability to balance scholarships within each tier difficult, especially if the institution sponsors football (pp. 219–23).

As an example of the dilemma faced by administrators, table 4.4.7 is a reconstruction of table 4.4.4, which accommodates an athletic program that has 50 percent men and 50 percent women. Scholarship allotments have been added with the assumption that scholarships don't differ for out-of-state and in-state students. In this case, the scholarship money should be split evenly between men and women. For the teams in table 4.4.2, let's assume that the athletic department is Division I and has attempted to create scholarship funding policies that have three conditions: (1) All tier I sports have funding to satisfy the maximum scholarship limits allowable under NCAA rules, (2) all tier II sports have funding to satisfy 50 percent of the maximum scholarship limits allowable under NCAA rules,

Table 4.4.7 Inequitable Team-by-Team Scholarship Allotments in a Three-Tier Model (207 Male Athletes and 207 Female Athletes, Unduplicated Count)

Tier I	Tier II	Tier III
M football (85)	M soccer (4.45)	M tennis (0)
M basketball (13)	W soccer (6)	W tennis (0)
W basketball (15)	M swimming (4.45)	M track (0)
W lacrosse (12)	W swimming (7)	W track (0)
W crew (20)	M fencing (2.25)	M volleyball (0)
W field hockey (12)	W volleyball (6)	W squash (0)
Scholarship total: 98 men's, 59 women's	Scholarship total: 11.15 men's, 19 women's	Scholarship total: 0 men's, 0 women's
SCHOLARSHIP TOTAL BY SEX: 109.5 MEN'S AND 78 WOMEN'S		

and (3) no athletic scholarships will be provided for tier III sports.

As demonstrated in table 4.4.7, under the current policy statements this institution could not possibly allot 50 percent of the scholarship dollars to women. A solution would be to change the second and third policy statement as follows: (2) All tier II sports have some scholarship funding up to the maximum allowable under NCAA rules, and (3) all tier III sports will be allotted some scholarship funding up to 40 percent of the maximum allowable under NCAA rules. Table 4.4.8 reflects a three-tiered program that would now be consistent with the established policies for scholarship allotment.

With a creative approach to policy making, equity regarding distribution of scholarship dollars can be achieved. Current NCAA legislation, however, may make this difficult at many institutions and, in essence, thwart the desire to treat female athletes and male athletes who occupy teams in lower tiers fairly. How and why has this happened? Two factors have contributed to this problem:

1. **Disparity in scholarship limits.** Historically, scholarship limits in football and basketball have been significantly higher than limits in other sports. These limits reflect the mentality of major versus minor sports. The maximum number of basketball scholarships poses less of a problem because both men and women compete in the sport. But philosophically it is hard to understand why almost every other sport has scholarship limits that equal the size of a starting lineup plus a few more for significant reserves whereas football and basketball have limits that are two to three times the size of the starting lineup. Football coaches argue that high injury rates necessitate having many athletes on the roster. According to Andrew Zimbalist (2002), an analysis of data from the NCAA Injury Surveillance Summary reports does not indicate that injury rates reinforce the need for 85 scholarships. He calls this argument a red herring. Over the past few years, in an effort to try to balance these scholarship offerings, the NCAA limits have risen for many women's sports while scholarship limits in men's minor sports have stayed the same or decreased. This strategy has been at best a Band-Aid approach to the problem. The reality is that excess spending on football continues not only to compromise gender equity but also to reduce access to scholarship dollars for males on lower-tier teams.

Table 4.4.8 Equitable Team-by-Team Scholarship Allotments in a Three-Tier Model (207 Male Athletes and 207 Female Athletes, Unduplicated Count)

Tier I	Tier II	Tier III
M football (85)	M soccer (2)	M tennis (1)
M basketball (13)	W soccer (12)	W tennis (3)
W basketball (15)	M swimming (2)	M track (1)
W lacrosse (12)	W swimming (14)	W track (4)
W crew (20)	M fencing (2)	M volleyball (1)
W field hockey (12)	W volleyball (12)	W squash (3)
Scholarship total: 98 men's, 59 women's	Scholarship total: 6 men's, 38 women's	Scholarship total: 3 men's, 10 women's
SCHOLARSHIP TOTAL BY SEX: 107 MEN'S AND 107 WOMEN'S		

2. **Different ways of measuring scholarship offerings.** Scholarship offerings for some sports are calculated as a head count, whereas other sports are permitted to offer scholarships that are equivalency based. The head-count measure means that each athlete who receives any athletic scholarship, even a partial scholarship, is counted in the number allowable. An equivalency-based scholarship allows coaches to divide the total amount of money allotted and offer it to as many athletes as they wish. Football and basketball are included in the head-count sports. Institutions could save a significant amount of money and provide more scholarship dollars for female athletes and males in lower-tier sports if the NCAA would reduce the allotted scholarship numbers in football and basketball and change them to equivalency-based sports.

Another problem related to the distribution of scholarships occurs when in-state tuition differs from out-of-state tuition. Theoretically, if policies are not discriminatory regarding the allotment of in-state versus out-of-state scholarships between men and women, programwide equity should be attainable. But in some situations more out-of-state scholarship dollars are needed to secure an adequate base of talent in one or more sports. If this situation relates primarily to a team or teams of one gender, a large disparity could develop in dollar-for-dollar equity. Administrators would have to be prepared to defend this perceived inequity as resulting from unique circumstances rather than gender-biased practices or policies.

Defining the Scope and the Expectations of the Recruiting Process As society's passion for winning sport teams grows, so does the pressure on coaches to attract the most talented athletes to their institutions. Even at smaller institutions, recruiting is one of the most significant parts of a coach's job. In a tiered athletic program model, the expectations and the level of funding provided to recruit players might differ between tiers. A correlation is usually present between the expectation of a team's success and the support provided for recruiting. Defining the scope and the expectations of the recruiting process for each tier is essential. Before that can be done, however, the administration must address a few philosophical questions:

- *What percentage of athletes should be recruited versus walking on from the student body?* Institutional administrators need to decide whether there is value associated with having athletes who are true representatives of the student body in contrast to those who have selected the institution largely because of the athletic program. Walk-on athletes can enhance the feeling of connection that nonathlete students feel toward teams. Walk-ons may also be less willing to devote all their time to athletics and, by example, can help a team reject the notion that they are or should be an isolated, elitist subgroup.
- *What percentage of athletes should be admitted under a policy that establishes special-talent slots?* It is no secret that colleges and universities have established practices that allow students who have special talents to matriculate even if they do not meet the prescribed academic requirements for admission. According to Shulman and Bowen (2001), these practices have filtered down from the large Division I programs and are prevalent among some of the most prestigious liberal arts institutions in the country. Administrators must confront the issues that surround the proliferation of special-talent slots. Additionally, Bowen and Levin contend that these athletes underperform academically more than they would have been expected to based on their incoming credentials (2011). Questions arise as to whether these athletes create an ethos that permits less attention or effort toward academics and subsequently reinforce the dumb-jock stereotype for all athletes. In addition, the administration must be prepared to offer academic services to enhance the ability of an academically underprepared student-athlete to succeed in the classroom. All these services cost money and must be considered as part of the equation.
- *What are the recruiting goals of the university or private school, and how should athletic recruiting support those goals?* One of the greatest components of sport is that

it is open to people from a variety of backgrounds. An educational institution may have better success attracting foreign students or ethnically diverse students by recruiting them into its athletic programs rather than through the regular recruiting process. Administrators may be wise to recognize and support those potential connections. In addition, for private schools and small colleges that have difficulty attracting enough students to meet their needed class size, athletic recruitment can play a significant role in fulfilling those objectives.

After these questions have been answered, athletic administrators must clearly delineate what the recruiting scope and expectations are within each tier. For example, because tier I teams are usually the most visible programs and are expected to be successful, they may have a budget that supports international recruiting. The full complement of coaches can possibly be on the road assessing and meeting with prospects whenever possible. Tier I teams may hold the majority of special-talent slots permitted, and the expectation may be that all athletes on the rosters are recruited. Tier II teams may be limited to recruiting regionally, have only a handful of special-talent slots, and be expected to leave 25 percent of their roster open for walk-ons. Tier III teams may have part-time coaches who do not have much time to recruit, and the expectation may be that they attract one or two impact players a year.

Regardless of what decisions are made pertaining to the scope and expectations of recruiting within each tier, they must be made in concert with other considerations. The availability of scholarship dollars, assignment of coaches, quality of facilities, and rigors of schedule are other factors that will undoubtedly affect recruiting.

Designing Coaches' Employment and Compensation Systems Designing employment and compensation systems for coaches is a complex process that requires input from a variety of administrative sources. Most universities and high schools have policies in place that must be adhered to regarding hiring, evaluation, termination, affirmative action, and the like. At some public institutions, salary scales are prescribed by the state. Unfortunately, this area is another in which many athletic departments have been permitted to work in a vacuum, and they have not been held to the same procedural standards as other campus departments. Therefore, the human resource director should be included in the process of creating or redesigning employment and compensation systems by tier.

Title IX law addresses "whether an institution has allocated sufficient resources to provide coaches who are equally qualified and equally available to female and male athletes" (*Achieving Gender Equity*, p. II-16). In other words, employment and compensation is analyzed by how it affects students rather than the employees themselves. If an employee wanted to claim gender discrimination during the hiring process, salary negotiations, termination, and so on, he or she would most likely refer to Title VII of the Civil Rights Act of 1964 or the Equal Pay Act. As a practical matter, if a complaint is lodged with the Office of Civil Rights regarding salary discrimination based on sex, it will usually be referred to the United States Equal Employment Opportunity Commission.

Many factors must be considered when determining how employment and compensation systems will or will not differ from tier to tier and how to ensure that they are meeting the provisions of gender equitable coach availability and quality for men's and women's teams in each tier. Several salient issues must be addressed:

- *How many coaches will be employed for each team?* This question can be answered in many ways. An institution may determine that tier I teams will be provided with the maximum allowable number of coaches under NCAA regulations, tier II teams will have a head coach and one assistant, and tier III teams will have a head coach only. Another solution may be to have a policy stating that every team has a head coach and will be assigned assistant coaches on an athlete-to-coach ratio of 1:12. That policy could apply to all teams regardless of tier, or the policy could include a 1:10 ratio for tier I teams, a 1:15 ratio for tier II teams, and a 1:20 ratio for tier III teams. This approach is an example of a truly gender neutral policy based on sheer numbers.

- *What will the provisions be for head and assistant coaches regarding full-time versus part-time employment and length of employment contracts (10 months, 12 months, multiyear)?* Part-time or full-time status of a coach is a significant factor pertaining to the availability of the coach to the athletes. Therefore, this measure should be consistent within tiers. For the higher-profile sports, all coaches may be expected to be 12-month employees, whereas lower-tier sports may have more part-time coaches. The consideration of multiyear contracts versus annual contracts would be a hiring incentive and may be reserved for coaches in higher tiers.
- *Will job descriptions and expectations for coaches be different?* This question is a critical element in designing coaches' employment packages that are fair, legal, and attend to gender equity. As discussed earlier in this chapter, different funding levels for each tier create a different set of expectations for the coaches. If the job or performance expectations of coaches are not different, creating tiered salary, benefits, and perquisite structures would be difficult. All these expectations must be articulated in the job descriptions and tied to compensation. For example, if tier I coaches are supposed to develop booster groups or fan clubs and coaches in other tiers are not expected to do so, that expectation should be clearly stated in the job descriptions and used as a rationale for pay differences between tiers. The expectation should be consistent among all tier I coaches. The second important part of this process is monitoring whether job and performance expectations are effectively being met. Athletic administrators are on shaky ground when they pay big salaries to coaches who do not meet the job or performance expectations specified in their contracts.

Additional responsibilities included in a coach's job description are another area that must be analyzed. An institution may decide that tier I coaches do not have to perform any duties outside those expected from coaching, whereas lower-tier coaches may have to teach physical education classes. Problems result when some coaches in the same tier have to perform a second duty, without additional compensation, while others don't. Another problem occurs when an administrative job, such as associate athletic director, is reserved as a second assignment for a tier I coach but is always given to the football coach regardless of whether other tier I coaches have better credentials to fill the post. This discriminatory hiring practice is often used as a strategy to inflate the salary of a specific coach.

- *Will differences occur in how the search process for coaches is conducted?* Many institutions already have policies in place that address employee levels and the extent to which more expensive national searches can be conducted. For example, according to the policies and procedures manual at Drew University (2001), a national search for a staff member can be conducted only for those at director level or higher. Special permission from a vice president must be obtained before a national search can be conducted for other employees.

In concert with their human resources department, institutions may want to develop the same types of policies in their athletic departments. National searches might be approved for the top two tiers, and regional searches might be the norm for lower tiers. After search policies are developed, administrators need to be careful not to compromise them. For example, too often athletic administrators conduct an extensive national search for a tier I men's basketball coach with the intention of getting the best possible candidate. The same administrator may look only around the corner for the tier I women's basketball coach. After not attracting a coach of the same quality for the women's program, the administrator will use the experience factor as justification to pay the women's coach significantly less.

- *What minimum qualifications will be required for coaches by tier? Will the preferred qualifications differ?* All job descriptions must include the qualifications that are required of any applicant. Additionally, many job descriptions also define preferred qualifications. Determining how these qualifications will differ for coaches in separate tiers is important in the employment process. For example, the number of years of experience as a head coach required for tier I coaches may be higher than that for coaches in other tiers. If coaches in tier II or tier III are expected to teach, they may be required to have a master's degree, and a PhD may be preferred. Measures that indicate prior coaching success (championships, coach of the year awards, and so on) are often included as necessary or preferred qualifications to support the salary differences between coaches in different tiers. As stated many times in this manual, there is no perfect model. Each institution has to decide what skills are necessary for a coach to be deemed qualified to meet the performance expectations defined for each tier.

- *What procedures will be used to determine salary and benefits? Will those procedures differ by tier?* Procedures for determining salary and benefits can differ dramatically from institution to institution. Many high schools and state colleges have a step system in place that clearly defines salary, annual increments based on the number of years of experience, and a standard benefits package available to all full-time employees. Other institutions may have the flexibility to negotiate salaries, include evaluation of merit in annual increases, and offer perquisites that go beyond the standard benefit package. Athletic administrators need to know what university parameters may exist regarding salary and benefit negotiations and design a compensation model that is compatible with the system. In a tiered athletic program, administrators must decide whether different procedures will be used to determine salaries and benefits by tier. In some cases, marketplace value may be a factor used to set a salary for a tier I coach but may not apply to coaches in other tiers. Tier I coaches may have access to bonuses based on team performance as well as country club memberships and other perquisites that are not available to coaches in other tiers. All these criteria should be clearly defined in the employment contract of each coach.

Quality of and Access to Practice and Competitive Facilities The quality of and access to practice and competitive facilities is another significant factor in determining tier distinctions and measuring gender equity. Playing soccer on a beautifully manicured grass field used solely by the soccer team is a different experience from playing on a multiuse field that has ruts and bare spots or on an Astroturf field that is primarily a football facility. Coaches can easily correlate team performance and ability to recruit with the quality of the facility.

The quality of practice and competitive facilities sends a strong message to coaches, athletes, parents, alumni, and fans regarding the commitment that an institution is making to a specific team. Facilities are a visible element that everyone can scrutinize. If the baseball team and the softball team are both tier II programs, but the baseball field has a permanent fence, new dugouts, and a scoreboard and the softball field has benches, no fence, and a flip-card scoring device, it is hard to say that parity exists based on tier distinctions or gender equity.

Facility decisions are often the hardest for administrators to make. Besides being expensive, facilities can quickly become obsolete. In addition, many constituent groups want regular access to athletic facilities. Constructing policies that seem fair to the campus and alumni community yet protect the facility from overuse and additional expense can be difficult at best.

Defining Access to or Quality of Other Program Variables Eight other program areas need to be assessed for compliance under Title IX, and these may have policy implications when constructing tiers. The remaining eight areas are

1. equipment and supplies,
2. scheduling of games and practice time,
3. travel and per diem allowances,
4. tutoring,
5. medical and training facilities,
6. housing and dining facilities and services,
7. publicity, and
8. support services.

After teams have been placed in tiers and the most salient policies have been formed regarding scholarship dollars, recruiting, availability and quality of coaches, and quality of practice and competitive facilities, it is a simpler process to decide whether any of the eight areas listed will have implications that affect tier distinctions or gender equity. The information that was gathered from the analysis of current policies and practices described earlier in this chapter can be used to see whether any outlying practices seem inconsistent with the emerging tiers. For example, let's say that the women's track team has been categorized as a tier I sport based on scholarship limits, recruiting dollars, availability and quality of coaches, and facilities. But the women's track team is the only tier I sport that doesn't have access to a training table. The administration has to decide whether there is a sound reason why this team is not included, and they must analyze whether this practice has implications regarding tier distinctions or gender equity.

Any deviations from policies in tiers must be gender neutral. For example, an administrator could not allow men's teams to stay two to a room in hotels while women's teams stayed three to a room based on the rationale that men are usually bigger and need more space. That policy is clearly not gender neutral. But a policy that states that athletes who are at least 5-feet-10 (178 cm) and 150 pounds (68 kg) will stay two to a room is an acceptable policy if it is applied equally to men and women. All these policy decisions should be practical and defensible.

Remember that Title IX does not dictate the structure of the athletic program in any way. In the November 2000 issue of *Title IX Q & A*, Bonnette states:

> There is no requirement under Title IX that any institution offer an athletic program. Institution officials make that choice. There is no requirement under Title IX that any athletic program offered be at any specific competitive levels such as NCAA Division I, II, or III. Institution officials make that choice. There is no requirement under Title IX that an institution join a particular national or regional athletic conference . . . or that any level of quality athletic program be offered. Institution officials make that choice. There is no requirement under Title IX that any specific benefits be offered in athletic programs regarding equipment, scheduling, modes of transportation, coaching, facilities, training services, housing, publicity, and so on. Institution officials make all of those choices. All Title IX requires is that female and male students be provided an equal opportunity to become intercollegiate athletic participants and that they be provided equal treatment, whatever that level of treatment might be. . . . With the vast number of choices that may be exercised by institution officials under Title IX, the one choice institution officials may not make is this: they may not choose to provide disparate treatment on the basis of sex. (pp. 5–6)

Section 7: Accommodating Differences in Each Tier

One of the questions often asked about a tiered model is whether differences between teams can exist when they occupy the same tier and the ramifications that those differences may have on gender equity. One of the major benefits of creating tiers is to help justify decisions that are made regarding treatment of each team. Therefore, administrators gain an advantage by creating consistent policies that apply to all teams in a tier. Having said that, however, many valid reasons can explain why teams in the same tier may be exempt from certain policies or practices. Three of the more common reasons include the uniqueness of specific sports, the role that marketplace value plays in determining coaches' salaries, and the short-term accommodation of historical inequities.

Uniqueness of Specific Sports When formulating policies that will be applied to teams that occupy a single tier, administrators may find that some of the policies are less applicable to the unique nature of one or more sports. For example, a policy may exist that all teams in tier II are required to travel by 15-passenger vans up to 150 miles (240 km) and may travel by bus to competition sites that are more than 150 miles away. That policy may work well for teams with little equipment, rosters of 26 or fewer, and two coaches who can drive. But in the case of a men's lacrosse team that may carry 40 players, employ two coaches, and have helmets, sticks, and protective equipment to transport, taking buses to all competitions may be more cost effective and realistic than renting four vans and hiring two more drivers. This practice would not be a violation of Title IX as long as the rationale was applied equally to women's teams.

A second example of a policy difference that could be caused by a unique situation may relate to recruiting. If all the teams in a specific tier are funded to recruit regionally only, an exception may be made for a coach to broaden the recruiting scope if the region does not have enough high school programs to create an acceptable talent pool. For instance, the majority of high school field hockey is played in the Northeast and Middle Atlantic regions. Therefore, an institution in the South may decide to increase the recruiting budget for the field hockey program to a level higher than that of any other men's or women's sport in that tier to accommodate this unique difference.

Role of Marketplace According to the United States Equal Employment Opportunity Commission guidelines (1997), marketplace value may be an appropriate defense for paying a coach of a men's team more than a coach of a women's team even if their experience, training, education, ability, job expectations, and working conditions are equivalent. Marketplace value is based on "the employer's consideration of an individual's value when setting wages" (EEOC, 1997, p. 9). In other words, the employer would have to prove that the particular person being recruited and offered the higher salary could not be hired because he or she commanded a higher salary in the marketplace based on current salary or a competitive offer to stay at his or her previous institution. The athletic director could not simply make a statement that whoever was hired for a position would get a higher salary because the marketplace in that sport was more competitive.

Thus, administrators should not attach a specific salary to a position. For example, if the median salary for men's basketball coaches in Division II is $90,000, an athletic director should not automatically pay whoever is hired that amount. Similarly, if the median salary for women's basketball coaches is $60,000, an athletic director would still have to assess the background of the individual. What would happen if the coach of the men's team has less experience and less success than the coach of the women's team? Significant evidence indicates that the pay differential between male and female coaches is a result of long-term discrimination. Therefore, attaching salaries to a position rather than a person would perpetuate discrimination based on sex.

Administrators also must not base a salary offer strictly on the amount that the new hire was paid in his or her last job. Before matching or exceeding that salary, an employer should "(1) consult with the employee's previous employer to determine the basis for the employee's starting and final salary; and (2) determine that the prior salary was an accurate indication of the employee's ability based on education, experience, or other relevant factors" (EEOC, 1997, p. 10).

Short-Term Accommodation of Historical Inequities Allowable accommodation of historical inequities often relates to personnel issues. For example, a coach whose team is placed in a lower tier may be given a salary and perquisites that exceed the identified pay range and the benefits that are normally available to coaches in that tier. This arrangement may be because of the longevity of the coach. Perhaps the coach was hired when that team occupied a higher tier. At any rate, a reasonable expectation is that the university will fulfill its established obligation to this employee with the intention to rectify the situation when a shift in personnel occurs.

A historical inequity may also be relevant when assessing scholarship allocations. If the university elects to reassign a scholarship-granting program to a lower tier, which in turn warrants a reduction or total elimination of scholarships, that team may not be expected to meet the new scholarship limitations until the current athletes have graduated or left the university.

Reasonable accommodations do not apply to discriminatory historical practices that have no effect on an individual's employment package or expectation of an education. For example, if the football team has always stayed in a hotel the night before a home contest and no female athletes have been afforded that opportunity, that arrangement cannot continue as a practice available only to the football team based on a historical inequity. The arrangement would clearly violate gender equity laws.

Other reasons besides the three listed may explain why institutions deviate from policies created for teams that occupy the same tier. The key is to try to build in as much consistency as possible and to deviate only when it makes much better sense to do so. Remember that gender equity assessments are programwide even when operating a tiered model. Some benefits afforded to men may be offset by other benefits afforded to women. For example, if the baseball team has a better scoreboard than any women's team, but a women's team has a better locker room than any men's team, an administrator could argue that these two inequities offset each other. According to Bonnette (2000), "This is acceptable if there is a balance of benefits in the overall intercollegiate athletic program." She cautions, however, that "weighting the effect of different types of benefits is difficult and would be a continuous challenge administratively" (p. 2).

4.6 MANAGEMENT TIP

Due Diligence When Adding New Sports

There are many conditions to be taken into consideration before institutions add new sports. Sport managers should understand the USDOE-OCR (2008) standards for considering an activity a varsity sport. DOE-OCR sent to the Minnesota High School League on April 11, 2000, in response to its inquiry about how to treat cheerleading, a definition of a sport that was reiterated in a 2008 *Dear Colleague* letter. It reads in part:

> In its case-by-case valuation of whether an activity can be counted as an intercollegiate or interscholastic sport for the purpose of Title IX compliance, OCR will consider all of the following factors:
>
> I. Program Structure and Administration—Taking into account the unique aspects inherent in the nature and basic operation of specific sports, OCR considers whether the activity is structured and administered in a manner consistent with established intercollegiate or interscholastic varsity sports in the institution's athletics program, including:
>
> A. Whether the operating budget, support services (including academic, sports medicine, and strength and conditioning support) and coaching staff are administered by the athletics department or another entity, and are provided in a manner consistent with established varsity sports; and
>
> B. Whether the participants in the activity are eligible to receive athletic scholarships and athletic awards (e.g., varsity awards) if available to athletes in established varsity sports; to the extent that an institution recruits participants in its athletics program, whether participants in the activity are recruited in a manner consistent with established varsity sports.
>
> II. Team Preparation and Competition—Taking into account the unique aspects inherent in the nature and basic operation of specific sports, OCR considers whether the team prepares for and engages in competition in a manner consistent with established varsity sports in the institution's intercollegiate or interscholastic athletics program, including:
>
> A. Whether the practice opportunities (e.g., number, length, and quality) are available in a manner consistent with established varsity sports in the institution's athletics program; and
>
> B. Whether the regular season competitive opportunities differ quantitatively and/or qualitatively from established varsity sports; whether the team competes against intercollegiate or interscholastic varsity opponents in a manner consistent with established varsity sports; when analyzing this factor, the following may be taken into consideration:
>
> - Whether the number of competitions and length of play are predetermined by a governing athletics organization, an athletic conference, or a consortium of institutions;
> - Whether the competitive schedule reflects the abilities of the team; and
> - Whether the activity has a defined season; whether the season is determined by a governing athletics organization, an athletic conference, or a consortium.
>
> C. If pre-season and/or post-season competition exists for the activity, whether the activity provides an opportunity for student athletes to engage in the pre-season and/or postseason competition in a manner consistent with established varsity sports; for example, whether state, national, and/or conference championships exist for the activity; and
>
> D. Whether the primary purpose of the activity is to provide athletics competition at the intercollegiate or interscholastic varsity levels rather than to support or promote other athletic activities.

When analyzing this factor, the following may be taken into consideration:

- Whether the activity is governed by a specific set of rules of play adopted by a state, national, or conference organization and/or consistent with established varsity sports, which include objective, standardized criteria by which competition must be judged;
- Whether resources for the activity (e.g., practice and competition schedules, coaching staff) are based on the competitive needs of the team;
- If post-season competition opportunities are available, whether participation in postseason competition is dependent on or related to regular season results in a manner consistent with established varsity sports; and
- Whether the selection of teams/participants is based on factors related primarily to athletic ability.

Please keep in mind that OCR's determinations based on these factors are fact-specific. Therefore, determinations may vary depending on a school district or postsecondary institution's athletics program, the nature of the particular activity, and the circumstances under which it is conducted.

Also noteworthy, as part of the rule-making process for the Equity in Athletics Disclosure Act (EADA), the secretary of education noted in 1999 that schools cannot count cheerleading or drill team members as varsity athletes. The department's guidelines for completing the annual EADA form also expressly state that schools cannot count cheerleading unless they have an approval letter from the DOE-OCR. The NCAA has also long notified its members that they cannot count cheerleading in the athletic participation data that they submit to the NCAA or on the EADA form. This position is printed on the front page of the NCAA data materials.

That being said, an organization, USA Cheer, and within it the College Stunt Association (CSA), is making a concerted effort to follow DOE-OCR guidelines (detailed previously) for counting stunt as a sport in the athletic program. Stunt is being developed as a new competitive team sport derived from cheerleading but removed from the crowd-leading element and focused on the technical and athletic components of cheer, including partner stunts, pyramids, basket tosses, group jumps and tumbling, and team performance. The current stunt competition structure defined by CSA national rules meets one of the definitions of a sport as advanced by OCR. The establishment of a stunt national championship in 2011 was an essential next step in fulfilling definitional requirements. Although it is not possible to assess whether the other OCR definitional requirements are being met until the sport is active on college campuses, a request by CSA is pending for stunt to be placed on the NCAA emerging sport list, a step that may advance this process.

The same status is true of acrobatics and tumbling, a partner sport based on dance, acrobatics, and tumbling defined by USA Gymnastics, most often referred to as acro-tumbling. The NCAA has recognized acrobatics and tumbling as an emerging sport.

Many girls and women who have expressed their stunt and tumbling skills through the student spirit activity of cheerleading do not have the desire to pursue traditional competitive gymnastics because of many factors, such as having to perform tumbling skills with higher levels of risk. The development of stunt or acrobatics and tumbling as a sport alternative can provide an important opportunity for this group. Because many athletic departments are already supporting cheerleading coaches and programs, administrators may be more inclined to add stunt or acrobatic gymnastics as a sport rather than more expensive or unfamiliar alternatives.

In this period of economic downturn and athletic program expense reductions in nonrevenue sports because of pressures of the football and basketball arms race, stunt or acrobatics and tumbling may be one of the few realistic possibilities for reigniting institutional commitments to Title IX compliance—a sorely needed movement. Title IX compliance efforts have stalled over the last decade, as evidenced by the still significant participation gap between male and female athletes. The addition of stunt or acrobatics and gymnastics as an emerging sport in the NCAA program and its eventual recognition by DOE-OCR may help close this gap in the future.

Two excellent resources should be reviewed by the athletic manager considering new sports to be added. The annual NCAA Sports Sponsorship and Participation Rates Report lists all sports sponsored by NCAA member colleges and universities, numbers of participants, average team sizes, and the number of institutions sponsoring the sport in each competitive division. It also lists emerging non–NCAA championship sports. The National Federation of State High School Athletic Associations annually publishes a similar listing of interscholastic sports by state and with participation statistics. In addition, the sport programs of all institutions and conferences within a school's or college's normal competitive region should be reviewed for sports that could be added and whether there is a sufficient number of opponents to offer a regular season schedule and postseason opportunities in such sports. Title IX requires that with regard to the selection of sports, the institution is not obligated to offer the same sports for males and females. Rather, the institution must provide a selection of sports that reflects the interest and abilities of each sex, respectively. Thus, the athletic administrator should review participation in the institution's club sport and intramural sports program, conduct student surveys, review high school sports participation and open amateur sport participation trends in geographical areas from which the institution recruits athletes, and review petitions or letters that request the addition of varsity sports.

4.7 MANAGEMENT TIP

Adding Esports to the Athletic Program: Is It the Right Fit?

The term *Esports* describes a specific type of competitive gaming. A debate is raging as to whether Esports should be considered "real" sports sponsored by interscholastic and intercollegiate athletic departments, or popular video game competitions sponsored by other departments on campus such as the club sports or student-life departments.

Despite a lack of unified support for Esports to qualify as a viable interscholastic or intercollegiate sport, there is a notable trend in the adoption of collegiate Esports programs across the country. According to *Athletic Director U*, Robert Morris University in Illinois, which was acquired by Roosevelt University in 2020, granted varsity status to its Esports program and awarded scholarships as early 2014. In 2019, ESPN.com published a list of more than 100 collegiate institutions sponsoring varsity Esports programs. The growth of varsity Esports programs has continued to rise:

- In 2015–16, Esports participants were awarded $2.5 million in college scholarships. By 2019 scholarship awards totaled $15 million, a 600 percent increase.
- Two long-standing governing bodies in college athletics, the National Junior College Athletic Association (NJCAA) and the Eastern College Athletic Conference (ECAC), created Esports associations for collegiate sports. From 2016 to 2019, their membership, which includes varsity programs and club sports programs, increased from 12 schools to more than 100 schools. These associations schedule schools into regular season competition and conference tournaments.
- In 2021, the governing associations mentioned above sponsored the Collegiate Esports National Championship, hosting 48 teams from across the country. Typical of other college sports, teams could qualify for the tournament through automatic bids determined by conference championships, at-large berths, or through a play-in invitational.

There is no doubt that institutions are creating competitive Esports programs to satisfy the business objective of attracting more students. The pandemic has been an accelerant that has forced higher education administrators to confront what might be their most significant financial challenge in recent history. According to Carey (2020),

> There has never been a crisis in American higher education like the one we are facing today. While fall enrollment numbers are still in flux as colleges scramble to deal with an out-of-control pandemic, there is no question that all but the wealthiest institutions are facing deep financial pain and potential catastrophe. Even relatively conservative estimates like those published by the college financial planning firm Edmit suggest that, thanks to declining revenue and investment returns, one-third of all private colleges are now on track to run out of money within six years—a nearly 50 percent increase in estimates from 2019—and many are vulnerable to bankruptcy much sooner. Public universities, meanwhile, are about to be hammered by steep cuts in government funding, forcing them to raise prices and cut services.

University administrators must find ways to identify, attract, and retain new pools of students. Esports appears to deliver the right demographic. According to Pew Research (2008), "Video gaming is pervasive in the lives of American teens—young teens and older teens, girls and boys, and teens from across the socioeconomic spectrum." Additionally,

- 97 percent of teens ages 12 to 17 play computer, web, portable, or console games
- 99 percent of boys and 94 percent of girls play video games. Younger teen boys are the most likely to play games, followed by

younger girls and older boys. Older girls are the least "enthusiastic" players of video games, though more than half of them play. Some 65 percent of daily gamers are male; 35 percent are female.

- 50 percent of teens played games "yesterday" (Pew Research, 2008).

It stands to reason that these numbers may increase among those gamers who play Esports (competitive play that usually has an audience) if there is a proliferation of college scholarships available to highly proficient Esports gamers. More important, the majority of Esport spectators connect culturally to Esports participants much like they do their favorite sports team and may be interested in attending a university that has a strong Esports program even if they do not participate in Esports. Therefore, the potential impact on enrollment, as well as retention and community engagement, is an interesting proposition that universities are exploring.

In 2019, Caldwell University combined the passion students have for gaming with the academic curriculum when it established the first Esports business management degree. The university has since woven its Esports curriculum into a variety of concentrations including business, digital marketing, sociology, and event planning. UNI Esports, a business that works with universities to plan, launch, and assess Esports programs, reports that 77 percent of students are interested in exploring the connection between Esports and classroom learning (Athletic Director U).

High schools have started exploring opportunities to provide Esports programs. In 2020, the NFHS (National Federation of State High School Associations) entered into an agreement with PlayVS to "introduce" Esports in 15 states. PlayVS and other Internet platform providers for gaming are funding such initiatives, including partnering with the California Interscholastic Federation (CIF) and the NFHS to promote high schools adding Esports, for their own commercial benefit. The student gamers (or schools on their behalf) pay these companies to play.

All this evidence suggests that educational institutions are exploring the benefits of offering Esports. Even if one is convinced that Esports is a viable activity that would enrich the high school and college experience and could positively affect university enrollments and budgets, the question of whether Esports should be offered as part of interscholastic and intercollegiate athletic departments is still debatable. Should it be treated the same as any other sport, and therefore counted as a participation opportunity when assessing Title IX compliance?

As of the writing of this book, the Department of Education Office for Civil Rights (OCR) has not issued any advice specific to counting Esports for Title IX participation compliance purposes. The applicable government guidance on the issue regarding what constitutes an interscholastic or intercollegiate sport is specified in OCR's September 17, 2008, *Dear Colleague Letter: Athletic Activities Counted for Title IX Compliance*. The *Dear Colleague* letter advises that OCR "does not have a specific definition of the term 'sport.'" Rather, OCR looks at the following specific factors and is available upon request to make a determination for a school on case-by-case basis. A summary of those factors include:

- Whether the operating budget, support services, and coaching staff are administered by the athletic department and provided in a manner consistent with established varsity sports;
- Whether participants are eligible for athletic scholarships and varsity awards and recruited in the same manner as other varsity sports;
- Whether the number, length, and quality of practice opportunities are available in a manner consistent with established varsity sports;
- Whether regular season competitive opportunities differ quantitatively and/or qualitatively from established varsity sports, specifically examining:
    - Whether the number of competitions and length of play are predetermined by a governing athletics organization, conference, or consortium of institutions;
    - Whether the competitive schedule reflects the abilities of the team;

- Whether the activity has a defined season;
- Whether the season is determined by a governing athletics organization, conference, or consortium.

- Whether pre-season and/or post-season competition exists consistent with that provided for established varsity sports (i.e., conference, state, or national championships);
- Whether the activity is governed by a specific set of rules of play adopted by a state, national, or conference organization and/or consistent with established varsity sports, which include objective, standardized criteria by which competition must be judged;
- Whether resources for the activity are based on the competitive needs of the team;
- If post-season competition opportunities are available, whether participation is dependent on regular season results in a manner consistent with other varsity sports; and
- Whether the selection of teams/participants is based on factors related primarily to athletic ability.

The following issues have been raised as to whether Esports would qualify under Title IX to count as a sport by meeting the criteria above:

- Whether Esports involve "athletic ability," namely the use of physical skills or capabilities such as strength, agility, or stamina. The California Interscholastic Federation (CIF) refers to Esports as "electronic" competitions rather than "physical" competitions.
- Whether the activity is governed by a specific set of rules. For example, if you play basketball anywhere, the rules are the same. There are more than 13 different video games recognized in Esports competition, with none of the rules for these games promulgated by an Esports national governing organization. The games are owned and created by a commercial vendor and leased to the players. Competition may also be owned or offered by the game publisher or those who offer Internet platforms to host the games. No Esports organization has been established for a single game.
- The activity is not yet widely recognized by collegiate athletics governance organizations as a varsity sport or by most of the state high school athletic associations.

Unrelated to the definition of a sport explained above and assuming theoretically that Esports met that definition, Title IX requires that the selection of sports for girls and boys meet their respective interests and abilities. Currently, while 41 percent of gamers of all ages are women, it is unclear what the percentage is among 14–22-year-olds. However, the Pew Research discussed earlier in this chapter does indicate that girls' interest in video games reduces as they get older and older girls are the least "enthusiastic" players of video games. Therefore, it is likely that Esports is an activity in which more males than females may express interest and thus could negatively impact Title IX opportunities for women.

Another consideration is that prize money is readily available. With regard to amateur status rules, CIF bylaws recognize the "professional athlete" definition of each sport's governing body. In the case of Esports, the AAU has partnered with the U.S. Esports Federation (USeF) with regard to open amateur sports governance. The Amateur Athletic Union (AAU) Code prohibits the participation of any athlete in any event that "presents any awards, prizes, or payments that would cause the athlete to be ineligible for high school competition or which would disqualify the athlete from receiving a college athletic scholarship" (Amateur Athletic Union, p. 23). The amount of prize money available in Esports is considerable and gambling is a significant concern, especially among high school boys. It would seem prudent for any national governing organization, all of which prohibit gambling and all of which prohibit pay for play, to have a strong anti-corruption mechanism in place.

To be clear, the authors of this book lean toward the traditional view that Esports should not be considered "real" sports because they do not involve athletic ability in the physical domain. More important, we have other concerns about whether Esports are appropriate activities to be sponsored at all in any educational institution. What message does it send when high schools or universities support activities that have the following ramifications?

- Many Esports games involve guns, violence, and sexism. While the games selected for school participation should unquestionably be "sanitized" (and not fall into these categories), awareness of the culture of gaming may be a consideration.
- Youth video game player addiction has been recognized by the American Psychiatric Association (2013) as a potential symptom of Internet gaming disorder (IGD). This disorder is defined as persistent and recurrent use of the Internet to engage in games, often with other players, leading to clinically significant impairment or distress. Gentile (2017) found a consistent link between IGD and poor school performance.
- Ten percent of gamers fall into the pathological video gameplay category (Coyne, 2020).
- Should sedentary activities be accepted as athletic activities or promoted as extracurricular activities given the declining regular physical activity of high school students? Choosing an electronic competition (an advanced version of a board game) over a physical skill-strength-stamina sport, club, or intramural program should be a consideration.
- Does competitive video gaming serve an educational function? Some state high school activity associations conduct competition in computer science that does not involve video games. Is there a better STEM connection than video gaming? Why wouldn't schools embrace specific video games with STEM connections such as Math Blaster, Reader Rabbit, National Geographic Challenge, World Rescue (climate change and other world issues), or the Portal Series? These are knowledge-testing, problem-solving games that are not disguised as sports. It is important to involve students in extracurricular activities, but is it appropriate to use the commercial entertainment–oriented video games currently embraced by the Esports movement?
- Has enough research been done to determine whether the negative effects of video gaming offset any positive effects? For example, some research indicates a negative correlation between video game participation and time spent on studies (Cabanas-Sanchez), time doing homework (Weis), reading performance (Cunningham), scores on pencil-and-paper tests (Borgonovi), and school competence (Hastings).

Educational administrators and athletic directors should think long and hard before they offer Esports. The potential for creating access to a dysfunctional activity that has questionable educational value for the purpose of recruiting new students must be considered.

BIBLIOGRAPHY

OPERATIONAL STRUCTURE OF THE ATHLETIC PROGRAM

Amateur Athletic Union. *Preamble to the AAU Constitution.* https://image.aausports.org/codebook/article_III.pdf.

American Psychiatric Association. (2013). *Diagnostic and statistical manual of mental disorders* (5th ed.). Arlington, VA.

Athletic Director U. *The rise of collegiate Esports programs.* https://athleticdirectoru.com/articles/the-rise-of-collegiate-esports-programs/.

Bonnette, V. (Ed.). (2000, November). *Title IX Q & A, 1*(2). San Diego, CA: Good Sports. https://titleixspecialists.com/title-ix-qa.

Bonnette, V. (Ed.). (2001, May). *Title IX Q & A, 2*(5). San Diego, CA: Good Sports. https://titleixspecialists.com/title-ix-qa.

Bonnette, V., & Daniel, L. (1990). *Title IX investigators manual.* Washington, DC: Department of Education, Office of Civil Rights. https://eric.ed.gov/?id=ED400763.

Borgonovi, F. (2016). Video gaming and gender differences in digital and printed reading performance among 15-year-olds students in 26 countries. *Journal of Adolescence, 48*, 45–61.

Bowen, W.G., & Levin, S.A. (2011). *Reclaiming the game: College sports and educational values.* Princeton, NJ: Princeton University Press.

Brown, G. (2000, October 23). A call to reduce arms. *NCAA News, 14.*

Cabanas-Sanchez, V., Garcia-Cervantes, L. et al. (2020, March). Social correlates of sedentary behavior in young people: The up & down study. *Journal of Sport and Health Science, 9*(2), 189–196.

California Interscholastic Federation. (2019). *Esports initiative guidebook.* https://www.cifstate.org/esports/resources/Guidelines_-PlayVS-.pdf.

Carey, K. (2020, September/October). How to save higher education. *Washington Monthly.* https://washingtonmonthly.com/magazine/september-october-2020/how-to-save-higher-education/.

Clotfelter, C.T. (2019). *Big-time sports in American universities* (2nd ed.). Cambridge, United Kingdom: Cambridge University Press.

Controversial tiering system rejected, UVA turns attention to fund raising. (2001, September). *Title IX Compliance Bulletin for College Athletics, 3*(9), 1.

Coyne, S., Stockdale L. et al. (2020). Pathological video game symptoms from adolescence to emerging adulthood: A 6-year longitudinal study of trajectories, predictors, and outcomes. *Developmental Psychology.* https://doi.org/10.1037/dev0000939.

Cummings, H., and Vandewater, E. (2007). Relation of adolescent video game play to time spent in other activities. *Arch Pediatric Adolescent Medicine, 161*(7), 684–689.

Drew University. (2007). *Department of Intercollegiate Athletics policy manual.* Unpublished manuscript. Madison, NJ.

Fulks, D. (2017). *Revenue & expenses: 2004–2016.* Indianapolis, IN: NCAA. http://www.ncaa.org/sites/default/files/2017RES_D1-RevExp_Entire_2017_Final_20180123.pdf.

Gentile, D., Bailey, K. et al. (2017, November). Internet gaming disorder in children and adolescents. *Pediatrics.* https://pediatrics.aappublications.org/content/pediatrics/140/Supplement_2/S81.full.pdf.

Hastings, E., Karas, T. et al. (2009). Young children's video game/computer game use: Relations with school performance and behavior. *Issues in Mental Health Nursing, 30*(10), 638–649.

Heilweil, R. (2019, January 21). Infoporn: College Esports players cashing in big. *Wired.com.* https://www.wired.com/story/infoporn-college-esports-players-cashing-in-big.

Hums, M.A., & MacLean, J.C. (2018). *Governance and policy in sport organizations* (4th ed.). Scottsdale, AZ: Holcomb Hathaway.

James Madison scraps plan to eliminate eight programs, decides to reallocate funds. (2001, April). *Title IX Compliance Bulletin for College Athletics, 3*(4), 1.

Miracle, A.W., & Rees, C.R. (1994). *Lessons of the locker room: The myth of school sports.* Amherst, NY: Prometheus.

Morrison, S. (2018, March 15). List of varsity Esports programs spans the US. *ESPN.* https://www.espn.com/esports/story/_/id/21152905/college-esports-list-varsity-esports-programs-north-america.

National Coalition for Women and Girls in Education. (2017). *Title IX at 45.* https://www.ncwge.org/TitleIX45/Title%20IX%20and%20Athletics.pdf.

National Collegiate Athletic Association. (1999). *Achieving gender equity: A basic guide to Title IX and gender equity in athletics for colleges and universities* (2nd ed.). Indianapolis, IN: NCAA. https://files.eric.ed.gov/fulltext/ED435362.pdf.

National Collegiate Athletic Association. (2012). *Equity and Title IX in intercollegiate athletics—a practical guide for colleges and universities*. Indianapolis, IN: NCAA. http://www.ncaapublications.com/p-4206-gender-equity-online-manual.aspx.

National Collegiate Athletic Association. (2020). *2020–2021 NCAA Division I manual*. Indianapolis, IN: NCAA. https://web3.ncaa.org/lsdbi/reports/getReport/90008.

National Collegiate Athletic Association. (2020). *2018–19 NCAA sports sponsorship and participation rates report*. Indianapolis, IN: NCAA. https://ncaaorg.s3.amazonaws.com/research/sportpart/2018-19RES_SportsSponsorshipParticipationRatesReport.pdf.

National Federation of State High School Associations. (2020). *2018–19 High School Participation Survey*. https://www.nfhs.org/media/1020412/2018-19_participation_survey.pdf.

National Federation of State High School Associations. (N.d.). *Esports*. https://www.nfhs.org/sports-resource-content/esports.

Pew Research Center. (2008, September 16). *Teens, video games and civics*. https://www.pewresearch.org/internet/2008/09/16/teens-video-games-and-civics.

Shulman, J.L., & Bowen, W.G. (2000). *The game of life: College sports and educational values*. Princeton, NJ: Princeton University Press.

Statista. (2021, May 5). *Gender split of US computer and video gamers*. https://www.statista.com/statistics/232383/gender-split-of-us-computer-and-video-gamers/.

Thelin, J. (1996). *Games colleges play: Scandal and reform in intercollegiate athletics*. Baltimore: Johns Hopkins University Press.

Title IX of the Education Amendments of 1972, 20 U.S.C. §1681 et seq.

United States Department of Education. (2008). *Dear colleague letter*. https://www2.ed.gov/about/offices/list/ocr/letters/colleague-201104.html.

United States Department of Education Office for Civil Rights. (1996). *Clarification of intercollegiate athletics policy guidance: The three part test*. (OCR-00016: OCR-00016A). https://www2.ed.gov/about/offices/list/ocr/docs/clarific.html#two.

United States Department of Education Office of Postsecondary Education. (2015). *User's guide for the Equity in Athletics Disclosure Act web-based data collection*. https://www.clearinghouse.net/chDocs/resources/article_USDepartmentofEducationOfficeofPostsecondaryEducation_1438204219.pdf.

United States Equal Employment Opportunity Commission. (1997, October 29). *Enforcement guidance on sex discrimination in the compensation of sports coaches in educational institutions*. https://www.eeoc.gov/laws/guidance/enforcement-guidance-sex-discrimination-compensation-sports-coaches-educational.

Weis, R., and Cerankosky, B.C. (2010, April 21). Effects of video-game ownership on young boys' academic and behavioral functioning: a randomized, controlled study. *Psychological Science 21*(4), 463–470.

Zimbalist, A. (1999). *Unpaid professionals: Commercialism and conflict in big-time college sports*. Princeton, NJ: Princeton University Press.

Zimbalist, A. (2005). Testimony before the Department of Education's Commission on Title IX, San Diego, CA. In Rita J. Simon (Ed.). *Sporting Equality*. London: Routledge.

Zotos, C. et al. (2016). *Creating gender neutral coaches' employment and compensation systems: A resource manual*. East Meadow, NY: Women's Sports Foundation. https://www.womenssportsfoundation.org/wp-content/uploads/2016/09/gender-neutral-compensation-guide-final-53016.pdf.

CHAPTER

5

Office Operations, Finance, and Budgeting

An efficient and respectful working environment that demonstrates fiscal and operational integrity in the daily operation of the athletic program does not occur by chance. To the contrary, it is a purposeful construction by an athletic director who anticipates and implements necessary policies and procedures that demonstrate compliance with standard institutional procedures, accountability, and fairness. The athletic director must ensure that staff members are adequately educated and trained to carry out their responsibilities. The documents in this chapter, in both the book and HK*Propel*, define how to conduct essential office operations including the orientation and training of new employees, internal and external communications, basic office operations, processing of contracts and agreements, execution of financial transactions, and the annual budgeting process. These areas are the nuts and bolts of conducting the daily business of athletics.

TYPES OF DOCUMENTS

Management tip—Factual background information, insights, problem-solving strategies, and suggestions for the athletic director

Planning tool—Steps to take or factors that should be considered in the development of strategic plans, action plans, professional development plans, or governance systems

Educational resource—Handouts that can be used to educate staff members, campus constituents, volunteers, or student-athletes

Policy—Sample policies and procedures that should be adopted by an athletic department after customization and review by appropriate expert institutional or school district officials

Form—Sample forms, letters, or job descriptions

Evaluation instrument—Administrative tools that help the athletic director, a supervisor, or an employee assess job performance and evaluate program content

Risk assessment—Checklists that help the athletic director, a supervisor, or an employee identify risks and prevent litigation

5.1 MANAGEMENT TIP

Orientation on Office Operations for New Employees

Never underestimate the importance of orienting every new employee—formally, in detail, and with supporting online reference documentation—about how the athletic department office operates. Internal operating systems need to be documented for several reasons:

1. **Information overload.** Employees experience considerable information overload during their first few weeks in a new job. They simply can't remember everything. They need reference materials in which they can look up everything that they are expected to know if they can't remember what they've been told.
2. **Accountability.** All policies and procedures for which an employee will be held accountable should be in writing and easily available online.
3. **Efficiency.** Employees do not need to memorize staff extensions or e-mail addresses. They just need to know where to go to access this information. An online user manual about how to operate a machine will save a new staff member from taking the time of another staff member to teach him or her how to perform a function.
4. **Accuracy.** Especially when it comes to critical functions such as cash management procedures, procurement procedures, and completing time sheets, reminders of the importance of accurate execution of tasks and forms to be used are essential.

To feel comfortable, confident, and part of the team, new employees need to understand the system and culture of the athletic department, from getting a parking permit and logging into the online department resources to the location of parking lots, the structure of the filing system, and a directory of who does what in the program. Form 5.2 is a sample orientation checklist that can be easily customized for use with any athletic program.

Thus, the athletic director should think through the documentation that must be accessible by each employee. Consider the following publications and decide whether they need to be at the desk of each staff member or accessible as PDFs on the employee's computer:

- **Institution's employee handbook.** Every high school and institution of higher education has a generic employee handbook containing policies and explaining procedures of which all employees must be aware.
- **Athletic department telephone and e-mail directory.**
- **Athletic department policy and procedures manual.** All policies governing the conduct of the athletic program (see Form 2.16 for a sample table of contents).
- **IT operating handbook.** Usually available online, a user manual showing the organization of all computer files, who has access privileges, and rules for entering information into and creating new files and records in various department databases.

5.2 Form—Checklist of Office Operations for New Employees

A sample form that defines initial meetings and training sessions that must be completed by each new employee and the person responsible for conducting these training programs.

Available in HK*Propel*.

- **Athletic department internal operations handbook.** Explanation of all office operating systems, policies, and procedures (see Form 2.17 for a sample table of contents with other policy and performance tool examples here in chapter 5).
- **Governance association rules manual.** The official athletic governance association (NCAA, NAIA, or other) handbook of rules and regulations.
- **Department events calendar.** A calendar showing all sport and other department-sponsored events.
- **Sports and department media brochures.** Media guides and the department's general public information piece.

Consideration should also be given to assigning a staff mentor to the new employee so that he or she always has someone specific to go to with questions. Being a mentor is a good leadership experience, and designating mentors allows a supervisor to spread out the extra duty of helping others. Supervisors should be asked to arrange or make sure that new employees participate in some type of social activity, whether it's a happy hour on a Friday afternoon after work or an invitation to have lunch or dinner at the home of the supervisor. Many cultures in an organization must be considered with regard to advancing employee acceptance.

Little things can make a real difference. For instance, never assume that acronyms commonly used by all staff are part of a new employee's vocabulary. From the NCAA to FBS to Division III, think about the vocabulary of sport culture acronyms that needs to be shared. Invite people to add to it every year. See Educational Resource 5.3 for a sample of an acronym vocabulary list.

Similarly, the communications unit or the receptionist might be charged with developing an FAQ document—a list of frequently asked questions starting with NCAA rules questions for representatives of athletic interest (see Educational Resource 7.8 for an example). Never assume that all employees understand how to initiate and sustain professional communications with their peers and superiors. Consider distributing an educational resource on this topic to motivate staff members to self-examine their everyday communication skills and aspire to be better. Educational Resource 5.4 is a sample resource on this topic.

Consider requiring every employee to maintain a "playbook" that explains to their temporary or permanent replacement exactly how to perform their everyday responsibilities. See Educational Resource 5.5 for employee instructions on preparing a playbook.

5.3 Educational Resource—Acronyms That All Staff Members Should Know

A sample acronym list that defines acronyms most commonly used by high school and college athletic departments. The list should be further customized to include institution-specific league, conference, and governance association affiliations.

5.4 Educational Resource—Professional Communication Guidelines

A sample handout that can be distributed to all employees to remind them of the keys to maintaining a professional atmosphere and the appropriate ways to resolve conflicts.

5.5 Educational Resource—Instructions on Preparing a Position Playbook

A sample handout that can be distributed to all employees to provide them with detailed instructions and examples of how to prepare a position playbook, including commonly asked questions and answers.

Available in HK*Propel*.

OFFICE OPERATIONS

The difference between good and great is attention to detail. This point is especially true regarding how employees communicate with each other and external constituents and the general cleanliness, look, and feel of the athletic department office environment. If these topics are not addressed with specific instructions regarding manager expectations, needless problems will be encountered that could have easily been avoided. Issues may range from stolen or lost keys and valuables to important people being put off by typographical errors or too-familiar forms of address. The documents in this section are designed to provide clear instructions and expectations regarding professionalism, neatness, and maintenance of an office environment that is impressive and welcoming to workers, recruits, and guests. All these policies are available in HK*Propel*.

5.6 **Policy**—Buildings and Grounds

A sample policy that details employee responsibilities related to keys, securing files, opening and closing office areas for business, ensuring that office machines are operational and fully supplied, general maintenance expectations, and employee safety.

5.7 **Policy**—Staff Meetings

A sample policy that informs employees about mandatory standing meetings of various department units and responsibilities related to agendas and meeting minutes.

5.8 **Policy**—Mail, E-Mail, and Social Media Communications

A sample policy that sets specific format, expression, and other communications standards for all employees related to all forms of business communication.

5.9 **Policy**—Computer and Software Use

A sample policy that designates electronic communication equipment and software provided to department employees, to whom requests should be directed, and security and use restrictions related to such devices.

5.10 **Policy**—Appearance Code

A sample policy that sets standards for professional dress while acknowledging that sport-related gear is permissible at certain times.

Available in HK*Propel*.

5.11 MANAGEMENT TIP

Production and Approval of Legal Agreements

Athletic departments enter into numerous contracts during the normal operation of the athletic program such as employment agreements with head coaches, game contracts with other educational institutions, purchase agreements, television contracts with commercial entities, and many others. These types of agreements are usually not covered by institutional standardized processes that normally govern the purchase of products and services. Most institutions do permit the athletic department, by position-designated signatories, to enter into contractual agreements for small purchases and transactions valued below an amount specified by the institution or for contest-scheduling contracts for which a previously approved agreement template designed by legal counsel is being used. All other agreements must be executed by the institution's chief financial officer or president. Most athletic directors are not attorneys, and if they are not, they should not be developing those documents without the assistance of the institution's legal counsel. These agreements constitute promises by the institution to perform a legal duty, and if that duty is not performed, the institution is subject to being legally compelled to perform it or can be assessed damages and other penalties.

Generally, there are several keys to internal controls. First, any athletic department policy dealing with the production or processing of contracts should be reviewed and approved by the institution's legal counsel. Policy 5.12 is such a model policy.

Keeping track of where contract documents are in the approval process and standardizing the requests for approval contributes to administrative efficiencies and enables the athletic director to relegate document handling to lower-level employees. Form 5.13 is a sample processing checklist that can be used to remind employees of institutional and athletic department policies and procedures governing contract processing and serve as a written record of document handling. Form 5.14 is a sample template for a cover document that can be used to request signature approval on contracts and other purchasing documents.

5.12 Policy—Contracts and Signature Authority to Expend Funds

A sample policy that governs the production and approval process for handling contracts or obligating the institution to the purchase of goods or services.

5.13 Form—Contract-Processing Checklist

A sample form used to track the processing of contracts and other purchasing documents that must be submitted to appropriate institutional officials for approval.

5.14 Form—Cover Memo: Request for Approval of Contract

A sample form to be used for requesting signature approval and transmitting contracts or other purchasing documents.

Available in HK*Propel*.

5.15 MANAGEMENT TIP

Insurance Issues Confronting Athletic Directors

Insurance is normally not the responsibility of athletic directors. Institutions usually retain experts for this purpose or have business office staff who handle those responsibilities. But athletic department staff members have responsibilities related to risk assessment, inspection of facilities and equipment, emergency treatment, and notification to the institution of practices that might not normally be covered by insurance policies. Every athletic director should consult with the school district, college, or university risk assessment manager or use those services as provided by the institution's insurance brokers. For those institutions that receive significant revenue through television contracts, game guarantees, and other revenue generated through game-day competition, athletic directors should work with experts to assess the need for event cancellation insurance. No one ever predicted that entire seasons would be canceled due to the COVID-19 pandemic.

Role of the Athletic Director

Most athletic directors assume that the school district or institution of higher education has made adequate provision for all insurance issues related to the athletic program. Although this is usually the case, it's not true 100 percent of the time. Unlike many programs that are run exclusively on the college campus, the athletic program conducts many parts of its program off campus, such as participation in away events, use of golf courses that may not be owned by the institution for golf and cross country, rental of a city-owned arena for the most highly attended basketball games, rental of indoor tennis courts or ice hockey facilities, or lease of part or all of boathouses for crew. Additionally, coaches may be allowed to use athletic facilities to conduct camps that they own. The institution may not be aware of such usage. Thus, the athletic director needs to have a general understanding of what risks exist in all these circumstances, whether they are insurable, and whether the institution is providing insurance coverage. Most important, the athletic director needs to use the risk assessment assistance provided by insurance brokers and the institution's business office to attempt to foresee possible areas of program weakness, act to reduce risk through employee training, and put in place strong policies that address employee responsibilities related to controlling risk.

Medical Insurance

Few athletic programs provide primary medical insurance coverage for student-athletes. The usual practice is to require that student-athletes be covered by their parents' policy or insurance programs available to all students at an institution. The athletic department then carries a secondary policy that covers charges not paid by the primary policy. The athletic department may also provide catastrophic injury and death coverage, or, in the case of NCAA member institutions, such coverage may be an NCAA member benefit. Several of the issues that should be addressed in such policies are whether the institution will reimburse for deductibles, what policies apply for athletes whose parents cannot afford health insurance, what athletic governance rules limit insurance benefits, and how long coverage continues after the student-athlete leaves the program (see Policy 9.5). For instance, in the case of the last issue, if an injury was incurred in the athletic program and treatment continues beyond graduation, how long is coverage applicable? Other key responsibilities of the athletic department include effective medical screening to determine preexisting conditions (see Policy 9.3 and Evaluation Instrument 9.4 in HK*Propel*), excellent record keeping for medical services and rehabilitation (see Policy 9.3), and efficient claim submission processes (see Policy

9.5 in HK*Propel*). The checklist contained in Risk Assessment 5.24 in HK*Propel* is a good review of insurance issues that require annual oversight.

Property Insurance

Property insurance is normally present for most educational institutions, covering buildings and building contents, for losses caused by theft, vandalism, fire, or destruction from other specified causes. Some causes might be excluded such as earthquakes, floods, or terrorism. A key responsibility of the athletic director is to maintain a complete inventory of the contents of athletic department areas (see Policies 11.21 and 11.24 and Forms 11.22, 11.23, and 11.25 in HK*Propel*) and to be sure that such inventory is either on the institution's mainframe computer system or backed up daily and secured off premises. It doesn't help to keep impeccable records and then have them destroyed by fire or other catastrophe.

General Liability Insurance

General liability insurance covers injuries to third parties or property losses by third parties who are users of school or university facilities such as spectators at athletic events, attendees at clinics or workshops, campers, and so on. Athletic department responsibilities in this area are primarily related to reporting and record keeping about injuries and medical emergencies that occur in campus buildings (see Forms 9.9 and 9.10 in HK*Propel*), approval of emergency medical plans for facilities operated by the athletic department (see Form 15.11 in HK*Propel*), and provision of adequate supervision of all physical activity areas (see Policy 15.10). Also key is proper signage in facilities that provide cautions and good instruction on the use and storage of equipment, especially in the weight room and swimming pool areas but also in conjunction with other facilities that are high risk (such as trampolines). Athletic staff should schedule annual walk-through inspections with university or school district risk managers to ensure that signage, supervision, emergency plans, and the location of emergency medical equipment meet standards. Again, a risk assessment checklist should be used on an annual basis to ensure adequate insurance oversight.

Employment Practices Liability Insurance

Employment practices liability insurance covers institutional costs related to employees damaged by discrimination, sexual harassment, wrongful termination, defamation, and other wrongful employment practices. Again, the institution carries this insurance, and it is not an athletic department cost. But athletic department policies and practices related to hiring, evaluation, treatment, and other employment practices serve to limit institutional risk in this regard. The athletic director needs to consult with the institutional human resources office on all situations related to corrective action and termination to ensure that these processes do not violate the law (see model Policies 6.5 and 6.10 in HK*Propel*).

Insurance Against Employee Crime

Although many school districts and colleges and universities carry insurance covering employee theft or criminal activity resulting in a loss of money or property, athletic directors should at least ensure that this is the case and should convey to the institution situations in which questions might arise about whether such policies provide coverage. Does the athletic department contract out all or some of its ticket sales, and is such insurance provided by the third party a condition of such use? Are volunteers or other nonemployees handling financial transactions or using computers or other expensive athletic department equipment, and does the university policy cover theft by these nonemployees? Does the athletic department have model cash-handling procedures and other financial policies (see Policy 12.13 in HK*Propel*)?

Workers Compensation Insurance

All employers are required to carry workers compensation insurance to cover the cost of injuries or medical treatment of employees who are injured while on the job. The athletic director's responsibility in this area is related to maintaining a safe working environment, conducting safety training sessions for employees, and especially ensuring that employees who operate cleaning or maintenance equipment, set up athletic equipment, or conduct activities on athletic equipment that require specialized skills (such as spotting techniques) get the training that they need to avoid injury. The athletic director must also consult with risk managers about the coverage of volunteers who may perform such functions (such as volunteers who might assist in maintaining the baseball field). The institution may decide that only paid staff should perform such functions or that volunteers must be covered by other insurance policies.

Professional Liability Insurance

Every lawsuit against the institution also holds the prospect of additionally naming individuals in the department for their accidental or negligent actions. Laws may protect state institutions from liability, but they do not apply to the negligent acts of individual employees. Professional liability insurance, also termed errors and omissions insurance, should be carried by coaches, athletic trainers, strength and conditioning coaches, and any professional staff member responsible for the care, health, and well-being of athletes. The athletic director should encourage professional members of the staff to understand this need and their potential exposure. Professional associations often offer such insurance at reasonable annual costs.

Product Liability Insurance

Many athletic departments conduct food and beverage sales or contract with concessionaires or volunteer groups to provide such services in conjunction with athletic competitions, camps, or other athletic events. Because most educational institutions run food service operations for the general student body, product liability insurance that covers accidents or negligence related to the sale of food and beverages is often in place. However, it is essential that athletic department staff or student-athletes who run concession stands be educated about and follow all safety protocols for handling food. Additionally, the athletic director must make sure that such policies apply to volunteers or charity groups that provide such services at athletic events or that health department inspection and insurance are required of such groups before they are allowed to operate on campus or at athletic events (see Policy 15.26 in HK*Propel*). Also, it is important to know that such insurance covers leasing or rental of sports equipment when such equipment is responsible for injury because of defects or improper maintenance. When the athletic equipment room allows the public to check out equipment, the athletic director should make sure that the institutional policy covers this practice.

Vehicle and Other Transportation-Related Insurance

Although school districts and colleges and universities carry insurance covering use, damage to, and liability for injury or damage to others for their own vehicles, such insurance is always conditioned on factors such as operation of such vehicles by qualified drivers. Thus, the athletic department must have policies that ensure compliance with all such requirements. Most athletic departments also rent vans, buses, and charter airplanes. Thus, clear policy instruction needs to be in place about insurance coverage of third-party service providers and the purchase of insurance when staff members rent and drive vehicles. The institution's risk managers need to be consulted regarding the development of such policies (see Policies 11.27, 11.28, and 11.29 in HK*Propel* about team travel).

FINANCIAL AFFAIRS

Although standardized institutional processes govern the purchase of products and services, a number of athletic department practices require additional financial and administrative policies and procedures or customized forms and instructions. For example, extensive team travel and coach recruiting travel may require the issuance of credit cards so that coaches do not have to carry large amounts of cash when on the road. On-site payment of game officials or vendors associated with special-event needs that may not be anticipated may require exceptions to institutional prior-approval policies. The operation of athletic events involves handling cash and checks and requires solutions to storing funds, handling negotiable ticket stocks, and securely transporting money to bank or business office depositories. Sample policies and forms that can be used to manage these processes are available in HK*Propel*.

5.16 **Policy**—Financial Policies

A sample policy that covers basic responsibilities and processes related to payment of salaries and wages, employee reimbursement of expenses, payments to vendors, cash and check handling procedures, petty cash funds, and the acceptance of gifts.

5.17 **Policy**—Staff Travel

A sample policy that governs the approval and payment of team and individual staff travel, hotel and meal expenses, use of department credit cards, restrictions related to family members accompanying employees on business trips, and other travel issues.

5.18 **Form**—Staff Travel Reimbursement Request

A sample form to accompany submission of receipts and invoices related to travel that records the purpose of all expenditures, whether paid with cash or credit card, serves as a request for reimbursement of expenses paid by employees, and ensures proper recording of budget line items to be charged.

5.19 **Form**—Advance Travel Authorization

A sample form to be used for travel preauthorization that requires a pretrip estimate of travel costs and enables the employee's supervisor to verify availability of budgeted funds.

5.20 **Form**—Request for Payroll Payment

A sample form to be used for payment of event or other part-time hourly wage or flat-stipend employees that requires supervisor validation of work performed, hours worked, and budget line items to be charged.

5.21 **Form**—Staff Nontravel Expense Reimbursement Request

A sample form to accompany submission of receipts to be used for reimbursement of non-travel-related expenses or record of credit card use for such purchases that ensures proper recording of budget line items used.

5.22 **Form**—Request for Payment to Vendor

A sample form to be used for payment to vendors that require the submission of invoice, explanation of purpose, and indication of budget line item to be charged.

5.23 **Form**—Report of Credit Card Use

A sample form to be used for reporting purchases made by credit card.

5.24 **Risk Assessment**—Checklist: Finance, Insurance, and Contracts

A sample risk assessment checklist to be completed by a staff member assigned the responsibility to examine best practices related to financial transactions, insurance coverage, and the processing of contracts.

Found in HK*Propel*.

5.25 PLANNING TOOL

Basic Characteristics of the Well-Conceived Budget

Integration With Goals and Objectives

Every well-managed athletic program has clearly delineated goals and measurable objectives for each of its sport teams and administrative support units. These goals and objectives, as well as any limitations imposed by a sport program's tiering system that specifies differentiation of support and practices based on program priorities, provides the foundation for building a budget. The budget also identifies the sources of financial support required to fund expenses necessary to achieve goals and objectives. The budget is a plan with the following characteristics:

- Is an accurate reflection of the cost of achieving current and future performance goals of the program
- Specifies the financial resources required to achieve those specific goals and the sources of those funds
- Covers a fixed period, usually one year
- Is based on past expenditures or experience
- Is based on accurate, current research on the costs of goods and services
- Projects the future based on stated assumptions

A well-conceived budget is a dynamic planning tool that matches resources with objectives and priorities. Thus, the budget of every team or support unit should be segmented according to stated measurable objectives and clearly stated assumptions (e.g., no significant increase in the cost of transportation will occur, based on projected decreases in fuel costs). The annual budget also provides a basis for controlling department activities and measures the efficient or inefficient use of department funds (i.e., actual expenses versus budgeted expenses).

Transparency and Collaboration

Sound budgeting takes time and collaboration. This annual exercise is a basic component of strategic planning, should involve all primary stakeholders, and should be as transparent as possible. Although the practice is not advisable, athletic directors commonly restrict budget creation and oversight to a select group of staff members. For example, in the traditional tiered funding model, head coaches of tier I high-priority sports often construct their own budgets, have full viewing access, and have modification privileges, whereas other coaches may have limited input or access to their budgets. Such practice usually occurs because the athletic director is trying to hide the effects of a tiered funding model or they want maximum flexibility to move money around without scrutiny. We believe that this practice is inefficient, creates a higher chance of reactive budgeting and overspending, and is in direct conflict with the basic principle of transparency. As discussed in chapter 4, clearly articulating the tiered program model promotes efficient and effective management strategies and serves to inform the entire staff of how and where their unit fits into the overall department mission. Additionally, athletic directors should be willing to explain decisions when moving money from one team or support unit to another. Evaluating the budget annually and constructing the following year's budget in a detailed and collaborative way is a great tool for reinforcing program-by-program goal alignment.

Commitment to Zero-Based Budgeting

Many athletic directors also make the mistake of simply adding a prescribed percentage increase or decrease to the budget every year.

With the possible exception of salaries, we do not recommend this incremental approach to budgeting. Even if the school district or university announces that no change will occur in the budget, we believe that the annual budgeting exercise (zero-based budgeting) is valuable and will provide information that can be used immediately and in the future. In addition, athletic department budgets are far too complex and include too many variations from year to year to rely on simple percentage increases. For example, a team may have two flights to away contests one year and none the next year. If a simple percentage increase is provided, money should be left over in the account that could have been used to offset a deficit by another team. We recommend that the athletic director require each budget manager to prepare a budget document annually using the zero-based budget approach (see Planning Tool 5.27, including table 5.27.1).

Clear Delineation of Budgetary Subunits by Program and Expenditure Type

Few departments in a high school or university have the budget complexity of an athletic department. Most athletic departments divide their overall budgets into salaries and benefits, team-by-team operating budgets, general administrative functions, and other administrative areas such as sports medicine, sports information, marketing, compliance, academic support, and the like. In addition, most teams have separate fund-raising expense and revenue accounts. Therefore, before the athletic director provides budget managers with instructions for completing their annual budgets, she or he should look at how the entire budget is separated into subunits. For instance, should the strength and conditioning program be separated from the sports medicine program? Then, the athletic director should ask staff whether budget inefficiencies or confusion is created by the operational expenditure typology under each subunit. Is this typology standard for all school or university departments, or can it be customized for the needs of the athletic program? For example, assume that all teams have a uniform budget line in their team budget. If all teams are getting new uniforms annually, having this budget line would make sense. But if some teams are getting uniforms every two or three years, then using two lines, one for new uniforms and one for uniform replacement, may be better to indicate when a team is in a uniform replacement year. Or, the athletic director could address this issue by having a general uniform budget not under the specific sport programs for those teams that do not order new uniforms yearly. This budget could be attached to a uniform replacement rotational chart (see table 5.25.1). This approach could clarify uniform purchasing schedules for coaches and equipment managers and may prevent funds from sitting in uniform budget lines unused during nonpurchase years.

Analyzing the subunit and line-item designations each year will result in an efficient, logical budget structure. Analysis also teaches budget managers how to identify structural inefficiencies that could result in waste.

Regularized Financial Reports

Another characteristic of a good budget is the mandate of viewing (online if possible) and reviewing budget reports at least monthly during the academic year. Such reports are required for adequate administrative oversight by the athletic director or designated senior staff member and for the use of each budget manager in determining whether funds will be sufficient to accomplish program goals. A review will also alert the budget manager to any administrative chargeback mistakes that may have been made (such as charging the cost of a bus to the wrong team).

Table 5.25.1 Sample Uniform Rotation Budget

	2022–2023	2023–2024	2024–2025	2025–2026	2026–2027	2027–2028
Field hockey						
Home shirts (25)			2000			2200
Away shirts (25)			2000			2200
Skirts/Shorts (25)			1800			1900
Outerwear			3000			3300
W lacrosse						
Home shirts (25)	2000			2000		
Away shirts (25)	2500			2500		
Skirts/Shorts (25)		1800			1900	
Outerwear		3000				3300
W soccer						
Home uniform (24)		2400			2600	
Away uniform (24)	2400			2400		
Warm-ups (24)					3300	
M soccer						
Home uniform (24)	2400			2400		
Away uniform (24)	2400			2400		
Warm-ups (24)			3000			
Cross country						
Singlet (24)			1000			1200
Shorts (24)			900			1000
Outerwear			2400			
W basketball						
Home uniform (16)	1800			1800		
Away uniform (16)		1800			1800	
Shooter shirt	1000			1000		
M basketball						
Home uniform (16)		1800			1800	
Away uniform (16)	1800			1800		
Outerwear, shooter shirt		1000				1000
M lacrosse						
Home jersey (30)	2400			12400		
Away jersey (30)			2400			2600
*Add 6 to outerwear		720		720		800
Baseball						
Home jersey (28)		2050			2200	
Away jersey (28)			2050			2200
Outerwear		2200				2400

(continued)

Table 5.25.1 ***(continued)***

	2022–2023	2023–2024	2024–2025	2025–2026	2026–2027	2027–2028
Softball						
Home uniform (20)			2300			2450
Away uniform (20)			2300			2450
Outerwear			1700			
W tennis						
Uniform (12)	1400			1400		
Outerwear		1600				1600
M tennis						
Uniform (12)	1400			1400		
Outerwear		1600				1800
Fencing						
Replacement Suits (8)	1200		1200		1300	
Outerwear (24)				2400		
Equestrian						
Outerwear (25)		2500				2500
Swimming						
Outerwear (36)			4000			
Bags (12)		500	500	500	600	600
Total	22,700	21,370	32,550	25,120	15,500	35,200

Uniforms are on a three-year rotation, and outerwear is on a four-year rotation.
Costs for items that are annually replaced are found in the individual sport team budgets.

5.26 PLANNING TOOL

Why Multiple Budget Managers Should Be Appointed

Why Multiple Budget Managers?

Assignment of responsibility for a budget is also the designation of accountability for the efficient and effective use of funds to accomplish specific goals and objectives. No matter what the size of the athletic department staff, thoughtfulness is required to ensure that accountability extends to the manager responsible for delivering results. If the athletic director or athletic business manager is designated as being solely responsible for budget production and oversight, it is virtually impossible for that person to be accountable for success in myriad sport and support programs. Thus, to support a budget process that has a high level of efficiency and accountability, multiple managers must be clearly and logically designated. Each should be responsible for a specific segment of the operating budget over which he or she has both supervisory authority and a high level of program expertise to be able to judge whether expenditures will produce desired results. Although the athletic director is ultimately responsible for the entire athletic budget and a senior staff manager who is expert in finance or business affairs can be assigned to coordinate budget preparation, reporting, and oversight, the accountability of each budget must lie with the person who administers the program.

Budget Manager Responsibilities

For example, assume that the following are generic manager titles for a large Division I athletic department. Each of these people would be considered budget managers. After each title is a typical designation of her or his respective budget responsibilities:

a. Head coaches: respective team operating budgets to include lines such as travel, uniforms, equipment, supplies, telephone charges, scholarships, and recruiting

b. Athletic director: coach and professional staff salaries

c. Associate director for business affairs: salaries of clerical, maintenance, and nonprofessional staff; benefits; utilities; debt service; capital equipment; administrative travel; construction and renovation

d. Assistant director for business affairs: insurance, awards, office supplies and services, vehicle maintenance

e. Assistant director for athletic facilities and equipment: operating budget to include hourly wages, maintenance and repair, supplies, equipment, uniforms

f. Director of dining hall: operating budget to include hourly wages, food, equipment, uniforms, maintenance and repair

g. Associate director for development: operating budget to include advertising, promotions, gift solicitation, donor cultivation activities, fund-raising events, licensed merchandise revenues and expenses, ticket office operations, hourly wages

h. Associate director for communications: operating budget to include media relations, publications, photography, website, television and radio production

i. Assistant director for athletic events: operating budget for all home events and tournaments including officiating expenses, ticket takers, ushers, security and other hourly wage employees, concessions, uniforms, ticket printing, band, cheerleaders, drill team

j. Assistant director for sports medicine: operating budget to include training room equipment and supplies, medical expenses, repairs and maintenance

k. Assistant director for student affairs: operating budget for basic skills and learning disabilities programs, summer school scholarships, hourly wages for tutors and other academic support staff, equipment and supplies

For smaller athletic departments, the same responsibilities (if they are applicable to the respective athletic program) would be spread across a smaller number of budget managers, many of whom would be managers with non-senior-level titles. For instance, in a small athletic program, the head coach might be responsible for conducting all home events in his or her sport. In larger departments, the managers designated in the previous listing might have middle managers below them prepare separate operating budgets for the specific unit under their respective supervision. For instance, the assistant director for events might have the head cheerleading coach prepare and be responsible for the cheerleading program annual budget and the band director and drill team director do the same for their programs.

Each budget manager is responsible for proposing a well-conceived budget for each assigned area. Each budget must include justification based on specifically stated department objectives. Each expense or revenue identified should be based on a past and assumed unchanging cost or a new currently researched cost projection. The budget manager is also responsible for detailing any factors that might influence the accuracy of estimates. All budget managers should have the expertise to defend their budget proposals. After the budget has been approved, the budget manager is accountable for oversight (monthly auditing of accuracy and submission of all receipts, revenues, and so on) and, if necessary, revision of estimates because of changing circumstances. If a revision is necessary, the budget manager must inform the athletic director or chief business officer immediately rather than risk an end-of-year deficit or opportunity to use full funding. Ultimately, at the end of each fiscal year, each manager is responsible for making sure that his or her budget is within approved limits.

5.27 PLANNING TOOL

Implementing the Budget Preparation Process

The budget process can be implemented in many ways. Regardless of the strategies employed, one constant is that a detailed, user-friendly plan must address how to complete the annual budget documents. What follows is a four-step approach to crafting annual budgets based on preliminary assessments, application of zero-based budgeting principles, a comparison of funding levels to desired objectives, and identification of other requests outside each budget area that may affect that program's budget.

Step 1: Preliminary Assessments

Each budget manager must produce a budget document that specifies and shows alignment with the stated objectives for his or her specific team or management area. The budget must be grounded in research and clearly articulated. The athletic director should be able to use each budget manager's document to compile an overall summary of department goal attainment. In addition, the budget document must reflect priorities and any concerns related to underfunding. Before assigning budget dollars to any individual budget lines, the budget manager must make several preliminary assessments and document them in the report.

a. **Review of the current budget.** Each budget document should begin with a review of the current year's budget. If the budgeting cycle is a year out, a review of the prior year's budget might have to suffice. Areas that were significantly overfunded or underfunded should be explained. For example, a baseball travel budget may have significant money left over if several games were rained out during the season. Similarly, the line for payment of officials may be in a deficit because more officials traveled farther to game sites, resulting in higher mileage costs. Analyzing these kinds of expenditures is important. Without doing so, an athletic director may assume that baseball is overfunded and reallocate those monies elsewhere. In the case of higher mileage costs for officials, the coach and the athletic director have the opportunity to look at the way in which officials are being assigned and make decisions about future assignments. The review also forces budget managers to take a second look at how they spent their money and decide whether they can be more efficient in the future.

   This review assumes that athletic directors do not allow budget managers to move money between lines. Unless the institution does not allow any specific budget line ever to show a deficit, we encourage athletic directors to prohibit movement of funds between lines in any account. This practice allows the budget manager and the athletic director to see where revenues and expenses differed greatly from those that were projected and puts a higher level of responsibility on the budget manager to be diligent in predicting each year's budget. If the institution prohibits showing a deficit on any line, then all internal money transfers should be approved by the budget manager's supervisor so that there is some internal knowledge of how money is being reallocated. This approach will also help budget managers reflect on decisions that they made during the budget process and allow them to be better informed for the next budget cycle.

b. **Assessment of goal attainment.** Each team and program area should have a specific set of goals and objectives. For example, the sports medicine department may have a goal of providing preparticipation physicals to all athletes free of cost. A sport program might have a goal of finishing in the top 25 percent of the conference. The athletic development office might have specific revenue objectives from each funding source. While constructing the budget document, the manager should include all goal statements and their respective measurable objectives that relate to the manager's program and reflect on whether objectives were met. If certain objectives that have budget implications were unmet, a clear explanation should be provided. For example, did other unanticipated expenses prevent this objective from being met? Will these unanticipated expenses be annual expenses going forward? Is this objective still realistic, or will additional funding be required to meet this goal? Each team will have specific objectives as well. Were recruiting objectives met? If not, does that have anything to do with the level of funding for recruiting travel or visits? Did a team's win–loss record meet expectations? If not, should scheduling changes be made? Do these changes affect next year's budget?

c. **Mandatory new expenditures.** Typically, some new expenditures each year are mandatory and should be noted clearly and accurately in the budget report. Some of these expenditures may be school- or university-wide such as salary scale increases or increases in employee benefits costs. Others may be relevant to the athletic department as a whole or to a specific team such as increases in dues for the governing body or in fees for basketball officials. Compliance with legal standards, such as new employment laws, may also create new mandatory expenditures. These mandatory expenditures must be well communicated among the staff and factored into the appropriate budgets because there is no flexibility related to their funding.

d. **Contractually determined revenues and expenses.** A review of expenses or revenues that are contractually defined and cannot be changed must be included in the budget document. For example, if a team has an annual contract with a shoe company, it must be reflected as a contracted expense. This point becomes particularly important when specific contracts are expenses in one year and revenues the next. For example, a team may receive a guarantee payment in one year in return for agreeing to travel to a specific opponent. In the opposite year, the team may be paying the guarantee to the visiting team. Contracts can create a surplus or a deficit in any given year with or without affecting other years. Keeping track of and documenting these contractual anomalies in the budget report is important.

e. **Other anomalies.** Each year, budget managers should identify any other anomalies that might be present in the upcoming year that could present another funding challenge or funding windfall. For example, a spike may occur in department-wide recruiting because of a large graduating senior class, which will have implications on the costs associated with student-athlete orientation. On the other hand, a team may receive a one-time gift from a parent to pay for spring break travel. The coach would want to note this as a one-time gift so that any monies reallocated elsewhere would not be lost in future years.

Step 2: Application of Zero-Based Budgeting

The definition of zero-based budgeting is as its title implies. Every year's budget must start at zero, and expenditures must be built anew according to anticipated expenses and revenues for every activity in the new budgeted year. In other words, the budget does not start with an anticipation of allocating the same amount that was allocated in the current budget or that was actually spent that year. But actual expenditures from the current or previous year are shown to provide a comparison on which to judge the new budget request. Table 5.27.1 is a sample of a line-by-line budget for a soccer team that reflects zero-based budgeting procedures.

Each budget line (travel, equipment, recruiting, and so on) has its own separate section, and every expenditure is clearly delineated. Using this method, the budget manager is expected to project and justify all expenditures for the following year. If expense headings need clarification, they should be noted at the bottom of the budget in the way that meals and hotels are described on the sample travel budget. Any significant changes in funds needed from the current year to the projected year should be described at the bottom of each chart as shown on the samples. Such a sample chart should be provided to each coach as an example of zero-based budgeting detail.

After all the resulting line-by-line budgets are completed, a summary analysis cover page showing all totals should be included as shown in table 5.27.2.

Table 5.27.1 Preparation of Zero-Based Budget Sample—Women's Soccer Budget, 2022–2023

TEAM TRAVEL BUDGET				
ACTUAL 2021–2022		PROPOSED 2022–2023 BUDGET		
Expenditure item	***Actual***	**Expenditure item**	**Proposed**	**Total**
Game at North Central		Game at Fairfield		$1,860.00
Bus	*$1,400.00*	Bus (based on current quote + 5%)	$1,470.00	
Dinner for 26	$390.00	Dinner for 26 ($15.00 per diem)	$390.00	
Tournament at Grand Junction		Tournament at Grand Junction		$3,435.00
Vans	*$700.00*	Van rentals (2 vans for 2 days, fuel at $175.00 each per day + 5%)	$735.00	
2 days of meals for 26	*$1,300.00*	2 days of meals for 26 ($25.00 per day)	$1,300.00	
14 hotel rooms	*$1,400.00*	14 hotel rooms ($100.00 per room)	$1,400.00	
Game at Montville		Game at South Central		$2,017.50
Bus	*$1,550.00*	Bus (based on current quote + 5%)	$1,627.50	
Dinner for 26	*$390.00*	Dinner for 26 ($15.00 per diem)	$390.00	
Tournament at West Arlington		Tournament at North Central		$6,955.00
Bus	*$3,600.00*	Bus (2-day rate + 5%)	$3,780.00	
2 days of meals for 26	*$1,300.00*	2 days of meals for 26 ($25.00 per day)	$1,300.00	
15 hotel rooms	*$1,875.00*	15 hotel rooms ($125.00 per room)	$1,875.00	
Tournament in Chicago		Tournament in Atlanta		$11,405.00
Flights for 26 ($250.00 fare)	*$6,500.00*	Flights for 26 (based on current fare of $285.00)	$7,410.00	
2 days of meals for 26	*$1,300.00*	2 days of meals for 26 ($25.00 per day)	$1,300.00	
Van rentals	*$700.00*	Van rentals (2 vans for 2 days, fuel at $175.00 each per day + 5%)	$735.00	
14 hotel rooms	*$1,960.00*	14 hotel rooms ($140.00 per room)	$1,960.00	
Game at Colts Neck		Game at Wycoff		$1,755.00
Bus	*$1,300.00*	Bus (based on current quote + 5%)	$1,365.00	
Dinner for 26	*$390.00*	Dinner for 26 ($15.00 per diem)	$390.00	
Game at Hampton		Tournament in Kansas City		$9,445.00
Bus	*$1,525.00*	Flights for 26 (based on current fare of $285.00)	$7,410.00	
Dinner for 26	*$390.00*	2 days of meals for 26 ($25.00 per day)	$1,300.00	
Van rentals	*$700.00*	Van rentals (2 vans for 2 days, fuel at $175.00 each per day + 5%)	$735.00	
Total	*$28,760.00*			$36,872.50

Notes:

Meal expenses assumes a travel party of 22 players, 3 coaches, and 1 trainer, same roster as this year; department per diem policy.

Hotel expenses assumes 11 team rooms, 2 coach rooms, 1 trainer room, and, if applicable, 1 room for driver, same as this year.

Hotel rates are based on 2020–2021 rates because future rates are unavailable.

The travel budget was much less this year because we had only one flight; next season will be our normal two-flight season; Atlanta is a more expensive trip than Chicago was this year.

No estimated increase in hotel rates; 5% increase in bus and van costs anticipated because of fuel cost increases.

Table 5.27.1 ***(continued)***

EQUIPMENT BUDGET				
ACTUAL 2021–2022		PROPOSED 2022–2023 BUDGET		
Expenditure item	***Actual***	**Expenditure item**	**Proposed**	**Total**
20 soccer balls	*$900.00*	20 soccer balls at $45.00 each	$900.00	
25 pinnies	*$150.00*	10 pinnies at $6.00 each	$60.00	
25 shin guards	*$625.00*			
25 fitted mouth guards	*$300.00*	25 fitted mouth guards at $12 each	$300.00	
50 game socks	*$600.00*			
Total	*$2,575.00*			$1,260.00

Note: Equipment expense is lower because we purchase shin guards and socks biannually and pinnies replacement stock annually.

RECRUITING						
ACTUAL 2021–2022		PROPOSED 2022–2023 BUDGET				
Expenditure item	***Actual***	**Expenditure item**	**Fees**	**Travel**	**Phone**	**Total**
Recruiting calls	*$1,200.00*	Recruiting calls			$1,200.00	$1,200.00
15 recruit visits	*$4,500.00*	Recruit visits (15 at $300.00 + 5%)		$4,725.00		$4,725.00
Piedmont Showcase (3 days)		Piedmont Showcase (3 days)				
Tournament fee	$400.00	Tournament fee (as posted)	$400.00			$400.00
Flight	*$275.00*	Flight (current fare + 5%)		$288.75		$288.75
Hotel, 2 nights	*$250.00*	Hotel (2 nights at $125.00 per night)		$250.00		$250.00
Rental car	*$125.00*	Rental car (2 days)		$125.00		$125.00
3 days of meals	*$105.00*	Meals (3 at $35.00 per diem)		$105.00		$105.00
		Dallas Showcase				
		Tournament fee (posted rate)		$350.00		$350.00
		Flight (current fare + 5%)		$341.25		$341.25
		Hotel (2 nights at current rate)		$395.00		$395.00
		Rental car (2 days)		$150.00		$150.00
		Meals (3 at $35.00 per diem)		$105.00		$105.00
Individual athlete assessment	$700.00	Individual athlete assessment		$735.00		$735.00
Total	*$7,555.00*					$9,170.00

Notes: Unless otherwise indicated and explained, no change in recruiting; proposed are based on last year's actual except a 5% increase projected for travel.

Addition of Dallas Showcase proposed to enhance recruiting effectiveness given poor quality of last year's class. Must extend recruiting reach; 5% increase projected for recruit visits because of estimated increase in travel costs.

GAME OFFICIALS						
ACTUAL 2021–2022		PROPOSED 2022–2023 BUDGET				
Expenditure item	***Actual***	**Expenditure item**	**Center official**	**Linespersons**	**Mileage**	**Total**
Carbondale	*$460.00*	Carbondale	$175.00	$250.00	$89.25	$510.00
Lion Weekend (4 games)	*$1,820.00*	Lion Weekend (4 games)	$700.00	$1,000.00	$178.50	$1,870.00
Farmingham	*$460.00*	Farmingham	$175.00	$250.00	$89.25	$510.00
Harrington–Bixby Weekend	*$970.00*	Harrington–Bixby Weekend	$350.00	$500.00	$178.50	$1,020.00
Maranca	*$460.00*	Maranca	$175.00	$250.00	$89.25	$510.00
Norris–Hanover Weekend	*$970.00*	Norris–Hanover Weekend	$350.00	$500.00	$178.50	$1,020.00
Carteret	*$460.00*	Carteret	$175.00	$250.00	$89.25	$510.00
Total	*$5,600.00*					$5,950.00

Notes: Proposed budget reflects $20 per game increase for the center official and $30 for linesperson per conference decision on fee increase. Mileage increased by 5% for anticipated increase in fuel cost over this year's actual.

MISCELLANEOUS				
ACTUAL 2021–2022		PROPOSED 2022–2023 BUDGET		
Expenditure item	***Actual***	**Expenditure item**	**Proposed**	**Total**
Video equipment (based on dept. allotment)	*$300.00*	Video equipment (based on dept. allotment)	$300.00	$300.00
Office supplies (based on dept. allotment)	*$200.00*	Office supplies (based on dept. allotment)	$200.00	$200.00
Conference coaches meeting		Conference coaches meeting		
2 day rental car (based on university rate)	*$80.00*	2 day rental car (based on current rate + 5%)	$84.00	$84.00
1 night in hotel (based on conference rate)	*$120.00*	1 night in hotel (same as this year's actual)	$120.00	$120.00
Tournament awards (based on last year's total)	*$300.00*	Tournament awards (based on this year's actual)	$300.00	$300.00
Total	*$1,000.00*			$1,004.00

Step 3: Comparison of Funding Levels to Desired Objectives

This section of the proposed budget submission should describe the level of achievement that the area can attain within the current funding level and the difference between that level and the desired objectives. A list of initiatives that the budget manager has implemented to provide a higher level of service with little to no cost should also be included. Finally, after these funding issues have been expressed, the budget manager should be asked to create a priority list of needs because only rarely are all budgeted requests granted. A thoughtful, detailed rationale for recommended priorities for addressing these needs should also be provided.

This section may also include an assessment and a comparison of competing institutions. Most athletic departments identify a set of peer institutions that they measure themselves against. If one of the primary goals is to be

Table 5.27.2 Sample Proposed Budget Summary Analysis Table
Women's Soccer Budget, 2022–2023

Line item	2021–2022	2022–2023	Difference
Team travel	$28,670.00	$36,872.50	$8,202.50
Equipment	$2,575.00	$1,260.00	($1,315.00)
Recruiting	$7,550.00	$9,170.00	$1,620.00
Officials	$5,600.00	$5,950.00	$350.00
Miscellaneous	$1,000.00	$1,004.00	$4.00
Total:	$45,395.00	$54,256.50	$8,861.50
Increase or decrease			19.52%

athletically competitive with these institutions, a periodic evaluation of how those comparable institutions are allocating their resources is necessary. Continuing to compete with an institution that is putting significantly more money into attracting the best coaches or recruiting the best athletes will be difficult. Are there other signs of financial support that will compromise the coach's ability to compete for top recruits, such as new facilities and more student-athlete support services? Each budget manager should have a finger on the pulse of funding priorities of peer institutions and reflect on how those priorities affect goal attainment both now and in the future. This information can be acquired through conference-wide surveys or school-initiated surveys. Relying on word of mouth is a dangerous approach, and we have found that most institutions are willing to share data when asked. Many conferences provide this survey service to member institutions on a regular basis.

Step 4: Identifying Other Needs Outside the Staff Member's Budget Area

Significant budget overlap occurs in the athletic department as well as with other campus departments. For example, athletic facilities budgets may be internal to the department, may be administered by the physical education or recreation department, or may be part of the overall institutional facilities budget. Thus, decisions made inside or outside the athletic department by a single budget manager could have dramatic effects on another budget manager's program. For example, a head coach may think that the sports information program is understaffed and cannot adequately promote her or his team and the individual athletes or that certain facility repairs need to be placed as higher priorities. Budget managers need to identify the needs external to their assigned budget responsibility and clearly describe the ramifications surrounding these issues. HK*Propel* contains a sample budget policy (Policy 5.28) and a sample form (Form 5.29) to use in implementing this budgeting process.

5.28 Policy—Policies Regarding the Development, Approval, and Control of the Annual Budget

A sample basic policy that details staff responsibilities for budget preparation and approval and the budget development process.

5.29 Form—Project Budget Form

A sample form that may be distributed to staff members to begin the zero-based budgeting process.

Found in HK*Propel*.

5.30 PLANNING TOOL

How to Cut a Budget

All but the most selective colleges and universities will be facing a decade or more of lower enrollment caused by the end of the baby boom generation, reductions in state funding, and the capping of student fees. Additionally, the pandemic not only revealed the unreasonableness of the expectation that athletic programs could continue unsustainable budget growth and maintain reliance on institutional subsidies, but also forced institutions to quickly adopt an increased capacity for online learning. It is clear that students do not expect to pay the same tuition dollars for online learning that they do for on-site education, and many will enroll in institutions that provide an array of online, blended, and on-site choices with different price points for each. This could significantly reduce institutional revenues.

When faced with budget reductions, athletic directors have to grapple with quality-versus-quantity decisions. Do you want to eliminate sports and preserve the funding levels of the remaining sports, or do you want to look for savings in a variety of areas to preserve all programs? The authors feel strongly that cutting teams and staff should be a last resort. More important, many athletic directors who have eliminated teams have openly regretted it, and in some cases have had to restore teams due to alumni unrest. Alumni rebellion and the bad press that accompanies cutting programs are not the only challenges. Often, dropping sports reduces alumni donations; brings about considerable pressure on trustees, legislators, the president, and the athletic director; and can result in Title IX lawsuits when women's sports are eliminated. For smaller institutions that do not give athletic scholarships and have an athlete population that comprises 20 to 30 percent of their undergraduate population, it may have a negative impact on the institution as a whole, reducing tuition dollars and negatively affecting retention and graduation rates. Eliminating teams also has a damaging effect on staff and student-athlete morale that cannot be overstated.

If you have a well-defined tiered structure in place as described in chapter 4, it will be much easier to analyze the department budget and identify potential savings. If you have never completed that type of analysis, it should be done now. It will provide practical solutions and policies to analyze and/or restructure the athletic department in a way that reflects a major–minor or multitiered sports system that would significantly reduce the overall operating budget, allow the athletic program to keep all currently sponsored sports, maintain priority funding levels for selected sports, and achieve full compliance with Title IX requirements. Additionally, it is imperative that all budget managers begin employing a zero-based budgeting approach as discussed earlier in this chapter. Too often, money is left unused in budget lines because annual across-the-board increases or decreases are implemented instead of using a zero-based budgeting process. It is amazing how reductions in many small-ticket items identified through zero-based budgeting can result in large savings.

Another reason to have a well-conceived budget based on a thorough analysis is to have the ability to provide detailed explanations of revenue and expenses to campus constituents. There is no doubt that athletic department budgets can be large and complex. Even in small institutions, the personnel costs, team operating and recruiting budgets, support services, facility revenues and expenses, game revenues and expenses, fund-raising budgets, and costs of alumni events can exceed the budget of almost any other department on campus. Large athletic departments that include television and vendor contracts in their budgets can well exceed any other school budgets (as opposed to department budgets) with the possible exception of a medical school. Therefore, campus administrators and other campus constituents may see the compelling size of an athletic department budget and assume that the department can afford to bear a larger percentage of overall university budget reductions compared to other departments. The athletic director must be able to present a cohesive, detailed budget that educates constituents on realistic needs of the department and ties the budget to the mission, goals, and objectives of the department and the institution.

Identification of Cost-Savings Strategies

Budget reductions could range from minimal to extreme. High schools and universities usually set reductions as a percentage of a department's operating budget (i.e., you must decrease your budget by 10 percent). Additionally, it makes a big difference if this reduction is for one year to make up for an immediate deficit, is part of a multiyear recovery strategy, or if it will be permanent. It is impossible to determine the best strategy for reducing a budget without knowing the specific circumstances and the percentage of reductions required. Instead, what follows is a general set of strategies that can be used during the budget reduction process to identify ways to trim expenses or increase revenues. It is also important to remember that the top three budget line items—personnel, scholarships, and transportation—is where the greatest savings will accrue.

- **Inclusion of All Staff.** Universities and high schools are insular communities that tend to share information among stakeholders. When budget reductions are being considered, word spreads quickly and most people start to worry about losing their jobs, which in turn leads to speculation, assumptions, and distractions that may be unwarranted. It is important that athletic directors are transparent about the situation as it evolves and assure staff that they will work as a team to identify the best process for making budget-reduction decisions. If the staff is aligned around a common vision of the organization, this process works well. Additionally, if there is a high level of trust in the athletic director and each subunit's budget manager, they will have an easier time in reaching consensus even when some reductions are distasteful. It is important that athletic directors keep the messages clear, be careful about what they promise, and don't expect to make everyone happy.
- **Reject Across-the-Board Cuts.** Using across-the-board cuts means that if an athletic department is asked to cut 15 percent from its overall budget, every subunit in the athletic department is directed to cut 15 percent from its budget. On the surface, across-the-board cuts appear to be fair and are much easier to administer than a deep-dive analysis resulting in targeted cuts. Sometimes leaders who use across-the-board cuts do so because they lack the information needed to do a thorough analysis or they lack the authority or trust from their employees to harness the support needed to implement a critical analysis of the budget. Neither of these reasons is good enough to take the easy way out. Many scholars state that across-the-board cuts are unsustainable, and Maddox (1999) calls them "indiscriminate." He states that across-the-board cuts "do not account for differences in units' ability to absorb cuts or in their starting level of budget flexibility" (p. 3). Leinwand and Couto (2017) claim that across-the-board cuts are unconnected to an organization's strategy and are difficult to justify. Given the complexity of an athletic department budget, these statements will reveal their accuracy when a thorough analysis is completed. Some units will have very little fat or ability to fund-raise while other units will have more flexibility to cut costs or increase revenue without altering the goals or objectives of the unit.
- **Use Targeted Cuts.** Targeted cuts are those that come from a complete budget analysis that takes into account the variables that follow in this section. Targeted cuts are based on justifiable reasons, are more sustainable than across-the-board cuts, and protect the primary goals and objectives of the department. If budget managers have been using zero-based budgeting, this should be an easier task. Identifying targeted cuts begins with a search for areas of funding that may have been nice to have in the past but are unnecessary to operate programs or services

at an acceptable level. Once those areas have been identified, calculations of cost savings should be made to determine next steps. If these reductions get the department close to its budget reduction goals, the athletic director may proceed straight to revenue-generation strategies to fill in the gap. If these reductions hardly make a dent, then a more thorough analysis will be necessary.

- **Personnel Savings.** Athletic staff employment contracts, salaries, and benefits are usually part of the institution's centralized employment system. The only exception may be revenue-generating athletic department programs that are administered as auxiliary enterprises of the university. Educational institutions tend to cut personnel as a last resort, and if possible will more often implement a wage freeze. However, if budget deficits mandate personnel reduction or pay cuts, the athletic director should be aware of any strategies the central administration is using or would find acceptable such as early retirement packages, buyouts of highly paid employees, hiring freezes, or reduction of salary through short furloughs. If there are head and assistant coaches who are making millions of dollars and have bonuses built into their contracts, they should be willing to forgo some percentage of their salaries and bonuses to help meet immediate needs. If none of these measures are acceptable or do not reach the mandated reductions in personnel, the athletic director should determine who are the "essential full-time workers" necessary to administering a functioning and effective athletic program. Undoubtedly, head coaches and some sports medicine personnel would be in that group and must be protected.

There are many other strategies that can help offset multiple terminations or the effect of terminations on how the department functions. If enrollment is down, are there ways to reduce salary but provide campus housing and food for young, single employees to make up the reduction in salary? Are there employees that could be eliminated by an investment in technology, such as eliminating some assistant coaches who do most of the recruiting by using online recruitment strategies rather than on-site recruitment? Are there support service employees such as an assistant equipment manager that could be replaced by a student intern who can be paid through the student work-study program? Can some support services be outsourced, such as contracting with a local physical therapy group to provide hourly services instead of maintaining salaries and benefits for the third and fourth athletic trainers? Are there ways to combine assistant coach positions within the department so one assistant coach works with two teams without doing too much damage to the quality of instruction or level of recruiting? Can the athletic director work with other campus departments to combine positions? For example, can an assistant coach also work as a resident director in a residence hall or fill a part-time position in alumni development? The possibilities are numerous and should be explored before an excellent employee is terminated.

- **Support Services Consolidation.** Almost every subunit that is considered a support service within a university athletic department has a counterpart department that provides many of the same services to the university population at large. Examples include sports medicine and health services, counseling services, career services, academic support programs, marketing and communications, fund-raising and alumni development, and targeted recruiting that leads to admissions and financial aid. Most athletic directors will tell you that they want complete control of these subunits, find oversight from central administration unacceptable, and even resist collaboration. During times of financial distress, athletic directors should be open to working with these departments to cut costs while continuing to provide quality services to student-athletes. In some cases, actual consolidation of two like subunits or departments may be necessary, and in the case of academic support, preferable.
- **Team Budgets.** No matter how many different types of teams are offered by an athletic department, team budgets look very similar.

Some common budget lines include travel expenses, game-day expenses, uniforms and outerwear, equipment, recruiting, office supplies, and professional development. There are several strategies an athletic director can use to reduce costs without affecting quality or quantity. One strategy is to centralize common purchases among all teams to increase purchasing power and reduce costs. For example, institutions often work with one apparel manufacturer to purchase all uniforms and outerwear. But do they think about contracting with a national hotel chain and dining chain to get discounts on meals for all team travel, as well as travel for recruiting and professional development? Can those same hotel deals be maximized when alumni come to campus for events or golf outings? Some of the larger athletic programs create deals with specific airlines that can cut costs by promising a significant amount of business and also monetizing frequent-flyer miles. Athletic directors should investigate any university-wide contracts, such as vending contracts and the food service contract, to determine if they can help offset concession expenses for events or summer camps.

Another way to cut costs while maintaining department quality and programming is to consolidate events. There may not be any other department on campus that hosts more on-campus events, off-campus events, or travels to more areas of the country than the athletic department. How can you maximize these events? For example, can a team trip also include an alumni event in that city rather than hosting separate alumni events? Besides saving on separate event costs, alumni will often host the event and serve dinner at their home for the team. Can the athletic department golf outing be the same day as the hall of fame induction dinner to generate more attendance at the dinner, which results in more revenue? The opportunities are endless and should be explored.

Strategies to save money or generate revenue for team budgets cannot always be done collectively. Some budget decisions will have to be completed team-by-team. Assuming all the unnecessary expenses described in the targeted cuts section have been accounted for, coaches and their supervisors may have to look for other ways to reduce their team budget. The athletic director must decide which teams will adopt one or more of the strategies listed below. If the athletic department is administering a major–minor sport model or a tiered funding model, it may be decided that tier I sports will not have to cut as much as sports in the other tiers. This can create some consternation among staff, but if there has been transparency about the different goals and objectives for sports in different tiers, decisions should be justifiable. Some team budget line items that could be considered for reduction include:

- *Fewer Contests*—Eliminating a few nonconference contests could dramatically reduce travel and game-day expenses, especially if those contests include flights or overnight stays. Most sports could do this without compromising their chances for postseason play.
- *Reduction of Financial Aid*—If student-athlete scholarships are actual dollars that come out of athletic department or team budgets rather than just a pass-through that is absorbed by the institution, a reduction in the number of full scholarships or partial scholarships could entail substantial savings.
- *Travel*—Travel reductions can be made by changing the nonconference schedule to reduce the distance to games so cheaper modes of transportation can be used and overnight stays would be eliminated. Additionally, per diem provided for meals could be reduced and the size of travel rosters could decrease. Staff travel for professional development could be eliminated or placed on a rotation of every two or three years rather than annually. Travel for spring break trips may have to be funded by student-athletes or trips canceled.
- *Uniforms and Outerwear*—Many teams may get new uniforms annually or every

two to three years. These time frames can be extended to save annual expenses or make up for a short-term budget reduction. This is an area similar to spring break travel where "pay for play" could be implemented, with student-athletes paying for certain items like athletic shoes, socks, mouth guards, or practice apparel.

- *Equipment*—Much like uniforms, equipment can be replaced less often or athletes can start paying for personal equipment like lacrosse sticks and baseball gloves.
- *Recruiting*—One of the only advantages of the 2020 pandemic is that it forced organizations to think about different ways to conduct business. There is no doubt this had a dramatic effect on recruiting. Athletic departments had to rely much more on social media, videos of student-athlete performances, online communications, and Zoom introductions and meetings. The cost of on-site recruiting was and can continue to be much reduced by using these strategies.

There may be other team budget lines that could be reduced. Each budget line needs to be analyzed. It is important to remember that if a reduction is permanent, it may also necessitate a policy change. For example, a current policy may state that teams will travel in university vans to contests up to two hours away and then will travel in buses for longer trips. If the practice changes to traveling in vans for contests up to three hours away, the written policy must be changed as well.

- **Athletic Conference Initiatives.** When the majority of institutions in the same athletic conference are under financial pressure, there may be several conference initiatives that could help relieve some of the burden. One strategy is the same one described in the team budget section that addresses consolidating common purchases across all schools. For example, the conference may be able to get better deals on apparel, equipment, hotel and restaurant discounts, and other common purchases by promising the business of 12 schools instead of 1.

  Another strategy is for conferences to analyze their current practices and see if there are embedded cost-savings measures. For example, a conference may have changed from a doubleheader schedule in baseball to a tripleheader schedule that necessitates an overnight stay for the visiting team. Reverting to the original game schedule could incur substantial savings. Some conference playoffs are multiday events at a single site. It might be more cost-effective if preliminary games were played on individual campuses.
- **Facilities Budgets.** Facilities budgets can be complex, have a wide range of expenses, and have multiple lines for significant revenue generation. Chapter 15 contains sections on fiscal sustainability, operating and deferred capital budgets, and personnel costs. A review of these sections can help athletic directors identify cost-savings measures or opportunities for revenue generation. Often, during times of financial stress, administrators tap deferred maintenance or capital reserve funds. This is risky because those funds must be available when facilities are in need of repair or replacement.
- **Increase Revenues.** When budget deficits are caused by a one-time occurrence or are minimal and can be corrected in one or two years, generating new revenue could be the sole solution and budget reductions may be avoided. A budget deficit that is substantial, permanent, and may increase over time makes total reliance on revenue generation difficult. This is especially true if revenue is "soft money" such as donations that cannot be counted on year after year. Chapter 13 contains 17 planning tools and management tips for revenue acquisition and fund-raising.

OFFICE OPERATIONS, FINANCE, AND BUDGETING

Canfield, C. (2011, August 24). Gov. LePage institutes "zero base" budgeting. *Bangor Daily News*. http://bangordailynews.com/2011/08/24/politics/gov-lepage-to-unveil-zero-based-budgeting-initiative.

Coyne, K., Coyne S. & Coyne, E. (2010, May). When you've got to cut costs—now. *Harvard Business Review*. https://hbr.org/2010/05/when-youve-got-to-cut-costs-now.

Drew University. (2007). *Department of Intercollegiate Athletics policy manual*. Unpublished manuscript. Madison, NJ.

Fried, G., Deshriver, T., & Mondello, M. (2020). *Sport finance* (4th ed.). Champaign, IL: Human Kinetics.

Lafaive, M.D. (2003, November 4). *The pros and cons of zero based budgeting*. Mackinac Center for Public Policy. www.mackinac.org/article.aspx?ID=5928.

Leinwand, P. & Couto, V. (2017, March 10). How to cut costs more strategically. *Harvard Business Review*. https://hbr.org/2017/03/how-to-cut-costs-more-strategically.

Maddox, D. (1999). *Strategic budget cutting*. Reprinted by the Grantsmanship Center. https://www.tgci.com/sites/default/files/pdf/Strategic%20Budget%20Cutting_1.pdf.

O'Brien, M. (2020, October 29). *Zero based budgeting revisited: a practical guide for 2021*. https://www.netsuite.com/portal/business-benchmark-brainyard/industries/articles/cfo-central/zero-based-budgeting.shtml.

University of Texas at Austin. (1992). *Intercollegiate athletics for women policy manual*. Unpublished. Austin, TX: Department of Women's Intercollegiate Athletics.

Zero based budgeting. (N.d.) Deloitte. https://www2.deloitte.com/us/en/pages/operations/articles/zero-based-budgeting.html.

CHAPTER

6

Managing a Staff to Accomplish Program Goals

Many variables must be addressed to provide an effective system of personnel management. Creating the organizational hierarchy, implementing strong hiring procedures that are tied to updated and specific job descriptions, administering a year-round system of departmental and individual performance evaluation, and linking compensation packages to performance are priority responsibilities of all athletic directors. The documents in this chapter, in both the book and HK*Propel*, provide a systematic way to construct and enhance employment practices, develop procedures and relevant documents, craft contracts and compensation packages, construct policies that will link the goals and objectives of the department to staff performance, and develop strategies for formative and summative evaluation.

TYPES OF DOCUMENTS

Management tip—Factual background information, insights, problem-solving strategies, and suggestions for the athletic director

Planning tool—Steps to take or factors that should be considered in the development of strategic plans, action plans, professional development plans, or governance systems

Educational resource—Handouts that can be used to educate staff members, campus constituents, volunteers, or student-athletes

Policy—Sample policies and procedures that should be adopted by an athletic department after customization and review by appropriate expert institutional or school district officials

Form—Sample forms, letters, or job descriptions

Evaluation instrument—Administrative tools that help the athletic director, a supervisor, or an employee assess job performance and evaluate program content

Risk assessment—Checklists that help the athletic director, a supervisor, or an employee identify risks and prevent litigation

6.1 MANAGEMENT TIP

Creating a Culture of Excellence

Recruiting new staff, motivating existing staff, and managing staff in an effective way are the most important tasks of any leader. But the ability to maximize staff performance and create a work climate that is enjoyable and inclusive should not rely completely on the inherent aspirations and work behaviors of employees. Proactive personnel management begins when the athletic director clearly articulates an expectation of excellence and inclusion that defines the working environment. A performance-based culture that generates enthusiasm, teamwork, and innovation is essential to maximizing employee success and satisfaction, both individually and collectively.

Changing the Work Culture

Whether the athletic director has occupied the same position for years or has taken a new position, he or she can always change a work culture that is deemed ineffective or low performing. Many new managers come in and start firing employees who don't seem to have the same vision or don't immediately meet their work expectations. That approach may seem like the easy thing to do, but it is patently unfair and may result in the loss of talented and committed employees. The better alternative is to educate staff and work collaboratively toward redefining goals and aspirations, as well as create new work structures that guide employees through the change process. Similarly, a long-standing athletic director may conclude that the current organizational culture is stagnant and needs revitalization. The first step may be as simple as just expressing this view aloud and making it clear that a commitment to change is required. In many cases, managers become so overwhelmed by the demands of day-to-day operations that they lose sight of opportunities to motivate staff or raise the performance bar. Thus, although building a culture of excellence from scratch is undoubtedly much easier than changing it, most managers must commit to proactive change as a way to enhance the performance culture over time. Key is the realization that accomplishing this goal requires built-in management systems that naturally support performance and innovation and don't rely heavily on the manager's ability to constantly motivate and direct employee behavior.

Connecting Compelling Vision With Goal-Directed Behavior

The first step in building a culture of excellence is building consensus through creation of a compelling vision. As described in chapter 3, a shared vision will be most effective, so collaborative determination of what constitutes excellence in the department is important. Unfortunately, many managers work with staff to develop vision, mission, goals, and objectives and then believe that their job is done. It is unrealistic to think that as long as clear performance goals exist, employees will naturally know how to reach them. This approach is no different from telling a coach to win games without discussing and identifying the key performance indicators that will result in success. Every goal must include a process for attainment that is both quantifiable and realistic. A well-defined process turns good intentions into goal-directed behavior.

Key Structural Elements of a High-Performance Culture

Several key elements are needed to build a culture of excellence and inclusion in which staff performance and satisfaction are maximized:

1. **Organizational structure**—Creating a department structure or organizational hierarchy as described in Planning Tool 6.2 that delivers clear decision-making authority, fair supervisory workloads, reliance on the contributions of senior managers, strong support for coaches, and respect for the role of support staff.
2. **Management style**—Insisting that all supervisors practice a daily management style characterized by open-door policies, intent listening and analysis of employee needs and requests, fairness, information sharing, and a commitment to conflict resolution. (Note: Chapter 1 is devoted to this topic, and Management Tip 6.3 discusses critical management behaviors.)
3. **Personnel hiring systems**—Developing clear job descriptions that are reflected in the posting of open positions, installing strong and comprehensive search processes including aggressive recruiting and well developed interview strategies, and providing comprehensive new employee orientation as described in Planning Tool 6.4.
4. **Personnel evaluation systems**—Ensuring that annual performance evaluations are integrated with measurable strategic plan objectives and executed by multiple stakeholders as described in Planning Tool 6.9.
5. **Compensation and benefit policies**—Ensuring fair and consistent compensation decisions, designing innovative reward and incentive systems, and providing mechanisms for job security as described in Planning Tool 6.32.
6. **Conflict resolution mechanisms**—Insisting on development of conflict resolution skills among employees, establishing fair disciplinary procedures, and providing wise termination processes as described in Management Tip 6.22.
7. **Professional development**—Establishing succession planning and demonstrating commitment to professional development for all employees as described in HK*Propel* Evaluation Instrument 6.14.
8. **Ethical behavior and professional conduct**—Providing comprehensive and clearly communicated standards, having low tolerance for unethical conduct, and requiring exemplary conduct of senior staff. (Note: Chapter 7 is devoted to ethical behavior and professional conduct.)

6.2 PLANNING TOOL

Organizational Chart and Supervisor Responsibilities

Organizational Chart

Many professionals believe that the best depiction of organizational structure as it relates to personnel management starts with the organizational chart. A realistic and accurate chart should reflect the hierarchy of positions with regard to decision-making authority and the reporting lines of all employees. Obviously, organizational charts vary in complexity as the size of the staff grows. Figures 6.2.1, 6.2.2, and 6.2.3 are typical organization charts for NCAA Division I, II, and III programs, respectively. Figure 6.2.4 is a typical organizational chart for a high school program.

Position Charts

Although organizational charts can correctly reflect hierarchies, the complexity of interrelationships between staff in an athletic department is often too difficult to depict. How senior management, coaches, and support personnel interact and conduct business varies significantly from institution to institution. This circumstance would be true even if the department operated under a sport equity model in which all sports were funded equally. The tiered models (in which some sports are treated differently from others) that are present in most athletic departments only create more ambiguity in structure and accountability. Thus, in addition to having in place the traditional organizational charts depicted in figures 6.2.1 through 6.2.4, the athletic director must create a position hierarchy that clarifies the status of positions that may have vastly different operating titles. Table 6.2.1 depicts such a position hierarchy.

Role of Senior Management

Another structural decision that must be made is the number and roles of senior management. Starting from the top, the athletic director has to decide which staff members should report directly to him or her. Of course, the size of the organization will dictate part of this decision. In a high school or small college, the athletic director may be the only person on staff with supervisory credentials. Coaches in these smaller athletic programs may hold second assignment titles as event managers, facility managers, physical education teachers, and the like, having responsibility for the day-to-day operations of their areas but no full-time staff supervision responsibility. But the athletic director in a larger, more decentralized department with several associate or assistant athletic directors has the flexibility to make more strategic decisions regarding personnel management.

One approach to making these decisions is to analyze four separate conditions.

1. **Priority athletic director responsibilities.** Compare the most important requirements of the athletic director's job against the need to supervise specific personnel. If external relationship building and fundraising are essential to the financial stability of the department, the athletic director may minimize the number of people who report directly to him or her so that he or she can spend a significant amount of time off campus meeting with donors, corporate sponsors, and the like.
2. **Power and visibility of employees.** Possibly a more important consideration is an analysis of the power and visibility of specific employees. Athletic departments are professional bureaucracies in which many employees (i.e., coaches) are experts in their areas. Such experts can be resistant to administrative oversight, and a select few, such as the head football or basketball coach, may wield significant power that includes support from trustees, important alumni, and vocal donors. Under such circumstances, the athletic director may have to be highly engaged with these employees,

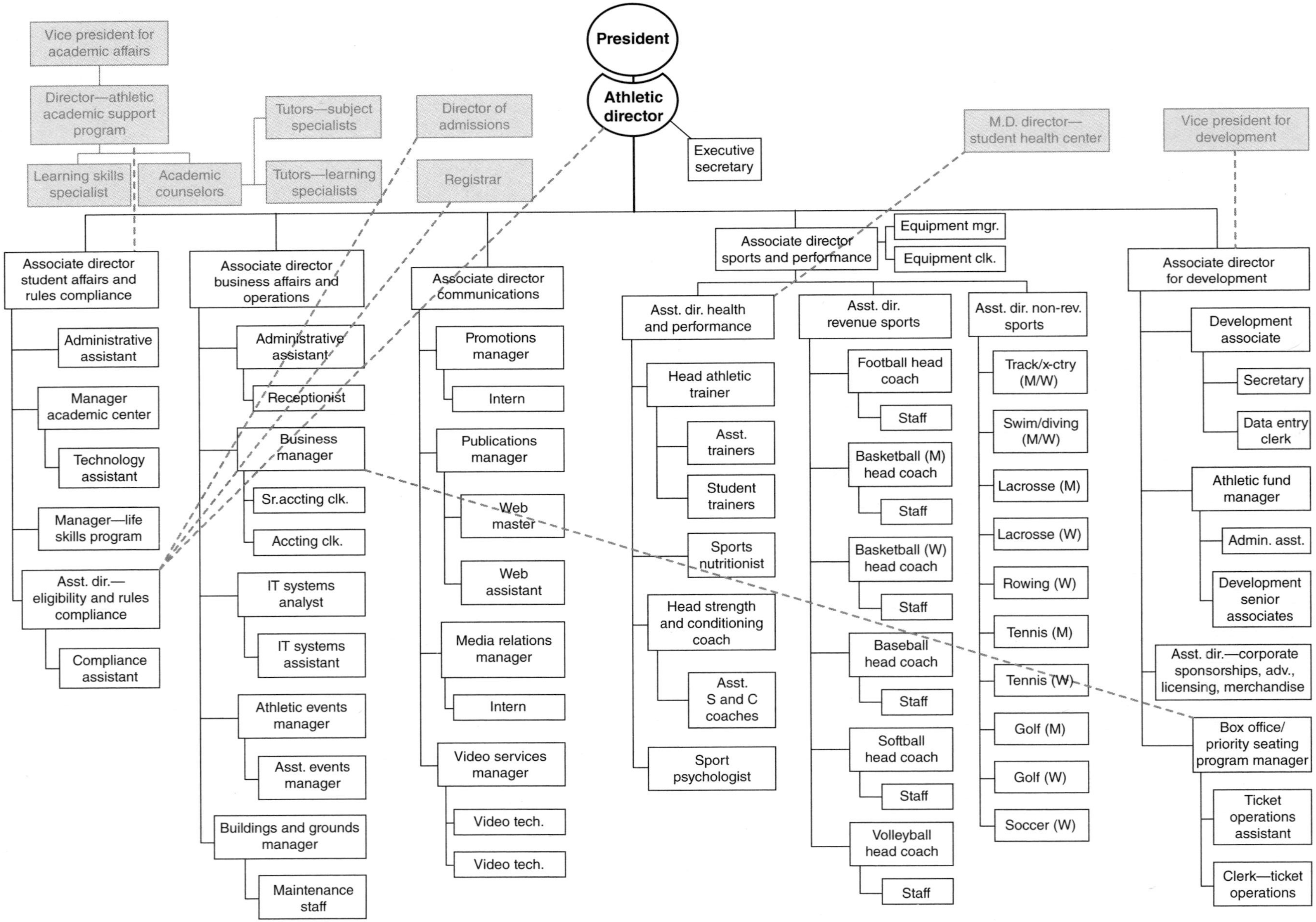

Figure 6.2.1 Sample organizational chart: Division I collegiate athletic program.

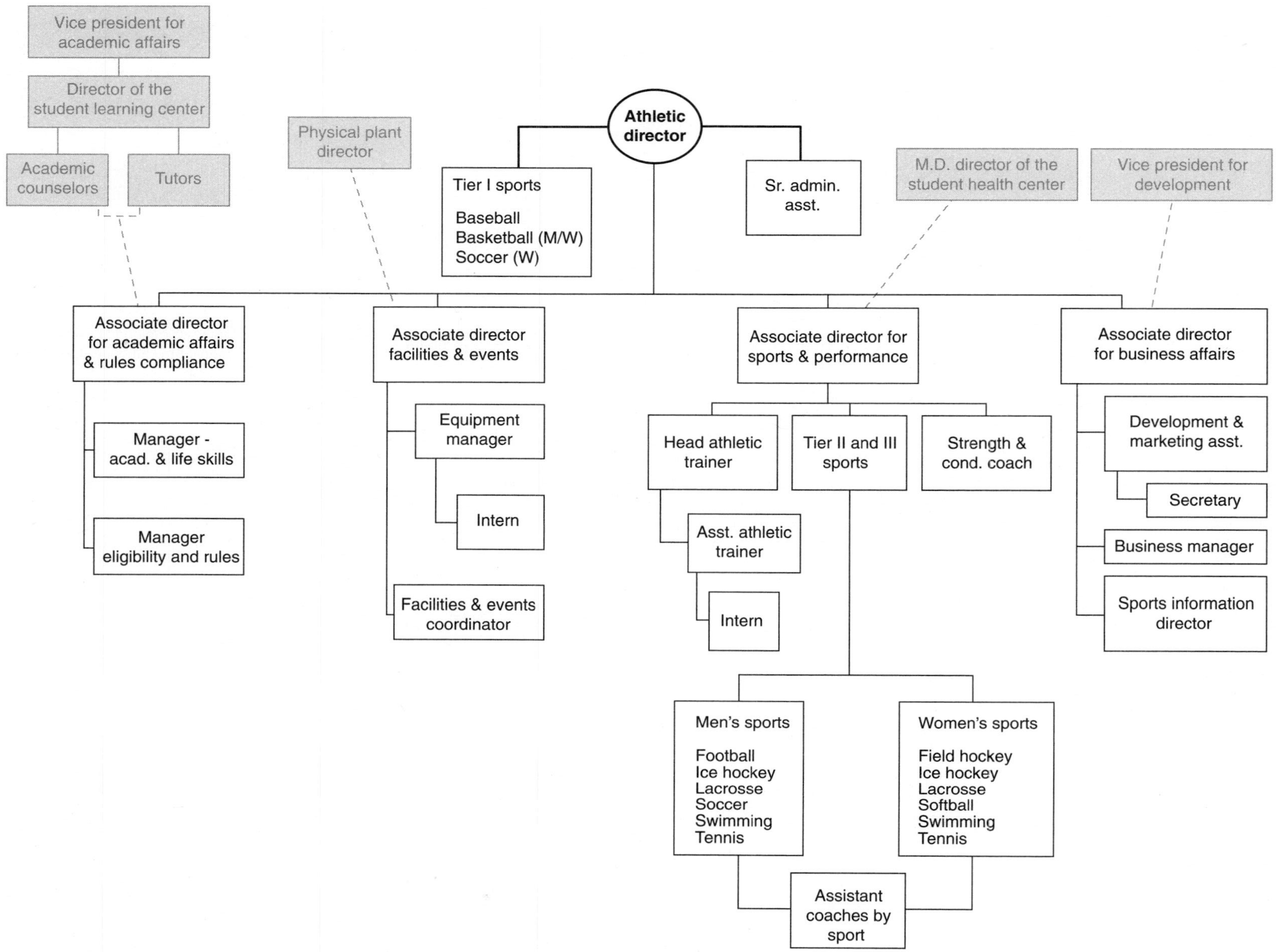

Figure 6.2.2 Sample organizational chart: Division II collegiate athletic program.

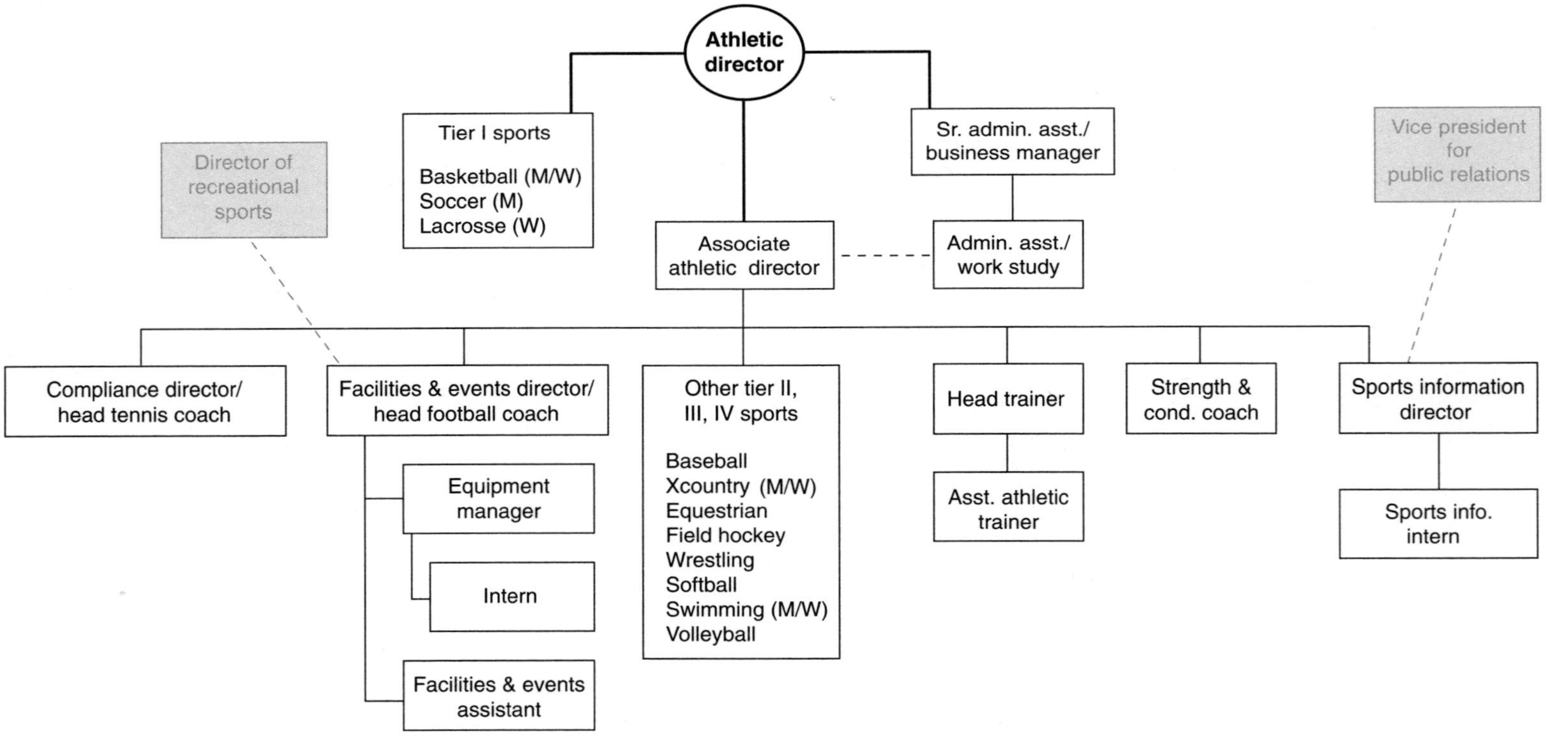

Figure 6.2.3 Sample organizational chart: Division III collegiate athletic program.

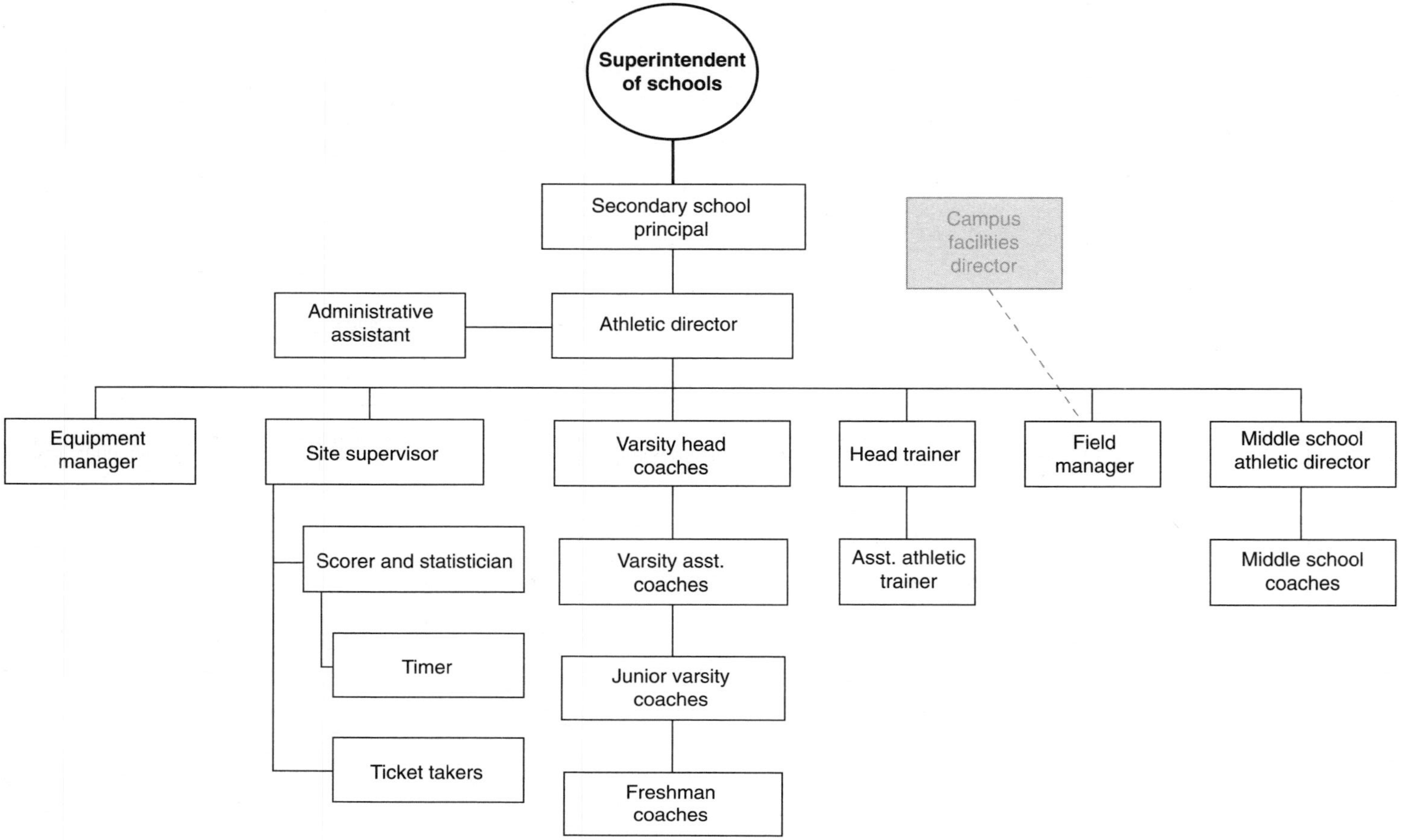

Figure 6.2.4 Sample organizational chart: High school athletic program.

Table 6.2.1 Sample Position Chart—Division I Athletic Department

Senior staff	Middle management	Exempt administrative and technical staff	Exempt professional staff	Nonexempt staff	Part-time or student workers
Athletic director	Manager, academic center	Assistant events manager	Head coach	Administrative assistant	Intern
Associate director for student affairs and rules compliance	Manager, student-life program	Web master	Assistant coach	Executive secretary	Graduate assistant
Associate director for business affairs and operations	Manager, eligibility and rules compliance	Video technician	Sport nutritionist	Secretary	Student trainer
Associate director for communications	Director, athletic academic support program	Recruiting coordinator	Head athletic trainer	Senior accounting clerk	Work-study student
Associate director for sport and performance	Business manager	Development associate	Assistant athletic trainer	Accounting clerk	Study hall supervisor
Associate director for development	IT systems analyst	Development senior associate	Head strength and conditioning coach	Receptionist	Technology assistant
	Athletic events manager	Equipment manager	Assistant strength and conditioning coach	Data entry clerk	Tutor, subject specialist
	Buildings and grounds manager	Compliance assistant	Sport psychologist	Ticket operations assistant	Tutor, learning skills
	Promotions manager		Learning skills specialist	Ticket operations clerk	
	Publications manager		Academic counselor	Groundskeeper	
	Media relations manager			Custodian	
	Video services manager			Equipment clerk	
	Sport operations director				
	Assistant director, health and performance				
	Assistant director, revenue sports				

Senior staff	Middle management	Exempt administrative and technical staff	Exempt professional staff	Nonexempt staff	Part-time or student workers
	Assistant director, nonrevenue sports				
	Sport operations manager				
	Athletic fund manager				
	Manager, corporate sponsorships, advertising, licensing, and merchandising				
	Box office and priority seating program manager				

Note: These job descriptions were selected because they reflect athletic staff positions with the highest degree of specialization, jobs most common among Division I athletic programs. In smaller athletic departments, positions might be combinations of two or three of these positions. Thus, in developing these job descriptions, responsibilities should be selected from among multiple position descriptions.

stay vigilantly aware of how they administer their programs, serve as a trusted collaborator, and know when to confront issues.

3. **Program priorities and risk.** The third condition is to analyze which program areas hold the highest level of priority or risk. If the department's physical plant is the largest barrier to success, the associate director for development may be instrumental in securing the funds needed for capital projects and should be a direct report to the athletic director. Similarly, the athletic director may determine that the inherent risks associated with sports medicine, coupled with a strained relationship between coaches who want their athletes back in action and a medical and training staff who refuse to clear them to play, is reason enough to have the assistant director for sports medicine report directly to him or her. This action would surely send a message to coaches that there is no gray area when determining the participation status of injured athletes.
4. **Supervisor capabilities.** The athletic director must assess who is capable of being the supervisor for the remaining senior managers. Is there an associate director of personnel or chief operating officer who has demonstrated high-level decision-making skills and the ability to mediate a variety of issues? Can this person serve as the second in command before she or he rises to the athletic director's level? If a person like this is not on staff, should one be added?

Supervisors as Teachers

Senior managers are typically in charge of a specialized area such as sports communication, event management, facility management, sports medicine, marketing and promotions, development, student services, and the like. Depending on the breadth of the athletic program, senior managers may each have a sizeable staff to supervise. Staff may include many part-time staff, interns, and student staff who need specific training and significant oversight. The athletic director should serve as a role model for these managers and make certain that they not only reflect the desired culture of the organization but also have the skill sets to both manage and teach people. Building both skill sets in practical ways is an ongoing leadership responsibility.

Distribution of Sport Program Supervision

Another important decision for the athletic director concerns the reporting lines for the head coaches who do not report directly to him or her. Some organizational charts show an equal distribution of sport programs among the associate and assistant athletic directors. In other words, each associate or assistant athletic director may be responsible for five teams. Others show only one direct report, often called the associate director for sports, responsible for all remaining sport programs. Still others have an almost scattergun depiction that places one team under one supervisor, four teams under another supervisor, and so on. The organizational chart does not tell the story of how or why these decisions were made.

Each athletic department is unique. Several factors should be considered when determining who should supervise head coaches. The most important factor is that the administrator must be self-confident enough to supervise coaches. As mentioned earlier, coaches are the experts in their sports and some have little tolerance for supervision. The administrator must recognize the importance of the coach's role but not be intimidated by it. Second, as few administrators as possible should be overseeing head coaches. An athletic department needs a consistent level of behavioral expectations and work performance from coaches. The ethos and the culture of the department rely heavily on the attitudes and actions of coaches. Therefore, consistent oversight is essential, and it may be compromised by supervision that is highly distributed among the senior staff. At the very least, if the sport programs are tiered with different levels of financial and other support and multiple supervisors are used, having the same person supervise all coaches of teams in the same tier may add some consistency to the mix.

Supervision of Strong Coaches

Even if reporting lines do not exist between coaches and some senior staff members, the athletic director must establish lines of control that clearly reinforce the role of management without compromising the positive influence of coaches. Coaches can be control freaks. They may want a say in all event decisions, the number of press releases sent out each week about their programs by sports information directors, scheduling of facilities for their teams, and a multitude of other decisions. Where are lines drawn between the wants and the needs of a coach and the expertise and decision-making authority of a manager? Determining a right or wrong answer for every situation is impossible, but a few rules of thumb may help. First, managers must be diligent about knowing and implementing policies that reinforce legal obligations, ethical decisions, and governing-body rules. In addition, managers are expected to reinforce department policies that are related to standardization of treatment of teams, consistency of quality of events, control of costs, duty of care for student-athletes, and other variables that should not be compromised. Athletic directors have to reinforce the importance of these variables, support senior staff efforts to control coach conduct, and consistently communicate why managers have both the right and the responsibility to make those decisions.

The importance of the coaching staff cannot be understated. At the end of the day, they are primarily responsible for making the most significant contributions to the success of the athletic program. They have the closest connections to student-athletes, their parents, donors, alumni, and other important constituents. Their winning percentages and the power that they wield are strongly correlated. This combination of power and ultimate responsibility creates a situation in which coaches want to run their own programs unilaterally, with little interference or oversight from anyone. They can become myopic and separate themselves from the rest of the department. In addition, like most human beings, as people become more enamored with them, their confidence can turn into arrogance. Often, the organizational structure of the athletic program supports this behavior by allowing winning coaches to work in a vacuum. A coach may not be held to the additional expectation of being a community member who is expected to reinforce department ethos and culture. In addition, coaches expect senior managers to play two vital roles: (1) boundary managers to protect them from outside interference and (2) budget managers and fund-raisers to secure the money they need for their programs. These roles are realistic and important, but senior managers must recognize that their responsibilities as they relate to coaches go beyond those of mere support. They must set expectations for coaches other than winning and have the courage to hold them accountable for meeting those expectations. Some coaches certainly have enough power to threaten an athletic director's or senior manager's job, but this circumstance does not release senior managers from doing their jobs as supervisors. Job descriptions and evaluation instruments and processes for coaches are important tools that help managers formalize the performance expectations of coaches while holding them accountable for meeting other expectations.

Supervisory Responsibilities of Coaches

An important responsibility of head coaches is to supervise assistant coaches. This starts with specific job descriptions and evaluation procedures. The head coach is also responsible for conveying the department's mission as well as goals and expectations of the program to her or his assistants and other staff members. The assistant coach needs to understand how s/he fits into the immediate and future needs of the program and must conform to the same ethical and professional responsibilities as the head coach. All job responsibilities, evaluation procedures, and ethical expectations must be clearly articulated and shared in writing. Head coaches must remain vigilant in monitoring the activities of assistants for rules compliance and integrity standards. Another responsibility of head coaches is to help assistants advance their careers. Head coaches must remember that they serve as mentors and must never lose sight of the significance of that responsibility.

Academic Unit Control of Student-Athlete Academic Support Programs

Control of athlete academic support programs should not reside in the athletic department for obvious conflict-of-interest reasons. But even though an academic unit controls the program, a close working relationship should exist between the athletic department and those responsible for the program with regard to student-athlete participation. The coach has a major and direct responsibility for recruiting student-athletes and supporting their academic success. The head coach controls whether a student participates or sits on the bench and is a key influencer whose encouragement is critical for attending class, study hall, and tutoring sessions and for engaging in other positive academic-related behaviors. Regular communication is needed between the academic support program staff and the coaching staff, either directly or through athletic personnel charged with that responsibility. Athletic program participation is time consuming. Academically at-risk students may need accommodations in scheduling or travel whenever sport participation and academic preparation conflict. Coaches may have to use the carrot of participation to reinforce class attendance or a student-athlete's participation in the academic support system.

Despite the forgoing discussion, some of the best and most ethical academic support programs in the country have been developed by athletic departments and are still controlled by athletic departments. What can the athletic director do in these cases to maintain program excellence while mitigating the appearance of impropriety? The solution is to move the entire program to control by an academic unit, being sure to retain the staff and organizational structure that made the program successful. In fact, moving the program would be a figure of speech. In all likelihood, the program would remain in the same physical space and continue to be funded by athletic department resources. All personnel would remain. The only change, though an important one, would be to whom the head of the program would report; that person would be outside the athletic department.

Development Relationships

Development or fund-raising creates an important organizational consideration. If the athletic program has any staff engaged in alumni and friend fund-raising, a dotted-line relationship should exist to the institutional development office and institutional policies that require athletic program development staff to collaborate in the cultivation and solicitation of gifts from high-wealth individuals, foundations, or corporations. Ultimately, in some cases the athletic department must be subservient to the larger interests of the university.

6.3 MANAGEMENT TIP

Critical Management Behaviors for Supervisors

Chapter 1 contains useful information that athletic directors can use to help train their management staff, including head coaches who supervise assistants. It may be prudent to have management staff read selected management tips and educational resources contained in chapter 1 and have a follow-up workshop to discuss essential skills and behaviors that will lead to everyone working in concert to build a culture of excellence. Although individual management styles may differ, a few management behaviors or policies should be consistent. The athletic director should consider mandating the following among all staff who supervise employees:

- **Open-door policy**. An open-door policy is an invitation for employees to approach their supervisors for advice at any time rather than requiring formal appointments or structured office hours. The time commitment that goes along with an open-door policy may be considerable, but employees who know that they can be heard when something important arises are more apt to avert crisis and be better team players. If employees sense that there is intolerance for sharing information or an attitude that employees are less competent if they can't solve their own problems, they will tend to work in a vacuum and minimize a problem until it reaches a boiling point. One strategy that a manager can use if he or she is busy is to ask the employee taking advantage of open-door access whether the conversation can wait until the manager completes his or her current task. Employees are often willing to wait and are happy that they were asked, and both the employee and manager are pleased when a short delay results in the problem resolving itself.
- **Listen, analyze, collaborate**. Having an open-door policy becomes useless if the manager is not a good listener. A certain amount of analysis has to take place while listening. Is the problem real or perceived? Is it important to this person but of no real significance to the program overall? Does the problem need to be addressed immediately, or is it something that may resolve itself just by waiting and watching? How much intervention is needed, and who is the best resource to help mediate the problem? Many times, when the manager listens and poses questions to the employee in an effort to analyze the nature of the issue, the result is collaborative problem solving that produces mutually beneficial results. Such collaboration also helps employees learn how to conduct their own problem solving for future situations. If the manager always provides the answer, employees become excessively reliant on the manager. Conversely, if the manager listens but then never gets back to the employee about the problem, the employee learns that trying to engage the manager is futile. He or she will tend to work in isolation. The manager needs to listen, ask questions essential to analyzing the problem, and collaborate with the employee to determine a solution.
- **Fairness**. Fair and consistent decision making is critical for all managers. People understand the word "no" when it can be explained reasonably and based on what is right or fair for the unit or department at large. Sometimes the presence of a tiered funding model may seem inherently unfair, but as long as the tiers and the rationale for a tiered system are clearly articulated, the manager should not be reluctant to make decisions that reflect those

differences and, while doing so, reemphasize why the differences must exist.

- **Information sharing.** Information sharing and transparency, except when the need for confidentiality exists, are essential components for building a team. Keeping people uninformed makes them feel disempowered, and they may ultimately see their manager as disingenuous. Keeping people informed gives them a sense of control and provides essential knowledge for good decision making, maximization of performance, and reinforcement of desirable work behaviors. To keep information flowing in all directions, having periodic, established staff meetings is important. When a staff meeting is scheduled every one or two weeks, managers will tend not to confront their supervisor for advice at every juncture but instead write down important issues as they arise for discussion in the next staff meeting. Staff meetings create regularized, proactive, and structured information sharing. If meetings are not on a set schedule, managers forget to share information at all levels and important information can be lost for certain subgroups.
- **Confrontation and problem solving.** The desire to be liked is present in most human beings. When the desire crosses over into a need, however, the ability to manage is often compromised. Managers must confront problems head-on. They must not bully or ever surmise that they know the motives that led to the problem but must engage in unbiased fact finding and be prepared to take the appropriate action. If a manager is ever unsure whether a problem warrants confrontation or feels intimidated by the employee, counsel should be sought from his or her immediate supervisor or the human resources department.

Valuing Staff Serving Support Services Roles

We believe that most people who work in athletics intuitively understand that employees who work in support services (sports medicine, sports information, academic support, administrative support, life skills, compliance, and so on) play vital roles in the lives of student-athletes, the success of the programs, and the culture of the department. Many athletic directors know that a great administrative assistant can be one of the most important people in the department. He or she can create and implement highly efficient day-to-day operations, avert crises on a regular basis, serve as a confidant to everyone in the department without compromising responsibilities or relationships, and bolster staff morale. In many athletic departments, however, the organizational structure of the department does not lend itself to an environment that fully appreciates the work of these important employees. They rarely get the recognition that they deserve, but more important they are often taken for granted. This circumstance is particularly true for athletic trainers, sports information personnel, and equipment managers. In many cases, coaches are permitted to create their in-season and nontraditional season training and game schedules with no regard for the effect that they may have on support staff. What makes matters worse is that coaches make last-minute changes to these schedules without asking support staff how such a change affects them. These last-minute changes are sometimes necessary, but at other times rescheduling may be on a whim or because a coach wants to punish a team by extending or adding another practice. In essence, staff in support services may be treated like indentured servants instead of valued colleagues.

A more compelling problem occurs when coaches impose pressure on support staff to behave in a certain way or to change a decision that creates ethical conflict. This issue can happen in a multitude of situations, but such conflict can bring about the greatest amount of risk and have serious consequences in three areas: rules compliance, academic support services, and sports medicine. Any pressure involving student-athlete participation as it relates to eligibility to play, academic success, or medical issues must be eliminated. Athletic directors must constantly reinforce that there are no gray areas in these three units and that coaches may not try to influence a decision in any way. In fact, as previously stated, this consideration is the rationale for removing academic support services from athletic department oversight.

The responsibility for creating an environment that recognizes support services staff members as expert and valued colleagues rests squarely on the shoulders of the athletic director. The athletic director must consistently mandate that all managers exhibit the highest respect for support staff. Athletic directors can use several strategies to set the tone for the treatment of staff in support services:

- Demonstrate respect for them by asking for feedback or their opinion when appropriate
- Take advantage of opportunities to thank them publicly
- Include them in staff meetings and ask them to report about their areas so that everyone can acquire an appreciation for what they do
- Create policies that demonstrate a concern for their seven-day-a-week, year-round schedule (e.g., by placing restrictions on Sunday practices unless a game is scheduled on Monday, giving them a seat at the table when nontraditional season practice schedules are being constructed, giving them the option to say no when schedules change unnecessarily)
- Remind coaches that by trying to control every aspect of their programs, they may be marginalizing some of the most important human resources available to them
- Create policies that give members of support staff the authority and right to make decisions

6.4 PLANNING TOOL

Assembling a Talented Workforce

Creating policies and procedures that will likely result in the hiring of highly qualified and talented employees while complying with laws that prohibit discrimination is the athletic director's most critical responsibility. Policy 6.5 found in HK*Propel* outlines a hiring approach that creates consistency and helps mitigate risk.

> **6.5 Policy**—Procedures Governing the Hiring of Employees
>
> Sample policies and procedures that address a step-by-step approach to hiring, including making a commitment to equal opportunity standards, posting job advertisements based on job descriptions, evaluating candidates, conducting interviews, evaluating finalists, conducting reference checks, and offering the job.
>
> Available in HK*Propel*.

The success of the athletic program depends on acquiring coaches who are master teachers; support personnel who are expert in responding to the academic, health, and developmental needs of student-athletes; and others who can acquire resources and fulfill responsibilities associated with conducting a successful athletic program. But program success is not enough. The athletic director is also seeking employees who demonstrate the highest standards of integrity and whose conduct and efforts are admired by the institution's faculty and staff, fans, alumni, and the public. Talented people who conform to the highest ethical and professional expectations are at the heart of the success of any organization. Although accurately judging the future success of any prospective employee is difficult, systems can be put in place to maximize this possibility. Following is a detailed discussion of model elements of a hiring process.

Job Descriptions

A basic and important piece of the personnel management system from both a hiring and evaluation perspective is the creation of detailed job descriptions that clearly express the responsibilities and work expectations of each employee. Job descriptions set the foundation that will affect hiring decisions, contract and compensation negotiations, annual performance evaluations, and daily supervision of personnel. Job descriptions should include at least all of the following elements:

- Title of the position
- Supervisor—who the position reports to
- The overall purpose of the position
- Employees supervised by the position
- An inclusive list of primary responsibilities including supervisory responsibilities
- Education and other formal certification requirements
- Experience required and preferred at a specific competency level

In essence, the job description serves as part of the employee's contract and determines employee accountability. Legally, the manager can expect the employee to perform only the duties listed on the job description and may be challenged by the employee if asked to complete other tasks. One way to create some flexibility is to include a line in every job description stating that the employee will be responsible for other tasks as assigned by the manager. If the job requires night or weekend work, that should be included in the job description as well. An example of a challenge based on a job description occurred when an athletic trainer asked the athletic director how she would be paid if the lacrosse team qualified for postseason competition. She was a nine-month employee whose contract ran from August 15 through May 15, and she refused to work the extra three days for the championship. When offered a later start the following year to make up for the three days worked, she refused. Therefore, the job description needs to be analyzed thoroughly so that it covers all demands of the job to the extent possible. A good management practice is to require supervisors and employees to update job descriptions annually. The employee and the manager should sign off on it for accuracy. This practice ensures that as a job grows or changes, the agreed-upon job description is up to date and the chance that an employee will challenge work expectations will be greatly reduced.

Job descriptions are time consuming to create because they partially reflect relatively detailed work contracts. Included in HK*Propel* are 44 job descriptions (Forms 6.42 through 6.85) common to a Division I athletic program. No job description is likely to be a perfect fit for an institution because the level of specialization in programs is extensive, but this collection can serve as a menu of job responsibilities and a starting point for athletic administrators to design their own job descriptions.

A significant position description anomaly in athletic programs is a common problem at many institutions. As described in Planning Tools 4.1 and 4.4, most athletic programs are tiered in that not all sports are treated equally. Yet many athletic departments have the same job description for all coaches although expectations of coaches from tier to tier are different, which often results in different responsibilities for head coaches and in some cases for assistant coaches as well. Therefore, athletic directors must be diligent about reflecting those differences in specific job descriptions. Failure to do so will create situations in which coaches can legally challenge compensation and treatment differences because coaching jobs appear to be equal based on the job descriptions. Careful attention should be paid to the sample job description for a head coach (Form 6.49 in HK*Propel*) to indicate criteria that might be different between coaches in various tiers.

A Model Hiring Process

Unfortunately, some athletic departments have been notorious for not following the hiring processes defined by the Equal Employment Opportunity Commission (EEOC) and observed by other campus departments, especially in the hiring of head coaches. Athletic directors claim that coaches are emergency hires because no one wants to lose recruits by going through a lengthy search process. This practice should be discouraged because it not only violates the spirit and letter of federal laws and can perpetuate years of discrimination in athletics with regard to the hiring of females and racial and ethnic minorities but also often results in bad-fit hires because due diligence was not taken to check references or have the candidate engage with a strong cross section of stakeholders before the selection decision was made. Thus, the hiring process should be respected, methodical, and focused on working to identify the right person for the position. Policy 6.5 is a sample policy and procedures document that clearly defines methodology for a model hiring process. Following is a practical discussion of the main steps, with an emphasis on important management tips.

Step 1: Reviewing the Job Description

Before any job is posted, the job description should be analyzed for accuracy and decisions should be made on necessary changes. These changes could result in a different reporting line, a different term of appointment, an adjustment in the compensation package, or new responsibilities. Any new hire may provide an opportunity for additional changes. The potential for change should always be explored, and the intent should be to provide an accurate description of the job responsibilities for the incoming position occupant.

Step 2: Forming the Search Committee

For department-specified non-entry-level professional positions (all head coach, senior staff, and middle manager positions with extensive supervisory responsibilities or significant duties), a search committee should be formed. Institutional or department policies may require representation on the search committee to be diverse in various ways. Chapter 10 on diversity, inclusion, and discrimination addresses these elements. If no policies exist, a good practice is to assemble a cross section of people from inside and outside the department and a committee composition that reflects gender and racial and ethnic diversity. If the athletic department workforce is significantly underrepresented with regard to gender and racial and ethnic minorities, consideration should be given to forming a search committee that has a majority of members from these minorities. Consider the following checklist for search committee composition:

- The direct supervisor of the position
- Athletic department employees whose jobs will be most affected by the new hire
- Athletic department peers of the new hire or those whose job will be minimally affected
- On-campus constituents outside the athletic department who have an interest in athletics, like the athletic policy board
- Faculty representatives (very important when hiring a head coach)
- On-campus constituents outside the athletic department who have minimal interest in athletics (as the most unbiased voice)
- Off-campus constituents who have an interest in the athletic department
- Student-athletes
- Representatives from underrepresented minority groups

Including a representative from each group for each position may not be necessary. For example, to hire a second assistant in compliance, the search committee may consist of the direct supervisor, one coach, one athlete, and a representative from a minority group. In contrast, a senior management or head coaching position should warrant a search committee that has a strong cross section of the groups listed earlier. In the case of a high-profile coach or athletic director, other people who are not part of the official search committee, such as the president or principal and members of the board, may meet with candidates.

Unfortunately, athletic department searches are often completed in-house with no outside voices. This circumstance occurs partly because of the emergency hire practice and partly because of long-standing cronyism. People with independent voices who are perceived as unbiased need to be included in searches so that the best hires can be made, hiring processes are diligently followed, and the manager is protected from accusations of selection bias. The chair of the search committee should have the confidence and trust of all members.

Step 3: Posting the Job The next step is for the institution's human resources (HR) office to use the job description to construct the job advertisement. If this task is not the function of HR but instead a responsibility of the athletic department, care must be taken to ensure that this posting announcement is accurate and functional. In some institutions, the hiring manager is an assigned HR office employee, whereas at other institutions, this responsibility is within the athletic department and performed by an assigned athletic business affairs employee or the direct supervisor for the position to be posted. Job advertisements are usually shorter and more concise than job descriptions because of the cost of posting in various print and electronic media and the size restrictions of such postings. See figures 6.4.1 and 6.4.2 for sample position postings of various sizes.

If the job description is comprehensive and complete, this process is much easier. The sections detailing education and experience required and preferred for the job and required skills, such as specific knowledge of computer programs, should be included. The job responsibilities, reporting line, and term of the appointment are already at hand in the job description. The hiring manager will have to decide whether to post a definite salary, a salary range, or leave compensation open ended and include a statement that salary is commensurate with experience. Remember that the salary range for coaching positions in men's and women's sports should be identical unless teams operate in different tiers and job descriptions and expectations are substantially different. Any difference in marketplace salaries offered must be based on the experience and qualifications of the individual, not the sex of the athletic team. In most instances, a brief description of benefits

Sample Position Posting: Long Form

*Position: Head Women's Lacrosse Coach at (*Name of Institution*)*

(*Name of institution*), located in the Philadelphia metropolitan area, is a comprehensive national university that supports 15 schools and divisions and provides graduate and undergraduate programs in 36 majors. The athletic department is a member of the NCAA (Division I) and the (*name of conference*) and supports 14 sports for men and 16 sports for women. All head coaches are expected to administer a sport program that promotes the educational goals of the institution, intentionally focuses on the growth and development of each student-athlete, and supports an ethical and fair sporting environment.

Duties

- In collaboration with the recruiting coordinator and the liaison from admissions, create and implement a comprehensive regional recruiting plan to attract athletically gifted student-athletes who match or exceed the academic profile of the student body
- In collaboration with the academic support staff, monitor and encourage the academic success of each lacrosse student-athlete, resulting in four- and five-year graduation rates that exceed those of the undergraduate student population
- In collaboration with the strength staff and sports medicine staff, construct a lacrosse training program that is safe and maximizes the athletic ability of each student-athlete, resulting in a win–loss record that, at the very least, secures a top-three finish in the conference annually and periodically (every three to four years) results in qualification for NCAA postseason championships
- In collaboration with the associate director for operations, complete the team game schedule annually
- Annually construct a zero-based budget for the lacrosse team that reflects sport program goals
- Oversee the implementation of the lacrosse team budget in accordance with university processes and procedures
- Administer one team community service project each year
- Supervise two assistant lacrosse coaches, one student-manager, and one work-study student
- Plan and implement fund-raising projects to offset the costs of the spring training trip and, if necessary, recruiting trips outside the Northeast and Mid-Atlantic regions
- Serve as the department liaison for all conference and national lacrosse coaches associations
- Oversee the implementation of all governing-body rules (lacrosse association, conference, NCAA) related to the lacrosse program
- Serve on a variety of campus committees
- Perform other duties as assigned by either the director of athletics or the associate director of operations, who serves as the direct supervisor to this position

Qualifications and Skills

Required

Bachelor's degree (preferably in education, sport management, or psychology)

Minimum of four years of experience as an NCAA Division I women's head lacrosse coach

Past record of improved team performance

Competent in Microsoft Word

Preferred

Master's degree

Coaching experience at a similar institution

Recruiting experience in the Northeast and Mid-Atlantic regions

Demonstrated success in NCAA postseason championship play

Competent in Excel spreadsheets

Submission of Materials and Deadline

Candidates must forward a cover letter, resume, and names of three professional references, including titles and contact information, by e-mail to

(*Name or title and e-mail address*)

The search will remain open until the position is filled.

(*Institution name*) fosters a diverse and inclusive working environment and is an equal opportunity employer. Qualified applicants from all racial, ethnic, or other minority groups are strongly encouraged to apply.

Salary is commensurate with experience and a comprehensive package of university benefits provided to all full-time employees is included.

Figure 6.4.1 Example of a position posting in long form.

offered is also included in the posting as well as statements related to the institution's commitment to equal opportunity employment processes.

At the first search committee meeting, committee members should review the job description and job posting. Questions or comments that may help inform thinking about the position should be invited. Collectively, the search committee should complete the posting document by determining what documents the applicants must submit (e.g., transcripts, resume, cover letter, three letters of reference), the closing date for application submission (or it can be left open until the position is filled if there is a concern that the talent pool will be limited), and where to send all applications.

Another important task of the committee is to decide where and when the posting will take place. Institutional policies often govern the level of the job and the scale of the search, and affirmative action policies ensure that advertising reaches minority candidates. The athletic department may have separate, institutionally approved policies that reflect what employee types require local, regional, or national searches, depending on the needs of the position

Sample Position Posting: Short Form

Head Coach, Women's Lacrosse

(*Name of institution*), located in the Philadelphia metropolitan area, is currently seeking a qualified head coach for the women's lacrosse team. The athletic department is a member of the NCAA (Division I) and the (*name of conference*) and supports 14 sports for men and 16 sports for women. Specific duties related to the lacrosse program include, but are not limited to, recruiting, academic advising, team training, scheduling, budgeting, fund-raising, implementing community service projects, monitoring governing-body rules compliance, and serving as the department liaison to campus and sport-specific committees. To be considered for the position, candidates must have a bachelor's degree (master's preferred) and at least three years of experience as a head women's lacrosse coach at an NCAA Division I member institution and a past record of improved team performance. Competency in Microsoft Word is required as well as a willingness to learn Microsoft Excel. Candidates must forward a cover letter, resume, and names of three professional references, including titles and contact information, by e-mail to (*name or title and e-mail address*). The search will remain open until the position is filled. (*Institution name*) fosters a diverse and inclusive working environment and is an equal opportunity employer. Qualified applicants from all racial, ethnic, or other minority groups are strongly encouraged to apply. Salary is commensurate with experience and a comprehensive package of university benefits provided to all full-time employees is included.

Figure 6.4.2 Example of a position posting in short form.

and the availability of talented people for those positions. For example, if the institution is in a well-populated area that is home to many businesses, excellent administrative assistants and personnel for the athletic business office may be easily found through local searches. If certain coaches are required to have teams ranked in the top 10 in the country, the search for those coaches may be extended to a national or international pool of candidates.

If the posting is subject to hard-and-fast institutional rules, the search committee does not need to decide where to post. But if flexibility is allowed because of the importance of the hire or a perception that the talent pool is small, members of the search committee need to help determine where the job will be posted. Feedback from the representatives of minority groups is especially important. Chapter 10 on diversity, inclusion, and discrimination contains detailed information pertaining to minority hiring strategies and practices.

Typically, before posting the job, the hiring manager must get approval to do so through the human resources office of the institution or school district and, if available on campus, the affirmative action officer. After those approvals are secured, the hiring manager may post the position at the sites agreed upon by the search committee.

Step 4: Defining Committee Operating Procedures After completing the work related to posting the position, other important agenda items to include at the first search committee meeting are as follows:

- Review policies and procedures related to the hiring process
- Create a schedule of meetings
- Establish deadlines for reading application folders
- Create a timetable for finalist interviews
- Designate the person responsible for producing the minutes of the meeting, emphasizing

the importance of detailing reasons that candidates are not selected or selected over each other

- Search committee function (to hire or to provide a ranked list to a senior manager)
- Agree on interview questions for references and committee members who will be authorized to contact references (draft to be prepared by supervisor for position to be hired)
- Agree on interview questions to be asked of all candidates (draft to be prepared by supervisor for position to be hired)
- Review and agree on a rating sheet to be used to compare candidates
- Decide whether background checks will be required of all finalists

All search committee members need to make their respective participation a priority so that when an agreed-upon schedule can be determined, they can participate as fully as possible. The search committee must also understand the role they play. Some search committees make the final hire based on majority vote. Other committees are responsible for providing a ranked or unranked list of finalists to a senior manager who ultimately makes the decision. In addition, minutes should be taken at all search committee meetings in case a complaint is lodged later in the process by a disgruntled applicant claiming biased selection. Another important point is to detail the reasons for not selecting candidates and selecting one candidate over another. These explanations are usually required by the institution's human resources office. Form 6.8 in HK*Propel* can be used to summarize information about each candidate and provide rationale for decisions.

Step 5: Engaging in Aggressive Recruitment Strategies Most important hires (senior managers, head coaches, and so on) do not rely on the typical job advertisement to create an excellent pool of candidates. Normal operating procedure is for athletic directors, presidents, principals, and the like to research winning programs or contact valued colleagues to identify the best talent in the marketplace. Personal solicitation of identified individuals and encouragement of their consideration not only happens all the time but is critical to identification of the most qualified and experienced applicants. Unfortunately, in athletics, recruitment often happens before the job description is even written or posted, and rumors abound that the job advertisement doesn't even appear until a secret candidate has been selected. As noted earlier, emergency hires should be minimized whenever possible. But we do encourage hiring managers to maintain succession lists and to expand the applicant pool through solicitation of applications from candidates who have demonstrated excellence. This strategy will help enrich the pool by soliciting strong minority and female candidates. There is nothing impermissible about encouraging prospective applicants to apply as long as the formal application, assessment, and interview process is fair and equal for all candidates who apply. A hiring manager should never convey that a candidate will get the job or that the process of interviewing other candidates is merely to demonstrate that institutional policy or state or federal laws are being followed.

Step 6: Assessing and Interviewing Candidates Litigation surrounding search procedures is commonplace. A number of hard-and-fast rules related to assessing and interviewing candidates and communicating with references provided by candidates must be followed.

Preinterview Assessment Rules

- Follow all affirmative action policies and procedures as provided by the institution.
- Make certain that everyone involved in the search as well as employees who process applications understand that candidate information must remain confidential at all times, even after a selection has been made.
- Make sure that every applicant has a file that is available to all approved readers and that every application file includes a record of when each document (resume, reference letters, and so on) arrived. A good practice is to send an e-mail or letter to all applicants thanking them for their interest and letting them know that their materials have been received. In the interest of efficiency, consider informing all applicants with a standard response acknowledging receipt of their application that also lets them know

that they will be contacted again only if they are selected for a telephone or on-campus interview. This practice will cut down on the number of applicants who call to see whether the materials arrived. Form 6.6 found in HK*Propel* is a sample acknowledgment letter.

- Create a rating sheet immediately after the job advertisement has been approved. The rating sheet should be based on the qualifications and job responsibilities listed on the job advertisement. Require every search committee member to complete a rating and mandate that the rating sheet must be used for every applicant. Form 6.7 in HK*Propel* is a sample rating sheet that is usable for all positions. For head coaches, elements such as years of experience as a head coach, years of experience as an assistant coach, competitive level of experience, win–loss records as head coach, and other important comparisons should be added to any general rating sheet.
- Be diligent about checking references and give special attention to the most recent direct supervisors of applicants. Employers hire an astounding number of people for new jobs without ever calling the most recent supervisor or listed references.
- Call only those references whom the applicant has provided. If the search committee wants to call other people who are not listed as references (e.g., a direct supervisor), the search committee chair should ask for the applicant's permission to call that person and place the applicant's e-mail or signed fax approval of such consent in the applicant's application file.
- Keep the number of people making reference calls to a minimum and prohibit anyone else from doing so, even off the record. All people making reference calls must understand rules related to permissible and nonpermissible employment or demographic questions.
- All references contacted should be asked the same questions to ensure the same breadth of information for all candidates. These questions should be collaboratively designed by the search committee or hiring manager, approved by a human resources staff member, and distributed to all those making reference calls if more than one person is making such calls.
- When calling a reference, never ask a question that does not relate to the job or is personal in nature (e.g., marital status, sexual orientation, age, number of children, race, ethnicity). Never pose a question from a negative perspective such as, "I've heard this guy can be lazy. What do you think?" It would be better to ask, "On a scale of 1 to 10 with 10 being the highest, how would you rate this applicant's work ethic?" Remember, most people serving as references are likely to call the applicant immediately and relate all

6.6 Form—Letter Acknowledging Receipt of Application

A sample form letter that lets applicants know which materials have been received, whether outstanding materials are needed, and what policies apply regarding follow-up contact.

6.7 Form—Candidate Evaluation Form

A sample rating sheet based on general qualifications such as education, years of experience, technical skills, and the like that could be used for any candidate.

6.8 Form—Summary of Candidates' Evaluations

This form is a template that can be used by the chair of the search committee or by the hiring manager to record average scores that search committee members assign candidates on a variety of qualifications, which should ultimately be used to determine the pool of finalists.

Available in HK*Propel*.

the details of the call, so care must be taken to remain impartial. An acceptable and recommended practice is to ask, as a standard reference question, whether there are any red flags related to the applicant that might compromise his or her ability to do the job.

- Resist speaking to applicants who call about the job because getting phone time with the hiring manager can be seen as an advantage to the applicant who does so. Merely direct them to the application procedures.
- If a deadline date has been set for submitting applications, it must be adhered to unless the search is reopened later. Therefore, applications that come in after the deadline may not be considered.
- Search committee meetings to evaluate applications can take one round or several rounds depending on the quality and the quantity of the applicant pool. Require all search committee members to have their rating sheets with them at each meeting. Ranking of candidates should be completed on paper, confidentially, so that committee members aren't swayed by other members' rankings. Again, be diligent that the minutes of the meeting reflect the process used and the ranking lists that were derived.
- After the search committee determines the final pool to be interviewed, the search committee chair should collect all the rating sheets. If an affirmative action officer or a human resources representative has to approve the finalists before interviews can be scheduled, he or she may want to review the rating sheets to see why some candidates were included and others were not. If that process does not exist, the search committee members may keep the rating sheets until all work is completed.
- Before interviewing finalist candidates, the search committee should create a slate of questions to ask all candidates so that they are on a level playing field. In addition, answers can be compared across those interviewed. Remember to include this slate of questions in the meeting minutes.
- The search committee should also create an interview rating sheet based on the questions, job requirements, and general demeanor such as poise, confidence, and enthusiasm.
- If preinterview assessment rating sheets were collected, hand the rating sheets of the selected candidates back to the respective committee members so that they have their own notes in front of them for the interviews.

Interview Rules

- After a finalist list of candidates judged to be qualified to advance to the interview stage of the hiring process has been determined, care must be taken to make sure that every candidate meets all the same people. Litigation risk is high whenever some candidates get to meet a dean, a principal, a board member, or another person in power while others don't. At times, some search committee members may miss an interview. That member may not take part in any ranking of the finalists unless the person they failed to meet is excluded from a ranking list determined by the rest of the committee. Remember to reflect this situation in the meeting minutes.
- Managers have asked whether videotaping a finalist candidate's interview is permissible if a search committee member is absent. This practice is not permissible unless all candidates had the same pressure of being videotaped during their interviews.
- Be diligent about asking all the same initial questions of each candidate. As the candidate speaks, other questions may arise. That kind of questioning is permissible.
- Never ask a candidate any personal questions (marital status, sexual orientation, age, and so on). Stay focused on the requirements of the job and the candidate's ability to perform the job.
- Allow time for the candidate to ask his or her own questions.
- Never share the names of other finalists.
- Never compromise the people who provided references by sharing information about those conversations with the candidate.
- End interviews by telling the candidate that if for any reason he or she decides not to continue pursuing the job, the candidate should let the search committee chair know

to withdraw his or her name. Conversely, if a candidate wants the job but in the meantime is offered another job, he or she should call the chair to find out where the search committee is in the process before accepting the other job.

- The recruiting process often focuses heavily on the applicant's background and does not provide the applicant with a clear understanding of the job and the working environment from a micro and a macro perspective. The search committee should specify that time will be set aside during every interview for the supervisor of the position to communicate exactly what it means to be part of the program, covering program goals, expectations, ethical underpinnings, and work climate. Applicants should be asked to reflect on how well their own aspirations, values, work behaviors, and work style fit with those elements. Inclusion of this interview element may cause some applicants to question whether the job is right for them and withdraw their names from consideration. But withdrawal is a much better alternative than hiring the person and finding out later that the person's goals, values, or work behaviors are incompatible with those of the department. Remember that many terminations are the result of bad fit rather than lack of skills or expertise. Assessing fit early in the process is imperative.

Postinterview Assessment Rules

- Determine whether any search committee members missed an interview and if so, eliminate them from ranking candidates unless the person he or she missed interviewing is excluded from the ranking list created by the rest of the committee. If a candidate was unable to meet with a person of importance (e.g., president, hiring manager), another meeting should be arranged. The human resource department will have to decide whether a phone interview would suffice.
- Similar to the preinterview assessment rankings, finalist assessments should be completed in a confidential manner and written on paper.
- Meeting minutes should reflect the processes used, the ranking lists, and the final slate of candidates to move forward to the hiring manager or the final selection, depending on the role of the committee.
- The committee should also discuss what-ifs. What happens if our selected candidate turns down the job? Do we automatically go to the second candidate? If so, what happens if the second candidate turns us down? Do we reopen the search?
- When the committee's work is completed, all rating sheets must be collected and included in the search file. All meeting minutes must be included in the search file as well. This practice will help protect the institution if someone challenges the process soon afterward or years later.
- As mentioned earlier, the hiring manager or chair of the search committee should complete Form 6.8 in HK*Propel*, which shows the reasons why all applicants were rejected, advanced to the interview stage, or ranked for the job offer.

Step 7: Offering the Job Standard procedure at most institutions is that certain individuals (e.g., a human resources representative, an affirmative action officer, a direct supervisor) must approve a hiring before the job is offered. The person offering the position must be armed with any information that was not provided during the interview such as final salary, contract elements, and the like. Standard form is to offer the position in writing with all critical elements reviewed and acknowledge that the hiring will not be complete until all formal letters of appointment or contracts are agreed upon and signed. This conversation is a good-faith job offer that includes as much detailed information as possible. Candidates often take a day or two to make their final decision.

Most managers are excited about informing a strong candidate that he or she was selected for the position. But this assignment can be frustrating when that person seems less than enthusiastic and asks for a significant amount of time to think it over. Managers must be prepared for this occurrence before even making the telephone call. Through consultation with appropriate others, the manager must be ready to respond with a deadline date based on myriad concerns that can range from worrying about losing other strong candidates to having to reopen the search, compromising the current program because no leader is in place (especially for a head coach hire), or other issues relevant to each situation. Regardless of the circumstance, the hiring manager should avoid frustration and be prepared to take the next step if necessary. The last thing a manager wants to do is hire a reluctant employee. Chances are that the person will stay for only a short time or create unnecessary problems.

Orientation of New Employees

New employees should be required to complete a well-constructed orientation program that provides information about institutional policies and procedures. The athletic department should construct an employee orientation checklist such as Form 5.2 to aid in this process. (Form 5.2 can be found in HK*Propel*.)

All new employees should be introduced to the full department policy manual and have a specified time to review it and meet again to ask questions. Of course, this process is ongoing, but having a required orientation of new employees may avert problems early in their tenure. Orientation also allows new people to meet each other, feel informed, and potentially feel less isolated in the first few weeks of a new job.

6.9 PLANNING TOOL

Program and Employee Evaluation and Corrective Action Techniques

Employee evaluation is an essential element of a strong personnel management system that also includes position descriptions, effective hiring processes, comprehensive orientation programs, model employment contracts, fair compensation packages, and other personnel policies. Without all these elements, personnel management becomes reactive rather than proactive and subjects the manager and the department to the potential for significant internal conflict that could ultimately result in reduced employee morale, grievances, or legal challenges. Evaluation plays a particularly important role because it holds the promise of motivating employees to improve and contribute more effectively to organizational success. Along with evaluation, the athletic department must have policies and procedures in place for employee improvement, reporting of grievances, and, if necessary, termination. It is important to remember that there is a distinction between annual evaluation and performance improvement plans compared to situations where the athletic director must address unacceptable employee misconduct or performance deficiencies that warrant immediate disciplinary or corrective action. Policy 6.10 found in HK*Propel* is a comprehensive approach to systematizing evaluation, implementing performance improvement plans, and taking corrective action in a variety of circumstances.

6.10 Policy—Evaluation, Corrective Action, and Termination

Sample policies and procedures that address department-wide expectations and ethical behavior, systematic evaluation, performance improvement plans, corrective action plans, termination, and employee grievances.

Available in HK*Propel*.

Healthy Performance Evaluation Perspective

If a room full of people are asked what they think about performance evaluation, the vast majority would undoubtedly say something negative. People react negatively to being evaluated for several reasons:

- Managers are basically uncomfortable in the evaluator's role and therefore tend to rush through the process without accomplishing specific objectives.
- Managers use evaluation in a punitive way to highlight employee weaknesses and demonstrate their own power.
- Employees are kept in the dark about what evaluation tools will be used, if any, and what will be measured until they walk into the evaluation meeting.
- Evaluation is purely subjective according to the ideas and inclinations of the manager.

The primary focus of performance evaluations should be a process that helps employees maximize their abilities, continue to grow in their positions, celebrate their accomplishments collectively and individually, and address a future professional development plan. Only when an employee refuses to listen to feedback, is resistant to change, is clearly a bad fit for the organization, or does something outside the boundaries of professional behavior should performance evaluation be used as a way to create a case for separation of service. In fact, when a strong performance evaluation system is in place—one that is fair, is well communicated, and provides employees with training and time to improve—most managers will rarely have to terminate anyone because ineffective employees will often seek and find another job before they are fired. Of course, this point does not apply to coaches with multiyear contracts who cannot resign while retaining their buyout packages.

Integrated Approach to Performance Evaluation

As with job descriptions, no single evaluation instrument is likely to be a perfect fit for a department. The athletic director needs to view a variety of approaches to performance evaluation from multiple perspectives: the overall athletic department, specific sport programs, specific support programs, individual staff members, student-athletes, and other stakeholders. Staff collaboration in the construction or revision of evaluation instruments is important. When staff members are permitted to discuss the reasonable performance indicators upon which they or their programs should be evaluated, a level of buy-in for the process develops that may not happen as easily when senior managers construct the instruments in a vacuum. Evaluation must be as objective as possible and not just a casual conversation at the end of the year. The use of well-constructed tools is essential, and evaluation meetings that are well documented must take place. An integrated three-step approach to department and individual staff evaluation as shown in figure 6.9.1 and described in the next section is suggested.

Step 1: Macro View The macro view of performance evaluation focuses on the collective achievements of the staff at large and has four basic purposes:

- Serves as an internal assessment of athletic department mission and goal performance
- Provides valid information for production of management reports that serve as value-added documents for university decision makers
- Creates a platform to celebrate department achievements and sell the program to important constituents (faculty, recruits, alumni, media)
- Creates motivational benchmarks for each staff member

Every athletic director must create annual management documents that reflect how well the department performed that year. This collection of measurements also applies to individual performance. Collecting data pertaining to multiple measures such as team winning percentage; league, conference, or national rankings; individual student-athlete awards; student-athlete academic performance; student-athlete satisfaction; coach awards; staff committee service and national, regional, and local appearances as speakers or authors; injury data; press coverage; fund-raising yields; community service projects; and other measurable performance indicators that can be directly tied to the mission, objectives, or performance expectations of the department is essential. That data, when compiled and presented,

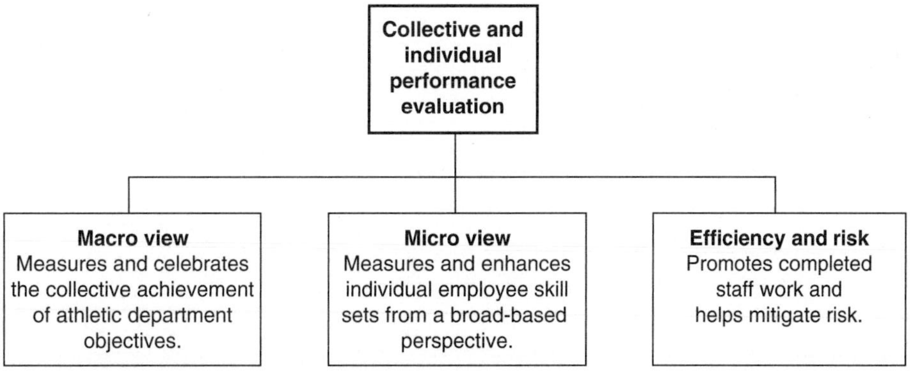

Figure 6.9.1 An integrated approach to performance management.

serves the basic purposes listed earlier and creates a positive approach to the evaluation process. Specific tools must be used to capture that data.

For example, year-end reports should be required of all head coaches and support-area program managers. Factual and quantifiable demonstration of achievements should be presented. Similarly, all employees should be asked to reflect on the specific elements of their respective job descriptions as well as common elements relevant to all staff for the purpose of communicating factual and quantifiable achievements. Athletic personnel take part in so many activities that it would be impossible to have a total appreciation of accomplishments and areas that need attention without asking staff members themselves. Excerpts from these reports should be used to develop an athletic department year-end report.

Overall department and specific program reports are macro views. Evaluation Instrument 6.11 is an example of a year-end summary of athletic department achievements that could be featured on a website, serve as part of the department's justification for the proposed budget, or be a focus for a year-end fund-raising initiative.

A report like this should be derived from all sport and support program submissions collected and should be a highly selective and impressive document of success and achievement. Evaluation Instrument 6.12 is an example of a sport program achievements report, and Evaluation Instrument 6.13 is a sample report from a specific support program area. These documents can be found in HK*Propel*.

Step 2: Micro View The micro view is a springboard from the collective accomplishments of the department described earlier to the specific skills, accomplishments, and possible weaknesses of each individual employee. In essence, individual employee evaluations should accomplish the following:

- Serve as a tangible link to job descriptions and reinforcement of specific duties and expectations
- Demonstrate that each person has an important role in the department
- Serve as a teaching tool to enhance employees' skills or improve identified weaknesses
- Serve to protect employees from complaining parents, other constituents, or even a new supervisor

Evaluation Instrument 6.14 found in HK*Propel* is a sample annual performance review instrument that could be used for every position within the athletic department.

Each instrument would be customized to include the specific job expectations for that position, which should be directly related to

6.11 Evaluation Instrument—Annual Athletic Program Achievement Report

Sample annual report that highlights overall department and student-athlete accomplishments related to athletic success, academic success, coach awards, fund-raising, and other important measures.

6.12 Evaluation Instrument—Current Year and Five-Year Sport Achievement Report

Sample template for collecting data relevant to the athletic, academic, recruiting, community service, and fund-raising accomplishments of one specific team annually and over a five-year period.

6.13 Evaluation Instrument—Current Year and Five-Year Development Program Report

Sample template for collecting data relevant to annual giving, major donations, ticket sales, and other income to measure the success of the development program annually and over a five-year period.

Available in HK*Propel*.

the department's stated performance objectives. Performance evaluations should be completely based on the responsibilities and expectations that are listed in the job descriptions as well as specific action plan responsibilities for which the employee is directly responsible for executing. This formalized annual evaluation performance assessment tool also contains a standard section that clearly reflects the types of team conduct and professional behavior expected from staff.

Besides the standard annual employee evaluation tool, other evaluation instruments should be considered for critical positions such as coaches. For example, Evaluation Instrument 6.15 is a coach practice assessment tool, and Evaluation Instrument 6.16 is a tool that can be used to obtain feedback from student-athletes about their instructional experiences. Both of these evaluation instruments can be found in HK*Propel*.

Another critical element of sound personnel management is being aware of how coworkers are getting along; collaborating on work projects; and adhering to policies, procedures, and the established ethos of the department. Therefore, conducting peer assessments can be a useful process that helps athletic directors understand the internal dynamics between employees. Evaluation Instrument 6.17 found in HK*Propel* is a sample peer assessment tool.

For athletic directors who believe in 360-degree evaluations, Evaluation Instrument 6.18 is a tool that senior-level managers in the athletic

6.14 **Evaluation Instrument**—Annual Performance Review

Sample individual employee evaluation form based on measurable objectives, specific job requirements, and general performance qualities with a section devoted to performance improvement plans.

6.15 **Evaluation Instrument**—Annual Coach and Team Practice Assessment

Sample team practice evaluation instrument that measures time on task, type and amount of individual feedback provided to student-athletes, practice management, instructional effectiveness, and the ability of the coach to create a positive practice environment.

6.16 **Evaluation Instrument**—Evaluation of the Coach by the Student-Athlete

Sample evaluation form that can be distributed to athletes for feedback regarding the coach's professionalism, instructional abilities, concern for academic success, and team-building ability.

6.17 **Evaluation Instrument**—Peer Assessment

Sample evaluation form that can be used to assess coworkers as positive representatives of the department who adhere to policies and procedures and work efficiently and collaboratively.

6.18 **Evaluation Instrument**—Evaluation of the Athletic Director by Senior Staff

Sample evaluation form that can be distributed to assistant and associate athletic directors, program managers, and head coaches to assess the communication and management abilities of the athletic director.

6.19 **Evaluation Instrument**—Staff Evaluation of the Athletic Director

Sample evaluation form that can be distributed to all other staff to assess the communication, management, and leadership ability of the athletic director.

6.20 **Evaluation Instrument**—Evaluation of Supervisor

Sample evaluation form that can be distributed to employees who have direct reports other than the athletic director.

Available in HK*Propel*.

department can use to assess the athletic director. The remaining staff can use Evaluation Instrument 6.19 to assess the athletic director. In larger athletic departments that have layers of assistant and associate athletic directors as well as program managers, Evaluation Instrument 6.20 can be used by employees to assess their direct supervisors. All these tools can be found in HK*Propel*. Note that when the athletic director or a senior manager invites staff to assess his or her performance, such a policy emphasizes that evaluation is for improvement, not punishment.

When a senior manager takes the time to sit down with individual employees to review all evaluation tools relevant to them, macro program assessments as well as micro individual assessments, the process demonstrates a commitment to celebrate what employees have done well. It also serves to identify areas for improvement while collaboratively inviting employee input on strategies to reach improvement goals. Additionally, one of the least talked about but most important reasons for strong personnel evaluation systems is that they can ultimately protect employees from individual constituents such as parents who complain about the competence of a coach or a support services staff member. When an athletic director is able to explain that the individual is evaluated on specific measures and has been evaluated highly by a variety of constituent groups, such accusations are quickly defused. Similarly, a file full of positive evaluations can protect an employee from being terminated on the whim of a new senior manager or at least put the person in a position to negotiate an excellent separation of service package.

Step 3: Building Efficiency and Mitigating Risk Performance evaluation should also include components that focus on increasing efficiency and mitigating risk. These components should serve several functions:

- To link department policy and procedures to completed staff work based on measurable key performance indicators
- To identify potential problems or concerns early and take corrective action in time to avoid a crisis
- To protect administrators from accusations of personal bias or wrongful termination through required documentation
- To turn most employee terminations into agreed-upon resignations

Every request for a year-end report should include a section that specifically asks the manager or employee whether he or she is aware of any program component, facility, or practice that might expose the department to litigation, is an unnecessary or excessive cost or waste, or might be an area in which the department can improve efficiency. When employees know that these areas will be reviewed annually, attention to efficiency-based performance will increase throughout the year.

Another example of an evaluation instrument that enhances efficiency is risk assessment checklists. Such instruments serve as reminders for staff to be alert to dangers or attend to common risks encountered in athletic programs, from equipment and facilities to event management. Staff in each program area should be encouraged to design their own checklists regarding efficiency or mitigation of risk to keep important duties or responsibilities from falling through the cracks. Thirteen risk assessment checklists for a variety of program areas are found in HK*Propel*. The seven-day-a-week nature of athletics often puts people in work overload mode, so anything that can be done to increase efficiency, which ultimately mitigates problems and risk, should be a welcome addition to a performance- and efficiency-based system.

Last but equally important is the fact that objective performance-based evaluation tools protect administrators from false claims that they have a personal bias against an employee or that they just don't like an employee. Fact-based measures and ongoing evaluation measures must be available to counteract these types of claims. In addition, when evaluation processes are strictly adhered to, methodical, and collaborative, many employees will leave a position well before the time comes to be terminated. Such tracking of nonperformance not only helps employees make departure decisions but also allows the rest of the staff to see that change and attrition are natural in any organization.

Improving Employee Performance

As evaluations are completed and areas of improvement are identified, administrators must work collaboratively with employees on performance improvement plans. The improvement plans must clearly link any deficiency to a direct job responsibility, and the administrator and employee should work together to design strategies and processes to work toward improvement and identify any challenges that may exist. Form 6.21 found in HK*Propel* is a sample performance improvement plan.

6.21 Form—Performance Improvement Plan

Sample form that can be completed collaboratively between an administrator and an employee after employee deficiencies have been identified through the evaluation process. The form facilitates clear identification of deficiencies, strategies for remedying deficiencies, additional training that may be needed, and other elements that will aid in the improvement process.

Available in HK*Propel*.

6.22 MANAGEMENT TIP

General Personnel Policies

Besides having comprehensive evaluation processes, every department should have other general overarching policies applicable to all employees that create consistent expectations among all staff regardless of position or standing. These common policies help to define the work environment and establish a common culture. No employee should be exempt from these policies. In addition, these policies enable the athletic director to address employment processes and practices that pose the greatest legal risk. Risk Assessment 6.23 in HK*Propel* is a checklist that can be used to ensure that all such employment areas are covered.

6.23 Risk Assessment—Checklist: Employment

A checklist that requires examination of policies and procedures to ensure that that areas posing the greatest risk for litigation are adequately covered.

Available in HK*Propel*.

Noticeably missing from the following discussion are policies that relate to ethical and professional behavior. We believe that the importance of this expectation cannot be overstated and have devoted chapter 7 to address issues of ethical and professional conduct. Although behavior that displays model personal and professional ethics can be hard to define and legislate, unethical behavior can be damaging to student-athletes, employees, the athletic department, and the institution at large. Therefore, continued diligence regarding expectations of ethical behavior and crafting policies and directives that define appropriate and inappropriate behavior to the extent possible is essential.

Also missing from the following discussion are policies dealing with compensation, benefits, and multiyear employment agreements, which are separately covered in Planning Tool 6.32.

Collegiality, Support, and Conflict Resolution

People who work in an athletic department should have a natural tendency toward teamwork and celebrating individual accomplishments as well as subunit success. At the same time, athletics promotes and values strong competition and attracts many people who are competitive by nature. In addition, the existence of a tiered funding model in most athletic departments, as described in chapter 4, can create a class system that may lead to discontent among staff. Therefore, the athletic department should have some formal directives about how employees treat each other independent of position or subunit. Policy 1.13 addresses these issues (found in HK*Propel*).

These expectations should also be part of the employee's annual performance review (see Evaluation Instrument 6.14 in HK*Propel* and highlighted earlier in this chapter), and the athletic director must orally reinforce the importance of these behaviors at staff meetings. At the staff meeting that occurs at the beginning of each academic year, the athletic director should personally voice the following expectations:

- Athletic staff members are expected to work toward common goals. Therefore, all employees must support each other, treat each other with respect, and maintain open channels of communication.

- If an employee has a problem or a disagreement with another employee, that employee is expected to resolve the issue with that person only. Do not share the problem with other employees. If the problem cannot be resolved between the two employees involved, they are both expected to seek counsel from their direct supervisors or an appropriate human resources mediator.
- All employees are expected to avoid gossip. If others are talking about a colleague or a department situation, remove yourself from the conversation.
- If time permits, offer to help others who appear to need an extra hand. This practice is especially important when the department is sponsoring a large number of events simultaneously (e.g., a golf outing, several home contests, and an alumni gathering).

Not all employees understand how to resolve conflicts. Thus, strong consideration should be given to adopting a conflict resolution policy similar to Policy 6.24 as well as a corrective action policy and procedure similar to Policy 6.10 and Form 6.25, all found in HK*Propel*. Employees need to understand the difference between the two. Conflict resolution is used by employees themselves to solve an issue whereas corrective action is the process used by an employee's supervisor to require correction of a performance deficiency.

Office Demeanor and Dress Codes

Policies regarding staff behavior and dress must be consistent with the image that the department wants to convey. Employees need to be reminded that they are department and community representatives who have a public relations responsibility. Policies 5.10 and 7.2 address professional conduct expectations relating to appearance codes and office demeanor. (These policies can be found HK*Propel*.)

Institutional and Departmental Professional and Ethical Conduct Rules

Most institutions have a faculty–staff handbook that describes rules or policies for all employees and is always located on the institution's website. At the very least, the athletic director should provide the link to this site and expect that employees will comply with these institutional policies. In addition, these policies or select policies could be added to the athletic department policy manual and the agenda for the annual meeting at the opening of the school year. Given the nature of athletics, additional department rules or policies may be needed. As mentioned earlier, Policy 7.2 in HK*Propel* addresses the obligation of all employees to comply with institutional and department rules or policies governing the ethical conduct of employees.

Sport Governing-Organization Rules

High school and college sport governing-body rules can be extensive, and some may apply to the entire staff. For example, no staff member at an NCAA member institution is permitted to provide benefits to student-athletes. Therefore, a policy should be in place that all personnel are expected to follow all governing-body rules, and a list of those common rules should be provided to reduce the chance that a violation will occur. See Policy 2.5 in HK*Propel* for an example.

6.24 Policy—Conflict Resolution

Sample policies and procedures that address timing, one-on-one meetings, demeanor, resolution strategies, and the role of the human resource department when issues arise between two or more employees.

6.25 Form—Corrective Action Record

A form to be used by a supervisor to create a written record of an employee's performance or behavior deficiency and expectations for correction.

Available in HK*Propel*.

Outside Employment of Personnel

Many athletic department personnel have skill sets that they can use to obtain outside employment as consultants or to create their own independent businesses. Therefore, policies or rules applicable to outside employment should be established as suggested in Policy 6.26 found in HK*Propel*. Also found in HK*Propel* are Forms 6.27 and 6.28, to be used to implement outside employment rules.

Such policies usually include the following prohibitions:

- Staff may accept short-term appointments as consultants outside the institution but may not accept regular employment from an outside company that may interfere with or be in conflict with their regular duties.
- No staff member may use his or her institutional address, stationary, business cards, e-mail, or phone number for a personal business with the exception of coach-owned sport camps that are held at the institution.
- No full-time member of the staff may be employed in any outside work or activity full time or receive a regular retainer fee before filing a description and nature of employment form with the appropriate institutional officials and receiving the necessary approvals.
- If a staff member is working as a short-term consultant or has received approval for outside employment that includes providing opinions about issues or supporting certain positions, he or she must communicate that such statements are his or her personal opinion and do not in any way reflect the position of the institution.
- Any consulting or approved outside work must be completed outside normal working hours or vacation time must be used.
- Employment by or volunteering for any open amateur athletic clubs, camps, workshops, or competitions must be consistent with governing-body rules.

More important, NCAA rules may prohibit college coaches from working in camps, clinics, clubs, and workshops where prospective student-athletes will be participating. Exceptions may be permitted for developmental clinics or competition or a national sport festival, a U.S. touring team selected in conjunction with a national sport governing body, or a U.S. team participating in the Olympics or world championships. Thus, care must be taken to install policies and procedures that are consistent with governance organization rules, specify such prohibitions, identify exceptions, and require coaches to obtain written certification from the camp owner that the camp or clinic meets such employment conditions. Form 6.29 found in HK*Propel* is a sample letter from the coach to the camp or clinic director that addresses this issue.

Overtime Policies

Overtime policies are usually divided between exempt staff (professional staff) and nonexempt

6.26 Policy—Outside Employment and Compensation of Personnel

Sample policies that address institutional and NCAA rules related to full-time staff members being employed or compensated by outside entities.

6.27 Form—Request for Approval of Outside Employment

Sample form to be used by the employee to request approval of outside employment.

6.28 Form—Acknowledgment of Outside Compensation Rules

Sample form used to comply with NCAA rules that require full-time staff members to report being employed or compensated by outside entities.

Available in HK*Propel*.

6.29 **Form**—Letter: Coach Participation in Camps or Clinics

Sample letter that serves as a request to camp or clinic directors to certify that the camp or clinic meets NCAA rules and regulations so that college coaches can participate without violating NCAA rules.

Available in HK*Propel*.

staff (hourly staff). By law, exempt employees are not entitled to overtime pay or compensatory time. But that doesn't mean that employers cannot voluntarily offer compensatory time or some kind of remuneration for work that goes beyond what is normally expected. Many exempt athletic department personnel work six to seven days per week as well as evenings. The sensible approach is to provide a system of straight compensatory time contingent on the approval of a direct supervisor when exempt employees work beyond what is normally expected. This policy will help relieve burnout and demonstrate that the administration realizes the extraordinary time commitment required from athletic department employees.

Under the Fair Labor Standards Act, nonexempt staff must be compensated for work in excess of 40 hours a week. If compensatory time is provided, it must be at a rate of 1.5 hours for each hour of overtime. If money is given, it must be paid at 1.5 times the normal hourly wage. Note that the common practice of providing small stipends to part-time coaches for full-time hours may be in direct violation of the Fair Labor Standards Act because part-time coaches in this situation are, in essence, working for much less than minimum wage. This circumstance may not be true at the high school level when a system is in place for all extracurricular activities in which flat stipends are the payment mechanisms for all advisors, head coaches, and assistant coaches, whether they are full-time employees of the school system or not. These legal questions are critical issues that vary by state and the system used to pay athletic coaches. Universities or school districts should consult with legal counsel on these issues.

Therefore, the burden is on the athletic department to have a system in place to track hours worked and make sure that employees are provided with salaries that meet labor laws or limit the time that they work to stay within the constraints of the salary offered. Time reports, overtime, and other issues are addressed in Policy 6.30 in HK*Propel*.

6.30 **Policy**—Time Reports, Overtime, and Outside Work

Sample policies and procedures that address the use of time reports, regulation and compensation for overtime hours, and staff participation in activities outside their normal work responsibilities.

Available in HK*Propel*.

Staff Involvement in Department Activities Outside of Job Responsibilities

Athletic departments sponsor many activities (camps, youth clinics, golf outings, alumni events, and so on) that may require more staff than are readily available, especially on weekends. Therefore, policies must be in place to address how staff may be involved in these outside activities and how they are going to be compensated. As stated earlier, Policy 6.30 in HK*Propel* addresses staff involvement in institutional or department activities outside the responsibilities stated in their formal job descriptions. In general, all supervisors should be aware of these points:

- Staff cannot be required to work activities that are outside their job descriptions.
- Any time that staff members work on department-sponsored activities that are not part of their job responsibilities, there must be a clear separation of services. The staff member cannot work on any tasks for this additional activity during normal working hours without taking vacation time to do so.
- Staff should be paid through the budget lines associated with the additional activity,

and payment should be requested through mandated institutional processes with a clear description of services rendered and hours worked.

- If receptionists receive calls about outside activities, they are permitted to provide basic information but should direct all specific questions to the voice mail of the appropriate activity director.

Solicitation and Acquisition of Volunteers and Paid Personnel

Athletic departments often solicit the services of many people who are not regular employees of the department. Therefore, policies that address the necessary controls and oversight of these additional personnel need to be in place. Policy 6.31 addresses employment of part-time personnel.

> **6.31 Policy—Work-Study, Volunteers, and Other Part-Time Personnel**
>
> Sample policies and procedures that address hiring of any part-time personnel as a paid employee or a volunteer including, but not limited to, student personnel.
>
> Available in HK*Propel*.

In general, the following rules should be made clear to all employees:

- No employee may hire any individual, whether paid or voluntary, to provide a service to the athletic department without obtaining prior written approval from the athletic director. Such people include, but are not limited to, assistant coaches, interns, broadcasting talent, massage therapists, and similar temporary service personnel.
- If the person is to be paid by the institution, the supervisor must submit the institutionally mandated approval of professional services form, get signature approval from the business manager, and process the form through the accounts payable office, as prescribed by institutional rules.
- The performance of these individuals must be under the constant supervision of the appropriate institutional employee to ensure the expected level of quality and professionalism.
- These individuals must have demonstrated knowledge of governing-body rules or must be educated by the institutional supervisor about the applicable rules before providing any services.
- To further the department's commitment to increase the number of women and racial and ethnic minorities in sport-related careers, all employees should be mindful that many of these positions are valuable entry-level opportunities for those in underrepresented groups and that searches for such assistance should include an effort to reach those populations.

Particular attention should be given to establishing a policy that prohibits former student-athletes from being hired for a paid position as an assistant coach immediately upon graduation. Authority issues related to supervising former teammates are difficult for inexperienced coaches. Many athletic departments mandate a three-year hiatus after graduation before such employment is permitted. Even if a former student-athlete serves as a volunteer or a graduate assistant coach while enrolled for an advanced degree, the hiring manager must take care to discuss his or her role and professional obligations and specifically educate the person about the potential issues of supervising student-athletes who were once teammates.

Assignment of Work-Study Students

The availability of work-study positions in the athletic department should be a process that is open to all university students who have work-study eligibility. An athletic department that is filtering those positions to athletes only may be in violation of governing-body rules by providing a benefit not available to all students. But if a job needs a special credential, such as water safety instructor and lifeguard certification, swimmers may be the only pool of candidates on campus who have the appropriate credentials. This scenario would not violate any governing-body regulations. To avoid privileged hiring, the responsibility for solicitation, interviewing, hiring, and wage reporting for work-study students should be placed in the hands of a single person (e.g., assistant business manager, executive assistant) who would have low potential for biased hiring. It is not a good practice to have every staff member hire his or her own work-study student. The hiring manager should interview all candidates to assess interest and skills and assign work-study students according to the number and type prescribed by department policies. For example, the department may have a policy that each head coach is eligible to receive one work-study student for 10 hours per week.

Legal Risks Related to Employment

Reducing risk related to allegations of employment discrimination requires constant diligence and adherence to institutional hiring and employment policies. The hiring process usually represents the greatest exposure. Policy 6.5 found in HK*Propel* and highlighted earlier in this chapter is a sample hiring policy and procedures document. After employees are hired, it is critical not to conflict with laws that require fair and nondiscriminatory termination and promotion processes (as highlighted earlier in this chapter and in Policy 6.10 in HK*Propel*) and compensation and benefits practices (provided in Policy 6.33 in HK*Propel*).

The expectations and supervision of coaches presents another layer of challenges for the athletic director because of the time that these employees spend with student-athletes, the intensity of the coaching function, the complexity of governing-association rules that they must follow, and the public visibility of these employees. Thus, athletic directors need to make sure that they convey these additional expectations, which are covered extensively in chapter 7. Coaches are also involved in instructional and conditioning activities that pose risks related to negligence. The athletic director should ensure a high level of communication between the athletic training staff, strength and conditioning coaches, and coaches of sport teams.

6.32 PLANNING TOOL

Designing Compensation, Benefits, and Employment Agreements

Numerous Institutional Differences

In some institutions athletic directors have little influence on compensation, benefits, and employment agreements because institutional policies totally prescribe them. Many public high schools and universities categorize all personnel positions into a progressive experienced-based system that determines an entry point into the system, predetermined compensation levels, benefit eligibility, and a step system for salary increases. Other institutions may have a strong formalized system but create leeway for documented merit increases, market-based compensation adjustments, or the addition of nonmonetary benefits such as courtesy cars or country club memberships. In other institutions, athletic departments may be considered auxiliary enterprises that are permitted to make highly flexible decisions when crafting employee contracts and the salary and benefits attached to each one. Some institutions allow such flexibility only for a limited number of high-level positions. The varieties of systems that exist are endless. Therefore, Policy 6.33 found in HK*Propel* offers general guides or examples for athletic directors who have the responsibility to articulate policies or determine compensation and benefits packages as well as create employee agreements and contracts.

> **6.33 Policy**—Compensation, Benefits, and Employment Agreements
>
> Sample policies and procedures that address institutional authority to establish compensation and benefit offerings, salary, merit pay, and grievance procedures.
>
> Available in HK*Propel*.

Ultimate Authority

The ultimate decision-making power regarding hiring approval, compensation, and benefits decisions and the types of contracts that may be executed seldom resides with the athletic director. That power usually rests with the presidents of institutions of higher education and principals at the high school level, acting on behalf of and with the approval of the board of trustees or school board, respectively. The board of trustees (or school district board of education) also determines which higher-level employees may have detailed contracts. Others, the vast majority of education employees, are at-will employees who do not have comprehensive employment contracts. Employees at will merely get a letter saying that they have a specific title and will be paid at a specific annual rate. That annual rate, however, does not always guarantee them even a full year of employment. When contracts for specified periods of employment exist in athletics, generally they are offered to head coaches of the most visible sports, and sometimes to the athletic director. Thus, the majority of coaches and other athletic personnel at most educational institutions are at-will employees. Therefore, athletic directors need to understand the difference between at-will employees and those who are employed by contracts and to focus on the typical construction of contracts as they apply to head coaches.

Employees at Will

Over 2,000 colleges and universities and over 25,000 high schools employ coaches for their athletic programs. At the high school level, coaches' salary schedules are most often addendums to full-time teacher and administrator salary schedules that list compensation for extra duties (band advisor, athletic team coach, and so on) and have provisions that similar stipends be paid to part-time personnel hired to coach.

These stipends differ by location and wealth of community. They typically range from $3,000 to $15,000 per sport for head coaching responsibility and provide lower sums for assistant coaches. These schedules are often subject to collective bargaining as part of teachers' union agreements. Typically, high school coaches and teachers receive a letter of appointment each year issued by the school district covering the upcoming academic year or containing no mention of the duration of the appointment. The appointment with an unspecified term simply continues until the school or the coach decides to make a change. The appointment letter specifies what the coach is being hired to do. Unless otherwise covered by a collective bargaining agreement, these coaches are employees at will, which means that the school can terminate the employee at any time and the employee can leave at any time. In these situations, the high school athletic director does not have to deal with developing the coach's contract. Coaching duties are simply part of the assignment made by letters of appointment issued by the school district.

The majority of colleges and universities operate similarly. Coaches are employees at will with appointment letters issued by the office of the president, chancellor, or provost. At the college level, however, coaches are more likely to have full-time or part-time coaching responsibilities with no or few teaching assignments. Also, at the collegiate level, coaches' salaries vary greatly and may be negotiated rather than be part of a public schedule or faculty collective bargaining agreement. But these practices vary from state to state with regard to public institutions, and the variability is even more evident at private institutions of higher education.

Standard letters of appointment for employees at will usually consist of one page that includes few details regarding the specific responsibilities of the position. Form 6.34 found in HK*Propel* is a sample appointment letter for an employee at will agreement. They often contain references to official job descriptions, which are normally detailed in athletic department policy manuals. Thus, these provisions in the athletic department policy manual regarding coaches' specific responsibilities and expectations for conduct and continued employment must be reviewed and approved by school district or university legal counsel because they reflect contractual obligations.

6.34 Form—Employee at Will Employment Letter

Sample of a typical letter of employment for at-will employees that clearly indicates that there is no guaranteed term of employment.

Available in HK*Propel*.

Many universities likely have some coaches who have multiyear agreements and others who are employees at will. The athletic director must always be sure that the department policy manual clearly acknowledges the type of employment agreements applicable to specific types of employees. Employment policies and individual employment agreements should be carefully reviewed and approved by legal counsel or other administrative authorities before being published and distributed.

Employment Contracts

Any form of contract that goes beyond the employee at will agreement described earlier can vary dramatically from institution to institution. Consultation with legal counsel or human resources administrators is essential in developing such agreements. It is also necessary to obtain the approval of higher authorities for contract terms, compensation provisions and benefits, and other terms that may differ from those offered to employees at will. Individually negotiated multiyear coaching agreements are generally accepted at institutions that hire full-time coaches for a single sport, have a high expectation with regard to competitive success, or expect the sport to produce significant revenues. These agreements are the opposite of employee at will appointments in that they have a specified duration, limited conditions under which employment may be terminated, and other terms that elevate the financial and other obligations of the institution and the employee. Such contracts are commonplace within the NCAA's Division I member institutions but also occur in selected sports at institutions in other competitive divisions and, less frequently, at the high school level. For example, high school football coaches in some states may be paid more than teachers are and have multiyear employment agreements, courtesy cars, and other perquisites more commonly found among college coaches. Even a small Division II or III athletic program may have a continuing expectation to be dominant in a sport unique to the history of the school. The coach may receive higher compensation and greater contractual assurances than coaches of other sports in the program. These multiyear coach employment agreements are discussed at length later.

Compensation Considerations

Some institutions have a hard-and-fast system of compensation and benefits that aligns with years of experience, educational credentials, and a step system for each year of employment. Salary increases to keep pace with cost-of-living increases or based on performance (merit pay) may also be institutionally prescribed. Typically, athletic department employees are treated the same as the faculty or other types of nonteaching employees at the institution, but athletic departments are allowed some departures for coaches. More flexible compensation and benefits permit the athletic department to keep pace with fluctuations in the marketplace or to maintain salaries and benefits on par with peer institutions in a conference or competitive division. Some institutions may even allow the athletic program to establish its own merit pay system.

Even if the institution does not compare salaries against those of peer institutions, the athletic department should acquire and maintain such data as justification for salary offers to new employees or as justification for salary adjustment requests that are not based on cost-of-living or performance criteria. Determination of peer institutions may vary by sport if the institution's conference members do not exhibit homogeneity in competitive strength. If the athletic department places a specific success expectation on a head coach, it should identify those institutions competing for such designation of success (top 25 percent of conference, top 50 nationally, and so on), and accumulate salary, compensation, benefits, and operating budget data for this group because those resources may need to be matched to keep a successful coach.

Although the athletic director cannot make promises covering future compensation (except as promised by a written employment contract), he or she should express the athletic department's philosophy regarding compensation with the disclaimer that applying it depends on the availability of financial resources as determined by the institution. This question often arises during the hiring process. Thus, the athletic director should get higher administration agreement with this expressed approach to keeping compensation competitive with institutions against which the institution is expected to be successful. For instance, an athletic director might express this philosophy in the following way:

> Dependent on availability of resources, the department tries to meet the following compensation goals:
>
> - Noncoaching personnel compensation should be comparable with like positions within the institution.
> - Coach compensation should be generally comparable to the mean salaries of like positions at conference institutions.
> - Compensation for employees at the associate director level or above and for head coaches whose teams occupy the tier I designation should be comparable with mean salaries of like positions at institutions that have their sport programs ranked in the top 20 nationally. (*Most institutions designate sports for which success is a priority and fund those sports at a higher level than other sports within the athletic program. Tier I refers to such a high-priority sport. See Management Tip 4.3 and Planning Tool 4.4 for a full discussion of tiered programs.*) Every employee receiving a satisfactory performance appraisal (final ranking of 5 or higher) shall receive the institution- and board-determined cost-of-living increase.
> - In addition to cost-of-living increases in salary, the department will make an effort to award merit pay increases based on performance. Employees are eligible to receive up to 5 percent of their previous year's salary in the form of a one-time merit payment (not added to the annual salary).

- Employees at the senior associate level or above and head coaches whose teams occupy tier I may be eligible for merit increases in excess of 5 percent awarded on the same basis (one-time award not added to salary).

When merit pay systems are developed, different rules and different conditions for implementation may apply to staff at various employment levels, all of which depend on institutional philosophy and circumstances. Policy 6.33 in HK*Propel* contains an example of a merit pay system policy.

Benefit Plans

Benefit plans at institutions vary greatly. Most include health benefits, disability benefits, and some form of pension or 401K option. Other full-time employee benefits may include some form of tuition remission for family members, use of institutional facilities at no cost or reduced cost, and a variety of other privileges. The basic institutional benefits package is usually offered to all full-time employees as institutionally prescribed. When athletic departments are permitted to offer additional benefits, those benefits are usually available only to senior administrators and selected coaches and require the approval of the institution. Such additional benefits might include courtesy cars, country club memberships, life insurance policies, annuities or other financial instruments, rent-free homes, use of private planes, and other perquisites designed to attract the best talent. These additional benefits are spelled out in detail within employment contracts. They should also be spelled out in the department policy manual if they are offered to multiple employees and require administrative oversight. Donor car programs are discussed in Management Tip 6.37 in the book and spelled out in Policy 6.38 and Forms 6.39 to 6.41 in HK*Propel*.

Multiyear Employment Contract Terms

Coaches' contracts at institutions with high-profile athletic programs usually include the greatest amount of additional dollars above and beyond the institutional salary along with many perquisites and incentives. *USA Today* regularly researches and obtains copies of hundreds of NCAA Division I head football and head basketball coaches' agreements that can serve as excellent examples (*USA Today,* 2020). Form 6.35 in HK*Propel* is a generic sample of a multiyear employment agreement.

6.35 **Form**—Multiyear Employment Agreement

A sample multiyear employment agreement that stipulates term, duties and responsibilities, base compensation, additional compensation, performance incentives, and many other elements.

Available in HK*Propel*.

Although a variety of considerations are covered within contracts, several elements are consistently included:

- Term (length of the contract)
- Duties and responsibilities
- Base salary provided by the institution
- Additional salary for other services provided or to cover duties and responsibilities
- Cost-of-living or other automatic escalations to salary
- Benefits to be provided by the institution
- Bonuses based on performance that are not additive to base salary
- Descriptions of standards of conduct expected for continued employment, typically based on institutional, department, and governing-body rules, and possible termination if violated
- Conditions under which employment and payments due the employee can be terminated, depending on type of termination
- Noncompete or other postseverance requirements
- Handling the issue of damages if one of the parties ends the employment relationship before the end of the agreement

Thus, athletic directors who must negotiate such agreements need to understand these contract elements, specify in writing institutional expectations for the sport program, and be versed in the history and format of existing coaching agreements within the institution. The legal counsel of the institution or school district should be a partner in this process.

The variety of employment agreements offered to coaches in high schools and universities appears to be endless. When athletic departments are permitted to construct agreements that aren't found in many other departments on campus and no internal guidelines are in place for their development, such contracts become an important responsibility that requires the athletic director to be knowledgeable about the sport business, even if he or she has the assistance of legal counsel. The following sections address the most important considerations in producing such agreements.

Term of Agreement Typically, the term of the employment agreement is addressed in one of three ways: (1) a specific number of years, (2) a specific number of years with a rollover provision specifying that the agreement continues for another term or specified number of years, or (3) a specific number of years with provisions for renegotiation during the term of the agreement at a certain time, at time intervals, or under certain conditions. Not recommended but frequently encountered in negotiations is a requirement that the institution provide advance notification of intent not to renew or noncontinuation by rollover. Such advance notice provisions can result in lame-duck coaches unless accompanied by the institution's right to transfer or reassign the coach to a different position during the lame-duck period. Athletic directors should take care to eliminate all ambiguities that relate to rollover clauses and the duration of agreements. Note that some universities and states have laws that prevent teachers at public education institutions or other state employees from having employment agreements in excess of one year in duration. In such cases, the institution must act to get special legislation permitting an exception.

Many coaches insist on agreements of a minimum of three to five years, recognizing that rebuilding a sport program requires multiple recruiting classes. The coach is normally able to replace players only as they graduate, and time is needed to install and teach skills and strategies as the coach wants them performed. Longer-term agreements are usually limited to coaches of proven value and performance. Shorter-term agreements may reflect the willingness of an institution to take a chance on a promising but unproven coach with limited or no experience as a head coach or an institution whose alumni do not tolerate a losing program over more than a three-year period. Again, speaking with athletic director colleagues at peer institutions or schools with programs of a quality level to which the institution aspires will give the athletic administrator a good idea of the duration, compensation, benefits, and other considerations that represent the marketplace in which the athletic director should be recruiting.

Although provisions for renegotiation during the term of an agreement appear unnecessary, they are common in long-term contracts because the coach wants assurance that his or her rate of compensation will keep pace with the marketplace. There are even some high-profile coaches who have difficult negotiations with athletic directors or presidents or are so comfortable working with people they like and trust that the departure of people in those positions can trigger a renegotiation provision that may or may not be limited to certain aspects of the agreement. Thus, these provisions are often included under term agreements.

Basic Coaching Duties and Responsibilities Employment policies and agreements should detail the basic duties and responsibilities of all coaches in their respective sports as listed in their job description, such as the following:

- Instruction of athletes
- Supervision of practice and conditioning sessions
- Instruction, supervision, and direction of athletes in competitive events
- Selection, supervision, and evaluation of assistant coaches, volunteers, student coaches, graduate assistants, interns, managers, and others assisting in the conduct of the sport program, including ensuring that such

personnel comply with athletic association rules and regulations
- Recruitment of athletes
- Budgeting
- Knowledge of and adherence to school or college policies and procedures
- Knowledge of and adherence to athletic governance association rules and regulations
- Scheduling of competitive events
- Media relations
- Fund-raising expectations or involvement
- Community service
- Conduct that advances or results in the academic success of athletes
- Obligation to report outside compensation (if required by governance association rules)
- Inclusion of NCAA or other governance association regulation language that subjects coaches to disciplinary action for rules violations.

Care should also be taken to detail prohibited activities. See the later section "Standards of Conduct."

Base Compensation Coaches' contracts normally separate base compensation from benefits, bonuses, deferred compensation, and other nonannually recurring compensation for several reasons:

- When coach salaries greatly exceed salaries provided to faculty, administrators, or even the chief executive officer, showing the lowest possible salary may have media relations benefits.
- Base salary may grow because cost-of-living increases are awarded on an annual basis, whereas bonuses or merit-based increases may not be additive to recurring annual base salary.
- Some compensation may not be dependent on the institution with regard to amount or if it is guaranteed, such as a coach's television or radio program, and thus is considered through separate provisions.
- Base compensation may have to meet standards set by collective bargaining or legislatively mandated salary schedules, but other compensation does not.

This section should also cover cost-of-living guarantees or any salary escalation automatically additive to base salary.

Whatever the reason, the athletic director must be able to justify both the base and total compensation package from both a philosophical and marketplace perspective. A marketplace that includes high-powered high school programs or NCAA Division I football and basketball coaches may be characterized by benefits and incentives that are inconsistent with educational philosophy, especially in situations where the athletic director, principal, superintendent, or college president believes that his or her position is in jeopardy if the community or alumni are not provided with winning teams. How can an educator justify having a coach earn 30 times more than an average full professor or 3 times more than the university president, especially in a tainted marketplace where wages to athletes are prohibited and most athletic programs operate at a net loss? Although the athletic director may find many of the key elements or benefits distasteful from an educational sport philosophical perspective, the fact remains that, right or wrong, they represent the reality of a marketplace in which failure to provide such elements may well signal the end of an athletic director's or college president's employment. The interinstitutional nature of athletics simply mandates that compensation to coaches not be considered in a vacuum. The athletic director must consult with colleagues at like institutions, preferably peer conference or similar competitors, to gain a clear understanding of the going rate for not only base compensation but also each contract element. These institutions should make up the marketplace in which the institution must compete for the employment of coaches.

Additional Compensation All compensation agreements related to the coach's employment at the institution should preferably come through the school district, college, or university. Coaches should not be allowed to leverage their position as a school coach for private gain without the express permission of the institution. The institution owns the rights to its name and logo, display of signage in school venues and on school uniforms, and numerous other properties that might be leveraged for sale of promotional or marketing rights of considerable value. Coaches do not have the right to sell these school property rights. The cleanest way to comply with these legal and ethical considerations is for all agreements related to the display of commercial logos on school property and the ownership of broadcast and telecasting rights for coaches' shows, call-in programs, postgame and pregame, Internet, or other use of other rights owned by the institution to be written between commercial sponsors and the educational institution. The educational institution receives all funds. The institution then writes a contract with the coach that pays the coach for performing certain duties related to such initiatives. Thus, coaches' agreements should address total compensation from all sources or have a section of the contract deal with other sources of additional compensation rather than just base salary. Similarly, the contract should contain a provision that prohibits the coach from entering into such outside agreements, especially agreements with companies that are competitors to sponsors of the athletic program.

Additional compensation may be guaranteed or not guaranteed, and the structure of such compensation must be specified in the contract. Several kinds of compensation provisions are typically addressed under the designation of additional compensation:

- Payment of a lump sum for all or designated amounts for each for personal services, which may be specified duties in addition to coaching and recruiting such as the following:
    - Coaches' television or radio shows, Internet chat rooms
    - Endorsing products of sponsors of the athletic program at the request of the athletic director
    - Consulting with apparel companies that provide institutional uniforms, shoes, and equipment at the request of the athletic director
    - Conducting summer camps or sport clinics
    - Rights to the coach's name, image, and autograph
- Payment of a lump sum for other duties that are typically included as normal coaching responsibilities but which might be pulled out from that designation because they are considered a larger or more burdensome responsibility or for other reasons:
    - Participation in athletic department or university fund-raising
    - Making appearances or speeches upon the request of the athletic department
    - Participating in media interviews or other public relations activities
- Pension or retirement plans that indicate annual employer contribution and the timing of the contribution (e.g., end of year) even if those are normal benefits provided to all employees
- Expense allowances for gasoline, clothing, family travel, personal cell phones, and athletic department–related entertainment of donors, prospective donors, or alumni
- Provisions related to deferred compensation, annuities, or other similar additional forms of compensation not received as cash in the current year

Bonus Payments This section covers cash payments in addition to base salary or additional guaranteed payments that depend on the achievement of specified performances ranging from the results of the coach's annual performance evaluation to the achievement of specified program objectives. Some examples of such bonus provisions are the following:

- Flat amount for conference or national championships or specified tournament finishes (e.g., Final Four, quarterfinals)
- Flat or graduated amounts for student-athlete graduation rates or academic progress rates
- Flat amount for winning specific contests (e.g., against archrivals)
- Flat or graduated amounts based on longevity (e.g., institutional contribution of a sum each year to an annuity or other financial vehicle that accumulates interest and becomes due to the coach after a specified period)

- Contract extensions tied to winning specific games or numbers of games
- Flat amount tied to achieving team behavior goals (no arrests or misbehavior damaging to institutional reputation)
- Flat amounts for coach accomplishments such as being named conference or national coach of the year
- Percentage of ticket revenues or increases in ticket revenues

Noncash Benefits The contract should also detail all noncash benefits provided, even if they are provided to all institutional employees. The coach is responsible for determining whether he or she must declare the value of such benefits as income according to state or federal IRS rules. Benefits that might be included in agreements are the following:

- Medical insurance, dental insurance, and other benefits
- Benefits of value that are paid for by the institution or its donors:
    - Provision of cars (see Policy 6.38 in HK*Propel*)
    - Country club or private club memberships, greens fees, carts
    - Personal use of private planes
    - Low-interest home loans
    - Use of vacation homes
    - Luxury suites in institutional or professional sport facilities
    - Tickets for conference, NCAA, or professional sport events
- Complimentary tickets for institutional events
- Free use of institutional facilities for summer camps
- Life insurance and disability insurance policies
- Insurance policies for courtesy cars provided by the institution or donors to the institution

Policies and conditions must also be developed for all material perquisites to guard against unintended use and to specify the coach's obligations in this regard.

Standards of Conduct Chapter 7 includes a comprehensive discussion of expected ethical and professional standards of conduct. The coach's agreement should detail conduct prohibited of all institutional employees and additional expectations. Under the category of typical prohibitions, the following should be considered:

- Use of institution funds (telephone, postage, and so on) to influence the outcome of any election or adoption of any legislative measure
- Acceptance of other employment as a paid lobbyist of any individual, firm, association, or corporation
- Use of official institution vehicles in connection with any political campaign or any personal or recreational activity
- Use of official institution vehicles for personal or recreational activities not related to the athletic program
- Acceptance of gifts in return for personal favors or acceptance of outside employment that would impair the discharge of institutional duties
- Lending, loaning, or selling institutional equipment or property to any outside individual or agency
- Removal of institutional property from campus without obtaining written approval from the institution according to stated policies and procedures

Additional conduct prohibitions that are more stringent than those listed in general institutional policies recognize that highly compensated coaches are constantly in the public eye and that their misbehavior adversely affects the reputation of the institution. The value of higher compensation and benefits demands these higher expectations. Thus, multiyear employment agreements may list any of the following practices as behaviors that could result in immediate corrective action including termination of employment:

- Falsification of or omissions from work, personnel, or other university records
- Failure to call in each day according to university and departmental policies when unable to report to work
- Working under the influence of illegal drugs or alcohol
- Neglect of duty to comply with athletic governance association policies and rules
- Insubordination
- Failure or refusal to perform assigned work or carry out management requests
- Dishonesty, including but not limited to plagiarism, falsification of academic credentials, gaining unauthorized access to or falsification of university reports or records, misappropriation or misapplication of university funds
- Rude or unprofessional conduct with students, faculty, staff, donors, or the public
- Any negligent act that might endanger one's own safety or life, endanger the safety or lives of student-athletes or others, or might result in damage to or destruction of institutional property (including driving institutional vehicles or donor-provided vehicles negligently, losing university property through negligence, and so on)
- Having unauthorized family members, friends, or animals in the workplace
- Misuse, abuse, unauthorized possession, removal, or use of university property or making unauthorized charges to university accounts
- Discrimination against or harassment of staff members, faculty members, students, or other constituents
- Conflicts of interest or the failure to resolve a conflict of interest
- Disclosure of confidential institutional or departmental information to unauthorized persons
- Arrests for or convictions of crimes committed at work or outside work that reflect unfavorably on a staff member's suitability for continued employment
- Violation of the civil or criminal laws on institutional property or while on institutional business
- The manufacture, possession, use, distribution, dispensation, or sale of illegal drugs or alcohol on university time or premises
- Violation of safety rules or procedures
- Engaging in or threatening physical violence
- Possession of firearms, explosives, flammables, or other weapons of any kind on institutional time or on institutional premises
- Carrying unauthorized persons in vehicles owned, leased, or rented by the institution
- Violations of coaches' code of conduct or ethics policy as highlighted in Policies 7.2 and 7.3 (found in HK*Propel*)

Additional examples are offered in the next section under conditions that result in immediate termination.

Termination Provisions Although talking about termination clauses may appear disadvantageous when a manager is trying to hire a new employee, the conditions for termination by choice of the coach or the institution are critical elements of the agreement. It is essential to think of worst-case scenarios and how the manner of a coach's exit before the end of the contract will do the least damage to the institution's relationships with donors, the image and pocketbook of the institution, and the reputation of the coach, if possible. A commonsense approach is to envision three scenarios in which the growth or quality of the sport program is not progressing according to plan or the coach is being dysfunctional in a minor or major way and then try to include provisions in the agreement that would permit termination to be handled in all or most of these situations.

Scenario 1

The coach is a good person, well liked within the institution and among alumni, and has a skill set that allows him or her to contribute to the athletic program in one or more ways other than coaching. Taking care of this person is important to donors and others who support the program, and the contributions of this employee to another area of the program would be equal to or better than hiring a different employee. In this case, the institution may wish to include a provision whereby the coach can be reassigned to another position in the athletic department or institution. Such a provision might be attractive to coaches nearing the end of their respective careers but not at all acceptable to coaches who wish to remain in the coaching profession.

Scenario 2

Either the coach wants to leave or the institution wants the coach to leave before the end of the term of the agreement and no violation of the terms of the agreement has otherwise occurred. Note that this scenario would apply when the institution is unhappy with a win–loss record (assuming that a specific standard is not included as a performance expectation in the agreement), the pace of development of the program, or the general quality of the program, all conditions that would not warrant termination for cause. In this case, a buyout or liquidated damages provision is usually in place whereby one party pays the other a specified and reasonable amount to exit the agreement in what could be a fairly cordial manner.

Scenario 3

The coach violates a performance standard contained in the contract by engaging in conduct that reflects unfavorably on the reputation of the institution (commonly referred to as a morals clause), criminal conduct, intentional violation of rules, or other specifically defined unacceptable conduct. Dismissal of the coach in this situation is commonly referred to as termination for cause. In this case, all compensation, benefits, and promises in the agreement become null and void at the date of termination.

Conditions that may result in termination for cause are usually detailed in the agreement. The following are some examples of contract provisions that would result in termination for cause if breached by the coach:

- Knowingly participating in violations of rules, policies, and regulations of the athletic governance association, school district, or college or university; knowingly allowing such violations by others; or failing to report such violations within a reasonable period from when he or she learns of such violations
- Failing to carry out duties and responsibilities specifically delineated in the agreement and, when informed of such failure by the institution, failing to remedy such deficiencies
- Conviction of felony
- Misconduct that offends the ethics or traditions of the institution or brings discredit or harm to the reputation of the institution
- Disability or death (usually accompanied by some kind of payment to coach or spouse covered by an insurance policy paid for by the institution)
- Violating state or institution ethics laws or policies
- Being fraudulent or dishonest in the performance of duties, including falsifying records or permitting or condoning falsification by an employee under his or her supervision
- Failing to instruct or counsel employees or student-athletes under his or her supervision, failing to respond fully and accurately or to appear upon request during investigations of rules violations by the institution or athletic governance associations of which the institution is a member
- Wagering on any amateur or professional athletic contest or consorting or associating with known gamblers or bookmakers
- Using controlled substances to such a degree that performance of duties is significantly impaired over a substantial period
- Failing to cooperate and enforce policies and procedures related to student-athlete drug-testing programs
- Committing acts of violence or condoning or encouraging employees or student-athletes in such conduct, which may not warrant criminal prosecution but results in public disrepute, contempt, scandal, or ridicule that reflects unfavorably on the reputation or mission of the institution
- Actions taken at other institutions that violate governance association rules and are not disclosed to the institution

It is important to anticipate conflict when termination of an employee occurs. The agreement should always include some type of due process provision whereby the employee is given the opportunity to present evidence refuting the reasons for termination. As a practical matter, an athletic director should never activate contract provisions to terminate employment without prior consultation with the institution's director of human resources and legal counsel. These provisions also specify what happens if such severance occurs with regard to payments under the remaining term of the agreement.

Noncompete and Other Closure Requirements Another common contract provision is a restriction placed on the coach from taking another coaching job at a competing university for a specified period if the coach leaves before the end of the agreement either with or without cause. Key to such noncompete provisions if they are ever challenged in the courts is that they must be (1) time limited (usually in the one- to two-year range) and (2) competitor limited (restricted to a small group of competing institutions such as institutions within the same athletic conference). Other types of noncompete provisions might be the promise not to recruit any athlete identified as a prospect by the institution while he or she was employed as a coach or not to use software, records, or other materials developed in the process of coaching at the institution. Similarly, contracts should specify the return of all playbooks, recruiting files, credit cards, keys, and so on upon the end of employment.

Liquidated Damages If the coach decides to leave before the end of the agreement or if the institution decides to terminate the coach's employment not for cause (no fault or breach of agreement by the coach) before the end of the agreement, one party must usually pay a specified compensation to the other for damages incurred because the full term of the contract was not fulfilled. These provisions are based on the notion that the early departure causes damage to the party responsible for not honoring the duration of the agreement. For instance, when the coach breaks the contract to go elsewhere, provisions like the following may be included:

- The coach must inform the institution of resignation in writing.
- The coach has no entitlement to any compensation or benefits detailed in the agreement following the termination date.
- The coach must pay a lump sum of a size reflective of the expenses that will be incurred by the institution in having to recruit another coach (note that this sum is often paid by the institution to which the coach is departing).

The stakes are often higher if the institution terminates the coach without cause. Provisions like the following may be included:

- The institution must pay the total compensation amount through the end of the agreement or a fixed (usually large) sum.
- Health care benefits must continue through the end of the contract term, paid by the institution or the coach, or until he or she obtains employment that provides such benefits.
- A clause that relates to the personal services part of the contract that obligates the coach to seek employment as a coach on a radio or television show or in some other capacity. If the coach becomes employed by another institution and starts to be paid for such personal services, the institution that terminated him or her would not be responsible for continuing those payments or other personal services terms of the agreement.
- As a condition of the institution's paying out the considerable sum representing the remainder of the agreement or a lump sum, the institution may be permitted to cease payment on any provision for life and disability insurance and the coach may be required to sign a comprehensive release that prevents him or her from making further claims on the institution.

Negotiating With Agents and Attorneys

Athletic directors now commonly deal with a coach's lawyer or agent in contract negotiations. In general, as the compensation, complexity, and sophistication of employment agreements increase and the negotiating process involves legal and business experts as representatives of the coach, an institution's legal counsel, human resources administrators, and other senior administrative officials should become involved. Athletic directors should focus on substantive deal points—a plain-language list of agreed-upon compensation, benefits, and responsibilities—and leave the actual drafting of the contract to the institution's attorney. Form 6.36 found in HK*Propel* illustrates a typical letter of understanding that lists deal points that will subsequently be memorialized by a formal, detailed, written employment contract. In fact, the coach may begin employment under the terms of such a letter while the employment contract is finalized, a process that may take months.

6.36 **Form**—Term Sheet Preceding Official Employment Agreement

Sample format and content of a memo of understanding detailing points that will be included in a subsequent formal employment contract.

Available in HK*Propel*.

The athletic director benefits by initially meeting with the coach and his or her agents without the institution's attorney being present. This sort of meeting deescalates the weight of such proceedings, permits the coach and athletic director to talk in plain language without attention to legal subtleties, and allows the initial meeting to focus on the needs and expectations of the coach and the athletic director rather than reaching an immediate agreement. The athletic director should explain that the purpose of an initial meeting is to put all needs and expectations on the table so that he or she can follow up with conversations with higher administrators to determine the elements and limits of compensations and benefits that he or she is authorized to include in any agreement. If the coach refuses to participate in such a meeting, indicating that he or she instead prefers to have an authorized representative work with the athletic director, the approach to the initial meeting, although it is with an agent, should not change. The athletic director should determine needs and expectations first, working toward agreement on a letter of understanding specifying acceptable deal points and terms under which employment may begin and designating those points that require continued negotiation to be finalized in the final contract document but upon which starting employment does not depend. Subsequent meetings between the institution's attorney and the coach's attorney will represent agreements on detailed language, negotiations on remaining points, and possibly a revision of the originally agreed-upon deal points to negotiate and balance other elements.

6.37 MANAGEMENT TIP

Donor Car Programs

A good example of an additional benefit is the use of donor cars. In a donor car program one or more local car dealers provide cars for the use of designated employees, usually head coaches but perhaps all coaches and top administrators, in return for sport event tickets, priority seating locations, or access to benefits afforded top-level donors. Policy 6.38 is a sample policy governing such a program. Forms 6.39 to 6.41 are samples of forms that can be used for administering a donor car program.

6.38 **Policy**—Donor Car Program

Sample policies and procedures that address the solicitation and assignment of donor cars, the contractual relationship between the donor or dealer and the institution, and the responsibilities of employees who are assigned donor cars.

6.39 **Form**—Request for Approval of Donor Car Assignment

Sample form letter that can be sent to the university's Office of the President to formally request approval of a donor car assignment.

6.40 **Form**—Employee Acceptance of Responsibilities for a Donor Car

Sample form that outlines the responsibilities of the recipient of the donor car and requires the recipient's signature.

6.41 **Form**—Monthly Report of Donor Car Use

Sample form that can be generated by the athletic department accounting clerk and is to be completed by the donor car recipient each month to record such data as business miles, personal miles, and total miles driven that month.

Available in HK*Propel*.

JOB DESCRIPTIONS

Developing job descriptions is a time-consuming responsibility of senior staff members. An easier and more efficient approach is to begin with a sample job description that includes the maximum number of possible job responsibilities and then edit to produce a document appropriate for the athletic program. Forms 6.42 through 6.85 are a compilation of such sample job descriptions for 44 different positions that are typically found in a Division I athletic department that administers a comprehensive program and reflects a high degree of staff specialization. The customization process for smaller athletic programs will likely result in collapsing two or three job positions into one by eliminating a number of responsibilities to create a less specialized position. This collection—found in HK*Propel*—can be helpful in developing appropriate job descriptions.

Form 6.42—Director of Athletics

Form 6.43—Associate Athletic Director for Compliance

Form 6.44—Associate Athletic Director for Sport Programs

Form 6.45—Associate Athletic Director for Development

Form 6.46—Associate Athletic Director for Student Affairs

Form 6.47—Associate Athletic Director for Business Affairs

Form 6.48—Sports Information Director or Communications Director

Form 6.49—Head Coach

Form 6.50—Assistant Coach

Form 6.51—Head Athletic Trainer

Form 6.52—Assistant Athletic Trainer

Form 6.53—Director, Athletic Academic Support Program

Form 6.54—Learning Skills Specialist

Form 6.55—Head Strength Coach

Form 6.56—Assistant Strength Coach

Form 6.57—Media Relations Manager

Form 6.58—Publications Manager

Form 6.59—Athletic Business Manager

Form 6.60—Events Manager

Form 6.61—Athletic Annual Fund Manager

Form 6.62—Basketball Operations Manager

Form 6.63—Information Technology Systems Analyst

Form 6.64—Academic Counselor

Form 6.65—Academic Tutor, Subject Specialist

Form 6.66—Academic Tutor, Learning Specialist

Form 6.67—Accounting Clerk

Form 6.68—Development Senior Associate

Form 6.69—Development Associate

Form 6.70—Facilities Manager

Form 6.71—Equipment Manager

Form 6.72—Assistant Events Manager

Form 6.73—Photographer

Form 6.74—Camp Director

Form 6.75—Executive Assistant

Form 6.76—Administrative Associate, Basketball (or Football)

Form 6.77—Information Technology Systems Assistant

Form 6.78—Senior Accounting Clerk

Form 6.79—Senior Office Assistant or Receptionist

Form 6.80—Administrative Assistant, Business Affairs

Form 6.81—Administrative Assistant, Student Affairs

Form 6.82—Administrative Assistant to Coaches

Form 6.83—Publications Technician

Form 6.84—Marketing Intern

Form 6.85—Student Trainer

Available in HK*Propel*.

BIBLIOGRAPHY

MANAGING A STAFF TO ACCOMPLISH PROGRAM GOALS

Bryan, L.L., & Joyce, C.I. (2007). *Mobilizing minds: Creating wealth from talent in the 21st Century*. New York: McGraw-Hill.

Chelladurai, P. (2017). *Human resource management in sport and recreation* (3rd ed.). Champaign, IL: Human Kinetics.

Collins, J. (2001). *Good to great*. New York: HarperCollins.

Covey, S.R. (2020). *The 7 habits of highly effective people*. New York: Simon & Schuster.

Cozzillio, M.J., & Hayman, R.L. (2005). *Sports and inequality*. Durham, NC: Carolina Academic Press.

Drew University. (2007). *Department of Intercollegiate Athletics policy manual*. Unpublished manuscript. Madison, NJ.

Drucker, P. (2008, March 1). *Classic Drucker*. Boston: Harvard Review.

Hayes, D.K., & Ninemeier, J.D. (2009). *Human resources management in the hospitality industry*. Hoboken, NJ: Wiley.

Jensen, C.R., & Overman, S.J. (2003). *Administration and management of physical education and athletic programs* (4th ed.). Prospect Heights, IL: Waveland Press.

Moorman, A.M., Claussen, C.L., & Sharp, L. (2014). *Sports law: A managerial approach* (3rd ed.). Routledge.

National Collegiate Athletic Association. (2010). *2020–2021 Division I manual*. http://www.ncaapublications.com/productdownloads/D121.pdf.

Pedersen, P.M., and Thibault, L. (2022). *Contemporary sport management* (7th ed.). Champaign, IL: Human Kinetics.

Silverstein, B. (2007). *Best practices: Managing people*. New York: HarperCollins.

Slack, T., & Parent, M. (2006). *Understanding sport organizations: The application of organization theory* (2nd ed.). Champaign, IL: Human Kinetics.

Spengler, J.O. et al. (2016). *Introduction to sports law* (2nd ed.). Champaign, IL: Human Kinetics.

United States Department of Labor. *Wages and the fair labor standards act*. https://www.dol.gov/agencies/whd/flsa.

University of Texas at Austin. (1992). *Intercollegiate athletics for women policy manual*. Unpublished. Austin, TX: Department of Women's Intercollegiate Athletics.

University of Texas at Austin. (2010). *Intercollegiate athletics policy manual*. Austin, TX. No longer available.

USA Today. (2020). Division I basketball coaches salaries. https://sports.usatoday.com/ncaa/salaries/mens-basketball/coach.

USA Today. (2020). Division I football coaches salaries. https://sports.usatoday.com/ncaa/salaries/.

Wong, G.M. (2010). *Essentials of sports law* (4th ed.). Santa Barbara, CA: Praeger.

CHAPTER

7

Ethics, Rules Compliance, and Professional Conduct

Athletics is the most visible and media-examined program of most educational institutions. Add the pervasiveness of social media and speed of Internet communication, and it is obvious that failure to attend to the ethical conduct of athletic staff and stakeholders holds the potential of inviting considerable damage to the reputation of the institution and the athletic program.

In the past, the athletic director's concerns centered on violations of recruiting and other governance association rules and regulations and control of alumni and fan involvement in the athletic program, especially in the area of providing prohibited benefits. Although these issues continue to be of concern and demand careful attention in the policy manual, additional challenges have become apparent in the past decade. Sexual abuse and harassment have always been issues, but in previous years incidents were often swept under the rug by campus police and higher administration. The use of physical punishment and verbal and emotional abuse, once accepted as coaching practices that create athlete toughness, are no longer acceptable. Retaliation against coaches who express gender equity concerns has become more artful because it is more likely to be legally challenged. Coach and athletic department attempts to control athletes' social media communications or social justice advocacy while in uniform are now scrutinized in the context of their free speech and expression rights. Academic fraud, from tutors doing student-athletes' work to placement of student-athletes in easy majors or courses, is more carefully examined. Thus, strongly expressed policies and education sessions that address ethical and professional conduct are essential.

The documents in this chapter, in both the book and HK*Propel*, provide model policies and forms that set expectations for the highest standards of ethical and professional conduct on the part of coaches and staff. Chapter 11, "Team Administration," addresses additional behavioral standards for and discipline of student-athletes. In addition, note that most policies contain some element of ethical instruction because their origins lie in mistakes made or attempts to prevent misconduct.

TYPES OF DOCUMENTS

Management tip—Factual background information, insights, problem-solving strategies, and suggestions for the athletic director

Planning tool—Steps to take or factors that should be considered in the development of strategic plans, action plans, professional development plans, or governance systems

Educational resource—Handouts that can be used to educate staff members, campus constituents, volunteers, or student-athletes

Policy—Sample policies and procedures that should be adopted by an athletic department after customization and review by appropriate expert institutional or school district officials

Form—Sample forms, letters, or job descriptions

Evaluation instrument—Administrative tools that help the athletic director, a supervisor, or an employee assess job performance and evaluate program content

Risk assessment—Checklists that help the athletic director, a supervisor, or an employee identify risks and prevent litigation

7.1 MANAGEMENT TIP

Setting Standards of Ethical Conduct

Integrity Education

"You can't legislate ethics" is a phrase that supervisors often use when an employee behaves in a way that a manager deems unethical, inappropriate, or unprofessional. To some extent, this posit is true, but it does not remove the responsibility for managers to create an environment where ethical constructs are conveyed and monitored and acts of unethical or unprofessional behavior are quickly addressed. Think of ethical conduct rules as educating employees about the meaning of integrity. Undesirable behaviors can range from illegal (e.g., sexual harassment, misuse of institutional funds) to embarrassing (e.g., a coach throwing a chair onto the basketball floor or swearing at fans). Whether behaviors are illegal or not, the institution has a right to protect its good name and reputation by not employing people who engage in behavior unbecoming to educators or educational institutions.

Sanctions as Deterrents

Athletics is usually the most public, visible, and media-examined program of an educational institution. If unacceptable behavior occurs, chances are good that many people will hear about it, especially in this age of instant communication. If the manager believes that the prospect of a negative consequence is an effective deterrent, clear communication of specific behaviors that will result in sanctions ranging from a formal warning to termination of employment is essential and elevates employee awareness of unacceptable conduct. At worst, when clear policies and sanctioning procedures do not deter such behavior, the institution has a mechanism to remove employees whose actions taint the reputation and integrity of the institution. Indeed, enforcement of these policies restores confidence in the institution by showing that the administration will not tolerate unacceptable behavior.

Complex Environment of Athletics

Issues of professional conduct in athletic departments are more complicated than those found in typical classroom environments. The standard expectations related to employee behavior and supervisor–subordinate relationships may be similar, but issues that are more complex arise related to the appropriate relationships between staff and student-athletes who spend an incredible number of hours together in practice, competition, and travel. In addition, numerous external stakeholders—sports officials, donors, vendors, alumni, and governing-body leaders—require maintenance of respectful relationships. Professional conduct in athletics involves adherence to numerous layers of laws, rules, and expectations: state and federal laws, institutional policy, rules of sport governing associations, concepts of sportsmanship and honoring the rules of the game, behavior appropriate to institutional leaders and spokespersons, behavior of public figures, and public expectations of role models. These expectations and their complexity make it essential that athletic managers build in as many mechanisms as possible to educate, define, and assess ethical behavior and professional conduct in the athletic setting consistent with, but in addition to, general institutional expectations for employees. Part of this process must include informing employees about sanctions that could result if policies or expectations are violated.

Positive Purpose of Ethics Education

Creating strong policies and expectations regarding ethical and professional behavior serves many positive purposes:

1. Educates the staff on how the administration, at both the institutional and department levels, defines ethical and professional

behavior, resulting in fewer errors in personal judgment and a system that helps protect staff from violations

2. Establishes a template for how employees should treat others and expect to be treated, regardless of position held in the administrative hierarchy or within the tiered funding hierarchy, which, in turn, creates a positive overall working environment
3. Reinforces how the department wants to be viewed in a manner similar to how the clear articulation of values, goals, and objectives creates departmental ethos and identity
4. Creates a set of common expectations for intraoffice and interoffice relationships among diverse constituent groups that help staff navigate complexity

As described in chapter 6, athletic administrators who seek to be outstanding personnel directors must approach policy making and defining expectations from a positive perspective that helps employees grow, feel empowered by understanding what is expected, and be less vulnerable to an environment filled with uncertainty. That said, managers are obliged to be clear about the types of behaviors that will result in immediate termination or significant sanctions, especially in the area of ethical conduct.

Policies Applicable to All Employees and Additional Conduct Rules for Coaches

The athletic department policy manual should include institutional ethics and conduct policies as well as those specific to the athletic department. The reality is that employees seldom read institutional policy manuals, whereas the athletic department policy manual is the handbook commonly and frequently referred to for daily operations. Also, one unfortunate fact is that a significant number of athletic departments have been allowed to work in a vacuum for many years and have been negligent in following the expectations or policies applicable to other departments. This isolation has clearly affected the reputation of athletics on some campuses; faculty and administrators complain that athletic departments have their own sets of rules. This practice has also left many athletic administrators and their supervisors vulnerable to complaints and lawsuits lodged by employees.

As stated earlier, the athletic department is much more complex than other departments on campus. Institutional policies may not address many of the issues that are relevant to the athletic department. Therefore, athletic administrators must be vigilant about creating additional policies and expectations to reinforce required and desirable practices and behaviors. The strategy for creating these additional policies and expectations should be approached in two ways:

1. Review common institutional policies to determine whether they are rich enough in content to address the needs of the athletic department. If some existing policies fall short of addressing the needs of the athletic department, ask the appropriate institutional administrator as well as the human resources director whether the policy can be reworded for athletic department staff. Legal counsel may not allow this, but it is worth investigating. Our experience as athletic directors and consultants has shown that athletic departments have often been allowed to strengthen institutional policies or at least create additional expectations of current policies given the unique nature of athletic programs.
2. Identify areas that are not covered by institutional policies but are necessary given the unique nature of athletics. Create detailed, specific policies and expectations for the athletic department as a whole, as well as for specific subunits (coaches, sports medicine personnel, academic support programs, and so on) and be sure that they are approved by institutional legal counsel or other risk management professionals.

Four basic policies and one code of conduct acknowledgment form, found in HK*Propel*, are offered as examples of how athletic departments might construct these important documents.

Although these policies focus wholly on ethical conduct, smaller parts of most policies do the same thing. For instance, consider the follow-

7.2 **Policy**—Ethical and Professional Conduct of Athletic Department Employees

Sample policy that covers issues such as confidentiality, compliance with NCAA and conference rules, sexual harassment, inappropriate student–staff personal relationships, conflict of interest, student-athlete well-being, sportsmanlike conduct, gambling and bribery, nepotism, drug use, criminal background checks, and prohibited activities.

7.3 **Policy**—Standards of Professional Coaching Conduct

Covers issues such as professional development, obligation to report violations, instructional safety, physical bodily contact with athletes, emotional and verbal abuse, proper error correction, equal treatment, coach–athlete relationships, peer pressure, social isolation, and interactions with other constituents.

7.4 **Form**—Coaches Code of Conduct Agreement

A ready-to-use form that verifies coach receipt and acknowledgment of the coach's obligation to comply with professional development and conduct policies, including the obligation to report violations committed by others.

7.5 **Policy**—Compliance With Athletic Governance Rules

Sample policy that details employee obligations related to rules compliance, reporting violations, and rules knowledge competency.

7.6 **Policy**—Gambling Prohibition

Sample policy that details student-athlete and staff involvement in gambling activities and sanctions for violating such policy.

Available in HK*Propel*.

ing examples of program-specific policies that include ethical guidance:

- Prohibitions related to doing assignments for athletes are part of academic tutor employment agreements (see Form 8.7 in HK*Propel*) and ethical conduct elements applied to the academic support program (see Policy 8.2 and Policy 8.11).
- Prohibitions related to provision of vitamin or nutritional supplements or other substances are included as part of drug distribution restrictions applied to coaches, athletic trainers, and strength and conditioning coaches (see Policy 9.17).
- Obligations to maintain accounting and financial records according to commonly accepted accounting principles are included under financial policies (see Policy 5.16).

A specific section of the athletic policy manual should highlight general expectations regarding ethical behavior and professional conduct. Within this policy section, considerable attention should be paid to compliance with governance association rules and regulations (see Policy 7.5 and accompanying documents in HK*Propel*).

Policies Applicable to Student-Athletes

Student-athletes also need to be educated about their responsibility to comply with rules. This obligation is usually communicated by the inclusion of a rules compliance policy in the student-athlete handbook. Policy 7.7 is a sample policy that accomplishes this purpose.

7.7 **Policy**—Rules Compliance for Student-Athletes

Sample policy that details student-athlete responsibilities related to compliance with athletic governance association rules and regulations.

Available in HK*Propel*.

Educating Representatives of Athletic Interests

Parents, alumni, faculty members, donors, and fans of the athletic program must also be educated about their obligations to comply with governance association rules and regulations. Educational Resource 7.8 is an example of a publication that can be sent to all former student-athletes, reprinted in the alumni magazine, included in game programs, inserted with donation acknowledgment letters, and posted on the athletic program website.

7.8 Educational Resource—Rules Advisory for Alumni, Donors, Friends, and Fans

Sample publication that details responsibilities related to compliance with athletic governance association rules and regulations for parents, alumni, donors, friends, and fans of the athletic program.

Available in HK*Propel*.

7.9 PLANNING TOOL

Compliance With Governance Association Rules

Rules Compliance Policies

Policies should clearly define the responsibilities of staff members and higher administration officials (registrar, director of admissions, and so on) in the determination of eligibility, the submission of supporting data, and the completion and submission of required compliance reports. Policies 7.10, 7.11, 7.12, and 7.13 are provided in HK*Propel* as examples of such documents.

Rules Compliance Manual

A critical management responsibility is the design and implementation of a comprehensive rules compliance system beginning with the development of a rules compliance manual. The rules compliance manual should include (1) deadlines and instruction for the preparation of each eligibility report required by the institution's state or national athletic governance association or athletic league or conference; (2) copies of forms, reports, and other documentation for all eligibility, financial aid, and other rules determinations; (3) copies of policies and accountabilities related to rules compliance; and (4) educational programs and resources to be delivered to staff, student-athletes, and representatives of athletic interests (parents, fans, and alumni). With regard to instructions for completion of each rules compliance report, such materials should contain the following information:

- Processing timetable
- Processing checklist
- Definition of terms
- Rules references to be followed
- Applicable rules or institutional policy interpretations
- Sample forms to use to obtain the information required for the report
- Designation of staff members involved in preparation of the report and each staff member's specific responsibilities, including the staff member with overall responsibility for ensuring completion of the report process
- Designation of required signatories

7.10 Policy—Academic Eligibility of Student-Athletes

A customizable sample policy that specifies institutional authorities regarding the determination and reporting of the academic eligibility of student-athletes.

7.11 Policy—Eligibility Lists and Participation Reports

A customizable sample policy that specifies institutional personnel responsible for specific elements of eligibility and contest participation records.

7.12 Policy—Ethical Recruiting

A sample policy that specifies the spirit and letter of ethical recruiting including full transparency of information to parents and prospects.

7.13 Policy—Report of Participation in Athletic-Related Activities

A sample policy that specifies the posting of rules about limits on the participation of student-athletes in athletic-related activities, how such activities are recorded, and who is responsible for completing and submitting required reports.

Available in HK*Propel*.

The appendixes of the rules compliance manual should contain a copy of all forms, cover letters, and educational resources used in compliance processes. Following is a sample table of contents for such a rules compliance manual:

Sample Table of Contents for Rules Compliance Manual

1.0 Duties and Responsibilities of Designated Individuals

2.0 Recruiting

3.0 Award of Financial Aid to Student-Athletes

4.0 Determination of Student-Athlete Eligibility

5.0 Admission of Student-Athletes

6.0 Certification of Continuing Eligibility

7.0 Obtaining Rules Interpretations

8.0 Monitoring Rules Compliance, Extra Benefits, and Eligibility

9.0 Obtaining Waivers

10.0 Investigation and Reporting of Rules Violations

11.0 Rules Education

12.0 Appendixes

A rules compliance manual is essential for several reasons:

- Whenever a report has critical compliance implications and deadlines that could result in student-athlete ineligibility for competition, the user manual becomes an essential risk-control mechanism.
- Eligibility reports depend on the academic idiosyncrasies and variable policies of both the institution and its numerous academic units (colleges, departments, and so on). After the correct application of governance association rules is determined for specific situations (transferable credits, noncountable electives, and so on), this information must be memorialized to ensure the consistency of future reports and documentation of formal decisions by academic authorities. These decisions must be supported by written proof of certification that must be produced if eligibility is ever questioned.
- Someone outside the athletic department is usually the required signatory (e.g., registrar, director of student financial aid, director of admissions) to ensure that the athletic department is not policing itself. Thus, these people must be taught about NCAA rules. Although meetings and governance association rules manuals are essential for this purpose, the report preparation material in the rules compliance manual must serve as the rules and decision-making anchor for the certifying authority.
- Several people are usually involved in preparation of the report. These people must know their lines of responsibility and respective deadlines, and one person must be designated to oversee the entire process.
- Highly detailed instructions and education systems are required to compensate for the inevitable staff turnover within and outside athletics.
- Degree requirements change all the time. Detailed documentation must be maintained of degree program requirements operable at the time student-athlete eligibility was determined.

Verification of Rules Compliance

Although many national governance associations and conferences assist their member institutions by providing the forms on which information is assembled and submitted along with instructions for completing those documents, this information is never fully institution specific. Thus, these documents and instructions must be supplemented with institution-specific processing details (who does what by when). Athletic directors or their directors of compliance should construct customized instructional manuals describing all processes used for each of the following critical reports if they are required by conference, league, state, or national governance association rules:

- Squad list (roster of eligible athletes)
- Report of athletic-related financial aid (not applicable for high schools)
- Satisfactory progress toward the degree

- Graduation rate report
- Report of athletic participation and seasons of eligibility completed
- Verification of full-time enrollment report

A formal verification document should be attached to each of these reports. The document should contain the signature of all institutional authorities who are responsible for preparing, reviewing, and verifying the accuracy of the report. Form 7.14 accomplishes this purpose.

In support of such reports, the administrator in charge of rules compliance should also be responsible for designating data collection and processing forms and educational resources to be used to support the documentation of these eligibility reports or communication of rules requirements. Examples of such documents include Form 7.15, Educational Resource 7.16, Form 7.17, Form 7.18, and Form 7.19.

Athletic Scholarships and Recruiting Documentation

Athletic scholarship agreements are legally binding contracts with student-athletes. The recruiting procedures and award of such scholarships should be clearly documented to ensure compliance with governance association rules. Policy 7.20, Form 7.21, and Form 7.22 in HK*Propel* can be used to ensure adequate documentation of these processes.

Other Forms Related to Rules Compliance

Additional rules-related forms and policies are explained in subsequent chapters and included in HK*Propel*:

- Documentation checklist for recruited and walk-on student-athlete selected for team

7.14 Form—Verification of Academic Eligibility Report

A sample form that includes all signatories responsible for the preparation, review, and validation of eligibility reports.

7.15 Form—Degree-Countable Coursework to Be Certified by Dean

A sample form that can be used to request verification by top-level academic administrators that courses taken by student-athletes are countable in fulfillment of degree requirements, as required by national governance association rules.

7.16 Educational Resource—Instructions for Hosting Visiting Prospects

A sample handout that can be given to the student-athlete who volunteers to host a visiting prospective student-athlete. It includes applicable rules governing the visit and a question-and-answer section to assist the host in responding to prospect inquiries.

7.17 Form—Official Visit: Prospect and Host Agreement

A sample agreement that would be signed by the visiting prospective student-athlete and his or her host for the purpose of advising both individuals of applicable governing association rules and institutional and athletic policies governing activities during such visits.

7.18 Form—Weekly Report of Athletic-Related Activities

A sample form to be used to report the participation of student-athletes in athletic-related activities that are time limited by governance association rules.

7.19 Form—Amateurism Questionnaire

A sample questionnaire to be used to question current and prospective student-athletes about receipt of government or other third-party subsidies or pay or other benefits of value in return for sport participation, relationships with agents, and participation in professional sport or drafts.

Available in HK*Propel*.

7.20 **Policy**—Athletic Scholarship Awards

A sample policy that provides for faculty oversight over the award of athletic financial aid and the withdrawal or reduction of athletic scholarships.

7.21 **Form**—Athletic Scholarship Agreement

A sample athletic scholarship agreement that can be used by colleges and universities but must be reviewed by institutional legal counsel and customized according to the national governance association or conference rules and regulations.

7.22 **Form**—Recruiting Log

A sample recruiting log to be maintained by coaches that requires the coach to record all telephone calls, evaluation visits, contacts, official visits, and materials sent to each prospective student-athlete.

Available in HK*Propel*.

(all required questionnaires and forms) (Section 2.0 of Policy 11.5)

- Walk-on student-athlete documentation checklist (all required questionnaires and forms) (Form 11.4)
- Notification of status of student-athlete: clearance to practice and participate (Section 5.0 of Policy 11.5)
- Consent forms for drug testing (Form 9.14) and allowing disclosure of health and other athlete information (Forms 9.6 and 11.7)
- Student-athlete completion of degree agreement (Form 8.5)

Invariably, the compliance director will design a number of data collection forms that provide the information needed to complete compliance reports. In addition, the athletic governance association or conference will provide forms to the institution such as those required to request waivers of rules or report rules violations. Typical additional forms include the following:

- Transfer Student-Athlete Information Form
- Application for Medical Hardship Waiver
- Approval for Outside Competition
- Notification of Official Visit
- Report of Completion of Official Visit
- Report of Unofficial Visit
- Complimentary Admissions Report
- Designation of Prospective Student-Athlete
- Prospective Student-Athlete Checklist
- Eligibility Worksheet
- Approval Form: Student-Athlete Receipt of Awards From an External Agency
- Coaches' Certification to Recruit Off-Campus
- Approval of Student-Athlete Participation in Speaking, Charitable, and Other External Activities

Rules compliance requires a staff that is highly organized, capable of attending to detail, and fully committed to following procedures. Rules compliance manuals are the playbooks that enable excellent performance by the compliance team.

BIBLIOGRAPHY

ETHICS, RULES COMPLIANCE, AND PROFESSIONAL CONDUCT

Clotfelter, C.T. (2011). *Big-time sports in American universities*. Cambridge, United Kingdom: Cambridge University Press.

Crowley, J. (2006). *In the arena: The NCAA's first century*. Indianapolis, IN: NCAA.

Drew University. (2007). *Department of Intercollegiate Athletics policy manual*. Unpublished manuscript. Madison, NJ.

Duderstadt, J. (2003). *Intercollegiate athletics and the American university*. Ann Arbor, MI: University of Michigan Press.

Ehrmann, J. (2011). *Inside out coaching: How sports can transform lives*. New York: Simon & Schuster.

Fraleigh, W.P. (1984). *Right actions in sport: Ethics for contestants*. Champaign, IL: Human Kinetics.

French, P.A. (2004). *Ethics in college sports*. Lanham, MD: Rowman & Littlefield.

Masteralexis, L.P., Barr, C.A., & Hums, M.A. (2015). *Principles and practice of sport management* (5th ed.). Sudbury, MA: Jones & Bartlett Learning.

Morgan, W. (2018). *Ethics in sport* (3rd ed.). Champaign, IL: Human Kinetics.

National Collegiate Athletic Association. (2010–2011). *Guide for the college bound student-athlete*. Indianapolis, IN: NCAA.

National Collegiate Athletic Association. (2020). *2020–2021 Division I manual*. Indianapolis, IN: NCAA.

Pedersen, P.M., & Thibault, L. (Eds.). (2022). *Contemporary sport management* (7th ed.). Champaign, IL: Human Kinetics.

Shulman, J.L., & Bowen, W.G. (2001). *The game of life: College sports and educational values*. Princeton, NJ: Princeton University Press.

Thelin, J. (1994). *Games colleges play: Scandal and reform in intercollegiate athletics*. Baltimore, MD: Johns Hopkins University Press.

University of Texas at Austin. (1992). *Intercollegiate athletics for women policy manual*. Unpublished. Austin, TX: Department of Women's Intercollegiate Athletics.

University of Texas at Austin. (2010). *Intercollegiate athletics policy manual*. Austin, TX. No longer available.

USOPC Coaching Ethics Code. (2017). https://www.teamusa.org/USA-Karate/Officials-and-Coaches/Coaches-Resources/USOC-Coaching-Ethics-Code.

Wieberg, S. (2009). NCAA study: Athletes continue to disregard rules, gamble on sports. *USA Today*. www.usatoday.com/sports/college/2009-11-13-ncaa-gambling-study_N.htm.

CHAPTER

8

Student-Athlete Support Programs

As pressure increases on student-athletes, coaches, and administrators to produce winning athletic programs, increases are also seen in student-athletes' time commitment to sport, the importance of maintaining academic eligibility, and the temptation to waive admissions requirements for athletes. Both the news media and social media can quickly spread news of low graduation rates, athlete ineligibility, and the routing of athletes into easy majors or courses or toward friendly professors willing to grade athletes generously for "independent study" credits. Instances of athlete misbehavior, from physical abuse of girlfriends to hazing and bullying, can become major stories. Thus, the pressure on athletic departments to provide academic services and educational programs to student-athletes to address those risks is considerable.

Service programs for student-athletes usually include academic support programs that offer access to tutors or other learning specialists, study halls, study skills programs, and computer labs that may be open to all students or restricted to student-athletes. Additional education programs offered under the rubric of student-life programs may include career counseling; workshops on sexual harassment, hazing, and bullying; programs that address the use of performance-enhancing and recreational drugs; leadership programs; and community service opportunities. In the past few years, many more athletic departments have begun to offer programming or other forms of support that address mental health issues. The documents in this chapter, in both the book and HK*Propel*, provide model practices, policies, and forms that define academic and student-life programs as well as policies that control the time that student-athletes spend on competition and involvement in external community activities.

TYPES OF DOCUMENTS

Management tip—Factual background information, insights, problem-solving strategies, and suggestions for the athletic director

Planning tool—Steps to take or factors that should be considered in the development of strategic plans, action plans, professional development plans, or governance systems

Educational resource—Handouts that can be used to educate staff members, campus constituents, volunteers, or student-athletes

Policy—Sample policies and procedures that should be adopted by an athletic department after customization and review by appropriate expert institutional or school district officials

Form—Sample forms, letters, or job descriptions

Evaluation instrument—Administrative tools that help the athletic director, a supervisor, or an employee assess job performance and evaluate program content

Risk assessment—Checklists that help the athletic director, a supervisor, or an employee identify risks and prevent litigation

8.1 PLANNING TOOL

Best Practices in the Development of Academic Support Programs

Historically, the design of academic support programs in college athletics has been more about responding to crisis than operating from a sound, proactive philosophical and educational perspective. The following examples demonstrate the point:

- A coach recruits a talented student-athlete who doesn't meet admissions standards. The institution makes an admissions exception and knowingly creates a situation in which an underqualified and academically unprepared student-athlete is at academic risk.
- A top athlete in the program becomes academically ineligible, and the institution has to explain why he or she is missing from the starting lineup. A faculty member on the athletic advisory council inquires about the situation, and the athletic department must demonstrate that it is providing the necessary academic support to enable the student-athlete to return to academic good standing.
- A newspaper reports that the basketball team has just qualified for postseason championships. Next to that article is a story about 60 percent of all qualifying teams having graduation rates below 40 percent, including your institution's team.

Because of the prevalence of these issues and other student-athlete academic concerns, the athletic department hires tutors, learning specialists, or other academic support personnel to help student-athletes who are having difficulties meeting academic expectations. The support system grows into an organized program as more athletes with similar problems are identified, so a person is appointed to direct the program on an ongoing basis. Then coaches realize the potential of the academic support program as a recruiting tool. A new arms race begins as state-of-the-art study areas, computer facilities, learning specialists, and academic services become part of a culture that defines athletes as special. The development of an academic support program that claims to "take care of our athletes better" becomes a significant recruiting asset.

Throughout this evolutionary process, chances are that the academic support program was

- initially or still is controlled by the athletic department;
- focused on the most important sports, which might have been more likely to recruit students at academic risk;
- developed through trial and error rather than acquisition of advice from academic experts;
- developed without reliance on fact-based data; and
- focused on serving the needs of the 5 to 10 percent of all athletes in the program who were at highest academic risk.

Many academic support programs are doing an excellent job, but others are just managing to stay one step ahead of the next academic crisis, thanks to the passionate commitment and hard work of dedicated staff members. These programs require ongoing and careful management attention that not only demonstrates a genuine concern for the academic success of student-athletes who are struggling academically but also minimizes the existing and growing high stakes of failure.

Today, institutional reputation risk related to academic integrity is at an all-time high because of the following factors:

- Media coverage of graduation rates and academic progress rates, publicly reported because of NCAA rules and legal open-records mandates, has become the rule rather than the exception.
- Academic progress rate failure poses the risk of loss of athletic scholarships or team ineligibility for postseason championship play as a penalty at NCAA Division I institutions, the most highly visible athletic programs.
- The revenue stakes of winning and lucrative coach contracts at Division I institutions show no signs of abating, putting more pressure on coaches in the recruiting process.
- The academic rigor at top institutions and the competition for the best students is escalating, putting more pressure on academically underqualified students in the classroom.
- Academic support programs controlled by athletic departments carry an inherent perception of a conflict of interest. Faculty and the public suspect that tutoring support may do more than help a student-athlete do his or her own work.
- As media reports come to light of student registration in selected easy courses, less demanding majors, or independent studies with less-than-rigorous professors, questions increase about whether student-athletes are receiving a meaningful education.
- Faculties, charged with preserving the academic reputation of the institution, become vocal critics of academic support systems that are controlled by athletic or nonfaculty personnel and not subject to faculty oversight.
- The NCAA mandates the existence of academic support programs for student-athletes in Division I, and these programs now come under regular certification review through a transparent on-campus evaluation process, the results of which are publicly released.

This environment creates even more pressure on academic support programs to prevent student-athlete failure, leading many observers to believe that athletic staff members serving in the role of academic advisors pressure student-athletes to take majors and courses in which they can be academically successful rather than follow career tracks and academic training that have useful future value. Thus, colleges and universities are beginning to take higher interest in these programs and use a more sophisticated approach to bringing them under faculty control and making them more effective and academically defensible. These factors also make it clear that the academic support program cannot be viewed in isolation from the admissions process, faculty oversight, or pressures on coaches.

Following is a discussion of the key elements and questions that should be considered in the development of effective and educationally defensible academic support programs.

Admissions Policy Exemptions

As soon as an academic institution grants a prospective student-athlete an exemption to the minimum academic standards established for admission applicable to all prospective students, two things happen: (1) its responsibility for the quality of the educational experience of the student-athlete increases because he or she will be challenged to compete in the classroom with better-qualified classmates, and (2) risk to institutional reputation increases. Although it is tempting to argue for no admissions exemptions, such exemptions are commonplace. Institutions often waive regular admissions requirements for students who are extraordinarily gifted in music, the arts, or other areas that defy traditional forms of standardized measurement. Institutions may also waive normal admissions standards for students with learning disabilities or from underrepresented minority populations whose socioeconomic status, past discriminatory treatment, lack of basic developmental skills, or other factors have prevented them from attaining the qualifications needed to meet normal admissions standards.

In many cases, the question is not whether such students are capable of graduation; rather, it is whether these students are provided with the programs that will enable them to acquire the study skills, learning strategies, and other advantages to which they have previously been denied so that they can compete in the classroom on a level playing field with their peers. Athletes, who are often classic overachievers, have many advantages in this regard if they can be surrounded with the right programs and environment. In fact, many institutions of higher education require specially admitted students to participate in academic support programming such as

- summer bridge programs offered before the first full semester of attendance,
- assessments of learning disabilities and basic reading and writing,
- remedial programming based on basic skills assessments or academic deficiencies identified during the admissions process, and
- academic support programs provided by the institution (as opposed to the athletic department).

Therefore, the first critical decision on the part of the university is whether athletes will receive admissions exemptions and, if so, under what criteria and according to what process. Additionally, the university needs to decide how many such exemptions will be granted. At what point does the number of special-talent admissions exceptions change the culture of a particular sport, the culture of the entire athletic program, or, at smaller institutions, the nature of the entire student body?

Academic Profiling

The athletic departments must backtrack and do research to identify the characteristics of (1) those student-athletes who were unable to graduate from the institution and (2) those who entered with characteristics predictive of academic failure but were able to succeed. What are the predictive criteria that define a student-athlete at high academic risk? What are the characteristics of at-risk students who succeed? Is a system in place whereby these criteria are used to influence recruiting decisions? Are coaches fully informed about the academic profiles of prospects? Does the academic support program maximize the production of the attributes of at-risk students who graduated?

Review of At-Risk Admissions

Some type of review mechanism, preferably by faculty members, should be in place to make decisions about whether scholarships or admissions exceptions should be offered to student-athletes with exceptionally high-risk profiles. A definite conflict of interest exists if the coach or athletic staff has the decision-making power over admissions, even if the registrar or other university administrators are part of the review system. Despite the fears of athletic administrators and coaches, faculty oversight committees are usually extraordinarily supportive of highly motivated student-athletes who have poor academic backgrounds. These faculty overseers not only support admissions exceptions but also, because of their decision-making responsibility, become invested in developing an academic support program that proves them right. Often, they take a personal interest in the academic success of these students. Athletic directors should consider establishing a structure in which a subcommittee of three to five faculty members of the intercollegiate athletic council is given this responsibility. No donors, coaches, or administrators should be a part of the recommending body. The coach and the athletic senior staff member overseeing academic affairs should be charged with presenting the case for such exemptions and responding to faculty queries regarding the reasons why the staff believes that the student-athlete will be successful.

Acknowledgment of Overall Faculty Control

Key to academic integrity for any athletic program is transparency of data and faculty control of academic performance tracking and oversight mechanisms, such as the suggested practice of reviewing and recommending admissions exemptions. The larger athletic policy structure (athletic advisory council, faculty athletic council, board of athletic policy committee) should always be faculty dominated (have faculty members make up the majority). All specially admitted student-athletes should be tracked throughout their collegiate careers. Regular academic progress and graduation achievement reports on this group as well as all student-athletes should be presented to the faculty senate or other appropriate faculty governance structure. Athletic department conformance with the institution's core belief in faculty control of academic integrity is essential. The extent to which the athletic department acknowledges this trust in faculty control and judgment by policy and through its governance structures defines the likelihood that coaches and athletic personnel will work together with the faculty to maximize the success of student-athletes.

Academic Unit Control of Student-Athlete Academic Support Programs

Control of athlete academic support programs should not reside in the athletic department for obvious conflict-of-interest reasons. But even though an academic unit controls the program, the athletic department should have a close working relationship with those responsible for the program with regard to student-athlete participation. The coach has a major and direct responsibility for recruiting academically capable student-athletes and supporting their academic success. The head coach controls whether a student participates in a game or sits on the bench and is a key influencer whose encouragement of attendance in class, study hall, or tutoring session and other positive academic behaviors is critical. Regular communication is needed between the academic support program and the coaching staff, either directly or through an athletic staff liaison charged with that responsibility. Participation in an athletic program is time consuming. Academically at-risk students may need accommodations in scheduling or travel whenever sports participation and academic preparation conflict. Coaches may have to use the carrot of participation to encourage a student-athlete's participation in the academic support system.

Some of the best and most ethical academic support programs in the country have been developed by athletic departments and are still controlled by athletic departments. What should the athletic director do in these cases to maintain demonstrated academic support program excellence while minimizing the appearance of conflict of interest? The solution is to move the entire program to academic unit control, being sure to keep the same staff and organizational structure that made the program successful. And "moving" is not meant in the literal sense: In all likelihood, the program would remain in the same physical space, continue to be funded by athletic department resources, and have all the same personnel. The only change, but an important one, would be to whom the head of the program would report. That person would be someone outside the athletic department.

Audience to Be Served by Academic Support Programs

Another key decision concerns who will benefit from the academic support program: (1) all student-athletes, (2) a subset of student-athletes at academic risk, or (3) all students on campus. The time commitment required for athletics should be considered a risk element for all student-athletes. Athletic departments should have policies in place that provide academic support benefits for all athletes in need rather than those who have been profiled as high risk. If all athletes must meet normal admissions standards, chances are good that no special academic support programs will be required. In that case, the athletic department is obliged to ensure that all athletes are aware of academic support programs available to all students and to ensure that athletic program obligations don't interfere with such access. The larger the population of student-athletes who do not meet normal admissions standards is, the more likely it is that the staffing, cost, and size of such programs will be considerable and the programs will become exclusive to student-athletes.

Early Assistance to At-Risk Students

First-semester performance sets the tone for academic success and should be an important focus for students at academic risk. If possible, high-risk student-athletes should enroll during the summer before their initial full-time semester to ease their adjustment to greater academic demands, provide time for the academic support program staff to assess their reading and writing skills or learning disabilities, undergo training in study skills, and participate in an academic support system that does not compete with the beginning of a sport season or a full academic course load. All program resources should be instituted at the beginning of the student-athlete's first full semester of work and in conjunction with monitoring programs that periodically assess progress or grades in each course during the semester. Chances are that at-risk students will require tutors for each of their courses in addition to general learning support (writing, reading, time management, note taking, studying, and test taking). Both programs should be instituted before signs of academic trouble appear.

Early Plug-In to Students With Disabilities Office

Students with learning disabilities receive many important services and accommodations that are unrelated to their status as student-athletes. Early identification of such students and establishment of connections with these services are essential.

Policy Support of Academic Achievement

Several critical areas of policy support need to be established by the athletic department or college:

- Notice to coaches that graduation rates and the academic success of student-athletes are among their critical responsibilities and that they are expected to adjust athletic demands toward that end
- Expectation that coaches will create disincentives for failure to attend class or scheduled academic support program obligations and will not hesitate to remove student-athletes from participation in practice or competition to provide them with necessary extra study time to remedy academic deficiencies
- Use of graduation rate and academic progress rate criteria as elements of evaluation in coach employment and factors considered for reappointment, contract renewal, or multiyear employment agreements
- Commitment to ethical and curricular integrity by coaches, other athletic personnel, and academic advisor personnel with regard to prohibitions against directing students to take or avoid particular courses, instructors, or majors to maintain athletic eligibility
- Prohibition of athletic competition during final exams when the institution controls the sport schedule
- Scheduling policies that limit missed class time and require the approval of athletic schedules by the faculty-dominated athletic policy board
- Specific procedures for approval by the athletic policy board for exceptions to missed-class limitations because of scheduling demands out of the institution's control (e.g., postseason championship play) and accommodation of academic needs during travel for such extra competition
- Prohibition of athlete enrollment in courses taught by coaches or, if such courses are required, mechanisms that prohibit coach involvement in determining an athlete's grade for that course
- Faculty governance control of course credits for varsity sport participation as part of physical education or sport-related majors and the maximum allowable hours accepted for such courses
- Required exit interviews with athletes that provide information on athletic department and coach support of the student-athlete's academic achievement
- Faculty governance prohibition of campus-wide cancellation of classes for athletic events
- Mechanisms for the regular collection and review of data by coach, by sport, and overall such as team GPAs, choice of major, athlete enrollment and grades by course section, academic progress (percentage of completion of units required for degree), graduation rate, and so on that enable administrative and faculty oversight
- Faculty majority composition of athletic policy and academic review committees
- Mandated reports to the faculty senate or other faculty governing body on the academic achievements of student-athletes with

comparisons with the regular student body, including data on specially admitted athletes

- Priority registration for athletes that will minimize lost class time and maximize their opportunity to register for classes required for progress toward their degrees
- Coach and athlete involvement in regular campus activities and programs that support the student's educational experience (community service, guest speakers, study abroad, and so on)
- Designation of a faculty member (faculty athletic representative) who is responsible for overseeing academically related athletic department policies, procedures, and programs
- Assessment of the academic skills and profiles of all newly enrolled athletes
- Monitoring and report preparation by a nonathletic entity to comply with rules of eligibility for athletic competition
- Training and supervision of tutors and employment agreements that define and require ethical conduct related to student-athlete production of all academic work product and student-athlete academic independence
- Provision of summer academic scholarship assistance for at-risk students
- Provision of assistance to students desiring to return to the university to complete undergraduate degree programs under appropriate circumstances
- Protection of athlete academic information in conformance with privacy laws and institutional policy

Elements of a Comprehensive Academic Support Program

College faculty, staffs of academic support programs administered by the office of the provost or other appropriate academic officials, and athletic personnel should work together to ensure that student-athletes, especially those at academic risk, have access to quality academic support programs containing the following programmatic elements:

- **Study skills learning support**—Training programs that help students improve skills in time management, writing, reading, note taking, prioritization of tasks, test preparation, and test taking
- **Tutoring**—Subject-matter tutors who help students with specialized course content
- **Mentoring**—Provision of regularly scheduled assistance to at-risk students with regard to reinforcement of study skills and strategies, monitoring of class attendance, and monitoring of grades on all assignments and tests
- **Accommodation of learning disabilities**—Assessment, support, and accommodation of students with identified learning disabilities by the appropriate campus office responsible for such programs
- **Technology access and training**—Access to, use of, and training on computers and other technologies essential for efficient production of academic work at times available to student-athletes
- **Study hall**—Access to study areas with a climate conducive to learning and with access to academic assistance

The extent to which the use of such programs is required by student-athletes should be dependent on their at-risk status and demonstrated academic performance. Programming mandates should be reduced as the student becomes academically and behaviorally more capable. The goal of all academic support programs should be to assist the student-athlete in achieving a level of academic competence that enables him or her to compete in the classroom in an independent, responsible, and mature manner.

All these practices are implemented through the adoption of policies and processes. The following documents in HK*Propel* are samples of necessary academic support system documentation.

8.2 **Policy**—Academic Performance of Student-Athletes

Sample policy that covers issues such as minimization of class absences because of competition; academic responsibilities of student-athletes; responsibilities of coaches related to the support of academics, relationships with the faculty, performance, tutoring and other academic support services; learning disabilities assessment; and academic advising related to selection of degree programs or classes.

8.3 **Policy**—Tutoring Services

Sample policy that sets standards and processes for the hiring and payment of tutors, procedures by which student-athletes may obtain tutors, evaluation of tutors, and accountability related to missed tutoring sessions.

8.4 **Form**—Request for Student-Athlete Academic Progress Report

Sample memo to professors of student-athletes asking for a midsemester progress report that will guide the design of a support program to address concerns about class performance.

8.5 **Form**—Student-Athlete Academic Contract

Sample academic contract typically used for student-athletes who make multiple changes in designation of an academic major or repeatedly exhibit academic deficiencies to ensure completion of an academic course of study that results in achievement of the baccalaureate degree within a reasonable period. The agreement is used to ensure accurate understanding over time of student-athlete decision making and promises of support by the athletic department.

8.6 **Form**—Tutor Application Form

Sample tutor application form to be used in the hiring process.

8.7 **Form**—Tutor Employment Agreement

Sample tutor employment agreement that details conditions of continued employment including prohibited activities, limitations on contacts with faculty, adherence to governance association rules and regulations, and maintenance of professional relationships with student-athletes.

8.8 **Form**—Payment and Verification of Tutoring Session

Sample form to be used by the tutor and signed by student-athletes to verify completion of a tutoring session and begin the process of tutor payment.

Available in HK*Propel*.

8.9 MANAGEMENT TIP

Assisting Academically At-Risk Student-Athletes

Student-athletes who are at risk academically need to be supported by an academic support system that (1) provides more structure of study time and more hours for academic preparation, (2) enables closer oversight of academic responsibilities and achievements to catch problems early and reward success, (3) provides assessments that may identify underlying learning disabilities or deficiencies in basic skills (reading, writing, note taking, and so on), and (4) surrounds the student-athlete with positive people who express confidence in the student-athlete's abilities. Following are program elements or practices that address those needs:

1. **Early tests of learning skills.** High school GPAs and SAT scores should be examined to determine whether students are entering the program at academic risk. This group should be tested for learning disabilities and basic reading and writing skills.
2. **Team academic coach.** If a team has a high number of at-risk students and the team is small enough, consideration should be given to assigning the team a full-time staff member. The academic coach will then have the option of coordinating teamwide solutions (study halls customized to match up to team practice and competitive schedules, study halls on the road, and so on) that are difficult to implement with larger squads. This academic coach model also minimizes the labeling of smaller groups of people as at risk and increases the prospect of academic success for all student-athletes on the team.
3. **Study hall time.** Consider moving study halls to immediately before team practice instead of after practice when student-athletes are usually both tired and hungry.
4. **Using sport participation as an incentive.** Coaches should consider implementing a team rule such as "We don't miss class, we don't miss study hall, and we don't miss practice" and instituting loss of playing time as a penalty. If such a rule is enforced early in every student-athlete's career, the desired result is quickly realized because the athlete knows that the coach is serious about the importance of all these expectations. Implementation of the penalty early in the season also ensures that player absences from competitions occur when game results aren't as critical.
5. **Reporting grades.** Consider having every team member take every graded quiz, test, and academic progress report to his or her academic coach upon receipt and communicating those achievements to coaches immediately to permit staff members to comment on and reward performance immediately through verbal recognition and compliments. This practice creates a culture of pride in academic achievement, acknowledgment of success, or early attention to and remediation of deficiencies.
6. **Experienced tutors.** Consider assigning more mature and experienced tutors who will be consistently available over three or four years to work with the same academically at-risk student-athletes. These tutors are more likely to provide a stable and predictable learning environment in which supportive, highly disciplined, and understanding relationships between student-athletes and tutors will evolve. The importance of tutor knowledge of student-athlete learning and studying patterns over time cannot be underestimated.
7. **Review of class notes.** Consider requiring tutors to begin every tutoring session by reviewing the student-athlete's class notes and discussing what the student retained from the class session. This review often provides critical insights on information retention, note-taking skills, and understanding of material.

8. **Profiles of academic success and failure.** Data on high school GPA, SAT scores, overall college GPA, and transfer status of all student-athletes should be analyzed over the immediate past 10 years to determine the relationship between academic success and these variables. These variables are often related to the quality of feeder institutions and vary greatly between institutions. For instance, many institutions have discovered that the quality of preparation of students from specific local high schools or of junior college transfers from certain states is a predictor of high academic risk or that the combination of a low SAT score and a low high school GPA is a significant risk predictor. Every effort should be made to give coaches the fact-based information that they need to assess the academic credentials of prospects. This recommendation is not to say that potentially at-risk students should not be recruited. Rather, efforts should be made to minimize their overall numbers so that the academic support system can provide adequate support for these students and coaches are prepared to make the commitment required to support such extra academic work.
9. **Clear expectations related to use of study halls and computer labs.** Creating a disciplined approach to study and a focus on academic responsibilities is advanced by a highly structured work environment that maximizes time on task and efficiency of effort. Implementing this environment requires clearly stated policies regarding study halls and computer labs and consequences for violating such policies. See Policy 8.10 for an example of such a policy.
10. **Faculty mentors.** We believe that the establishment of a faculty oversight structure that is a standing committee of the athletic advisory council is a critical element in successful programs for academically at-risk student-athletes (see Policy 8.11). These faculty members can assist in identifying faculty interested in mentoring student-athletes.

8.10 Policy—Study Hall and Computer Lab Rules

Sample policy that defines the structure and rules governing study environments, including sanctions for violating such policies.

8.11 Policy—Oversight of Student-Athlete Academic Performance

Sample policy that defines the functions and operation of a faculty standing committee charged with oversight of student-athletes' academic performance, including the development of a faculty mentor program.

Available in HK*Propel*.

8.12 PLANNING TOOL

Design of Model Student-Life Program

History

The formalization of student-life programs sponsored by athletic departments is a relatively recent occurrence. Faced with criticism that high-powered Division I athletic programs were using athletes to win championships and raise millions in revenues while their student-athletes were not getting a similar return on investment from their institutions (graduation with meaningful degrees, good jobs, and useful preparation for life after sport), in 1991 the NCAA Foundation initiated efforts to create a total development program for student-athletes. Through the collaborative efforts of the NCAA Foundation and the Division 1A Athletics Directors' Association, the CHAMPS/Life Skills Program was created. In 1994 the NCAA introduced the CHAMPS/Life Skills program to all NCAA members. The purpose of the program was to promote the personal, educational, and career development of student-athletes. That NCAA program has now been renamed NCAA Life Skills (NCAA, 2021), and most NCAA member institutions sponsor some form of a planned life-skills program in their athletic programs. Some institutions, however, philosophically insist that student-athletes participate in the same academic, career, and personal development programs offered to all students at the institution.

Time Challenges

One of the difficulties that must be navigated with any student-athlete support program is time. Because student-athletes spend three to four hours or more a day on their sports, spend another four to five hours a day attending classes, dedicate their weekends to competitions, and have to place a high priority on daily study time, any new program has to be reasonable in terms of time demands. Thus, a premium must be placed on program design that creates value while limiting delivery time. Also, student-life programming (with the exception of academic support programs) should be thought of as extending over the four-year eligibility period of the athlete.

Priorities

Few will argue that the highest priority in student-athlete support programs must be in the area of academics. For the student-athletes with the highest academic risk, the priority and time commitment for study hall and special academic assistance is even greater. Also, the types of student-life programs that can be offered are almost limitless. Thus, the most effective student-life programs are those that are highly customized to meet the needs of individual student-athletes. Delivering cookie-cutter programs in which participation involves all teams or entire teams may not be the best idea. Similarly, the number of programs delivered should not be a critical consideration. Quality and customization according to individual athlete needs should be the primary considerations.

Replication and Excess

An inherent dilemma for all athletic departments is the issue of special treatment of student-athletes, especially when that treatment replicates an institution program available to all students. Although universities support computer labs, athletic departments offer that same service with better equipment, in a plusher environment, during better hours, and with more individualized staff support. Although study areas are located all over campus, few are reserved for student subgroups, and few are as attractive as athletic department study halls. This situation is more likely to be an issue in Division I programs where those programs are used as recruiting incentives than it will be for Division II or III or high school programs. An arms race is underway among the big-time programs about who has the finest computer labs, study areas, locker rooms, and socialization areas. But choosing to go over the top has the downside of creating a campuswide perception of athletic excess.

Academic Support Programs

Although academic support programs were among the first student-life programs developed, these programs have become necessities rather than optional enhancements. Planning Tool 8.1 and Management Tip 8.9 in this book and Policies and Forms 8.2 through 8.8, 8.10, and 8.11 in HK*Propel* are devoted to this student-athlete support program.

Peer Mentoring Program

An important element of a student-life program is giving student-athletes the opportunity to mentor younger players and providing younger players the opportunity to learn from upperclasspersons. These programs should be structured by policy and should include training programs for student-athlete mentors. Educational Resource 8.13 is a sample document to be distributed to all peer mentors as a reminder of responsibilities and important points highlighted in a training program.

8.13 Educational Resource—
Guidelines for Student-Athlete Peer Mentors

Sample educational resources that could be distributed as part of a training program for student-athlete peer mentors and highlights important responsibilities and skills.

Available in HK*Propel*.

Other Program Elements

Following is a menu of possible student-athlete development programming in addition to academic support programming.

Career Development

Best delivered as one-on-one counseling with small group workshops.

- Mentoring
- Creating an online brand
- Career assessment and planning
- Job interview skills
- Networking skills
- Negotiating salaries
- On-campus interviewing and career fairs
- Information interview program and corporate visits
- Posteligibility job placement assistance
- Internship assistance
- Graduate internship and assistantship placement
- Resume writing, reference plan, and cover letter writing

Life Skills Seminars and Workshops

Lectures and small-group seminars or workshops about personal and social issues delivered by top speakers, optional programs or required attendance at a minimum number over a four-year period, or a combination of mandatory and optional.

- Goal setting
- Values leadership
- Dealing with grief
- Dealing with diversity
- Handling money and credit
- Alcohol and drug education
- Manners and etiquette
- Media relations
- Decision making in the clutch
- Personal image, presentations, and dressing for success
- Confidence and self-esteem
- Positive personal relationships
- Time and stress management
- Sexual responsibility (sexual harassment, sexual abuse, sexual misconduct)
- Eating right and personal nutrition

Formal Leadership Experiences

Student-athletes should be encouraged to develop their leadership skills by serving on committees and advisory councils, especially when those experiences include the opportunity to watch adult role models who are also serving on those committees.

- Captains program—For team captains and those being groomed as team captains
- Student-athlete advisory committee
- Athletic advisory council—Athletes serving with faculty, alumni, and so on
- Involvement in student government
- Diversity council—Student-athlete, coach, and staff addressing department diversity issues
- Mentors against violence program—Student-athletes playing a campus leadership role in preventing violence and sexual abuse on campus (Northeastern University, 2011)

Community Service

Rather than having each team pick its own community service program, consideration should be given to a year-round department-wide program in which all teams participate in the same program but do so at a time of the year or for a length of time that best suits that team or the individuals on that team. The advantages of such an approach are that (1) teams perform their community service outside their competitive seasons, (2) effective scheduling limits the time that any one team spends off campus, and (3) the athletic program can more easily become branded for its community service affiliation through a year-round program.

- Elementary school or nonprofit organization reading program
- Habitat for Humanity
- Adopt a school (each team)
- Campus community service programs
- Community or neighborhood cleanup programs
- Mentoring or tutoring disadvantaged populations

Consideration should also be given to having the athletic department partner with student government, the local school district, and the larger institution's diversity and community relations office to offer the type of community service program that no athletic department could logistically or financially support but one in which student-athletes could easily participate. The award-winning University of Texas at Austin Neighborhood Longhorns program is one such program. It has been in existence for over 20 years and is fully integrated with multiple campus departments (University of Texas at Austin, 2011).

A sample policy describing a possible student-life program, its structure, and requirements is contained in Policy 8.14.

8.14 Policy—Student-Life Program

Sample policy that describes a multiple-element student-life program that includes such requirements as career development, life skills workshops, formal leadership experiences, and community service.

Available in HK*Propel*.

Exit Interviews

Some athletic governance associations like the NCAA suggest that institutions conduct exit interviews of student-athletes upon their completion of eligibility for athletic participation. Many institutions conduct annual surveys of all student-athletes covering all aspects of their athletic experience. No matter what the guiding policy, exit interviews are important tools with which to evaluate the athletic experience of the primary athletic program consumer. Policy 8.15 provides an example of an exit interview policy, and Evaluation Instrument 8.16 is a sample instrument that might be used.

8.15 **Policy**—Student-Athlete Exit Interviews

Sample policy that describes an exit interview requirement for all student-athletes who complete athletic eligibility.

8.16 **Evaluation Instrument**—Student-Athlete Exit Survey

Sample evaluation instrument that can be used to assess the student-athlete experience upon completion of athletic eligibility.

Available in HK*Propel*.

8.17 PLANNING TOOL

Student-Athlete Community Service and Fund-Raising Issues

Teams and individual student-athletes are increasingly being asked by institutional and community stakeholders to perform on-campus and off-campus community service projects. In some cases, the athletic department requires teams to conduct fund-raising activities to offset expenses for team training trips or team operating budgets. Although it is reasonable to expect student-athletes to contribute to campus life and community-at-large projects and to help fund certain athletic experiences or team extra benefits, these activities can become excessive without proper approvals and procedures in place. One athletic administrator should always know what fund-raising and community service projects are being completed at all times and have the responsibility to approve or disallow any project. Without strong oversight, some of the following problems may occur:

- Involvement in charities or community service projects that may be contrary to the mission of the institution or the department
- Involvement in charities, community service projects, or fund-raising projects that would be in conflict with activities sponsored by the institution, its development office, or the athletic department
- Involvement in charities, community service projects, or fund-raising projects that could be seen as a conflict of interest for a coach, staff member, or student-athlete
- Involvement in charities, community service projects, or fund-raising projects that come with unacceptable strings attached
- Unknowing encroachment by one team on another team's project (asking the same businesses for money, contacting Special Olympics to serve as volunteers, and so on)
- Teams conducting too many similar projects, lessening the effect of all projects
- Poor financial procedures in place regarding cash handling, logging gifts, and so on, which could result in breaking governing-body rules, creating the perception of money mismanagement, an actual occurrence of money mismanagement, or donors not receiving gift receipts
- Teams or individual student-athletes conducting projects on their own without coach approval
- Teams or student-athletes being asked to spend too much time away from studies to work on these projects

Policy 8.18 is an example of a policy approach to avoiding these anticipated problems, and Forms 8.19 and 8.20 are examples of how to respond to outside requests for the participation of coaches or student-athletes in community service and fund-raising projects.

8.18 **Policy**—Participation in Events Sponsored by Outside Organizations

Sample policy that describes the process that must be followed to request and receive approval for participation of coaches or student-athletes in events sponsored by outside agencies, including restrictions related to participation in charity events.

8.19 **Form**—Response to Requests for Participation in Outside Events

Sample cover letter, to which Form 8.20 is attached, which is a standard response to community requests for participation by coaches and student-athletes in outside events that explains athletic department policy, states the requirement to complete a written application, and describes the department's decision-making procedure.

8.20 **Form**—Request for Coach or Student-Athlete Participation in Outside Event

Sample standard application form to be used to request the appearance or participation of a coach or student-athlete in a third-party event that collects all pertinent information about the event and permits the athletic department to make a decision based on department policy.

Available in HK*Propel*.

8.21 MANAGEMENT TIP

Addressing Student-Athlete Mental Health Issues: Prevention, Access to Services, and Treatment

Addressing student-athlete mental health in the final section of this chapter does not mean the issue is of lesser importance. In fact, the authors believe it is extremely important. However, attention to mental health has been overlooked by many coaches and athletic administrators. A review of NCAA rules manuals indicates that it wasn't until 2019 that Divisions I, II, and III adopted rules requiring mental health services to be available to athletes.

Athletic departments have come to realize that student-athletes' mental health can no longer be ignored, and we believe this will be one of the biggest challenges athletic departments must face. More and more studies are being conducted related to student-athlete mental health. For example, Cox et al. (2017) found that 33.2 percent of 950 Division I student-athletes reported symptoms of depression, with female athletes reporting higher rates than male athletes. Putukian (2020) links physical health with mental health, stating that "for some student-athletes, the psychological response to injury can trigger or unmask serious mental health issues such as depression, anxiety, disordered eating, and substance use or abuse" (p. 1). In 2020, the NCAA commissioned a study on how the pandemic was affecting student-athletes. A survey was e-mailed in the spring and a similar survey was sent again in the fall. Almost 25,000 athletes completed the survey. In both semesters, athletes indicated elevated rates of depression, mental exhaustion, anxiety, and hopelessness. Mental health concerns were highest among women, those living alone or away from campus, those on the queer spectrum, and those reporting family economic hardship.

Strategies to address student-athlete mental health concerns should begin with an examination of behavioral practices within the sport culture that may exacerbate mental health issues. Additionally, institutions must clearly communicate how athletes can access the mental health services available to them and must have strict protocols in place for actual treatment.

- **Sport Culture.** There is no doubt that the sport culture is fraught with perceptions and practices that can undermine the physical and mental health of student-athletes. The expectation that athletes must be strong, resilient, and never show weakness encourages a culture in which athletes often hide injuries or feelings of emotional and mental distress. This is exacerbated by the fact that many coaches use abusive strategies and practices to "toughen up" athletes. Reardon et al. (2019) found that psychological abuse, physical abuse, and sexual abuse were the three most common forms of nonaccidental violence committed by adults with power over athletes. Unfortunately, the only cases of abuse that people become aware of are those that make national media headlines, such as the avoidable death of University of Maryland football player Jordan McNair, the women's soccer players at the University of Houston that suffered from rhabdomyolysis after being subjected to grueling workouts, and the hundreds of gymnasts at Michigan State University and USA Gymnastics that were sexually abused by team physician Larry Nassar.
- These cases are the tip of the iceberg. Many head coaches, assistant coaches, and strength coaches routinely use verbal and physical abuse and circumvent policies and rules regarding time spent in athletic activities that result in athlete depression, loss of confidence, overuse injuries, eating disorders, lack of sleep, and many other physical, emotional, and mental issues. These coaches live by the mantra "more is better" and reject evidence or science that does not support their narrative. They put athletes in untenable situations

where they cannot keep up with their studies yet they also pressure them to get grades that will maintain eligibility to participate. Coaches justify these practices as imparting the discipline and control that is needed to create a winning program. There is no sign that these abusive practices are abating. A primary reason for this abuse is that the United States, unlike many other developed countries, does not require any nationally accredited educational standards or certifications to become a coach. Some states require courses for high school coaches but the quality of those programs varies greatly. Typically, college coaches only need a college degree, even if that degree is unrelated to teaching, sports physiology, sports psychology, or other relevant fields of study. Therefore, without the appropriate education and a recognized professional organization like the National Education Association or the American Medical Association that could provide professional development and monitor abuse, these practices are perpetuated.

A second reason that this abuse prevails is because some athletic directors fail to: (1) establish standards of professional conduct, (2) monitor staff conduct, (3) act decisively when coaches or other support staff use abusive tactics, and (4) establish systems for reporting abuse and protecting whistleblowers. Athletic directors may believe that coaches need complete autonomy and that the athletic director should not interfere in team administration. Some coaches wield enough power with alumni or boards of trustees that supervisory oversight is difficult. Other athletic directors may want to protect the brand of the department, team, or coach and refuse to take action that may induce a critical review of the program. Chapters 6, 7, and 11 provide information that will help the athletic director establish standards of professional conduct and implement policies and procedures that work toward eliminating student-athlete abuse.

- **Communicating Access to Mental Health Services.** Most student-athletes have access to sports medicine facilities that are staffed with certified athletic trainers and, in some cases, team doctors. Coaches and athletes rely heavily on these professionals to tend to athletes' physical injuries and rehabilitation needs. In contrast, many athletic departments have never addressed the mental health or counseling needs of student-athletes. Coaches or administrators have rarely promoted the mental health services that are provided to all students on campus and only encouraged student-athletes to utilize these services when they were faced with serious mental health issues. The stigma attached to emotional or mental health concerns as signs of weakness made it a topic that was avoided or ignored.

  As noted, in 2019 all NCAA member institutions adopted legislation to make the provision of mental health services for athletes required. The 2020–21 NCAA Division I rules manual states:

> An institution shall make mental health services and resources available to its student-athletes. Such services and resources may be provided by the department of athletics and/or the institution's health services or counseling services department. Provision of services and resources should be consistent with the Interassociation Consensus Report: Mental Health Best Practices. In addition, an institution must distribute mental health educational materials and resources to student-athletes, including those transitioning out of their sport, coaches, athletics administrators, and other athletics personnel throughout the year. Such educational resources must include a guide to the mental health services and resources available at the institution and information regarding how to access them. (p. 254)

The Interassociation Consensus Report mentioned above was created by members of the NCAA Sport Science Institute and leading mental health organizations across the country to understand and support student-athlete mental wellness. All athletic directors, coaches, and staff that work directly with athletes should read this comprehensive report and access the NCAA Sports Science Institute website, which includes numerous resources and educational materials related to mental health and other student-athlete wellness and safety protocols. However, it is important to note that this NCAA resource falls very short in addressing the elephant in the room: the proclivity of coach abuse that can lead to student-athletes' physical, emotional, and mental health issues. The authors concur with a Drake Group position statement (2019) suggesting that the Sports Science Institute should develop and require every coach to take an online mental health training program and coaches should be expected to comply with an NCAA code of conduct that prohibits physical, psychological, and sexual abuse.

The consensus report does address the need for coaches to be supportive of student-athletes when they become aware of emotional or mental concerns. Providing mental health resources to student-athletes will not have much effect on behavior if coaches continue to demonstrate frustration with athletes who are struggling or if they fail to openly espouse trust in the mental health services provided. The important role coaches play in reducing the stigma associated with mental illness and appearing weak cannot be understated. This is particularly true for Black athletes. A study completed by Evans (2017) found evidence that Black student-athletes resisted addressing mental health issues because mental health services have been stigmatized in the African American community; time is limited to access services due to athletic, academic, and social obligations; and Black athletes already are dealing with the combined stigmas perpetuated by some students and faculty that marginalize them because they are Black and a student-athlete.

- **Protocols for Treatment**. Treatment should only be provided by clinical licensed mental health care professionals. The authors feel strongly that these professionals should not report directly to anyone whose primary employment is in the athletic department. There is too much at stake to risk a conflict of interest that results in a coach digging for information or putting pressure on an athlete's counselor because s/he is frustrated with the athlete's performance. We have seen this dynamic far too often between coaches and athletic trainers, so we can safely assume it would happen with mental health professionals. Counselors must be free to resist any interference by athletic department staff. It is also important to create a situation where confidentiality is less likely to be breached and student-athletes feel safe to share their experiences with someone outside the control of the athletic department. This does not mean that the licensed professional cannot be housed in a discreet location in the athletic department. In fact, Gill (2020) contends that some athletes will not go to campus-based counseling centers out of fear of being recognized or for other reasons. The NCAA also recommends that student-athletes should be provided with a list of licensed practitioners so they can self-refer to someone who is completely outside of the athletic department if they desire. We believe such a policy will increase the chances of student-athletes asking for help.

STUDENT-ATHLETE SUPPORT PROGRAMS

Associated Press. (2020, August 4). How the Larry Nassar scandal has affected MSU, others. *Oakland Press.* https://www.theoaklandpress.com/sports/how-the-larry-nassar-scandal-has-affected-msu-others/article_6c2930f2-d67f-11ea-89b1-77dd77fe8d53.html.

Britto, B. (2019, June 13). UH launches investigation into rhabdo cases as new details emerge related to life-threatening condition. *Houston Chronicle.* https://www.houstonchronicle.com/news/education/article/UH-launches-investigation-into-rhabdo-cases-as-13992419.php.

College athlete health and protection from physical and psychological harm. Position Statement. (2019, October 1). The Drake Group. https://www.thedrakegroup.org/2019/10/01/college-athlete-health-and-protection-from-physical-and-psychological-harm.

Cox, C.E., Ross-Stewart, L., & Foltz, B.D. (2017). Investigating the prevalence and risk factors of depression symptoms among NCAA Division I collegiate athletes. *Journal of Sports Science, 5*(1).

Dinich, H. (2018, August 11). Maryland OL Jordan McNair showed signs of extreme exhaustion. *ESPN.com.* https://www.espn.com/college-football/story/_/id/24343021/jordan-mcnair-maryland-terrapins-died-heatstroke-team-workout.

Evans, I. (2017, February). Mental health and the black student-athlete. Hogg Foundation for Mental Health. http://hogg.utexas.edu/black-student-athlete-mental-health/.

Faculty Athletic Representatives Association and National Collegiate Athletic Association. (2013). *Faculty athletics representatives handbook.* https://www.ncaapublications.com/productdownloads/FAR13.pdf.

Gill, E.L. (2020, November). *2020 Power five conference: Behavioral/mental health providers race & gender report card.* Athletes and Advocates for Social Justice in Sports. https://socialjusticeinsports.org/report-cards%2Ftestimonies.

Johnson, G. (2021, February 16). Pandemic continues to affect student-athletes' mental health. *NCAA.org.* https://www.ncaa.org/about/resources/media-center/news/pandemic-continues-impact-student-athlete-mental-health.

Koehler, M., & Giebel, N. (1997). *Athletic director's survival guide.* London: Prentice-Hall.

National Collegiate Athletic Association. (2009, June 30). *Academic support services evaluation guide.* http://fs.ncaa.org/Docs/AMA/Athletics%20Cert/N4A-NCAA%20Academic%20Support%20Services%20Eval%20Template%20JP-6-09.pdf.

National Collegiate Athletic Association. (2010). *Division I athletics certification self-study instrument.* www.ncaapublications.com/p-3986-division-i-athletics-certification-self-study-instrument.aspx.

National Collegiate Athletic Association. (2010). *Division III institutional self-study guide.* http://fs.ncaa.org/Docs/AMA/DIII%20Membership/ISSG.pdf.

National Collegiate Athletic Association. (2015–16). *Division II institutional self-study guide.* https://www.merrimack.edu/live/files/2614-self-studypdf.

National Collegiate Athletic Association. (2020, January). *Interassociation consensus document: Mental health best practices.* NCAA Sport Science Institute. https://ncaaorg.s3.amazonaws.com/ssi/mental/SSI_MentalHealthBestPractices.pdf.

National Collegiate Athletic Association. (2020–21). *NCAA Division I manual.* https://web3.ncaa.org/lsdbi/reports/getReports/90008.

National Collegiate Athletic Association. (2021). *NCAA life skills.* https://www.ncaa.org/about/resources/leadership-development/life-skills.

National Collegiate Athletic Association. Sports Science Institute. https://www.ncaa.org/sport-science-institute.

Northeastern University Center for the Study of Sport in Society. *Mentors in violence prevention.* https://www.northeastern.edu/sportinsociety/program/mentors-in-violence-prevention/.

Putukian, M. *Mind, body and sports: How being injured affects mental health.* NCAA Sport Science Institute. https://www.ncaa.org/sport-science-institute/mind-body-and-sport-how-being-injured-affects-mental-health.

Reardon, C.L., Hainline, B. et al. (2019). Mental health in elite athletes: International Olympic Committee consensus statement. *British Journal of Sports Medicine.* https://bjsm.bmj.com/content/bjsports/53/11/667.full.pdf.

University of Texas at Austin. (1992). *Intercollegiate athletics for women policy manual.* Unpublished. Austin, TX: Department of Women's Intercollegiate Athletics.

University of Texas at Austin. (2010). *Intercollegiate athletics policy manual.* Austin, TX. No longer available.

University of Texas at Austin. (2011). *Neighborhood Longhorns program.* https://diversity.utexas.edu/neighborhoodlonghorns/.

CHAPTER

9

Sports Medicine and Athletic Training Programs

Athletic training policy development requires the combined experience and expertise of an athletic trainer certified by the National Athletic Trainers' Association and licensed by the state, a team physician, and the athletic director. The athletic director alone simply does not have the sports medicine expertise to develop adequate policy oversight over this specialized area. Because actions related to preventing and treating injuries, handling and distributing drugs and other ingestible substances, and making decisions related to returning to play after injury are areas fraught with legal risk from the standpoint of negligence, athletic department policies in this area must be comprehensive and an annual formal risk assessment must be performed (see Risk Assessments 9.16 and 9.25 in HK*Propel*). National athletic governance organizations have strict rules regarding concussion protocols that must be utilized by all members and there are many states that have laws to enforce similar mandates. Another issue of importance is whether the athletic program has a sufficient number of certified athletic trainers to cover team practices and competitions. The National Athletic Trainers' Association has an assessment instrument designed for this purpose, which is available online (search www.nata.org for *Recommendations and Guidelines for Appropriate Medical Coverage of Intercollegiate Athletics*). The documents in this chapter provide sample model policies and forms to implement best practices in sports medicine and athletic training.

TYPES OF DOCUMENTS

Management tip—Factual background information, insights, problem-solving strategies, and suggestions for the athletic director

Planning tool—Steps to take or factors that should be considered in the development of strategic plans, action plans, professional development plans, or governance systems

Educational resource—Handouts that can be used to educate staff members, campus constituents, volunteers, or student-athletes

Policy—Sample policies and procedures that should be adopted by an athletic department after customization and review by appropriate expert institutional or school district officials

Form—Sample forms, letters, or job descriptions

Evaluation instrument—Administrative tools that help the athletic director, a supervisor, or an employee assess job performance and evaluate program content

Risk assessment—Checklists that help the athletic director, a supervisor, or an employee identify risks and prevent litigation

PROGRAM AND FACILITY OPERATIONS

Proper lines of authority and the separation of responsibilities between administrators, supervising medical doctors, and certified athletic training staff must be documented by written policy. Similarly, rules regarding the operation of the athletic training and strength-training facilities, especially those rules related to storage and issuance of drugs and maintenance of medical records, must be developed and implemented. The documents in this section are contained in HK*Propel* and are sample model policies for implementing best practices in these areas.

9.1 **Policy**—Sports Medicine and Athletic Training Program and Authority

A sample policy that defines administrative, medical, and athletic training staff authorities and responsibilities, program scope and operating policies related to use of allied health professionals, second or conflicting medical opinions, coverage of practice and competitive events, and responsibility for medical expenses.

9.2 **Policy**—Athletic Training Room Operations

A sample policy that specifies standards for cleanliness and supervision; requirements related to equipment, consumable supplies, and safety signage; and rules of conduct for student-athlete users.

Available in HK*Propel*.

PREPARTICIPATION REQUIREMENTS

Before allowing any student-athlete to participate in interscholastic or intercollegiate sport, the institution must protect both the student-athlete and itself by ensuring that (1) no preexisting health conditions would preclude such participation, (2) the student-athlete (and parents if under the age of 18) understands the risks associated with athletic participation, (3) both parties (the institution and the student-athlete and his or her parents) understand insurance obligations and payment responsibilities for treatment of athletic injuries if such treatment is required, (4) the student-athlete waives his or her privacy rights associated with health and eligibility information so that athletic personnel may share such information with physicians or athletic governance associations, and (5) the student-athlete understands other conditions that must be met to participate. The documents in this section are contained in HK*Propel* and are sample model policies, evaluation instruments, and forms used to obtain such information, inform the student-athlete of participation requirements, and obtain student-athlete and parental consents.

9.3 **Policy**—Medical Screening, Records, and Emergencies

A sample policy that defines medical screening requirements, medical records that must be maintained by the sports medicine or athletic training staff, alignment of medical records with privacy laws, maintenance of emergency action plans specific to each athletic facility, and availability of emergency medical equipment.

9.4 **Evaluation Instrument**—Student-Athlete and Family Medical History

A sample evaluation instrument that requires the student-athlete to provide essential information related to family contacts in the event of a medical emergency, student-athlete and family medical histories, and medications and supplements currently being used.

9.5 **Policy**—Student-Athlete Insurance Coverage and Treatment of Athletic Injuries

A sample policy specifying (1) insurance coverage, (2) coverage of expenses for athletic-related and non-athletic-related injuries, (3) participation in a required drug abuse prevention program, (4) forms and other conditions for clearance to participate, (5) insurance claims processing, and (6) student-athletes' obligation to report athletic injuries.

9.6 **Form**—Insurance Authorization, Medical and Health Treatment, Informed Consent, and Release of Liability

A sample form to be used to obtain (1) written student-athlete (and parent if under the age of 18) acknowledgment that he or she has been informed of insurance coverage and coverage of expenses for athletic-related and non-athletic-related injuries, (2) permission for the athletic department to obtain medical treatment in the event of injury, and (3) voluntary release of the athletic department from being liable for any loss or damage created by participation in the athletic program.

9.7 **Form**—Proof of Insurance

A sample form to be used to obtain written student-athlete (and parent if under the age of 18) acknowledgment that (1) participation in tryouts requires that the student-athlete be insured under his or her own insurance policy and (2) the athletic department is not responsible for medical expenses in the case of injury during tryouts. The form also requires information about the student-athlete's insurance coverage.

9.8 **Form**—Preparticipation Physician's Examination and Participation Clearance

A sample form to be used by the student-athlete's physician to record a physical examination and physician clearance for participation in athletics.

Available in HK*Propel*.

INJURY DOCUMENTATION

Documentation of medical and rehabilitation treatment provided by physicians and athletic training staff is essential for insurance purposes, initial care, and referral care and may be required in the case of litigation. The four forms in this section and contained in HK*Propel* address the most common situations requiring record keeping.

9.9 **Form**—Emergency Case Report

A sample form to be used for all cases in which a student-athlete is taken to a hospital or emergency medical services provider for treatment of an athletic-related injury.

9.10 **Form**—Nonemergency Injury Report and Treatment Record

A sample form to be used for all cases in which a student-athlete is injured to record causative factors or playing surface conditions, type of injury, and initial diagnosis and treatment. The form is also used to record all subsequent treatment until the student-athlete is cleared for return to participation.

9.11 **Form**—Medical Referral Form

A sample form to be used when a student-athlete is referred to a specialist by the team physician.

9.12 **Form**—Medical and Participation Status Report to Coach

A sample form to be used to communicate the type of injury suffered by a student-athlete and any restrictions on practice or competition participation to his or her coach for the purpose of ensuring no misunderstanding with regard to participation limitations.

Available in HK*Propel*.

DRUG-TESTING PROGRAM

Clear policies and procedures governing the conduct of any required drug-testing program are essential to prevent samples from being contaminated or tampered with and to protect student-athletes from being wrongly declared users of prohibited drugs and, as a result, ineligible. Because athletes may be taking prescription drugs that may produce positive drug tests, such permissible drug use must be documented for declaration before producing drug test samples. Even more important is requiring and defining the scope of a comprehensive drug education program. The following documents available in HK*Propel* provide model policies and forms and a risk assessment checklist to ensure the conduct of a model drug-testing program and the offering of a drug education program focused on prevention of drug use.

9.13 **Policy**—Drug Education, Testing, and Rehabilitation Program

A sample policy that describes the elements of a comprehensive drug education, testing, and rehabilitation program including (1) scope of a required education program, (2) procedural protections for student-athletes, (3) sanctions for positive results, (4) appeal opportunities, (5) a safe harbor program, and (6) responsibilities of staff members and student-athletes.

9.14 **Form**—Informed Consent for Institutional Drug Testing

A sample form that requires the student-athlete (or his or her parents if under the age of 18) to acknowledge (1) receipt and understanding of the drug-testing policy, (2) obligation to report taking prescription drugs or supplements, (3) sanctions for positive results, (4) appeal opportunities, (5) a safe harbor program, and (6) responsibilities of staff members and student-athletes.

9.15 **Form**—Request for Documentation of Prescribed Medications

A sample form letter to physicians of student-athletes advising them of drug prohibitions and requesting that they report all medications prescribed.

9.16 **Risk Assessment**—Checklist: Drug Testing and Education

A sample checklist that can be used to conduct an annual assessment of policies, procedures, and programs related to drug testing and education.

Available in HK*Propel*.

CRITICAL SPORTS MEDICINE ISSUES

Most athletic directors have minimal knowledge in the areas of sports medicine and athletic training, but these areas hold the highest risk for potential litigation and professional misconduct. Thus, ensuring that the head athletic trainer, team physician, and institutional director of student health services are competent and experienced in the oversight and operation of sports medicine and athletic training programs is essential. In addition, attention to detail in these policy areas is essential for risk prevention. Past litigation shows that the areas of highest risk include training-room operations (especially ensuring that personnel are not operating beyond the parameters in which they are state licensed and certified), treatment of pregnant or parenting student-athletes, treatment of eating disorders, practices related to treatment of athletes participating in extreme heat or cold, the treatment of concussions, and preventative measures that address the transmission of blood-borne pathogens and infectious diseases. The following documents available in HK*Propel* provide model policies and forms to help the athletic director address these issues, including a comprehensive risk assessment checklist governing the operation of the entire sports medicine and athletic training program. In addition, Planning Tool 9.26 discusses responding to concussion in a way that protects student-athletes from this serious injury.

9.17 **Policy**—Distribution of Drugs, Supplements, and Other Ingestible Substances

A sample comprehensive policy that specifies staff members permitted to administer prescription and over-the-counter drugs and supplements, documentation requirements for purchase and distribution of such substances, inventory audit and storage requirements, and procedures to be followed upon issuance of drugs to student-athletes.

9.18 **Policy**—Treatment of Pregnant or Parenting Student-Athletes

A sample policy in full alignment with Title IX, a federal law that prohibits discrimination based on pregnancy or parenting status, that also addresses retaliation, athletic staff counseling prohibitions, determination of participation restrictions, and coverage of medical expenses.

9.19 **Policy**—Treatment of Eating Disorders

A sample policy that assists staff in dealing with the potentially serious medical consequences of eating disorders and addresses issues such as weighing of student-athletes, comments related to weight and body type, dietary supplements, identification, screening, participation limitations, and confidentiality.

9.20 **Evaluation Instrument**—Screening Tool for Eating Disorders

A sample evaluation instrument that could be added to the medical history form required as a condition of athletic participation or used specifically for student-athletes suspected to be suffering from an eating disorder.

9.21 **Form**—Eating Disorder Contract 1

A sample agreement to be signed by a student-athlete with an identified eating disorder to specify the conditions upon which return to athletic participation will be granted, including adherence to a treatment plan with measurable outcomes.

9.22 **Form**—Eating Disorder Contract 2

Another sample agreement to be signed by a student-athlete with an identified eating disorder to specify the conditions upon which return to athletic participation will be granted, including adherence to a treatment plan with measurable outcomes.

9.23 **Policy**—Blood-Borne Pathogens and Infectious Diseases

A sample policy that specifies the permissibility of participation restrictions in cases of HBV, HIV, MRSA, and other infectious diseases; standards for immediate care; personnel training; and required equipment and supplies.

9.24 **Policy**—Dehydration and Heat- and Cold-Related Illnesses

A sample policy that specifies required coach education about dehydration and heat- and cold-related illnesses and specifies hydration policies and protocols and required preventive measures in the event of conditions of extreme heat or cold.

9.25 **Risk Assessment**—Checklist: Sports Medicine and Athletic Training

A sample risk assessment checklist that covers all major areas of concern related to sports medicine and athletic training.

Available in HK*Propel*.

9.26 PLANNING TOOL

Concussion: Protecting Student-Athletes and the Institution

During football season, it's not unusual to read about a teenage football player collapsing several weeks after suffering a concussion. Afterward the athletic director may learn that the player returned to competition claiming no symptoms, when in fact he continued to experience headaches but told no one because he was afraid of missing playing time. Or the athletic director may walk into the principal's office with an advertisement for a coach-administered computer-based program promoting neurocognitive testing of athletes. He or she may tell the administrator how important it is to have baseline data before returning a player to competition after a head injury. How should the manager of an educational institution deal with the potentially life-threatening consequences of head injury?

The athletic director can take several steps to make sure that coaches and staff members are prepared to respond to concussions:

1. At the beginning of every season, the school's team physician should present an in-service program for coaches and athletic event staff about recognizing the observable behaviors and student-reported symptoms that are signs of concussion. Most important, the team physician is responsible for sending a clear message: "When in doubt, sit the athlete out!" Such in-service programs recognize the fact that a certified athletic trainer or team physician is not in attendance at every practice and emphasizes the school policy directing staff to err on the side of student safety.
2. On the issue of whether a school should have protocols for baseline concussion testing or neurocognitive evaluation in response to suspected concussions, the answer is yes, and most athletic governance organizations have rules and many states have laws that detail such concussion protocol mandates. Such testing programs should be administered by a certified athletic trainer, a physician, or other qualified personnel and never by a coach. The coach will always be in a conflict-of-interest position and thus should not be involved in athlete treatment, testing, or the decision to return an athlete to play after a concussion, which may very well rely on comparisons to such baseline data. Although the coach plays an important role in recognizing behavioral symptoms or listening to an athlete describe his or her symptoms, assessments of physical condition and decisions to return from injury rightfully belong to trained certified medical or athletic training personnel.
3. The decision to return to competition should not depend solely on athlete-reported symptoms because the athlete also has a conflict of interest. Research demonstrates that athletes underreport their conditions because of a desire to return to competition (Conway et al., 2020). Although athlete reporting plays a role, neurocognitive testing must ultimately guide any such decision.
4. Following a concussion, the athlete should be referred to a physician for medical evaluation, on the same day as the injury if any of the following occurred: loss of consciousness; amnesia lasting longer than 15 minutes; vomiting; motor, sensory, or balance deficits; or symptoms that worsen. Immediate transport to the hospital emergency room should occur in the case of pulse or respiration irregularity or decreases; unequal, dilated, or unreactive pupils; lethargy; confusion; seizures; and other symptoms. All these operating rules should be covered in the physician education program at the beginning of the season and be given to coaches and staff in writing. Clear protocols for responses to concussion must be communicated to coaches and staff.
5. The school should have conservative policies in place to deal with athletes who suffer repeated concussions, from removal for the

rest of the game to disqualification from participation for the rest of the season to complete disqualification from participation in contact sports. These policies should be established in consultation with a physician and be based on continuation of symptoms, repeated concussions, and other physician-determined factors.

6. Policies should exist that require a physician or certified trainer to give oral and written instructions to parents regarding home care after an athlete suffers a concussion, especially with regard to ingesting alcohol, drugs, or other substances that affect cognitive functioning.

One of the best resources for the athletic director and school administrator is the *Consensus statement on concussion in sport—the 5th international conference on concussion in sport held in Berlin, October 2016* (McCrory, 2016) and the NCAA Sports Science Institute's collection of concussion resources (NCAA, 2021).

In summary, responsible handling of concussions means

- assessment of neurocognitive baseline data by qualified personnel,
- adequate preparation of on-the-field staff in symptom recognition and conditions for emergency treatment versus physician referral,
- oral and written communication with parents and caregivers regarding home care of the athlete following a concussion, and
- conservative decisions about returning to play only after qualified medical personnel are sure that the athlete is symptom-free.

See Policy 9.27 in HK*Propel* for a sample model policy regarding concussion.

9.27 Policy: Concussion

A sample policy specifying a concussion management plan consistent with national guidelines, requirements for staff training, and responsibilities of the team physician and athletic training staff.

Available in HK*Propel*.

SPORTS MEDICINE AND ATHLETIC TRAINING PROGRAMS

American Academy of Family Physicians, American Academy of Pediatrics, American College of Sports Medicine, American Medical Society for Sports Medicine, American Orthopaedic Society for Sports Medicine, and American Osteopathic Academy of Sports Medicine. (2010). *Pre-participation physical participation clearance form*. https://www.aafp.org/dam/AAFP/documents/patient_care/fitness/ppeclearanceform2010.pdf.

American College Health Association. (2021). *Immunization recommendations for college students*. https://www.acha.org/documents/resources/guidelines/ACHA_Immunization_Recommendations_Feb2021.pdf.

Austin Independent School District. (2018). *Athletic department pre-participation physical packet*. https://www.austinisd.org/sites/default/files/dept/athletics/docs/2018_Physical_Form_English.pdf.

Cappaert, T.A. et al. (2008). National athletic trainers' association position statement: Environmental cold injuries. *Journal of Athletic Training, 43*(6). https://www.ncbi.nlm.nih.gov/pmc/articles/PMC2582557/.

Casa, D.J. et al. (2012). Inter-association task force recommendations for preventing sudden death in collegiate conditioning sessions: Best practices recommendations. *Journal of Athletic Training, 47*(4). https://www.nata.org/sites/default/files/preventingsuddendeath-consensusstatement.pdf.

Casa, D.J. et al. (2015). National athletic trainers' association position statement: Exertional heat illnesses. *Journal of Athletic Training, 50*(9). https://pubmed.ncbi.nlm.nih.gov/26381473.

Centers for Disease Control and Prevention. (2021). *Recommended immunization schedule for adults (according to age requirements)*. https://www.cdc.gov/vaccines/schedules/hcp/imz/adult.html.

Centers for Disease Control and Prevention. (2021). *Recommended immunization schedule for children and adolescents*. https://www.cdc.gov/vaccines/schedules/.

Centers for Disease Control and Prevention. (2011). *Universal precautions for preventing transmission of bloodborne infections*. www.cdc.gov/niosh/topics/bbp/universal.html.

Conley, K.M. et al. (2014). National Athletic Trainers' Association position statement: Preparticipation physical examinations and disqualifying conditions. *Journal of Athletic Training, 49*(1). https://www.ncaa.org/sites/default/files/NATA-Position-Statement-PPEs-and-Disqualifying-Conditions.pdf.

Conway, F.N. et al. (2020). Concussion symptom underreporting among incoming National Collegiate Athletic Association Division I college athletes. *Clinical Journal of Sports Medicine: Official Journal of the Canadian Academy of Sport Medicine, 30*(3). https://europepmc.org/article/PMC/6488438.

DeFranco, M.J. et al. (2008). Environmental issues for team physicians. *American Journal of Sports Medicine, 36*(11). https://pubmed.ncbi.nlm.nih.gov/18978185.

Hainline, B. et al. (2016). Interassociation consensus statement on cardiovascular care of college student-athletes. *Journal of the American College of Cardiology, 67*(25). https://www.jacc.org/doi/full/10.1016/j.jacc.2016.03.527.

Hogshead-Makar, N., & Sorensen, E.A. (2008). *NCAA pregnant and parenting student-athletes: Resources and model policies*. Indianapolis, IN: NCAA. https://www.ncaa.org/sites/default/files/PregnancyToolkit.pdf.

Joy, E. (2013). *Heat illness: Gatorade Sports Science Institute sports medicine tip sheet*. www.amssm.org/MemberFiles/Heatillness.pdf.

McCrory, P. et al. (2016). Consensus statement on concussion in sport—the 5th international conference on concussion in sport held in Berlin, October 2016. *British Journal of Sports Medicine, 51*(11). https://bjsm.bmj.com/content/51/11/838.

McDermott, B.P. (2017). National Athletic Trainers' Association position statement: Fluid replacement for the physically active. *Journal of Athletic Training, 52*(9). https://pubmed.ncbi.nlm.nih.gov/28985128.

National Athletic Trainers Association. (2015). *Emergency action plans*. https://www.nata.org/sites/default/files/white-paper-emergency-action-plan.pdf.

National Athletic Trainers Association. (2018). *Recommendations and guidelines for appropriate medical coverage of intercollegiate athletics*. https://www.nata.org/professional-interests/job-settings/college-university/resources/AMCIA.

National Collegiate Athletic Association. (2014). *2014–2015 NCAA sports medicine handbook*. Indianapolis, IN: NCAA. http://www.ncaapublications.com/productdownloads/MD15.pdf.

National Collegiate Athletic Association. (2020). *Concussion safety: What coaches need to know*. https://ncaaorg.s3.amazonaws.com/ssi/concussion/SSI_ConcussionFactSheet_Coaches.pdf.

National Collegiate Athletic Association. (2020). *Concussion safety: What educators need to know.* https://ncaaorg.s3.amazonaws.com/ssi/concussion/SSI_ConcussionFactSheet_Educators.pdf.

National Collegiate Athletic Association. (2020). *Concussion safety: What student-athletes need to know.* https://ncaaorg.s3.amazonaws.com/ssi/concussion/SSI_ConcussionFactSheet_StudentAthletes.pdf.

National Collegiate Athletic Association. (2020). *NCAA drug testing program.* https://www.ncaa.org/sport-science-institute/ncaa-drug-testing-program.

National Collegiate Athletic Association. (2020). *NCAA sport science institute health and safety resource catalog.* Indianapolis, IN: NCAA. https://ncaaorg.s3.amazonaws.com/ssi/publications/SSI_HealthSafetyResourceCatalog.pdf.

National Collegiate Athletic Association. (2020–21). *NCAA division I drug testing consent.* https://ncaaorg.s3.amazonaws.com/compliance/d1/2020-21D1Comp_Form20-1b-DrugTestingConsentBannedList.pdf.

National Collegiate Athletic Association. (2021). *Cardiac 3-minute drill.* Indianapolis, IN: NCAA. https://www.ncaa.org/sites/default/files/Cardiac_3minDrill_Web10102011.pdf.

National Collegiate Athletic Association. (2021). *Concussion.* https://www.ncaa.org/content-categories/health-and-safety/topics/concussion.

National Collegiate Athletic Association. (2021). *A fact sheet for coaches: Sickle cell trait.* https://www.ncaa.org/sites/default/files/NCAASickleCellTraitforCoaches.pdf.

National Collegiate Athletic Association. (2021). *NCAA sickle cell trait (SCT) testing—What you need to know.* https://www.ncaa.org/sites/default/files/SCT%20testing%20brief%202014.pdf.

Ohio High School Athletic Association. (2020–21). *Physical examination form.* OHSAA: Columbus, OH. https://www.ohsaa.org/medicine/physicalexamform.

Shirley, E., Hudspeth, L.J., & Maynard, J.R. (2018). Managing sports-related concussions from time of injury through return to play. *Journal of the American Academy of Orthopaedic Surgeons, 26*(13). https://journals.lww.com/jaaos/Abstract/2018/07010/Managing_Sports_related_Concussions_From_Time_of.5.aspx.

United States Department of Labor Occupational Safety and Health Administration. (2021). *Bloodborne pathogens and needlestick prevention.* https://www.osha.gov/bloodborne-pathogens/standards.

University Interscholastic League. (1999). *Cold weather illness: Recognition, management, and prevention of cold exposure.* Austin, TX. www.uiltexas.org/health/info/cold-weather-illness.

University of Iowa. (2019). *2019–2020 Department of intercollegiate athletics student-athlete handbook.* https://static1.squarespace.com/static/5b68c118c3c16a24e756f022/t/5d5ac169c4eeb000015f7f7f/1566228843745/2019-2020+Student+Athlete+Handbook.pdf.

University of Texas at Austin. (1992). *Intercollegiate athletics for women policy manual.* Unpublished. Austin, TX: Department of Women's Intercollegiate Athletics.

University of Texas at Austin. (2020–21). *Intercollegiate athletics student-athlete resource guide.* Austin, TX. https://texassports.com/sports/2019/8/9/GEN_0729133817.aspx.

CHAPTER

10

Diversity, Inclusion, and Nondiscrimination

Diversity, *inclusion*, and *nondiscrimination* are terms often used interchangeably. *Diversity* refers to differences that may be ethnic, racial, sex, age, or socioeconomic in nature but always include the notion that a variety of differences within groups, societies, or institutions is a good thing that leads to more points of view, opinions, and solutions. *Inclusion* adds the notion of acceptance of additions to the group—the acceptance of diversity. *Nondiscrimination* adds the concept of fairness and the absence of prejudice. All three are important. To have diversity without acceptance and fairness is not a desirable outcome. To have diversity and fairness without accepting and welcoming those who may be different from us is similarly dysfunctional. Thus, the goal of the athletic director should be to assemble a staff and group of student-athletes that not only reflects the incredible variety of people in our society but also ensures that the organizational culture values this diversity, welcomes all into the organizational family, and treats everyone with respect and fairness.

With regard to fairness and nondiscriminatory treatment of current employees, chapter 6 addresses individual employee hiring, evaluation, improvement, and corrective action systems that advance this commitment (see Policies 6.5 and 6.10 in HK*Propel*). The documents in this chapter, in both the book and HK*Propel*, recognize that most athletic departments fall short in the areas of diversity and nondiscrimination. Women, persons of color and different ethnicities, and people with disabilities are underrepresented, and the vestiges of historical discrimination remain. Thus, policies, strategies, and initiatives to remedy such underrepresentation must be put in place.

TYPES OF DOCUMENTS

Management tip—Factual background information, insights, problem-solving strategies, and suggestions for the athletic director

Planning tool—Steps to take or factors that should be considered in the development of strategic plans, action plans, professional development plans, or governance systems

Educational resource—Handouts that can be used to educate staff members, campus constituents, volunteers, or student-athletes

Policy—Sample policies and procedures that should be adopted by an athletic department after customization and review by appropriate expert institutional or school district officials

Form—Sample forms, letters, or job descriptions

Evaluation instrument—Administrative tools that help the athletic director, a supervisor, or an employee assess job performance and evaluate program content

Risk assessment—Checklists that help the athletic director, a supervisor, or an employee identify risks and prevent litigation

10.1 PLANNING TOOL

Elements of a Model Diversity and Inclusion Program

Athletic programs that demonstrate a commitment to social justice, social responsibility, respect for individual differences, and nondiscrimination have specific policies and programs in place that enhance the racial, ethnic, age, disability, and gender diversity of their student-athletes, staffs, and athletic policy boards. A predicate to developing and implementing these programs is assembling fact-based data that demonstrate to staff and student-athletes that most athletic departments fall short in the areas of diversity and nondiscrimination and that the institution's athletic program is not dissimilar. Moving forward toward successful correction of historical discrimination begins with the athletic director's leadership. He or she needs to create an atmosphere of social justice and responsibility rather than confer blame or suggest intentional discrimination. This process begins with educating hiring supervisors and coaches who are recruiting prospective student-athletes about (1) evidence of continued historical discrimination nationally and at the institution, making the case for affirmative action; (2) reasons why diversity and inclusion will improve performance of staff, student-athletes, and teams; and (3) why the majority need not fear that correcting historical discrimination is a zero-sum game, that they will lose if underrepresented groups gain. An initial responsibility of the athletic department leader is to address this issue by direct communication with staff and student-athletes as an expression of program and personal values. If staff and student-athletes do not think that diversity, inclusion, and nondiscrimination are important to the boss, those concerns will not be a priority for stakeholders.

Communicating Evidence of Continued Historical Discrimination

The athletic director should not assume that staff and student-athletes are educated about issues related to discrimination based on race, gender, disability, sexual orientation, or other factors. U.S. Census estimated 2019 population data indicate that 60.1 percent of the U.S. population is white and the remaining nonwhite and mixed categories represent 39.9 percent (U.S. Census Bureau, 2019). However, we must recognize that prior to the mid-1970s, higher education institutions met the needs of an 85 percent white/15 percent nonwhite student population, not reaching 55 percent white/45 percent nonwhite until 2018 (U.S. Dept. of Education, NCES). Diversity has lagged among the college athlete population (63 percent white), athletic department employees (85 percent white [NCAA]), and college faculties (75 percent white [U.S. DOE/NCES]). Facts should be used to make the case. National sport participation and employment diversity data is easily presented, such as that appearing in tables 10.1.1, 10.1.2, 10.1.3, 10.1.4, and 10.1.5.

Table 10.1.1 Gender and Persons of Color in NCAA College Sport Leadership, 2020

Position	Male	Female	White	Persons of color
Athletic director*	76.1%	23.9%	85%	15%
Associate director of athletics	64.1%	35.9%	85%	15%
Assistant director of athletics	65.1%	34.9%	84%	16%
Business manager	38.4%	61.6%	83%	17%
Fund-raising/development mgr.	64%	36%	84%	16%
Sports information director	85.3%	14.7%	91%	9%
Head athletic trainer	66.1%	33.9%	90%	10%
Head coach	75.1%	24.9%	84%	16%
Assistant coach	71.7%	38.3%	75%	25%
Strength coach	85.6%	14.4%	79%	21%

Data from NCAA Demographics Database (2021).

Table 10.1.2 Gender and Persons of Color in Professional Sports Leagues—NBA, WNBA, 2020

Professional Sports League	Male	Female	White	Persons of color
NBA League Office	59.7%	40.3%	60.6%	39.4%
NBA–Team CEO	89.1%	10.9%	89.1%	10.9%
NBA–Team Management	67.0%	33.0%	69.5%	30.5%
NBA–General Manager	100.0%	0.0%	72.0%	28.0%
NBA–Head Coach	100.0%	0.0%	70.0%	30.0%
WNBA–League Office	39.1%	60.9%	50.0%	50.0%
WNBA–Team CEO	41.7%	58.3%	75.0%	25.0%
WNBA–Manager/Sr. Director	53.3%	46.7%	65.1%	34.9%
WNBA–General Manager	72.7%	27.3%	72.7%	27.3%
WNBA–Head Coach	58.3%	41.7%	75.0%	25.0%

Data from Lapchick et al., *TIDES Race and Gender Report Card* (2020).

Table 10.1.3 Gender and Persons of Color in Other Professional Sports Leagues—MLB, MLS, NFL, 2020

Professional Sports League	Male	Female	White	Persons of color
MLB Central Office	59.9%	40.1%	61.8%	37.5%*
MLB–Team CEO	100.0%	0.0%	96.7%	3.3%
MLB–Team Sr. Management	71.2%	28.8%	79.8%	19.4%*
MLB–Team General Manager	100.0%	0.0%	86.7%	13.3%
MLB–Head Coach	100.0%	0.0%	80.0%	20.0%
MLS–League Office	60.7%	39.3%	58.4%	41.6%
MLS–Team CEO	100.0%	0.0%	82.6%	17.4%
MLS–Team Sr. Management	76.4%	23.6%	82.9%	17.1%
MLS–Team General Manager	100.0%	0.0%	78.6%	21.4%
MLS–Head Coach	100.0%	0.0%	59.3%	40.7%
NFL–League Office	61.8%	38.2%	64.8%	30.5%*
NFL–Team CEO	93.9%	6.1%	84.8%	12.1%*
NFL–Team Sr. Management	76.1%	23.9%	81.2%	18.0%*
NFL–Team General Manager	100.0%	0.0%	93.6%	6.5%
NFL–Head Coach	100.0%	0.0%	87.5%	12.5%

*remaining percentage is voluntary nondisclosure

Data from Lapchick et al., *TIDES Race and Gender Report Card* (2020).

Table 10.1.4 Persons of Color in Sports Media Positions, 2010–17

	PERSONS OF COLOR		
Position	2010	2014	2017
Sports editor	3%	8.5%	15%
Assistant sports editor	15%	9.8%	13.6%
Columnist	14%	16.5%	19.7%
Reporter	14%	15%	17.9%
Copy editor and designer	10%	16.7%	12.3%

Data from Lapchick et al. (2011, 2018).

The situation is no different among student-athletes except historical discrimination favoring white athletes is more easily masked. For instance, examine table 10.1.5, which shows national percentages of white and nonwhite male and female athletes when athletes participating in all NCAA sports are aggregated. Nonwhite athletes are clearly underrepresented.

When the data are examined by sport, the underrepresentation is more startling. Sports in which athletes of color are overrepresented are among those with the highest participation numbers—basketball (61 percent) and football (55 percent) for men, and basketball (50 percent) for women. These figures significantly skew the

Table 10.1.5 2020 NCAA Student-Athlete Sport Participation by Race or Ethnicity and Gender

Gender	White	Nonwhite
% male	33.2%	22.6%
% female	30.0%	14.1%
% total	63.3%	36.7%

Data from National Collegiate Athletics Association (2021).

aggregated total athlete population numbers, giving the impression of higher nonwhite participation than is actually the case. A nonwhite participation gap (percent of nonwhites in the sport is less that the percent of nonwhites general population of 39.1 percent) occurs in 11 of the 19 sports for men and 19 of the 21 sports for women. Sharing data such as those depicted and, as important, sharing actual data for the specific institution is both easy to do and necessary to make a compelling case. See Evaluation Instrument 10.2 in HK*Propel* for suggestions about how to collect and display data on institutional diversity.

10.2 Evaluation Instrument–
Diversity Evaluation Based on Key Performance Indicators

A model evaluation instrument that demonstrates how to collect and display diversity data to track athletic department progress against diversity goals and objectives.

Available in HK*Propel*.

Why Diversity Will Improve the Athletic Department

The more diverse an organization's workforce is, the more varied the points of view and the greater the range of experience that will be brought to solving organizational challenges. When all employees see themselves represented among senior staff members, their motivation to perform and achieve advancement within the organization will be greater, the possibility of which has been demonstrated. When all employees feel included, valued, and respected, their loyalty and commitment to organizational success is strengthened. Employee diversity compels all employees to improve their communication skills so that they can successfully interact with people who are not like them. When all student-athletes see people like themselves serving important roles at every level of the organization, they see their own future possibilities and aspire to higher career goals. The athletic director must make statements like these to supervisors responsible for hiring to reinforce the importance of the athletic department's diversity goals.

Obtaining assistance in the delivery of staff and student-athlete diversity education programs from specialist third parties is a good idea and a wise use of resources. Scheduling at least one workshop for student-athletes and new staff each year is a good strategy. The athletic director should always be the first to speak during such programs and should strongly espouse the diversity value orientation of the department.

Such workshops should always address the myths and stereotypes about underrepresented groups that are commonly advanced by families and homogeneous groups as reasons for lack of interest or qualifications.

Addressing Fears of Majority Groups

Athletic departments are predominantly white and male (in the NCAA, 75 percent among head coaches; 65 percent among assistant coaches; and 64 to 76 percent among athletic directors, associate athletic directors, and assistant athletic directors [NCAA, 2021]). The higher the status and pay of the position, the more likely it is that a white male will be the occupant. Because this group dominates with regard to hiring authority, it is important to address the fears of these stakeholders, who may believe that equal opportunity is a zero-sum game—that is, if women, persons of color, or other members of underrepresented groups receive preference, then those in the majority will lose. This fear must be addressed head-on. The athletic director must point out that educational systems and athletic programs are in a perpetual state of growth. As the U.S. population grows, schools are added, sports are added, and new jobs and participation opportunities are the reality. Simple evidence of this natural growth is found by looking at growth in high school and college athletic participation over the last 48 years, as depicted in table 10.1.6.

Alternatively, look at the growth in the number of college athletics professional jobs (18 job titles tracked by the NCAA, such as assistant athletic directors, athletic trainers, compliance directors, facilities directors, etc.) from 26,565 in 2015 to 30,670 in 2020, a 16 percent increase that does not include normal attrition from retirements and career changes (NCAA Demographics Database, 2020). A similar examination of NCAA coaching jobs reveals that from 2015 to 2020, the number of head coaches, assistant coaches, and strength coaches increased from 65,920 to 69,142 (5 percent) (NCAA Demographics Database, 2020). Whether it is coaching positions or other jobs within athletics or participation opportunities for student-athletes, the number of employment and participation opportunities is constantly growing, and those within the existing job pool are retiring or leaving for various reasons. The notion of not working to distribute those opportunities more fairly among underrepresented groups is selfish and self-centered. We can do better, but only if athletic directors insist that we do better by reinforcing an opportunity environment of sufficiency for everyone rather than scarcity.

No one is suggesting that current job occupants or student-athletes who are members of majority groups be replaced with members of underrepresented groups. Neither is anyone suggesting that applicants for new positions or new student-athletes from underrepresented groups be hired or offered scholarships or positions on a team if they are less skilled than applicants from majority groups. What should be stated as a department policy is that the department is committed to making a diligent and persistent effort to identify qualified job applicants and talented student-athletes who are members of underrepresented groups because fairness and nondiscrimination is about making sure that the finalist pool and the composition of staff and student-athlete populations reflects the diversity of our society. A fair, nondiscriminatory environment is the goal. Research shows that we are more likely to discriminate because we hire and recruit people who look like us and with whom we feel most comfortable, exercising an unintentional bias, but a bias nonetheless. If we don't commit to combating this bias by embracing, valuing, and aggressively seeking diversity, we will unintentionally continue to do what athletic departments have done in the past, which is to be homogeneously white and male. Table 10.1.1 provides a clear picture of this homogeneity.

Specifically, every athletic department should have the following diversity program elements in place:

- A written diversity, inclusion, and nondiscrimination policy (see Policy 10.4 in HK*Propel*)
- Measurable objectives that are part of the athletic department's strategic plan or a separate diversity plan (see Planning Tool 10.3 in this book for a sample diversity strategic plan)

Table 10.1.6 Growth in High School and College Athletic Participation: 1972–2020

	HIGH SCHOOL		NCAA COLLEGE	
Years	Male	Female	Male	Female
1972–73	3,666,917	294,015	170,384	29,977
2018–19/HS 2020/NCAA	4,534,458	3,402,733	281,699	222,920
% growth	+ 24%	+ 1057%	+ 65%	+ 643%

Data from National Federation of High Schools (2019); Data from National Collegiate Athletics Association (2021).

- Ongoing, systematic, and evidence-based evaluation practices based on key performance indicators that target diversity goals (see Evaluation Instrument 10.2 in HK*Propel*) using aggressive marketplace search and recruiting mechanisms targeting underrepresented populations (see Planning Tool 10.5 in the book)
- Ongoing educational programming about student-athlete and staff diversity and inclusion (see Planning Tool 10.6 in the book)
- Specific retention and inclusion strategies and tracking of key performance indicators (see Management Tip 10.7 in the book)
- Expansive role and involvement of the athletic policy board and minority faculty in hiring, recruiting, and retention (see Management Tip 10.8 in the book)
- Staff incentives and disincentives to demonstrate diversity improvement (see Planning Tool 10.9 in the book)
- Athletic department involvement in general university diversity programs (see Planning Tool 10.6 in the book)
- Use of alumni assets to assist in educational programs and recruiting (see Planning Tool 10.6 in the book)
- Clear understanding of issues and required practices related to fair treatment of people with disabilities (see Management Tip 10.10 in the book)
- An evaluation tool to be completed annually to determine compliance with Title IX gender equity requirements (see Evaluation Instrument 10.11 in HK*Propel*)
- Clear definitional statements of sexual harassment and abuse prohibitions as required under Title IX (see Management Tip 10.12 in the book)
- A policy to ensure a safe and welcoming environment for LGBT student-athletes and staff members (see Policy 10.13 in HK*Propel*)

10.4 **Policy**—Diversity, Inclusion, and Nondiscrimination

A model policy that defines the scope of the athletic department's diversity commitment, persons responsible for leadership and oversight, a requirement for a diversity plan, and complaint procedures to be used to address harassment or discrimination, including redress and appeals.

10.11 **Evaluation Instrument**—Title IX Compliance (Gender Equity)

A model evaluation instrument for the collection of data necessary to determine Title IX compliance, including instructions about how to analyze the information. Includes a Title IX Assessment Workbook with 27 Excel spreadsheets for data collection and analysis of Title IX compliance.

10.13 **Policy**—Inclusivity and Nondiscrimination for LGBTQ Individuals

A model policy that sets standards for a safe, welcoming, and equal-opportunity environment for LGBTQ students, staff, and spectators, including a prohibition against negative recruiting, the eligibility of transgender student-athletes, and dealing with harassment or threats to the safety of LGBTQ individuals.

Available in HK*Propel*.

10.3 PLANNING TOOL

Strategic Planning for Diversity: Goals and Objectives

Setting goals and measurable objectives is a key first step in achieving diversity outcomes. In general, a goal should be a broad, narrative, and visionary expression of the athletic program's commitment to diversity, whereas objectives are specific and measurable and may include a timeframe for achievement. Typically, a diversity goal is one of many goals established by the athletic department and a part of the athletic program's strategic plan. Alternatively, or in addition, the athletic department may have a separate diversity plan with its own goals and objectives.

Sample Strategic Plan

Following is an example of a diversity goal and measurable objectives that would be appropriate for a strategic plan.

Goal

The composition of the athletic department staff and student-athletes and its organizational climate shall reflect the highest commitment to diversity and respect for individual differences.

Measurable Objectives

Annually, the athletic department shall strive to achieve the following objectives:

1. The racial, ethnic, and gender composition within all categories of staff and all student-athlete teams shall annually improve until they generally achieve national census proportions.
2. The recruitment of staff and student-athletes shall ensure an adequate pool of candidates from underrepresented groups and conform to institutional policy, governance association rules and regulations, and state and federal laws.
3. Selection or retention of staff and student-athletes shall be based on skill and competency criteria and shall not be based on race, religion, color, national origin, gender, sexual orientation, age, disability, or status as a military veteran except as permitted by the offering of sex-separate sport programs or as required by law.
4. The organizational climate of the athletic program shall be perceived by staff and student-athletes as welcoming to all people and reflective of fair treatment and decision making.
5. Athletic department staff and student-athletes shall be knowledgeable of diversity issues, and individuals shall be acknowledged for their diversity efforts and initiatives.
6. The athletic department shall support special programs and efforts that demonstrate success in increasing employment and participation opportunities for underrepresented groups.
7. The athletic department shall annually conduct educational programs for first-year student-athletes and new athletic department employees that address the benefits of diversity.

Appropriate Comparators

Careful consideration must be paid to the question of appropriate comparators for goal setting. For institutions of higher education that recruit staff and student-athletes nationally, a national census population comparator is recommended. For institutions dedicated to serving local needs (i.e., community colleges or high schools), regional or local population demographics would be more appropriate. Administrators should not use the larger institution's current student or faculty demographics as a comparator because institutions of higher education commonly have percentages of racial and ethnic minorities and female faculty and staff that are lower than the national average. Thus, setting athletic department goals based on general institutional percentages may be an inherently flawed strategy.

Overall Versus Distributed Diversity

Typically, racial and ethnic minorities are significantly overrepresented in sports like football, basketball, and track and field and underrepresented in almost all other sports. Similarly, racial and ethnic minorities and females have higher representations in the lower-paid or lower-status positions than in the higher-paid and more senior professional levels (Lapchick et al., 2020; NCAA, 2020, *Demographics Database*). Simply computing overall representation, therefore, hides these serious inequities within sport and senior job categories. Thus, it is highly recommended that the stated commitment to diversity be specified as distributed within all teams and employment categories rather than overall.

Student Population as the Athletic Program Gender Comparator

Title IX establishes the general student-body proportions of males and females at each institution as the required comparator for the athletic program at each institution under prong 1 of its participation requirements. Even if the institution uses prong 2 (consistent effort to increase opportunities for the underrepresented sex) or prong 3 (complete fulfillment of interest and ability at or below the general student-body proportion) defense for not meeting the proportionality standard, the institution is still obligated to make efforts to remedy historical discrimination and continue to strive for proportionality. Note that this proportionality based on the institutional general student-body comparator is appropriate because Title IX requires this measure for athletics.

10.5 PLANNING TOOL

Aggressive Marketplace Search and Recruiting Practices

If the number of minority applicants in the overall applicant pool or those who make it to the finalist interview stage is small for open staff positions, as typically is the case, the athletic department should install more aggressive search and recruiting practices. Following are several suggestions in this regard:

- Develop multiple prospect lists. The staff member or committee responsible for the search should be asked to develop three prospect lists (overall, nonwhite, and female) by making telephone calls to trusted professionals in the area of the position opening. For instance, if the department needs a lacrosse coach, the hiring supervisor should call the top lacrosse coaches in the country and get recommendations. Every conversation should specifically ask about coaches of color and female coaches.
- Even before a position becomes open, the athletic director should be assembling lists of minority group talent in various sport program positions and should seek to establish relationships with those people. At every conference, NCAA meeting, or professional association meeting, the athletic director should query colleagues about talented, up-and-coming women and minority men and women.
- Requiring every head coach and every senior staff member to list the top three women, nonwhite men, nonwhite women, and overall best replacements should they themselves decide to retire or leave the institution—a good succession-planning practice—is an excellent way to develop these prospect lists over time.
- Because fewer prospects in the marketplace are typically from underrepresented minority groups, the hiring supervisor should assume that the best candidates will not come from the applicant pool; rather, those candidates will need to be persuaded to apply for the position and must be hired away from their current positions. Identification of these prospects is not enough. The athletic director and hiring supervisor must make a commitment to making personal phone calls and visits to these minority group prospects to persuade them to enter the applicant pool.
- The institution should be prepared to offer higher salaries to minority group prospects as a matter of supply and demand. Getting someone to leave his or her current position will take a competitive salary offer. If increasing minority group representation is an important commitment, the saying "You have to be willing to put your money where your mouth is" will likely be applicable.

With regard to recruiting minority student-athletes, a more aggressive approach is similarly necessary. Remember that male and female nonwhites are overrepresented in football, track and field, and basketball. Therefore, the focus must be on sports in which minorities are traditionally underrepresented. Following are three suggestions that would have a long-term positive effect on recruiting minority student-athletes:

- Typically, hotbeds are located in various places in the country where nonwhite coaches have developed outstanding developmental programs for nonwhite youth in their respective communities (for example, Peter Westbrook's fencing program in New York City) (Peter Westbrook Foundation, 2012). Work to identify these programs by developing relationships with staff members of national sport governing bodies who are knowledgeable about their national junior and senior teams and Olympic development programs. Strong relationships with these hotbed coaches should be established in the same manner that strong relationships are built with coaches of high school programs that have produced successful recruits in other sports. The athletic director should work with coaches to monitor the identification of these programs and the size of the nonwhite recruiting pool for each sport early in the recruiting season.

- Consider changing the institution's approach to offering local clinics to youth from lower socioeconomic groups. Target sports in which minorities are underrepresented and offer to conduct free coach-training programs for community agencies conducting those sports (giving a fishing rod instead of a fish) who promise to recruit coach prospects, including nonwhite prospects. Maintain relationships with those programs over time by having teams return to run clinics and exhibitions in conjunction with the coach-training program.
- Establish a diversity commitment policy for summer camp programs. For every sport camp conducted at the institution, require coaches to offer at least a minimum number of free scholarships to applicants from lower socioeconomic levels (nonwhites are overrepresented in lower socioeconomic groups), assuming that such summer camps are conducted for age groups below the NCAA definition of recruits and are in full compliance with NCAA or state high school federation rules.

10.6 PLANNING TOOL

Staff and Student-Athlete Diversity Education

Long-Term Planned Approach

Student-athlete turnover every four to five years requires a short-term and long-term approach to educational programming. Over the short term, every new class of student-athletes and every new employee should have a meeting with the athletic director during which he or she addresses the issue of diversity, program values, and expectations regarding respect for differences. The topic should also be a part of every orientation program. Strategic plans and diversity plans should be distributed in writing, as should the institution's policy statements on harassment, prohibited personal relationships between coaches or staff and student-athletes, and so on.

Presenters Must Connect

The success of in-service diversity programs increases in relation to the perceived utility of the information presented to the user, respect for the expertise of the presenter, and the strength of the emotional connection between the presenter and the audience. Thus, great care should be taken in the selection of presenters and the composition of the audience for every educational program. Professional presenters who specialize in the area of diversity workshops should be considered.

Meeting the Practical Needs of Coaches

Coaches are often the most literal among athletic department employees with regard to needing to see the practical application of theory. Traditional diversity workshops are often led by presenters who do not connect with coaches about the practical realities of coaching. Thus, the athletic director should design in-service diversity training sessions that are specifically targeted to meeting the needs of coaches. These sessions should also be attended by personnel from student life, athletic training, strength training, and academic support programs. Consider staggering the following three programs so that they are offered once every three years:

- Identify a minority coach recognized for his or her minority recruiting success to participate in a presentation and discussion with head and assistant coaches about successful practices and priority considerations when recruiting minority student-athletes. This program should include practices to increase minority retention.
- A respected male coach of a men's team who has hired a female assistant and can comment on the value and utility of such gender diversity should present on this topic.
- A respected minority student-athlete graduate or panel of such graduates should be asked to present a session on the minority athlete experience and provide recommendations for improving that experience.

Management Reports as Part of an Educational Program

An often-unrecognized form of educational programming is practicing transparency through the wide dissemination of management reports. For instance, sharing key indicator reports with all staff creates the impression of a caring and open organization that isn't afraid to examine its practices or share information.

Mentoring Programs

An ongoing mentoring program for student-athletes who wish to pursue careers in sport and other industries is an important educational initiative that is critical for minority student-athletes. This type of program is the perfect place to involve and connect with successful institutional alumni. Consider adding to the duties of head coaches and other senior athletic personnel the obligation to mentor minority assistant coaches, interns, graduate assistants, and junior professional staff in the athletic department. Each mentor would be required to have an annual meeting with his or her junior staff member to produce a written professional development plan that would include

- identification of next-step opportunities in the athletic department if feasible;
- identification of career goals;
- further education (degree, certificate, conference, workshop, or other professional work) to be accomplished over the short term and long term;
- designation of three people per year outside the athletic department to whom the mentor would provide introductions and arrange a formal information interview or other relationship-building experience;
- recommended membership in professional organizations; and
- other recommendations related to building intrapersonal and other competencies.

Consider subsidization of membership dues in professional organizations or travel to professional meetings for (minority) junior staff members.

Consider establishing a "Meet Top Professionals" program. On a monthly or quarterly basis, organize the campus visit of a respected female or nonwhite coach or professional to engage in an informal or formal presentation or activity, including a separate activity that targets minority junior staff members. The latter should be a mentor–mentee invitation-only activity that is in addition to a general open session for all staff or student-athletes.

The athletic director should have a conversation with mentors about the difference between mentoring and sponsorship. The former consists of advice, identification and implementation of educational experiences, and other forms of professional development. Sponsorship requires the mentor to take the extra step of using his or her connections and reputation to get a new position, salary increase, or promotion for the person being mentored. Sponsorship requires an investment of the mentor's capital in the young professional. Female and minority staff are often overmentored but undersponsored.

Use of Alumni

Most athletic programs have internships, graduate assistantships, student coach positions, and other programming that are ideal for the support of diversity objectives. Converting those programs to important diversity initiatives that leverage alumni relationships usually involves the following:

- Setting goals for overrepresentation of minority groups in these programs
- Assigning current employee or alumni mentors to each student in the program
- Including information interviews with alumni as part of the program
- Using alumni connections for career placement following the athletic department experience
- Bringing in alumni as speakers for educational programming related to career advancement
- Requiring that each student in the program have written career and professional development plans

Within 5 to 10 years of the establishment of such minority development programs, the athletic department will be in a position to point with pride to the number of former interns, graduate assistants, and others who have secured good jobs in the sport industry. Such success would be a significant recruiting asset. More important is that the athletic department acknowledges and remedies the fact that the time commitment and financial aid limitations of student-athletes prevent them from developing an employment resume during their collegiate careers. In the case of women and nonwhite student-athletes, they often do not have the community connections and are faced with postgraduate job barriers that are more significant than those of their male and white counterparts. Further, time constraints often limit their access to general university career development services.

Leadership of University Diversity Efforts

Most athletic departments have the potential to position the athletic program as a leading proponent and exemplar of racial and ethnic diversity in their wider university communities, and they should do so. Often, the proportion of racial and ethnic representation in the athletic program is greater than that across the university itself. Efforts to promote greater visibility of student-athletes on campus to model diversity and deliver diversity education messages to the wider university community should be considered. Consideration might also be given to establishing programs in which student-athlete leaders are trained to discuss diversity issues with students on campus. Even if the athletic program does not fully conform to national demographic proportions of staff and student-athletes by race and sex, being an example by openly discussing efforts to achieve diversity demonstrates leadership to the larger university family.

10.7 MANAGEMENT TIP

Retention Strategies and Inclusion Issues

Athletic departments often focus on bringing in minorities to fill apprentice, intern, or entry-level positions, forgetting the importance of having same-sex or same-race mentors available. Every minority should see a role model in positions above him or her, a person who has achieved advancement in every level of the organization. Thus, making sure that minority representation is present in every job category (entry level to senior staff) is critical. Similarly, athletic administrators should examine years of service or significant salary gaps in position categories for whites and nonwhites, and males and females, as important retention indicators. Often, an employee earns a promotion to a higher level but does not receive the same message of respect and competence when it comes to an accompanying salary increase.

The existence of financial support for professional development activities is important to retention. Even if financial support of professional development activities is limited, making sure that minority group employees receive such benefits is essential. An annual information interview with an accomplished role model is a simple and cost-effective objective for every employee and sends the message that the athletic department cares about employees' professional advancement. Genuine caring will contribute to retention of employees.

Exit interviews, preferably by same-sex, same-race, or same-ethnicity faculty or administrators outside the athletic department, should be conducted. These interviews can provide valuable information about retention and organizational climate objectives.

Regular examination of all of the key performance indicators (KPIs) listed in the athletic department diversity plan (see Evaluation Instrument 10.2 in HK*Propel*), being sure to use the filters of sex, race, and ethnicity, will provide the administrator with valuable information about retention-related factors for both minority-group staff and minority student-athletes.

With regard to student-athlete retention, particular attention should be paid to success in the classroom: graduation rates, GPAs, and APRs, especially of at-risk students (students who have low GPAs or have been specially admitted). Typically, minority students are overrepresented in these at-risk categories. Providing academic tutors and counseling services to reduce such academic stress is key to retention.

Another key area of minority student-athlete retention is adequate scholarship support because of the higher percentage of nonwhites in lower socioeconomic groups. For instance, it is important to examine equivalency sports when it comes to scholarship distribution. Making a concerted effort to attract minorities may require greater scholarship commitments to athletes in lower socioeconomic levels.

Last, a clearly defined approach should be used to identify the risk factors related to dropping out before graduation, especially among high-risk groups such as specially admitted students (admissions granted even though the student does not meet admissions standards applicable to prospective students generally). For instance, a prominent NCAA Division I institution found a 100 percent failure rate among student-athletes who had all of the following risk factors: (1) a history of chronic injury, (2) junior college attendance in that state, and (3) a high school GPA below 2.25. Often these risk factors can be identified as high school or preenrollment red flags that should influence recruiting decisions. At the very least, these risk factors identify student-athletes who need to be carefully monitored and specially supported.

10.8 MANAGEMENT TIP

Role of the Athletic Policy Board in Advancing Diversity

In higher education, an athletic policy board, usually named the athletic advisory council and consisting of faculty, administrators, and alumni from outside the athletic department, is often a governance association requirement. Even if it isn't, having an objective, faculty-majority oversight board in place to review key indicators of diversity performance each year and to be invested in the achievement of diversity objectives is beneficial. Consideration should be given to establishing a goal for this group to be 40 to 60 percent minority (female and nonwhite), because it should play a major leadership role in increasing diversity. Establishing the composition of appointed committees is much easier than changing the composition of a staff or student-athlete population. A committee that is majority female and nonwhite will be more likely to attend to diversity program initiatives.

The athletic director should consider creating a diversity subcommittee of the athletic policy board that consists of three faculty, alumni, or administrator members, again with a majority of persons of color or female. Its function would be to serve as a standing search committee to assist in filling all department position openings. The search committee would meet with each athletic department employee responsible for hiring whenever a position becomes open to (1) review that unit's diversity assessment report, (2) review the job advertising plan and minority prospect list, (3) make suggestions about increasing the minority applicant pool, and (4) participate in the interview process with finalists. The athletic department should embrace a policy requiring that every pool of finalists for open positions include at least one minority applicant, that all finalists participate in formal face-to-face or telephone interviews, and that the athletic director or his designee participate in finalist interviews. This committee would also be responsible for annually reviewing progress on the department's diversity plan.

A faculty academic affairs subcommittee of the athletic policy board should also be established, consisting of three members who should be responsible for meeting with each head coach at the end of each academic year to (1) review the academic progress of all athletes, (2) review the academic credentials of all incoming recruits, (3) review the team's diversity assessment report, and (4) offer assistance to the head coach in creating a faculty–staff mentoring and support system for each minority student-athlete on the team. The faculty members involved in such support structures should assist the head coach in recruiting when minority prospects are on campus visits. This faculty subcommittee should also be responsible for reviewing the credentials of prospective students with below-average admissions records and making recommendations to the director of admissions. Student-athlete diversity should be examined by sport in meetings with the head coach, and the athletic policy board should ask how it could be of assistance in increasing these numbers.

Another primary responsibility of the entire athletic policy board or advisory committee would be to review reports from those standing committees and to analyze annual department diversity reports on student-athletes, coaches, and staff in formats similar to those previously recommended. These tasks should be done formally and in consultation with the athletic director.

10.9 PLANNING TOOL

Staff Incentives to Advance Diversity Objectives

The athletic director should consider establishing all of the following practices to encourage diversity in hiring, recruiting, and retention:

- In sports in which the maximum limit of NCAA scholarships is not awarded, make known the availability of additional athletic financial aid to recruit minority student-athletes who might otherwise not be able to afford to attend or consider attending the institution.
- Publicly recognize and express appreciation in staff meetings to coaches and staff who have contributed to employment diversity or increased student-athlete diversity on their teams.
- In sports in which head or assistant coaches are not full time, permit increased percent time appointments for minority coaches if necessary for hiring or retention. For all coaches and staff, seek institutional approval for salaries necessary to compete in the marketplace, especially for minority employees.
- As a condition of receiving funding for attending professional conferences, insist that the staff member attend diversity sessions on the conference program and share such content with all staff upon his or her return to campus.
- Each year, plan an event with each head coach (at least one team per season or three per year) to have an informal conversation ("Cokes with the athletic director" or "Milk and cookies with the athletic director") in which the athletic director specifically addresses the value orientation of the program—diversity, respect, integrity, leadership, and service—and how each student-athlete can contribute to those values. Never underestimate the leadership power of the athletic director.
- Annually review the staff diversity assessments at a meeting of the full department each year. The athletic director should lead a discussion on specific ways to improve diversity.
- In the case of employees who have not yet achieved success in increasing staff and student-athlete diversity, consider using the following mechanisms:
    - Asking for the reconstitution of a finalist pool that includes more and better-qualified minority applicants
    - Not recommending a cost-of-living or merit increase for that employee
    - Not offering a multiyear employment agreement for that employee
- Establish a policy to add a criterion such as "contributes to the recruiting or employment of minority job applicants" to the annual employee evaluation instrument used for all athletic department coaches and staff.
- Establish an award named after a respected former athlete or coach of color and bring that person back to campus to present the award at the annual awards banquet. Such public celebration of the achievements of graduates or coaches of color is an important demonstration of respect that may contribute to minority staff and student-athlete retention.

10.10 MANAGEMENT TIP

Issues Related to Individuals With Disabilities

The Rehabilitation Act of 1973 (RA) and the Americans with Disabilities Act of 1990 (ADA) are federal laws that prohibit discrimination against people with physical or learning disabilities. To use the protection of these laws, the person must be able to prove that she or he is (1) disabled (has a physical or mental impairment that substantially limits one or more major life activities), (2) would be otherwise qualified to participate if he or she weren't disabled, and (3) was excluded solely on the basis of the disability. Note that participation in sport is not considered to be a major life activity. Rather, the courts have interpreted major life activity as basic tasks central to daily life (*Toyota* v. *Williams*, 2002). But a student with a disability who meets the required level of skill or ability of a student without the disability must be allowed to participate in intramural, club, or interscholastic or intercollegiate varsity and junior varsity programs with students without disabilities even if such participation requires an accommodation of rules or aids as long as such accommodation does not fundamentally alter the sport or program (US DOE-OCR, 2013). If such mainstreaming is not possible and the number of interested and qualified (comparably skilled) students with disabilities is sufficient, the educational institution should offer separate and possibly different sports or teams.

What are the implications of these laws and Office for Civil Rights guidance documents with regard to access to varsity athletic participation? Although many issues have yet to be resolved by the courts, the following general guidance should be followed:

1. **Obligation to provide individualized evaluation.** Key is the establishment of a policy designating an employee responsible for conducting an unbiased assessment for each person with a disability who wishes to participate to determine whether a modification or accommodation is necessary and required for participation in an existing sport program or, if mainstreaming is not possible, whether a separate or different athletic opportunity needs to be created for skilled students with disabilities when interest and numbers of disabled students indicate the need for such separate and different sport teams or activities (e.g., wheelchair basketball, wheelchair tennis).
2. **Tryouts for athletic team.** Any student with a disability must be allowed to try out for an athletic team as long as such participation does not result in risk of harm to that student or those whom he or she is playing with. The assessment of harm must be objective and specific to the student with the disability. For instance, a student with one leg can participate in wrestling, a student with diabetes wearing an insulin pump can try out for football, and a deaf student can participate in basketball. Any action to deny participation must not be based on a stereotype. Rather, it must be based on a medical expert's recommendation specific to a student's disability and the sport in which the student wishes to participate.
3. **Selection of sports.** The athletic department should consider adding an adapted sport(s) for students with disabilities (e.g., wheelchair basketball). Even if such an adapted program is initiated, students with disabilities must be allowed to try out for and participate in mainstream sports.
4. **Accommodations for individuals with disabilities.** The athletic department should be prepared to make a reasonable accommodation that would allow a student with a disability to participate, such as allowing a one-handed touch of the wall in a swimming breaststroke race for a student with only one hand or allowing the use of a golf

cart when others are required to walk in the case of a student with a condition that limits ambulatory ability. Or, as an alternative when mainstreaming is not possible or when the number of interested and skilled students is sufficient, a separate sport team or program should be established including the consideration of developing (1) districtwide or regional teams instead of school-based teams, (2) mixed male and female students with disabilities on teams together, or (3) "allied" or "unified" sport teams on which students with disabilities participate with students without disabilities (US DOE-OCR, 2013).

5. **Stereotypes about prostheses.** Prostheses do not give athletes with disabilities an advantage. Athletes with prostheses must be allowed to participate with the prostheses against nonamputee participants.
6. **Stereotypes about facility damage.** Athletes in wheelchairs and athletes competing with prostheses cannot be denied participation because of any fear of damage to playing surfaces.
7. **Learning disabilities.** Although the courts have not agreed on handling cases of learning disabilities, the same approach of conducting an objective individual analysis of the situation is essential. The most common situation occurs when a student is held back in school because of a learning disability and then suffers the discrimination of an age limit eligibility rule established by an athletic governance association. Ethically, the institution should support the application for a waiver if waiver of the rule does not impose a danger of injury risk to others, which is the fundamental purpose of age limit rules that prevent older athletes who are physically more mature from injuring younger, less physically mature athletes.
8. **Access to facilities.** All athletic facilities, even those that are not used for athletic competition (e.g., use of private clubs or restaurants for fund-raisers) should be in full compliance with RA and ADA requirements regarding handicapped access.
9. **Employment.** People with disabilities cannot be discriminated against with regard to employment (see sample Policy 6.5 in HK*Propel*). The athletic department must be willing to accommodate employees with disabilities by modifying work areas, equipment, work schedules, training materials and user manuals, and so on to enable the employee to fulfill job responsibilities. Accommodation does not require the department to tolerate misconduct or absenteeism.

Most important, the athletic administrator should consider the need for a change in the mindset of athletic directors. Right now, neither the NCAA nor the National Federation of State High School Associations officially sanctions any intercollegiate program, event, or competition for individuals with disabilities. Students with disabilities are on the outside looking in. When one in five people in the United States has a documented disability, the educational institution is ethically obligated to make sure that all educational aspirations of this group, including the desire to participate in varsity sport, are seriously considered. Although athletic directors are probably not intentionally discriminating based on disability, they appear to be simply ignoring the issue in the hope that they won't have to deal with it. Following the guidelines by which the administrator's mindset is "I have the responsibility to create varsity athletic opportunities for this group that has been historically discriminated against" is far different from hoping that the issue will go away.

In addition to requiring participation opportunities, disabilities laws require that all athletic facilities and events be accessible to spectators and participants with disabilities. Athletic administrators should seek help from the institution's administrative office overseeing buildings and grounds to conduct an audit of all athletic facilities to determine compliance with the RA and ADA. In addition, this campus office should provide the athletic department with a summary of RA and ADA rules as they apply to facility access. In consultation with the institution's legal counsel, a letter should be developed to (1) inform third-party facility operators used for athletic events (competitions, fund-raisers, and so on) that institutional policy requires use of ADA-accessible facilities and (2) request that the third party reply with an assurance that their facility complies with these rules.

The institution is also obligated to have a process for investigating and responding to complaints related to handicapped access to facilities and program access by students with disabilities. The institutional process should be used for such complaints rather than an independent process conducted by the athletic department.

Special care must be taken in the hiring process not to ask the applicant or his or her references nonpermissible questions related to health or disability. No queries should be related to whether the applicant has physical or learning disabilities, medical conditions, history of mental illness or sickness, prescription drug use, or similar questions. If concerns about employee performance or absenteeism arise after hiring an employee, asking such questions and even requiring a medical examination are permissible.

These RA and ADA obligations must translate into athletic department policies. Following are examples of such policies.

Tryouts for Students With Disabilities

Any student with a disability must be allowed to try out for an athletic team as long as such participation does not result in a risk of harm to that student or the others whom he or she is playing with. The assessment of harm must be objective and specific to the student with the disability. Any action to deny participation must not be based on a stereotype. Rather, it must be based on a medical expert's recommendation specific to a student's disability and the sport in which the student wishes to participate. Coaches are required to inform the head athletic trainer if students with disabilities wish to try out for an athletic team and the coach has any concerns with regard to the possibility of injury or harm to that student or others. The head athletic trainer shall be in charge of completing the required assessment.

Reasonable Accommodation of Student-Athletes With Disabilities

Federal law and ethical obligations require that the institution make every effort to accommodate student-athletes with disabilities (e.g., applying for a waiver of swimming breaststroke rules that require a two-handed wall touch to allow a one-handed swimmer to compete, applying for a waiver of an age limit rule for a student with a learning disability who was held back in secondary school). Coaches should consult with the head athletic trainer and the athletic director regarding the submission of such waivers. With regard to competition, inclusion in the same event with athletes without disabilities is the first choice if fair and safe competition can result (e.g., if a prosthesis does not confer advantage or create a safety consideration). The second choice would be participation in the same competition via a separate event and the third choice would be inclusion via a separate and/or hybrid (including athletes with and without disabilities) team.

Mandated Use of Facilities Accessible to the Handicapped

All institutional facilities must comply with federal laws requiring accessibility by the physically handicapped (see Policy 12.20 in HK*Propel*). By policy, the athletic department shall not schedule an athletic, fund-raising, or other public event at any noninstitutional facility that does not meet these standards of federal law. The events manager shall be responsible for ensuring that such third-party facilities meet this requirement.

Equal Opportunity Employment Commitment

The institution, including the athletic program, is fully committed to assembling a diverse workforce in a manner that does not unlawfully discriminate against any person based on race, color, religion, sex, national origin, age, disability, veteran status, sexual orientation, or gender identity or expression (see Policy 6.5 in HK*Propel*).

Impermissible Questions in Checking References of Job Applicants

When calling a reference, questions that do not relate to the job or are personal in nature should not be asked (e.g., marital status, sexual orientation, age, disability, number of children, race, ethnicity, medical conditions, history of mental illness or sickness, prescription drug use). Similarly, the hiring manager should not pose a question from a negative perspective. Questions should be formatted in a positive way, using a rating scale if possible (e.g., "On a scale of 1 to 10 with 10 being the highest, how would you rate this applicant's work ethic?"). It is acceptable and recommended to ask, as a standard reference question, whether any red flags related to the applicant might compromise his or her ability to do the job.

Impermissible Questions When Interviewing Job Applicants

Candidates shall not be asked any personal questions (e.g., marital status, sexual orientation, age, disability, number of children, race, ethnicity, medical conditions, history of mental illness or sickness, prescription drug use). All questions should focus on the requirements of the job and the candidate's ability to perform the job. Never share the names of other finalists or information provided by the candidate's references.

Accommodation of Employees With Disabilities

The athletic department shall accommodate employees with disabilities by modifying work areas, equipment, work schedules, training materials and user manuals, and so on to enable the employee to fulfill job responsibilities (see Policy 6.5 in HK*Propel*).

Formal Complaint Process Alleging Discrimination

The athletic department shall not tolerate discrimination affecting any employee or student-athlete. Further, the department will not tolerate harassment of any employee or student-athlete. Discrimination and harassment are actions that create hostile, offensive, or intimidating work environments. Discrimination and harassment include but are not limited to sexual and racial harassment or harassment because of disability. Harassment may include derogatory comments, jokes, or threats. Any employee or student-athlete who believes that he or she has been discriminated against or harassed in the workplace may seek redress. The procedures for redress following discrimination or harassment are progressive with regard to documentation and severity of action. The procedures for corrective action following complaints of discrimination or harassment are progressive and follow the guidelines for other institutional disciplinary and corrective actions.

- **Informal complaint.** Individuals seeking redress for discrimination or harassment may choose to seek informal conflict resolution. To issue an informal complaint, the individual must approach her or his work supervisor or other impartial ranking administrative official within the athletic department. All people involved, including the impartial administrative official, will meet to discuss how the offending individual's actions are perceived. All those involved should identify ways to make positive changes in the workplace and strive to achieve those changes. Those seeking redress have the right to bypass the informal complaint procedure.
- **Formal complaint.** People seeking redress for discrimination or harassment may issue a formal complaint. A formal complaint must be issued in writing to the person's direct supervisor. In cases that involve harassment of employees by work supervisors, the person experiencing harassment may bypass the direct supervisor and issue a formal written complaint to the institution's human resources director. In cases involving student-athletes, the complaint should be submitted to the assistant athletic director for student affairs or to the institutional office of student affairs. Pursuing a complaint does not compromise a person's right to seek legal action on the state and federal level for discrimination or harassment.
- **Disciplinary action.** On receiving a formal complaint of discrimination or harassment, work supervisors, the human resources director, or other institutional officials receiving such a complaint must thoroughly investigate the occurrence. If it is determined that discrimination or harassment has occurred or continues to occur, progressive disciplinary action must be taken following the policies and procedures for corrective action.
- **Nonretaliation.** Any employee or student-athlete who submits a complaint regarding

discrimination or harassment in the workplace or who participates in the investigation of a discrimination or harassment complaint may do so without fear of retaliation. Notwithstanding this policy, the athletic department may issue corrective action to employees who abuse the complaint procedure by knowingly bringing false complaints.

10.12 MANAGEMENT TIP

Sexual Abuse and Harassment

In the spring of 2011 the investigation of Yale University for violation of sexual harassment prohibitions under Title IX of the Education Amendments of 1972 made national headlines (Yale, 2011). Investigations of other Ivy League and other prominent institutions of higher education followed soon thereafter. In April 2011 the Department of Education (DOE) issued a *Dear Colleague* letter to clarify the obligations of educational institutions. DOE instructions were clear. When any school, college, or university becomes aware of the occurrence of sexual harassment or abuse (or sexual violence of any kind), it must respond "promptly and effectively" to eliminate its occurrence and address its effect. The institution must take such action even if the victim of the action does not wish to file a formal complaint and even if a criminal investigation is ongoing. Every educational institution that receives federal funds must comply with Title IX, including the obligation to have a Title IX coordinator and a widely distributed Title IX policy.

The athletic department cannot see itself as operating in isolation in this area. If anyone in the athletic department becomes aware of sexual harassment, sexual abuse, or sexual violence of any kind, the case should be reported to the institution and handled according to established institutional Title IX policy and procedures. Title IX prohibits sexual harassment based on race, color, national origin, sex, and disability. Many school districts and institutions of higher education have adopted antibullying policies that are handled similarly and have added protected categories to the traits expressly protected by Title IX to include sexual orientation and religion.

As national media attention is focused on this issue, the time is ripe for athletic department leaders to devote time in staff meetings and student-athlete orientation programs to reviewing Title IX sexual harassment policies and procedures and the definitions of prohibited activities. This media focus should also give every sport manager pause and a reason to examine athletic department practices. Here are some questions that should be addressed:

- Does the athletic department have an annual education program for all staff and student-athletes that addresses sexual harassment, bullying, sexual abuse, quid pro quo harassment, Title IX policy and procedures, and the ethical responsibilities of all staff members and educators with regard to relationships with their students? Does this education program include information on "grooming," the artful cultivation of the victim by a pedophile?
- Does every member of the athletic staff understand his or her immediate obligation to report any instance of sexual harassment or abuse whether or not the victim wishes to file a formal complaint?
- Do coaches' employment agreements and athletic department policy clearly state that intimate relationships with students, even if they have reached the age of consent and even if the relationships do not meet a technical definition of sexual harassment, are expressly prohibited because they undermine impartiality and trust and that, in the case of violation of such policy, such actions are cause for termination of employment (see Policies 7.2 and 7.3)? Are coaches and athletes in the same room with the athletic director when forms of verbal, physical, and emotional abuse are detailed via explicit prohibitions (e.g., no use of conditioning as physical punishment, no touching an athlete without asking for permission, etc.)?
- Do policies on student-athlete conduct and team rules clearly address zero tolerance for sexual harassment, hazing, bullying, and similar forms of conduct that create hostile environments (see Policy 11.18)?

Sexual harassment and sexual abuse are different. Sexual harassment is unwanted and often persistent sexual attention. It may include written or verbal abuse or threats; sexually oriented comments or jokes; lewd comments or sexual innuendoes; taunts about body, dress, marital status, or sexuality; shouting or bullying; ridiculing or undermining of performance or self-respect; sexual or homophobic graffiti; practical jokes based on sex; intimidating sexual remarks, invitations, or familiarity; domination of meetings, training sessions, or equipment; condescending or patronizing behavior; physical contact, fondling, pinching, or kissing; sex-related vandalism; offensive phone calls or photos; or bullying on the basis of sex (WomenSport International, 2004).

Sexual abuse often occurs after careful grooming of the athlete until he or she believes that sexual involvement with the abuser is acceptable, unavoidable, or a normal part of the athlete's training or everyday behavior. It may include exchange of rewards or privileges for sexual favors; groping; indecent exposure; rape; anal or vaginal penetration by penis, fingers, or objects; forced sexual activity; sexual assault; physical or sexual violence; or incest (WomenSport International, 2004). While recent highly publicized cases of sexual abuse in sport have involved male coach abuse of male athletes, 90 percent of all incidents involve older males harassing or abusing younger females. The remaining 10 percent of sport incidents is split evenly between older male and younger male, older female and younger male, and older female and younger female across all types of sexual abuse in sports (Kirby, Greaves, & Hankivsky, 2000).

Unfortunately, the world of sport has been riddled with sexual abuse and harassment of young athletes by their powerful and publicly respected coaches (respected for producing performance results) for many decades, across all sports, and regardless of sex. Although data on the prevalence of these transgressions have not been consistently collected, evidence indicates that news reports may be the proverbial tip of the iceberg:

- "In 2003, the *Seattle Times* reported that 159 high school coaches in Washington were fired or reprimanded for sexual misconduct ranging from harassment to rape. Nearly all were male coaches victimizing girls. At least 98 of these coaches continued to coach or teach" (Willmsen & O'Hagan, 2003, para. 9). "Even after getting caught, many men were allowed to continue coaching because school administrators promised to keep their disciplinary records secret if the coaches simply left. Some districts paid tens of thousands of dollars to get coaches to leave. Other districts hired coaches they knew had records of sexual misconduct" (Willmsen & O'Hagan, 2003, para. 11). In 2019, *Athletic Business* reported that the Anaheim (Calif.) Union School District agreed to pay $7.9 million to five former Kennedy High School female water polo players to settle a sexual abuse lawsuit against their male coach (Steinbach, 2019).
- Media reports are also replete with stories of college athlete sexual abuse. In March 2020, three former college athletes sued their track coach and the NCAA for sexual abuse while at the University of Arizona and University of Texas from 1996 to 2000. In April 2021, a federal lawsuit alleged that Canisius College allowed sexual harassment and rape on its men's and women's cross country teams, ignoring reports of sexual assault and fostering a hostile environment (Specht, 2021). Team doctor Larry Nassar was sentenced to 40 to 175 years in prison in 2018 for using his sports medicine position to abuse hundreds of college athletes at Michigan State and in the USA National Gymnastics team program (History.com editors, 2018). Over a 20-year period, Ohio State University team doctor Richard Strauss sexually abused at least 177 male athletes, mostly football players and wrestlers (Witz, 2020).

Athletes are often drawn into keeping the sexual abuse secret against their better judgment for the sake of protecting the team from public embarrassment (Women's Sports Foundation, 1999). Or, athletes may not understand the quid pro quo nature of athlete–coach relationships. Quid pro quo sexual harassment occurs when submission to such conduct is explicitly or implicitly made a term or condition of the victims' participation in the sport or is used as the basis for decisions affecting that person. In the coach–athlete relationship, quid pro quo harassment occurs when a coach grants or withholds benefits (such as coaching attention, a scholarship, starting position, or playing time) as a result of an athlete's willingness or refusal to submit to the coach's sexual demands, whether this expectation is obvious or not. The silence of athletes because of these factors greatly reduces the amount of data available to understand the scope of the problem.

Like schools, colleges, and universities (and their athletic departments), sport organizations from privately owned local sport clubs and teams to national sport governing organizations and national coaches associations have not been effective in responding to this issue. Although many sport organizations have policies in place that prohibit such conduct, little success appears to have occurred with regard to (1) taking action against coaches who violate these policies, (2) implementing consistent programs that educate athletes and parents about sexual harassment and abuse and dealing with such situations, and (3) creating a climate in which athletes feel safe in reporting such incidents.

Thus, these crimes and abuses of power of the teacher or coach often go unreported. When they are reported, few coaches are terminated from employment or banned from the profession for violation of professional rules of conduct; in the case of criminal acts, few are brought to justice from a legal standpoint. This failure to stop such unethical or criminal coach activity is because of myriad factors:

- Athletes and parents not being educated about the nature of sexual abuse and harassment and the fact that such conduct is unethical or criminal
- Athlete embarrassment
- Lack of physical evidence
- Time lapses in reporting
- Coaches owning their own sport clubs and having no oversight body to receive such complaints
- Young athletes who seek attention and approval of their coaches or who do not understand the quid pro quo nature of sexual abuse by a teacher, coach, or someone in authority
- Parent denial
- Lack of effective reporting and investigatory mechanisms
- Conflict of interest seen in coaches being asked to judge their colleagues or institutions when they might rather protect the reputation of their institution than the safety of the athletes they are serving (Starr, 2011)

The result is that athletes across all sports are becoming victims of sexual exploitation as consenting or nonconsenting minors or adults. Meanwhile, coach perpetrators are caught only after numerous transgressions or are continuing to coach after deals are struck to protect the organization employing them.

"It is probably the biggest problem confronting sport today," says professor Celia Brackenridge, who has been researching sex abuse in sport for more than 15 years. "Everyone talks about the perils of doping, but if there were 100 drugs cases under investigation in football, or 60 in swimming, or 40 in tennis, there would be uproar. Yet, that's the scale of the problem with sex abuse today" (Downes, 2002, para. 11).

Although sport governance organizations and clubs have either added a code of conduct to their policies (see USOC, 2000, for an example), implemented policies that require coaches to pledge not to engage in intimate relations with athletes, or established policies that outright state that no such relationships are permitted, those efforts have not stopped the occurrence of sexual abuse or harassment of athletes by coaches (see Sandler & Shoop, 1996; Women's Sports Foundation, 1999; U.S. Department of Education Office for Civil Rights, 2011).

Even when strong policies exist, many organizations fall short on policy implementation. In the case of a number of colleges and universities, the excuse of waiting for the results of a criminal investigation by local authorities has been used by the institution to delay action, in many cases resulting in the victim's continuing to have to attend class or practice with an offending professor, peer student, athlete teammate, or coach. This practice has been expressly prohibited by the Office for Civil Rights, which has clearly mandated prompt proceedings and a preponderance of evidence standard that is a much lower bar than that used by many institutions (U.S. Department of Education Office for Civil Rights, 2011).

Sexual harassment and abuse are serious matters that deserve the careful attention of the sport manager. Given the media's current focus on this issue and its ongoing interest in all matters related to the integrity of sport programs, now would be a good time to take a careful look at how athletic programs deal with this issue.

DIVERSITY, INCLUSION, AND NONDISCRIMINATION

Acosta, R.V., & Carpenter, L.J. (2012). *Women in intercollegiate sports: A longitudinal national study—35 year update 1977 to 2012*. www.acostacarpenter.org. Unpublished data provided by e-mail about sports information director and head athletic trainer position growth between 1998 and 2012.

Age Discrimination in Employment Act of 1967, 20 U.S.C. § 621 et seq.

Americans With Disabilities Act of 1990, 42 U.S.C. § 12101 et seq.

Americans With Disabilities Act Regulations, 28 C.F.R. § 36.104. (2005).

Bonnette, V.M., & Daniel, L. (1990). *Title IX athletics investigator's manual*. U.S. Department of Education Office for Civil Rights. http://fs.ncaa.org/Docs/gender_equity/resource_materials/AuditMaterial/Investigator%27s_Manual.pdf.

Brooks, D.D., & Althouse, R.C. (Eds.). (2007). *Diversity and social justice in college sports*. Morgantown, WV: Fitness Information Technology.

Butler, J., & Lopiano, D. (2003). *Women's Sports Foundation report: Title IX and race in intercollegiate sport*. Eisenhower Park, East Meadow, NY: Women's Sports Foundation.

Cheslock, J. (2008). *Who's playing college sports, parts II and III: Trends in funding and diversity*. Eisenhower Park, East Meadow, NY: Women's Sports Foundation.

Cheslock, J.J., & Anderson, D.J. (2004, October 21). *Racial issues relating to Title IX and intercollegiate athletics*. Unpublished working paper. University of Arizona.

Civil Rights Act of 1964, 42 U.S.C. § 1981.

Civil Rights Act of 1964, 42 U.S.C. § 1983.

Cozzillio, M.J., & Hayman Jr., R.L. (2005). *Sports and inequality*. Durham, NC: Carolina Academic Press.

Cunningham, G.B. (2011). *Diversity in sport organizations*. Scottsdale, AZ: Holcomb Hathaway.

Equal Pay Act of 1963, 29 U.S.C. § 206(d)(1).

Downes, S. (2002, April 7). Every parent's nightmare. *Observer Sports Monthly*. https://www.theguardian.com/observer/osm/story/0,,678189,00.html.

Gill, E., Lopiano, D., Smith, B., Sommer, J., Gurney, G., Lever, K., Porto, B., Ridpath, D.B., Sack, A., Thatcher, S., and Zimbalist, A. (2021). The Drake Group Position Statement: A Continuing Disgrace—Intercollegiate Athletics Race Issues. https://www.thedrakegroup.org/2021/05/31/a-continuing-disgrace-intercollegiate-athletics-race-issues/.

Griffin, P., & Carroll, H.J. (2010). *On the team: Equal opportunity for transgender student athletes*. National Center for Lesbian Rights and Women's Sports Foundation. www.nclrights.org/site/DocServer/TransgenderStudentAthleteReport.pdf?docID=7901.

History.com editors. (2018). Larry Nassar, a former doctor for USA Gymnastics, is sentenced to prison for sexual assault. *History.com*. https://www.history.com/this-day-in-history/larry-nassar-usa-gymnastics-doctor-sentenced-prison-sexual-assault.

Kirby, S.L., Greaves, L. & Hankivsky, O. (2000). *The dome of silence: Sexual harassment and abuse in sport*. Black Point, Nova Scotia: Fernwood.

Lage, L. (2020). Ex-track athletes detail alleged sex abuse by college coach. *ABCNews.com*. https://abcnews.go.com/Sports/wireStory/track-athletes-detail-alleged-sex-abuse-college-coach-69572004.

Lapchick, R. et al. (2011). *The 2010–11 Associated Press sports editors racial and gender report card*. Orlando, FL: Institute for Diversity and Ethics in Sport, University of Florida. www.tidesport.org/RGRC/2011/2011_APSE_RGRC_FINAL.pdf.

Lapchick, R. et al. (2018). *The 2018 Associated Press sports editors racial and gender report card*. Orlando, FL: Institute for Diversity and Ethics in Sport, University of Florida. https://43530132-36e9-4f52-811a-182c7a91933b.filesusr.com/ugd/7d86e5_9dca4bc2067241cdba67aa2f1b09fd1b.pdf.

Lapchick, R. et al. (2020). *The 2020 racial and gender report card: College sport*. Orlando, FL: Institute for Diversity and Ethics in Sport, University of Florida. https://43530132-36e9-4f52-811a-182c7a91933b.filesusr.com/ugd/8af738_3b5d1b6bdb10457ebe8d46cc5a2fcfd0.pdf.

Lawrence, S. (2011). NCAA transgender policy approved. *National Collegiate Athletic Association*. www.ncaa.org/wps/wcm/connect/public/NCAA/Resources/Latest+News/2011/September/Transgender+policy+approved.

National Collegiate Athletic Association. (2018). *Instructions for completing the 2018 Division III institutional self-study guide*. https://www.ncaa.org/sites/default/files/d3-online-issg-instructions.pdf.

National Collegiate Athletic Association. (2019). *User's Guide for Division II institutional self-study guide to enhance integrity in intercollegiate athletics.* https://ncaaorg.s3.amazonaws.com/membership/d2/D2Mem_ISSGUserGuide.pdf.

National Collegiate Athletic Association. (2020). *2019–20 NCAA sports sponsorship and participation rates report.* https://ncaaorg.s3.amazonaws.com/research/sportpart/2019-20RES_SportsSponsorshipParticipationRatesReport.pdf.

National Collegiate Athletic Association. (2021). *NCAA demographics database.* https://www.ncaa.org/about/resources/research/ncaa-demographics-database.

National Federation of State High School Associations (NFHS). (2019). *2018–19 high school participation data.* https://www.nfhs.org/media/1020412/2018-19_participation_survey.pdf.

Peter Westbrook Foundation. (2021). www.peterwestbrook.org.

Pregnancy Discrimination Act, 42 U.S.C. § 2000 e(k).

Rehabilitation Act of 1973, 29 U.S.C. § 701 et seq.

Sandler, B.R., & Shoop, R.J. (Eds.). (1996). *Sexual harassment on campus: A guide for administrators, faculty and students.* Boston: Allyn and Bacon.

Sharp, L.A., Moorman, A.M., & Claussen, C.L. (2007). *Sport law: A managerial approach.* Scottsdale, AZ: Holcomb-Hathaway.

Specht, C. (2021). Lawsuit accuses Canisius College of allowing rape culture on running teams. *WKBS.com.* https://www.wkbw.com/news/local-news/lawsuit-accuses-canisius-college-of-allowing-rape-culture-on-running-teams.

Spengler, J.O., Anderson, P.M., Connaughton, D.P., & Baker III, T.A. (2009). *Introduction to sports law.* Champaign, IL: Human Kinetics.

Sports Business Journal (SBJ). (2002, May 27). *2002 Sports Business Journal salary survey.* Street & Smith's Sports Group. www.sportsbusinessdaily.com/Journal/Issues/2002/05/20020527/Special-Report/Making-Comparisons.aspx?hl=2002%20Salary%20Survey&sc=0.

Starr, K. (2021). Empowering athletes to win from within. *Safe4Athletes.* https://safe4athletes.org.

Steinbach, P. (2019). District to pay victims of coach's sex abuse $7.9M. *AthleticBusiness.com.* https://www.athleticbusiness.com/civil-actions/district-to-pay-victims-of-coach-s-sex-abuse-7-9m.html.

Title VII of the Civil Rights Act of 1964, as amended by the Civil Rights Act of 1991, 42 U.S.C. § 2000e et seq.

Title IX Athletics Regulations, 24 CFR Part 106.

Title IX of the Education Amendments of 1972, 20 U.S.C. § 1681 et seq.

Toyota Motor Mfg. v. *Williams,* 122 S. Ct. 681 (2002).

U.S. Bureau of Labor Statistics. (2020). *Labor force characteristics by race and ethnicity, 2019.* BLS Reports: December 2020. https://www.bls.gov/opub/reports/race-and-ethnicity/2019/home.htm.

U.S. Census Bureau. Quick Facts: Population estimates, July 1, 2019 (V2019). https://www.census.gov/quickfacts/fact/table/US/PST045219.

U.S. CONST. amend. I.

U.S. CONST. amend. IV.

U.S. CONST. amend. XIV.

U.S. Department of Education, National Center for Education Statistics, Digest of Education Statistics, 2013, NCES 2015-011 (2015), Table 306.10, "Total Fall Enrollment in Degree-Granting Postsecondary Institutions, by Level of Enrollment, Sex, Attendance Status, and Race/Ethnicity of Student: Selected Years, 1976 through 2012." http://nces.ed.gov/fastfacts/display.asp?id=98, and 2017 Population Estimates, retrieved September 5, 2017, https://www.census.gov/data/datasets/2016/demo/popest/nation-detail.html. See Digest of Education Statistics 2017, table 101.20.

U.S. Department of Education Office for Civil Rights. (1979, December 11). A policy interpretation: Title IX and intercollegiate athletics. *Federal Register, 44*(239). www2.ed.gov/about/offices/list/ocr/docs/t9interp.html.

U.S. Department of Education Office for Civil Rights. (1996). *Policy clarification of intercollegiate athletics policy guidance: The three-part test.* www.nacua.org/documents/IntercollegiateAthleticsPolicyClarification.pdf.

U.S. Department of Education Office for Civil Rights. (2001, January). *Revised sexual harassment guidance: Harassment of students by school employees, other students, or third parties—Title IX.* www2.ed.gov/offices/OCR/archives/pdf/shguide.pdf.

U.S. Department of Education Office for Civil Rights. (2008). *Dear colleague letter: Athletics activities counted for Title IX compliance.* www2.ed.gov/about/offices/list/ocr/letters/colleague-20080917.html.

U.S. Department of Education Office for Civil Rights. (2010, April 20). *Dear colleague letter re: intercollegiate athletics policy clarification: The three-part test—Part III.* www2.ed.gov/about/offices/list/ocr/letters/colleague-20100420.pdf.

U.S. Department of Education Office for Civil Rights. (2011, April 4). *Dear colleague: Sexual violence.* www.whitehouse.gov/sites/default/files/dear_colleague_sexual_violence.pdf.

U.S. Department of Education Office for Civil Rights. (2013, January 25). *Dear colleague: Students with disabilities in extracurricular activities.* http://www2.ed.gov/about/offices/list/ocr/letters/colleague-201301-504.html.

U.S. Equal Employment Opportunity Commission. (1997, October 29). *Enforcement guidance on discrimination in the compensation of sports coaches in educational institutions.* EEOC Notice Number 915.002. http://archive.eeoc.gov/policy/docs/coaches.html.

United States Olympic Committee. (2000). *Coaching ethics code*. www.usacoaching.org/resources/Coaching%20 Ethics%20Code_new.pdf.

Willmsen, C., & O'Hagan, M. (2003, December 14). Coaches who prey: The abuse of girls and the system that allows it. *Seattle Times*. https://archive.seattletimes .com/archive/?date=20031214&slug=coaches14m.

Witz, B. (2020, May 8). Ohio State Pays $41 Million to Settle Claims From Doctor's Abuse. *New York Times*. https://www.nytimes.com/2020/05/08/sports/ohio-state -strauss-settlement.html.

Women's Sports Foundation. (2002). *It takes a team. An education kit and program*. East Meadow, NY: Women's Sports Foundation. https://eric.ed.gov/?id=ED473448.

Women's Sports Foundation. (2011). *Physical activity and athletic competition for individuals with disabilities. A Women's Sports Foundation position statement*. East Meadow, NY. https://www.womenssportsfoundation .org/advocacy/physical-activity-athletic-competition -individuals-disabilities.

Women's Sports Foundation. (2011). *Race and sport: The foundation position*. https://www.womens sportsfoundation.org/advocacy/race-sport-foundation -position.

Women's Sports Foundation. (2016). *Sexual harassment and sexual relationships between coaches, other athletic personnel and athletes: The foundation position*. https:// www.womenssportsfoundation.org/advocacy/sexual -harassment-sexual-relationships-coaches-athletic -personnel-athletes.

Women's Sports Foundation. (2019). *Homophobia and sport policy recommendations: The foundation position*. https://www.womenssportsfoundation.org /advocacy/homophobia-sport-policy-recommendations -foundation-position.

WomenSport International. (2004). *WSI position statement—Sexual harassment and abuse of girls and women in sport*. http://womensportinternational.org /index.php/wsi-position-statement-sexual-harassment.

Wong, G.M. (2010). *Essentials of sports law*. Santa Barbara, CA: Praeger.

Yale is subject of Title IX inquiry. (2011, March 31). *New York Times*. www.nytimes.com/2011/04/01/us/01yale .html?_r=1.

CHAPTER

11

Team Administration

Many athletic directors allow coaches to administer their sport programs in a vacuum. Giving coaches unilateral decision-making authority over the administration of their teams will most assuredly lead to inconsistent treatment of student-athletes within the department, which, in turn, may lead to student-athlete discontent or an increased risk of coach or athletic department liability. The documents in this chapter, both in the book and in HK*Propel*, help the athletic director standardize policies and procedures related to roster management, student-athlete selection and participation, unsupervised conditioning programs, and coach-athlete relationships and conduct. In addition, there are separate sections that address consistent policies and procedures for the issuance and use of equipment and uniforms, efficient and safe team travel, and the eligibility and selection of athletic department award winners.

TYPES OF DOCUMENTS

Management tip—Factual background information, insights, problem-solving strategies, and suggestions for the athletic director

Planning tool—Steps to take or factors that should be considered in the development of strategic plans, action plans, professional development plans, or governance systems

Educational resource—Handouts that can be used to educate staff members, campus constituents, volunteers, or student-athletes

Policy—Sample policies and procedures that should be adopted by an athletic department after customization and review by appropriate expert institutional or school district officials

Form—Sample forms, letters, or job descriptions

Evaluation instrument—Administrative tools that help the athletic director, a supervisor, or an employee assess job performance and evaluate program content

Risk assessment—Checklists that help the athletic director, a supervisor, or an employee identify risks and prevent litigation

ROSTER MANAGEMENT

11.1 MANAGEMENT TIP

Athletic Director's Role in Team Roster Decisions

Many issues are associated with selecting players for a team and effectively managing roster changes. A commonly accepted practice is that the coaches of each team have the responsibility and full prerogative to decide which players are selected for the team, which players can be added to the roster at various intervals during the season, and, if necessary, which players are removed from the team because of team rules violations, inappropriate behavior, or a host of other unacceptable circumstances. The coaching staff undoubtedly has the expertise and the right to make these decisions. The opportunity to play, however, is highly coveted by the vast majority of student-athletes and their parents. Student-athletes and parents often challenge coaches' decisions and wage campaigns to have those decisions overturned by the athletic director, another institutional administrator, or, in some cases, the courts. Therefore, the athletic director and coaching staff must craft policies that are fair and consistent regarding tryouts, adding players to the roster after cuts are made, and removing players from the roster, all while remaining in compliance with governing-body rules that may limit roster size or player eligibility.

Controlling the size of rosters may be important not only from a financial perspective but also from an equal opportunity gender equity perspective. The athletic department may inadvertently create large discrepancies in participation opportunities if roster limits are not established. Policy 11.2 addresses roster management issues.

11.2 Policy—Roster Management and Tryouts

Sample policies and procedures that address team tryouts, eligibility for tryouts, selecting the team, and meeting with student-athletes who are not selected.

Available in HK*Propel*.

After policies are established and communicated, they must be consistently upheld. Too often, policies are overlooked when a decision will affect a star player. Conversely, at times decisions may be too severe because the player affected is a nonstarter. Therefore, the athletic director needs to be involved in every substantial decision regarding a change in a team's roster. This policy will serve to protect the coach from making a hasty decision. In addition, it will allow the athletic director to weigh the potential repercussions of the decision, gain the support of other administrators before the final decision is made, and promote department-wide consistency in handling roster management issues.

11.3 MANAGEMENT TIP

Proper and Improper Use of Roster Management

A frequently used strategy known as roster management has significant implications for achieving gender equity, stabilizing athletic program expenditures, and conducting an ethical sport program. Roster management is a way to establish a maximum limit on the number of players that are allowed on the roster of a sport team or program. The uses, both proper and improper, of roster management are discussed in the following sections.

Honor to Be Selected

Historically, most high school and college programs practiced roster management without using that particular label. Practically every athlete remembers trying out for the varsity or junior varsity team and anxiously waiting for the coach to post the names of students who made the team. Interscholastic and intercollegiate athletics have traditionally been viewed as elite programs for the most highly skilled. The most highly skilled students would be selected for a team, which would have the opportunity to play against the best players from other institutions. Participation in varsity sport is equivalent to selection to an honors program, the school debate team, the choir, or the marching band.

Determination of Proper Team Size

The limits on the size of varsity debate teams or athletic teams are usually determined in relationship to competition rules. How many players are required to compete? How many substitute players are needed in case of illness, injury, or fatigue because of the nature of the sport or similar sport-related factors? How many players can the teacher or coach reasonably be expected to instruct, given the need for a significant and positive athletic experience? Many high school and college athletic governance associations (conferences, leagues, national championship fields) have set limits on the size of a team permitted to compete to legislate fairness and financial restraint. Some conferences do not limit the size of a team that the institution can sponsor, but many limit the number who can travel to away contests. Reasonable and commonly acceptable maximum roster limits can be identified by looking at those legislated numbers, such as the size of a team allowed to participate in an NCAA championship or the travel squad limits of a conference.

Philosophical Approaches

In sports like football, having large squads and never cutting the size of a team has become a tradition. At many educational institutions, giving as many students as possible a varsity experience is philosophically important. For instance, football as a sport caters to a wide range of body types and even to participants with limited skill (e.g., the very large and overweight individuals who are not quick or mobile being used as offensive linemen). At schools with such participation philosophies, either no limits are imposed on the size of any sport program, or junior varsity and freshman squads have been added to encourage more participation.

Stockpiling

In some highly competitive college programs, large squads are a way of keeping talent away from other institutions (known as stockpiling) or making sure that sufficient "tackling dummies" are available so that more valued players won't have to sacrifice their bodies during practice.

Legitimate Financial Purpose

Some schools use roster management as a legitimate way to control costs. They want the team or program to be of sufficient size to offer a quality experience to all participants but not so large that many players are unlikely ever to get a chance to play.

Title IX Implications of Large Teams

Before Title IX, when athletic programs primarily consisted of men, roster size was not a gender equality issue. But when Title IX imposed the obligation of equal participation opportunities, roster size became a critical factor. Keeping a football team of 100 players instead of the 65 or 70 that might really be needed meant adding another two to four sports for women, a considerable financial outlay. Hard financial times for athletic programs and educational institutions added to these pressures, as did the arms race to put extravagant sums of money into men's football and basketball programs.

Managing the Size of Men's Teams Only

In the late 1990s many schools implemented a practice that became known as roster management. To avoid cutting men's teams, the schools cut back on the number of male participants who would be allowed on existing teams. Often, football and men's basketball did not have roster limits. By placing limits on squad size on some or all men's teams and subsequently reducing the total number of male athletes, institutions increased the percentage (but not number) of female athletes in their programs. Although this practice would help an institution meet the Title IX prong 1 proportionality standard, it would not help an institution meet the prong 2 (continuing program expansion) or prong 3 (fully met interest of underrepresented sex) standard.

Unrealistic Squad Sizes Imposed on Women's Teams

As more women enrolled in college and demanded opportunities to participate in athletics, institutions faced larger opportunity gaps that roster management could not solve. Schools did not want to cut men's sports but also could not cut any more men from the existing teams without severely affecting their competitiveness. To meet prong 1, they had to add opportunities for women. Adding new sports costs money and places demands on facilities. Schools that did not want to reallocate the resources necessary to do this looked for ways to increase participation on existing women's teams either in fact or in appearance. The goal for many schools was to devise ways to add participation numbers without adding new women's sports. Some schools set new and higher minimum squad limits for women's teams, some of which were unreasonable with regard to normal team size and optimum coach–athlete teaching ratios.

"Ghost" Participation Slots

These unreasonable size expectations for women's teams ran afoul of Title IX requirements. Some schools were found to report female participation based on the squad sizes they created rather than the number of female athletes who were participating. Courts ruled that counted athletic participation opportunities must reflect opportunities filled by actual students (*Cohen* v. *Brown University*) and could not be "ghost slots" or opportunities that a school claims to offer but are not filled by students. For example, a school cannot count 18 softball players when, in fact, it has only 15 players, even if the school wanted to have 18 players and even if the school told the coach to find 18 players. If only 15 athletes actually exist, then the school cannot count more than those 15 athletes. This counting method was also expressly upheld when the U.S. Office for Civil Rights rejected a Title IX Commission recommendation that would have permitted the counting of such "ghost slots." As stated on page 4 of the *Dear Colleague Letter* of the 1996 OCR Clarification, "Athletic opportunities must be real, not illusory."

EADA Participant Data Manipulation

Some schools have gotten into the habit of focusing on numbers that they are required to submit under the Equity in Athletics Disclosure Act (EADA) and manipulating those numbers rather than achieving actual gender equity. Incredibly, some schools count male practice players used for women's teams as female participants. Other schools manipulate their rosters around the date of their first competition, which is the date on which participants are supposed to be counted. For example, they may have 18 female athletes (underrepresented sex) show up for practice at the beginning of the season, but they do not remove them from the roster after they quit or are not selected for the team or even when they cease participation before the first competition. Or, they intentionally keep them on the team until after the first competition and then cut them to produce a more manageable roster size of actual participants. In both cases, the EADA female participation number is artificially increased to include more athletes than those that actually participate because the institution manipulates the instruction to report the number of participants on the first date of competition.

Conversely, some schools drop men (the overrepresented sex) from the sport roster before the date of their first competition so that they do not count them on the EADA and then add them back to the roster after the date of their first competition. Alternatively, they intentionally keep male athletes out of the first game and do not add them to the team roster until the next day. Doing so has no athletic purpose. Schools do it to make their numbers look better.

When schools count male and female athletes differently in these ways, they violate the purpose and intent of Title IX and, by definition, they discriminate on the basis of sex. They do so to avoid adding new women's sports and, in so doing, they artificially limit women's athletic participation opportunities. This practice is the essence of sex discrimination and the problem that Title IX was intended to fix.

Proper Counting

Accordingly, to assess actual participation opportunities, one must carefully look at the numbers to determine how many athletes exist and how many receive the benefits of varsity participation. The 1979 policy interpretation explains that counted participants are those athletes

a. who are receiving the institutionally sponsored support normally provided to athletes competing at the institution involved (e.g., coaching, equipment, medical and training room services) on a regular basis during a sport's season; and

b. who are participating in organized practice sessions and other team meetings and activities on a regular basis during a sport's season; and

c. who are listed on the eligibility or squad lists maintained for each sport; or

d. who, because of injury, cannot meet a, b, or c but continue to receive financial aid on the basis of athletic ability.

OCR also uses this definition to determine the number of athletic participation opportunities provided for purposes of prong 1. Whether a student meets this definition is fact specific. In most circumstances, reviewers would assume that a student who is listed on a team roster is a participant. But given the increasing manipulation of roster and squad lists for the EADA, it is becoming more important to look behind the numbers to investigate which students are actually receiving a meaningful varsity experience.

Establishing Proper Team Sizes

A good strategy to determine optimal team size is to compare the number of athletes on each team to the number of athletes who would reasonably be expected to be on such a team given the nature of the specific sport. For example, most people would understand that because a basketball team can play only 5 athletes at a time, a varsity team of 25 is so large that most of those athletes would not ever compete or receive a varsity experience. This concept applies to all sports.

If a school carries 20 women on a cross country team, but the nature of the sport is such that only 12 of those women actually practice and compete, then the extra 8 athletes likely do not receive a genuine varsity experience—and likely are not expected ever to compete, especially if they were not recruited and do not receive athletic aid. By padding the number of participants on women's teams, schools not only fail to provide varsity benefits to the extra women but also devalue the varsity experience of all women on the team by spreading resources and playing time too thin. Women on such padded teams receive less coaching because of higher coach-to-athlete ratios, fewer benefits, and less (if any) playing time compared with men who play on smaller, more reasonably sized squads.

Although participation analysis is fact specific, coaches and other people who understand the nature and operation of each sport generally have clear views about the number of athletes they want on a team or that they believe they can reasonably carry on a team. They do not want to carry athletes who will never compete or who do not have the athletic ability to contribute to the team overall. True varsity teams are elite by nature, and thus such cuts must be made. Reasonable squad size is often a function of both the nature of the sport and the school's funding of the team. A school that fully funds a team and provides a large travel budget and a large coaching staff may be able to carry one or two more athletes than schools that have lean and mean budgets with high coach-to-athlete ratios. NCAA squad sizes provide excellent guidance about reasonable squad sizes. Average conference squad sizes are also usually reasonable comparators. The NCAA regularly issues updated athletic participation reports that include average squad sizes.

When Questions Should Be Raised

Whenever women's squad sizes are unusually large but men's squad sizes are not, or women's squad sizes are average and men's squad sizes are smaller than usual, the size of individual teams should be investigated to learn whether legitimate athletic reasons account for the differences (e.g., a team has a high number of injured or redshirt athletes that year). If legitimate reasons do not explain large differences or if those large differences persist over many years and many teams, the school is manipulating its women's participation numbers to feign prong 1 compliance without providing genuine varsity athletic participation opportunities to women. Ultimately, the analysis is fact specific, but such red flags should prompt further investigation of the reported numbers.

Need to Examine Recruiting Practices

When investigating the squad numbers, considering how the schools find their athletes is also important. If men's teams fill their rosters by recruiting high school athletes with the athletic ability to play at the school's competition level (e.g., junior college, Division I, Division III), then women's teams should find their athletes in the same way. If, instead, women's coaches must fill their mandatory minimum squad sizes by recruiting students from the dining hall or physical education classes, then the additional athletes may not have the skills necessary for varsity participation. This approach to filling a roster is evidence that the school does not provide recruiting or scholarship resources or that it does not intend to provide the additional athletes with the expected benefits of varsity participation. If a team has many extra athletes or if the program overall has many extra athletes who are not recruited, do not have the same skills as the recruited athletes, and do not receive athletic scholarships, they are likely there to fill an artificial quota, not to contribute to the team. This practice devalues the varsity experience for everyone. A recruited athlete with high-level sport skills does not want to waste valuable, NCAA-limited practice time training with students who have substantially less skill and who will never compete.

Manipulating Indoor and Outdoor Track Teams

Some schools go so far as to eliminate a men's sport season such as men's indoor track as a designated team, so that they can reduce the number of male participants in the athletic program by not counting the indoor and outdoor team twice (a currently permissible but questionable practice). Even so, the men's team can compete in indoor track meets as part of its maximum number of permissible competitions in outdoor track (an interesting historical loophole in NCAA rules).

Summary

In summary, a good management practice is to set a maximum limit on the number of participants in a varsity sport program based on the normal size of a team related to the rules and the nature of the sport to control costs and establish a coach-to-athlete instructional ratio that will support an elite-level athletic experience. It is an unacceptable management practice to set different limits for the same men's and women's sport or to set higher limits for women's sports than men's sports when the purpose of such roster manipulation is purely to meet a participation proportionality goal and doing so results in discriminatory treatment of the underrepresented sex. The intent of the athletic director is crucial when it comes to ethical conduct in sport.

ATHLETE SELECTION, PARTICIPATION, AND PREPARATION

After tryouts are completed and the final team roster has been determined, student-athletes must submit additional documents before they participate in practice. In addition, coaches, appropriate support personnel, and sport program supervisors must formalize planning and supervisory responsibilities of conditioning programs and practice sessions to provide safe training environments and ensure systems of accountability. Eight forms, policies, and risk assessments found in HK*Propel* and listed below address these issues.

11.4 **Form**—Clearance to Participate in Tryouts

Sample form that requires the signature of the academic services director and the head athletic trainer confirming that all required documents such as, but not limited to, proof of physician's clearance, academic eligibility review, and release of liability have been submitted before a student-athlete can participate in tryouts.

11.5 **Policy**—Clearance for Athletic Participation

Sample policy that details all information that must be submitted before an athlete who has been selected for a team may commence practice.

11.6 **Form**—Student-Athlete Participation Agreement

An agreement that student-athletes are required to read and sign outlining their responsibilities related to academic commitment, behavioral expectations, physical conditioning and training, and teamwork.

11.7 **Form**—Limited Privacy Waiver (FERPA and HIPAA Release)

Sample form that can be used for student-athletes to waive their rights under FERPA and HIPAA regulations related to specific personal information, educational records, and medical records.

11.8 **Form**—Unsupervised Preseason Conditioning Agreement

Sample agreement that student-athletes are required to read and sign outlining their understanding of the intent of unsupervised preseason conditioning and their responsibilities associated with participating in unsupervised preseason conditioning.

11.9 **Policy**—Athlete Preparation: Conditioning and Practice Sessions

Sample policy and procedures that address the planning and supervisory responsibilities of conditioning programs and practice sessions, as well as withholding student-athlete participation when appropriate.

11.10 **Form**—Preseason Conditioning Program Communication

Sample letter sent to student-athletes along with an unsupervised preseason conditioning program that describes the intent of the conditioning program and how to participate in it safely.

11.11 **Risk Assessment**—Checklist: Athlete Preparation and Participation

Sample checklist for an administrator overseeing a specific sport team that evaluates whether proper policies and procedures have been followed related to student-athletes' physical preparation for preseason, in-season, and nontraditional season conditioning programs and practice sessions.

Available in HK*Propel*.

COACH AND STUDENT-ATHLETE CONDUCT

11.12 MANAGEMENT TIP

Managing the Coach–Athlete Relationship

High school and college coaches interact with and establish strong relationships with student-athletes, as well as other children and young adults whom they may work with at summer camps and clinics. In essence, coaches are teachers and educational mentors, much like faculty members. The coach–athlete relationship, however, can be much more powerful than the relationship between students and classroom teachers because of the amount of time that a coach spends with the team and the emotional intensity of practice and competition. Although coaches use instructional and motivational strategies similar to those used by other teachers to help students overcome barriers that limit performance, many commonly accepted coaching techniques are at the edge of propriety. In addition, coaches establish team and individual athlete expectations to promote collective discipline and unity. Unfortunately, unreasonable expectations that go unchecked can result in intimidation, conditioned compliance, inappropriate methods of control of student-athletes, or creation of a group with a pack mentality. For these reasons, all athletic directors need to establish policies that address appropriate oversight of coaches related to the instruction of student-athletes, define coaches' proper and professional mentorship roles, require senior staff who supervise coaches to observe practices regularly, and use various assessment tools to measure student-athlete satisfaction. These policies will go a long way to establishing the culture of the department and creating an ethos of treating student-athletes with respect.

Coaches will undoubtedly consider this kind of oversight a form of micromanaging. The reality is that many coaches have been permitted to work in a vacuum and define the athletic director's role in two ways: (1) to guard the walls from outside intruders (parents, media, and so on) and (2) to secure more resources for their programs. Unfortunately, many athletic directors adopt this mentality and, in essence, do not lead their programs. The result is a fragmented culture that becomes highly dependent on the individual behavior of staff members who face the highest pressure, namely coaches. Managing coaches and the coach–athlete relationship is a form of protection for the coaches, for the department, and most important, for the student-athletes.

Another important responsibility of the athletic director is risk management in the area of student-athlete conduct. Athletic governance associations (state high school associations, the NCAA, and so on) and their member educational institutions are permitted to establish and enforce rules necessary to conduct athletic activities as long as these rules are not arbitrary or capricious and, in the enforcement of these rules, the athletic governance association or institution abides by its own policies and procedures. Note that the courts consider participation in athletics a privilege rather than a right, the latter of which would be strictly protected by the due process and equal protection clauses of the Fourteenth Amendment. The courts have even agreed that the most exceptional athletes, those who might be professional sport prospects, do not have a property interest in varsity interscholastic or intercollegiate sports.

Thus, the courts have upheld the right of institutions to establish codes of conduct and team rules for athletes and the right of athletic associations to limit or prohibit the participation of athletes who do not meet eligibility, recruiting, amateur status, or other rules that establish the conditions for fair competition between member institutions. But this consistent enforcement of institutional control by the courts does not mean that institutions will not face lawsuits. Common sense dictates that lawsuits will be less likely if institutions make sure that (1) rules created by coaches or teams are not arbitrary or capricious; (2) student-athletes and their parents are fully informed of expectations regarding conduct and rules compliance; and (3) fair complaint, waiver, and appeal processes exist even if those procedures are not required and do not meet the more formal and higher standards of due process. Risk Assessment 11.13 is a tool that the athletic director can use to ensure that model policies and procedures exist in this area.

11.13 Risk Assessment—Checklist: Student-Athlete Discipline and Behavior

An assessment tool that assists the athletic director in determining policy and procedural deficiencies in the areas of student-athlete discipline, behavior, and rules compliance.

Available in HK*Propel*.

11.14 PLANNING TOOL

Handling a Complaint Related to Coach Behavior

The athletic director must establish a fair process for handling complaints by student-athletes or parents related to the instructional ability or behavior of a coach. This process must be consistent with standard procedures for handling employee conflicts or performance issues but must also include more stringent procedural requirements when dealing with sexual harassment or grievances that might result in suspension or termination of employment of a coach or suspension or termination of participation by a student-athlete. The institution should engage its legal counsel to craft relevant policies and procedures or use established institutional procedures that guarantee due process and adjudication by unbiased personnel from outside the athletic department.

In general, the athletic director should be committed to the following general principles of action:

- The opportunity for a student-athlete to report cases of abuse to a neutral third party outside the athletic department
- Procedures that protect the privacy of the athletes and coaches involved including appropriate limitations on confidentiality
- Procedures for determining whether abuse has occurred that protect the legal rights of coaches and players until an investigation has been completed
- An appeals procedure in the event that the accused or the alleged victim is dissatisfied with the outcome of the investigation or hearing
- A requirement to inform those involved about statutes of limitations and opportunity for redress in a court of law
- Procedures that protect coaches and athletes from retaliation before, during, and after a hearing or appeals process; view retaliatory behavior as serious as the abuse itself; and acknowledge that there is zero tolerance for retaliation independent of whether a charge of abuse is substantiated
- A requirement for immediate action to ensure that the environment is free of abuse and ensure that an investigation proceeds in a timely manner
- Investigatory guidelines to ensure that investigators follow proper procedures for a fair and effective investigation

In the instance of any situation for which the institution has established a specific reporting and investigation procedure (sexual harassment, hazing, initiation rituals, Title IX complaints, designated employee issues, and so on), that process should take precedence over the athletic department's investigation or adjudication of the complaint. This default to institutional processes serves to protect the athletic department from allegations of bias. This dependence on institutional process, however, does not affect the obligation of the athletic department to correct any hostile environment immediately and give notice to appropriate parties of zero tolerance for retaliation against a complainant.

11.15 PLANNING TOOL

Student-Athlete Handbook, Team Rules, and Athlete Rights

The athletic department policy handbook is a complete collection of all policies and procedures guiding the conduct of the athletic program. The student-athlete handbook includes all the policies contained in the athletic department policy handbook that deal with student-athletes. Team rules, conditioning programs, playbooks, and other sport-specific information are not included in either the department handbook or the student-athlete handbook. Thus, student-athletes should receive the student-athlete handbook, team rules, and any other sport-specific documents so that they fully understand both their rights and their responsibilities. Transparency is integral to the integrity, success, and cohesiveness of an intercollegiate athletic program.

One of the first things that the athletic director and staff must decide is what information to include in the student-athlete handbook versus the team-by-team policies and rules documents. The following is a list of elements that typically appear in department-wide student-athlete handbooks:

- A statement about the department's philosophy of educational sport, including vision, mission, and goals
- General behavioral expectations of student-athletes as representatives of the institution, usually taken from the athlete participation agreement
- Academic and athletic association eligibility requirements for participation
- Financial aid rules and regulations
- General tryout and team selection standards
- Training-room rules and procedures
- Study hall and academic support programs rules and requirements
- Care and responsibility for uniforms and equipment
- Departmental, conference, and governing-body drug-testing and substance abuse policies
- Prohibitions from gambling and other behaviors that would result in serious sanctions
- Statement of zero tolerance for discrimination, sexual harassment, and hazing along with sanctions for such behaviors
- Professional conduct expectations of coaches including prohibition of sexual misconduct with student-athletes, maintenance of a safe and nonhostile environment, and so on
- Expectations for student-athlete development and community service
- Rules governing transportation to contests (unless a tiered model reflects different travel policies, in which case transportation policies are covered in sport-by-sport policies and rules)
- Permission forms, release from liability, assumption of risk
- Conditions under which the right to participate or an athletic scholarship may be terminated
- Grievance and appeals procedures

Formal team rules and other sport-specific supplementary information should be separately provided to student-athletes. This information should include the following:

- Specific behavioral expectations as a team representative
- Academic expectations
- Time commitment
- Self-discipline
- Coach, athlete, and team relationships
- Specific travel policies (dress, departure times, and so on)
- Game-day policies (curfews, apparel, and so on)
- Role of parents
- Conflict resolution

Both of these resources—the student-athlete handbook and team rules—should be annually reviewed with student-athletes. Policies must be in place that require coaches and other appropriate specific personnel (strength coaches, trainers, substance abuse counselor, and so on) to deliver this review. In addition, allowing athletes to collaborate on the construction of team codes of conduct is an educationally sound approach. Student-athlete involvement advances the prospect of accountability, fair treatment, and team building while contributing to students' educational experience. Policies 11.16, 11.17, and 11.18 found in HK*Propel* address student-athlete handbook and team rule issues.

Many athletic departments have well-documented policies and rules for student-athletes but rarely consider or address the rights of athletes. Within our Team Rules and Disciplinary Procedures document (11.16 in HK*Propel*) and our Student-Athlete Participation Agreement (11.6 in HK*Propel*) the following athlete rights are addressed:

- Coach conduct expectations that prohibit abusive, hostile learning environments and intimate relationships between coaches and athletes
- The creation of a safe learning environment where athletes can and should self-report any physical, mental, or emotional issues or forms of abuse without fearing retaliation from coaches
- A requirement that team rules should be developed with student-athlete input
- A clear prohibition of hazing, intimidation, or sexual harassment of athletes
- Support for students to report violations of governing body rules or coach/team misconduct without fear of retaliation
- A system of due process that will be followed if a student-athlete is accused of a policy or rules violation that could suspend or terminate participation.

Throughout this book, we have included policies and procedures that not only protect student-athletes' rights to participate in a fair, safe, equitable, and nonthreatening athletic environment but also provide athletes with the opportunity to voice concerns and share in decision making. For example:

- In our chapter on governance, we promote the need for a student-athlete advisory council.
- In our chapter on ethics, we have strong policies on standards of professional coaching conduct that include a professional code of conduct agreement all coaches must sign and a section on the expectations of ethical recruiting.
- In our chapter on student-athlete support services, we make strong arguments that the manager in charge of the academic support unit should report to an administrator outside of the athletic department to maintain academic integrity and reduce conflicts of interest. Additionally, we address the need for model student-life programs and for strong mental health support services where counselors do not report to anyone in the athletic department so student-athlete confidentiality is protected.
- In our chapter on sports medicine, we include clear policies that give trainers and team doctors full authority to make medical decisions, return-to-play decisions, and decisions about prescription drugs and supplements with no interference from coaches.
- In our chapters on the operational structure of the athletic program and on diversity, we describe Title IX compliance so women and men enjoy the same benefits of participation.
- In our chapters on event management and on facilities operations, there are numerous procedures, policies, and risk assessment checklists that help athletic staff provide a safe playing environment.

There are other issues related to athletes' rights that are harder to address through policies and procedures. One of those issues is how to determine what qualifies as constitutionally protected speech and expression rights for college athletes. Many people remember Colin Kaepernick, the NFL quarterback who knelt during the playing of the national anthem to protest social injustice, especially the killing of Black people by police.

What about college athletes? To what extent should athletic departments control athlete behavior on social media or in connection to political or social activism? Are requirements to stand during the national anthem, to cover body tattoos, to take off armbands, or to have athletes provide the athletic department with social media passwords violate First Amendment rights? In a landmark Supreme Court case, *Tinker* v. *Des Moines Independent Community School District,* a high school principal suspended students for wearing black armbands in school, stating that it would disrupt learning. The Supreme Court ruled that neither students nor teachers "shed their constitutional rights to freedom of speech or expression at the schoolhouse gate. The Court took the position that school officials could not prohibit only on the suspicion that the speech might disrupt the learning environment" (United States Courts). These are tough issues that all athletic directors will face and will necessitate that they work with institutional legal counsel to address situations as they arise. However, there have been situations in college athletics that have tested the waters. For example:

- In 2021, the Bluefield men's basketball team was sanctioned by the university president, David Olive, with a one-game suspension for kneeling during the national anthem. Olive wrote: "The basis for my decision stemmed from my own awareness of how kneeling is perceived by some in our country, and I did not think a number of our alumni, friends, and donors of the College would view the act of kneeling during the anthem in a positive way" (Castaneda, 2021).
- In 2017, the Albright College football team voted to kneel during the coin toss before a game and stand during the national anthem. Their message was one of team unity that respected racial differences. A backup quarterback decided to kneel on his own during the playing of the national anthem. The players had been told that there could be consequences if they decided to kneel during the anthem. The player was dismissed from the team.
- In 2015, the president of the University of Missouri System, Tim Wolfe, came under fire for failure to respond to a series of racist incidents on campus including the drawing of a swastika with human feces on a residence hall wall. Student body protests ensued and 30 athletes from the University of Missouri football team announced that they would not practice or play in games until Wolfe was fired. Wolfe resigned and the football players returned to the team.

It is important to note that not all speech and behavior is protected. The First Amendment does not protect speech that could be categorized as "fighting words" that can inflame or incite violence. Speech or behavior that constitutes threats of imminent harm to another person, involves patently offensive sexual material, or is used in committing a crime such as sexual harassment is not protected. Higher education institutions have been quick to penalize teams that have engaged in non-protected speech. For example:

- In 2020, Amherst College suspended its men's lacrosse team through the 2021 season for bigoted language that ridiculed the transgender community and included racial slurs. Additionally, a player painted a swastika on the face of a teammate who had passed out at a party. The entire team was sanctioned because the team would not identify which team member was responsible.
- In 2018, a football player was dismissed at the University of Arizona when a video he recorded was circulated on social media that showed him referring to teammates as monkeys.
- In 2016, Harvard University discovered a "vulgar" scouting report in which men's soccer players rated the sexual appeal of members of the women's soccer team and provided explicit descriptions of their physical traits and preferred sexual positions. The university found evidence that this practice had gone on for at least four years and the documents were publicly accessible on Google. The university canceled the remainder of the men's soccer season and denied the team participation in any postseason play.
- In 2016, the Columbia University men's wrestling season was suspended due to text

messages sent by members of the team that were described as racist, misogynistic, and homophobic. Similarly, the Amherst College men's cross country team was disciplined due to a series of emails and messages that were deemed racist, misogynistic, and homophobic and included references to women as "meat slabs" or a "walking STD." A third situation in the same year occurred at Princeton University, where the administration suspended the men's swimming and diving season after it discovered material on a university-sponsored team LISTSERV that it deemed vulgar, offensive, misogynistic, and racist.

To believe that these examples are isolated instances would be naïve. Peer pressure and group dynamics coupled with the proclivity of young people to frequently express themselves on social media is a recipe for disaster. So what should an athletic director do? The Drake Group published a position statement titled *College Athlete Codes of Conduct and Issues Related to Freedom of Speech and Expression.* The authors believe that many of the recommendations listed below can help athletic directors navigate freedom of speech and expression issues. The Drake Group position statement includes the following recommendations:

> *Although the First Amendment only applies to public institutions, public and private institutions alike should honor First Amendment rights because freedom of inquiry lies at the heart of higher education.*
>
> *When considering restrictions on athletes' viewpoints expressed by speech or behavior, institutions should answer these test questions: (1) does the restriction prevent a significant material disruption of the educational environment, (2) is the prohibited activity directed at others (individuals or groups) causing harm or a hostile or chilling educational environment, and (3) are other reasonable time, place, and manner restrictions available that could satisfy both the school's interests and athletes' interests.*
>
> *Athletic directors should identify as "red flags" and evaluate especially carefully any proposed restriction of athlete viewpoint expression that is justified by the following: (1) "protects the brand"; (2) is imposed in the name of "team uniformity"; (3) advances "team chemistry"; (4) protects a sponsor relationship; (5) "saves the athlete from making a mistake on a social media platform"; (6) makes sure donors don't get angry or diminish their financial support; or (7) "promotes sportsmanship". Athletic departments should consider whether athlete education programs, rather than restrictions of speech and other expression, are not more appropriate response to such concerns.*
>
> *Athlete education programs on codes of conduct and First Amendment rights should occur annually and should cover unprotected activities (such as threatening speech or physical assault, bullying, hazing, sexual harassment, violations of law such as drug use or confidentiality of teammates medical information, etc.)*
>
> *Lawyers not employed by the athletics department should review proposed restrictions of athlete speech and behavior.* (The Drake Group, pp. 2–3)

Another Drake Group recommendation that the authors agree with and have mentioned several times in this book is that student-athletes should be treated in the same way that all university students are treated. Therefore, disciplinary actions regarding athlete participation rights, investigations, and adjudications should follow the same processes established for all students.

11.16 Policy—Team Rules and Disciplinary Procedures

Sample policies and procedures that address team and department-wide rules, strategies for handling violations, potential sanctions, student-athlete appeals, and due process.

11.17 Policy—Alcohol, Tobacco, and Drug Use

Sample policies and procedures that address the responsibilities of specific personnel for educating student-athletes about alcohol, drug, and tobacco use as well as potential sanctions for violations and the process that must be used for appeals.

11.18 Policy—Hazing, Sexual Harassment, and Other Intimidation Tactics

Sample policies and procedures that address the definitions of hazing, sexual harassment, and other intimidation factors; the responsibilities to report violations committed by personnel or student-athletes; possible sanctions for violations; and the process that must be used for appeals.

Available in HK*Propel*.

11.19 MANAGEMENT TIP

Consider Retaining a Substance Abuse Counselor

Issues related to student-athletes and substance abuse can be complex and at times dangerous. Over-the-counter supplements have compounded these problems. Many supplements cause dehydration or other side effects that could be harmful or even deadly during intense training. In addition, serious substance abuse is often a result of emotional problems. Student-athletes are reluctant to share information about substance abuse with their coaches, and even if they did, coaches, and to some extent athletic trainers, are ill equipped to counsel student-athletes who have substance abuse issues. Therefore, the athletic director must identify a qualified professional on campus outside the athletic department who can serve as the substance abuse counselor. The responsibilities of the substance abuse counselor would be as follows:

- Administer educational seminars for student-athletes and staff annually
- Disseminate information to staff, student-athletes, and parents about current research and findings on tobacco, alcohol, and drug abuse
- In collaboration with the sports medicine staff, annually review and edit the policies on tobacco, alcohol, and drug abuse
- Disseminate the athletic department's tobacco, alcohol, and drug abuse policies to student-athletes and parents annually
- Monitor and ensure the implementation of the athletic department's tobacco, alcohol, and drug abuse policies

11.20 MANAGEMENT TIP

Uniforms and Equipment: Model Practices and Risk Mitigation

Equipment Inspection, Maintenance, Repairs, and Replacement Schedules

Damaged, broken, or defective equipment poses significant risk for participant injury and the potential for litigation. Thus, policies and procedures related to equipment inspection, instruction on the proper use of equipment, ensuring the proper fit of protective equipment, maintenance, repairs, and replacement schedules are critical responsibilities of the athletic director. Policy 11.21 is a sample policy that addresses each of these elements.

Record keeping is particularly important in this area to demonstrate that the athletic department is following manufacturers' instructions, making necessary repairs, and following replacement schedules consistent with industry recommendations. These elements are critical in controlling risk. Forms 11.22 and 11.23 are sample forms that perform this function.

Proper Storage and Signage

Facility storage and safety signage is an often forgotten area of administrative policy. For instance, it is important to mandate that free weights be racked and that strength and conditioning–room equipment and mats be wiped down after use. Foils used by the fencing team must be removed and returned to storage in a methodical way so that they are not left out for any person to pick up and use. Trampolines need to be folded and closed with chain and lock following use. One senior staff member should be assigned the responsibility to audit all equipment that requires special storage, locking arrangements, or safety signage.

Student-Athlete Notification and Responsibility

Policies and procedures must be established that ensure student-athlete accountability for the care and return of equipment and uniforms. More important, these processes should inform each student-athlete of his or her responsibility to report damage or concerns with any equipment immediately and to cease using it until such equipment is inspected. Such policies also ensure that athletic governance association rules related to the provision of nonpermissible benefits (such as student-athletes keeping uniforms or equipment

11.21 Policy—Equipment Selection, Purchase, Maintenance, Issuance, and Safety

Sample policy that details all elements of a comprehensive policy on equipment selection, purchase, inspection, inventory, and safety.

11.22 Form—Equipment Inventory and Replacement Schedule

Sample form to use for equipment inventory, which also serves the function of designating a replacement schedule, recording replacements, and specifying access restrictions.

11.23 Form—Equipment Inspection, Repair, and Maintenance Record

Sample form to use for equipment inventory, which also serves the function of providing a repair and maintenance record.

Available in HK*Propel*.

in violation of such rules) are followed. Obviously, such policies also have financial significance from the standpoint of preventing loss, planning for replacement expenditures, and reminding employees of their obligation to follow institutional purchasing procedures. Another ancillary by-product of such policies is the establishment of standards regarding the design, color, and display of proper logos for the selection of uniforms. Policy 11.24 and Form 11.25 enable those functions.

Risk Management

Key to the management of risk and reducing potential liability is the regular use of risk assessment checklists to make sure that policies and procedures exist, that staff and student-athletes are adhering to those policies, and that required signage and other safety mechanisms are in place. Risk Assessment 11.26 represents such an evaluation instrument that should be used on an annual basis.

11.24 **Policy**—Uniform Selection, Purchasing, and Issuance

Sample policy that establishes standards and processes to be used for the design, purchase, and issuance of team uniforms.

11.25 **Form**—Student-Athlete Equipment and Uniform Checkout and Return Record

Sample form to use for the issuance and return of equipment and uniforms to student-athletes that includes the obligation of student-athletes to report damaged equipment immediately.

11.26 **Risk Assessment**—Checklist: Athletic Equipment and Apparel

Sample risk assessment checklist that reviews equipment policies and practices that should be in place.

Available in HK*Propel*.

TRAVEL

Team travel arrangements need to be standardized to ensure that male and female athletes are treated equally and that travel is as safe as possible. Many elements such as modes of transportation (bus, airline, van), quality of hotels, per diem food allocations, and number of athletes assigned to a room must be examined to ensure equal treatment by establishing policies that are either not gender based (e.g., all teams traveling more than 200 miles [320 km] must use a chartered bus) or mandate the same treatment for male and female athletes. HK*Propel* contains the following sample policies, forms, and risk assessments that can be used to administer all elements of team travel logistics.

11.27 **Policy**—Team Travel

A sample policy that covers head coach responsibilities, documentation of travel itineraries, use of a travel coordinator or agency, rules regarding departures and returns, driver or travel vehicle insurance, and student-athletes who do not travel with the team.

11.28 **Policy**—Ground Transportation

A sample policy that governs nonairline travel including acquisition of vehicles, driver requirements and responsibilities, coach responsibilities, mandatory rest stops and drive time, accident and emergency procedures, violations resulting in loss of driving privileges, guidelines for use of noninstitutional vehicles, and required documentation.

11.29 **Policy**—Air Transportation

A sample policy that governs airline travel including flying decisions when noncommercial aircraft are used and requirements for the use of chartered aircraft.

11.30 **Form**—Travel Arrangements Request Form

A sample form to be used by the travel coordinator that requires the coach or other designated staff member to indicate destination, preferred mode of transportation, authorized drivers, preferred lodging, and rooming lists.

11.31 **Form**—Hotel Confirmation Request and Rooming List

A sample form to be used by the travel coordinator to confirm all hotel arrangements with the hotel being used for a team trip.

11.32 **Form**—Team Travel Itinerary

A sample form to be completed by the coach or traveling administrator that includes all information about the trip including emergency contact numbers.

11.33 **Form**—Approval of Student-Athlete Not Traveling With Team

A sample form to be used to obtain athletic department permission for a student-athlete not to travel with the team. A reason for the special travel arrangement is required.

11.34 **Policy**—Band and Cheerleader Travel

A sample policy that specifies the contest for which band and cheerleaders may travel to away events and the size limitations of the travel party.

11.35 **Risk Assessment**—Checklist: Team Travel

A risk assessment checklist that enables the athletic director to confirm that model policies and procedures are in place with regard to team travel.

Available in HK*Propel*.

AWARDS

All interscholastic and intercollegiate athletic programs have annual participation awards, and awards may be given for league or conference championships and state or national championships. Awards may be presented in conjunction with an annual awards banquet or a special gathering for the team. Policies must exist to govern these awards because athletic governance associations usually have established limits on the value of such gifts and Title IX requires that male and female athletes be treated equally. Similarly, gender equity laws mandate that awards events for male and female athletes be comparable. Thus, it would not be permissible to have an annual awards dinner for the football team at the finest steakhouse in the city and then have all other men's and women's sports be feted with a chicken buffet catered by Kentucky Fried Chicken.

The athletic director also needs to address the question of whether staff members besides the members of the team will receive championship rings and address similar questions regarding controls on the number of recipients. In addition, the selection process needs to be defined for special awards such as the team most valuable player and most improved player. Sample policies 11.36 through 11.40 in HK*Propel* are examples of the types of policies that should be put in place.

11.36 **Policy**—Annual Participation Awards

A sample policy that demonstrates the types of eligibility criteria that should be established for annual participation awards and the types of awards.

11.37 **Policy**—Special Awards

A sample policy that demonstrates the types of annual special awards (MVP, scholar-athlete of the year, and so on) that may be established and the criteria for each award.

11.38 **Policy**—Conference Championship Awards

A sample policy that defines eligibility for conference or league championship awards, the maximum value of such awards, and individuals other than team members and coaches who may receive such awards.

11.39 **Policy**—National Championship Awards

A sample policy that defines eligibility for state or national championship awards, the maximum value of such awards, and individuals other than team members and coaches who may receive such awards.

11.40 **Policy**—Annual Awards Banquet

A sample policy that mandates an annual all-sports awards event open to the public and the prohibition of individual team events. The policy also specifies who receives complimentary tickets.

Available in HK*Propel*.

BIBLIOGRAPHY

TEAM ADMINISTRATION

Alfred University. (1999). *Initiation rites and athletics: A national survey of NCAA sports teams.* https://eric.ed.gov/?id=ED463713.

American Sport Education Program. (2007). *Coaches' guide to team policies.* Champaign, IL: Human Kinetics.

Associated Press. (2016, December 13). Amherst College suspends cross-country team for sexually explicit messages. *USA Today.* https://www.usatoday.com/story/sports/college/2016/12/13/amherst-college-cross-country-suspended-sexually-explicit-messages/95367570.

Berkman, Seth. (2016, November 14). Columbia suspends wrestling season over lewd and racist text messages. *New York Times.* https://www.nytimes.com/2016/11/15/sports/columbia-suspends-wrestling-season-lewd-text-messages.html.

Boston University. (N.d.). *Student-Athlete Code of Conduct.* https://www.bu.edu/policies/student-athlete-code-of-conduct.

Branch, John. (2017, September 7). The awakening of Colin Kaepernick. *New York Times.* https://www.nytimes.com/2017/09/07/sports/colin-kaepernick-nfl-protests.html.

Castaneda, Bea. (2021, February 12). Bluefield College suspends basketball team for kneeling during anthem. *The College Post.* https://thecollegepost.com/bluefield-basketball-team-suspension-kneeling.

Ciccotta, Tom. (2020, April 6). Amherst College suspends entire lacrosse team after 3 players accused of racism. *Breitbart.* https://www.breitbart.com/tech/2020/04/06/amherst-college-suspends-entire-lacrosse-team-after-3-players-accused-of-racism.

Cohen v. Brown University. http://caselaw.findlaw.com/us-1st-circuit/1368039.html.

Covell, D., & Walker, S. (2016). *Managing intercollegiate athletics.* New York: Routledge.

Drew University. (2007). *Department of Intercollegiate Athletics policy manual.* Madison, NJ. Unpublished manuscript.

Duke University. (2019). *Student-athlete handbook.* Durham, NC. https://goduke.com/documents/2019/8/7/638784.pdf.

Ehrmann, J. (2011). *Inside out coaching: How sports can transform lives.* New York: Simon & Schuster.

Gleeson, S. (2015, November 8). Missouri football players to boycott until president Wolfe resigns. *USA Today.* https://www.usatoday.com/story/sports/ncaaf/2015/11/07/missouri-tigers-football-players-boycott-tim-wolfe-president-resigns/75399504.

Lake Forest High School. *Parent/Athlete Handbook.* Lake Forest, IL. https://www.lakeforestschools.org/schools/lfhs/athletics/parentathlete-handbook.

Lewis, M. (2005). *Coach: Lessons on the game of life.* New York: Norton.

Louisiana State University. (N.d.). *LSU compliance: Student-athletes.* Baton Rouge, LA. http://www.compliance.lsu.edu/studentathletes-intro.

Louisiana State University. (2019, July 11). *Strategic plan book.* Baton Rouge, LA. https://lsusports.net/sports/2019/7/11/204774365.aspx.

Martens. R. (2012). *Successful coaching* (4th ed.). Champaign, IL: Human Kinetics.

Mele, C. (2016, December 15). Princeton is latest Ivy League school to suspend team over vulgar materials. *New York Times.* https://www.nytimes.com/2016/12/15/sports/princeton-mens-swimming-suspended.html.

National Collegiate Athletic Association. (2016). *NCAA goals study of the student-athlete experience.* https://www.ncaa.org/sites/default/files/GOALS_2015_summary_jan2016_final_20160627.pdf.

National Collegiate Athletic Association. (2017). *NCAA student-athlete substance use study.* Indianapolis, IN: NCAA. https://www.ncaa.org/about/resources/research/ncaa-student-athlete-substance-use-study.

National Collegiate Athletic Association. (2021). *2020–2021 NCAA Division I manual.* Indianapolis, IN: NCAA. https://web3.ncaa.org/lsdbi/reports/getReport/90008.

National Highway Transportation Safety Administration. (N.d.). *15 passenger vans.* https://www.nhtsa.gov/road-safety/15-passenger-vans.

Oklahoma State University Athletics. (2015). *Oklahoma State University policy and procedures: Team travel.* https://okstate.com/documents/2015/10/29/Team_Travel.pdf.

Schlabach, M. (2017, October 11). Division III Albright College cuts player for kneeling during anthem. *ESPN.com.* https://www.espn.com/college-football/story/_/id/20988938/division-iii-albright-college-cuts-player-kneeling-anthem.

Seelye, K. & Bidgood, J. (2016, November 4). Harvard men's soccer team is sidelined for vulgar scouting report. *New York Times.* https://www.nytimes.com/2016/11/05/us/harvard-mens-soccer-team-scouting-report.html.

The Drake Group. (2018). *Position Statement: College Athlete Codes of Conduct and Issues Related to Freedom of Speech and Expression.* https://www.thedrakegroup.org/2018/11/15/college-athlete-codes-of-conduct-and-issues-related-to-freedom-of-speech-and-expression.

United States Courts. (1969, February 24). *Facts and cases summary: Tinker v. Des Moines.* https://www.uscourts.gov/educational-resources/educational-activities/facts-and-case-summary-tinker-v-des-moines.

University of Texas at Austin. (2010). *Intercollegiate athletics policy manual.* Austin, TX. No longer available.

WomenSport International. (2004). *Report on sexual harassment and abuse in sport.* https://womensportinternational.org/index.php/1998-2004-task-force-on-sexual-harassment.

Wooden, J., & Jamison, S. (2005). *Wooden on leadership: How to create a successful organization.* New York: McGraw-Hill.

CHAPTER

12

Event Management and Scheduling

No department on a high school or college campus conducts more events open to the public than the athletic department. Most athletic programs host 150 to 200 home competitions per year, several postseason conference or state or national championship events, workshops, clinics, summer camps, and fund-raising events that use 8 to 15 different physical activity facilities, which must also be scheduled for practices and community events. For each of these events, functions such as facility setup, ticket selling, security, crowd control, concessions, hiring of officials, media accommodations, emergency medical arrangements, and postevent breakdown and cleanup must be executed. Undoubtedly, event management is one of the most important administrative responsibilities of the athletic department staff. The documents in this chapter, in both the book and HK*Propel*, focus on sample policies, forms, and other tools that will help the athletic director put model systems in place to perform those functions.

TYPES OF DOCUMENTS

Management tip—Factual background information, insights, problem-solving strategies, and suggestions for the athletic director

Planning tool—Steps to take or factors that should be considered in the development of strategic plans, action plans, professional development plans, or governance systems

Educational resource—Handouts that can be used to educate staff members, campus constituents, volunteers, or student-athletes

Policy—Sample policies and procedures that should be adopted by an athletic department after customization and review by appropriate expert institutional or school district officials

Form—Sample forms, letters, or job descriptions

Evaluation instrument—Administrative tools that help the athletic director, a supervisor, or an employee assess job performance and evaluate program content

Risk assessment—Checklists that help the athletic director, a supervisor, or an employee identify risks and prevent litigation

SCHEDULING OF PRACTICES AND CONTESTS

Although the scheduling of all facilities on high school and college campuses has been greatly enhanced by a variety of exceptional software programs, scheduling athletic facilities is a much more complicated process than managing classroom or single-purpose facilities. Responding to changes in practice times; accommodating requests of visiting teams constrained by travel limitations; accommodating important community events that are essential for maintaining institutional town and gown relationships; establishing academic, cocurricular, extracurricular, and noncurricular program priorities; and dealing with the effect of weather on an extensive array of outdoor facilities are daily challenges. The first step is making sure that all athletic staff understand institutional scheduling priorities and the process to be followed for scheduling athletic program activities. Policy 12.1 is such a document, and Form 12.2 is a sample facility request document. Policy 12.3 communicates scheduling guidelines to coaches that limit classes missed and the quality and quantity of events that may be scheduled. Policy 12.4 contains instructions to coaches that segment responsibilities for scheduling and executing contracts related to such schedules, and Form 12.5 is a sample contest agreement. Form 12.6 enables an organized process to report and handle requests for schedule changes. Policy 12.7 provides instructions related to the offer of guarantees (e.g., cash, free hotel rooms) as a scheduling incentive.

12.1 **Policy**—Facility Scheduling for Athletic Activities

A sample policy that explains institutional scheduling priorities and basic athletic department scheduling policies.

12.2 **Form**—Facilities Request

A sample form to submit practice, competition, and other facility use requests.

12.3 **Policy**—Competition Schedules

A sample policy to establish guidelines on the quantity and quality of competitions to be scheduled, limits on classes missed, travel limitations, and responsibilities of coaches related to submission of requests for use of facilities.

12.4 **Policy**—Contest Contracts

A sample policy that segments responsibilities for creating the contest schedule and processing contracts that obligate parties to participate in such contests.

12.5 **Form**—Contest Agreement

A sample agreement that can be used to obligate both teams to the scheduling of a contest and specifies the rules, officiating provisions, provision of complimentary tickets, and financial considerations, if any.

12.6 **Form**—Request for Schedule Change

A sample form that can be used to process requests for changes in practice or competition schedules.

12.7 **Policy**—Offering and Accepting Guarantees

A sample policy that specifies department rules related to the approval of an offer of cash, room nights, transportation, or other incentives of value to enable the scheduling of an athletic contest.

Available in HK*Propel*.

EVENT OPERATIONS

The athletic department's event management responsibilities are extensive with regard to the volume of events conducted and the complexity of functions associated with managing events. A series of sample policies and forms are offered in HK*Propel* to assist the athletic director in managing these processes. Policy 12.8 and Forms 12.9 and 12.10 are a suggested organized approach to the hiring, assignment, evaluation, and payment of contest officials. Policy 12.11 specifies responsibilities associated with the accommodation of visiting teams. Policy 12.12 is a model approach to dealing with all issues related to the management of event ticketing. Policy 12.13 specifies best practices related to handling cash at athletic events or other activities such as summer camps or workshops. Form 12.14 supports such a policy. Policy 12.16 defines rules related to bidding to host special events such as tournaments and postseason championships. Policy 12.17 is a model approach to handling the media at athletic events, and Policy 12.18 is a model approach to rules related to the display of signage and distribution of commercial products at athletic events.

12.8 Policy—Hiring, Assignment, and Evaluation of Sports Officials

A sample policy that can be used to communicate responsibilities related to the acquisition, payment, and evaluation of officials.

12.9 Form—Official's Payment Voucher

A sample form that can be used to verify the provision of officiating services and to request the payment of fees and expenses to officials.

12.10 Form—Evaluation of Contest Officials

A sample form that can be used to evaluate the performance and professionalism of game officials.

12.11 Policy—Arrangements for Visiting Teams

A sample policy that specifies coach and staff member responsibilities related to accommodating the needs of visiting teams.

12.12 Policy—Tickets

A sample policy that deals with multiple ticketing issues such as ticket pricing, complimentary and promotional tickets, lost or stolen tickets, and conditions constituting a revocable license.

12.13 Policy—Cash-Handling Procedures at Events and Summer Camps

A sample policy that deals with model practices regarding the handling and security of cash collected in relation to athletic events, summer camps, and other activities.

12.14 Form—Cash Box Request and Reconciliation

A sample form that can be used to request a cash box and subsequently used to reconcile cash upon return of the box.

12.16 Policy—Bidding to Host Special and Championship Events

A sample policy that specifies the conditions required to bid for hosting special events or championship events and the approval process for such bids.

12.17 Policy—Support of Print and Electronic Media

A sample policy that specifies responsibilities related to meeting the needs of print and electronic media covering athletic events such as parking, credentials, accommodations, provision of statistics, and interview rules.

12.18 Policy—Signage, Distribution of Commercial Products, and Promotional Activities

A sample policy that specifies prohibitions related to employee and student-athlete participation in promotional activities, prohibited fund-raising, permissible and nonpermissible signage, and rules regarding signage and commercial product sampling.

Available in HK*Propel*.

12.15 MANAGEMENT TIP

Alternatives to Concessions Outsourcing

Many potential liabilities are associated with hosting an event. Managing concessions may carry significant risk regarding cleanliness, food-handling issues, properly trained staff, accuracy of preevent and postevent inventory, inappropriate consumption of product, and cash-handling procedures. Athletic directors must weigh the risks against the projected concessions revenue. Of course, the size and scope of concessions play a big role in determining whether to outsource concessions operations. If a team wants to set up a table with candy, bags of chips, and soda using all packaged goods and no food preparation for an event that is projected to draw 300 people, the decision is easy. But a packed stadium that holds thousands of people brings about a set of problems that may include not only regular concessions stands but also catered services for suites, media rooms, and so on.

According to Fried (2010), approximately 30 percent of colleges with substantial concessions operations elect the outsourcing option and pay between 25 percent and 40 percent of the concessions revenue to do so. In addition, many educational institutions are creating internal policies that prevent employees from being involved in any food-handling operations unless all the food is prepackaged. This approach is particularly common in institutions that have an outside vendor for all their dining hall and catering needs. The athletic director should be part of the negotiations when campus food service contracts are being constructed or are up for renewal so that options for including part or all of athletic events concessions are considered for inclusion in a broad institutional contract. Including athletic events in a larger concessions agreement makes outsourcing for small events more likely.

If the concessions operation is going to be administered by the athletic department, the following procedures should be followed:

- Make a commitment to train workers annually on food-handling and cooking procedures and monitor those procedures to ensure that they are followed diligently. This task is particularly difficult if the athletic department is using student workers or volunteers (see Policy 15.26 for sample policy governing the use of volunteers to run concessions).
- If training is not feasible, sell only prepackaged foods.
- Sell unwrapped (bagels, donuts, and so on) or cooked food (hot dogs, hamburgers, and so on) only if the concessions stand is within a closed structure that is on both a regular and an event-based cleaning schedule. Preevent and postevent cleaning must be completed and diligently monitored.
- Purchasing of products, preevent inventory, and postevent inventory should be completed only by full-time staff. Do not allow students or volunteers to handle these responsibilities.
- Ensure that the concessions area is kept clean and free from insects throughout an event.
- Follow appropriate inspection schedules for cleanliness, equipment maintenance, and bugs.
- Proper storage of products at the end of an event should be monitored by a full-time employee.
- Products with expiration dates must be checked before being sold and discarded no later than the expiration date, even if the food seems fine.
- If concessions are handled by several constituents (different teams or volunteer groups), assign one full-time staff member to oversee management so that there is consistency from one group to the next.
- If anyone complains about the taste of food or feels sick after eating something, discontinue selling that product immediately from all concessions areas.

12.19 PLANNING TOOL

Factors Dictating Preevent Risk Assessment

Whenever the athletic department is going to administer a major or new event, significant planning takes place that includes input from a variety of campus and department personnel. More often, mistakes occur because people tend to follow the script when an event has already been administered once. Assuming that similar events, such as all men's lacrosse games, will require the same preevent setup and procedures is not safe. Although similarities will be present, a small difference in one particular event could create unpredicted problems. For example, most weeknight games may not include a large number of student fans from the opposing institution. But will that be the case if the contestants are particularly strong rivals? Should different decisions about security be made? Therefore, a worthy exercise is to go through the following list of questions before each event and try to foresee problems before they arise.

- What are all the facility areas that will be used by this event? For each of these areas, what are the concerns about how the facility will handle the corresponding demands? For example, the visitors' locker room may be fine for every team on the schedule except one that has a particularly large roster, or outdoor areas may not have wheelchair pathways.
- Are there any special concerns about moving fans and participants (including officials, the band, and so on) from their starting points and into, through, and out of the facility? For example, if an event will require off-site overflow parking, are specific plans in place to deal with the volume of people who must be shuttled to and from the site at the beginning and end of the game? More buses would likely be needed after the game when everyone is leaving at the same time.
- Does the day of the week, the time of day, or the day of the year change any decisions about event management and security? For example, night and weekend games may demand higher security because of the potential that fans will be drunk on arrival. Rental stands may not be available the day after Thanksgiving for the soccer championship if the institution is located near New York City and the Macy's Thanksgiving Day parade rents stands from all the local vendors.
- Is the event part of a specific rivalry or is the event itself politically charged in a way that would demand different decisions about event management and security? For example, will a player who was recently charged with steroid use be competing? Could this circumstance cause unruly fan behavior such as taunting? Does the outcome of this particular event determine qualification for postseason play?
- Will the profile of the spectators or participants create the need for different event management and security decisions? For example, if a heavy metal band is performing in the stadium rather than the jazz artist that performed last month, different protocols, setups, and procedures may have to be implemented.
- Does this particular event carry a higher risk of medical concerns than other similar events? For example, one Division III school always had the required certified trainer at its men's lacrosse games. One team from its conference, however, sponsored a Division I men's ice hockey program. Some of these bigger, stronger hockey athletes also played on the lacrosse team, and the injuries in those games were potentially more severe. This circumstance warranted the presence of a team doctor on the sideline for that game only.
- Is all staff employed for this particular event appropriately trained for their duties? Are there reasons to change the mix of staff usually hired for events? For example, if an event may be more contentious because of rowdier fans, perhaps more athletic department

employees rather than work-study students should serve as sideline monitors.

- Have enough staff for this event been trained on emergency response procedures? Are there any reasons to review specific emergency response procedures for this event? For example, is the extended weather forecast calling for bad weather? Should the sideline monitors and press box employees be reminded about protocols involving lightning?

Policies 12.20 and 12.21 in HK*Propel* provide sample approaches to confronting these issues. Policy 12.20 addresses event accessibility and safety, and Policy 12.21 presents model security management procedures.

12.20 **Policy**—Event Accessibility and Safety

A sample policy that specifies ADA and other conditions of event accessibility and safety considerations, including facility action plans and emergency medical access.

12.21 **Policy**—Security Management

A sample policy that specifies the conduct of event security meetings, campus policy training, and required preevent security preparations.

Available in HK*Propel*.

12.22 MANAGEMENT TIP

Effective Crowd Control

Most states have laws, many of which are part of the state's education code, that control the behavior of spectators attending athletic events. These laws provide specific guidance with regard to athletic department policies and procedures related to the production and sale of tickets and crowd control policies during events. In short, institution officials usually have full legal authority to ask spectators to leave a facility when their behavior is interfering with the competition or interfering with the ability of others to watch that competition.

Preventative crowd control action is often implemented in rivalry contests, upcoming athletic events in which crowd behavior in the past has been a problem, or unexpected incidences of unacceptable crowd behavior. The athletic director should work with local media to disseminate announcements regarding zero tolerance for unacceptable behavior, communicating the athletic department's policy about revocation of attendance, and educating the public about acceptable and unacceptable fan behavior. The athletic director should always strive to distinguish spectator conduct at educational sport events from what might be acceptable conduct at professional sport events. A strong public address system and printed program statements should state that spectators are being invited into the classroom, albeit an educational sport event. The athletic competition is a learning environment, and spectators are expected to respect coaches' and officials' decisions related to controlling the game environment. Sample Policy 12.23 in HK*Propel* is a model crowd control policy.

One of the most difficult tasks involved in addressing unacceptable spectator behavior is to define what is unacceptable and to convince all security personnel to address this behavior uniformly. Too often, some security staff will let things slide while others take a no-nonsense approach. This inconsistency can create havoc at an event, erode the authority of even the most diligent event staff and security officials over time, and serve to escalate fan resistance to crowd control efforts.

> **12.23 Policy—Crowd Control**
>
> A sample policy that specifies prohibited items that cannot be brought into an athletic event, required spectator conduct announcements, responses to spectator misconduct, and prohibitions related to the use of alcohol, tobacco, and tailgating.
>
> Available in HK*Propel*.

Getting security personnel to respond in a consistent way is difficult for several reasons:

1. Every individual has a personal tolerance for what constitutes acceptable versus unacceptable behavior, which influences how he or she may respond to a given situation.
2. Some people believe that fan behavior can affect the outcome of a game by intimidating opponents. Therefore, if the game is winding down and the outcome is in the balance, security personnel may allow more unruly fan behavior to try to tip the scales in favor of the home team.
3. When working security, every employee must answer the "Is it worth it?" question. Is it worth it to confront a relatively minor spectator conduct problem, or will doing so just cause a larger issue? If the behavior is not confronted, might it escalate? The answers to these questions will differ from person to person, and so will the response.
4. Almost anyone who has worked in security for any length of time has been in a situation that has been somewhat intimidating. For example, it can be difficult to confront an unruly group of drunken college students by yourself in an authoritative way.

Each of these hypothetical circumstances must be addressed in a required training session for security personnel. Getting campus or city police to buy into training from the athletic department can be difficult, but at the very least they should be presented with a clear list of unacceptable fan behavior that they must confront when they work athletic department events, as well as the policies associated with responding to issues. They are being paid for their services, so the events manager, facilities director, or the athletic director should not be reluctant to hold them accountable for doing a good job. Any on-campus or off-campus officer who demonstrates reluctance to get on board should be blacklisted from working future events.

Unacceptable Spectator Behavior

The first issue that must be resolved is what constitutes unacceptable fan behavior. The athletic department must create a working definition for unacceptable spectator behavior that will not be tolerated. The Iowa Girls Athletic Union has listed the following definitions of unacceptable behavior pertaining to spectator conduct on school premises during all school sponsored and cocurricular activities:

1. Abusive verbal or physical conduct of spectators directed at participants, officials, or sponsors of the event or at other spectators
2. Verbal or physical conduct of spectators that interferes with the performance of students, officials, or sponsors of the event
3. The use of vulgar, obscene, or demeaning expressions directed at students, officials, or sponsors participating in the event or at other spectators (para. 5)

Defining what is abusive, vulgar, or demeaning can be a challenge. Is "You suck, ref" abusive or vulgar? It does sound demeaning, but is it demeaning enough to warrant a response? Does "You stink, ref" demand a different response? What happens if a group is chanting the insult rather than a single person yelling it? What happens if the expression is a constant refrain from a specific group or individual rather than a one-time occurrence? What happens if the insult is directed at a single player repeatedly instead of the referee? Although there are no hard-and-sure answers to these questions, they have to be addressed nonetheless. Tackling these definitions as a group problem-solving exercise may be the best way to handle it. Discussing the pros and cons of various reactions and the tipping points when action must be taken is a useful strategy. The security official needs to go right to the source of the problem. Chastising a group, which feels like an easier thing to do than confronting a single person, can create pushback from members of the group.

All security personnel must be reminded that they are present to ensure a safe and family-friendly environment that protects all participants (players, officials, event employees, and spectators) and promote a positive experience. Their job is not to protect the rights of rowdy or unruly fans to have fun. Nor are they to permit behaviors that are typically allowed at professional sporting events. These school-based events have different sets of rules that should be supported by educational principles rather than by business principles and revenue generation.

Influence of Fan Behaviors on the Outcome of a Game

Whether fan behaviors targeted at intimidating opponents or game officials can influence the outcome of a game is debatable. When it comes to security management, however, it just doesn't matter. Security personnel must respond to intimidating fan behavior consistently, whether it occurs on the opening play or in the last two minutes. There are no upsides to allowing the crowd to "get in the game" inappropriately to help secure a win. In fact, unchecked fan behavior later in the game increases the possibility of a postgame brawl. Security personnel must also remove themselves from caring about the outcome of the game. Doing this can be difficult because the security staff is usually composed of campus employees and local officers. Nevertheless, execution of their duties has to take precedence over any emotional attachment to the team.

The "Is It Worth It?" Factor

Except in clearly abusive, demeaning, or dangerous situations, the answer to this question will be left to the total discretion of the security officer. Is it worth it to confront this issue, or will I be seen as overreacting to a minor situation that could escalate the problem? On the other hand, what are the ramifications of doing nothing? Occasionally, doing nothing is the right decision, but more often than not giving fans a pass on inappropriate behavior usually just results in more inappropriate behavior. A security officer can use various strategies for lower-level offenses before delivering an official warning or reprimand or removing the fan from the contest. Establishing eye contact with a rowdy fan and making a little shake of the head sends a message to cool it. At the very least, this action lets the unruly person and those nearby know that the security officer is aware of the situation and is prepared to act if necessary. This message can be much better than just ignoring the problem. Sometimes telling a fan, "I'm going to let that behavior go this time, but I don't want to see it again" serves to deter continued problems. Another strategy is to signal to another security guard or call for backup. Just the presence of more security officers or other event administrators can accomplish much without having to ignite a confrontation.

When the Situation Is Intimidating

Feeling intimidated in a potentially hostile environment is never a good situation for a security officer. To allay some of those feelings, security personnel should be instructed to call for backup any time they feel the least bit uncomfortable. Security personnel should be assured that calling for backup is an expected first-stage deterrent rather than a weakness. In addition, as mentioned earlier, just the presence of more security officers sometimes defuses a situation that could have resulted in a terrible incident if one person tried to handle it alone.

No matter what the circumstance, the best prevention for unruly crowd behavior is consistent, decisive action by security personnel. All security officers must realize that they have a responsibility to create a culture of respect for all event participants. They must also realize that when they fail to act, they not only exacerbate a problem but also may negatively affect the ability of other security personnel to do their jobs. Forms 12.24 and 12.25 are sample documents suggested for use in reporting security incidents and dealing with spectators removed from events because of misconduct.

Risk Management

Key to managing risks associated with the conduct of athletic events is having policies and procedures in place that anticipate what can go wrong, how staff and spectator misconduct can be prevented, and how athletic and security personnel will respond if such management challenges are encountered. Risk Assessment 12.26 in HK*Propel* is a checklist that the athletic director can use to ensure that the athletic department is prepared to address most occurrences.

12.24 **Form**—Security Incident Report

A sample form to be used to report any security incident that occurs at an athletic event.

12.25 **Form**—Letter to Spectators Removed for Misconduct

A sample letter to be sent to spectators removed from an athletic event because of misconduct that informs the spectator of future penalties.

12.26 **Risk Assessment**—Checklist: Event Management

An assessment tool used to audit policies and procedures surrounding the conduct of athletic events that identifies potential risks and whether the department is prepared to address them.

Available in HK*Propel*.

12.27 MANAGEMENT TIP

Fan Engagement and Broadband Capability

For those institutions that have large stadia and arenas that hold thousands of spectators, athletic directors must be prepared to meet the demand for broadband capability and immediate distribution of information. Technological advances and shifts in media consumption have changed fan expectations of engagement when attending sporting events. They want more than a bird's-eye view of the game. According to Maddox, 57 percent of millennials prefer to watch sports at home on their smart TV or by live-streaming events that include different camera angles, replays, updates, and expert analysis. When watching at home, they are simultaneously operating other digital devices to look up statistics, check e-mail or social media, or communicate with friends during commercial breaks. They expect to be able to do the same during their attendance at live events. College students report they are leaving stadiums at halftime if they don't have reliable and fast connectivity or if they can't upload photos to send to their friends (Maddox, 2014).

The millennial generation has grown up with technology that keeps them connected and mobile. They are always looking for ways to enhance their experiences and to share those experiences with others. They resist being a passive participant in almost anything they do, especially when it comes to entertainment. According to Live Production, fans who attended the 2015 Super Bowl transmitted 395,000 tweets per minute during the event. Wagner (2018) reported that "digital intelligence provider Zoomph found that 83% of adults check their mobile phones while attending a live sporting event" (para. 2).

Fans are passionate about sports and even more passionate about their cell phones, which have become highly sophisticated digital devices through which they access social media platforms to feel closer to their teams and individual players, share information, and express opinions and emotions. Fans don't want to lose that connectivity when they walk through the stadium gates. Leagues and teams are finding ways to capitalize on this relatively new reality. A multimedia operation planned around the 2014 FIFA World Cup resulted in the "download of more than 10 million apps, with as many as three million users a day, choosing to enrich their experience through second screen services. Over the course of the tournament, more than 24 million unique users watched content through the multimedia solutions" (Live Production, para. 6).

The ways in which fans consume sports continue to evolve. Understanding their preferences and attitudes toward access of information during sporting events is important for athletic directors. A study was conducted by EVS that included in-person fan interviews across four countries to measure the importance and type of digital media availability and video consumption while watching sporting events. The results were as follows:

- 77 percent of season ticket holders use their mobile devices during a game, so strong Internet access must be available
- 73 percent of fans would like to watch multi-angle replays from their smartphone; nearly half of season ticket holders would pay to have replay access on their phones and 83 percent would accept advertisements to access that content
- 60 percent consumed sports news
- 49 percent watched match highlights
- 41 percent watched a live event stream
- 65 percent were using technology to consume content and monitor activity on social media (EVS)

Overall, fans want immediate access to all types of information that may be affecting the game in front of them such as team lineups, statistics from previous games, and updates on injuries. They also want access to concession menus and food delivery. Many venues are using apps for ticketing, directions, parking, upgrading seats, and access to game-day special events or activities.

Sports venues are taking different approaches on fan engagement through digital and social media. Some have their own branded apps that give them total control of content. Some use Facebook or other social media platforms. No matter which option is used, it is clear that attention to this type of engagement is critical and provides universities the opportunity to offer exclusive information for a personalized fan experience.

12.28 PLANNING TOOL

Management of Camps and Clinics

Policy Documentation

The operation of camps and clinics by school and college athletic departments is almost universal practice. Given the fact that these programs most often deal with minors, it is critical to have a comprehensive written policy and well-thought-out procedures that document all staff, participant, and parent responsibilities. The camp or clinic policy should include the following topics:

- A requirement to assemble and distribute parent information packets containing all forms and policies
- Required consent, authorization, and information forms
- Minimum age, skills, and experience of staff members who work camps
- Required background checks and references
- Required staff training
- Cell phone requirement
- Professional conduct
- Duties and responsibilities
- Parent involvement and support
- Policies governing the pick-up and drop-off of participants

Policy 12.29 in HK*Propel* is a sample of such a policy.

12.29 Policy—Camps and Clinics

A sample policy that specifies the manner in which camps and clinics are administered.

Available in HK*Propel*.

Communication With Parents

The camp director must engage the support of the parents in a partnership to provide a camp or clinic experience that is positive and safe. The first step in this process is the presentation of a camp or clinic information packet that contains all required forms, important policies such as participant behavior, and drop-off and pick-up expectations. If parents refuse to complete any of these forms, their child should not be allowed to participate. Sample required forms that must be completed as a condition of participation are contained in HK*Propel* and include the following:

1. Camp or Clinic Participant Acknowledgments, Authorizations, and Releases (Form 12.30)
2. Camp or Clinic Participant Proof of Insurance (Form 12.31)
3. Medical Information and Physician Clearance for Camp or Clinic Participation (Form 12.32), which includes a list of prescription medications and allergies
4. Parent Acknowledgment of Drop-Off and Pick-Up Policies (Form 12.33)
5. Parent Acknowledgment of Participant Behavior Expectations (Form 12.34)

In addition to required forms, the parent packet should include all of the following:

- Letter from the camp director
- Statement of the instructional philosophy and purpose of the camp or workshop
- Daily camp schedule
- Campus map indicating pick-up and drop-off areas, office for public safety, and camp director's office

12.30 **Form**—Camp or Clinic Participant Acknowledgments, Authorizations, and Releases

A sample form to be signed by the participant or parent that authorizes emergency medical treatment and disclosure of health information, acknowledges that the athletic department will not administer nonprescription medications or provide insurance, and releases the institution from liability arising from camp or clinic activities.

12.31 **Form**—Camp or Clinic Participant Proof of Insurance

A sample form that requires the participant or parent to acknowledge responsibility for payment for medical service and provision of health insurance and to provide health insurance policy information.

12.32 **Form**—Medical Information and Physician Clearance for Camp or Clinic Participation

A sample form that requires the participant or parent to provide information on medical history, immunizations and medications, and proof of physical clearance for participation.

12.33 **Form**—Parent Acknowledgment of Drop-Off and Pick-Up Policies

A sample form that must be signed by the parent of the participant that specifies pick-up and drop-off rules and locations and penalty fees and procedures for children not picked up on time.

12.34 **Form**—Parent Acknowledgment of Participant Behavior Expectations

A sample form that must be signed by a parent that specifies participant behavior expectations and prohibited behaviors and a range of sanctions up to and including revocation of camp participation.

Available in HK*Propel*.

- Times at which parents are invited to observe instruction or competition
- List of contact numbers for camp director and other important people
- Residence hall policies (if the camp includes an overnight experience) (Policy 12.35)
- Department camp or clinic policies (Policy 12.29)
- General information summary containing information on participant attire, footwear, towels, bathing suits, sunscreen, cash for concessions or apparel, required personal sports equipment, and so on
- List of camp or clinic fees and refund policies

Staff Employment Training

Policy 12.29 in HK*Propel* emphasizes that staff members employed for camps should be at least 18 years old, should possess the instructional or supervisory skills necessary for their positions, and have criminal background and reference checks. A formal training meeting should be con-

12.35 **Policy**—Residence Hall Policies for Overnight Camps

A sample policy distributed to staff and parents that specifies the rules related to use of residence halls including security rules, participant responsibility for room damage, and documentation of disciplinary incidents.

12.36 **Policy**—Protocol for Missing Child During a Camp or Clinic

A sample policy distributed to all camp or clinic staff members that details expectations regarding child supervision and the process that should be followed if a child is discovered missing from a participation group.

Available in HK*Propel*.

ducted to review all camp or clinic and residence hall policies. In addition, a missing child protocol should be carefully reviewed. Policy 12.36 details such a protocol.

At the end of the orientation or training meeting, all staff members should be required to sign acknowledgments attesting to the fact that they have reviewed all policies and had questions answered. They should sign another form verifying that they understand their responsibilities related to instruction and supervision of participants and reporting medical and disciplinary incidents. Sample Forms 12.37 and 12.38 are examples of such documents.

Risk Assessment

An important management responsibility is to anticipate and prevent problems. Risk Assessment 12.39 is a checklist of model policies and practices related to the operation of camps and clinics.

12.37 **Form**—Camp or Clinic Staff Acknowledgment of Policy Review

A sample form to be used for staff to acknowledge that they have received and understand all camp or clinic policy documents.

12.38 **Form**—Responsibility for Participant Safety

A sample form to be used for staff to acknowledge that they have received a list of all their responsibilities related to participant instruction and safety.

12.39 **Risk Assessment**—Checklist: Camps and Clinics

A sample checklist to be used to assess whether model policies and procedures are in place.

Available in HK*Propel*.

EVENT MANAGEMENT AND SCHEDULING

Ammon, R., Southall, R.M., & Nagel, M. (2016). *Sports facility management: Organizing events and mitigating risks* (3rd ed.). Morgantown, WV: FIT Publishing.

Bell, A., & Ball, B. (2018). *Basic camp management* (9th ed.). Monterey, CA: Healthy Learning.

Chernushenko, D., van der Kamp, A., & Stubbs, D. (2001). *Sustainable sport management: Running an environmentally, socially, and economically responsible organization*. United Nations Digital Library. https://digitallibrary.un.org/record/453171?ln=en.

City of Virginia Beach. (N.d.). *Unattended children policy*. https://www.vbgov.com/government/departments/libraries/about-us/Library%20Policies/20120416-LIB-OSC-Unattended%20Children%20Policy.pdf.

Drew University. (2007). *Department of Intercollegiate Athletics policy manual*. Unpublished manuscript. Madison, NJ.

EVS. (2015, March). *Connected fan: Return on emotion*. https://evs.com/en/connected-fan.

Fried, G. (2021). *Managing sports facilities* (4th ed.). Champaign, IL: Human Kinetics.

Glassman, T. et al. (2007). Alcohol related fan behavior on college football game day. *National Library of Medicine*. https://pubmed.ncbi.nlm.nih.gov/18089506.

Iowa Girls High School Athletic Union. (N.d.). *Spectator conduct policy*. https://ighsau.org/about/policies-guidelines/spectators.

Jensen, C.R., & Overman, S.J. (2003). *Administration and management of physical education and athletic programs* (4th ed.). Prospect Heights, IL: Waveland Press.

Karp, Russell. (2019, April 6). How technology is changing the sports fan experience. *Start it up*. https://medium.com/swlh/how-technology-is-changing-the-sports-fan-experience-6f32a5bf921d.

Lawrence, H., & Wells, M. (2015). *Event management blueprint: Creating and managing successful sports events* (2nd ed.). Dubuque, IA: Kendall Hunt.

Live Production. (2016, January 31). *Creating an immersive experience for connected fans*. https://www.live-production.tv/case-studies/sports/creating-immersive-experience-connected-sports-fans.html.

Maddox, T. (2014, April 11). Stadiums race to digitize: How sports teams are scrambling to keep millennials coming to games. *TechRepublic*. https://www.techrepublic.com/article/how-sports-teams-are-scrambling-to-keep-millennials-coming-to-games.

Muret, D. (2011, May 9). Centerplate investing 2 million in Notre Dame concessions. *Sports Business Journal*. https://www.sportsbusinessjournal.com/Journal/Issues/2011/05/09/Colleges/Notre-Dame.aspx.

Pedersen, P.M. & Thibault, L. (Eds.). (2022). *Contemporary sport management* (7th ed.). Champaign, IL: Human Kinetics.

Solomon, J. (2002). *An insider's guide to managing sporting events*. Champaign, IL: Human Kinetics.

Stoldt, G.C. et al. (2021). *Sport public relations*. Champaign, IL: Human Kinetics.

Supovitz, F., & Goldblatt, J. (2013). *The sports event management and marketing playbook* (2nd ed.). Hoboken, NJ: Wiley.

University of Texas at Austin. (1992). *Intercollegiate athletics for women policy manual*. Unpublished. Austin, TX: Department of Women's Intercollegiate Athletics.

University of Texas at Austin. (2010). *Intercollegiate athletics policy manual*. Austin, TX. No longer available.

Wagner, Z. (2018, August 14). Millennials expect more out of their game day experience. *Lumavate*. https://medium.com/lumavate/millennials-expect-more-out-of-their-game-day-experience-89c410e31f11.

Weiner, J. (2008, October 20). Have fans gone too far? *Sports Business Journal*. https://www.sportsbusinessjournal.com/Journal/Issues/2008/10/20/SBJ-In-Depth/Have-Fans-Gone-Too-Far.aspx.

Williams, L. (2018, February 15). How sports teams engage fans with their venue experiences. *Marketing Insider*. https://www.mediapost.com/publications/article/314634/how-sports-teams-engage-fans-with-their-venue-expe.html.

CHAPTER

13

Revenue Acquisition and Fund-Raising

Every athletic program, large or small, interscholastic or intercollegiate, needs to maximize acquisition of revenues. Institutionally provided funds are simply insufficient to cover most program expenses. Even if such allocations were sufficient, every unit in an educational institution has a responsibility to maximize its revenue possibilities either to reduce pressure on general institutional funding or to provide for the special or growing needs of that program. As a general management rule, every effort should also be made to diversify revenue sources to maximize protection against years in which revenue projections from primary sources may not be realized. If an athletic department has all its eggs in one basket, such as football or basketball, recovering from a shortfall will be difficult. The documents in this chapter, in both the book and HK*Propel*, focus on developing staff capability and other predicates to successful revenue acquisition as well as planning and executing the five major sources of athletic revenue: (1) annual giving and major giving, (2) fund-raising campaigns, (3) corporate giving and sponsorship programs, (4) athletic events income, and (5) multimedia rights and advertising income. As we enter a new era of digital technology and social media communication, it is critical to emphasize the importance of relationship building and relational giving as the underpinnings to all sources of revenue production. Issues such as pay to play, launching new revenue sports, and developing licensed merchandise and smaller revenue opportunities are also addressed.

TYPES OF DOCUMENTS

Management tip—Factual background information, insights, problem-solving strategies, and suggestions for the athletic director

Planning tool—Steps to take or factors that should be considered in the development of strategic plans, action plans, professional development plans, or governance systems

Educational resource—Handouts that can be used to educate staff members, campus constituents, volunteers, or student-athletes

Policy—Sample policies and procedures that should be adopted by an athletic department after customization and review by appropriate expert institutional or school district officials

Form—Sample forms, letters, or job descriptions

Evaluation instrument—Administrative tools that help the athletic director, a supervisor, or an employee assess job performance and evaluate program content

Risk assessment—Checklists that help the athletic director, a supervisor, or an employee identify risks and prevent litigation

OVERVIEW OF GENERAL CONSIDERATIONS

13.1 PLANNING TOOL

Elements of a Model Revenue Acquisition and Fund-Raising Program

Revenue Distribution Authority

The most important philosophical predicate to the development of a sound revenue acquisition program is establishing the premise that all revenues generated by the athletic program belong to the institution and not the athletic department, the program that raises those funds, or the person who raises the money or coaches the team. This concept of institutional ownership of all revenues is important to transmit to all coaches and staff. This premise does not prevent the institution from creating a policy that allows units that raise funds to retain such funds in whole or in part or provide salary or bonus incentives for those who raise significant funds. In fact, many institutions and most athletic programs have such policies in place. But the critical part of the premise is that the authority to determine the use of raised funds lies with the institution, not the program generating the funds.

This ownership of revenues is also significant with regard to compliance with state and federal laws, such as the Title IX requirements for gender equity. No matter what the source of funds, after the institution accepts revenues for use in providing for educational programs and activities, it must ensure that no discrimination occurs on the basis of sex in the provision of participation opportunities, scholarships, or treatment (from equipment, uniforms, and supplies to the quality of coaches provided). An institution can legally accept a gift restricted for the use of a men's team, as long as the benefits provided to male athletes resulting from such a gift are also provided to female athletes. In such a circumstance, providing the comparable benefit to the women's program would have to be funded from other sources. Similarly, these legal obligations exist with regard to ensuring nondiscrimination on the basis of race and ethnicity, disability, and other factors. After these basic legal obligations are met, the institution's governing board ultimately determines how earned or donated revenues are going to be used to accomplish optional institutional goals.

In essence, the educational institution could be likened to a united fund in which as much money as possible is collected from all sources and then such funds are distributed according to a master plan that supports the basic operation of all program and service delivery units and enhanced operation of programs or purposes that may be considered priorities. Thus, the institution ultimately decides whether it wants to have a nationally ranked top 50 engineering program, an adequate foreign language program, or a nationally competitive athletic program. Similarly, within the athletic department, the athletic director, with the approval of higher administration, may determine sport priorities.

Mission, Goals, Objectives, and Values

Whatever the place of athletics within the larger institutional mission or the priority of sport within athletic program priorities, a predicate to successful revenue acquisition is expressing mission, goals, objectives, and values and communicating this vision to stakeholders. Chapter 3 addresses how to develop a basic document that is a compelling story of why donors and funders should support athletics.

Revenue Priorities

From a practical standpoint, the athletic director needs to establish priorities in the development of various revenue streams. At a minimum, a well-organized program should first be established in each of the following five areas: (1) individual giving (booster clubs, direct mail, major giving, and so on), (2) athletic event ticket sales, (3) fund-raising campaigns (building construction or significant special purposes), (4) corporate giving and sponsorships, and (5) multimedia rights and advertising, if applicable. The athletic director should also emphasize the importance of relationship building through regular nontransactional social media communications with all current sponsors, donors, and other revenue generators and building the largest possible reach with prospects. The digital era of communication makes extraordinary reach possible and the next generation of consumers (millennials and Gen-Y) are multitaskers and residents of the Internet and untethered to print and cable delivery systems.

This priority list may not be applicable to all athletic programs. For instance, summer camp programs or athletic facility rentals may be among the top three or four revenue streams. Each of these primary areas has the potential for the development of multiple revenue streams, but an anchor program of high quality should exist in each area before expansion within the area is considered. The reason for this emphasis on quality first is simple. If a donor, fan, or sponsor is not treated well, the program risks the loss of the revenue provider and must expend additional effort to retrieve the lost customer. If the anchor program is successfully implemented and well administered, the positive experience of the customer will be a good stepping-stone for moving that customer into other programs that will increase his or her revenue donation.

Staff Capabilities

Another practical consideration is having sufficient dedicated staff to produce revenues. Although head coaches and the athletic director will be the primary relationship builders with donors, fans, and sponsors, the consistent care of these customers and the mechanical communication with and daily handling of these people must fall on the shoulders of others dedicated to that work. Human capacity is especially critical in fund-raising because people give to people. Relationships are everything. Relationship building is at the heart of all successful revenue programs. Ultimately, the size of a development program is related to the institutional commitment to staff devoted to this task.

Integration With Institutional Development

Last but not least, the athletic program resides within a larger educational institution and holds the potential for competing with institutional fund-raising priorities. The athletic director must always strive to integrate athletic and general institution development efforts. Integration requires regular communication and consultation and joint initiatives with major donors and vendors. If the athletic department operates without regard to the rest of the institution, conflict is inevitable.

Given all these considerations, what does a model revenue acquisition and fund-raising program look like? Following is a list of revenue acquisition and fund-raising elements that must be carefully evaluated and prioritized and for which explicit strategies should be developed.

- Staffing, technology, and organizational structure considerations. Are sufficient staff and the necessary technological capacity available to execute a quality effort in all revenue acquisition or fund-raising programs in which the department is involved? (See Planning Tool 13.2 in the book.)
- Relationship building by coaches and staff. Is "friend-raising" required of all staff members, and are training programs in place to improve those face-to-face, cell phone, e-mail, and social media skills? (See Planning Tool 13.3 in the book.)
- Fund-raising events. Are there limits on the number of fund-raising events that the department will sponsor and criteria for the evaluation of those opportunities? Do these events include crowd funding and online video meetings with donors and donor prospects? (See Planning Tool 13.4 in the book.)
- Annual giving and booster clubs. Does a well-organized annual giving or booster club umbrella program exist with a detailed plan for growing membership? (See Planning Tool 13.6 in the book and sample Policy 13.7 in HK*Propel*.)

- Major donor and endowed gift programs. Does a major donor program exist that includes a research component and opportunities to make endowed or other planned gifts? (See Planning Tool 13.8 in the book.)
- Building construction and other major multiyear campaigns. If such fund-raising campaigns exist, do they include case statements, leadership committees, gift rate charts, and solicitation action plans? (See Planning Tool 13.11 in the book.)
- Corporate giving, sponsorships, and advertising. If such programs exist, are they based on sponsorship needs and do they include proof of performance requirements? (See Planning Tool 13.13 in the book.)
- Maximizing income related to athletic events (ticket sales, parking, concessions, and so on). Do admission fees exist for multiple sports in which spectator access and seating can be controlled? Are detailed policies in place governing discounted and complimentary tickets, concessions, and parking? (See Planning Tool 13.17 in the book.)
- Seating priority points systems. If such a system exists, do specific rules exist for date-certain retroactive accumulation of points, specification of who receives credit for spouse or business checks, designated cutoff dates for annual point accumulation, and other similar issues? (See Planning Tool 13.18 in the book.)
- Packaging and marketing events and multimedia rights. If this program exists, was a request for proposal issued that included a clear delineation of all athletic assets? (See Planning Tool 13.19 in the book.)
- Diversification. Do specific detailed plans exist for launching new sports as revenue producers? (See Planning Tool 13.22 in the book.)
- Licensed merchandise. Does the athletic program have its own logo and the right to license its use on various products under agreements approved by school district or institution legal counsel? (See Planning Tool 13.23 in the book.)
- Student fees and pay to play. If either of these programs exists, has consideration been given to the seven points that should be reviewed before implementing such programs? (See Planning Tool 13.24 in the book.)
- Potential sources of additional institutional support. Have tuition waivers, facility rentals, land leases, and vending machine income been evaluated as potential sources of additional athletic revenues? (See Planning Tool 13.26 in the book.)
- Summer camps. Have multiple options for the structure of summer camps been explored to determine revenue potential? (See Planning Tool 13.27 in the book.)

Although Division I collegiate athletic programs will have a significant number of staff members working to maximize all these opportunities, Division III and high school programs will engage in only a few programs and seldom devote a full-time position to the entire fund-raising area. Key to developing a sound program is (1) carefully considering all possibilities to determine which hold the potential for the most significant revenues and therefore warrant spending time and resources to develop them and (2) fully developing high-potential programs before adding less lucrative ones. Quality execution includes a high standard of care of donors, spectators, and customers and is an essential predicate to program expansion. If these consumers are unhappy, the fund-raising program will not be successful.

13.2 PLANNING TOOL

Critical Staffing, Technology, and Integration Issues

Basic Technology and Staff Support

Most intercollegiate athletic programs enjoy the technological support of institutional finance or development offices. Thus, institutional databases and accounting systems are used to support individual and corporate donor revenue initiatives including donations, event ticket sale purchases, and perhaps even a contact management system. School districts that are less dependent on individual donations and more dependent on tax dollars for operating revenues are not as likely to possess donor, ticket, or contact management software. Extremely large NCAA Division I athletic departments may have their own customized donor and ticketing databases that are more sophisticated than institutional software. Even if the athletic program is so small that it has no designated fund-raiser other than the athletic director and no institutional database support, serious consideration should be given to having at least one full-time clerical position whose primary responsibility is maintaining an off-the-shelf integrated fund-raising and event ticketing database. Such technology and staff support is now a necessity. Numerous off-the-shelf products are designed to meet the sophisticated needs of athletic programs. Key is making sure that a single database can fully integrate all software applications to handle the individual, corporate, and event-related needs of the athletic department. In addition, sufficient clerical staff must be available to relieve more highly paid relationship builders and fund-raisers from the time-consuming tasks of database entry and maintenance. If the general institution has a donor database and the athletic department possesses different donor fund-raising software or ticketing software, such databases must be fully integrated with each other.

Integration With the Central Development Office

Almost all institutions of higher education have centralized development offices that serve all units of the college or university. The athletic program is an amazing front-porch asset for an institution of higher education because it conducts hundreds of sport events at home and away that bring alumni and friends into contact with the university on a regular basis. Because of the high interaction with alumni, donors, and others that regularly occurs in conjunction with the athletic program, consideration should be given to housing dedicated central development office staff within the athletic department to work hand in hand with ticket managers, the athletic director, marketing and sponsorship personnel, and coaches in donor identification, cultivation, and solicitation efforts. Such an integrated staff structure will go a long way toward preventing miscommunication and successfully addressing larger university and athletic program needs without such efforts competing with each other. Unfortunately, such a staffing approach is not politically viable at many institutions because of historical or personnel circumstances. In such situations, at the very least a university policy should govern notification of intent to contact any individual donor classified as a major donor, whatever that definition is, based on either an annual or overall donor amount. The institution and the athletic department must carefully plan six- and seven-figure requests for support and cannot risk giving donors the impression that the right hand doesn't know what the left hand is doing.

In the case of school districts, the development or fund-raising function is usually based in the office of the superintendent of schools and is extremely limited in nature. This circumstance is primarily because of the school district's dependence on tax dollars as the primary revenue source. At the high school level, the primary athletic development issue is the operation and control of booster clubs that are separately incorporated as nonprofit organizations external to the school district. These groups may exist separately at each high school, or one districtwide booster club may be formed by citizens to provide support for athletic programs in the district. Because booster clubs developed as external independent entities controlled by influential citizens, most school districts have been forced to create a policy that sets conditions for their recognition and operation in return for approval of the use of the school name and fund-raising purpose. Planning Tool 13.6 in the book and sample Policy 13.7 in HK*Propel* address these issues in more detail.

Consolidation of Ticketing and Fund-Raising Functions

In larger, more sophisticated Division I collegiate athletic programs, especially those with seating priority points systems (see Planning Tool 13.18), consideration should be given to housing the athletic ticket manager in the athletic development unit rather than in the athletic finance, event management, or business office unit. Ticketing and seat locations are critical donor interface opportunities that should be handled by fund-raisers and coordinated within a larger relationship-building and cultivation strategy.

Capacity Investment Priorities

An important financial issue is how to prioritize the athletic department's capacity investments—people, technology, third-party direct mail, Internet site development, fund-raising events, and so on. The first priority must be infrastructure: (1) database technology that enables quality administration, (2) people to operate and maintain the database, and (3) establishment of a basic individual giving program. The basic individual giving program defines the case for support, or why the athletic department needs money, how people can give, and what benefits donors receive beyond the tax deduction for their gift. After these structural and "sales" benefit elements are in place, the issue of staffing priority lies in the simple fact that in most annual giving campaigns, 60 percent of the donation revenues come from the 10 percent of donors who have the higher capacity to give. Between 15 and 25 percent of donation revenues will come from 20 percent of all donors who comprise midrange givers and 15 to 25 percent of revenues will come from small gifts from 70 percent of all donors (Averill, 2019). Thus, after the infrastructure is in place, the focus should be on the staffing needed to provide leadership to the program and to cultivate and care for the 10 to 30 percent of donors who are contributing at the higher gift levels.

The most important piece of the staffing puzzle is the head of the athletic development program, who will serve as chief strategist. This person, normally at the associate athletic director level, is the "point guard" who must direct all aspects of the program: (1) accumulating lists of friends or donor prospects from many sources, (2) establishing quarterly or other regularized direct mail campaigns to mine new prospects and increase the giving of existing donors, (3) researching the financial status of prospects to determine who has the capacity to be a major donor, (4) determining who should be cultivated and developed into major donors and by whom, and (5) implementing the individual contact strategies and meetings that will deliver development results. Describing this person using the analogy of the basketball team's point guard is accurate. He or she may not score the points, but this is the person responsible for making everyone else look good and perform well. This person is dedicated to orchestrating the fund-raising effort, from ensuring compelling and consistent storytelling in communicating with donors to directing the relationship-building efforts of head coaches and the athletic director. This development program leadership position is key.

The basic annual giving program will grow through list accumulation, mass events, and mass mailings. One full-time-equivalent (FTE) position should be able to handle this program. As the number of those giving or capable of giving higher amounts grows, staff must be added to focus on cultivating this major donor group. The athletic department or institutional development office should have an operating ratio to determine when new staff members are required. For instance, in larger institutions of higher education the ratio might be one FTE position in fund-raising assigned to cultivate every 50 to 100 qualified major donor prospects. At smaller institutions, the ratio might increase to 1:150. A qualified major donor is a label placed on a person based on an estimate of the donor's capacity for annual giving. In some smaller athletic departments that figure might be $1,000 to $5,000 per year, and in larger programs it might be $10,000 to $25,000 per year. These figures vary depending on the quality and scope of the donor pool and the maturity of the development program. As the average annual gift per donor increases over time, this definition of qualified major donor will change accordingly.

The next priority for staffing is the caretaking of corporate and business relationships, which is another type of prospecting of qualified major donors that requires specialized staff knowledge in the areas of advertising, marketing, and event sponsorship. In small programs, the athletic director may be in charge of caretaking these relationships and creating these programs, whereas in larger athletic departments, a multiperson staff that has a separate director of marketing and director of annual giving may carry out these tasks. The priorities for corporate and business relationships are the same as those for the individual donor program: (1) ensuring that the software and staff infrastructure is in place, (2) concentrating on the cultivation of businesses or corporations that will yield larger revenues, and (3) working on gradually expanding the size of the sponsorship prospect pool and the growth of the average sponsorship package. Staff should be added at the beginning of a fiscal year so that they have time to earn their own salaries and then start developing new unallocated dollars.

Visionary Revenue Czar

Developmentally, athletic programs grow almost haphazardly when staff members reveal various fund-raising skills and create their own fiefdoms based on their success. One staff member may be great at advertising sales, another at sponsorships, another at major and planned gifts, and another at handling ticket sales. As early as possible, a full-time leader of all development business units should be appointed to ensure integration, balance, and a team approach in the development of this staff talent. Whoever occupies the revenue czar position should be responsible for (1) expanding all existing revenue programs, (2) creating new revenue streams, (3) ensuring the highest standard of care and communications with donors and sponsors, and (4) maximizing the use of every athletic event that could be used for donor cultivation. Most important, the revenue czar is responsible for insisting that the athletic director and head coaches make fund-raising and donor relationship building their number two priority behind the success of the sport program.

Cautions in a Declining Economy

A declining economy, an institutional financial crisis, or the financial uncertainty created by unanticipated events (e.g., COVID-19 pandemic, donor reaction to improper employee or athlete behavior, etc.) requires early efforts to *expand* investment in development staff and initiate more aggressive relationship building and maintenance initiatives. More effort and more time are needed simply to maintain revenue streams in such an environment. At the very least, fund-raising staff should not be cut. The financial risk of investing in additional fund-raising staff is extremely limited if such investments are made early in the fiscal year because all new FTEs should easily earn their salaries and benefits in new revenues that each should be expected to generate. In a tough economic climate, even more communication with donors and supporters is needed, so more hands are needed on deck to overcome giving declines in some areas.

Importance of Internet Presence

Most athletic program websites are primarily structured to communicate rosters, results, and statistics. Little attention is devoted to telling the compelling stories of program purpose, such as the student-athlete experience, the postgraduate success of former athletes, or the enthusiasm of donors who serve as examples of numerous ways to make gifts. Without these compelling stories that either encourage donor investment or, in the case of higher education, assist coaches in recruiting prospective student-athletes through a sophisticated marketing approach, the website is little more than a statistics sheet and photo album. A person seeking donation information and desiring to make an online donation or wanting to purchase a ticket to an event should not have to struggle to accomplish these tasks. In this Internet-enabled society in which going to the movies or a professional sport event means printing out your ticket at home, technological sophistication is expected. Increasingly, third-party vendors provide these web services as turnkey operations, from provision of a secure payment area for making online donations and purchases to website design and hosting. No athletic program needs to spend $25,000 setting up a website anymore. Having a sophisticated web presence is a basic expectation rather than a luxury option.

13.3 PLANNING TOOL

Relationship Building by Coaches and Staff

"Friend-Raising" as a Responsibility of All Staff

The donor cultivation opportunities presented by athletics are so extensive that fund-raising responsibilities must not be limited to development staff or the athletic director. Every senior staff member and full-time head coach should be responsible for donor cultivation and "friend-raising." Every staff member should be asked to contribute lists of prospects. Such assignments would be made by the head of athletic development, but the athletic director is ultimately responsible for changing athletic department culture and job responsibilities to include these expectations for all full-time employees. Relationship building should be viewed as a game changer or tipping-point strategic necessity.

Specific Expectations for Coaches, Teams, and Other Athletic Department Employees

The athletic director should be specific in communicating relationship-building expectations. Following are several examples of such expectations.

Away Event Engagement Assignment Each full-time head coach should be responsible for engaging at least 10 alumni donors or donor prospects annually in conjunction with away athletic events, 40 percent of whom should be major donor prospects. Such engagement would translate into the following responsibilities:

a. Send a personal letter (approved by development staff) advising the donor prospect or existing donor that the team will be in the area and inviting the prospect to be a guest coach at the game.
b. For donors who accept the invitation, the coach should do the following:
    - Meet the donor at the event; give a personal scouting report before the game; arrange for seating at the event; and invite the donor to join the team for pregame, halftime, and postgame locker room meetings.
    - In the locker room or at an appropriate time prior to the game, have each team member introduce himself or herself (year, hometown, major, position).
    - Invite the donor to the postgame meal if one is being arranged.
    - Assign a staff member or player who won't be playing to chaperone the guest coach during the event.
    - Follow up after the event with a thank-you card signed by the team, the gift of a guest coach T-shirt, or an autographed team photo.

Home Event Guest Coach Program Each full-time head coach should also be responsible for conducting a guest coach program at each home event, engaging in the same donor activities as they do at away events with help from the senior staff administrator assigned to cover that event. Instead of having an administrative staff member assigned simply to oversee an event, he or she should also be responsible for duties related to chaperoning donors. When initially implementing home or away donor entertainment experiences, care should be taken to establish operational criteria such as the following to provide the donor a quality experience:

- Construct a game timetable that is transmitted to the guest coach with the invitation to attend. The timetable would give a rundown of what the guest coach experience includes.
- Make sure that each head coach has a game program or roster that has the name and number of every player and individual player statistics if those are available.
- Have a one-page handout that includes factoids about the program from team and

program grade point averages to graduation rates, championship success, and a list of former players now successful in life after sport.

- Have the head coach or an assigned assistant coach give a pregame scouting report.
- Before going to the gym or playing field, have coffee and sandwiches in the athletic director's office where the scouting report and other information about the program can be delivered.
- Make sure that the head coach greets and speaks with guest coaches during the pregame warm-ups and points out starting players to watch.
- If a statistics summary is prepared at halftime for home and visiting team coaches or media, make sure that the guest coaches get a copy.
- At the end of the game, make sure that each player goes up to the guest coaches and thanks them for coming to the game.
- Make sure that chairs are available for the guest coaches to sit on that are located immediately behind the team bench so that they can listen to team huddles and coach instructions.
- Caution guest coaches that because they are sitting right behind the bench, they should not criticize officials or opponents. Rather, like coaches, they should exhibit good coach decorum.
- If available, arrange for soda or popcorn to be delivered to the guest coaches during the game.

Attention to detail is essential. Quality execution becomes simple after the coach and supervising staff get one or two of these experiences under their belts.

Parent Cultivation Each coach should be required to write a personal letter or email to the parents of each student-athlete in that sport at the beginning of the season, thanking them for supporting the attendance of their daughter or son, inviting them to attend games compliments of the athletic department (as permitted by athletic governance association rules), and inviting them to be a guest coach if they haven't done this before. Parents are important prospective donors. A short once-a-week e-mail to the families of players updating them on the progress of the team is a solid relationship builder. A report to the development staff on the coach's estimate of the parent's ability to make a donation should also be required.

Summer Campers Each coach should be required to send a personal communication to the parents of all campers who attended the coach's summer camp that year, inviting them to attend regular season games and have their children meet the players before or after the game. Parents should be asked to sign up their children to become members of the booster club, and the parents should be invited to donate to the booster club.

Community Group Cultivation Full-time employees should be asked to participate in prospective donor cultivation. If a staff member is a member of a church or community service group, he or she should be asked to organize such groups to attend a game as a guest of the athletic program. The price of admission would simply be adding their names to the athletic department mailing list. Staff members should be asked to identify who among their acquaintances might be major donor prospects. When staff members share lists, they should be assured that none of their friends will be solicited for anything without the staff member's permission.

Customer Service Training Administrative, clerical, ticket office, and all employees with public interface responsibilities should receive training in customer service, satisfaction, and relationship building.

Rewards Annual evaluations and merit awards should include an assessment of contributions to revenue generation, number of new friends introduced to the program, and development activities.

All staff should be educated about how to be successful in building relationships. Scott (2009) offers 10 keys:

1. **Grow and engage with your contact list.** Ask donors, mentors, and friends whether they can help you better express the athletic program story, strategic plan, or the importance of scholarships. Keep in regular contact with

key people and ask how you can help them. People are more apt to assist you later when you have offered aid for their projects. Volunteer to be on committees or help others. Send out meaningful updates and stories of your work on a quarterly basis. Identify key skills, supports, or tangible donations that you need and ask people who they know who might be interested in learning about the athletic program and helping you. Think now about who is on your holiday card list.

2. **Ask questions and follow through.** Every time you communicate with someone, be mindful of how often you share your perspective versus asking what is happening in the supporter's life and how he or she feels about what you are doing. Remember, if you ask for money, you will get advice, and if you ask for advice, you will get money. Asking for input and authentically inquiring about another person's work, home, or passions are essential for building strong relationships. By listening, listening, and listening some more to what is said and not said, you can follow through with personalized and meaningful information. If you do this, people will ask how they can help you. Then you can tell them about the resources needed by your organization.
3. **Bring forth a strong work ethic.** People invest in leaders whom they see are hungry and working hard to be successful. When they can see your persistence and authentic belief in what you are doing, they are more apt to support you. Impeccable attention to communication is essential. Always follow up conversations or personal meetings with personalized notes or customized partnership proposals. Provide details about your work and have a plan for sequential and coordinated engagement (e.g., meet with top contributors twice per year, e-mail them monthly, call them quarterly) with key supporters.
4. **Believe and act in partnership.** If you are truly listening and engaged with people, you will hear what their dreams and desires are. At the same time, they will hear yours. By asking people to partner with you on your dreams, understand that this request will be easiest when you genuinely want to help build their dreams, too. Know that this philosophy can be applied to coworkers, investors, boosters, athletes you coach, and others.
5. **Use gifts or sales to secure more funds.** Whenever a gift is secured or requested, work with the supporter to ask how public he or she will let you be with the gift. Often the gift will allow you to seek a matching gift or create a challenge for others, thereby doubling or tripling the person's investment. Always think in terms of a gift rate chart and share this with supporters (e.g., we need 10 gifts at $10,000 or $100,000 to do this project) even if you know the supporter can give you the entire amount. Ideally, you want the supporter to give you more than $10,000 and the names of nine others who can help raise the $100,000. Minimally, get permission to publicize the story of the gift with or without the person's name attached because people want to give to success.
6. **Build a circle of leaders and experts.** Whether it is staff, an advisory council, or an athletic policy board, building a successful fundraising program requires a trusted group of advisors from a variety of key fields (finance, legal, digital marketing, communications). Be sure to give each volunteer a specific assignment through which he or she will feel capable of engaging with others. People want to use their talents in a way that is a considerate and efficient use of their time.
7. **Focus time on the top 20 percent.** Most nonprofits are funded with 80 percent of the money coming from 20 percent of the donors. Building trust and rapport with this top 20 percent should take 80 percent of your time. These high-wealth relationships will inevitably lead you to their peer groups, and more donors, over time.
8. **Build a list of benefits for exchange.** Before going into the marketplace for donors or sponsors, compile a list of benefits that the athletic department can offer in exchange for sponsorship. With a menu of opportunities for partnership, you can customize a meaningful relationship. Never overlook the opportunity to provide something of value

that can't be bought, such as an autographed item from a sport legend or a behind-the-scenes experience with a leader or coach.

9. **Mimic practices of the university development office to build brand.** Analyze the tools used by the institutional development office and model them where appropriate. Invite leadership (deans, coaches, or top thought leaders) to speak at events or hosted parties (in campus settings or esteemed private homes) to engage with key audiences (alumni lists or people profiled by technology sources on income or affinity) on a relevant topic. Know that all significantly funded organizations have people designated to do research on prospects and donors and their ability to give. When dealing with major donors, it is important to understand their giving focus and life passions and determine where athletics can fit within those interests.
10. **Build visibility with technology.** Use new media to tell your story and make timely updates to your mission and the contributions made by the athletic department staff, coaches, and student-athletes to the community and society. Continually review your website to ensure that relevant information is present. Think of your website as your living room where you will entertain investors whom you have invited to dinner. With this practice, you will offer an impressive, elegant, and impeccable environment to any web visitor. Master the art of storytelling on your website and in web communications as an essential element in asking for involvement and gifts.

Building the Fund-Raising Base

Staff and families of student-athletes and summer campers can make up a substantial part of a pool of new athletic program friends. The larger the pool of donor prospects is, the larger the potential is for discovering major donor prospects. Cultivating, engaging, and capturing a new major donor takes two to three years. The giving capacity of the people who can make major gifts is often not evident at the time they are initially engaged. People give to people. Friends help friends. Donors give to people they know, trust, and think are doing a good job. Creating this "friend-raising" climate needs to be the responsibility of everyone in the athletic department.

13.4 PLANNING TOOL

Fund-Raising Events That Make Sense

Many athletic departments get sidetracked by inefficient fund-raising events. Everyone appears to be doing a particular type of event such as golf tournaments or clinics, and people simply assume that these efforts are cost-effective profit makers. Special events in general are notorious for consuming staff time, especially on top of conducting more than 100 home athletic competitions that keep all staff members busy. Fund-raising events should have criteria that mandate producing a profit considering the cost of staff time and effort involved. Consider the difference between a $200 per person golf tournament that costs the department $100 per person and requires the time of 15 staff members and 40 volunteers to execute and a $2,500 per ticket benefit performance with a free big-name celebrity that costs the department $300 per person and the same number of staff members to execute. Moreover, such high-ticket events can often generate additional revenue of $100,000 or more by including a quality auction. These events can be such successful profit makers that the athletic department can afford to save staff time by having a third-party event organizer do the bulk of the work while most staff and volunteers work primarily only on the night of the event. Therefore, it is essential to reexamine the cost–benefit relationship of existing events and contrast them with other event possibilities that offer more revenues at lower cost and effort. For instance, the athletic department should increase the number of smaller, more sophisticated events hosted by high-wealth donors in their homes. Such events require the presence of only the athletic director, the head coach, and maybe one or two athletes. The guest list consists of the peers of the high-wealth donor, and the donor pays all expenses.

Limits should be placed on the number of annual events that are offered. Event quality and staff workloads need to be considered. Donors to the athletic program, in a desire to help, often suggest events like golf tournaments. If rules about adding new events are not in place, refusing a suggestion is difficult, especially if it is from a major donor. Thus, minimum criteria should be established for offering such events, such as the following:

1. Events require 16 weeks of lead time (or other number) to ensure quality execution.
2. The host or host committee members define and deliver a fund-raising goal as follows:
    a. A private reception has a minimum goal of $__,000 (above expenses) secured on site or defines and delivers a fund-raising goal of $__,000 within one year of the event by those attending the event.
    b. A regional or public event has a minimum goal of $__,000 (above expenses) from the event or delivered within one year of the event by those attending the event.
3. The size of the function (number of attendees and hard costs to put on the event) is determined by development staff.
4. Host or host committee members shall make two or more of the following commitments:
    a. Contribute a personal list and commit to making personal calls to follow up
    b. Make a personal contribution to offset event expenses (see item 5)
    c. Make a personal commitment to purchase a table or tickets to the event
    d. Deliver one or more significant friends to the event capable of making a major contribution (corporate, foundation, personal) in the future
5. The host or host committee delivers the following resources at no or reduced cost through personal contributions or their

connections; quality and details are to be approved by athletic development staff:

a. Catering services where needed
b. AV services
c. Payment of travel and entertainment for AD, coaches, and athletes
d. Design and production costs for print materials
e. Management of invite list and RSVP responses
f. Photographer
g. Public relations support for preevent and on-site execution where applicable

6. The athletic department agrees to provide the following:

a. Leadership to speak at the event
b. Student-athletes to appear and speak at the event (mutually agreed upon number and names of athletes before event commitment)
c. Mailing list to supplement host or host committee list
d. Assistance with creation of invitations and print materials
e. Applicable educational and visual resources on site
f. Follow-up for event attendees including, for instance, photos for event attendees
g. Ongoing consultation with host or host committee members
h. Public relations and web support to communicate and support promotions, messaging, and media relations

The main points are (1) the athletic director must insist on a business analysis of the real cost of every event that is not a sport competition and must never say yes on impulse, (2) before offering an event, alumni or volunteers must make a commitment to deliver invitation lists and their connections to increase revenues and decrease expenses, (3) alumni and friends should commit to supporting the event through personal contributions or ticket sales, and (4) quality event execution requires adequate lead time.

Team Fund-Raising Activities

On occasion teams may be allowed to conduct minor fund-raising activities to support specific needs. To ensure that these activities do not conflict with other athletic fund-raising events, each team must be required to obtain athletic department approval before conducting such events. Form 13.5 is a sample form that can be used for this purpose.

13.5 Form—Approval for Team Fund-Raising Activity

A sample form that enables the athletic director or person in charge of development to be aware of, approve, and oversee all fund-raising initiatives.

Available in HK*Propel*.

13.6 PLANNING TOOL

Annual Giving Programs and Booster Clubs

Booster Club Program

A booster club individual annual giving program is simply a storytelling framework combined with a graduated categorization of donation levels and benefits associated with each level with which to solicit and receive gifts. Institution X establishes the X Athletic Fund. Anyone who donates to the fund becomes an X Athletic Fund or booster club member and receives benefits that are laddered in value according to the amount of the gift. For example, a $25 donor receives a membership card, a $100 donor receives a T-shirt, and a $1,000 donor receives a seat assignment at the 50-yard line when he or she also buys a football season ticket. Almost every athletic program has some type of individual giving framework like this that promotes the feeling of being a part of the team and helps raise funds for scholarships or supports the athletic program in other ways.

In general, when establishing benefits, they must be perceived by donors as having higher value at the higher giving levels. Careful attention should be paid to not offering too much value at lower giving levels and reserving significant premiums or exclusive benefits to higher giving levels. The purpose is to grow all giving levels and be able to afford to offer the benefits. Therefore, benefits should entice donors to stretch to give at the top of their ability to give. To maintain a sense of exclusivity, pre- and postgame donor entertainment areas, pregame scouting reports delivered by an assistant coach, postgame analysis from the head coach, and meeting and interacting with the popular head coach in a one-on-one or small-group setting must remain premium experiences. Successful individual giving programs usually make benefits associated with the most popular sport programs available at the higher levels rather than trying to treat all sports the same way. The higher prices for the benefits associated with the most popular sport are a function of both limited capacity as well as public demand.

Single Sport Versus Umbrella Clubs

Historically, booster clubs started as single-sport entities, most commonly for the benefit of football or boys' or men's basketball and were established and run by alumni or parents outside the institution. Over time, booster clubs were formed for other sports including those for newly emerging female programs. Problems with such single-sport structures soon became apparent:

1. **Gender inequities.** Large amounts of money raised for high-profile male sports like football created imbalances in the treatment of male and female sports. This situation put the athletic director in a difficult position of continually having to use institutional funds to balance the benefit differential while having little control over the benefits provided by external groups. On one hand, the athletic director who informs parents that any funds raised by the single-sport booster club will go into a central fund for distribution to all the sports as determined by the administration might incur the wrath of many parents who will not understand why they can't support their child in his or her sport. On the other hand, if the athletic director doesn't provide equivalent treatment to participants of men's and women's sports, a Title IX violation may occur. But the bottom line is that under current federal law, using a special source of funds or donor-restricted donations for men's sports is not a violation of Title IX unless the benefits provided to male athletes by that donation are not provided to females through funding from another source.

2. **Multiple solicitations of businesses and individuals.** When separate sport support groups (e.g., the football booster club, the basketball booster club) are operating, each group undertakes its own solicitation efforts. Businesses and individuals could be asked five or six times a year to support a sport program. In effect, each booster club is in competition for the same dollars from the same donors.
3. **Inefficient use of parents' and volunteers' time.** If a child is involved in multiple sports, parents are asked to volunteer to work for each sport's booster club, creating pressure and stress on parents.
4. **Lack of professional development leadership.** With multiple fund-raising groups operating external to the institution, a strategic leader is not in place to determine the capacity of prospective donors, the method in which they should be solicited to create the greatest yield, or funding priorities. As dependence on external funding grows, this situation becomes less tolerable.
5. **Lack of common messaging.** With multiple groups representing the athletic program but operating without its full authority, there is no common messaging to donors and no opportunity to communicate priorities.
6. **Financial improprieties or lack of transparency.** The risk for mishandling of funds increases as volunteers handle money without strict financial controls, as does the public relations risk of lack of transparency in communicating with donors.

The solution to all these issues eventually evolved through the creation of an umbrella, or all-sports, booster club administered by the institution. With this structure, the institution has the opportunity to have everyone on the same page doing what is best for all student-athletes. When a booster club is controlled by the institution, it is easier to be sure that booster club giving is fully integrated with ticket priority, major giving, and other department fund-raising programs and subject to strict financial controls.

Cautions Concerning External Booster Clubs

Booster clubs and private foundations at some universities and colleges still exist outside their institutions. Although most college and university athletic governance associations require institutional oversight of athletic fund-raising to ensure that monies are used in ways that are permitted by their rules and regulations, this control may mean only that the external club or foundation is subject to annual reporting. Thus, exceptional diligence must occur in working with these external enterprises that have established their own 501(c)(3) status (nonprofit organizations that permit the acceptance of tax-deductible gifts) for the purpose of raising funds to support the educational sport activities of their institutions. Because these groups of volunteers are perceived by both donors and the public as being administered by the institution, if they do not do a good job of maintaining proper records or caring for the donated funds, the institution's reputation may suffer. Fortunately, more educational institutions, school districts, and governance associations are now requiring institutional control of booster club activities, including mandating audits of externally operated clubs or bringing all financial transactions inside the institution itself—processing checks, acknowledging all donations, making decisions regarding the distribution of funds, and conducting annual year-end audits.

High school athletic directors have greater reliance on externally governed booster clubs than colleges and universities, who have a broader geographical reach for donors, larger donor pools, and more diversified revenue sources (radio, television, and so on). Thus, the prudent high school athletic administrator needs to assess the risks involved with booster clubs and be certain that thoughtful policies and procedures are put in place to minimize those risks.

The first step in assessing the risk related to booster clubs is defining the institution's obligations as prescribed by institutional and school district policy and statutory and regulatory requirements. This task would be done in conjunction with school district or university legal counsel. Several questions need to be asked:

- What are the applicable policies of the school district with regard to the designation of gifts to particular programs, where are funds deposited, and what are the rules that govern the use of such funds?
- What are the policies of the state high school activities association related to such funds? As an example, the University Interscholastic League (UIL) in Texas has developed a comprehensive set of booster club guidelines for all UIL members to follow and has clearly delineated all the restrictions and the penalties for violating those guidelines (UIL, 2011).
- What state and federal statutes affect booster clubs?
- What U.S. Internal Revenue Service regulations apply to fund-raising?
- What are the National Federation of High School Associations (NFHS) regulations?

These are just some of the many questions that need to be asked in assessing the risks associated with booster clubs.

The next step is to look at the existing booster club structure and policies and to ask whether they meet all of these legal and policy requirements. If not, what needs to be revised? Start with the premise that separate sport fund-raising clubs are dysfunctional to the integrity and long-term fund-raising health of the institution and the assumption that an all-sports, or umbrella, booster club should be mandated.

Structuring the Umbrella Booster Club

Because the athletic program is a legitimate part of the academic mission, the all-sports booster club should be structured in a manner that ensures complete support and concurrence with the institution's core values, financial integrity, and institutional control. To align the club with these principles, consider establishing the following mandates:

1. **Define the purpose of the club.** The club should exist to enhance the student-athlete's involvement in sport as part of the pursuit of academic and athletic excellence that is consistent with the school's mission. The following purposes are usually identified:
    a. Promoting fan support, school spirit, and community pride
    b. Providing supplemental financial support and services to all sports programs
    c. Enhancing the opportunities for honest and open communication between coaches, parents, and administrators
    d. Providing educational opportunities for members to learn about the rules of games, coaching strategies, nutritional needs of the athletes, Title IX, and other athletic issues
    e. Promoting sportsmanship and ethical conduct among student-athletes, coaches, parents, and fans
2. **Mandate and approve a governing document (constitution and bylaws).** Legal counsel should be used to develop a policy document that clearly defines authority, responsibilities, and the way that the club functions. If the club is external, a formal constitution and bylaws together with articles of incorporation will also be required. The policy document should include but not be limited to covering the following topics:
    a. Clarify that the club's role is to support all sports and student-athletes
    b. State that the conduct of all sport activities are under the total control and direction of the school district administrators (superintendent, principal, athletic director, or president)
    c. Specify the person within the school administration who will have final approval on all fund-raising activities
    d. Provide for an election of officers, their duties, and their terms
    e. Establish an advisory board with a parent or other representative from each of the sport teams and a determination of how that representative will be selected
    f. Establish the athletic director as a liaison to the advisory board

g. Establish how often the advisory board will meet

h. Establish the number of general booster club meetings

3. **Establish written guidelines for most of the club's operating functions.** Guidelines should minimally cover the following functions:

a. Fiscal controls. These extremely important policies and procedures specify how cash or checks will be handled for such activities as concessions and the sale of T-shirts and other merchandise. Tight controls need to be established to reduce the risk of fraud or embezzlement.

b. Fund-raising activities. The kinds of fund-raising activities that are acceptable and those that are prohibited need to be specified. Will student-athletes or coaches be allowed to participate in fund-raising activities, and if so, what restrictions will apply? Will businesses be asked more than once for contributions? Do such solicitations require athletic department approval?

c. Banquets and awards. What is the club's role in the conduct of postseason banquets for each team or an end-of-year event for all sports? If awards are given at such events, what types of awards will be given to student-athletes and what is the value limit for the award? Will guest speakers be at each banquet? Title IX requires equitable treatment in those areas as well.

d. Conduct policies. Fan conduct at home and away games and booster club trips to away games are two items that need written documents to encourage proper conduct on the part of the booster membership. Whenever an external group is allowed to use the name of the educational institution, their actions will reflect the brand and reputation of that institution. Therefore, the institution has the right to demand such controls.

Policy 13.7 is a sample policy defining the governance elements of a booster club.

13.7 Policy—Governance of External Booster Clubs

A sample policy that defines the function and operation of a booster club, participation by third parties in an advisory capacity, and mechanisms that advance full alignment with the institutional mission, legal requirements, athletic governance association rules, and institutional policies regarding financial affairs.

Available in HK*Propel.*

The athletic director should wield a significant role in setting the tone for the booster club by attending all of its meetings for members as well as governing or advisory board meetings, always being positive and supportive but also being insistent on adherence to policy.

Dealing With the Challenges of Change

If a school has multiple single-sport booster clubs and is making the change to an all-sports booster club because inequities result from disparate funding, bringing the administration of the club into the athletic department, although highly advised, may be difficult. But if it must be done, it should be done with courage, conviction, and straightforward communication. Several steps should be considered to advance this effort in a positive, constructive manner:

- The athletic director should get the support of two or three key alumni or parent booster club leaders by having individual meetings to explain the need for change and discuss the process of getting parents invested in a successful transition.
- All booster club leaders should be assembled to learn about the institution's or school district's fiduciary commitment to strong fiscal controls and its obligation to comply with Title IX. There should be a comprehensive explanation of how Title IX applies to booster clubs.
- The advantages of an umbrella structure with regard to program unity and fiscal controls should be explained. Questions

should be invited. A written summary of these advantages and a summary of questions and answers should be distributed to all club members, alumni, and parents after the meeting.

- Sport-specific groups and their leaders do not need to be discarded. Their volunteer support of events and other efforts are valuable. Rather, the central control of fund-raising and the use of such revenues will change. In fact, each sport club leader can be invited to sit on the athletic director's advisory board so that alumni and parents are regularly informed about the use of funds and program needs.
- Communication and explanations are critical. The athletic director should share social justice analogies related to the designation of funds to provide advantages to one group and not another. For instance, the athletic director might use race as an example by saying, "The Civil Rights Act would not permit a separate booster club for white and Black athletes. Why should we send the message that male and female athletes should be treated differently?" Further, the athletic director might suggest that alumni and parents be challenged to use the change to an umbrella structure as a real-life values lesson for their children, demonstrating parents' commitment to treating their sons and daughters equally. And inevitably, this statement will be made: "Men's sports bring more money to the department." Although men's sports generate revenue, for the most part they still spend more than they bring in. But that isn't the point. The point is that there cannot be an economic justification for discrimination. No school is allowed to say that it will treat boys better than girls because it will make more money that way.

Bringing people together and providing honest answers about doing the right thing for the right reason is paramount. The bottom line message of this discussion is that booster clubs and their fiscal and branding opportunities are more successful for all when they are brought under the control of the institution.

Building the Donor Prospect and Annual Donor Pool

The process of converting a prospective donor to a donor (someone who gives any amount of money to the athletic program) is very different from the process of converting a donor into a major donor (a donor who is among the top 20 percent of all donors with regard to total annual contributions). Getting first-time donations requires numerous strategies such as multiple list acquisition mechanisms and sales tools such as direct mail, e-mail, online, telephone, fund-raising events, and opportunities to cultivate athletic event groups. Conversion to the major donor level is an intensive personal cultivation process that focuses on having one-on-one meetings, offering exclusive entertainment privileges such as guest coach experiences or lunch with the coach and athletic director, maintaining a social media presence that constantly grows followers, and executing personalized communications by phone calls, e-mails, and even handwritten notes.

From a fund-raising accountability perspective, the athletic director should always ask the head fund-raiser to track key performance indicators (KPIs) and to show solid growth on designated parameters. Thus, monthly reports on the following individual giving program KPIs are critical and measurable performance objectives for staff:

- Total number of donors and the percentage increase over the same month in the previous year.
- Total number of meetings (one on one in person and phone calls) with current major donors and the percentage increase over the same month in the previous year.
- Total number of donors in selected donor categories (less than \$100, \$101–\$250, \$251–\$500, \$501–\$1,000, \$1,001–\$2,500, \$2,501–\$5,000, over \$5,000, or similar categories) and the percentage increase over the same month in the previous year.
- Number of staff relationship initiatives by type within each donor category (direct mass mail, individual note, personal phone call, face-to-face meeting). Note that direct mass mail is used for lower donor levels whereas personal written notes, phone calls, and

meetings are typically reserved for major donor prospects.

- Total number of gifts and average gift in the current month compared with the same month in the previous year.
- Total number of planned gifts or planned gift material requests or conversations.

Ideally, a healthy fund-raising program demonstrates steady growth on all these parameters, especially on "sales" contacts. Meeting these record-keeping and performance expectations requires not only good database and contact management, record keeping, and a meeting reminder system (basic fund-raising technology available off the shelf) but also a staff member to orchestrate staff contacts and communications. An effective annual giving program also includes a well-laid-out annual plan that outlines efforts to collect new prospect lists, distribute communications (print and electronic) to prospects and donors, and accomplish one-on-one meetings with major donor prospects.

Legal Considerations

The ability to use athletic department contributions as tax-deductible donations carries the potential for abuse. The athletic program therefore needs to be careful in acknowledging such contributions. In general, it is best to follow several rules:

- Acknowledge all monetary contributions in writing and state, "This contribution is tax deductible to the extent permitted by law."
- Whenever the donor receives something from the institution in return for a contribution, the value of that benefit should be stated by the institution in the acknowledgment. For instance, a ticket to a fund-raising event might be $100, but the value of the meal is $22. The acknowledgment should include the stated value of the meal because the donor needs the information to determine his or her tax deduction.
- When the donor gives the athletic department a gift-in-kind (a service, a piece of equipment, and so on), the donor is responsible for determining and reporting the value of that item, not the institution. The athletic department should send the donor a letter thanking the donor for the gift and naming the gift but should not indicate a value even if the donor makes a specific request to the institution to do so and provides a suggested specific value amount.
- Athletic departments may encounter donors who would like to give the athletic department money to support a specific individual known to the donor such as an athlete, student trainer, or intern. The law does not allow the donor to designate recipients in this manner. But the donor could be appointed as a member of a selection committee that determines the recipient of a postgraduate scholarship or other type of grant, and that level of involvement would be proper.
- The institution may have policies governing acceptance of gifts of stock or real estate, but if it does not, the athletic department would be well served by having a policy that requires the immediate liquidation of such gifts upon receipt. Implementing this policy is especially important if such funds are being used to establish an endowment or attain a certain giving category to obtain higher benefits. There is no need to risk the wrath of a donor or the inability to maintain an endowment because of unanticipated declines in the value of such gifts over short or long periods.

Advisory Versus Fiduciary Boards of Directors

If the booster club is a separately incorporated 501(c)(3) nonprofit organization, its board of directors has fiduciary or legal decision-making responsibility for the operation of the organization. The only way that the institution (or school district) can control the operation of this external group is to condition use of the institution's name, provision of benefits related to the athletic program, and acceptance of contributions from the organization on adherence to institutional policy regarding the operation of the club. Sample Policy 13.7 is an example of such an approach. But even if the club's board has full authority for the operation of the club, the board has no control over the operation of the athletic program. Thus, as the policy notes, all club board recommendations regarding athletic program operation or benefits to club members are advisory. The tension in this arrangement is obvious, but manageable. When the club is operated by the athletic program with no separately incorporated external entity, the board, if the athletic department decides to have one, is really an advisory committee that has no fiduciary authority. To avoid the perception that a board has fiduciary authority, this group should be titled a committee, such as the development committee suggested in Planning Tool 2.11 and sample Policy 2.12. If a booster club does not exist, such a development committee is a proper way to involve external stakeholders in fund-raising activities.

13.8 PLANNING TOOL

Major Donor and Endowed Gift Programs

Definition of a Major Donor

The definition of a major donor with regard to gift amount is relative to the maturity of the fund-raising program and the capacity of alumni and friends. Generally, a good definition is the average total amount of the annual contribution of the 10 individuals who fall in the low end of the top 20 percent of all givers to the program. This term, *major donor*, is used internally to describe prime fund-raising targets and those who should receive premium treatment. The term should not be used externally.

Research Investment

One of the easiest and most essential investments for any individual giving program is the regular use of donor qualification or wealth-screening research services that enable the fund-raising staff to prioritize contacts with the best prospects and identify prospective major donors. The institution simply sends its list of current donors and its prospect lists to a service (such as Wealth Engine or Donor Search), which, on the basis of zip code and other factors, matches public records (LexisNexis, real estate ownership lists, Dun & Bradstreet business lists, Who's Who directories, Federal Election Commission political donor lists, and so on) with athletic department lists on indicators of wealth. The institution's main development office should be contacted for firms that it uses for such services. These firms return the athletic department list with rankings or ranges that indicate the giving capacity for each donor. Such services may cost as little as $1 per record if done for a large quantity of names. Detailed research on a prospect that includes biographical data and income information will be more costly.

This type of donor research will detect people who may be giving very little to athletics or are simply prospects who have not yet made a contribution but who have the capacity and philanthropic intent to give substantially. These factually qualified prospects or donors should be the focus of regular communication and personal contact relationship-building efforts. Time is needed, in most cases 18 to 24 months involving three or four face-to-face meetings per year, to build the trust and relationship required for the donor to make a substantial gift. These meetings require a high level of planning, persistence, and patience. In the interval between meetings, personal telephone calls or written notes should provide program updates or simply acknowledge birthdays, awards, and so on. Gatherings associated with athletic events can provide exposure to athletic program excellence, institutional leadership, and many other excellent relationship-building opportunities.

Endowed and Other Planned Gifts

Clear policies are required to control the establishment of endowed funds. An endowed fund is money that cannot be spent but is invested to generate interest income that can be spent. Legal instruments are required to establish these permanently restricted nonrevocable funds, and they normally require the formal acceptance and approval of the institution's board of trustees or the board of education for a school district. In most cases, such legal documents have been developed by the institution or school district, and the athletic department simply needs to use existing templates from the institution's development office. If these policies and instruments don't exist, they need to be developed with the assistance of legal counsel. Policies need to consider issues such as (1) the minimum amount required to establish an endowment; (2) whether the donor would be allowed to contribute the gift over time and, if so, the minimum amounts and time limits for such giving plans; (3) what happens if the donor does not fulfill his or her donation obligations; (4) if the endowment is to be established upon death and wholly or partially by a bequest, the conditions of such a gift; (5) whether the institution will allow the operation of a program that will eventually be funded by an estate gift before the death of the donor and, if so, under what temporary funding conditions; (6) what happens if investment interest is insufficient to fund the purpose of the endowment; and (7) what happens if the purposes of the endowment are no longer feasible. See Policy 13.9 for a sample policy that addresses all these issues and Form 13.10 for an example of a legal agreement that might be used to establish an endowed fund.

13.9 Policy—Permanently Restricted Endowments

A sample policy that details the conditions under which a permanently restricted endowment may be established or changed.

13.10 Form—Establishment of an Endowment

A sample legal agreement that establishes a permanently restricted endowment.

Available in HK*Propel*.

Other sophisticated forms of planned giving offer major tax benefits that require the expertise of a trained development officer and may even require the services of a lawyer to establish. These types of giving vehicles include but are not limited to the following:

- **Charitable gift annuity.** The donor contributes funds or assets to the educational institution, which in turn makes fixed annuity payments to the donor from the institution's general assets. The donor receives an immediate income tax deduction for a portion of the gift, and a portion of each annuity payment is treated as a tax-free return of the investment. The portion of the gift not used for payments benefits the nonprofit organization.
- **Charitable remainder trust.** The donor establishes a trust for the donor's lifetime or for a period of years not to exceed 20, and the donor (or beneficiaries) receives income from a trust during this period. At the end of that time, the balance of the trust is transferred to the educational institution. The donor is permitted to take a charitable deduction for a portion of the gift made to the trust in the year the trust is established.
- **Charitable lead trusts.** The donor establishes a trust and designates the educational institution to receive a regular, fixed amount from the trust for a specified period or for the lifetime of the donor. At the end of that period or upon death of the donor, the remainder of the trust passes to the donor's designated heirs or other beneficiaries.
- **Charitable bequests.** The donor leaves money or nonmonetary assets to the educational institution from the donor's estate through a will or a revocable living trust.
- **Life insurance policies.** The donor designates the educational institution as the beneficiary of an insurance policy and receives athletic department annual giving credit, tax deductions for yearly premiums, and tax credit for the full value of the insurance policy upon his or her death.

Key for the athletic administrator is preidentification of a trained financial professional, lawyer, or institutional development officer who can be immediately contacted when a donor indicates that he or she wants to make a substantial gift but needs tax or other special advantages or has concerns regarding additional gift beneficiaries. The athletic director or staff fund-raiser does not have to understand the intricacies of these tools but must know that these tools exist and have a general idea of the advantages that might be compelling to a donor. With donors of substantial capacity, the function of the athletic fund-raiser may be simply to convince the donor to explore special tax and other possibilities through a conversation that includes the athletic department's expert advisor and the donor's accountant or other financial advisor.

13.11 PLANNING TOOL

Building Construction and Other Major Fund-Raising Campaigns

Building and other project campaigns with significant fund-raising goals require detailed preparation, a high level of organization, an educated and committed volunteer leadership committee, and a sustainable level of patient and persistent effort. If no one on the staff or in the institutional development office has expertise in the conduct of major fund-raising campaigns, serious consideration should be given to hiring a fund-raising consultant. A fund-raising consultant would be charged with (1) doing the research necessary to determine the ability and capacity of the athletic department to undertake a successful campaign at the level desired and (2) teaching the athletic department staff and leadership committee how to do it. This is a fund-raising area in which the athletic director should not assume that he or she can go it alone.

Building and special project campaigns should be approached like a high-stakes competition such as a conference or national championship. From selecting the players on the team (campaign committee) to preparing the team and coaching them every step of the way, the athletic director has to approach such a project as a critical program competition. These campaigns place a great deal of pressure on the athletic director and his or her chief development staff member to maintain current giving levels while obtaining commitments for additional gifts over and above such normal giving. An investment in obtaining a top consultant will reduce this pressure considerably. Although a consultant won't reduce the staff or committee effort required to achieve the campaign goal, his or her presence will increase everyone's confidence in reaching the goal, prevent unnecessary mistakes, ensure the undertaking of adequate donor research and donor meeting preparation, and provide efficiencies and assistance that save staff time. This assistance is critical because the major gifts campaign is conducted on top of continuing normal tasks of operating an athletic program, selling tickets, and maintaining annual goals for individual and corporate giving.

Major gift campaigns are specialized, highly sophisticated undertakings. After such campaigns are publicly announced, the athletic department must be confident that everything has been done to reduce the risk of failure. That being said, the following is a general outline of the steps involved in executing such a campaign:

1. **Determine campaign capacity.** If the athletic department has not received gifts of more than $20,000 from at least 10 people, chances are good that the individual-giving program is not mature enough to undertake a seven- or eight-figure capital campaign. The first thing that a fund-raising consultant will do is assess current capacity and define the donor growth parameters required before initiating the proposed campaign. After it is determined that the capacity for the campaign is present, then the following steps need to be accomplished.
2. **Develop the case statement.** Every successful campaign requires a compelling story that articulates the need for the project. The case statement communicates the effect of the project on the department and its student-athletes. The story needs to be embraced by the people who will be telling it (the campaign leadership committee) as well as the donors who will be inquisitive and want to understand the value of their gifts.

3. **Obtain commitments of people to serve on the campaign leadership committee.** These are the people who will do the asking. They need to be the group that is excited about the case statement, willing to have personal face-to-face meetings with prospects, and be perceived by donors as trustworthy, hard-working, and committed. Most important, they will be successful in their role to the degree that they are educated about the prospects and ways to approach them. Committee members need to be convinced that their role is, initially, (1) to tell a compelling story, (2) to ask the donor for advice, and (3) to be a careful listener. If they do these things well, the donor will ask how he or she can help and enlist the help of friends. See Educational Resource 13.12 for a handout that can be distributed to campaign leadership committee members to prepare them for their duties.
4. **Develop the gift rate chart and benefits afforded donors at each giving level.** The gift rate chart is a graduated list of gift amounts, from high to low, that includes the desired number of donations of each amount, all adding up to the total amount required for the campaign. At every level, the athletic department needs to have three to five or more times as many qualified prospective donors from whom it will seek gifts. Each level also needs to list donor benefits (naming rights, seating priority, and so on). This document also details the length of the period over which pledges can be paid. This element of the campaign includes the development of high-quality printed materials that tell the campaign story in a compelling way.
5. **Create the solicitation action plan.** This is the game plan of who is going to be asked to give what amount by whom. The amount and the person asking are determined by a variety of factors including factual analysis of giving capacity, knowledge of the person through visits or conversations, wealth assessment, and past giving history. The solicitation action plan would also include a timetable for the campaign that has benchmarks for fund-raising goals, dates of leadership committee reporting meetings, events, and more. Finally, campaigns and volunteers are more successful when each committee member has a goal. A specific goal should be set for each committee member regarding the number of prospect visits during each week of the campaign, and the emphasis should be on personal visits rather than phone calls or letters.
6. **Initiate the quiet phase of leadership gifts.** Before the campaign is publicly announced, the goal should be to secure leadership gifts or pledges that total 50 to 70 percent of the eventual total campaign goal. The larger the goal is, the larger this percentage should be. The entire focus of this part of the campaign is to obtain gifts at the highest levels of the gift rate chart, methodically starting by completing visits with prospects at the top level and working down. This aspect of the campaign is the most critical in that achieving this goal almost guarantees campaign success because it will indicate to subsequent donors the viability of the fund-raising effort and create an impetus to achieve success.
7. **Execute the public launch and complete the campaign.** With the bulk of the campaign goal in place (50 to 70 percent pledged), executing the launch and remainder of the campaign is a bit easier because of the increased confidence of the campaign committee, community momentum, and high staff and institution morale. Campaign completion, however, requires persistence, focused effort, and a continued sense of urgency to want to win for the team and institution.

13.12 Educational Resource—
Campaign Leadership Committee Guidelines

A sample handout that inspires and instructs committee members how to ask for campaign contributions.

Available in HK*Propel*.

13.13 PLANNING TOOL

Sponsorship and Corporate-Giving Programs

Policy Considerations

Corporate sponsors can represent a significant potential revenue stream by providing cash or promotional sponsorships, purchasing advertising, buying tickets, and contributing services or products. But the athletic department, as an educational not-for-profit organization, must be extremely cautious about its association with commercial for-profit entities. There must be clear understanding of the benefits that the nonprofit athletic program can provide to commercial entities and those it cannot. What benefits are prohibited by law or institutional policy? What benefits might be inconsistent with the athletic department's educational mission? For instance, institutions may not permit a car dealer to display an automobile on the university campus or to film a commercial advertisement on campus. State laws may prohibit the conduct of an auction or raffle featuring a sponsor's product except under limited circumstances. Limitations may govern the display of signage in school buildings or the distribution of commercial advertisements at school events. Would the institution enter into a relationship with a sales corporation that uses a pyramid sales scheme, a company that sells diet or vitamin products of questionable origin or integrity, a business that sells alcohol products, or a sex club? What happens if the corporate sponsor wants to say that the athletic department endorses the use of its product? All these issues need to be addressed by adopting a policy that has been reviewed by legal counsel and approved by higher administrative authorities. See Policy 13.14 for a sample policy that deals with these issues. Giving a copy of this policy to sponsors is important.

13.14 Policy—Corporate Sponsorships

A sample policy that defines the conditions under which the athletic program will accept corporate sponsorships and advertising.

Available in HK*Propel*.

Benefits-Based Sponsorship Program Framework

Just as individual-giving programs have a menu of donor opportunities that delineates the benefits for each level of giving, the corporate-giving program must have a similar framework. When these parameters are clear, the athletic director or head of marketing must go through an exercise of identifying possible areas of corporate interest and specifying how the athletic program might be able to fulfill that interest (e.g., see table 13.13.1).

The initial conversation with a sponsor prospect should always start with a focused effort to determine sponsor needs and desired outcomes of a partnership within the established framework so that the language of the proposal matches "corporate speak." Every effort should be made to integrate into the sponsorship agreement as many of these sponsor benefit elements as possible because the prospective sponsor must see how he or she can justify a significant expenditure of company funds. See Form 13.15 for an example of a sponsorship proposal format. See Educational Resource 13.16 for a handout to remind the institution's staff, graduate student, or volunteer workforce about the keys to developing successful corporate sponsorship programs.

Table 13.13.1 Matching Sponsorship Benefit With Sponsor Need

Sponsor need	Type of sponsorship program
Identification with athletic or institutional brand	Advertising, titled event, official product, corporate signage at event, cobranded merchandise
Exclusivity among producers of similar product	Official product or supplier, institutional vendor agreement
Consumer affinity	Media exposure, redemption of discount or rebate coupons
Consumer reach	Media exposure, redemption of discount or rebate coupons
Product sales	Rebate or donation with purchase
Trial use or sampling of product	Event sampling, donation with trial
Customer entertainment	Premium tickets, VIP event in conjunction with athletic event, head coach appearance at corporate VIP event
Employee entertainment or involvement	Group tickets, discounted tickets, employee volunteers at athletic department community service event
Media exposure	Advertising, event signage, title sponsorship, consumer promotions

13.15 Form—Corporate Sponsorship Proposal

A sample proposal that defines the terms of corporate sponsorship of an athletic event with regard to benefits provided by the athletic department and value to be received from the business.

13.16 Educational Resource—Guidelines for Soliciting Corporate Sponsors

A sample handout for staff and volunteers that addresses the balance of receivables and benefits delivered and other structural components of sponsorship proposals as well as key considerations in how to approach businesses for sales pitches.

Available in HK*Propel*.

Quality Execution and Proof of Performance

Key to maintaining successful sponsorship agreements is working to maximize the success and quality execution of such relationships, keeping in mind that the corporation is seeking all or some of the following benefits: (1) visibility and credit with a consumer public, (2) appreciation from its employees, and (3) a factual demonstration that such sponsorship is directly related to increased consumer sales or increased employee or consumer corporate affinity. Although the corporate sponsor can easily track the effect on consumer sales with product-related promotions, increases in employee or consumer affinity may require the athletic department to arrange for the conduct of market research. Resources to do this are available on campus at little or no cost if the athletic department engages its advertising, marketing, or business school faculty and graduate students to assist in demonstrating the effectiveness of these sponsorship programs. Cultivating relationships with the institution's sport management program can even provide the workforce to produce and sell sponsorship and promotional proposals.

Accountability and Key Performance Indicators

The head of fund-raising may also be in charge of building corporate giving, which could include advertising, ticket sales, and sponsorships in addition to the annual giving and major giving programs. Alternatively, another person may be responsible for leading the corporate sponsorship program. In either case, the structure of the sponsorship and corporate-giving program is similar to individual-giving fund-raising programs. It is necessary to determine key performance indicators (KPIs), manage regular communication and personal contacts to build relationships, and demonstrate growth on all parameters over time. As revenues and numbers of contacts increase, more staff is required. Sample KPIs for a corporate-giving program are as follows:

- Number of corporate sponsor proposals delivered year to date and compared with the same date in the previous year
- Number of accepted proposals year to date and compared with the same date in the previous year
- Number of prospective corporate sponsor in-person visits to date and compared with the same date in the previous year
- Total cash and in-kind value of corporate sponsorships year to date compared with the same date in the previous year—total and by product category
- Total advertising revenues (separate from or inclusive of those included in sponsorship proposals) year to date and compared with the same date in the previous year—total and by product category
- Corporate season-ticket and entertainment suite sales to date and compared with the same date in the previous year

Integration of Individual- and Corporate-Giving Programs

Whether speaking to an individual or corporate donor prospect, the fund-raiser must have (1) a menu of all possible giving opportunities, (2) a good idea of the giving capability of the donor, (3) a sense of what is important to the donor, and (4) the answer to the donor's question of the athletic representative, "Where do you most need help and why?" The fund-raiser never knows when an individual donor can become or lead to a corporate donation and vice versa. A common challenge for athletic departments is whether or what part of corporate sponsorship dollars should generate credit for the determination of booster club benefits or individual seating priorities that might carry renewal rights. These issues can be addressed in many ways (see the discussion of priority-seating systems in Planning Tool 13.18), but the point is that these questions need to be answered. The athletic department should have a compilation of common questions and answers that are accumulated over the years to ensure consistent treatment of donors and sponsors. The menu of all possible giving opportunities should be an internal written document that carefully details benefits, donation or sponsor levels, and so on.

Leveraging Institutional Vendor Programs

Athletic departments should make every effort to have the larger institution's vendor requests for proposals (RFPs) include an obligation to consult with the athletic department for opportunities beneficial to the vendor. The athletic department should recommend the establishment of an institutional business office policy requiring that all businesses seeking a commercial relationship with the institution or submitting a response to an RFP consult with the athletic department to determine whether their submissions can offer added value through an athletic department relationship. This simple provision can provide the athletic department with increased sales contacts and appropriate but invaluable leverage with which to generate increased advertising and sponsorship sales.

13.17 PLANNING TOOL

Maximizing Event Income: Ticketing, Concessions, Parking, and Guarantees

Besides offering opportunities for athletic event sponsorship programs with athletic event benefits (see Planning Tool 13.13) and individual-giving programs tied to seating priorities (see Planning Tool 13.18), athletic events present myriad other revenue generation possibilities that should be exploited if possible. These opportunities include event ticket sales (season, individual game, and special or postseason events), concessions, guarantees, and parking. Another source of income is including event program and signage opportunities in a multimedia rights package (see Planning Tool 13.19 in the book and Form 13.20 in HK*Propel*).

The Decision to Sell Tickets

The first revenue decision to be made for any sport program is to answer the question of whether tickets could be issued and a fee charged for admission to a sport event. The answer to this question depends on whether the sport is being contested in a controlled-access facility that has spectator seating. If the answer to this question is yes, the next question is whether admission *should* be charged. Before answering this question, the administrator should consider the following:

- The public will place a higher perceived value on events for which an admission fee is charged as opposed to free events. Thus, the decision to charge for admission is a decision by the athletic department to place a value on the sport program.
- Admission fees can always be waived for special populations such as parents, members of the current student body, or faculty upon presentation of an institutional ID or courtesy pass.
- The cost of charging for an event is minimal: the price of roll tickets (cheap generic paper tickets that are numbered for accounting purposes but not printed specifically for the event) and the hourly wages for a ticket seller and a ticket taker to thank the fan for his or her support (usually a task that can be performed by a person working at minimum wage, a volunteer, or an existing staff member).
- The greater the involvement of a person in a program and the closer his or her perceived relationship is to the coach, players, and institution, the more likely it is that the person will make a donation to the program on top of the price of admission. Ticketing is the first step in developing a sport into a revenue producer. Donor gifts are often more important than ticket revenues.
- Diversification of revenue sources is a characteristic of successful fund-raising programs. If a program depends on revenues from only one or two sports and one of those sources fails or has a down year, the financial stability of the athletic program may be endangered. Every effort should be made to develop every sport as a revenue producer, if not through the sale of event tickets, then at least in the development of donors who have an affinity for that sport.
- Fan and friend attendance at athletic events, which naturally occurs as an element of the athletic program, is the most cost-effective mechanism for the development of donors. Athletic events bring donors to interact with the program in large numbers at their own expense.

If the leadership thoroughly examines the preceding considerations, it is difficult to justify a decision not to charge admission. Sometimes these decisions depend on the energy and passion of the athletic administrator to develop a program, but at other times such decisions depend on the availability of human resources to administer and promote the ticketing program.

Season-Ticket Considerations

After establishing a mechanism for the purchase of walk-up tickets as the first step in developing game revenues, the second step is determining how to market season-ticket sales. Season-ticket sales increase revenues because the money is received in advance and retained whether the purchaser uses the tickets or not. Tickets could be redeemable based on one per game, exist as a season-ticket pass, or exist as a book of general admission tickets that could be used at any event when the customer wants to bring friends and family, depending on decisions related to public demand. Ticket books are not necessary when a season-ticket pass card that is punched for each of a maximum number of games is just as functional and more cost effective. The advantage of individual tickets for each game is that they can be given to others. And, of course, premium fees can be charged for the best seat locations, the nicest seats, tournaments, special events, or postseason championship play. Promotional imagination is the only limitation on the types of season tickets that can be offered.

Discounted and Complimentary Tickets

Care must be taken in offering discounted and complimentary tickets. The number of seats offered of each type and the seating location of students, faculty, and staff must be carefully thought out, especially when the size of the facility cannot fully accommodate ticket demand. Student, faculty, and staff involvement in the program must often be balanced against pressure to produce revenues. These decisions have significant political and philosophical implications that must be carefully weighed. The distribution and identity of persons receiving complimentary tickets should be recorded for every athletic event, and such practices should be reviewed every season. Complimentary ticket promotions will always be more prevalent when developing a new revenue sport than with a mature, high-demand revenue sport. When seats are available, "papering" the house with youth groups, community service organizations, and other groups can be an effective promotional effort in introducing a sport to prospective fans and creating an exciting game atmosphere.

Concessions

Historically, concessions at high school and college athletic events have been operated either by volunteers (booster clubs, parents, and so on), student groups, or charitable organizations. Such groups keep a percentage of the profits of such operations for their charitable purposes. In these circumstances, the institution is responsible for the volunteers working in these areas and the safety and health-related concerns of food operations. These volunteers are not eligible for workers compensation benefits.

As health and food safety laws and regulations have become more stringent, the operation of concessions has increasingly moved to third-party operators who are food service experts and are insured to manage these operations at little or no risk to the educational institution. Many of these third-party operators continue to use the same volunteer groups, but the training obligation and risk has effectively been transferred to the concessionaire. In many cases, the concessionaire is the same company that provides student union, cafeteria, or other food service operations on campus. Ideally, such third-party execution of concessions is desirable. When concession rights are sold to a third party that executes the food, beverage, or merchandise services, a percentage of gross sales is negotiated as the return value to the athletic department. The concessionaire is responsible for everything from staffing concession booths to the purchase and preparation of products to be sold. These third-party turnkey vendor opportunities are viable only when athletic event attendance reaches significant levels in the view of the concessionaire or at smaller institutions where operating the food service for all university events makes sense with regard to amortizing staff and operating costs.

At many high schools and small colleges where attendance at athletic events is not substantial enough to warrant the business interest of third-party concessionaires, the institution is still faced with administering and supervising these operations and the athletic department has the primary responsibility for doing so. In today's litigious culture, policies, procedures, and training programs for these volunteer and concession operations are essential. A common practice at smaller high schools and colleges is for the athletic department to allow student clubs or local community service organizations to run concession booths and turn over a percentage of the gross to the athletic department. The community group keeps a larger share. Alternatively, the athletic department can make all arrangements (provision of booth, product, and so on) and allow volunteer groups to provide staffing in return for receiving a smaller percentage of the gross. Key to implementing these types of concessions services is having strict policies and procedures to ensure that each vendor meets local health and other regulations. For samples of essential policies, a volunteer release and consent form, and a charitable organization application for a concessions booth, see Policy 15.26, Form 15.27, and Form 15.28, respectively, in HK*Propel*.

Guarantees

Institutions often have difficulty scheduling nonconference home competitions. As a result, an athletic department might offer a financial incentive, commonly called a guarantee, for another institution to come to its institution to play. In the case of NCAA Division I institutions, such guarantees may be six-figure sums that are critical to the budget of the institution being enticed to play an away event against what is often a better team.

Parking

When parking is limited, institutions often charge for access to convenient parking areas or give the premium parking areas to major donors as a benefit associated with high annual contribution levels or to fans who have purchased larger numbers of higher-priced season tickets. The decision to charge for parking depends on both demand and the ease and expense of controlling access to a parking area.

13.18 PLANNING TOOL

Seating Priority Points Systems

Definition, Purpose, and Advantages

Seating priority points systems (SPPS) are common mechanisms used across the country by athletic programs to determine ticket purchasing and seat location priorities for collegiate athletic events. These systems are designed to create incentives for ticket buyers to increase donations to the athletic annual fund or major giving programs in exchange for better seat locations. Seats are assigned based on total number of points earned, and points earned are heavily weighted toward total annual donations. For example, 1 point may be awarded for each $100 donated to the annual fund and 2 points may be awarded for each season ticket purchased. The purposes of an SPPS are threefold:

- Establish a fair and transparent system underlying all decisions related to seat location
- Thank and give preference to those who make the greatest contributions to the success of the university and its athletic program
- Encourage increased donations to the athletic annual fund that support student-athlete scholarships for an education and workplace preparation, salaries that will enable the university to attract the finest coaches who are master teachers central to the success of the program, and maintenance costs of athletic facilities and programs that serve the entire university community

These systems are in stark contrast to seat-licensing systems that place a tax on top of the price of a season ticket based on the premium location of a seat. Seat licenses are most often used by professional sport franchises that have high market demand. Priority point systems are a better philosophical fit for universities in that they honor and thank donors who do the most to advance the mission of the department rather than make the more commercial statement that "this is the price you pay to get a good seat."

With an SPPS, the spectator is under constant pressure to give more money and get more points to retain his or her seat location or get a better seat location. Seat licenses, on the other hand, are like taxes. They increase every so often, and taxpayers usually aren't happy about the increases. Because the SPPS seat price never really exists as an identifiable amount, the ticket buyer doesn't get the impression of increased costs. Priority points are accumulated beginning at a time that usually corresponds to the earliest year of giving and ticket purchase records that are presumed accurate and continues indefinitely into the future, until the account holder (or spouse) dies.

Another characteristic of SPPS is that seats can change every year. Points are recalculated every year, and seat locations are assigned accordingly. In reality, however, after the first few years during which fans figure out the system and their ability to afford a certain point level, seating becomes relatively stable.

An SPPS is more transparent and fairer than a seat-licensing system. In a seat-licensing system, everyone in a certain section pays the same license fee, but issues of priority occur within the section. Many times these issues are settled by longevity (years holding the tickets), but this method does little to provide incentives for increased giving. Most athletic directors agree that an SPPS is transparent and therefore perceived as fair because everyone knows the rules. Of course, the year in which the rules of the seat location game are changed is difficult in regard to ticket buyer relations.

Most important to remember is that an SPPS is not a ticket sales tool; it is a development or fund-raising mechanism. Implementing an SPPS presents a valuable opportunity for the athletic department development staff to interact through a personal meeting with a season-ticket holder, ostensibly to explain the new system but in reality to seek increased financial commitment to the institution and its athletic program.

Critical Steps in Creating a Ticket Priority System

The following steps should be taken to create an SPPS:

- Create a point system that expresses institutional values and creates incentives for the most valued behavior (e.g., growing annual gifts versus selling the greatest number of season tickets). For example, see figure 13.18.1.
- Address the need to balance the athletic department interest with the greater institutional interest. The larger the expectation is that athletics will produce increased revenues and carry its own funding burden, the greater the emphasis should be on points for athletic giving and the less the emphasis should be on points for nonathletic giving.
- When developing the point system, recognize that some people will always try to beat the system. Commit to figuring out what the loopholes are and how to eliminate them.
- Examine how the establishment of such a system to exploit an athletic asset might have an unanticipated effect on nonathletic giving and how that can be minimized. All communications about implementing the system must contain a request that increased giving to athletics not come at the expense of giving to other university departments.
- Before instituting the system, take the previous year's actual season-ticket purchasers and apply the system to them to assess the real effect of the system on all stakeholders. Adjust the system based on factual data rather than fears.
- Before instituting the system, create a master list of expected questions and answers to anticipate the problems. The people who will have to answer those questions need to have answers. Invariably, this exercise results in the establishment of good policy before the rollout of the new program and makes for a less-stressful transition.
- Commit to meetings with the most important stakeholders and create a communications piece that introduces the system in a personal way that will result in gaining the greatest support for the system.

Issues That Must Be Addressed by the Point System

Closing loopholes before they are discovered by donors and ticket buyers is crucial. Be sure to consider the following point calculation and ticket purchase issues and make policy decisions or SPPS rules that accompany all formal statements about the SPPS program:

- **How far back will you go with regard to accumulating points?** This decision is based on record keeping. A policy statement such as the following example should be created: "Points are accumulated over time, starting with June 1, 1992, the earliest year in which we are most confident of having accurate donor records and, for season-ticket points, starting in August 1, 2001, the earliest year in which we are most confident in athletic department season-ticket records, and continuing through the end of the previous fiscal year (May 31) for all tickets to be purchased in the current fiscal year."
- **Who gets credit in the case of spouses' or business checks?** Consider the following policies:
    - Calculation is on a per account basis. Whoever sends the check to purchase one or more tickets or make a donation is the account holder.
    - Unless specifically requested to keep accounts separate, both spouses get points for donations that they may make individually and points are combined into one account that shall be held in both names. But points will always be calculated and maintained for each individual.
    - Accumulated points are nontransferable upon death, except to one's spouse.
    - For corporate sponsorships, the account holder is the corporation and not an individual.

Sample Point System

In thanks for your support of our XU athletic program . . .

Cumulative Point Allocations

- 1 point for each $100 donated to athletics, including the cash value of any insurance policy donated to the institution and interest generated by any endowment
- 1 point for each $500 of deferred gifts
- 1 point for each $100 donated to athletics in the first year by a new XU booster club member whom you have recruited as indicated by your name inserted as sponsor on the new member's booster club membership application or in writing on the contribution check (only one sponsor designation by any new booster club member)
- 2 points for each season ticket purchased for any XU sport

. . . especially for your loyalty

Cumulative Point Allocations

- 3 points for every year that you have been a booster club member
- 2 points for every year in which you have purchased one or more season tickets in any sport

One-Time Point Allocations

- 10 points if you were a letter winner at XU in any sport

. . . and for your investment in XU

Cumulative Point Allocations

- 1 point for every year in which you have been an XU faculty or staff member
- 1 point for every year that you have been a dues-paying member of the XU Alumni Association
- 1 point for each $100 donated each year to the XU chancellor's club (annual contribution of $25,000 or more to any XU academic or other program), president's club ($10,000–$24,999), provost's club ($5,000–$9,999), or to the capital campaign

One-Time Point Allocations

- 1 point if you ever attended XU

Figure 13.18.1 A sample point system for priority seating that rewards valued behavior.

From D. Lopiano and C. Zotos, *Athletic Director's Desk Reference*, 2nd ed. (Champaign, IL: Human Kinetics, 2023).

- **What cutoff dates apply to points calculations?** Consider the following policies:
    - Any donation to the institution before the actual purchase of season tickets counts in that year.
    - Pledges must be paid before the end of the previous fiscal year (May 31) to have the donation counted for priority points considered for ticket purchases in the current year.
    - The current-year institution donation required for the purchase of any seat in a priority point premium section must be paid before or with the season ticket. The value of that donation, however, is not included in the priority point calculation until the following year.
- **Will current membership in the booster club be a requirement for purchase of premium seats?** A policy statement such as the following might be considered: "To buy a basketball season ticket in any designated premium seating section, the account holder must be a current (year in which ticket is purchased) athletic department booster club member at the minimum designated level for each ticket purchased in that section." For example, if a section is open to individuals who make at least a $200 annual contribution to the athletic fund, buying four tickets in that section requires an $800 contribution to the athletic fund.
- **Will incentives be created for per game or nonpremium seating season tickets?** A policy statement like the following might be considered: "Per game or season tickets located outside premium seating sections that are ordered at the same time as season tickets for premium seating sections have priority over public purchasers and are given location priority according to priority point totals within priority point account holders."
- **How are special types of gifts credited?** The following types of policies should be considered:
    - Matching gifts from the employer of the account holder (or spouse) shall count as if such gifts were from the account holder.
    - For corporate sponsorships, points are awarded for each $100 in sponsorship or advertising dollars excluding the cost of any tickets or hard costs to the athletic department of any sponsorship package.
    - For gifts-in-kind accepted by the athletic department, points are awarded for each $100 in value only if the gift offsets a budgeted expense and excluding the cost of any tickets or hard costs to the athletic department involved in accepting or using the gift.
- **Will a major annual donor be permitted to purchase an unlimited number of tickets?** Institutions should consider the following policy: "An account holder is limited to a purchase of no more than eight season tickets in any priority point premium seating section."

Model Systems

Searching the website of any major Division I institution for its priority points system will provide an example of points systems and policies that should be considered. Remember that keeping the system simple ensures better donor and customer understanding and acceptance as well as ease of athletic department administration. There is no one right way to design an SPPS.

13.19 PLANNING TOOL

Selling Event and Multimedia Rights

Multimedia Rights and Advertising Sales

Another approach to corporate giving is an advertising and sales approach that involves commercial leveraging of athletic program multimedia assets either in addition to sponsorship sales or instead of such sales depending on market interest in multimedia rights. There are three basic ways to use athletic product rights commercially with advertisers:

- Sell the rights to the athletic program properties to a third party to sell commercially, receiving a fixed rights fee amount per year
- Hire a third party to sell advertising and sponsorships to exploit athletic program assets, paying the third party a commission on sales
- Sell to sponsors and advertisers directly by dedicating a full-time or part-time staff position to this effort

Why Package Multimedia Rights?

Developing multimedia rights related to sport program products has been the source of considerable revenue growth for numerous collegiate programs and is beginning to filter down into scholastic athletic programs. The reason for this is simple. When distribution of content (radio play-by-play, television programming, uniform logo rights, licensed merchandise, and so on) was limited to a few broadcast television stations, a limited number of radio stations in the local market, or a limited number of retail outlets, only the product perceived by the limited number of distributors as having the highest public interest and value was marketable. This meant that only the top college programs with the highest number of followers or highest interest to the public were able to sell these assets. Today, the means of content and product distribution has expanded exponentially because of the growth of the Internet and the proliferation of cable television distributors. For example, televised product distributors have grown from broadcast television only to broadcast plus regional sport cable channels to broadcast, regional sport cable, satellite television, and hundreds of cable channels and finally to almost unlimited distribution opportunities through the Internet. Thus, instead of going to the broadcast operator with the greatest reach to promote their product, advertisers are now dealing with a highly fragmented communications universe in which they must work with third parties who are responsible for aggregating audiences derived from doing numerous deals with many rights holders.

This fragmented distribution system has placed a huge value on content. More distributors than ever before need to fuel their 24/7 existence with sport products. Members of the public do not go to the television set or the Internet to seek advertising; they go seeking content. Advertising attaches itself to content to get the viewer or listener to see or hear the message. Broadcast television stations, radio stations, cable and satellite television companies, and so on need content to attract money from advertisers, and as a result many may be willing to pay for the rights to distribute certain content. These distributors receive greater or lesser amounts of money from advertisers based on the number of viewers they can deliver. The result of this market fragmentation has been the development of a new middleman—the aggregator of sport content who sells exposure to advertisers across multiple content distributors. For example, one college in a small town airing a local athletic event isn't worth much to an advertiser. A middleman can accumulate rights for 100 such institutions in 100 markets and then seek to provide factual proof of significant audience reach.

A middleman who can prove that advertising is seen by everyone that receives the institution's football schedule card multiplied by 100 institutions, a schedule poster multiplied by 100 institutions, an Internet site multiplied by 100 institutions, and so on can sell advertising opportunities at higher rates because the company is able to guarantee greater reach. The purpose of this lengthy explanation is simple. Athletic programs, no matter their size, should assess whether any third-party content aggregator is interested in obtaining the rights to sell sponsor or advertiser exposure to some or all of their athletic program products.

Who Should Sell Advertising and Sponsorships?

Exploring an athletic program's multimedia rights sales possibility requires the athletic director to define all athletic program assets that could be sold. First, the athletic director should seek a third-party aggregator. Even if an aggregator has no interest in purchasing all these rights, this exercise will give the athletic director a clear understanding of what can be sold to advertisers. Better yet, by going through this process, the athletic director is more likely to see opportunities to bundle program assets to create greater reach or exposure for advertisers, thereby generating more revenues than could be gained by selling one asset at a time or only the most desirable asset. Most athletic directors are not experienced commercial salespeople. Thus, recognizing limits of time and expertise, the athletic director should always seek to commission a local advertising sales agency (which keeps a percentage of whatever it sells) to market the athletic product. If no one is interested in paying the institution for the right to sell advertising associated with athletic content, the athletic director may take the fallback position of hiring someone to sell directly to advertisers, assigning a staff member to perform this function, or doing it him- or herself.

Identify Athletic Program Assets

Key to exploiting this potential revenue source is identifying potential commercial opportunities. The following is an example of what that list of opportunities (commercial inventory) might look like. The next step for the salesperson is to define how many people attend, receive, listen to, or watch each product. Based on the numbers generated, the next step is to bundle and value the advertising or sponsorship package, and the last step is to go into the marketplace and attempt to sell it.

- At every athletic event open to the public, by sport:
    - All permanent and temporary signage within the facility
    - Product displays at the event
    - Sampling, couponing, and product distribution at the event
    - Public service announcements as promotional opportunities
    - Opportunity to host a hospitality event
    - Title and presenting sponsorships
    - Pregame, postgame, halftime, and timeout promotions, contests, mascot appearances, corporate recognition and presentations, and giveaways
    - Tailgate areas and fan fair
    - VIP hospitality areas
- All athletic program printed materials:
    - Football game program and per game roster inserts
    - Men's and women's basketball game programs and per game roster inserts
    - Baseball season program and per game roster inserts
    - Softball game program and per game roster inserts (and any other sports for which such materials are produced)
    - Athletic event tickets (advertising available on ticket back)
    - Game promotional flyers
    - Schedule cards
    - Schedule posters
    - Backs of parking passes
    - Media guides
- Football stadium sponsorship:
    - Scoreboards (or video boards)
    - Sideline signage
    - Field-level signage
    - End zone signage

- Goalpost pads
- Field goal nets
- Team bench backs
- Concourse displays, temporary signage and displays for special events
- T-shirts of sideline and concession employees
- Plastic souvenir cups and concession containers
- Message center and public address announcements

- Basketball arena sponsorship:
    - Scorers' table, press row, and courtside table advertising panels
    - Message center and public address announcements
    - Team bench and floor seating chair backs
    - Shot clock advertising panels
    - Basketball goal pads, stanchions, and so on
    - Concession, entry and exit, and restroom signage
    - Concourse displays, temporary signage, and displays for special events
    - Scoreboard (or video board) sponsorship and promotions
    - Wall-mounted scoreboards and fascia strip scoreboards and signage
    - Plastic souvenir cups and concession containers
    - Restroom signage
    - Seatback drink cup holder signage
    - All permanent and temporary signage
    - Courtside employee (e.g., ball boys and girls, scorer's table crew) clothing
    - Branded vending opportunities
- Baseball and softball stadium sponsorship:
    - Video board or scoreboards signage
    - Outfield wall signage
    - Dugout back signage
    - All permanent and temporary signage
    - Plastic souvenir cups and concession containers
- Radio events:
    - Radio play by play
    - Coaches' radio call-in shows
    - Daily report
    - Satellite radio
- Television events:
    - Daily report
    - Coaches' shows
    - Live or delayed play-by-play coverage not included in conference or other rights packages
    - Pre- and postseason specials
- Promotional tags and credits such as "brought to you by" or "made possible through the generous support of"
    - Radio event promotions
    - Television event promotions
    - Ticket mailer inserts
    - Athletic ticket envelopes
    - Media backdrop at press events
    - Coaches' headsets
    - E-mail blast promotions
- Official supplier rights (logo on product, exclusivity) as approved by institution:
    - Isotonic beverage (e.g., coolers, cups, towels, squeeze bottles)
    - Athletic apparel
    - Athletic shoes
    - Royalty-free use of marks and logos
- Official athletic website:
    - Banners, buttons, features
    - Online store
    - Auctions
    - Photo store
    - Subscription revenue
- Merchandising opportunities:
    - Affinity products
    - Specialty merchandise
    - Highlight videos and CDs

The commercial exploitation of these assets is often limited by institutional policy and philosophy. To what extent does the institution wish the public to perceive its athletic program as commercially motivated? Or, using a more positive approach, to what extent does the institution want the public to perceive such efforts as offsetting costs through public contributions that help support and expand educational programming? How the athletic administrator positions such sales efforts can make a world of difference in public perception and public and commercial support.

Issuing a Request for Proposal

After the athletic department determines the assets it wishes to sell, seeking an aggregator will require the preparation of a request for proposal (RFP) to determine the company that will be given the exclusive right to produce and sell or package and sell these assets. The institution's procurement office has the expertise to assist the athletic director in structuring a comprehensive RFP. See Form 13.20 for an example of such a proposal.

13.20 **Form**–Request for Proposal: Athletic Event and Multimedia Rights

A sample RFP that specifies the inventory of athletic program assets that are available, the proposal submission and selection process, and a financial quotation form that dictates the type of offer expected.

Available in HK*Propel*.

After the responses to the RFP are received, the decision on the aggregator agency should be made not only on the basis of the guaranteed fee and breadth of coverage promised but also on the reputation of the agency with regard to financial stability; proof of performance with similarly situated institutions; and relationships with broadcast, cable, Internet, and satellite partners (Foster, Greyser, & Walsh, 2006).

13.21 PLANNING TOOL

Assessment of Radio, Television, and Internet Streaming Production Capability

Self-Supporting or Profit-Making Radio and Television Programming

If the right to telecast or audiocast an athletic event is drawing no commercial interest or some of this inventory is remaining after exposure by the institution's national or regional sports channel packages, the institution can often produce its own programming without difficulty and pay for it through the sale of program advertising. The institution would arrange for production of the game, live or delayed delivery to the distributor, carriage on a television or radio station, and the sale of advertising to offset the costs of these elements. Alternatively, because the cost of video equipment and uploading such content to the athletic department website is reasonable, any high school or college athletic program can produce its own advertising-supported or advertising-free online content.

What Questions Should Be Asked to Determine Feasibility of Selling Content to a Commercial Distributor?

Several costs and issues need to be considered before deciding to undertake producing such programming:

1. Will the quality of the production be satisfactory to the radio or television distributor with regard to numbers of cameras used, graphical treatments, ability to display statistics, professionalism of commentators and camera crews, and so on?
2. What quality of production can be afforded? The institution can easily contract for expensive high-quality production by a third party, but the sale of the advertising inventory must support it. The price of advertisements depends completely on average ratings—the number of households who will see it—which is a function of the reach of the carrier, which in turn is a function of the day and time slot of the programming.
3. Can live broadcast be afforded? This involves the cost of a satellite truck or microwave connection. Can the advertising necessary to fund this cost be sold?
4. Does the athletic program have the bandwidth or is it willing to purchase the bandwidth or platform to air the program, audio or video, on its own or a third-party website? What additional reach might that provide to an advertiser? Does the institution have the donor and fan interest to subscribe to such Internet broadcasts or the advertising interest to support free access?
5. Is the carrier able to provide an optimal day and time slot (which may be a function of its willingness or authority to displace existing programming for live coverage), or will the event have to be on a delayed broadcast? What will the cost of this time be? Producing delayed telecast events with local reach is relatively inexpensive, but producing live programming with regional or national reach is difficult and expensive. And, of course, radio is less complicated and expensive than television. Given the single or multiple carriers willing to air the event, what is the reach of such carriers?
6. How much can be charged for advertising given the going rate for advertising for the audience projected?
7. Can event-related signage, tickets, or other athletic program benefits be packaged with the advertising to increase the current rate charged for these nontelevision or nonradio advertisements?

8. Is it possible for any of these elements to be joint ventures? For example, the radio or television carrier could provide the time at no cost to the institution, the institution could provide the cost of production, and each party could agree to sell and keep the proceeds of half of the television or radio advertising inventory. The prospect of such joint ventures or getting a third-party packager to invest in the programming increases as the value of benefits that could be added for the advertiser increases.

In the worst-case scenario, the institution would have to incur the expense of elements 1 through 5 listed earlier.

Why Is Radio and Television Carriage Important?

An institution might want to make the effort and investment to audiocast or videocast its athletic events for numerous reasons:

- Establish product credibility. The public thinks that an event that is televised or on radio must be a good product.
- Recruiting and sport participation benefits. Many coaches believe that recruiting is enhanced when they can promise parents that they can see their child on television or represent to an athlete that his or her future career is better advanced by high media exposure.
- Product advertising. Having an event on television or radio is the equivalent of athletic program advertising. Such exposure promotes the sport covered and its availability as an event attendance choice and donor support option.
- Investment in future commercial viability. Proving the viability of the product with a well-produced program that shows fan attendance, audience enthusiasm, advertising support, and an overall high-quality athletic product increases the possibility of getting TV rights fees in the future or future interest in carriage as a joint venture.
- Enhance title sponsor and other corporate sponsor proposals. Offering advertising inventory on such radio or television broadcasts as part of a game or season sponsorship proposal enhances the value of that package.
- Coach retention. Producing a coach's show to enhance the coach's brand or supplement his or her income by programming profits may contribute to coach retention.

Weighing the Risks

Of course, financial risks and other cautions need to be considered as part of the decision-making process related to having the athletic program produce its own media product. To reduce financial risk, the athletic director must understand the economics of such projects. If the program production is poor, the program suffers loss of credibility, which could damage gate receipts and advertiser interest. Is the communications department or radio, television, and film department of the institution or another local institution capable of providing production? Several elements are required to make a production professional, from graphics to the number of cameras used. The program must present a product that meets viewer expectations, including showing a good crowd and generating expected game noise (band, music, cheerleaders). Last, the institution should be selective about which games it chooses to air to protect game-day attendance. In general, live telecasts in the local market should be avoided because they may have a negative effect on ticket sales. Likewise, games versus poor opponents should not be aired because the audience may think it's not worth it to go to the game and thus choose to watch on television. But highly anticipated games should be aired, whether live or delayed, because the in-arena experience at such events is always superior to the televised or radio broadcast product.

13.22 PLANNING TOOL

Launching a New Sport as a Revenue Producer

Success Requires Full Support of the Athletic Department

At many institutions little effort has been made to develop a fan base or generate significant revenue in some sports. Coaches may have been asked to raise revenues, but left to their own limited experience and having little time, they typically don't do much more than produce an annual alumni direct mail solicitation, organize an alumni game, or host a golf tournament. Administrators should consider a more methodical approach to revenue development that will result in sustained growth over the long term. Coaches can and should be given a primary role, but administrators must be involved in assuring fans and donors that the entire athletic department is committed to supporting the sport. Sports initially selected for such development should be those that have a controlled-access playing facility where tickets can be sold for admission, reasonable seating for the event, parking adjacent or close to the facility, and access to a pre- and postcompetition meeting place for fans and donors.

Identification of Core Supporters as a Year-One Priority

Among the coaching staff, a sufficient number of personal friends, parents of summer campers and student-athletes, and whatever small fan base as currently exists should be identified. This list is then personally solicited by the coaches. The goal is to generate 50 to 100 initial prospective season-ticket buyers and members of that sport's booster club, which should be a subunit within the larger umbrella annual donor organization of the athletic department. The season-ticket price would be reasonable and would include charter membership in that sport's booster club. The bulk of these friends will most likely not be alumni. The members of this group likely have an existing affinity for the sport, close friendships with the coaching staff, or are relatives and friends of student-athletes. All good fund-raising starts with existing relationships and continues with friend-raising. The goals in year one are to (1) build around a solid core of supporters, no matter how small the number, and ask them to introduce the sport to their friends, (2) establish the existence and awareness of a season-ticket purchase opportunity, and (3) establish the existence of an enjoyable booster club experience with the coach and student-athletes.

Booster Club Home Game Experience

Beginning in year one, the sport-specific booster club should meet before every home game to receive a scouting report from an assistant coach. After giving the scouting report, the assistant coach should introduce one key concept lesson about the sport that booster club members would be asked to look for during the game. For example, "Number 5 is their best offensive player and our best defensive player is number 6. I want you to watch this matchup to see how many times number 6 is successful in denying number 5 from getting a pass from her teammates." The coach should not assume that a new audience understands the sport. If possible, this pregame meeting should allow for the purchase of a pregame snack and drinks in a social setting. The club should also gather immediately after every game to meet the coach for a short postgame report and to meet selected or all players, who will be asked to comment on the game. The head coach and players would also participate in a postgame audience question-and-answer session. These activities are designed to establish strong affiliation relationships, which are key to increasing donor support and spectator commitment. The size of the first-year group doesn't matter. A donor and fan program must start somewhere, and a smaller group allows a more intimate experience. This premium gathering is essential to developing a season-ticket base.

Introduce-a-Friend Ticket Books

Also beginning in year one, each season-ticket holder–charter booster club member would receive an Introduce-a-Friend ticket book in addition to his or her season tickets. This book, a gift to the season-ticket buyer, would contain 20 tickets that could be used at any home game during the season. Each ticket holder–booster club member would be asked to use the tickets to introduce new friends to the sport program. The ticket holder–booster club member would also be asked to bring their guests to the pre- and postgame booster club events. These guests would form the core for the following year's season-ticket solicitation. If season tickets have seat locations and the ticket books are for general admission (nonreserved) seating, having friends sit in a location removed from the season-ticket holder presents a dilemma. But creative solutions can solve most problems. For instance, if a season-ticket holder is entertaining a large group, seating them in a more premium general admission area or providing reserved seats for all on a personalized request basis is possible given enough advanced notice. Early in the development of a fan base, numbers are so small that this kind of personal attention is possible and advances the goal of developing close relationships with the people who are going to be the prime volunteers and leaders in the development of a fan and donor base.

Guest Coach Program

Faculty and key donors should be invited to be guest coaches at each home game. They receive an informal scouting report from the head coach during pregame warm-ups, meet the team in the locker room and listen to the pregame talk, sit behind or on the bench during the game, and attend the postgame booster club meeting. A development staff member or athletic department administrator should be assigned to chaperone this group and participate in the postgame booster club meeting as a donor cultivation assignment.

Year-Two Season-Ticket Drive

Two months before the start of the second year of the program, an annual season-ticket drive should be organized using the most committed sport supporters. The primary targets for the drive are those people who came to games in the previous year using Introduce-a-Friend tickets. A local hotel sponsor would be asked to sponsor the season-ticket drive by hosting six weekly wine and cheese receptions for the team draft (week 1), sales materials and rules session (week 2), and four subsequent weekly ticket sales reporting receptions. Five to six teams would be assembled through a fun draft reception in week 1. Captains would be preidentified and would engage in a formal draft for team members; each team would select 5 to 10 members. The teams would convene at the second reception in week 2 to be introduced, receive team T-shirts, and receive season-ticket brochures and sales report materials. At this meeting, rules would be reviewed regarding the team and individual sales competitions. At each of the next four receptions, teams would convene to deliver their checks and completed season-ticket applications. Weekly individual sales winners and team winners would be announced and receive prizes (licensed merchandise, donated gifts such as dinner for two at local restaurants, and so on). At the last reception, overall individual sales and team sales winners would receive awards (such as plane tickets for two to anywhere in the United States donated by a travel agency). The highlight at each reception would be a returning player introducing a new freshman recruit and the coach commenting on his or her expectations for both players during the coming season. An informal Q&A session would follow. Again, as in year one, each season-ticket holder would receive an Introduce-a-Friend ticket book. Committed execution of such a plan, repeated for four to five years, will result in exponential growth of season-ticket holders each year.

Role of Development or Administrative Staff

Although the coaching staff needs to take major responsibility for the execution of this plan, general athletic department support is required as follows:

- The athletic director and development staff must attend the home games and booster club events. New prospective donors and ticket buyers develop their affinity for the program and are cultivated at these games and events, and it will take more than the coaching staff to develop these relationships.
- Sports communication staff or other athletic department staff should be assigned to serve as emcees for pregame and postgame events and participate in cultivation activities. The sports information director or a member of his or her staff is the perfect person to deliver a pregame scouting report if an assistant coach is not available to do this.
- Event management staff should be assigned to arrange for pregame and postgame events, sale of food and refreshments, and so on. These arrangements do not have to be elaborate; they can be as simple as hot dogs, chips, and soft drinks or, for outdoor sports, coffee, hot chocolate, and donuts. What is important is establishing a social event and area where people are treated as special guests. A tent or other designated area that is protected from the elements is helpful.
- The athletic director or sponsorship staff would be assigned to obtain a hotel sponsor, prizes for the season-ticket drive, and bookstore donations of licensed merchandise for team T-shirts and prizes. Obtaining the hotel sponsorship is not difficult because wine and cheese or vegetable trays are not an expensive outlay and the hotel is introduced to donors as a friend of the program. A hotel representative would be asked to attend and speak at a ticket drive event so that the athletic director can thank the representative of the property in person and in front of prospective hotel customers.
- The ticket office should be assigned to produce Introduce-a-Friend ticket books. Printing tickets is an important and essential expense that indicates an elevation in the status of the program. If the event is important enough to print and sell tickets for, it is important enough for people to want to attend.

A commitment of time and staff is required to develop a new sport as a revenue producer. Coaches alone should not be accountable for making all these initiatives happen. The heart of developing a fan base is having people in the community who can talk about being at the game last night, about having personally spoken with the coach and players after the game. In effect, they will be telling their friends about an athletic event experience that is special and desirable. The athletic department is selling this affinity or connection as the most valued asset. The fan is purchasing this special status.

13.23 PLANNING TOOL

Licensed Merchandise

Selling the right for a third party to use the athletic program or institutional logo on products (apparel, coffee cups, and so on) is a lucrative revenue source for many institutions. The first issue is ensuring that the institution has registered its marks with the United States Trademark Office. Incredibly, many institutions have not done this or have done it only for the institutional seal and not for athletic department logos and depictions of mascot images commonly used as athletic program marks. The legal counsel or business manager of the institution or school district should be contacted for this information. Registering marks is an inexpensive and simple process. If marks have not been registered, chances are that the athletic department may have used several different marks or numerous versions of the same mark over the years. Before registration, decisions might have to be made on which marks to register. Policies should be established that require a more disciplined approach to using acceptable depictions. Typically, athletic departments need multiple designs that can be used in square, rectangular, or digital formats, with and without the name of the institution and the name of the sport. Alumni or friends of the program associated with graphics or advertising agencies should be asked to contribute such work as a gift to the institution or the school district, as opposed to paying for such professional services.

After the educational institution owns the right to all its marks, the next issue is whether and what portion of revenues from the sale of such rights should go to the athletic program. At some institutions, the institution retains rights to the use of its name alone or the institutional seal, and the athletic department gets to keep all revenues associated with use of the name in conjunction with a sport, the athletic program, or the sport mascot (e.g., XU Bears, XU Hawks). Exploitation of the name and marks of the institution or athletic program is a business initiative that requires the involvement of legal counsel. Typically, revenues are generated as a percentage of gross sales of all products bearing the marks. No such fees are required if the athletic department is ordering and selling the items itself.

The athletic department will have to consider tax implications if it wants to get into the business of selling products and acting like a commercial retail entity such as a bookstore or novelty store (mail, online, or offline) in addition to running its educational sport program. These product sales by a nonprofit entity may be considered unrelated business income and thus be taxable. Although government publications can be reviewed (see www.irs.gov/pub/irs-pdf/p598.pdf), consulting with legal counsel is advisable because exceptions may apply to educational institutions when the sale of such product is directly related to an educational purpose. Just because the profit from the sales is used to support athletics is not a sufficient reason to be exempt from such taxes. Also, if the athletic department runs a store to carry on such business on a regular basis, these operations may have to be separately incorporated as a business. As with any retail business entity, product sales would be taxed. Legal advice is essential in this area.

Some institutions have given the exclusive right to sell products with institutional logos on campus to an entity like their own bookstore, thereby preventing the athletic program from even selling such products. If this is the case, the athletic program may wish to explore the possibility of a joint program with the bookstore that results in a portion of any bookstore income generated by athletics being returned to athletics. The bottom line for the athletic director is that this revenue source needs to be explored. Mechanisms need to be identified to generate income for athletics when athletics uses its events or access to donors and fans to produce sales. Agreements with third parties who are experts in retail sales and fulfillment of online and mail orders should be considered because this activity is not the primary business of educational sport. Often, the best approach is to hire an expert to exploit a commercial possibility. The athletic department takes a sizable cut and does not have to worry about the retail business. The alternative is for the athletic department to try to run a retail operation that comes with significant costs in terms of staff time and attention.

13.24 MANAGEMENT TIP

Student Fees and Pay to Play

Student Fees

At most institutions of higher education, student fees specifically designated for the support of athletic programs are the most significant revenue source supporting varsity athletics. These fees are also traditional sources of funding for recreation, intramural, and other student programs. These athletic-designated taxes may be levied by credit hour (such as a $2 per credit hour student fee) or by semester and can be as high as $2,000 per year for a full-time student. The NCAA reported that in 2018, colleges and universities collected $1.2 billion, a 51 percent increase over the previous 10 years (NBC News, 2020). The fee may give the student free or reduced-rate access to athletic events or the right to draw for athletic event tickets from a limited number of available tickets in a student section. Such student fees may also be levied to fund special building campaigns such as building a new student recreational center that is also used for athletics or a new basketball arena or football stadium. Referendums often include provisions whereby student fees are not levied until the building is accessible to students, which means that students voting on the measure may not even pay the fee if the facility does not come online until after their graduation.

Cautions on Increasing Student Fees

The athletic department frequently considers asking for increases in student fees to fund higher athletic aspirations within its current competitive division or to enable a move to a higher competitive division. These requests should be considered with caution. With the exception of 15 to 25 NCAA Football Bowl Subdivision (FBS) institutions, members of NCAA Division I are heavily subsidized by their institutions, running average annual operating deficits of $8.5 to $9.5 million per year even without football programs (Fulks, 2010). Although the NCAA Division I philosophy is to have self-supporting athletic programs, this goal has not been met. In fact, although the largest and richest athletic programs are in this division, programs in this division are the ones most likely to drop sport programs. As competitive aspirations lead schools into the Division I football or men's basketball arms race, a greater proportion of the men's athletic operating budget is funneled in this direction (78 percent of budgets in the Football Bowl Subdivision are spent on just these two sports). Men's minor sports either get a small piece of the financial pie or are eliminated (Fulks, 2010). Thus, an institution whose intercollegiate sport program accommodates a large number of student participants that asks for and gets student fee dollars and then is subsequently faced with the need for program contraction to keep pace with its competitors may face considerable criticism from the faculty and student community.

The larger and more competitive the athletic program is, such as Division I Football Bowl Subdivision and Football Championship Subdivision programs, the lower the student fee income is as a percentage of the total athletic budget (6 to 19 percent) (Fulks, 2010). At Division III institutions, student fees and institutional subsidies account for almost the entire athletic budget as well as fully fund intramurals and recreational sport. As these fees increase over time and represent a larger proportion of tuition and fees, especially during challenging economic times when faculty salaries are affected and tuition is raised, such taxes become more unpopular. At many institutions, although the president may have final authority to approve setting such fees, such actions are usually preceded by student referendums or review by student committees. Thus, attempts to establish or increase student fees are not simply a matter of budgetary requests to the president. Student fee initiatives are highly political and require the considerable attention and political acumen of the athletic director. On the plus side, whenever these fees are the subject of student votes or referendums, because of low participation by the student body in such balloting and the ability of the athletic department to mobilize 500 to 1,000 voting student-athletes, student-athlete votes often control the outcome of such initiatives.

Pay to Play

The equivalent of student fees at institutions of higher education to support athletic programs is pay to play at the high school level. Public high school education is supported primarily by local tax dollars. When these revenues are insufficient to support after-school activities, local school districts may decide to levy user fees as a partial or whole financial solution to support sport or other after-school programs. Fees for students who cannot pay such fees are usually waived or substantially discounted. Eligibility for federally subsidized school lunch programs is the primary criterion for offering such waivers or discounts. Often, additional appeals for waivers are considered. These fees may be minimal, in the range of \$25 to \$75 per activity, or substantial, sometimes exceeding \$300 to \$600 per activity. Athletics isn't the only extracurricular activity charging participation fees. Average school participation fees were \$161 for sports, \$86 for arts, and \$46 for clubs and other activities in 2018 (Mostafavi, 2019). The lower the fee is, the less the effect is on participation, and the inverse is true for higher fees. See Policy 13.25 for a sample policy for a pay-to-play program.

Athletic directors forced to consider implementing such programs should consider the following factors:

- Keep fees as low as possible.
- Offer discounts for multiple-activity participants (e.g., \$100 for the first sport, \$75 for the second, \$50 for the third, and so on).
- Consider imposing lower fees for middle schools than for high schools. Those programs are usually less expensive to run because fewer competitions occur in a season and travel is more local.
- Specify that the fee becomes payable only if the student makes the team and determine when failure to pay results in ineligibility to participate.
- Ask parents and others who can afford to do so to make additional contributions to support waivers for less fortunate families.
- Establish policies to deal with injured student-athletes who are no longer able to participate, such as refunds keyed to length of season played. Establish policies that prohibit refunds for voluntary cessation of participation or ineligibility because of academic performance or violations of school policy or athletic governance association rules.
- Decide whether pay for play includes the right to playing time, because some communities have sought to require such assurances.

Note that such programs often result in the establishment of a parents' group to engage in efforts to (1) raise funds for the purpose of supporting waiver programs or even the entire athletic program, (2) pressure school boards to rescind such programs, (3) lobby local governments to increase tax rates for the specific purpose of funding after-school programs, or (4) lobby state representatives to pass laws prohibiting such charges for extracurricular activities. Policy 13.25 represents a sample approach to such a program.

13.25 Policy—Pay-to-Play Program

A sample policy that defines the parameters for a high school pay-to-play program, including fee structure, eligibility for waivers or discounts, payment plans, and requirements for obtaining refunds.

Available in HK*Propel*.

13.26 PLANNING TOOL

Tuition Waivers, Facility Rentals, Land Leases, Vending Machines, and Other Income Sources

A declining economy, state budget deficits, or the need to achieve gender equity has prompted many institutions to search for additional ways to support athletic programs. The following revenue possibilities may provide income that can be dedicated to support athletics or mechanisms that provide relief from expenses. All these programs require careful review by legal counsel to ensure minimization of legal risk. Also important is the need for the athletic director to (1) perform due diligence with regard to applicable business models and (2) not to undertake such program extensions without adequate administrative and program staff support.

Tuition Waivers

Scholarships represent the second or third largest expense item after salaries in most higher education athletic programs, but the actual cost to the institution of one or two more students in a class is minimal. The institution could easily absorb tuition costs. Asking the institution to absorb the tuition cost of scholarships (tuition waivers) and to mandate that these cost savings be used to support gender equity is a reasonable request that should be explored.

Vending Machine Income

Vending machines located all over campus often represent discretionary ancillary revenues for the institution. These revenues could be funneled to the athletic program.

Land Leases

Institutions often purchase or receive gifts of property and may exploit such assets through short- or long-term leases. If the property is large enough, development into a golf course might be possible. The property could produce revenue as a golf course, or it could be leased for that purpose. The annual lease fee plus percentage of gross revenues and free-use rights for the institution's golf teams could produce stable long-term funding for the athletic program. Again, these revenues represent institutional income that could be given to athletics at the discretion of the institution.

Facility Rental and Fee-Based Use Programs

Sport facilities are often in great demand for use by external entities because institutional facilities are usually superior to what community recreation programs are able to build. The extent to which institutions make their facilities available to external entities is usually a function of availability and quality of physical activity facilities and the willingness of institutions to develop and operate such programs. In the case of school districts, these school physical plants are built and supported by local taxes, so the community expects to have access during nonschool hours when school programs are not using these facilities.

Rental Programs Especially if the athletic department is charged with administering the facility rental program, the athletic director should ask for the right to use this income. Care must be taken to set up transparent procedures and systems that fairly consider applications for use, protect the institution from liability, provide the necessary maintenance following occupancy by external users, require supervision by institutional representatives, and address other important issues. See Policy 15.22 and Forms 15.23, 15.24, and 15.25 for sample policies and procedures, application forms, and agreements that could be used to administer such a rental program.

Community Fitness Programs Many public and private institutions of higher education open selected athletic facilities for use as community fitness centers in much the same way as a private fitness club might operate by providing fitness classes, swimming lessons, and access to strength and conditioning areas. These fee-based community service programs not only provide revenues but also represent an opportunity for the institution to develop relationships with community residents, cultivate new friends, and extend its donor base. If the athletic department operates this type of program, it should be set up as a full-fledged separate business entity with adequate administrative and instructional staff, recognizing that this activity is different from operating a scholastic or collegiate athletic program.

Youth Age-Group Programs Some institutions operate lucrative age-group swimming or other youth sport programs or allow third-party agencies to do so under long-term lease agreements. In the case of the former, care must be taken to ensure that these programs conform to NCAA or other recruiting rules. Similar to a community fitness program, these youth programs are significant business undertakings that require specialized business experience and adequate administrative and instructional staffs. Monthly and annual fees, especially for the highest-skilled groups, can be considerable, but the real profit is derived from having a significant volume of regular participants in the younger age groups.

Team Fund-Raising Activities

Individual sport teams may engage in fund-raising activities either because they are required to bring in a certain percentage of their operating revenues or because their operating budgets are not sufficient to cover special competitions or activities like a spring-training trip, a trip to an out-of-state tournament, or international competition. A gender equity caution is important. Title IX requires that no matter what the source of revenues, male and female athletes must be provided with equal opportunities, benefits, and treatment. For example, if the baseball team is allowed to raise funds for a spring break trip and participate in such activity, a corresponding number of female participants must be provided with the same type of additional participation activity whether or not the female team is able to raise the same funds to do so. The rationale behind this requirement is simple. A long history of discrimination has affected the ability of women's teams to raise funds in the same way that men's teams might. A good solution to this type of situation is for the athletic administrator to pair men's and women's teams to do fund-raising together, equally splitting the proceeds. Or, each team has their special trips funded by the athletic department every set number of years but must engage in a fund-raising activity that goes into a common special trip fund on a scheduled basis.

After gender equity considerations have been satisfied, the athletic director or athletic department development officer needs to be aware of all fund-raising efforts and ensure that they do not conflict with other fund-raising efforts. Thus, a mechanism must be in place to gain approval for such team fund-raising activities. See Form 13.5 in HK*Propel* for a sample approval form.

13.27 PLANNING TOOL

More Than Summer Camps for Children

Sport Summer Camps

Summer camps represent potentially lucrative revenue opportunities. At many institutions they are essential mechanisms used to supplement coach's salaries, thereby increasing the prospect of retaining good coaches. Such programs can be structured in many ways:

- The institution owns and operates the program, keeps all revenues, and pays all salaries from proceeds.
- The institution leases the facility to the coach for full or discounted facility rental fees. The institution keeps the rental fees, and the coach operates the camp and keeps all income over expenses.
- The coach and the institution operate the program as a joint venture. The institution provides the facilities at no charge and receives a fixed percentage of gross income in return.

Again, advice of legal counsel is essential to ensure that the arrangement does not violate institutional policy or state and federal laws. See chapter 12 (documents 12.27 to 12.38) for additional information concerning the operation of summer camps.

Back-to-University Programs

A relatively new trend for athletic departments is to operate family summer camps for alumni families and friends that combine (1) lectures on current topics from noted faculty, (2) math and science experiences for children, and (3) sport and other leisure activities for the entire family. These back-to-university programs are often developed in conjunction with the alumni association and the university development office because they offer valuable opportunities to enhance relationships with alumni and other prospective donors.

Adult Fantasy Sport Camps

Another relatively new trend is weekend or weeklong fantasy sport camps for adults. A popular head coach and staff run what resembles a youth sport camp but gear the program for adult participants. These programs are often priced at a premium level ($3,000 to $5,000 per week) and use high-end hotels. The operation of these programs can even be outsourced to a specialized third-party company that exists for this purpose.

REVENUE ACQUISITION AND FUND-RAISING

Averill Fundraising Solutions. (2019). *Build a successful annual fund campaign: The essential guide.* https://averillsolutions.com/annual-fund-campaign-guide.

Drew University. (2007). *Department of Intercollegiate Athletics policy manual.* Unpublished manuscript. Madison, NJ.

Enright, M. et al. (2020). *Hidden figures: College students may be paying thousands in athletic fees and not know it.* NBCNews.com. https://www.nbcnews.com/news/education/hidden-figures-college-students-may-be-paying-thousands-athletic-fees-n1145171.

Foster, G., Greyser, S.A., & Walsh, B. (2006). *The business of sports: Text and cases on strategy and management.* London: Thompson-South-Western.

Fullerton, S. (2010). *Sports marketing.* New York: McGraw-Hill.

Graham, S., Neirotti, L.D., & Goldblatt, J.J. (2001). *The ultimate guide to sports marketing.* New York: McGraw-Hill.

Koehler, M., & Giebel, N. (1997). *Athletic director's survival guide.* London: Prentice-Hall.

Lopiano, D. and Zotos, C. (2021). *Restructuring a college athletic program to protect Olympic sports during financial uncertainty.* Champaign, IL: Human Kinetics.

Mostafavi, B. (2019). Does "pay-to-play" put sports, extracurriculars out of reach? *University of Michigan Health Blog.* https://healthblog.uofmhealth.org/lifestyle/does-pay-to-play-put-sports-extracurriculars-out-of-reach.

Mullin, B.J., Hardy, S., & Sutton, W.A. (2007). *Sport marketing.* Champaign, IL: Human Kinetics.

National Collegiate Athletic Association. (2019). *2004–19 NCAA revenues and expenses reports by division.* Indianapolis, IN: NCAA. https://www.ncaa.org/about/resources/research/archives-ncaa-revenues-and-expenses-reports-division.

Pedersen, P.M., & Thibault, L. (Eds). (2022). *Contemporary sport management* (7th ed.). Champaign, IL: Human Kinetics.

Pike Masteralexis, L., Barr, C.A., & Hums, M.A. (Eds.). (2014). *Principles and practice of sport management.* Sudbury, MA: Jones and Bartlett.

Scott, T. (2015). *Keys to successful relationship building.* https://www.tutiscott.com/articles-1/10-tips-for-relationship-building.

Shank, M.D., & Lyberger, M.R. (2015). *Sports marketing: A strategic perspective.* London: Routledge.

University Interscholastic League. (2011). *Booster club guidelines.* https://www.uiltexas.org/policy/booster-club-guidelines.

University of Texas at Austin. (1992). *Intercollegiate athletics for women policy manual.* Unpublished. Austin, TX: Department of Women's Intercollegiate Athletics.

University of Texas at Austin. (2010). *Intercollegiate athletics policy manual.* Austin, TX. No longer available.

University of Wisconsin–Milwaukee. (2010). *Types of giving.* Milwaukee: University of Milwaukee Foundation. www4.uwm.edu/give_to_uwm/planned_giving/types.

CHAPTER

14

Communications, Media Relations, and Promotions

The larger and more visible the athletic program is or the greater its importance is to the institution or community, the more responsive the athletic department must be to providing timely and rich content to satisfy the public and various stakeholders. The production of content is not an easy proposition when an institution offers 15 to 30 sports; when immediate reports of results and updates of statistics are expected; when an insatiable media demands access to coaches, administrators, and players; and when the institution expects the highest standards of accuracy, spelling, and grammar to be upheld. Added to this demand is the requirement that the communications staff support athletic department fund-raising programs, corporate-sponsored event promotions, and the recruiting efforts of coaches.

The documents in this chapter, in both the book and HK*Propel*, are intended to help the athletic director develop policy documents that clearly define staff service responsibilities and expectations of coaches and student-athletes. Numerous sample forms are provided to assist in collecting information, documenting copyright permissions, and helping staff execute action plans that result in timely production of extensive publications.

TYPES OF DOCUMENTS

Management tip—Factual background information, insights, problem-solving strategies, and suggestions for the athletic director

Planning tool—Steps to take or factors that should be considered in the development of strategic plans, action plans, professional development plans, or governance systems

Educational resource—Handouts that can be used to educate staff members, campus constituents, volunteers, or student-athletes

Policy—Sample policies and procedures that should be adopted by an athletic department after customization and review by appropriate expert institutional or school district officials

Form—Sample forms, letters, or job descriptions

Evaluation instrument—Administrative tools that help the athletic director, a supervisor, or an employee assess job performance and evaluate program content

Risk assessment—Checklists that help the athletic director, a supervisor, or an employee identify risks and prevent litigation

14.1 PLANNING TOOL

Getting the Message Out Versus Selling

Critical Definitions

Definitions are important to distinguish between getting the message out and selling. Fund-raising and marketing (the packaging and actual sale of assets) are the selling functions, whereas communication, media relations, and promotion are activities that get the message out and make donors, sponsors, and fans aware of and impressed by the athletic program and more likely to buy the athletic product. A successful athletic program requires excellence in both sales and communications. Unfortunately, seldom does the athletic director have one staff member who excels at both functions. As well, most high school and collegiate athletic programs in this country do not produce significant revenues and cannot afford to have more than one employee working in these areas, usually with the job title of sports information director (SID). In these programs the SID performs necessary communications tasks, and the athletic director assumes the role of marketing and sales manager. As a program becomes more popular and more successful as a revenue producer or the level of the program indicates higher levels of fan awareness and affiliation essential to fund-raising success, the institution may add more communications or sales staff. In this case, numerous ways of segmenting the staff can maximize the specialized skills of staff members.

Importance of Integrating Communications and Sales

As soon as the athletic department is able to add staff specialists so that multiple people are working in both areas (communications and sales), a single leadership position should be controlling all elements: fund-raising, marketing, communications, promotions, and media relations. This senior staff member should be responsible for the athletic department's brand and positioning and accountable for conducting a fully integrated communications and sales program that reaches all athletic program consumers from faculty and administration to parents, fans, donors, corporate sponsors, and the media. We live in a media culture characterized by a huge amount of knowledge and information bombarding everyone every day. The athletic program risks getting lost in this chaos if its messages are fragmented, inconsistent, or not prioritized. Having one person working on communications, promotions, and media relations while another does marketing and fund-raising is fine, but one person needs to be designated as the development and communications czar.

Functional Categorization

Although the popular definition of marketing now seems to encompass marketing, communications, media relations, and promotions, we prefer the following definitions because they make it easier for the athletic director to understand, segment, and make staff accountable for each element. The athletic director may want to use the following functional categorization of these elements and measurements of key performance indicators (KPIs):

Communications

Communications—Defining and policing use of the athletic brand (name, logo, colors, graphical look, and messaging) to ensure its consistent portrayal in every athletic department communications vehicle from stationery, e-mails, and Internet sites to radio and television advertising, uniforms, merchandise, media guides, and event promotions.

KPIs

- Consumer awareness of brand identity and purpose (what it is—e.g., Longhorn = winning collegiate athletic program) among those who successfully identify the logo
- Consumer satisfaction with program purpose and reputation
- Coach and AD satisfaction with content and quality of print and electronic publications

Media relations—Identifying, establishing, and maintaining relationships with the media; increasing media exposure to the public; and fulfilling all media and public requests for information from interviews, rosters, and statistics to photographs and video.

KPIs

- Exposures by media category (print, Internet, radio, television)
- Consumer awareness and recognition of brand (Longhorn = University of Texas) as a percentage of all respondents
- Consumer awareness of brand identity and purpose as a percentage of all respondents (Longhorn = winning collegiate athletic program)
- Consumer approval of brand or product—percentage who approve of program
- Media members' satisfaction with athletic department service

Promotions—Produce advertising, obtain free publicity, increase consumer awareness of home events, and enhance the in-arena consumer experience to drive fan attendance and satisfaction at events.

KPIs

- Attendance at home events (paid and unpaid)
- Walk-up ticket sales (paid attendance)
- Fan satisfaction

Sales

Marketing—Defining, pricing, selling, and evaluating sports products offered to consumers from licensing and merchandising to advertising, season-ticket sales, sponsorships, and media rights.

KPIs

- Revenues generated from each category of sport product
- Sponsor or customer satisfaction with program execution

Fund-raising—Annual giving, major gifts, endowments, and multiyear fund-raising campaigns

KPIs

- Total number of donors and percentage increase over the same month in the previous year
- Total number of meetings (one on one, in person, and phone calls) with current major donors and percentage increase over the same month in the previous year
- Total number of donors in selected donor categories, total number in each category, and percentage increase over the same month in the previous year
- Number of staff relationship initiatives by type within each donor category, total number of gifts, and average gift in the current month and compared with the same month in the previous year
- Total number of planned gifts and planned-gift material requests or conversations

Staff Limitations

Even if one employee covers all these areas, all functions have to be executed to some degree. With one or a small number of employees working in these areas, the issue is how the number and competencies of staff employed will limit the number of activities in each of these areas. For instance, with a communications unit of one or two staff members, the athletic director may take total responsibility for marketing while the unit's staff members handle all other areas for basketball, football, and volleyball only. There may be no paid advertising at all, and free publicity efforts may be extremely limited. Media guides may be produced for only one or two sports, if at all. Under these circumstances, the athletic director must determine whether the unit will serve all sports in the program with minimal effort in each or operate according to priorities based on opportunities for the greatest reach with the least cost and fewest staff. Alternatively, the athletic director may create a system somewhere in the middle whereby every sport receives a minimal level of service and certain activities are designated as priority initiatives. These decisions depend on what the program philosophy is, whether these efforts are critical to revenue generation, and whether such revenues are essential to program success or existence.

14.2 PLANNING TOOL

Branding: Why Expert Help Is Necessary

Most athletic directors have limited training in communications-related areas and therefore don't understand the critical importance of branding. Every athletic department should have a brand manual that gives precise instructions on all the following elements:

- The values and attributes that the athletic department wants associated with the image of the program
- Precise colors to be used for the logo
- The precise font to be used
- How the logo should appear as a horizontal or vertical image
- The logo that must be used for all digital communications (website, e-mail, and so on)
- Whether the logo could appear with another logo as a composite logo
- Whether a tagline can appear in conjunction with the logo and if so, what the tagline is
- What neutral colors can be used with school colors on home and away uniforms
- Whether the school or mascot name can be abbreviated (e.g., Chevrolet to Chevy)
- What permissions and approvals are required for use of the logo
- Design of banners (headers) for all publications—newsletters, website, and so on
- Stationery, business card, note card, press release, presentation folder standard designs, rules of formatting, and content

All these issues should be considered in advance. Rules should be determined and clearly stated in a rules manual as precisely as the rules for the game of football or soccer are stated.

Such identity and use guidelines form the critical first step in consistent messaging. Consumers and all athletic department stakeholders must know who is delivering the message and who is producing the athletics product.

The second and simultaneous step is ensuring that the name, logo, and any tagline generate positive and high-quality feelings on the part of the consumer, are authentic, and differentiate the athletic program from others in the marketplace in a way that is meaningful to all the targeted audiences—prospective athletes and their parents, donors, parents and families of current athletes, alumni, and members of the community who will attend events or follow the teams (Paun, 2018). These feelings and attributes are critical because they establish credibility, market status, and consumer loyalty. Whether it is using poor-quality artwork or an ugly or too-vicious character, or whether referring to the boys as "Pirates" and the girls as "Lady Pirates" will result in allegations of sexism, or whether the use of "Indians" will generate controversy, these types of branding issues must be considered. What consumers think and feel when they look at the brand reflects on the public reputation of the program and ultimately their decision to be affiliated as fans, donors, or supporters.

The third step in creating a successful brand is gaining maximum exposure—consistent and repetitive delivery of the brand to the public. Remember that brand awareness builds over time and brands are created to last the lifetime of the program. That is not to say that the brand doesn't change. If a brand has been in use for years and is outdated, of poor quality, or lacking for other reasons, it can be tweaked or updated so that font, colors, and graphic style give a different and more positive feel to the same words or names.

Note that most athletic programs can get free expert help and advice in this area from volunteer professionals who are alumni or parents of children in the program or from faculty members at the institution. At the college level, plenty of faculty in communications or marketing departments would be happy to help. Getting good advice should not cost money. Defining the use of the athletic brand (name, logo, colors, graphical look, and messaging) so that it is consistently portrayed and perceived to be of the highest quality is a major administrative responsibility. A comprehensive brand manual must exist.

So, the athletic director's role is clear—get expert help to make sure that the brand is distinct and compelling, establish clear rules on use, and implement a plan to get maximum exposure for the brand. Someone should be held accountable for tracking increases in public awareness of the brand and evaluating whether the public understands the athletic program's purpose, values, and attributes. Measuring the success of the athletic department communications unit by key performance indicators, another task that communications, advertising, or marketing classes or a graduate student can help with at little or no cost, is essential. See Planning Tool 14.5 for sample performance indicators and more information on assessment of effectiveness of the communications unit.

14.3 MANAGEMENT TIP

Establishing Guidelines for Social Media

Restrictions on Use of Social Media

Athletic departments tend to place stringent restrictions on the use of social media by student-athletes. On one hand, social media should not be used to violate athletic department or institutional policies on such standard subjects as sexual harassment, bullying, respectful conduct, or conformance with NCAA or governance association rules. On the other hand, all student-athletes and staff members have a right to free speech. The authors believe that the athletic department should use educational efforts as its primary mechanism to encourage responsible use of social media, emphasizing that every student-athlete and employee has a right to free speech but that no social media posting can violate existing institutional, athletic department, or team rules of conduct. Thus, rather than create new policy to control social media use, staff and student-athletes should be educated that existing policy applies to social media use. Then, student-athletes and staff should be informed of the dangers of social media and be encouraged to exercise common sense in their use. Educational Resource 14.4 is a good example of such an educational document.

14.4 Educational Resource—Wise Use of Social Media

A sample handout that is designed for distribution to staff and student-athletes to educate them about the dangers of social media and their responsibilities to ensure that social media use does not violate existing institutional or athletic governance association policies or rules or state or federal laws.

Available in HK*Propel*.

Social Media as a Communications Strategy

Although social media present certain challenges regarding negative use, they have significant positive uses as an integral part of the athletic department's communications and marketing strategy. Most athletic departments are already using social media as a relationship-building technology that better enables them to connect with their stakeholders—fans, alumni, prospective student-athletes, donors, parents, the campus community, and the public. Key to this use are rules for prior approval before launching any social media site that uses the name or marks of the athletic program or institution. Another key is designating a specific individual responsible for any official athletic department social media site—the person allowed to post comments, check the site every day, and respond to comments and inquiries. A team or athletic department social media presence, like any athletic publication, must also conform to branding rules. Those responsible for operating such sites should be prohibited from posting any athletic department or team document that is confidential or sensitive and should conform to all institutional policies. Because the site is an official athletic department publication, care must be taken to avoid political or religious content, off-color humor, disrespectful comments, or any subject that would never be included in an athletic department document, such as public criticism of officials or denigration of opponents. Special care must be taken to educate the appointed custodian of the site that opinions and views need to be properly attributed and approved by the individual providing the opinion. If an opinion is rendered, it must be attributed to an individual.

14.5 PLANNING TOOL

Media Relations, Promotions, and Public Relations

Policy Requirements

Three basic areas require specific policies to define and segment staff responsibilities and ensure accountability related to media relations, promotions, and public relations: (1) media relations staff organization and responsibilities, (2) media responsibilities of coaches, and (3) crisis communications. Policies 14.6 and 14.7 in HK*Propel* are intended to help the athletic director customize a broad media relations policy appropriate to his or her program and media environment and define the responsibilities of the communications staff and the coaches.

Information Collection

In addition to volumes of highly detailed and sport-specific contest data (performance statistics, wins and losses, and so on), the communications staff is responsible for maintaining up-to-date information on the backgrounds and interests of coaches and student-athletes. Forms 14.8 and 14.9 in HK*Propel* are sample tools for collecting coach and student-athlete background information.

Media Operations

In addition to maintaining a database of media contacts, the communications staff is responsible for meeting the needs of members of the media who attend athletic events. Form 14.10 in HK*Propel* is a sample mechanism for communicating policies related to media attendance at athletic events, gathering information for the media contact database, and determining the specific on-site accommodations required by media representatives.

14.6 **Policy**—Media Relations

A sample umbrella policy that covers communications staff responsibilities for maintaining statistics and player files, providing results to the media, obtaining credentials for athletic events, controlling media work and interview areas, instituting media interview rules, writing and disseminating press releases, arranging press conferences, and producing publications.

14.7 **Policy**—Media Responsibilities of Coaches

A sample policy that specifies coach responsibilities related to participating in media and community events, media training requirements, duty to keep media staff informed, and limitations related to transmitting health and injury information or statements more appropriately under the jurisdiction of higher management.

14.8 **Form**—Media Relations: Student-Athlete Information

A sample form to be used for the collection of basic information on past academic and sport participation and interests of student-athletes necessary for the preparation of media guides and websites.

14.9 **Form**—Media Relations: Coach Information

A sample form to be used for the collection of basic information on past employment, sport background, coaching achievements, and interests of members of the coaching staff to be used in the preparation of media guides and websites.

Available in HK*Propel*.

Crisis Communications

A critical responsibility of the communications unit is to manage all communications during a crisis. Policy 14.11 in HK*Propel* represents a typical crisis communications process.

Evaluation of Communication Program

Many athletic programs believe that they don't have the resources to measure the effectiveness of their communications units because of the cost of research and especially the cost of public surveys. At collegiate institutions, however, research and annual public surveys can be conducted at little or no cost through agreements with academic departments or faculty on campus (marketing, advertising, communications departments). Those relationships simply must be developed.

Most programs are primarily concerned with getting the athletic program message to four target audiences: (1) the media who will help disseminate the message; (2) the local public who are prospective event spectators, ticket buyers, donors, and parents of athletes or prospective summer campers; (3) current donors; and (4) local and nonlocal alumni who are prospective donors. Thus, the athletic director should identify key performance indicators (KPIs) and establish measurable objectives for each. Key is the establishment of current base measurements so that progress can be tracked. After those base measurements and a growth or attrition measurement have been made, an objective might be to increase the measurement by a specified number or percentage (e.g., 10 percent growth in public awareness). The following KPIs should be considered (not in rank order of importance):

1. **Public awareness**—percentage of public surveyed who are aware of the athletic program brand and purpose
2. **Public approval**—percentage of public surveyed who support or fully support the athletic program purpose
3. **Print and electronic media impressions**—number of annual overall and positive print and electronic (including web traffic) media impressions specific to each sport and the athletic program by media type
4. **Media representative satisfaction with communications service**—percentage of media representatives on communications media lists who are satisfied or very satisfied with communications unit service and responsiveness
5. **Media relations**—number of (*a*) face-to-face meetings and (*b*) telephone calls with media representatives
6. **Walk-up ticket sales**—walk-up ticket sales for all sports and overall
7. **Web traffic**—the number of unique visitors to the athletic department website
8. **Online transactions**—(*a*) number of online donor transactions, (*b*) photo orders, and (*c*) downloads
9. **Parent awareness**—percentage of parents with children who play sports who (*a*) are aware of athletic program summer camps, (*b*) have one or more family members who have attended an athletic event in the past year, or (*c*) have one or more children who have attended an athletic department summer camp or clinic

14.10 Form—Request for Media Credentials

A sample form to be used for media to request credentials to cover an athletic event that also includes policies on priorities for the issuance of credentials.

14.11 Policy—Crisis Communications

A sample policy that specifies the structure and function of a crisis management committee, preparation of formal statements and other materials, and the conduct of news conferences.

Available in HK*Propel*.

10. **Prospective donor awareness**—percentage of local and nonlocal alumni surveyed who are (*a*) aware of the athletic program brand and purpose and (*b*) aware of the annual athletic donor fund
11. **Prospective donor approval**—percentage of local and nonlocal alumni surveyed who support or fully support the purpose of the athletic program
12. **Timely production**—percentage of athletic publications produced by the deadline originally established for production
13. **Quality production**—number of factual or typographical errors in a publication
14. **Coach and staff satisfaction**—percentage of all head coaches and senior staff who are very satisfied, satisfied, or not satisfied with athletic department publications

14.12 PLANNING TOOL

Checklist: Basic Communications Vehicles

Four basic areas require specific policies and procedures that define and segment staff responsibilities and ensure accountability related to athletic department publications: (1) delineation of athletic department publications, (2) copyright releases, (3) website publishing, and (4) photography services. Following is a comprehensive list of common communications vehicles for a Division I athletic program that need to be branded with a consistent look and feel and produced on a detailed annual publication schedule. For other competitive divisions or for programs with smaller staff and budgetary resources, the list should be culled accordingly. Most institutions are required to follow general university guidelines regarding official university stationery, business cards, and so on. Many athletic departments seek special exceptions to such policies so that they can include special taglines or team nicknames (e.g., Sooners, Vikings, Red Storm).

Stationery

- Regular business stationery and envelopes
- Notecards and envelopes
- Holiday and other cards and envelopes
- Business cards
- Press release template
- Event credentials: media, photographer, staff, student-athlete
- Media kit cover with pockets

Electronic Publications

- E-mail template
- E-newsletter template
- Website
- Social media

Print Publications

- Sport media guides
- Sport game programs
- Sport yearbooks
- Year-end annual report
- Awards banquet program

Fund-Raising Materials

- Annual fund and booster club brochure
- Major donor program and endowed fund brochure

Event Publications

- Swim event heat sheets
- Track event heat sheets
- Event statistics and results report

Promotional Materials

- Sport schedule posters
- Billboards
- Pocket schedule cards
- Season-ticket brochures
- Season-ticket order forms
- Tickets for athletic events
- All-American press kits

Video

- All-sports program video
- Sport-specific recruiting video
- All-American nominee video

Basic Publications Policy

A department policy should be produced that details every publication that the communications unit is responsible for producing. This policy makes two things clear to all coaches and staff members: (1) resources are not unlimited and (2) the publications burden of the communications unit is substantial. Policy 14.13 in HK*Propel* represents such a document.

14.13 **Policy**—Athletic Department Publications

A sample policy that defines publications to be produced, including Internet and video publications, and production responsibilities.

Available in HK*Propel*.

Copyright Releases

The communications unit is responsible for ensuring that all publications and materials produced by the athletic department become the intellectual property of the institution. Thus, a policy requiring coaches and student-athletes to give their consent to the use of their images, photos, content, relevant intellectual property, name, likeness, biography, and recordings by the athletic department and acknowledge that any content produced is the property of the athletic department is essential. Policy 14.14 and Forms 14.15, 14.16, and 14.17 in HK*Propel* represent such documentation.

Staff Action Plan

Many publications produced by the communications unit are time sensitive (e.g., game programs, media guides, recruiting brochures), so it is essential to have a master list of publications, each publication's deadlines for review by coaches and other employees, dates when the publication must be delivered to the printer, and dates when the publication must be ready for release or distribution. For each publication, one employee should be designated as accountable. Form 14.18 is a sample form included in HK*Propel* that provides a management tool for tracking such production action plans.

Website Publishing

The development and daily maintenance of the athletic program website is a huge and time-consuming responsibility that has a significant impact on student-athlete recruiting, donor relations and fund-raising, and event revenue

14.14 **Policy**—Copyright Releases

A sample policy that defines information or copyright releases that must be obtained consistent with athletic governance association and institution policy and state and federal laws.

14.15 **Form**—Student-Athlete Communications Copyright Release

A sample form that gives permission for the institution to use and own all copyrights associated with print and electronic media content produced by the institution involving the name, image, reputation, quotes, messages, and other materials associated with a student-athlete.

14.16 **Form**—Employee Communications Copyright Release

A sample form that gives permission for the institution to use and own all copyrights associated with print and electronic media content produced by the institution involving the name, image, reputation, quotes, messages, and other materials associated with coaches and other employees.

14.17 **Form**—Visiting Student-Athlete and Staff Copyright Release

A sample form that gives permission for the institution to use and own all copyrights associated with print and electronic media content produced by the institution involving the name, image, reputation, quotes, messages, and other materials associated with student-athletes, coaches, and other employees of visiting teams.

Available in HK*Propel*.

success. Fortunately, commercial templates are readily available that enable the communication staff to accomplish these responsibilities with minimal technological skills. Establishing a policy that addresses privacy issues, sharing user information, and requiring coach review and approval of content is necessary. Policy 14.19 in HK*Propel* provides such a sample document.

Photography

A policy regarding the production and use of photographic imagery for athletic department publications, maintenance of print, negative, and digital archives, and procedures for fulfilling media and general requests for photographs is essential. Policy 14.20 in HK*Propel* represents such a document.

14.18 **Form**—Publications Production Action Plan

A sample form that designates one employee to be responsible for the production of each athletic department publication to be produced during the academic year and includes deadlines for review and approval of each publication before release or distribution.

14.19 **Policy**—Website Publishing

A sample policy that defines responsibilities associated with development and maintenance of the athletic department website including approval processes required before posting any content related to photos or information about children.

14.20 **Policy**—Photography Services

A sample policy that defines photography services including staff responsibilities for the maintenance of digital files and the provision or sale of photographs to student-athletes and external third parties.

Available in HK*Propel*.

COMMUNICATIONS, MEDIA RELATIONS, AND PROMOTIONS

Boudreaux, C. (2012). *Social media governance: Policy database*. http://socialmediagovernance.com/policies.php.

Clemson University. (2018). *Student-athlete code of conduct*. https://clemsontigers.com/student-athlete-handbook.

College Sports Information Directors of America. (2013). *CoSIDA code of ethics*. https://cosida.com/sports/2013/2/6/GEN_0206132054.aspx.

Dartmouth College Department of Athletics and Recreation. (2018). *Student-athlete social media policy*. https://dartmouthsports.com/documents/2018/6/4/Social_Media_Policy.pdf?id=12139.

Foster, G., Greyser, S.A., & Walsh, B. (2006). *The business of sports: Text and cases on strategy and management*. London: Thompson-South-Western.

Fullerton, S. (2016). *Sports marketing*. Chicago, IL: Chicago Business Press.

Koehler, M., & Giebel, N. (1997). *Athletic director's survival guide*. London: Prentice-Hall.

Lehigh University Athletics Department. (2015). *Social media policy and guidelines*. https://www1.lehigh.edu/communications/resources/socialmedia.

Mullin, B.J., Hardy, S., & Sutton, W.A. (2014). *Sport marketing*. Champaign, IL: Human Kinetics.

Paun, G. (2018). Brand authenticity: Why differentiation is a game changer. *Forbes*. https://www.forbes.com/sites/forbesagencycouncil/2018/11/16/brand-authenticity-why-differentiation-is-a-game-changer/?sh=40b70dd0560b.

Pike Masteralexis, L., Barr, C.A., & Hums, M.A. (Eds.). (2014). *Principles and practice of sport management*. Sudbury, MA: Jones and Bartlett.

Shank, M.D. (2015). *Sports marketing: A strategic perspective* (5th ed.). London: Routledge.

Stoldt, G.C., Dittmore, S.W., Ross, M., & Branvold, S.E. (2021). *Sport public relations* (3rd ed.). Champaign, IL: Human Kinetics.

University of Texas at Austin. (1992). *Intercollegiate athletics for women policy manual*. Unpublished. Austin, TX: Department of Women's Intercollegiate Athletics.

University of Texas at Austin. (2010). *Intercollegiate athletics policy manual*. Austin, TX. No longer available.

CHAPTER

15

Facilities and Operations

No department on a high school or college campus has more daily responsibility for the inspection and supervision of institutional facilities and arranging for maintenance and repair of those facilities than the athletic department. Similarly, no department accommodates greater numbers of students who participate in physical activities, members of the public who participate as spectators at athletic or special events, or third-party users who rent athletic facilities for community events. Such use involves significant responsibility for the safety of all users in an environment that holds considerable inherent risks. Thus, from the initial conceptualization of a new facility or renovation of older facilities to the daily operation of facilities, great attention must be paid to safe design and operation. The documents in this chapter, in both the book and HK*Propel*, are intended to help the athletic director meet all responsibilities associated with the building and operation of athletic facilities.

TYPES OF DOCUMENTS

Management tip—Factual background information, insights, problem-solving strategies, and suggestions for the athletic director

Planning tool—Steps to take or factors that should be considered in the development of strategic plans, action plans, professional development plans, or governance systems

Educational resource—Handouts that can be used to educate staff members, campus constituents, volunteers, or student-athletes

Policy—Sample policies and procedures that should be adopted by an athletic department after customization and review by appropriate expert institutional or school district officials

Form—Sample forms, letters, or job descriptions

Evaluation instrument—Administrative tools that help the athletic director, a supervisor, or an employee assess job performance and evaluate program content

Risk assessment—Checklists that help the athletic director, a supervisor, or an employee identify risks and prevent litigation

15.1 PLANNING TOOL

First Step: Facility Planning Committee

The first step in planning for a new or a significantly renovated facility is to form a committee of important stakeholders who will help formulate the mission, objectives, and parameters of the building, which will ultimately result in a facility project plan. This plan will be provided to outside contractors when requests for qualifications and requests for proposals are required. The committee should represent a cross section of constituents who have various interests in the project. The athletic director and other campus decision makers should consider whether one or more representatives from the following groups are important based on their expertise, the need for project support, or for political or fund-raising reasons.

- **Local or state government officials.** Will this facility affect the community in any way? Will community events or activities be scheduled in this facility? Will services provided in this facility (e.g., swimming lessons) affect other community facilities such as the YMCA? Will government officials want access to this facility for special events? Is there any potential for the city planning board to block construction of this facility? Can this facility significantly contribute to the overall community and therefore strengthen town and gown relationships?
- **Campus experts.** Experts from the campus facilities department usually play a significant role throughout the entire process from project inception to completion. But what other people on campus who have a specific expertise could contribute to the planning stages? For example, a professor who teaches facility management may have research interests in the effect and funding of green construction (see Management Tip 1.29).
- **Local experts.** Depending on the size of the campus, the internal facilities department may not have the needed expertise to analyze construction proposals. Therefore, a prudent approach may be to identify local experts (construction, plumbing, electrical, and so on) who will not be in a position to bid for the project but would enjoy the opportunity to serve and provide reality checks regarding project plans and costs.
- **Facility users.** This often-overlooked category may be the most important. Users would include employees who will work in the facility; students and other members of the campus community, including alumni, who use the facility; and, if applicable, outside users such as visitors or renters. In a multiuse facility, each campus department that will use the facility should have some form of representation. Too often, athletic department representatives make all the decisions about a facility without including employees of the recreational sport program or physical education department.
- **Campus or community resisters.** Almost every project plan will mobilize a subset of people on or off campus who will resist the project for a variety of reasons such as cost, environmental concerns, disruptions to the area during and after construction, mission incompatibility, and the like. Often, a good strategy is to identify those who could potentially create havoc within the project and invite them into the process so that their concerns can be addressed from the beginning.
- **Donors and corporate partners.** Few projects are built solely with institutional funds. Most large projects are funded through targeted capital campaigns that may include large gifts from individuals and businesses,

as well as postconstruction revenue streams from corporate partners (naming rights, outsourced concessions, and so on). Is it important to include any of these financial contributors in the planning process? By doing so, would any concerns about conflicts of interest arise?

- **Important others.** Construction or significant renovations of athletic facilities are usually high-profile projects. Participation in planning these projects can bring a certain level of status to committee members. Has a subset of people made important contributions to the institution in a variety of ways over the years? Have they been significant donors, leaders, mentors to the student body, or valued employees? Would their presence bring a certain level of credibility to the project? Would the institution's commitment to these people be strengthened by inviting them into the planning process of this important project?

Overall, committee selection is an important first step in the planning process for a new or significantly renovated facility. Including everyone who would have interest or expertise in the project will be impossible, but the selection of committee membership must be well conceived and strategic. One way to include others in the process without assigning them to the committee is through focus groups. Small groups of constituents (alumni, students, community residents, and so on) meet with a member of the committee and have the opportunity to weigh in on facility design, uses, concerns, and so on. Another good strategy to include more voices is an online survey. People appreciate being asked and may support a project more fully if they are involved in some way. Of course, you always run the risk of someone being disgruntled because you did not use his or her advice. The advantages of these processes, however, usually far outweigh the disadvantages.

15.2 PLANNING TOOL

Justification for a New Building or Renovation Project

Before a facility construction plan can be addressed, the mission, objectives, and rationale for the project must be articulated and bolstered by a full and thorough needs assessment. The needs assessment should also include a SWOT (strengths, weaknesses, opportunities, and threats) analysis. The following questions will help the committee appointed to oversee the construction or renovation of a building identify the elements that can be used to create and articulate a clear and concise mission, establish measurable objectives, and provide a well-conceived rationale for the project:

1. What type of facility is this (single use, multipurpose, blended use)?
2. Is there any chance that this facility will be expanded in the future to increase the projected use or to serve other purposes? If so, what future changes in the facility need to be planned and analyzed in this phase of the project?
3. Whom will this facility serve now and in the future? (List all internal and external constituents and users and activities that will take place in the facility.) It is important to remember that the potential need for broadband capability has to be included in the early planning stages of any new facility or renovated facility. Section 12.27 in this book discusses fan engagement and broadband capability and should be reviewed to determine the extent and type of Internet access and streaming capabilities needed for all users in each area of the facility. Fans are only one type of user that may need extensive broadband capability. Classrooms in multiuse facilities would have special needs, as would conference rooms, security offices, and the like.
4. What are the desired benefits from constructing or renovating this facility? How realistic is each one, and how does each relate to the institutional or department mission?
5. Are there desired benefits that cannot be met? Why not?
6. What compromises will have to be made (e.g., noise around residence halls during events, lights that shine into a neighborhood) that must be articulated as unavoidable from the very beginning of this process?
7. Do the demographics of campus users and external users clearly support construction of this facility? How?
8. Are market data (local comparisons or comparisons with like institutions) available to support the need for this project? Should further studies be conducted before construction to create data sets that may provide stronger rationale for this project or create questions that need to be addressed?
9. Why does this project make sense at this time?
10. What is the potential economic impact of this project?
11. What is the potential social impact of this project?
12. What are the predictable challenges facing this project related to construction and postconstruction funding of the facility, size of the facility, site selection, user satisfaction, internal and external politics and support, timing, insurance costs during construction, insurance costs and risk assessment of activities that will take place in the new facility (e.g., is a climbing wall really worth the associated risks?), and any other relevant variables? How will each one be addressed?
13. What other information do we need to gather to ensure the viability of this project?

15.3 PLANNING TOOL

Site Selection for a New Facility

Site selection for a new facility is a critical decision. The site options for a campus-based facility may be limited, but looking at every possible location and analyzing suitability based on several variables is still important. An architect should work collaboratively with the campus-based committee appointed to oversee the construction or renovation of a building to determine site options before facility design commences. The following considerations must be addressed to determine whether a site is a viable option and how a facility may be positioned on a specific site.

Size

A few mistakes related to the size of the selected site are often made when constructing houses, office complexes, restaurants, sport facilities, and other buildings. The size of the basic footprint of the building or field is rarely miscalculated, but attention given to the ancillary components of the building site is often insufficient. For example, elements such as walkways, concessions stands, restrooms, fencing, landscaping, parking lots, outdoor lighting, and so on may not be fully taken into account when the site is selected. The result is that when these elements are introduced into the project plan, the size of the primary facility may have to be reduced. Another element of size that must be considered is the level of certainty to build up rather than out. Has sufficient analysis been done to determine whether to add levels rather than construct a single-level facility with a larger footprint? Those decisions must be made before site selection even begins. A third consideration is expansion. Even if there is no current plan to expand in the future, would the expansion option be limited by the site that is selected or would maximum expansion opportunities remain available in the future?

User Needs

A full analysis of who will be using the facility, what their needs are today, and what they may be in the future is critical to site selection. For a multiuse facility, will it be necessary to have a variety of entry points into various parts of the facility? Can this site accommodate multiple entrances? If children's camps will be held at this facility, is safety a concern given the location of the site and the adjacent community? Will the institution be renting this facility? Does this site lend itself to ample parking for a variety of rental groups or events? Is the site large enough to accommodate portable stands if the institution is selected to host a state or national championship? Is the site large enough to allow the facility to be rented out for larger events? Do the surrounding roads and highways provide reasonable access to the facility? An important point is to look at the potential use of a facility throughout the entire process rather than focus only on the primary use. That approach will also help avoid making mistakes regarding size of the site as discussed earlier.

Surrounding Communities

Many campuses sit within a local community and must therefore accommodate community concerns whenever building on a site that in any way infringes on neighborhoods or local businesses. Events in athletic facilities can create annoyances related to traffic, tailgating, rowdy behavior, bright lights, and significant noise. When selecting a site, decision makers must consider what events will take place at the site (athletic contests, rock concerts, graduation, and so on), how those events will affect the surrounding communities, and what kind of resistance they may create to the project. Decision makers must also take into account the campus community. Do they want to build an athletic facility near the health center or the president's office? Will the pregame music of a multiuse athletic field bother graduate students whose residence halls are adjacent to the field? Will the incoming traffic for an afternoon event at this site create chaos for faculty and students leaving at the end of the school day?

Utility, Cable, and Internet Access

The expense of bringing utilities and cable to a site that has no current access can be enormous. Perhaps the institution is constructing intramural fields and doesn't need any electricity, water, or cable. What will happen if those fields need to be reconfigured in the future for varsity competition? How much will it to cost to build restrooms, concessions stands, and a press box with computers or even light up a scoreboard if there is no electricity, plumbing, or cable access nearby?

Environmental Considerations

Athletic facilities are being increasingly scrutinized because of environmental concerns. Golf courses use an enormous amount of water. Significant energy is needed to heat pools and light stadiums. Clearing acres of trees for construction can have a dramatic effect on wildlife in the area or create problems with rainwater runoff. Analyzing how the environment around a construction site will be affected is an important factor in selecting the right property. Also important is thinking about how the site can accommodate green building components. For example, can this athletic facility be positioned on this site in a way that maximizes the use of solar panels (see Management Tip 1.29)?

Site Preparation, Zoning, and Building Permits

An essential part of the process is getting an accurate assessment of the cost to ready a site for construction and meet all obligations pertaining to zoning, building permits, and other legal considerations. Will the grading be minimal or extensive? Does the grading create extra concerns about being compliant with ADA (Americans with Disabilities Act) laws? Is the site readily accessible to construction equipment? Will clearing costs be significant? Is any of the land protected, a circumstance that will require more inspections, ultimately increase costs, and possibly cause delays? Does the site have poor drainage, which will result in more upfront costs to remedy the problem? Will this problem be further exacerbated if lots of rain falls before or during construction? Has anyone tested this land for underground waste hazards? Have all zoning and building permit requirements been investigated?

15.4 PLANNING TOOL

Feasibility Study Part I: Facility Cost

Several steps can be followed to determine ballpark costs for building a new facility before hiring architects and builders. Much can be learned by researching the cost of recent similar projects at other institutions and on campus. The following action steps will help the committee appointed to oversee the construction or renovation of a building determine a ballpark cost estimate for the project and decide whether the project is worth pursuing given the magnitude of the cost.

Research the Cost of Recently Built Similar Facilities Identifying institutions that have built similar facilities in the past few years and knowing the overall costs of those facilities is the first step in gathering data. This process may be simple if the institution is building a single-use facility like a field hockey field with no press box, locker rooms, or concessions stands. If the institution is building a multiuse athletic and recreation center, the committee may have to look at buildings in piecemeal fashion. For example, if a similar facility is found on another campus but it does not include the aquatics center that will be in the proposed building, the committee may have to identify a stand-alone aquatics center as well.

Visit Recently Built Similar Facilities A subcommittee of construction experts and primary users must visit the facilities. These visits may be time consuming and somewhat costly, but the process will definitely save money in the end. The visitors need to call ahead and ask to tour the facilities with the person who led the construction process for that building. Meeting with the current facilities director to gather information about annual operating expenses is also important.

Prepare a Master List of Spaces Before the visit, the committee should create, with the help of other resource people who may not be serving on the committee, a master list of each space that will be included in their facility, approximate square footage desired, all nonmoveable structures (flooring, built-in seating, lockers, and so on), and all moveable structures (desks, goals, baskets, and so on). For example, the page for the swimming pool may describe a 25-meter tiled swimming pool with eight lanes, eight diving blocks, 20 feet (6 m) of tiled and heated deck space on all sides, a 100-square-foot (9.3 sq m) storage room, a 120-square-foot (11.1 sq m) office for two people with rubber tile flooring, a timing system, lane separators, two lifeguard chairs, six rows of bleachers, and so on.

Prepare On-Site Tour Questions Before the on-site tour begins, the host should be asked about the need for and the cost of readying the site for construction. This question may or may not yield much useful information, but it is a reasonable question. Another important question would concern the cost for architectural renderings and whether building a green facility was explored along with those associated costs.

Identify External Features Before the tour, the group should also note the exterior features of the building that could affect cost. Is the entire front entrance floor-to-roof glass? Is it brick or cinder block?

Conduct a Comparative Analysis of the Master List of Spaces During the visit, at least one person must be responsible for conducting a comparison of the master list to this facility. Staying with the example of the swimming pool, it may be noted that this facility has a 25-meter pool, six lanes, no diving blocks, 15 feet (4.5 m) on each end of the pool, and 10 feet (3 m) on the sides. A small amount of storage space is located against one wall in the same room as the filter and mechanicals. The office is 72 square feet (6.6 sq m), and the floor is covered by a water-stained carpet. In addition, the person responsible for the list has to look around the facility. He or she needs to ask and record which moveable structures were included in the construction price and which ones had to be bought separately. For example, were components such as the timing system, the lifeguard chairs, the pool lane separators, and the ADA platform included in the overall construction price?

Query Building Successes and Mistakes When visiting each part of the facility, the group should ask the host what they did right and what they would change. You may find out that coaches need bigger offices because the space doesn't accommodate a recruit, two parents, and one sibling on campus visits. This question should also be asked of the facility director and any area managers that the group may run into during the tour. It is completely appropriate to call a variety of people after the group returns to campus. For example, a head trainer should be more than willing to discuss the upsides and deficiencies of the facility's training room.

Estimate Annual Operating Costs After touring the facility and recording as much comparative information as possible, the committee should meet with the current facilities director and request information regarding employee costs (full-time, part-time, work-study); utility expenses by area if possible; annual equipment inspection, repair, and replacement costs; basic cleaning and maintenance costs; insurance costs; contingency budgets; and deferred maintenance and capital budgets. Detail is great, but even learning only that it costs $850,000 to run the building annually is helpful. It is important to find out whether that figure includes debt service and annual funds set aside for large capital replacement costs like a new roof or a new surface for the five indoor tennis courts.

Add Estimates of Furnishing and Equipment Upon returning to campus, the committee needs to analyze each component of the master list for differences between the facility visited and the one proposed. From that analysis, research by the most appropriate person on the committee or another staff member must be completed to project cost increases or decreases based on the differences noted to get a better projection of overall cost. Each area of the facility needs to be analyzed for all moveable elements that will not be included in construction costs. The costs of those elements (e.g., desks, computers, treadmills, trophy cases, batting cage) must then be included in building completion estimates.

Estimate Ancillary Costs Other costs that must be calculated include readying the site for construction (discussed in Planning Tool 15.3), local or state building permits and inspections, local insurance rates, labor costs (local rate and any requirement for using union labor only), increased costs based on when the comparative facility was built versus when the proposed facility will be constructed, and commitments to green initiatives if they exist.

Find Construction Costs of Recent On-Campus Projects Assuming that other buildings have been constructed on campus within the last several years, the campus facilities department may have expertise and baseline data on projected costs for readying the site for construction and architectural renderings. The facilities representative can supplement that knowledge with advice from local contractors who have done work on campus in the past few years, or estimates could be requested at any time during the process if such work is not too complex or time consuming.

Estimate the Cost of the Land If the land for the project must be acquired, those costs would have to be estimated and factored in as well.

After all the costs have been added together and a ballpark project cost has been estimated, the committee needs to investigate the funding options for completing this project. Potential revenue streams are covered in Planning Tool 15.5.

15.5 PLANNING TOOL

Feasibility Study Part II: Facility Financing

After a ballpark estimate has been established for architectural renderings, readying the site for construction, the purchasing of land (if necessary), construction costs, and costs for moveable elements inside the facility, the committee appointed to oversee the construction or renovation of a building must analyze the potential revenue streams that might be used to cover construction costs or meet debt service payments after construction is completed. Rarely is a multimillion-dollar athletic facility funded by one source of revenue. Therefore, many building projects use multiple sources of revenue to cover these costs. Revenue sources often include several options.

Government Subsidies

State institutions may be provided with government subsidies to help offset the cost of construction. These subsidies may be in the form of grants with no repayment necessary, or they may be in the form of tax-exempt bonds whereby the institution must pay back the loan over a designated period. Tax-exempt bonds can also be provided to private institutions.

Institutional Endowment Funds

Almost all private high schools and public and private colleges and universities have endowment funds that have been acquired through fund-raising initiatives throughout the history of the institution. Some of these funds have restricted use, and others may be used at the discretion of the school's or university's board of trustees. An institution with a large endowment may have significant institutional dollars to put toward facility construction.

Institutional Deferred Capital Replacement Accounts

A second source of institutional funds may come from deferred capital replacement accounts. For example, when an institution constructs a turf field that is projected to last eight years, it may put aside $100,000 annually into a turf replacement account so that the money is available when needed. These accounts often have significant balances that can be used for other capital projects.

Department or Subunit Operating Budgets

Department or subunit operating budgets may also offset some of the expenses for a new facility, especially in the area of moveable objects. For example, the cost for treadmills in the weight room may be subsidized by the campus facilities equipment budget, or the varsity soccer team's equipment budget may be tapped for the soccer goals. The technology division may use annual budget dollars to purchase the computers and phones for the new facility, and all office equipment may be provided through an existing contract with the campuswide office equipment and supplies vendor.

Institutional Capital Campaign

Almost all institutions administer planned campaigns to raise money for facilities. These campaigns occur periodically according to projected facility needs. Campaigns may focus on a single facility or include several facilities. For example, a school may announce that over the next seven years it will conduct a capital campaign to raise $500 million to fund a new residence hall, a new athletic and recreation center, and a new library. Thus, athletic directors need to be knowledgeable about all facilities needs on campus and work with the director of development so that athletic facilities are not overlooked in capital campaign planning. Capital campaigns usually have several layers of fund-raising initiatives. The fund-raising possibilities usually include identification of single donors (individual or corporate) to fund an entire project; gifts for naming rights of the facility or specific parts of the facility (e.g., the Comcast

Athletic Center or the Carter Dance Room); lead gifts by one donor who in turn solicits the same level of gifts from others; annual pledged gifts over a specified period; gifts of stocks, real estate, art, or other items that can be liquidated; gifts for specific items that may include a naming right (e.g., buy-a-locker campaign or buy-a-brick campaign); or one-time donations. Most capital campaigns start with a silent phase during which a sizable predetermined percentage of the project cost is raised before the campaign is announced. This practice is designed to establish confidence that the project is fundable, which in turn motivates others to give. A more comprehensive description of capital campaigns can be found in Planning Tool 13.11.

Athletic Department Fund-Raising Initiatives

Some athletic programs have demonstrated the capacity to raise a significant amount of money through television contracts, corporate sponsorship support, and licensing deals as well as ticket sales and significant annual gifts from wealthy alumni or friends of the program. These sophisticated athletic programs have the staff and resources to administer their own capital campaigns using the same strategies described earlier for university capital campaigns. Departments that cannot raise significant dollars may be asked to sponsor several types of fund-raising initiatives, such as golf outings, to buy scoreboards or other items for a new facility.

Third-Party Vendor Contracts

Before or during construction, institutions may negotiate contracts with third-party vendors who will ultimately be responsible for operating part of the facility. For example, an outside concessions company may partner with the university to run the concessions for 10 years. The contract may include a stipulation that the concessions company makes a lump-sum payment to offset the building costs of the concessions areas.

Postconstruction Revenue

Chapter 13 contains a detailed description of athletic department revenue streams that can be used to fulfill debt service obligations. When a new facility is financed through bonds or loans, annual revenue that will be used to pay back the debt must be identified. For example, the athletic department may project that it will make $375,000 a year on basketball ticket sales. That money may be earmarked to repay part of the facility debt service every year. Another revenue stream that may offset significant debt is a fee assessed to students and faculty for the use of the new facility. This practice is often used for a campus recreation center. If the facility is going to include rental or third-party vendor agreements, a specific percentage of debt service may be funded by assessments on third-party contractors.

Bank Loans

Bank loans are the least desirable way for an institution to fund a capital project. Interest rates can be high, and obtaining loans over long periods can be difficult. Some project costs (usually a small portion of the overall facility cost), however, may have to be funded through bank loans. Occasionally, a short-term bridge loan might be required to cover expenses when pledged gifts do not come in as scheduled.

15.6 PLANNING TOOL

Feasibility Study Part III: Fiscal Sustainability

Before construction, the committee appointed to oversee the construction or renovation of a building must exercise due diligence by assessing whether the institution can afford to operate the facility after it is constructed. This analysis can be done by creating a postconstruction business plan and budget that provides ballpark figures for expenses and reasonable projections for revenue. This plan should reflect answers to the following questions:

Management and Personnel

1. Will the operation of this facility be kept in-house, or will it be outsourced to a management company? If the overall facility is managed in-house, will certain sections be outsourced (e.g., the ice rink or the store)?
2. What will the cost be to outsource all or part of this facility? Will shared revenue from outsourcing agreements cover all costs and even generate a profit? How much profit will be generated?
3. If operations are managed in-house, are all staffing needs already met through current employees, or will more full-time, part-time, or work-study employees need to be hired? What are the projected costs for additional salaries and benefits?

Operating Expenses (Nonevent)

1. What is the projected annual debt service for this building?
2. What are the projected taxes, if any?
3. What are the projected utility costs?
4. What are the projected insurance costs?
5. What are the projected costs for cleaning and basic building maintenance?
6. How reliable was the information received on visits to other facilities regarding operating costs for annual inspections, repairs, and replacement expenses? Is more research needed to get figures that are more accurate, or are the data collected sufficient?
7. Based on the data collected on visits, what is a reasonable contingency budget for this facility?
8. What are the big-ticket items (e.g., resurfacing the turf, replacing the roof) that will necessitate monies being deposited into deferred capital accounts? How much will those costs be annually?

Event and Rental Expenses

1. Will the institution be hosting events in the new facility that it has hosted before? If so, will the events budget cover all the expenses, or will there be additional costs that were not incurred at the previous facility (e.g., the new baseball stadium has lights and 50 percent of the practices and games have been moved to evening hours, so the projected energy costs will be higher)? If there are additional expenses, how much will they be?
2. Will new events be held in the facility? What new costs will be incurred (e.g., part-time event staff, shuttles to off-site parking lots, security costs)?
3. Will marketing expenses be incurred to promote the new facility to a variety of users or renters? If so, what are the projected costs?
4. Will legal expenses be incurred to create contracts for outside renters? What are the projected costs? Will rental fees cover all renter costs?
5. Will additional insurance costs be incurred because of rentals? Will additional insurance costs be built into third-party rental agreements?
6. Will the extended use of the facility based on increased events and rentals necessitate an increase in the dollar amounts allotted for

contingency budgets and deferred capital budgets? If so, how much?

Revenue Streams

All expenses estimated from asking the previous questions must be compared with projected revenue. Besides the revenue streams outlined in the financial feasibility study (see Planning Tool 15.5), will any part of the building campaign revenues (see Planning Tool 13.11) be designated for operating costs or will an endowment (see Planning Tool 13.8) to fund some or all operating costs be part of the campaign? Chapter 13, "Revenue Acquisition and Fund-Raising," contains complete descriptions of many other potential revenue sources that should be analyzed to determine whether they can contribute to the financial sustainability of the new facility.

15.7 PLANNING TOOL

Outsourcing Facility Construction and Operations

Most facility renovation and construction projects are not completed by on-campus facilities staff. They are outsourced to design and construction companies that have building-specific knowledge and experience as well as knowledge of laws related to inspections, permits, ADA (Americans with Disabilities Act) requirements, union labor, and so on. Outsourcing the project has many advantages that go beyond expertise and experience:

- Current facilities staff can keep up with their normal duties so that other campus priorities are not compromised.
- An enormous amount of liability and risk is transferred to the third-party contractor (but the appropriate campus representatives must be vigilant to ensure that construction quality doesn't suffer as the outside contractor looks for ways to cut expenses and maximize profits).
- Timelines are more likely to be met (an area easily compromised by other priorities when projects are being handled in house).
- The institution has recourse if jobs are not completed to the specifications.

Most institutions or school districts will be mandated by policy to put the project out for bid even if they have had an excellent relationship and a positive experience with an architect or builder who has completed other work on campus. There are several steps to follow to complete the bid process:

1. **Project scope.** The institution must create a document that is a detailed narrative of the project including a statement of need; the scope of the project; and detailed descriptions of the space needed and the furnishings, equipment, and features (lighting, surfaces, finishes, and so on) for each area. Much of this information should already have been compiled when the committee appointed to oversee the construction or renovation of the building created the mission statement, objectives, and rationale for the project as described in Planning Tool 15.2 and conducted the feasibility study as described in Planning Tools 15.4 through 15.6.
2. **Request for qualifications.** If the project is complex or may attract a large number of contractors interested in bidding for the project, the institution may start the process by advertising the project and issuing RFQs (requests for qualifications). The institution would prepare a smaller summary document of the project to distribute to vendors and ask them to submit credentials and letters of recommendation that demonstrate the level of knowledge and experience that their firm has for this type of project. This step allows the institution to decrease the pool of companies bidding on the project to a reasonable number made up of those that are clearly most qualified.
3. **Contractor prospect pool.** After the RFQs are submitted, the institution selects the most qualified contractors to bid for the project.
4. **Request for proposal.** The project scope document (step 1) is sent to the selected contractors along with an RFP (request for proposal), which asks the contractors to submit a detailed proposal for their services to complete the project and outlines instructions and timelines for submission. In most instances, the contractors will have individual meetings with campus decision makers to clarify issues, look at the potential or selected site, and ask targeted questions before they decide whether to pursue the bid. The contractors have to decide whether it is in their best interest to spend the time and the money to bid the project. They must weigh several variables such as, but not limited to, the following:

- Do they know or can they predict who they will be bidding against? What are the chances that they can bid the project at a competitive rate? In other words, they must compare the pursuit costs against the potential for being awarded the contract.
- If they complete the project, can they expect to gain future business through other campus building projects or through partnerships? For example, some sport facility construction companies also have concessions management divisions. Can the contracts be written to include post-construction partnerships? Would any of these partnerships require upfront fees before construction completion?
- Can they realistically meet the timelines?
- Are they required to use union labor only, or can they work with their own subcontractors?

5. **Submission of bids.** Each firm, at its own expense, creates a detailed document of services, timelines, legal requirements, and any other elements relevant to project completion and submits it to the institution. During this process, the institution may also invite all the contractors to campus for a prebid meeting to clarify information and answer questions. To have a fair bidding process, every contractor must receive the same information and have the same opportunities to ask questions.
6. **Presentations.** After the proposals are submitted, contractors will have the opportunity to come to campus, meet with decision makers, and conduct a sales presentation to try to win the contract. All projected costs are included in the sales presentation.
7. **Negotiation and selection.** A negotiation phase may take place, and a contractor will then be selected.

This seven-step outsourcing process can also be used to complete specific areas of a facility. For example, the institution may want to partner with an outside contractor to run a restaurant within the facility. That contractor may be given the space in the building and have the opportunity to complete the finish work so that the restaurant meets the specifications of the brand, especially if it is a franchised restaurant that requires a standard appearance. The outside contractor may have to bear the expense of finishing the restaurant and be required to include all details regarding the postconstruction contract (revenue sharing, fees, labor, and so on) in the RFP.

15.8 PLANNING TOOL

Virtual Walk-Through: Functionality, Efficiency, and Safety

Before facility construction, a worthwhile exercise is to do a virtual walk-through of the facility to assess functionality, efficiency, and safety. Even if a facility is already completed, an actual walk-through to identify possible trouble spots and establish plans to mediate those issues is an important strategy. The virtual or actual walk-through starts on the drive onto the site. Every part of the facility should be analyzed by identifying all elements that should be present if the facility

- is truly functional for all projected users,
- lends itself to be used in the most efficient way,
- is constructed in the most cost efficient way, and
- is as safe as possible.

For example, the parking lot would be evaluated for the following elements:

- The parking surface (which may be different in frigid or intensely hot weather) and the size of parking spots
- The access to the facility from the parking lot including the location and surface of walkways (a potential safety concern if people have to walk through the parking lot to get to the facility)
- Access roads and facility entry points for medical vehicles
- The number of spaces relative to projected needs based on daily operations and all possible events
- The number of spaces that may be in risky areas (e.g., vehicles subject to being hit by balls hit over an outfield or sideline fence)
- The number and location of handicap spaces
- The number and location of electric car docking spaces
- Drop-off and pick-up locations
- The number, quality, and locations of lights (and the possibility of needing more lights because many children will be using the facility for camps and clinics)
- The numbers and positioning of surveillance cameras
- The width, surface, and turning radius of parking areas to handle all types of vehicles (buses for visiting teams, flatbed trucks for big equipment, police vehicles, television trucks, shuttles from overflow parking lots, helicopter pad, and so on)
- Areas for tailgating
- Landscaping around the parking lot (the possibility that it will infringe on walkways, hang over roofs of cars, or create hiding areas for unsavory people)

This list can go on and on depending on the size and location of the facility as well as the number and types of activities sponsored and the diversity of users of the facility.

Although this process may be time consuming, it can help prevent errors such as, for example, putting a catwalk for fans directly over the edge of a pool or placing carpet, which is now stained and moldy, in locker rooms. In those situations, people weren't conducting the level of analysis needed to ensure maximum functionality, efficiency, and safety. Even when a building committee does due diligence in the analysis, the walk-through may be overlooked or purposely skipped when the committee believes that changes to the original facility design will not be considered because of concerns about funding or meeting the timeline. Anticipating everything that might turn out wrong is nearly impossible, but attempting to identify as many shortfalls as possible is important. Addressing these potential issues will result in users who are more satisfied and a facility that is more efficient and harbors fewer risks.

15.9 PLANNING TOOL

Adequate Supervision of Sport Facilities

Decisions about the number and type of supervisory staff in a sport facility, as well as the level of supervisory responsibilities, can be complex, especially in a multiuse facility. Important personnel decisions need to be made about full-time, part-time, or work-study staff, the number of employees needed for each area, and the level of expertise or maturity needed for each position. Cost is always factored into these decisions, but safety should not be compromised to save money. The facilities manager must address the following questions about staffing and supervision for everyday operations.

- **Entry points.** What are the entry points into the facility, and who will be using each entrance? Do these entry points need monitors? Will the process for checking IDs, membership cards, tickets, or using a sign-in sheet be relatively easy? How important is consistency of using the same person? Will someone need to handle a significant number of complaints or confrontations that will demand a more mature person? Will someone need to conduct searches that would demand a trained public safety officer? What are the risks if the wrong person gains access to this facility?
- **Required credentials.** Which parts of the facility must be supervised by personnel with required credentials? For example, pool supervisors may need certifications in water safety instruction, a certified pool manager's license, a lifeguard certification, and basic first aid certification. Fitness room supervisors in the free-weight room may need strength-training certifications, but a work-study student may suffice to monitor the cardio and weight-machine room.
- **Required expertise.** Which parts of the facility must be supervised by personnel with established levels of expertise? For example, a gymnastics facility may have to be supervised by the gymnastics coaching staff.
- **Level of leadership.** Which parts of the facility need full-time, experienced managers who have immediate decision-making authority? For example, the ice hockey rink may need two full-time managers because of the high use, cost of the facility, number of hours of operation, number of children using the facility, safety considerations, and other factors that necessitate maximum on-site and expert supervision.
- **Walk-through areas.** Which areas can be left unmanned through most of the open hours but will need daily walk-through inspections by a supervisor? For example, squash and racquetball courts may not need a supervisory presence, but periodic walk-throughs may be needed to make sure that users are wearing their goggles or are not using the courts inappropriately (e.g., kicking a soccer ball against the wall). Can this be done by other employees who will be entering and exiting the building and walking by the courts many times during the day?
- **Unmanned areas.** Which areas can be left unmanned because of lack of concerns for safety or improper use? For example, classrooms, office areas, and the aerobics dance room that must be reserved to be open may be areas that are generally left unsupervised.
- **Multiple employee areas.** Which areas of the facility will need more than one employee supervising at all times or at specific times? For example, a pool will usually need more than one lifeguard on duty even during hours of low participation because the pool deck cannot be left unmanned, even for bathroom

breaks. The gymnastics facility may need only one supervisor until 4:00 but may need two from 4:00 to 8:00 because of high usage.

- **Other risk management concerns.** Are there any other variables that must be addressed regarding supervision of certain parts of the facility that may have been overlooked, especially those that would carry a medium to high level of risk? For example, if a small section of a walkway around the facility is adjacent to a neighborhood known for gang-related activity, should a security guard be posted in that area after dark?

Note that many of the answers to these questions may have to be reevaluated during events or when the facility is being used by outside third-party renters. If the president of the United States is going to give a speech in a facility, entry point supervision, law enforcement presence, and many other practices will change. Even facility employees may not be permitted in the building. If the facility is rented to a professional team for a practice session, the facilities director may elect to monitor the practice area that day rather than leave it to a work-study student.

Answers to these questions must be consolidated into a clear policy document that addresses the priority of safety, certifications and credentials of supervisors, facility emergency action plans, inspection and maintenance responsibilities of supervisors, and ratios of participants to supervisors. Policies 15.10 and 15.11 address all these areas.

Making sure that each facility has a separate emergency medical plan is also a critical responsibility. This plan should be distributed to all supervisors working in the facility, all staff should be trained in execution of the plan, and a copy of the plan should be posted within the facility.

15.10 Policy—Supervision of Sport Facilities

A sample policy that deals with the proper supervision of facilities.

15.11 Form—Facility Emergency Action Plan

A sample of a facility emergency action plan that should be developed for each facility.

Available in HK*Propel*.

15.12 PLANNING TOOL

Facility Operating and Deferred Capital Budgets

Constructing an operating budget for a small, single-use facility is a relatively easy process, but the complexity of the process grows with a multiuse facility. One of the best ways to attack this process is to separate out the costs for the daily operations of a facility from special-event costs, to the extent possible. Event costs are covered in chapter 12. Categories to consider when constructing the day-to-day operating budgets of a single- or multiuse facility are outlined in the following sections. Also addressed are considerations for analyzing specific categories for inclusion in the overall facility budgets or in area-by-area budgets.

Debt Service

As with owning a home and having a mortgage, one of the primary expenses of any facility is the debt service. If the facility is completely paid off, there is no debt service. As described in Planning Tool 15.5, however, the facility may have been financed in various ways. Bond or loan agreements have built-in payment schedules that will affect short-term or long-term balance sheets. An educational institution may place the debt service expense of a sport facility in an overall institutional facilities budget rather than reflect that expense in the operating budget of the facility. Still, the facilities director and the athletic director should know how that expense is accounted for, what revenue streams are being used to pay the annual debt service, and what the length of the loan is.

Fixed Predictable Expenses

Expenses such as utilities, taxes, and insurance may be part of the facility budget, but similar to debt service, these expenses are often absorbed into a campuswide facilities budget.

Office Supplies and Other Inventory Items

A line item for basic office supplies is essential. In many cases, the institution has a single vendor contract for campuswide office supplies. The expenses for office supplies within the sport facility may be tied to the facilities budget or may be part of the campuswide office supplies budget. Other inventory types of expenses must also be analyzed for inclusion in the overall facilities budget or an area budget. For example, a store may have many inventory items such as apparel and trinkets. The sports medicine area supplies budget may be included in the athletic department budget, or a portion of it may be included in the facilities budget.

Personnel Expenses

Personnel expenses (salary and benefits) in a single-use facility with a small staff are usually separated into full-time staff, part-time staff, and student work-study allotments. In a large multiuse facility, the administrators who oversee the entire facility (e.g., director, associate and assistant directors) along with certain support staff (e.g., equipment manager, secretaries) may be included in the overall facilities budget, whereas other managers (e.g., ice rink director, aquatics director) and their staffs may be separated into program budgets for each activity area.

Contract Labor

Some institutions elect to outsource some work rather than support those positions internally. For example, the facilities director may contract with a management company to oversee the fitness areas because the institution offers a community fitness club membership that requires a specialized marketing and management staff. The expense associated with those contracts may be recorded in an overall facilities budget or may be separated into area budgets.

General Facility Maintenance

This category should include the costs for basic maintenance of the facility including cleaning, trash removal, ice rink maintenance, pool maintenance, grass cutting, and so on. Each maintenance category must be analyzed for any associated expenses related to labor and supplies.

Nonmoveable Structures, Systems, and Hardware

This category includes built-in sound systems; surfaces (tile, carpet, turf, wood floors, and so on); elevators and escalators; railings; built-in spectator seating; and any other nonmoveable structures, systems, or hardware that need to be placed on inspection, maintenance, and replacement schedules. These estimates need to be both short term and long term. Form 15.13 is an example of how a short-term schedule can be developed for a basketball facility, and Form 15.14 is an example of how these expenses can be budgeted on a rotational basis over a 10-year period. Many of these items will be included in the overall facility budget, but some, such as scoreboards and sport-specific surfaces, may be recorded in area-by-area budgets (e.g., athletics versus recreation versus physical education).

Moveable Equipment

This category includes equipment such as moveable soccer goals, moveable baskets, treadmills, desks, computers, moveable bleachers, and any other pieces of moveable equipment that need to be placed on inspection, maintenance, and replacement schedules. Again, Form 15.13 is an example of how these schedules can be developed, and Form 15.14 is an example of how these expenses can be budgeted on a rotational basis. Many of these expenses may be reflected in area-by-area budgets.

Lease Agreements

The facilities director may decide to lease rather than purchase some equipment. For example, fitness equipment such as treadmills, stair steppers, and stationary bikes is often leased and may include inspections, repairs by certified specialists, and replacement deals.

Small Equipment

Some other types of sports equipment are rarely placed on inspection schedules and will just be replaced when they look worn, such as balls, kickboards, nets, and so on. The replacement cycle for each item should be determined. For example, if the facility has 25 basketballs available to check out, should the annual operating budget include the cost of replacing five basketballs per year? When will the indoor tennis nets be replaced? Perhaps all four will be replaced every three years. Form 15.14 addresses small equipment in a rotational budget for a basketball facility.

Contingency Funds

Every facilities budget must include a general or area-by-area contingency fund. This fund is for the unexpected or unpredicted circumstances. There is no perfect way to determine how many dollars should be allocated for contingency budgets. Contingency funds are often determined by considering factors such as (1) the history of contingency spending, (2) the age of the facility, (3) a percentage of the annual operating budget, or (4) a percentage of the capital assets. Many unexpected expenses will vie for contingency dollars. Facilities managers must attempt to protect that fund throughout the year and use it only for

15.13 Form—Basketball Gymnasium Maintenance, Inspection, Repair, and Replacement Schedule

A sample form to be used for estimating costs and frequency of expenditures for items included in a typical basketball gymnasium.

15.14 Form—Basketball Gymnasium Rotation Budget

A sample form to be used for estimating costs over a 10-year period for replacement of various items included in a typical basketball gymnasium.

Available in HK*Propel*.

necessary items so that it is not depleted too early in the budget cycle.

Deferred Capital Replacement Accounts

Facility directors must plan for the replacement of big-ticket items so that a significant amount of money is already set aside when the replacement is needed. To accomplish this, a specific amount of money is annually allotted to deferred capital replacement accounts. For example, when 10 tennis courts are built, a fund should be established to resurface the courts in a specific number of years based on the typical life of the surface, the expected level of use, and the effects of weather on the surface. The projected expense for resurfacing the courts should be based on contractor estimates and projected inflation. If the estimate for court resurfacing is $350,000, then $35,000 can be allotted to the deferred capital replacement account annually for 10 years. Unfortunately, institutional decision makers often fail to make a commitment to fund deferred capital accounts. The result is that facilities cannot be repaired or replaced when needed, a situation that can create an unsafe environment that increases liability exponentially.

15.15 PLANNING TOOL

Mitigation of Risk Through Proper Facility Management

Most sport facilities include equipment or structures that create a high degree of risk. Among the many forms of risk to consider are (*a*) user or employee injury or death; (*b*) loss of significant revenue from downtime; (*c*) theft; (*d*) unpredicted costs because of improper use, maintenance, or repairs and the user's perception of poor facility quality; and (*e*) discriminatory behaviors which, in turn, negatively affect institutional image. Fully anticipating all negative occurrences is impossible, but it is essential to foresee as many potential problems as possible based on the nature of the facility and its use so that actions can be taken to mitigate those problems.

Facility maintenance, including basic cleaning and upkeep, timely repairs, and well-crafted replacement schedules is an essential element of facility management. A well-maintained facility has a positive effect on several important aspects:

- **Cost efficiency.** Diligently following prescribed maintenance schedules will extend the life of the facility and equipment and minimize the cost of repairs.
- **Image of the building and the institution.** Many campus visitors tour the athletic and recreational facilities, and their perception of the quality of those facilities often affects their perception of overall institutional quality and financial health.
- **Safety and liability.** A high degree of risk is associated with sport participation. Accidents will occur, but there must be a commitment to anticipate and prevent as many accidents as possible through prescribed facility inspection, maintenance, scheduled repairs, quick responses to unscheduled repairs, and adherence to replacement schedules.
- **User satisfaction.** Athletic and recreation facilities serve multiple purposes. They serve as recruiting incentives for prospective athletes and nonathletes. A facility can also serve as a campus center that brings together diverse people from campus and the community. By their very nature, the activities that take place in athletic and recreation facilities support the notion of good health and positive use of leisure time. A poorly maintained facility will affect user satisfaction and compromise many of those benefits.

Facility Audit

The first step in committing to facility maintenance is to conduct an area-by-area audit. First, the facility should be dissected into subareas: playing field, locker rooms, restrooms, storage closets, maintenance closets, patron seating areas, pool, squash courts, hallways, concessions areas, and so on. For each area, a list is made of every nonmoveable or moveable structure or piece of equipment that could possibly be put on a maintenance, inspection, repair, and replacement schedule. Each item is placed on a schedule that reflects the need and the timing for maintenance, inspection, repair, and replacement. A sample of an audit schedule for a basketball gymnasium is included in Form 15.13, which can be found in HK*Propel*.

After costs are estimated in this part of the audit process, the next step is to project the costs over time for each action needed, which in turn will help the facilities director create annual rotational budgets associated with the maintenance, inspection, repair, and replacement of all nonmoveable and moveable structures and equipment. Form 15.14 is a sample rotational budget form for a basketball gymnasium.

Facility Policy

A basic necessity is the development of written policies that require regular facility inspections, specify staff with inspection responsibilities, and mandate the use of inspection checklists. The same requirements should be specified for maintenance and repair. Policy 15.16 is a sample of such a policy.

15.16 Policy—Facility Inspection and Maintenance

A sample policy that specifies athletic facility inspection, maintenance, and repair responsibilities of staff.

Available in HK*Propel*.

Proper Usage

Facilities managers and schedulers must be fully aware of how a facility can be used and what activities must be prohibited. For example, a turf soccer field may not have the appropriate Gmax rating to support a collision sport like football or rugby. An injury suffered by a player on the rugby club team when playing on this field could easily result in a negligence lawsuit. Determining which activities are allowable is only one piece of the puzzle. The manager must also determine whether signage and supervisor training must address requirements for participation in allowable activities. For example, weightlifting is allowable in the free-weight room, but health codes mandate that shirts must be worn and safety standards require that qualified spotters must be used at the bench press station. Fully analyzing activities that will take place in a facility must be part of the due diligence for rentals or special events as well. If a rock band is going to perform at the stadium, will pyrotechnics be permitted? Having a general list of prohibited activities is recommended. The following is an example of a general list of prohibited activities:

- Any activity that violates institutional policy or local, state, or federal law
- Use or possession of alcoholic beverages and controlled substances
- Smoking, chewing, or any other use of tobacco products within or outside the building
- Fighting, gambling, or other disruptive or illegal activities
- Use of flammable substances or materials
- Open flames (candles, cooking tools, and so on), fireworks, or pyrotechnics
- Attendance at events exceeding approved occupancy limits
- Use of trampolines, climbing walls, enclosed or air-supported structures of any type, climbing ropes, firearms or shooting activity, bow and arrow shooting activity, or related equipment or devices

Hours of Operation

Opening and closing (locking down) various areas of a facility during posted hours of operation should be one of the easiest forms of mitigating risk. But this practice can be one of the biggest problems for facilities managers who rely on a variety of people to unlock and lock doors and monitor supervisors. If campus public safety officers are responsible for opening the building every morning at 7:00 a.m., who is checking on whether all area monitors are on time and present? Did the swim coach tell the lifeguard the night before that he would lock up when he left and then forget to do it? Strict procedures and policies must in place and an assigned staff member must be responsible for ensuring that areas are open and closed on time and that supervisors are present.

Qualified Users (Nondiscriminatory)

Are there any parts of the facility where participation is limited to those who have specific skills, qualifications, or training? For example, should access to the fitness rooms be allowed only to users who watch an instructional video and get a sticker on their ID or membership cards? Should the platform diving well be used only by divers who have the appropriate and proven level of experience? Are certain pieces of equipment in the gymnastics room off-limits to general users and provided only for gymnastics team members because of the need for experience and trained supervision? Is a senior staff member assigned to be an overall facility director charged with the responsibility of being vigilant about these issues? Also, the means used to qualify users must be legally acceptable so that qualification standards do not discriminate against people.

Environmental Factors

Outdoor facilities must have clear policies related to weather concerns, and the supervisor of each outdoor activity area must have the responsibility and authority to cancel or suspend activities when appropriate. Of critical importance is dealing with lightning and other dangerous weather (see Policy 12.20 in HK*Propel* for more discussion).

Signage

Signage in all athletic venues is an essential element in ensuring the safety of all participants and spectators. Signage is useful in providing safety information, evacuation instructions, severe weather and lightning warnings, and important items in the emergency action plan (EAP). Managers of each facility must be assigned to create a written checklist of required signage and the specified location of such signage. An inspection of signage should occur on a regular basis depending on the nature and usage of the facility.

Insurance Coverage

The senior staff member in charge of facilities should meet annually with the institution's legal counsel to review insurance coverage for all institutional facilities, which should include the purchase of a general liability policy (umbrella) to cover unforeseen events. A full disclosure of all activities that take place in the facility is essential because some activities (wall climbing, platform diving, and so on) may necessitate additional forms of coverage. In addition, outside groups that use institutional facilities must be required to obtain a policy or policies for general liability insurance that provide coverage for personal injury and property damage and name the institution as coinsured. This point is covered more fully in Policy 15.22 in HK*Propel* (Use of Sport Facilities by Community Groups) and Management Tip 5.15 (Insurance Issues Confronting Athletic Directors) in this book. Each activity should be analyzed for the need for additional insurance.

Waivers

The use of waivers, releases, and informed consent forms will not protect the institution from all liability, and they will not stop an attorney from filing a lawsuit. Thus, they should never be relied on as the only risk management techniques to prevent claims or litigation. Coaches, teachers, and administrators should not carry out their duties under the mistaken assumption that these documents eliminate the need for sound accident prevention programs and the adoption of an injury-prevention environment. These documents, however, will help in the defense of a claim or litigation if the plaintiff alleges that no warning was provided or that he or she did not know of the risks involved in the activity. In addition, the laws of the state may allow a reduction in liability if the plaintiff executed a release or waiver before participating in an activity. A properly constructed waiver, release, or informed consent form can help reduce liability by documenting that the plaintiff–participant

- was informed of the risks involved in an activity,
- voluntarily gave consent to participate,
- assumed the risks involved with the event or activity,
- waived his or her rights to sue in the event of an injury while participating,
- released the sponsoring organization,
- stated that he or she was physically able to participate in the event or activity, and
- stated that the institution sought and was provided with important medical or other information.

Although a waiver for student-athletes is available as Form 9.6, consider using a more general version such as Form 15.17 for non-student-athlete participants who may be using facilities for other purposes.

15.17 Form—General Release, Waiver, and Consent

A sample consent and release from liability form to be used when community groups or individuals use the institution's athletic facilities.

Available in HK*Propel*.

Incident Report Forms

Incident report forms are extremely important documents. Generally, incident reports are discoverable in litigation, which means that a judge will direct a school or college to produce the report for the plaintiff's attorney if a report exists. Depending on the information on the report and the manner in which the report is drafted, a report can either help or hurt the defense of a case involving an injury to a student or athletic participant. Injury reports must be completed accurately and objectively only with information known to the person completing the report. The report should indicate whether a third party provided information; for example, "Coach Michael Smith reports that Len Jones hurt his right leg while sliding into second base during the afternoon baseball game." Forms 9.9 and 9.10, found in HK*Propel*, represent injury report forms that are recommended for athletic events. See Form 15.18 for a general incident or injury report form that could be used in any facility for any activity.

15.18 Form—General Incident or Injury Report

A sample report form to be used by facilities supervisors or event personnel when any participant or spectator is injured while using an athletic facility or attending an athletic event.

Available in HK*Propel*.

Emergency Action Plans

Emergency action plans (EAPs) are clearly documented, step-by-step procedures for handling the unexpected such as injury, violent weather, active shooter, and so on. Creating these plans is time consuming and should not be completed in a vacuum. The sport facilities director should be a member of the campuswide risk management team that develops, discusses, and tests EAPs. From there, the sport facilities director must analyze each area within the facility and determine what may have to be added to the facility's EAPs. For example, campuswide plans may address how to proceed when a person is injured on campus, but some sport facilities such as pools may have phones that ring directly to the campus public safety office. The EAP in the pool will have to reflect that difference. Campus EAPs may not cover lightning or other weather anomalies, but any outdoor sport facility must have an EAP for bad weather. Covering all types of EAPs is impossible, but each one must be well documented, available to all employees, fully covered in the training of designated personnel, and posted in the facility as needed.

Shared, Rented, or Free Facilities

In many instances the athletic department may use facilities that are not under the total direction of institutional employees. In some cases, institutions have agreements with local governments or outside owners to share or rent facilities. When teams travel for spring break and other school holidays, they often rent facilities in other cities. In some cases, institutions are permitted to use outside facilities free of charge, such as a local golf course for a fund-raising event. The campus sport facility director must make sure that all the considerations mentioned earlier are present in these noninstitutional facilities. In addition, the institution should adopt a policy that the athletic department, or any department, cannot use any private club or facility that has discriminatory membership policies that are inconsistent with the nondiscrimination policy of the institution.

Annual Risk Assessment

Risk assessment checklists are excellent management tools for the athletic director to use as an additional method to ensure sufficient consideration of facilities issues. A comprehensive facility risk assessment such as Risk Assessment 15.20 should be completed at least once annually. Facility-specific checklists such as Risk Assessment 15.19 (for ball fields) in HK*Propel* should be performed more frequently. Every coach and facility supervisor should do a preactivity observation walk-around to identify potential hazards or concerns. Such a checklist can also be used to develop a routine maintenance schedule. Risk Assessment 15.20 in HK*Propel* is a sample of a comprehensive facility policies and procedures checklist that can be easily customized for use.

15.19 **Risk Assessment**—Checklist: Ball Fields Inspection

A sample athletic ball field risk assessment checklist that should be completed by a senior staff member or facilities director on a monthly or semester basis, depending on frequency of use.

15.20 **Risk Assessment**—Checklist: Facility Safety and Supervision

A sample athletic facilities policies and procedures risk assessment checklist that should be completed by a senior staff member or facilities director on an annual basis.

Available in HK*Propel*.

15.21 PLANNING TOOL

Considerations in Scheduling a Multiuse Facility

Scheduling each unit of space in a facility (e.g., playing field, locker room, ticket office) is a relatively easy process in a single-use facility. But institutions are increasingly finding ways to maximize the use of all facilities as a way to serve more constituent groups, create community bonds, and generate revenue. More and more athletic departments are using their pools to provide children's swim lessons, restriping tennis courts for community pickleball lessons and tournaments, renting their turf fields to other institutions when too much rain or snow has made grass fields unplayable, and scheduling large outdoor and indoor spaces for concerts, noted speakers, and other mass community events. As universities and high schools are building new facilities, they are reimagining ways to maximize their use. This can generate significant revenue and create stronger connections within the community at large that may positively affect fan base size, summer camp attendance, enrollment, and donations to the athletic program. The biggest challenge in renting facilities is meeting the need for revenue generation while addressing the expectations of campus constituents who want uninterrupted access. Therefore, managers need to direct attention to the following points when scheduling a facility that has multiple users.

Priority Use

Too often, conflicts arise regarding use of facilities because no hard-and-fast rules are in place to identify which constituent group has priority over each space. On a campus, a sport facility may be frequently used by the athletic department, the physical education department, and the department of campus recreation. In addition, the facility manager may want to maximize revenue through rentals. In this example alone, four different managers could be involved in negotiating for time and space. This process can be contentious if priority use has not been determined. Therefore, each space in a facility must be analyzed to determine who has first priority on that space. But it can't stop there. Several other questions must be addressed as well:

- **How deep does the priority list go?** Does the athletic department have priority, while everyone else is scheduled on a first-come, first-served basis? Or is physical education second on the list, recreational sport third on the list, open campus access fourth, and outside rentals fifth? If outside rentals or lesson programs have been factored into the facilities revenue and expense budgets, do campus constituents have to be educated on why outside community use may be high on the priority list even if it limits use by students and other campus constituents? This can be a very contentious issue that needs to be considered and addressed in the planning and policy-making process.
- **Who are the part-time users of the facility, and how do they affect priority use?** For example, does the admissions department use the gymnasium for an open house when the number of visitors reaches a certain threshold? Does the admissions department automatically get priority use of the space when that happens? If so, anyone who schedules that space on an admissions open-house date must understand that the event might have to be canceled at the last minute based on the number of visitors for the open house. That stipulation must be put in writing on the form used to apply for facility use.
- **Is each space being analyzed separately?** For example, the basketball team may have priority use of the gymnasium for practices and games, but do they always have priority use of the two classrooms that they normally use for halftime chalk talks? Or does physical education have priority use of classrooms, thus requiring the team to look for alternative space when games conflict with scheduled classes?

What happens when unscheduled classes are added later in the semester as makeup sessions? Does physical education have to work around the basketball team's schedule, or does the basketball team have to accommodate the change?

- **Are specific timelines involved in priority use?** For example, campus recreation may have priority use over the indoor multipurpose field. But does the priority switch to the athletic department from January 15 to March 1 so that the spring teams can practice indoors when it snows?
- **Do special events need to be factored into the schedule regardless of priority use?** For example, does the indoor multipurpose field, which doubles as an indoor tennis center, have to be scheduled as a backup site for graduation if it rains, even though the tennis team, which normally has priority use, would also need it if it rains during the first round of the NCAA tournament that same weekend?

Creating a priority-use document is a time-consuming and complex process. The document will never fully address every situation, but it will help eliminate and mediate many potential conflicts. Constituents should be involved in the process of creating this document by selecting a committee of various stakeholders (administrators, department chairs, students, faculty, alumni, unbiased others). Taking this approach will protect the athletic director or the facilities manager from accusations of making decisions based on self-serving interests. Use of a stakeholder committee will also help create more buy-in for established priority use and begin to build collegial relationships that will help in the negotiation processes when they are needed.

Master Calendar

One of the biggest problems in educational institutions is creating a master calendar that reflects all facility use and then getting all departments to adhere to it. Too often, facility users change dates for an event indiscriminately before checking on facility availability. For example, admissions may change an open-house date without checking the gymnasium schedule and then expect their priority use to trump the havoc that was caused because of the date change. Sometimes a user will check on the primary facility but may not check on ancillary facilities. For example, the admissions department may have checked on the gymnasium but not on other campus activities and therefore did not realize that parking was going to be a challenge because three other events were being held on campus that weekend. A sport facility manager must do everything in his or her power to support a campuswide facility master calendar, which will reduce many conflicts. If the institution does not create the campuswide master calendar, the sport facility manager must at least create one for the facilities under his or her purview. Among the components of maintaining a master calendar are the following:

- **One person must be responsible for scheduling** and keeping the calendar up to date; a second person serves as a backup when the primary scheduler is unavailable.
- **All commitments to campus-only use should be scheduled.** Sometimes, campus decision makers elect to have specific sport facilities open only to the campus community. For example, a policy may state that students, faculty and staff, and alumni must have open access to the indoor multipurpose surface and the fitness centers from 4:00 p.m. through closing on weekdays and 1:00 p.m. through closing on weekends whenever school is in session. This provision should be noted on the master calendar so that when the Amateur Athletic Union (AAU) calls the basketball coach and asks to rent the facility to host a basketball tournament all weekend, the coach knows that it can't be done or, at the very least, that such use will have to be negotiated as an exception to the current policy.
- **All primary and ancillary facilities must be included on the calendar.** For example, for an NCAA championship soccer match, scheduled facilities may include the stadium, two team locker rooms, an officials' locker room, parking lots, a press room, a room for an alumni reception, a practice field, a meeting room for the NCAA committee, and so on.
- **Each scheduled facility use must include time for setup, breakdown, or turnover**

when needed. This requirement may necessitate taking a facility offline for a longer period than it is actually needed because the facilities manager may not want to pay overtime charges to clean a facility and may just shut it down until the next day when it can be cleaned during normal working hours.

- **All blackout days should be included on the master calendar.** Schedulers should not assume that people realize that the fitness facilities will be closed during school breaks (winter holidays, spring break, and so on) because no student work-study employees are available to monitor the facility.
- **All anticipated offline days should be included on the master calendar.** Maintenance, repair, and replacement schedules often affect whether facilities can be left open or must be shut down. If the pool is always drained and cleaned two weeks before school starts, that entry should be made on the calendar every year.
- **All contingency schedules should be noted on the calendar.** For example, if the athletic center is a rain site for all alumni weekend events, that point should be noted on the master calendar. The scheduler may allow a small student group (such as the Frisbee club) to schedule space in the athletic center during that time as long as they realize that their practice may have to be canceled if it rains.

Identification of the Decision Maker

Even if an institution does an outstanding job of creating priority-use policies and maintains a comprehensive master calendar, disputes will arise between facility users. Therefore, one individual must be given the authority to handle disputes and make final decisions. Of course, campus politics will affect who is appointed as the decision maker. To protect that person from extremely contentious or political situations, a committee-based appeals process could be incorporated to promote a sense of fairness.

FACILITY RENTALS

The use of athletic facilities by community groups and other external third parties is commonplace. Such use is a community responsibility at public education institutions and an important relationship-building tool at many private institutions. The athletic department is often responsible for managing these relationships. Thus, fair rental or use fees and efficient processes must be installed with safety, insurance, and legal liability as primary considerations. Often, community groups provide volunteers as ticket takers, event management assistants, or spotters on the golf course. Volunteers may perform those or numerous other functions related to athletic events. Groups provided by nonprofit organizations may staff food or souvenir concessions stands to earn money for their respective organizations. When these people set foot on campus, they represent risks for injury to themselves or pose the potential to act in a way that causes injury to others. Form 15.17, General Release, Waiver, and Consent, and Form 15.18, General Incident or Injury Report, can be used with non-student-athlete-participants. In addition, the following policies, forms, and risk assessment checklists are provided in HK*Propel* to deal with these responsibilities.

15.22 Policy—Use of Sport Facilities by Community Groups

A sample policy that prioritizes facility use by institutional and community entities, defines prohibited activities, specifies use fees, details application and decision-making procedures, and informs prospective users of insurance and other conditions of use.

15.23 Form—Application for Use of Facilities

A sample facility use application form to be used for institutional or community entities that provides all details required to make use decisions.

15.24 Form—Notification of Decision for Facility Use Application

A form letter to be used to respond to applicants for use of athletic facilities to inform the applicant of the decision.

15.25 Form—Facility Use Agreement

A sample agreement for use with athletic facilities users that details dates and facilities approved, fees to be charged, deposits required, setup arrangements, location restrictions, prohibited activities, and other essential details.

15.26 Policy—Volunteer Groups and Concessions at Home Athletic Events

A sample policy governing the use of volunteer groups to operate concessions booths at athletic events when nonprofit charities receive a portion of sales proceeds.

15.27 Form—Volunteer Consent and Release From Liability

A sample release form to be signed by volunteers working at athletic events that specifies limits of insurance coverage and the obligation to report injuries or other incidents that may result in institutional liability and training obligations.

15.28 Form—Charitable Organization Application for Concessions Booth

A sample application form to be used by charitable organizations to apply for acceptance as the operator of a concessions booth at an athletic event.

15.29 Risk Assessment—Checklist: Facility Use by Third Parties

A sample checklist to be used by the athletic director to determine whether proper policies and procedures exist for facility use by third parties and the use of volunteers at athletic events.

Available in HK*Propel*.

BIBLIOGRAPHY

FACILITIES AND OPERATIONS

Ammon, R., Southall, R.M., & Blair, D.A. (2016). *Sports facility management: Organizing events and mitigating risks* (3rd ed.). Morgantown, WV: FIT Publishing.

Chernushenko, D., van der Kamp, A., & Stubbs, D. (2001). *Sustainable sport management: Running an environmentally, socially, and economically responsible organization.* Nairobi, Kenya: United Nations Environment Program.

Drew University. (2007). *Department of Intercollegiate Athletics policy manual.* Unpublished. Madison, NJ.

Fried, G. (2021). *Managing sport facilities* (4th ed.). Champaign, IL: Human Kinetics.

Glassman, T. et al. (2007). Alcohol related fan behavior on college football game day. *Journal of American College Health*, *56*(3), 255–261.

Jensen, C.R., & Overman, S.J. (2004). *Administration and management of physical education and athletic programs* (5th ed.). Prospect Heights, IL: Waveland Press.

Muret, D. (2011, July 25). Decisions, decisions, decisions. *Sports Business Journal.* www.sportsbusinessdaily.com/Journal/Issues/2011/07/25/In-Depth/Elements.aspx?hl=college%20stadiums&sc=1.

NIRSA. (2009). *Campus recreational sports facilities.* Champaign, IL: Human Kinetics.

NIRSA. (2009). *Space planning guidelines for campus recreational sport facilities.* Champaign, IL: Human Kinetics.

Pederson, P., & Thibault, L. (2022). *Contemporary sport management.* (7th ed.). Champaign, IL: Human Kinetics.

Peterson, J.A., & Tharrett, S.J. (Eds.). (2007). *Health/fitness facility standards and guidelines* (3rd ed.). Champaign, IL: Human Kinetics.

Sawyer, T.H. (Ed.). (2019). *Facility planning and design for health, physical activity, recreation, and sport* (14th ed.). Urbana, IL: Sagamore.

Schwarz, E.C., Hall, S., & Shibli, S. (2010). *Sports facility operations management: A global perspective.* Burlington, MA: Elsevier.

Smith, M. (2008, August 27). IMG venture to offer private financing for college sports facilities. *Sports Business Journal.* www.sportsbusinessdaily.com/Journal/Issues/2008/08/20080825/This-Weeks-News/IMG-Venture-To-Offer-Private-Financing-For-College-Facilities.aspx?hl=IMG%20venture%20to%20offer%20private%20financing&sc=0.

University of Texas at Austin. (1992). *Intercollegiate athletics for women policy manual.* Unpublished. Austin, TX: Department of Women's Intercollegiate Athletics.

Index

Note: Figures and tables are indicated by *f* or *t* following the page number.

A

abuse 14, 264-265, 266, 288, 304-307, 321, 326
academic profiling 251, 257
academic review committee 75
academics
  Esports and 148, 150
  graduation rates 30, 73, 75, 250, 253
  integrity and reputation 72-73, 249-250
  policies supporting achievement 253-254
  progress rates 73, 75, 250, 253
  strategic plan for excellence 107, 108*t*
  student-athlete eligibility 18, 137, 241, 242, 249
academic support programs 249-257
  academic profiling 251, 257
  admissions policy exemptions 250-251
  at-risk students 251, 252-253, 256-257, 296
  audience served 252
  class note reviews 256
  conflicts of interest 73, 193, 250, 252
  control of 251-252
  development of 249-255
  documentation 254-255
  elements of comprehensive 254
  ethical conduct 239, 254
  faculty role 250, 251-252, 257
  grades, reporting 256
  learning disabilities 251, 253, 254, 256
  mentoring programs 254, 257
  operational program structure and access to 123-124, 127*t*
  organizational structure 193
  overview 247, 259
  policy support 253-254, 255, 257
  prioritizing 258
  recruitment and 249, 250
  remedial programming 251
  retention with 296
  sport participation as incentive 256
  study halls 254, 256, 257
  study skills learning support 254
  summer bridge programs 251
  team academic coaches 256
  technology access and training 254, 257
  tutoring 123-124, 127*t*, 239, 254, 255, 256
accreditation 9, 64-65
action plans
  developing 101-102
  emergency 272, 341, 438, 445
  fund-raising 105-106, 106*t*
  team 103, 104*t*
administration. *See* higher administration
administrative support services 125, 195-196
admission fees. *See* ticketing
admissions 92, 250-251
advertising
  corporate sponsorship 355, 377-379, 378*t*, 388-389, 395
  job postings 199, 200*f*-201*f*, 201-202, 202*f*
  multimedia rights and 387-390
  promotions 408
  radio, television, streaming 391-392
alcohol. *See* substance use/abuse
alumni
  athletic advisory council role 74, 78
  athletics increasing involvement 93
  budget cut responses 175
  coach recruitment response 48
  diversity education role 288, 294
  donors 78, 79, 360
  ethical conduct education 240
  governance 74, 78-80
  rules compliance 79, 240
Amateur Athletic Union (AAU) 149
American Management Association 17
Americans with Disabilities Act (ADA, 1990) 299, 300-301
assistant coaches 53, 122, 138-139, 177, 193, 218
Association for Christian College Athletics (ACCA) 67
athletes. *See* student-athletes
athletic advisory councils
  alumni and donor 74, 78, 80
  authority and purpose 72
  composition 72-74, 297
  diversity role 288, 297
  functions 72, 74
  fund-raising 80
  governance role 61, 72-78, 80, 81-82
  sport performance 81-82
  standing committees 74-75
  student-athlete 73-74, 76-77
  term limits 74
athletic departments
  admissions department and 92, 251
  directory 155
  diversity leadership 294-295
  events calendars 156
  fund-raising and revenue production 13-14, 92-93, 431
  mission and vision. *See* mission; vision of organization
  office operations 153-180
  operational program structure 113-152
  organizational structure. *See* organizational structure
  in professional bureaucracy 8, 31
  relationship building 37-38
athletic directors 1-56
  athletic advisory council role 74
  athletic event management 14
  athletics integration in education 29-30, 89-93
  attributes 4-5
  budget responsibilities 167
  change management 3, 32-36, 41-46
  coach recruitment 47-49, 117, 203
  coach terminations 50-55, 177, 228-230
  communicating performance expectations 27-28
  critical thinking 6-7
  decision making 6-7, 15
  educational credentials 8, 9-10, 29
  employee management training 31
  employee relationships 15-18, 38
  environmentally responsible actions 56
  ethical conduct standards 3, 14
  governance role. *See* governance
  insurance issues 159
  leadership 1, 3
  learning environment 3, 25-26, 84
  longevity of 22
  media management 12-13
  ongoing training 11-14
  political acumen 3, 19-20
  power, wise use of 21-22
  problem-solving strategies 39-40
  qualifications 8-10
  relationship building 15-18, 37-38
  revenue production 13-14
  risk management 11-12
  rules compliance 61, 67-68
  skills 3
  sports management training 8-9
  strategic planning 25, 27, 35-36
  team roster management role 313
  Title IX challenges 41-46
  values and principles 3, 23-24
athletic event management 335-350
  bidding to host 338
  broadband capability 345-346
  budgeting and cost-cutting 167, 178
  cash handling 338
  concessions 339
  crowd control 342-344
  event cancellation insurance 159
  facility scheduling 337
  fan engagement 345-346
  finances 162, 167, 178, 338
  fund-raising and revenue production 355, 356, 357, 360-361, 380-382, 393-395, 431
  game officials 338
  guarantees 382
  media and promotion 338, 342, 345-346, 413
  operational policies 338
  overview 335
  parking 382
  risk assessment and management 66, 339, 340-341, 344, 349
  security issues 340, 341, 342-344
  sports camps 347-349
  ticketing 338
  training in 14
  visiting teams 338
athletic program governance. *See* governance
athletics
  adding or eliminating sports 116, 129, 144-150, 175, 355, 393-395
  alumni involvement 93
  competitive success 126, 128
  education role and function 29-30, 89-93
  funding 13-14
  local, state, national exposure 92
  media coverage 12-13
  participation in. *See* sport participation
  philosophy of educational 14, 89-93
  purpose of 94-95
  varsity. *See* varsity sports

athletic scholarships
academic status and 250
cost-cutting by lowering 178
Esport 147
gender equity and 41, 42, 45, 134-137, 135*t*, 136*t*
loss of 73
minority access to 296, 298
operational program structure and 121-122, 126*t*, 127*t*, 134-137, 135*t*, 136*t*, 142, 147
retention with 296
rules compliance 243, 244
tuition waivers 400
athletic training 269-280. *See also* sports medicine
concussion protocols 269, 277-278
critical issues 275-278
equipment storage and signage 328
ethical and professional conduct 81, 239
facility operations and 124, 127*t*, 271, 328
injuries. *See* injuries
insurance coverage 272
operational program structure and 124, 127*t*
overview 269
preparticipation requirements 272, 318
rules compliance 269
sport performance advisory group 81-82
at-will employees 220-221
awards 78, 298, 331. *See also* hall of fame

B

background checks 203
back-to-university programs 402
benefits. *See* compensation and benefits
board of education 69-70, 69*f*, 220
board of trustees 54, 69-70, 69*f*, 74, 220
bonuses 226-227
booster clubs
board of directors 371-372
building donor pool 370-371
change management 369-370
external 367-368, 369
fund-raising and revenue production 354, 357, 366-372, 386, 393-394
gender equity and Title IX 366, 369-370
governance 78-79, 367, 368-369
legal considerations 371
new sport home game experience 393-394
operational guidelines 369
purpose of, defining 368
relationship building 79
seating priority points systems 386
single sport 366-367, 369-370
structuring 368-369
umbrella clubs 366-367, 368-370
brand identity 13, 363
brand positioning 407-411
brand awareness 410, 411
expert help 410-411
instructional manual 410, 411
logos 14, 225-226, 329, 355, 389, 396, 410-411
messaging vs. selling 407-409
staff for 407, 408-409
statement of 94, 96
budgeting
basic characteristics 163-164
budget managers, multiple 167-168
budget preparation process 169-174
cost-savings strategies 176-179
cutting or reducing 175-179
delineation of subunits 164
facility 179, 430-433, 439-441
gender equity 45-46
goals and objectives integration 163, 169-170, 173-174
identifying external needs 174
peer institution comparison 173-174
policies 174
preliminary assessments 169-170
review and reporting 164, 168, 169
sample 165*t*-166*t*, 171*t*-174*t*
team 177-179
transparency and collaboration 163, 176
zero-based 163-164, 170, 171*t*-174*t*, 175
buildings. *See facility entries*
bullying, prohibitions 304

C

California Interscholastic Federation (CIF) 148, 149
camps. *See* sports camps
career development programs 259
certifications 9-10, 29, 64-65
chain of command 69-71, 69*f*
chancellors. *See* higher administration
change management
athletic director's 3, 32-36, 41-46
booster clubs 369-370
gender equity 41-46
inevitability of change 32
navigating change 32-33
resistance, considerations 33-34, 41, 43-44
resistance, preventing 35-36
responses to change 32
charitable gifts 374. *See also* donors
class system 120
clinics. *See* sports camps
coaches
ability of 128
assistant 53, 122, 138-139, 177, 193, 218
budget responsibilities 167
compensation and benefits 122, 138-140, 142, 177, 199, 220-231
conflicts of interest 17-18
diversity training 293
donor relationship building 360-363
employment contracts 47-48, 50, 52-53, 139, 220-231, 304
firing/terminating 50-55, 177, 228-230
fund-raising responsibilities 360-363
gender of 44, 199
guest 360-361, 394
job descriptions and expectations 139, 193, 197-198
media responsibilities 413
operational program structure and 122, 126*t*, 127*t*, 128, 138-140, 142
power and visibility of 185, 191, 192-193
program merits communication to prospective 117
qualifications 29-30, 139-140, 265
recruitment of 47-49, 117, 203
search for 139
sexual misconduct and abuse 14, 264-265, 266, 304-307, 321
standards of conduct 227-228, 238-239
student-athlete relationship with 319-320
supervision of 192-193
as supervisors 193
transition planning 55
collegiality 214-215
Commission on Colleges of the Southern Association of Colleges and Universities 64
Commission on Sport Management Accreditation (COSMA) 9
communications
brand positioning. *See* brand positioning
budgeting 167
camp-parent 347-348
crisis 414
donor, fan, and alumni 80
First Amendment rights 323-325, 412
functions of 407
guidelines for professional 156
key performance indicators 408, 414-415
media. *See* media; media relations
mental health service access 265-266
operational program structure 115-119
overview 405
performance expectations 27-28
policies 157
program evaluation 414-415
publications 155-156, 388, 416-418
sales integration with 407
social media strategy 412
staff for 407, 408-409
termination decision 52-55
community groups
as donors 361
facility rentals 400-401, 450
community service 25, 26, 91, 260, 262-263
compensation and benefits
additional 225-226
at-will employees 220-221
base 225
benefit plans 223
bonuses 226-227
coach 122, 138-140, 142, 177, 199, 220-231
considerations 222-223
contracts 220-231
cost-cutting 177
cost-of-living increases 222, 225
game official 338
goals for 222-223
institutional differences 220
liquidated damages 229, 230
marketplace influences 142, 199, 222, 224, 225, 291
merit pay 222-223, 225
minority group prospects 291
noncash benefits 227
outside activities 217-218
outside employment 216
overtime 216-217
payroll 162
peer institution comparison 222, 225
personnel management 184, 199, 216-218, 220-231
renegotiation provisions 224
ultimate authority 220
concessions 161, 178, 339, 381-382, 431, 450
concussion protocols 269, 277-278
conference affiliation 67-68, 120
conference cost-saving initiatives 179
conflict resolution 184, 215
conflicts of interest 17-18, 73, 193, 250, 251, 252
contingency funds 440-441
continuing education credentials 10. *See also* professional development
contracts
athletic scholarship 243, 244
budgeting based on 170, 178

contest 337
employment 47-48, 50, 52-53, 139, 220-231, 255, 304
lease 400, 440
production and approval of 158
vendor 178, 431
copyright releases 417
corporate giving 355, 377-379, 378*t*, 384, 386, 387-390, 395
corrective actions 208, 215, 302-303. *See also* disciplinary actions
crisis communications 414
critical thinking 6-7
customer service 361

D

decision making
athletic director's 6-7, 15
compensation and employment contract authority 220
facility scheduling 449
fairness in 194-195
governance. *See* governance
philosophy 15
return to play after injuries 18, 269, 277-278
deferred capital replacement accounts 430, 441
development. *See* fund-raising and revenue production
dining facilities 124, 127*t*
disabilities, people with
accommodation 299-300, 301, 302
discrimination complaint process 302-303
diversity, inclusion, and nondiscrimination 288, 299-303
employment 300-302
facility access 300, 301, 341
facility damage fears 300
individualized evaluations 299
learning disabilities 251, 253, 254, 256, 300
prostheses 300
sport selection 299
team tryouts 299, 301
disciplinary actions 302-303, 324-326. *See also* corrective actions; sanctions
discrimination. *See also* diversity, inclusion, and nondiscrimination
continued historical 283-286, 284*t*-286*t*
disciplinary actions 302-303
employment 44, 219
formal complaint process 302-303
hiring process 198, 199
laws prohibiting 11
nonretaliation 302-303
sex 41, 119, 138, 316
diversity, inclusion, and nondiscrimination 281-310
addressing fears 286-288
athletic advisory council role 288, 297
athletic department improvement with 286
continued historical discrimination 283-286, 284*t*-286*t*
defined 281
education on 288, 293-295, 298
elements of model program 287-288
gender-based 281, 288, 290
hiring process 198, 199, 202, 203, 288, 291-292, 301-302
LGBTQ individuals 288, 304
overall vs. distributed diversity 290
overview 281
peer institution comparisons 289-290
people with disabilities 288, 299-303
policies 287, 288
retention strategies 288, 296
search and recruitment mechanisms 288, 291-292
sexual harassment and abuse prohibitions 288, 304-307
staff incentives 288, 298
strategic plans 287, 289-290
Division I-III organizational charts 186*f*-188*f*
Division I position chart 190*t*-191*t*
donor car programs 232
donors. *See also* fund-raising and revenue production
annual giving 78, 354, 357-358, 366-372
away event engagement 360
building base/pool 363, 370-371
coach termination communication 52, 54
database of 356
endowments 355, 373-374, 430
ethical conduct education 240
facility planning committee role 423-424
governance 78-80
home event guest coaches 360-361, 394
legal considerations 371
major 16, 21, 37, 45, 50, 52, 54, 78-80, 105-106, 355, 358, 362-363, 370, 373-374, 386
power of 21
program awareness and approval 415
relationship building 78, 80, 354, 358, 360-363, 373
research on 373, 375
rules compliance 79, 240
dress codes 157, 215
drop-out risk factors 296
drugs. *See* substance use/abuse

E

Eastern College Athletic Conference (ECAC) 147
educational credentials 8, 9-10, 29-30, 265, 437. *See also* professional development; training
educational institutions
accreditation 9, 64-65
alumni. *See* alumni
athletic departments in 8, 31, 69*f*
athletics' educational role at 29-30, 89-93
bureaucratic structure 8, 31
in formal governance environment 62*f*
online programs 10
property rights 225-226, 227, 396
reputation 61, 72-73, 235, 249-250
revenue distribution authority 353
educational materials 28
emergency action plans 272, 341, 438, 445
employee handbooks 155
employees. *See also* coaches; personnel management; supervisors
accountability 84
at-will 220-221
crimes of, insurance against 160
with disabilities 300-301, 302
diversity incentives 288, 298
dress/appearance code 157, 215
education. *See* professional development; training
exempt vs. nonexempt 216-217
facility planning committee role 423
fund-raising and revenue production 354, 356, 357-358, 360-363, 394-395
leadership 5
management training 31
navigating change 32-33
new employee orientation 155-156, 207
part-time 218
performance evaluations. *See* performance evaluations
performance expectations 27-28, 139, 193
policies for. *See* policies
power and visibility of 185, 191
relationships 15-18, 38
risk management 12, 13
selling strategic plan to 35-36
staff meetings 157, 195
trust-creativity-efficiency balance 16-17
work environment. *See* work environment
employment contracts
at-will employees without 220-221
coach's 47-48, 50, 52-53, 139, 220-231, 304
compensation and benefits 220-231
designing 220-231
duties and responsibilities 224-225
institutional differences 220
liquidated damages provision 229, 230
multiyear 221-222, 223-230
negotiations 230-231
noncompete and other closure provisions 230
sexual misconduct clauses 304
standards of conduct 227-228
termination provisions 228-230
term of agreement 224
tutoring 255
ultimate authority 220
employment practices liability insurance 160
endorsements 226, 377
endowments 355, 373-374, 430
environmentally responsible organizations 56
Equal Employment Opportunity Commission 138, 142, 198
Equal Pay Act 44
equipment and supplies
budgeting 172*t*, 179, 439, 440
cost-cutting on 179
inspection, maintenance, repairs, and replacement 328
insurance 161
leased 440
moveable 440
operational program structure and 123, 125*t*, 126, 127*t*
record keeping 328
risk management 329
safety signage 160, 328
small 440
student-athlete accountability 328-329
use and storage 160, 328
Equity in Athletics Disclosure Act (EADA) 145, 315-316
Esports 147-150
ethical and professional conduct 235-245. *See also* principles; values
abusive conduct vs. 14, 265
academic integrity and 73
academic support programs 239, 254
athletic director's standards 3, 14
in athletics' complex environment 237
athletic training 81, 239
coach standards 227-228, 238-239
of educational sport 14
education on 237-238, 240

ethical and professional conduct *(continued)*
employee applicability 238-239
employment contracts 227-228
governance with 62
institutional and departmental rules 215
integrity education 237
overview 235
personnel management 184, 214, 215, 227-228
rules compliance 215, 239, 240, 241-244
sanctions and enforcement 237
student-athlete applicability 239, 319-320, 324-325
ethics committee 75
event management. *See* athletic event management
exit interviews 253, 260, 261, 296
expense allowances 226. *See also* per diem allowances
expense reimbursements 162
experts 61, 81-82, 410-411, 423

F

facility access
handicapped 300, 301, 341
operational program structure and 123, 140
facility budgets
contingency funds 440-441
contract labor expenses 439
cost-cutting 179
debt service 431, 439
deferred capital replacement accounts 430, 441
event and rental expenses 432-433
fiscal sustainability 432-433
fixed expenses 439
lease agreements 440
maintenance expenses 439-440
management and personnel expenses 432, 439
moveable items 440
new facility financing 430-431
nonmoveable items 440
office supplies and inventory costs 439
operating expenses 432, 439-441
revenue streams 431, 433
small equipment 440
facility construction 423-436
ancillary costs 429
bid process 434-435
building permits 427
comparative analysis 428-429
costs 428-429
environmental issues 427
feasibility studies 428-433
financing 355, 375-376, 430-431
fiscal sustainability 432-433
furnishings and equipment 428, 429
justification for 425
land costs 428
master list of spaces 428-429
on-site tours 428
operating cost estimates 429
outsourcing 434-435
planning committee 423-424
resistance to 423, 426
site preparation 427
site selection 426-427
size 426
surrounding communities 426
survey taking 424
users 423, 425, 426
utility, cable, Internet access 427
virtual walk-through 436
zoning 427
facility financing
bank loans 431
capital campaigns 355, 375-376, 430-431
deferred capital replacement accounts 430, 441
department fund-raising 431
endowments 430
government subsidies 430
postconstruction revenue 431
vendor contracts 178
facility operations 437-449
athletic training, sports medicine, and 124, 127*t*, 271, 328
audits 442
cost efficiency 442
credentials and expertise 437, 443
damage fears from assistive devices 300
deferred capital budgets 439-441
emergency action plans 438, 445
entry points 437
environmental factors 444
equipment storage 160, 328
gender equity and 123, 124, 127*t*, 140
hours of operation 443
image perceptions 442
incident reports 445
inspection and maintenance policy 442-443
insurance coverage 160, 444
leadership 437
locker rooms 123, 448
maintenance 439-440, 442-443
operating costs 429, 432, 439-441
operational program structure and 123, 124, 126*t*, 127*t*, 128, 140
outsourcing 432, 434-435, 439
overview 421
prohibited activities 443
proper usage 443
qualified users 443
quality of facilities 123, 124, 126*t*, 128, 140
risk assessments 445-446
risk management and mitigation 11, 12, 66, 438, 442-446
safety and liability 437-438, 442, 444
scheduling use. *See* facility scheduling
shared, rented, or free facilities 445
signage 160, 328, 377, 444
supervision 437-438
user satisfaction 442
waivers 444
walk-through and unmanned areas 437
facility rentals
expenses 432-433
policies 450
proper use requirements 443
revenue production 400-401, 402
risk assessments 450
scheduling use 447
facility scheduling 447-449
decision maker for 449
games and practices 123, 127*t*, 337
master calendar 448-449
priority use 447-448
rentals 447
faculty
academic achievement policies 253-254
academic support program role 250, 251-252, 257
accountability to 117
admissions consultation 251
athletic advisory council role 72-73, 74-75, 297
athletic representative 73, 75
ethical conduct education 240
minority 288
search committee role 199
fair competition doctrine 47
fair decision making 194-195
Fair Labor Standards Act 217
fans. *See also* booster clubs
crowd control 342-344
engaging via technology 345-346
ethical conduct education 240
governance 78-80
influence on game outcome 343
rules compliance 79, 240
unacceptable behavior 343, 344
finances. *See also* budgeting; compensation and benefits; fund-raising and revenue production
athletic event management 162, 167, 178, 338
cost-savings strategies 176-179
ethical and professional conduct 239
facility construction 355, 375-376, 430-431
office operations 162
team roster management and 314
travel 123, 127*t*, 162, 171*t*, 178
First Amendment rights 323-325, 412
food and beverage services. *See* concessions
funding structure. *See* operational program structure
fund-raising and revenue production 351-403. *See also* donors
annual giving 78, 354, 357-358, 366-372
athletic department 13-14, 92-93, 431
athletic events 355, 356, 357, 360-361, 380-382, 393-395, 431
booster clubs 354, 357, 366-372, 386, 393-394
budgeting and 167, 179, 431, 433
capacity investments 357-358
capital campaigns 355, 375-376, 430-431
compensation for 226
consultants 375
corporate giving, sponsorships, and advertising 355, 377-379, 378*t*, 384, 386, 387-390, 395
distribution authority 353
elements of model program 354-355
endowments and planned giving 355, 373-374, 430
facility rentals 400-401, 402
gender equity and 45, 353, 366, 369-370, 401
governance 78-80
guarantees 382
integration with institutional 354-355, 356-357, 363
key performance indicators 105-106, 106*t*, 370-371, 379, 408
land leases 400
leadership 357, 358, 367, 376
legal considerations 371
licensed merchandise 355, 388, 395, 396-397
major donor programs 373-374
mission, goals, objectives, and values underlying 353
multimedia rights 355, 387-390
new sports launches 355, 393-395
organizational structure 193
overview 351
parking fees 382
policies 80

priorities 353-354, 357-358
publications 388, 416
radio, television, streaming production 389, 391-392
relationship building 78, 80, 354, 358, 360-363, 373
research 373, 375
sales function 408
seating priority points systems 355, 383-386
special events, sensible 364-365
sports camps 355, 361, 402
staff capabilities 354, 356, 357-358, 394-395
strategic plans 105-106, 106*t*
student-athlete role 262-263
student fees and pay to play 179, 355, 398-399, 431
team activities 365, 401
technology use 354, 356, 357, 358-359, 363, 391-392
ticketing and 356, 357, 380-381, 393, 394, 395, 431
tuition waivers 400
vending machine income 400
websites and 358-359

G

game officials 173*t*, 338
games
away events 360
cost-cutting with fewer 178
fan behavior influencing outcome 343
home events 360-361, 393-394
scheduling 123, 127*t*, 337
gaming, competitive 147-150
gender equity and diversity committee 75
gender equity and Title IX
accommodating interests and abilities 121, 130, 132-134, 134*t*
adding new sports and 144-146, 148-149
athletic director's challenges 41-46
athletic scholarships 41, 42, 45, 134-137, 135*t*, 136*t*
booster clubs 366, 369-370
coaches and 44, 122, 138-140, 199
continued expansion demonstration 132
continued historical discrimination vs. 283-286, 284*t*-286*t*
diversity, inclusion, and nondiscrimination 281, 288, 290
elements required 121-125, 127*t*
Esports 148-149
facility access and quality 123, 124, 127*t*, 140
fund-raising and revenue production 45, 353, 366, 369-370, 401
governance compliance 66
hiring process 198, 203
historical inequities 142-143
operational program structure and 116, 118, 119, 121-125, 126, 127*t*, 129-146, 130*t*, 131*t*, 135*t*, 136*t*, 148-149
participation opportunities 119, 129-134
participation statistics 41-42, 42*f*, 43*f*, 116, 133, 285-286, 286*t*, 287*t*
proportionality standard 130-132, 130*t*, 131*t*, 290, 315
recruitment 42, 137-138
resistance to change 41, 43-44
sex discrimination vs. 41, 119, 138, 316
sexual abuse and harassment prohibitions 288, 304-307
strategies to achieve 45-46
support for change 44
team roster management and 132, 313, 315-316
travel 330
general liability insurance 160
goals and objectives
budgeting integration with 163, 169-170, 173-174
compensation and benefits 222-223
crafting specific 87
diversity, inclusion, and nondiscrimination 287, 289-290
fund-raising based on 353
operational program structure supporting 118, 129
philosophy of educational sport and 89-90
strategic plans 97-110, 99*f*-100*f*, 104*t*, 106*t*, 108*t*, 287, 289-290
student-athlete growth and development 115
team 103, 104*t*, 115-116
vision connected to 183
governance 59-85
accreditation and certification 64-65
alumni and fans in 74, 78-80
athletic advisory councils 61, 72-78, 80, 81-82
booster clubs 78-79, 367, 368-369
chain of command 69-71, 69*f*
defined 61
experts 61, 81-82
formal governance environment 62*f*
legal counsel 63, 66
navigating layers 61-63
overview 59
policies 61, 65, 68, 72, 77, 80, 83-84
rules compliance and 61, 67-68, 79, 215
rules manuals 156, 241-242
sport performance advisory group 81-82
student-athletes in 73-74, 76-77
team 62-63
government subsidies 430
grades, reporting 256
guarantees 382

H

hall of fame 78, 79, 80
harassment 14, 264, 266, 288, 302, 304-307, 321, 326
health issues. *See* athletic training; injuries; mental health services; sports medicine
higher administration
athletic advisory council role 74
chain of command 69-71, 69*f*
coach termination role 50, 52, 54
compensation and employment contract authority 220, 221, 231
gender equity plan 45
governance role 61, 62-63, 69-71, 74
new sport support 393
preferential treatment influence 128
vision of organization 35
high school level
academic integrity 73
accreditation 64
adding new sports 144-145, 146, 148-150
booster clubs 367-368
coach qualifications 29, 265
coach recruitment 47
compensation and employment contracts 220, 221, 222
concessions 381-382
disability-accommodating events 300
Esports 148-150
fund-raising and revenue production 355, 356-357, 367-368, 399
gender equity and Title IX 41-46
operational program structure 115, 133, 144-145, 146, 148-150
organizational structure 69-70, 69*f*, 189*f*
pay-to-play programs 399
relationship building 37-38
rules compliance 67, 215
sexual harassment and abuse 305
sport participation by gender 41, 42, 42*f*, 133, 287*t*
strategic plan 36, 100*f*
team roster management 314
hiring process
background checks 203
candidate assessments 203-206
coach recruitment 47-49, 117, 203
diversity and inclusion 198, 199, 202, 203, 288, 291-292, 301-302
impermissible questions 204, 205, 301-302
interviews 205-206, 302
job descriptions 197-198
job offers 206-207
job postings 199, 200*f*-201*f*, 201-202, 202*f*
legal risks 219
model process 198-207
operating procedures 202-203
personnel management 184, 197-207, 218-219
rating sheets 203, 204, 205, 206
reference checks 204-205, 301-302
search committee formation 198-199
work-study positions 218-219
housing arrangements 124, 127*t*
human resources
coach termination consultation 50, 230
employment contracts 221, 230-231
governance role 63
hiring involvement 199, 202, 203, 206

I

inclusion. *See* diversity, inclusion, and nondiscrimination
information sharing 195
injuries
athletic scholarships and 136
concussions 269, 277-278
documenting 273
reporting 445
return to play decisions 18, 269, 277-278
risk management 66
sport performance advisory group 81-82
insurance 124, 159-161, 227, 272, 348, 374, 444
intellectual property rights 396, 417
intercollegiate athletic councils 78
IT operating handbooks 155. *See also* technology

J

job descriptions 27, 139, 193, 197-198, 233
job offers 206-207
job postings 199, 200*f*-201*f*, 201-202, 202*f*

K

key performance indicators (KPIs)
academic excellence 107, 108*t*
communications 408, 414-415
corporate sponsorships 379
developing 101-102
diversity 286, 288, 296

key performance indicators (KPIs) *(continued)*
fund-raising 105-106, 106*t*, 370-371, 379, 408
governance 65
marketing 408
media relations 408
promotions 408
sales 408
team 103, 104*t*
knowledge 3, 22. *See also* learning

L

land leases 400
laws
antidiscrimination 11
concussion 269
disability 299, 300-301
gender equity. *See* gender equity and Title IX
governance under 61, 62*f*, 66
labor 217
sport 11, 12
lawsuits 11, 44, 47, 119, 319-320
leadership
athletic director's 1, 3
attributes 4-5
communications 407
of diversity efforts 294-295
employee's 5
facility operations 437
fund-raising 357, 358, 367, 376
gender and persons of color in 284*t*
student-athlete 259
learning 3, 25-26, 84. *See also* knowledge; professional development; training
learning disabilities 251, 253, 254, 256, 300
lease agreements 400, 440
legal agreements. *See* contracts
legal counsel consultations
booster club structure 367, 368
coach terminations 50, 230
complaint management 321
employment contracts 221, 224, 230-231
governance 63, 66
insurance 160
intellectual property rights 396
licensed merchandising 396
sports camps 402
student-athlete speech and conduct restrictions 325
legal issues
contractual 47, 221
employment discrimination 219
fund-raising 371
gender equity and Title IX 44
governance compliance 61, 62*f*, 66
operational program structure for compliance 119
overtime 217
risk management. *See* risk management
sports medicine and athletic training 269, 275
tortious interference 47
LGBTQ individuals 288, 304
liabilities
facility risk and 442, 450
insurance 160-161
risk management. *See* risk management
licensed merchandise 355, 388, 395, 396-397
life skills programs 259
listening skills 194
locker rooms 123, 448
logos 14, 225-226, 329, 355, 389, 396, 410-411

M

management
athletic director's philosophy 3
change 3, 32-36, 41-46, 369-370
effective and efficient strategies 118
personnel 181-234
theory 16
training, for employees 31
marketing 407, 408. *See also* advertising; brand positioning; promotions; publicity
media
abuse and harassment coverage 14, 264, 304, 305, 307
academics of student-athletes coverage 250
athletic events 338, 342, 345-346, 413
athletics coverage 12-13
coach recruitment leaks 48
coach termination communication 51, 54
gender and persons of color in 284*t*
governance under scrutiny 61
guides and brochures 156
multimedia rights 355, 387-390
privacy issues 13, 66
publicity 124-125, 127*t*, 226, 338, 362, 408
responding to aggressive 117
social. *See* social media
Title IX coverage 42
media relations
functions of 408
information collection 413
key performance indicators 408
media operations and 413
overview 405
policies 413
program evaluation 414
staff for 407, 408-409
medical insurance 159-160, 227
medical issues. *See* athletic training; injuries; mental health services; sports medicine
mental health services 264-266, 327
mentoring programs 254, 257, 259, 260, 293-294
minorities. *See* diversity, inclusion, and nondiscrimination
mission
athletics as extension of educational 90–92
defining 89
fund-raising based on 353
goals and objectives reflecting 97, 99*f*-100*f*, 118
operational program structure supporting 129
statement of 87, 94, 95
strategic plans 97-98, 99*f*-100*f*
multimedia rights 355, 387-390

N

NAIA institutions 42, 67, 156
National Association for Intercollegiate Athletics 67. *See also* NAIA institutions
National Association for Sport and Physical Education (NAPSE) 9
National Athletic Trainers' Association 269
National Christian College Athletic Association (NCCAA) 67
National Collegiate Athletic Association 67. *See also* NCAA institutions
National Federation of State High School Athletic Associations 146, 148, 300, 368
National Interscholastic Athletic Administrators Association (NIAAA) 9
National Junior College Athletic Association (NJCAA) 67, 147
NCAA institutions
academic integrity 73
academic support program mandates 250
adding new sports 145-146
athletic scholarships 135-137
certifications 64-65
coach employment and compensation 138, 221-222, 223, 225
coach recruitment 47
concussion protocols 278
disability-accommodating events 300
diversity, inclusion, and nondiscrimination 284*t*, 287*t*
exit interviews 261
fund-raising and revenue production 356
gender equity and Title IX 41-46
governance 64-65, 67-68, 73
graduation and progress rate reporting 250
insurance coverage 159
mental health services 264, 265-266
organizational charts 186*f*-188*f*
outside employment policies 216, 217
position charts 190*t*-191*t*
revenue and expenses reports 92-93
rules compliance 67-68, 215, 216, 217, 242, 319
sexual harassment and abuse 305
sport participation by gender 41-42, 43*f*, 133, 287*f*
strategic plan 99*f*
student-athlete codes of conduct 319
student fees 398
student-life programs 258, 260
team roster management 314, 317
new employee orientation 155-156, 207
new sports 116, 144-150, 355, 393-395
nonathlete students, on athletic advisory council 74
noncash benefits 227
noncompete clauses 230
nondiscrimination. *See* diversity, inclusion, and nondiscrimination
North American Society for Sport Management (NASSM) 9

O

office demeanor 215
office operations 153-180
budgeting 163-179
contracts and legal agreements 158
financial affairs 162
insurance issues 159-161
new employee orientation 155-156
overview 153
policies 157
open-door policies 194
operational program structure 113-152
accommodating differences in tiers 141-143
accommodating interests and abilities 121, 130, 132-134, 134*t*
adding or eliminating sports 116, 129, 144-150
articulating tiered funding model 115-117
assessment and formalization 116-117
athletic scholarships 121-122, 126*t*, 127*t*, 134-137, 135*t*, 136*t*, 142, 147
budgeting and 175

challenges, confronting 120
coaches and 122, 126*t*, 127*t*, 128, 138-140, 142
communicating benefits of tiers 118-119
defining current model 125-126, 125*t*, 126*t*, 127*t*
determining program differences 121-125
Esports 147-150
evaluating current model 129
facility access and quality 123, 124, 126*t*, 127*t*, 128, 140
four-tier model 126, 127*t*
gender equity and 116, 118, 119, 121-125, 126, 127*t*, 129-146, 130*t*, 131*t*, 135*t*, 136*t*, 148-149
guide to creating 121-143
job descriptions and 139, 198
overview 113
participation opportunities 119, 129-134
policies and practices by tier 134-141
preferential treatment factors 126, 128-129
recruitment and 122, 126*t*, 127*t*, 137-138, 142
team objective variance 115-116
three-tier model 126, 126*t*, 130*t*, 131*t*, 134*t*, 135*t*, 136*t*
operations handbooks 83-84, 156
organizational charts 27, 69*f*, 185, 186*f*-189*f*
organizational culture. *See* work environment
organizational structure
academic support programs 193
chain of command 69-71, 69*f*
culture of excellence and 184
development office 193
organizational charts 27, 69*f*, 185, 186*f*-189*f*
personnel management 184, 185-193, 186*f*-189*f*, 190*t*-191*t*
position charts 185, 190*t*-191*t*
supervisory roles 185, 191-193
organization resiliency 32
outsourcing. *See also* vendors
concessions 339, 381-382, 431
facility construction and operations 432, 434-435, 439
licensed merchandise 395, 396-397
multimedia and advertising sales 387, 388, 390
sports camps 402
overtime policies 216-217

P

parents
booster club involvement 367, 370
coach termination communication 52, 55
as donors 361
ethical conduct education 240
gender equity support 44
program awareness 414
sports camp communication 347-348
student-athletes as 276
parking 382, 436
participation. *See* sport participation
part-time employees 218
payroll 162. *See also* compensation and benefits
pay-to-play programs 179, 355, 399
peer mentoring 259
pension plans 226
per diem allowances 123, 127*t*
performance-enhancing drugs 11
performance evaluations
corrective actions 208, 215
diversity objectives 298
efficiency and risk mitigation 209*f*, 212
evaluation instruments 27, 210, 211
fund-raising 361
game officials 338
healthy perspective on 208-209
improving performance 213
integrated approach 209-212, 209*f*
macro view 209-210, 209*f*
micro view 209*f*, 210-212
performance tools 27
personnel management 184, 208-213
professional development 31
relationship building 38
succession planning 31
performance expectations 27-28, 139, 193. *See also* key performance indicators
personnel management 181-234. *See also* employees
collegiality and support expectations 214-215
compensation and benefits 184, 199, 216-218, 220-231
conflict resolution 184, 215
corrective actions 208, 215
culture of excellence 183-184
demeanor and dress codes 215
donor car programs 232
employment contracts 220-231
ethical and professional conduct 184, 214, 215, 227-228
hiring process 184, 197-207, 218-219
job descriptions 193, 197-198, 233
legal risk mitigation 219
organizational structure 184, 185-193, 186*f*-189*f*, 190*t*-191*t*
outside activities involvement 217-218
outside employment 216, 217
overtime policies 216-217
overview 181
performance evaluations 184, 208-213
policies 214-219
professional development 184
rules compliance 215, 216, 217
supervisor's management behaviors 184, 194-196
support service roles 195-196
volunteer solicitation 218
work-study assignments 218-219
philosophy
compensation 222-223
decision making 15
of educational sport 14, 89-93
management 3
team roster management 314
values, principles and 23
photography 418
physical education 29, 43
policies. *See also under specific topics*
exceptions 83
manuals 83-84, 155
review 83
values and principles via 23
political acumen 3, 19-20
position charts 185, 190*t*-191*t*
position descriptions. *See* job descriptions
position playbooks 156
power 21-22, 185, 191, 192-193
practice times 123, 127*t*, 337
pregnant student-athletes 276
prescription drugs 274
presidents. *See* higher administration
principals. *See* higher administration
principles 3, 23-24. *See also* ethical and professional conduct; values
privacy issues 11, 13, 66, 272, 318, 321
problem-solving strategies 39-40, 195
procedures 83
product liability insurance 161
professional conduct. *See* ethical and professional conduct
professional development 10, 25-26, 28, 31, 184, 296. *See also* training
professional liability insurance 161
professional organizations 9, 25, 294
promotions
athletic event 338, 342, 345-346
functions of 408
key performance indicators 408
overview 405
publications 416
staff for 407, 408-409
property insurance 160
proportionality standard 130-132, 130*t*, 131*t*, 290, 315
publications 155-156, 388, 416-418
publicity 124-125, 127*t*, 226, 338, 362, 408
public pressure 13, 18
purpose, statement of 94-95

R

radio programming 389, 391-392
rating sheets 203, 204, 205, 206
recruitment
academic support programs and 249, 250
athletic department role 92
budgeting 172*t*, 179
coach 47-49, 117, 203
conflicts of interest 18
cost-cutting on 177, 179
diversity, inclusion, and nondiscrimination 288, 291-292
ethical and rule-compliant 241, 243, 244
gender equity 42, 137-138
operational program structure and 122, 126*t*, 127*t*, 137-138, 142
team roster management and 317
recruits
accommodating interests and abilities 121, 130, 132-134, 134*t*
coach termination communication 55
program merits communication 117
walk-ons vs. 137
reference checks 204-205, 301-302
Rehabilitation Act (RA, 1973) 299, 300-301
relationship building
athletic director's 15-18, 37-38
booster club 79
in chain of command 70-71
donor 78, 80, 354, 358, 360-363, 373
employee 15-18, 38
friend-raising 360, 363
keys to successful 361-363
reputation
academic integrity and 72-73, 249-250
athletic director's 22
educational institution's 61, 72-73, 235, 249-250
ethical and professional conduct 235, 237
retention strategies 288, 296
revenue production. *See* fund-raising and revenue production

risk assessments
athlete preparation and participation 318
athletic equipment and apparel 329
checklists 12
drug testing and education 274
employment 214
event management 344
facility 445-446
facility rental 450
finance 162
insurance 159, 160
preevent, factors dictating 340-341
sports camps 349
sports medicine and athletic training 269, 276
student-athlete discipline and behavior 320
team travel 330
risk management
athletic event 66, 339, 340-341, 344, 349
crowd control 344
equipment and uniforms 329
facility construction 434
facility operations 11, 12, 66, 438, 442-446
governance and 66
insurance for. *See* insurance
radio, television, streaming production 392
training needs 11-12, 13
risk mitigation
employment discrimination 219
facility management 442-446
performance evaluations 209*f*, 212
role models 19, 191, 296
roster management. *See* team roster management
rules compliance
alumni, fan, and donor 79, 240
athletic director's responsibilities 61, 67-68
athletic training and sports medicine 269
Esports 149
ethical and professional conduct 215, 239, 240, 241-244
forms 243-244
governance and 61, 67-68, 79, 215
manuals 156, 241-242
policies 241
scholarship and recruitment 241, 243, 244
sports camp employment 216, 217
student-athletes 239, 319-320, 322-323, 326
team rules 322-323, 326
verification 242-243

S

safety
accessibility and 341
athletic events 340, 341, 342-344
facility 437-438, 442, 444
signage 160, 328, 444
sales 407-408. *See also* licensed merchandise; ticketing
sanctions 21-22, 237, 324-325
scholarships. *See* athletic scholarships
search committee 198-199. *See also* hiring process
seating priority points systems (SPPS) 355, 383-386, 385*f*
security
athletic events 340, 341, 342-344
facility operations 437-438
self-evaluations 5, 64, 65
senior management. *See* supervisors
service organizations 15-16
sex discrimination 41, 119, 138, 316. *See also* gender equity and Title IX
sexual misconduct
abuse and harassment 14, 264, 266, 288, 304-307, 321, 326
complaint management 321
definitions and distinctions 305
ethical conduct vs. 14
failure to stop 306
media coverage 14, 264, 304, 305, 307
policies and policy implementation 304, 306-307, 326
quid pro quo harassment 305-306
reporting 305-306, 321
sexual orientation 288, 304
social media
athletic event broadband capability 345-346
communications strategy 412
employee policies 157
fund-raising relationship building via 351, 354, 370
publications 416
restrictions on use 412
student-athlete use 235, 324-325, 412
speech, freedom of 323-325, 412
sponsorships 294, 355, 377-379, 378*t*, 384, 386, 388-389, 395
sport culture 264-265
sport law 11, 12
Sport Management Program Review Council (SMPRC) 9
sport participation
as academic incentive 256
gender equity and opportunities for 119, 129-134
"ghost" slots 315
preparticipation requirements 272, 318, 348
statistics by gender 41-42, 42*f*, 43*f*, 116, 133, 285-286, 286*t*, 287*t*
team administration 318
sport performance advisory group 81-82
sports. *See* athletics
sports camps
adult fantasy 402
cash handling 338
coach–athlete relationship 319
compensation and benefits for 226, 227
diversity, inclusion, and nondiscrimination 291
forms 347-348, 349
fund-raising and revenue production 355, 361, 402
management of 347-349
NCAA rules 216, 217
parent communication 347-348
policies 347, 348
relationship building 361
risk assessments 349
staff training 348-349
sports management training 8-9
sports medicine 269-280. *See also* athletic training
athletic event presence 340
blood-borne pathogens and infectious diseases 276
budgeting 167, 439
concussion protocols 269, 277-278
critical issues 275-278
drug distribution 276
drug testing 11, 244, 274
eating disorders 276
facility operations and 271
heat, cold, and hydration issues 276
injuries. *See* injuries
insurance coverage 272
mental health services 264-266, 327
overview 269
pregnant or parenting students 276
preparticipation requirements 272, 318, 348
sport performance advisory group 81-82
staff meetings 157, 195
stakeholders
accountability to 117
budgeting collaboration 163
coach termination communication 52, 54-55
facility planning committee role 423-424
search committee role 199
selling strategic plan to 36
strategic plans
for academic excellence 107, 108*t*
budgeting and 163
defined 27
developing 97-98, 99*f*-100*f*
diversity, inclusion, and nondiscrimination objectives 287, 289-290
for fund-raising 105-106, 106*t*
implementation 36
long-range 102, 107, 108*t*
performance expectations 27
review and revision 97-98, 109-110
selling to staff 35-36
selling to stakeholders 36
shared learning environment 25
strategies, KPIs, and action plans 101-103, 104*t*, 105-107, 106*t*, 108*t*
for teams 103, 104*t*
vision of organization 35, 97-98
student-athlete handbooks 322-323
student-athletes
academics. *See* academics
athletic advisory council role 73-74, 76-77
athletics enhancing overall development 91
coach relationship with 319-320
coach termination communication 51, 52, 53-54
disciplinary actions 324-326
drug testing 11, 244, 274
ethical and professional conduct 239, 319-320, 324-325
fairness to 118
fund-raising involvement 262-263
gender equity for. *See* gender equity and Title IX
governance role 73-74, 76-77
growth and development objectives 115
handbook 322-323
harassment and abuse of 14, 264-265, 266, 288, 304-307, 321, 326
hiring postgraduation 218
housing and dining 124, 127*t*
injuries. *See* injuries
insurance coverage 124, 159, 272
participation. *See* sport participation
pregnant or parenting 276
privacy issues 11, 13, 66, 272, 318, 321
recruitment of. *See* recruitment; recruits
rights of 323-325
rules compliance 239, 319-320, 322-323, 326

scholarships for. *See* athletic scholarships
search committee role 199
social media use 235, 324-325, 412
support programs. *See* academic support programs; student-life programs
team rules 322-323, 326
walk-on 137, 243-244
student fees 355, 398-399, 431
student-life programs 258-266
academic support 259
budgeting 167
career development 259
community service 260, 262-263
exit interviews 260, 261
fund-raising involvement 262-263
history 258
leadership experiences 259
life skills 259
mental health services 264-266
overview 247
peer mentoring 259
priorities 258
replication and excess 258-259
time challenges 258
study halls 254, 256, 257
study skills 254
substance use/abuse
counselors 327
drug distribution 276
drug testing 11, 244, 274
policies 274, 276, 326
succession planning 31, 203
summer bridge programs 251
summer camps. *See* sports camps
superintendents. *See* higher administration
supervisors
capabilities 191
change management 33
of coaches 192-193
coaches as 193
confrontation and problem-solving 195
distribution of sport programs under 192
facility operations 437-438
fairness 194-195
function of 16
information sharing 195
listening, analysis, and collaboration 194
management style 184, 194-196
new employee welcome 156
open-door policies 194
organizational roles 185, 191-193
strategic planning 35-36, 109-110
as teachers 191
valuing support services 195-196
support programs. *See* academic support programs; student-life programs
support services 125, 195-196
sustainable sport initiatives 56
SWOT analysis 35, 109, 425

T

teaching 25-26, 191
team academic coaches 256
team administration 311-333
athlete selection, participation, and preparation 318
awards 331
coach–athlete relationship 319-320
complaint management 321
equipment and uniforms 328-329
overview 311
roster management 132, 313-317
student-athlete codes of conduct 319-320
student-athlete handbook, rules, and rights 322-326
substance abuse counselors 327
travel 330
team budgets 177-179
team fund-raising activities 365, 401
team roster management 132, 313-317
team rules 322-323, 326
team strategic plans 103, 104*t*
team tryouts 299, 301, 313, 318
technology. *See also* social media; websites
access and training 254, 257
broadband capability 345-346
fund-raising use of 354, 356, 357, 358-359, 363, 391-392
IT operating handbooks 155
radio, television, streaming production 391-392
television programming 389, 391-392
terminations 50-55, 177, 208, 228-230
ticketing
database 356
discounted and complimentary 381
facility financing debt service 431
fund-raising and 356, 357, 380-381, 393, 394, 395, 431
introduce-a-friend 394, 395
new sports 393, 394, 395
policies 338
season tickets 381, 393, 394
tiered funding structure. *See* operational program structure
Title IX. *See* gender equity and Title IX
Title VII 44
tobacco. *See* substance use/abuse
tortious interference 47
trademarks 396
training. *See also* professional development
abuse, harassment, and bullying prevention 304
athletic. *See* athletic training
concession 339
customer service 361
diversity 288, 293-295, 298
educational administration 8
ethical and professional conduct 237-238, 240
management, for employees 31
ongoing 11-14
relationship building 361-363
risk management 11-12, 13
sports camp staff 348-349
sports management 8-9
transition planning 55
transportation insurance 161
travel
finances 123, 127*t*, 162, 171*t*, 178
gender equity 330
operational program structure and 123, 127*t*, 141-143
per diem allowances 123, 127*t*
policies 162, 330
staff 162
team administration 330
transportation insurance 161
tuition, and athletic scholarships 137
tuition goals 92
tuition waivers 400
tutoring 123-124, 127*t*, 239, 254, 255, 256. *See also* academic support programs

U

uniforms 125*t*, 126, 164, 165*t*-166*t*, 178-179, 328-329
U.S. Esports Federation (USeF) 149

V

values. *See also* ethical and professional conduct
athletic director's 3, 23-24
defined 23
fund-raising based on 353
organizational 87, 94, 95-96
statement of 23-24, 94, 95-96
varsity sports
adding new 144-150
defining true experience 120
educational role and function 29, 30
Esports 147-150
rules compliance 67
team roster management 314, 316-317
vending machines 400
vendors 162, 178, 379, 381-382, 431. *See also* outsourcing
vision of organization
fund-raising based on 353
goal-directed behavior and 183
overview 87
philosophy of educational sport and 89-93
proving achievability 35
statement of 94, 95
strategic plans 35, 97-98
visiting teams 338
volunteers 218, 367, 381-382, 450

W

waivers
facility use 444, 450
privacy 318
tuition 400
walk-on athletes 137, 243-244
websites
fund-raising support 358-359
importance of Internet presence 358-359
publications 416, 417-418
sponsorship and advertising 388
traffic on 414
weight-training 124, 127*t*, 271, 328
women, equity for. *See* gender equity and Title IX
Women Leaders in College Sports (WLCS) 9
work environment
changing 183
conflicts of interest and 17-18
culture of excellence 183-184
employee relations and 17-18
fair and nondiscriminatory 287, 289
hiring interview description of 206
integrity in 237
office operations and 153
shared learning in 25-26
values and principles affecting 23
workers compensation insurance 160-161
work-study positions 218-219

Y

youth sport programs 401. *See also* sports camps

Z

zero-based budgeting 163-164, 170, 171*t*-174*t*, 175

About the Authors

© Donna Lopiano

Donna A. Lopiano, PhD, is president of Sports Management Resources, a consulting firm that draws on the knowledge of experienced former athletic directors to assist scholastic and collegiate athletic departments in solving challenges in growth and development. She served for 18 years as the director of women's athletics at the University of Texas at Austin and is a past president of the Association for Intercollegiate Athletics for Women. During her tenure at the University of Texas, she built what many believe to be the premier women's athletic program in the country, twice earning the award for top program in the nation.

Lopiano was the chief executive officer of the Women's Sports Foundation from 1992 to 2007 and was named one of the 10 most powerful women in sports by Fox Sports. The Institute for International Sport also named Lopiano one of the 100 most influential sport educators in America. She has been recognized for her leadership as an athletic administrator and for advocating for gender equity in sports by the International Olympic Committee, National Collegiate Athletic Association, National Association for Girls and Women in Sport, National Association of Collegiate Women Athletics Administrators, and National Association of Collegiate Directors of Athletics.

She has been a coach of collegiate men's and women's volleyball and women's basketball and softball and has coached the Italian national women's softball team. As an athlete, she participated in 26 national championships in four sports and was a nine-time All-American in four positions in softball, a sport in which she played on six national championship teams. She is a member of the National Italian American Sports Hall of Fame, National Softball Hall of Fame, Connecticut Women's Hall of Fame, and Texas Women's Hall of Fame, among others.

Courtesy of Kathryn Hoolan

Connee Zotos, PhD, retired from her position as associate dean of academic and faculty affairs and clinical associate professor of sports management in the School of Professional Studies at New York University. She is currently a senior associate for the consulting firm Sports Management Resources.

Zotos has over 38 years of experience in scholastic and collegiate athletics as a basketball and field hockey coach, Division II and Division III athletic director, and professor. Zotos served as the director of athletics at Drew University and William Smith College and director of women's athletics at Philadelphia College of Textiles and Science. She has published numerous articles in refereed and nonrefereed journals and is a noted speaker and author on tiered funding models in collegiate athletics, coaches' employment and compensation packages, coach evaluation systems, and gender equity in sport.

Zotos has served on the NCAA Division III Management Council, is a past president of the Collegiate Athletic Administrators of New Jersey, and was a member of the board of directors for the National Association of Collegiate Women Athletics Administrators.

She received a Division III Administrator of the Year award from the National Association of Collegiate Women Athletics Administrators. She was recognized for her enduring contributions to collegiate athletics with the Garden State Award from Collegiate Athletic Administrators of New Jersey. In 2021, Zotos received a Nike Lifetime Achievement Award from Women Leaders in College Sports. As a faculty member, she received a Teaching Excellence Award from the School of Professional Studies at New York University. Zotos is a member of the Glassboro State College–Rowan University Sports Hall of Fame and the Drew University Athletic Hall of Fame. She resides in Leland, North Carolina.